WESTMAR COLLEGE LIBRARY

P9-DMG-108

Fundamentals of Child Development

Second Edition

Fundamentals of Child Development

Second Edition

HARRY MUNSINGER
University of California, San Diego

HOLT, RINEHART AND WINSTON

New York   Chicago   San Francisco
Atlanta   Dallas   Montreal   Toronto
London   Sydney

BF
721
.M83
1975

Cover illustrations by Suzanne Szasz.

"Differences in Structure and Differences in Early Training..." on p. 55 is from J.B. Watson: *Psychology from the Standpoint of a Behaviorist*, 3rd ed. (Philadelphia: J.B. Lippincott Company), 1929. The article on Binet, p. 255, is from R.J. Herrnstein's *IQ and the Meritocracy* (Boston: Little, Brown and Company), 1973. "Second Thoughts about Man: What the Schools Cannot Do," p. 283, is from *Time* Magazine (April 16, 1973). "Rules for Rulers," p. 373, is from Desmond Morris' *The Human Zoo* (New York: McGraw-Hill, Inc.), 1969.

Library of Congress Cataloging in Publication Data

Munsinger, Harry.
  Fundamentals of child development.

Includes bibliographies and index.
  1. Child study. I. Title. [DNLM: 1. Adolescent psychology. 2. Child development. WS105 M969f]
BF721.M83 1975   155.4   74-23601

Copyright © 1971, 1975 by Holt, Rinehart and Winston
All rights reserved
Library of Congress Catalog Card Number: 74-23601
ISBN: 0-03-091881-2
Printed in the United States of America
5 6 7 8 9   032   9 8 7 6 5 4 3 2 1

103337

To Kim and Brita

Preface

To the Student and the Instructor

People enter a course in child development with diverse backgrounds and varying interests. There seems to be no "typical" student. Yet the needs of all students should be considered when teaching or when writing a textbook in child development. Some people in child psychology courses are education majors; while others may have backgrounds in biology, physics, or mathematics. Some students want to understand their own childhoods; others are concerned with rearing children of their own or beginning a career in teaching. Instructors, too, have different goals in their courses. One might stress theory, another fact, and a third might concentrate on practical applications.

While the main purpose of a text is to teach, the divergent needs of students and instructors must also be met. In order to do this a text must be carefully constructed and the aim of the textbook writer must be to be clear, comprehensive, easy-to-understand, interesting, and correct. In addition to attempting to meet these goals, I have tried to make the second edition of *Fundamentals of Child Development* flexible by organizing it into self-contained units. Each of these units — or chapters — covers a single subject area throughout the course of a child's life from the moment of its inception through the period of adolescence. Because these units are self-contained, the instructor need not follow the order of the textbook but can arrange to teach the subjects included in the child development course in the order that suits him or her best.

But *Fundamentals of Child Development* was also revised with the student in mind. It is organized so that people with different backgrounds can easily comprehend the material included in the text. Each chapter opens with a detailed outline of its contents, so as to allow the range of material to be seen at a glance, and with a preview which emphasizes the important points discussed in the chapter. Each chapter also points out theories, facts, and the practical applications that are most important to the subject matter. Technical terms are underlined and explained in the context of the chapter, as well as in an extensive Glossary at the back of the book. Also included is a Selected Bibliography for further reading.

All views of child psychology are represented in this text, and it is balanced by the vast body of research being done in the field. Thus, experimental and observational data, human and animal studies, cross-cultural research, as well as data from so-called normal and clinical populations are given and are supplemented by opposing interpretations of the data. I have tried to evaluate such material in the most objective way possible, given the current state of our knowledge.

The Appendix of advanced topics will interest some students, or may be assigned for extra credit. Such topics include the ethics involved in studying children; the history of the field of child psychology; the use of statistics; the scientific method; and specific theories about sensation, memory, grammar, and emotion.

Summary sentences along the margin throughout the book appear beside each paragraph. They not only provide a ready index to the contents of the book but also will prove to be a help when it is time to review before examinations. Each chapter contains citations of important research, and ends with additional recommended readings. Chapter 1 presents a framework of child development—the description of normal human development from before birth through adolescence. Subsequent chapters treat specific topics in depth.

The "Portraits," which appear in all chapters except the first, are arranged with biographical and professional material on the first page; a visual presentation of the work of the subject and his or her photograph; and an excerpt or reading from the person's work on the facing page. The excerpt will often run for several pages and can be distinguished from the text by its two-column setting.

Until experts in the English language find a suitable and graceful substitute for constant repetition of he/she or him/her, the generic use of the masculine pronoun seems to be a less awkward solution. This is not chauvinistic bias on my part and I have tried to avoid using feminine and masculine pronouns wherever possible. But sometimes—for clarity and to avoid clutter—I have fallen a victim of our mother tongue.

The book was written for you, the student and the instructor. If you have questions or comments, my publishers and I would appreciate hearing from you.

Everyone knows that a modern text requires many people's combined skills, but no one is more aware of that fact than the author himself. This book is the joint result of my discussions with colleagues and students in child development, the constant reading of literally hundreds of original research papers, and the patient editing of my wife and my publisher. I owe a special debt to my editors at Holt, Rinehart and Winston: Richard Owen and Louise Waller, who have demonstrated again and again the intelligence, foresight, and sensitivity that all authors hope for and few receive. The quality of this finished text owes much to their judgment and taste.

In addition to sources noted in the figure legends throughout the book, credit is due to many for permission to reproduce or adapt material.

January 1975
La Jolla, California   —H. M.

Contents

Preface   vii

Part I   The Bases of Human Development   1

1   NORMAL HUMAN DEVELOPMENT   3

    Conception   4
    The Newborn   6
    The Neonate   7
    The Infant   7
    The Toddler   11
    The Preschool Child   16
    The School Child   22
    The Adolescent   26
    Summary   31

2   THE BIOLOGICAL BASES OF DEVELOPMENT   32

    The Mechanisms of Evolution   34
    The Evolution and Development of the Human Nervous System   34
    Conception   38
    Genetics and Behavior   41
    Portrait: Francis Galton   52
    Reading: "Differences in Structure and Differences in Early Training
       Will Account for All Differences in Later Behavior" by John S. Watson   55
    Stages of Prenatal Development   60
    Prenatal Influences   64

Birth   70
The Newborn   72
Summary   81

3   SENSORY-MOTOR GROWTH   82

Physical Growth   84
Sensory-motor Integration   99
Portrait: Jean Piaget   100

4   PERCEPTUAL DEVELOPMENT   122

Vision   124
Audition   126
The Chemical Senses   128
Kinesthesis and Balance   129
The Skin Senses   130
Attention   132
Theories of Perception   137
Portrait: George A. Miller   138
The Perception of Space   145
Object Perception   147
Perceptual Constancy   151
Errors of Perception   154

Part II   Cognitive Development   159

5   LEARNING AND REMEMBERING   160

Behaviorism   162
Portrait: B.F. Skinner   168
Human Memory   185

6   LANGUAGE ACQUISITION   193

The Biological Bases of Language   195
Early Vocalizations   200
Grammar Acquisition   204
Portrait: Noam Chomsky   210
Speech   218
The Development of Meaning   219
Nonverbal Communication   221

7   COGNITIVE DEVELOPMENT   223

Cognitive Processes   225
Portrait: Jerome Bruner   228
Stages of Children's Thought   238

8 INTELLIGENCE AND CREATIVITY   250

   The Intelligence Test   252
   Portrait: Alfred Binet   254
   Test Characteristics   262
   Tests of Ability   266
   Group Differences in IQ   274
   The IQ Debate   277
   Creativity   285

Part III Personal, Social, and Emotional Development   291

   9 MOTIVATION AND EMOTIONS   292

   Innate Behavior Patterns   295
   Biological Drives   297
   Human Motives   306
   Portrait: Niko Tinbergen   308
   Emotions   322
   Reading: "Sleep" by Julius Segal   327

   10 PARENT-CHILD RELATIONS   333

   How Parents Influence Their Children   335
   Parent-child Interaction   343
   Variations in Family Relations   350
   Practical Child-training Suggestions   359
   Portrait: Benjamin Spock   360

   11 SOCIAL RELATIONS AND THE SCHOOL   367

   The Peer Group   369
   Reading: "Rules for Rulers" by Desmond Morris   373
   Portrait: Kurt Lewin   383
   The Teacher   392
   The School   399
   Educational Problems   404

   12 PERSONALITY   409

   Factors in Personal Development   412
   The Measurement of Personality   418
   A Theory of Personality Development — Sigmund Freud   424
   Challenges to Personal Growth   428
   Portrait: Margaret Mead   430
   Reading: "Human Sex Roles" by Tom Alexander   440

13   ABNORMAL DEVELOPMENT AND THERAPIES   452

    Causes of Abnormal Behavior   455
    Neuroses   461
    Childhood Disturbances   461
    Portrait: Sigmund Freud   467
    Personality Disorders   472
    Psychoses   474
    Psychological Therapies   477
    Individual Psychotherapy   482
    Group Therapies   487
    Evaluation of Therapies   489

Part IV   Adolescence   493

    14   ADOLESCENCE   494

    A Definition of Adolescence   496
    Portrait: Erik Erikson   500
    Physical Development during Adolescence   507
    The Peer Group   511
    Vocational Choice   519
    Problems of Adolescent Development   523

Appendix   ADVANCED TOPICS IN CHILD DEVELOPMENT   534

    The Ethics of Studying Children   536
    A History of Child Psychology   537
    Some Statistics for Child Psychology   540
    The Scientific Methods   549
    Theories of Sensation   556
    Theories of Forgetting   561
    Some Theories of Grammars   563
    Theories of Emotion   567

Glossary   571
Selected Bibliography   584
Name Index   593
Subject Index   599

Fundamentals
of Child
Development

part I

The Bases of Human Development

(Photo by Erika Stone)

I Normal Human Development

Conception (0-9 months)
The Newborn (birth-1 week)
The Neonate (1 week-1 month)
The Infant (1 month-1 year)
  Growth of Sensory-motor Coordina-
    tion
  Formation of Social Interactions
    Verbal Communication
  Voluntary Behavior and Play
The Toddler (1 year-3 years)
  Beginnings of Independence
  Cognition and Language
  Social Relations
    Aggression
    Sex-role Development
The Preschooler (3 years-6 years)

Intuitive Thought
Development of Perception
Changes in Social Relations
  Nursery School
Personality Development
The School Child (6 years-12 years)
  Moral Development
  Personal Development
    Peer Groups and Teachers
    Prejudice
The Adolescent (12 years-17 years)
  The Growth Spurt
  The Development of Abstract Thinking
  Social Change
  Adolescent Values
Summary

All the world's a stage,
And all the men and women merely players:
They have their exits and their entrances;
And one man in his time plays many parts,
His acts being seven ages. At first the infant,
Mewling and puking in the nurse's arms.
Then the whining school-boy, with his satchel
And shining morning face, creeping like snail
Unwillingly to school. And then the lover,
Sighing like furnace, with a woeful ballad
Made to his mistress' eyebrow. Then a soldier,
Full of strange oaths and bearded like the pard,
Jealous in honour, sudden and quick in quarrel,
Seeking the bubble reputation
Even in the cannon's mouth. And then the justice,
In fair round belly with good capon lined,
With eyes severe and beard of formal cut,
Full of wise saws and modern instances;
And so he plays his part. The sixth age shifts
Into the lean and slipper'd pantaloon
With spectacles on nose and pouch on side,
His youthful hose, well saved, a world too wide
For his shrunk shank; and his big manly voice,
Turning again toward childish treble, pipes
And whistles in his sound. Last scene of all,
That ends this strange eventful history,
Is second childishness and mere oblivion,
Sans teeth, sans eyes, sans taste, sans every thing.

As You Like It

Human development
is a sequence of
stages.

Children change dramatically as they mature, a fact that this first chapter will illustrate, as the reader is introduced to the various stages of infancy, childhood, and adolescence. There is fair agreement among psychologists about the sequence of human development, but little consensus about the causes for these changes. The sequential stages outlined here should serve as a basic framework for understanding the course of human development. It is also with this framework in mind that the basic processes—like physiology, perception, learning, motivation, and so on—can be looked at and learned in detail. We begin with the earliest event in human development—the moment of conception.

Conception

Human life begins at
conception.

Human life begins when one of many available sperm from a male succeeds in penetrating the wall of an ovum (egg) inside the female (*see* Figure 1.1). The combination of material from the two parents, which determines what characteristics the new individual will inherit, begins a complicated sequence of development which will one day produce a mature human adult. The interval between conception and birth is called the *prenatal* period and on the average it lasts nine months. The prenatal stages of human development are: the *germinal phase,* which lasts from conception until two weeks, the *embryonic phase,* from two weeks to eight weeks (*see* Figure 1.2), and the *fetal phase,* from eight weeks to birth (*see* Figure 1.3). The germinal phase is a time when the fertilized egg travels down a

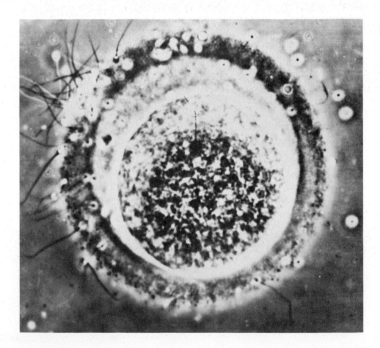

FIGURE 1.1
Living human ovum at the moment of fertilization. Note the entire fertilizing sperm in the egg proper at 11 o'clock. (Courtesy Landrum B. Shettles, M.D., F.A.C.S., F.A.C.O.G.)

FIGURE 1.2
The human embryo at twenty-one days.
(Courtesy Landrum B. Shettles, M.D.,
F.A.C.S., F.A.C.O.G.)

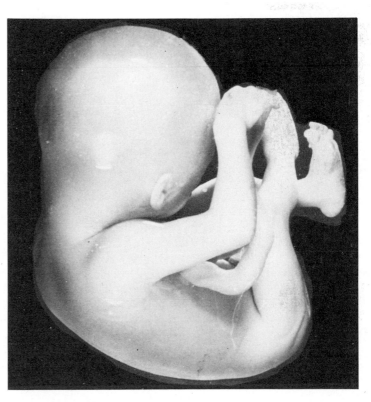

FIGURE 1.3
The human embryo at eighteen weeks.
(Courtesy Landrum B. Shettles, M.D.,
F.A.C.S., F.A.C.O.G.)

female Fallopian tube and implants itself in the wall of the mother's womb (uterus), where it will remain until birth. During the embryonic phase differentiation and maturation of major organ systems occur in the new human, while during the fetal stage of development before birth minor systems develop and general physical growth occurs. Little important behavior takes place during this prenatal period. Most descriptions of infant behavior begin with the characteristics that can be seen in the actions of a newborn baby.

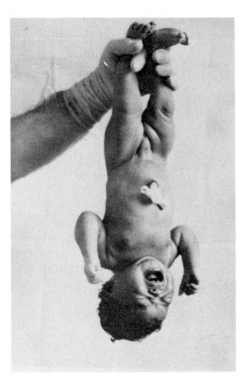

FIGURE 1.4
A full-term infant right after delivery.
(Courtesy Landrum B. Shettles, M.D., F.A.C.S., F.A.C.O.G.)

The Newborn

Newborn behavior is reflexive.

A newborn human enters this world with a cry (*see* Figure 1.4). It is well equipped to survive in a protected environment, but could not live on its own. For the most part, the behavior of a newborn is reflexive; that is, involuntary. For example, it does not have to be taught to suck in order to obtain food; it contracts its pupil to avoid bright light without anyone showing it how to do so, and it startles when a loud noise is sounded, grasps objects which are thrust into its hand, withdraws its body from painful stimuli, and if touched on one side of the face turns its head in that direction and roots for a nipple so as to suck — all by automatic response. These reflexes help the infant satisfy such basic needs as breathing, sleeping, eating and eliminating, and escaping from pain.

Simple reflexes handle many of these needs automatically; the remainder are satisfied in cooperation with the mother or father. Human babies are called newborns for about one week after birth, when they are recovering from the rigors of being born. After the first week the baby is called a neonate, until it is one month of age.

The Neonate

The neonate begins adaptation to life.

Several changes occur during the neonatal period. For one thing, the baby grows in physical size and its body proportions alter. Specifically, the average newborn in the United States weighs about 7.5 pounds and measures around 20 inches from head to toe. However, by the time it is one year old, a healthy infant weighs almost 20 pounds and averages 28 inches in length. At birth the baby's head accounts for almost one-fourth of its total length, but by the time the child is ten years old the head measures only about one-seventh of the total height. Near the end of the neonatal period, at about one month, an infant develops new skills, like the ability to remember what happened a few minutes before and the ability to become bored by repeated stimulation. Many psychologists believe that these new skills signal the beginning of memory.

The neonate shows classical conditioning.

Also during the neonatal period a baby begins to inhibit the reflexes when they are repeatedly stimulated, and it connects old reflexive responses to new stimuli by a process called classical conditioning (*see* Chapter 5). Many psychologists believe that this inhibition and classical conditioning of reflexes is the beginning of adaptation, and that these two processes signal a transition from passive reaction to more active interaction with the environment.

The next period of human development is called infancy and lasts from one month to around one year of age. During this time the baby's primary task is to coordinate the sensory abilities and the growing motor skills.

The Infant

Growth of Sensory-motor Coordination

The infant shows sophisticated sensory-motor abilities.

The most significant changes during this period are the growth of sensory-motor coordination and the formation of social attachments. On the basis of recent research psychologists now believe that infants are much more perceptually sophisticated than was formerly thought. We now know that infants are attracted by stimuli that move, are intense, or have contrasting areas of light and dark. Perhaps even more remarkable is the fact that around seven months of age, when the average baby begins to move about on its own, it possesses the ability to perceive three-dimensional space (*see* Figure 4.20). In all mammals depth perception is

FIGURE 1.5 As the child grows, he follows a typical sequence of motor development beginning by moving his head and limbs and finishing the first year of life by being able to walk.
(Featherkill Studio)

available to the organism when it begins to move about in the environment. Once they begin to move, all normal human babies follow a typical sequence of motor development, although the particular age for each stage varies among infants. The typical motor sequence begins with moving the head and limbs during the neonatal period; sitting up at about six months of age; crawling at around eight months; standing at about eleven months; and walking with help by one year of age (*see* Figure 1.5).

Visually-directed reaching matures by 1 year of age.

In addition to motor and sensory development, the coordination of perceptions and responses grows during infancy. One sensory-motor ability that has been studied in detail is looking at, reaching for, and grasping an object. Observers report that before about five months of age most babies simply stare intensively at an object when it is held in front of them, but they do not reach for it. However, by one year of age they actively reach for objects and can successfully grasp many of them on the first try. While the infant coordinates seeing and grasping, it also interacts socially.

Formation of Social Interactions

Smiling is a baby's first social act.

The infant's first social interaction is probably a smile of recognition of any object that resembles the human face. The face does not have to be well formed, because anything that is round, has two spots (like eyes) and a dark bit of hair on top will elicit a smile at this stage. All over the world parents are delighted by this smile of social recognition when their baby is about four months of age.

Fear of strangers appears around 8 months of age.

However, when this same infant is eight months old it will show strong signs of wariness or fright around strangers. Fear of strangers appears when the infant becomes attached to its parents (*see* Figures 1.6 and 1.7) and begins to differentiate strangers from those who are more familiar. Later, at about one year of age, the infant shows separation anxiety whenever its mother and father leave it alone in a strange place. Separation anxiety does not occur if a baby crawls away from its parents but has clear access to them. However, if the baby is in a strange room without the comfort of one or both parents, the one-year-old becomes noticeably frightened.

Cooing, crying, and smiling are the baby's first language.

VERBAL COMMUNICATION Next to smiling and eye-to-eye contact, the most important symbol of attachment for the infant is verbal communication. The baby begins making noises from the moment of birth. Its early communications are cries of discomfort or pain or hunger when it needs attention. At around two months of age the baby adds a second sound to its vocabulary: It coos when happy or excited. Both crying and cooing are innate responses to specific stimuli rather than language in a technical sense. Neither crying nor cooing has grammatical rules or meaning beyond a simple signification of mood. Also, these early signals of happiness or distress are controlled by the baby's internal state and are unrelated to its environment. We know this because deaf children show exactly the same patterns of early crying and cooing as children who can hear. However, at about three months of age, the hearing and deaf children begin to diverge in their development of language.

FIGURE 1.6
When an infant becomes attached to the adults around him, he may also become afraid of strangers. (Featherkill Studio)

FIGURE 1.7
Young animals, like this monkey, can become very attached to a comfortable cloth surrogate mother.
(Courtesy Harry F. Harlow, University of Wisconsin Primate Laboratory)

Babies babble at around six months of age.

At around six months of age babbling begins, and many parents notice that their infants begin experimenting with new sounds and sound combinations. Recording of infant's vocalizations during the period between six months and one year of age shows stretches of babbling longer than an hour in length, when a baby is simply babbling to itself, as if practicing the sounds which will be language. Some psychologists believe that although babbling is not yet language, it is the root of later language development. Probably babbling is related to speech development rather than to the acquisition of grammatical rules. Babbling is how the baby practices sounds and learns to relate these sounds to breathing, tongue movements, and other aspects of speech production. Even during this very early period, infants produce the sounds of all languages, and only later do they drop those which are not used in their own linguistic community. Children from all language groups begin making sounds in much the same way, and these early babbles are unrelated to what they hear. Vowels outnumber consonants during these early stages, but later consonants begin to dominate, because there are more of them. At the end of infancy the baby begins to construct sequences of sounds which will eventually form meaningful units of language. By one year the baby has distinguished vowels from consonants and begins to combine them into meaningful units like Ma Ma and Da Da. These first words appear around one year of age in all cultures; many psychologists and psycholinguists believe that their appearance is caused by maturation rather than experience. Although a one-year-old infant can say only a few simple words, it understands many things. In general, the child's comprehension of language is much more sophisticated than its ability to speak.

Voluntary Behavior and Play

Voluntary actions begin around seven months of age.

Near the end of infancy most babies begin to show voluntary behavior rather than just simple reactions to external stimuli. The psychologist Jerome Bruner argues that voluntary behavior requires the anticipation of a goal, the selection of a way to reach that goal, freedom from immediate sensory control, the ability to maintain a sequence of behavior, the skill to order responses, and the desired motor acts. Bruner believes that the seven-month infant can initiate and carry out voluntary acts like reaching for an object without having to see both his hand and the object.

Play is an important voluntary action.

One particularly important voluntary behavior is play. The basic function of play is not yet clearly understood. Some psychologists believe that play is important for later development of understanding and knowledge, while others think that children play to compensate for weakness or lack of skills. Much recent research has concentrated on the former, or cognitive, aspects of play. The common observation that children always examine a new toy first before using it supports the notion that play is directed toward understanding the world. Additional support for a cognitive theory of play comes from the fact that children who use toys imaginatively turn out to be more creative as adults than children who are not imaginative with toys. By the end of its first year of life, the baby knows that what it sees close at hand can also be touched, that sounds have meanings, and that parents or those who take care of them are important. In addition to sensory-motor coordination, language development, and social attachment the average one-year-old can move about on its own two feet, and so can enter the stage of toddlerhood, a remarkable time that lasts until the child is three years of age.

The Toddler

Beginnings of Independence

Independence begins around 1 year of age.

The interval between one and three years of age contains many of the greatest changes of an infant's entire life. This period marks the transition from the dependent infant to the independent child. During toddlerhood the child becomes mobile; no other achievement has quite the same impact on its life. Parallel with this increased ability to move about are the toddler's expanding social, linguistic, and cognitive abilities. During the second and third years of life the toddler shows signs of what will later be called intelligence, and constructs sentences of two or three words which have meaning and a grammatical structure. Along with the toddler's new found freedom of movement comes an ambivalence between being an independent bully or mother's baby. Toddlerhood is a time of contrast between brave ventures into the unknown and frantic flights back to mother's skirts.

Toddlerhood is a time of rapid growth.

Consider first what happens to the child's growth and motor abilities during toddlerhood. The average three-year-old is 38 inches tall and weighs about 33 pounds. During early life the limbs and trunk grow faster than the head and the resulting changes bring the child's proportions closer to adult shape. During toddlerhood he develops good large muscle control and strength, but his small muscles remain immature. As a consequence, the toddler is better at running than at picking up a pebble. Not only are the muscles growing at a rapid rate, but his lungs, heart, and circulatory system keep pace to give him increased energy and stamina. During toddlerhood the child acquires almost 80 percent of his total brain weight. Partly because of this physiological maturation, his motor and sensory coordination is improved, so he can make a stack of seven or eight blocks instead of the three or four of his earlier years. He can also begin to make crayon strokes on paper which are bolder and more continuous than the scribbles of a one-year-old.

Cognition and Language

Two-year-olds can symbolize.

The infant is preoccupied with acquiring sensory-motor coordination, but the toddler is more concerned with developing language and thought. For example, Jean Piaget, the Swiss psychologist, believes that by the end of the second year a young child can symbolize events with motor movements, perceptual images, and the beginnings of language. Professor Piaget also thinks that the toddler can use these new tools to generate solutions to problems and to begin manipulating events mentally rather than by physical trial and error. Once the toddler begins to use language and thought, psychologists cannot resist trying to measure his intellect.

Tests of toddler IQ do not correlate with adult intelligence.

Most tests for toddlers require him to follow verbal commands, recall strings of numbers or letters, and use thinking to solve simple problems. For example, the Stanford-Binet test asks the two-year-old to describe common objects, fit three blocks into matching holes in a form board, put together a simple puzzle, indicate the major parts of a doll's body, and repeat two digits spoken by the tester. Tests for toddlers are called intelligence measures, but they rely primarily on simple abilities; there is no significant relationship between the toddler's score on such a test and his adult IQ measure. Only after a child enters school does his intelligence during childhood correlate highly with his adult IQ. The tests for toddlers are also inaccurate because of poor motivation, distractability, and lack of interest in doing well.

Language grows rapidly in the second year.

Exciting evidence of a toddler's growing abilities comes with his language use during the second and third years of life. By the time he is two years of age the average toddler can use 250 words correctly; and at the end of three years he will utter as many as 1000 different words. Not only can the toddler use more words as he grows older but he begins to construct sentences with this expanding vocabulary. By the end of his third year the child can use three or four words in a single utterance. These early sentences contain two types of words: the pivot word, which is used to begin the sentence, and a string of possible X-words, which can appear after the initial pivot word. Example of two-word sentences are *Daddy go, Pretty Mommy, Hit it, See them.* Most of the child's vocabulary is composed of X-words, with only a few designated as pivot words in his early grammar. A main feature of this early grammar is its telegraphic form. Only important elements of the sentence are used, so the listener must interpret or replace missing parts.

Piaget believes that cognition develops before language.

There are many theories about the relation between language and cognition. For example, Piaget argues that cognition comes first and language develops from cognition. On the other hand, some psycholinguists believe that language is the first ability, and that cognition develops as an outgrowth of linguistic skill. Another theory argues that language and cognition develop independently and become coordinated as the child matures.

Social Relations

Social relations are important in toddlerhood.

During the second and third years of life a toddler's personal and social relations expand in range and complexity. Because the toddler is much more mobile he can interact with peers, parents, and objects. There is strong individual variation among toddlers' social and personal relations. Some are active and aggressive, while others are quiet and shy. These early years are critical times for the later development of personality, because the child is acquiring a sex role, aggressiveness, and curiosity or indifference about his social and cognitive environment. The toddler's family atmosphere strongly affects his self-concept. Depending partly on his parents and others in the home, he may see himself as a competent, desirable human being who is maturing normally, or as an incompetent, rejected, undesirable brat who is constantly failing to meet his parent's expectations. The two important determinants of a child's social and personal development are his genetic inheritance and his home environment. The child's genetic endowment partially determines whether he will be introverted or extroverted, and normal or neurotic. The family atmosphere of love or hate and control or permissiveness may

FIGURE 1.8
Toddlers imitate adults around
them and may even exaggerate
their actions.
(Magnum Photos)

modify these early genetic tendencies. Specifically, restrictive parents can produce dependency or neuroticism. By contrast, permissive parents are more likely to produce a healthy child if they are loving or a delinquent if they are hostile and rejecting.

Children identify with their parents.

A fundamental part of family life is the identification of a child with his parents or others in the home. In this way he incorporates values into his own character. Identification begins when the toddler starts to comment on the similarities between himself and his parents. He may notice that their eyes are the same color; one of them has the same haircut; and that the young child is beginning to look just like Mommy or Daddy. The toddler not only incorporates the actions and values of his parents into his own character, he exaggerates them. Some results of this identification with parents are the acquisition of a conscience, a sex role, and aggression. Consider how the parents might influence the development of aggression in the child.

Two-year-olds have frequent tantrums.

AGGRESSION.   Aggression by the toddler begins in response to socialization. Specifically, if he is subjected to severe toilet training or other restrictions, the child may try to retaliate by temper tantrums or verbal attacks. Temper tantrums are most frequent in the two-year-old, and they remain a major means of aggression for the next year. During the third year of life verbal attacks increase, as the child shifts from diffused rage into aggression aimed at the source of his frustration. The way in which a child reacts to frustration is determined by a number of variables: age, sex, frustration tolerance, amount of punishment or reward associated with aggression, and the models of parental aggression to which he has been exposed. In general, boys are more aggressive than girls; older children are more likely to aggress than their younger peers; children who are punished for aggression will often inhibit their anger, while children who are rewarded for expressing aggression or are exposed to models of aggression will imitate those models and produce many aggressive responses. Investigator Gerry Patterson and his colleagues found that in the nursery school aggression is often its own reward. They report that a permissive atmosphere leads children to increase their attacks on peers. However, they also discovered that children who counterattack the aggressor significantly decreased aggression against themselves compared with children who were passive when attacked. Apparently the aggressor will attack a safe victim if given the choice.

SEX-ROLE DEVELOPMENT.   Next to aggression, the most significant challenge facing the average toddler is his sex-role development. All babies come into the world with a chromosomal sex determination, and they gradually develop a hormonal sex pattern, a genital sexual development, and, finally, a social sex role. Usually, there is agreement among these various determinants of sex. However, if there is disagreement, then the social role acquired during the first three years of life seems to be the primary determinant of a person's sexual identity for life.

There are three important theories about sex-role development. One was suggested by Sigmund Freud and is called the identification theory of sex-role development. Another is based on social-learning theory; and the final hypothesis about sex-role acquisition is based on a cognitive model. Let us first consider Freud's theory and then look at the learning and cognitive theories of sex-role acquisition.

Sigmund Freud first used the term identification to explain sex-role development. He assumed that a child adopts the traits of his same-sexed parent, and that by identifying with the parent, the child acquires the sexual role of a male or female. Thus, Freud proposed that children acquire sex roles by identification with a parent or other model of appropriate behavior. The social-learning theorists adopted Freud's notion of identification, but proposed that instead of simply using the same-sexed parent as a model, the child acquires appropriate sex-role behaviors by being reinforced or rewarded when he acts like a man or she acts like a woman. In addition, the learning theorists assumed that little boys are discouraged from doing things which are considered feminine—like crying or grimacing when something hurts—and little girls are discouraged from climbing trees or playing rough-and-tumble games like boys. The other theory of sex-role development, the cognitive theory, assumes that

Sex roles begin in toddlerhood.

There are three theories about sex-role development.

Freud felt that sex roles develop by identification with parents.

the child first acquires the idea of boy or girl, and then develops other behaviors consistent with this notion of maleness or femaleness.

Cognitive theories of sex role exist.

The main difference between these theories is that the cognitive model assumes that a child acquires the idea of boy or girl first and then develops behaviors which are congruent with that idea; while the first two theories assume that behavior appears, and then the idea of male or female is derived from these behaviors. We will return to these theories in Chapter 12.

The 3-year-old has many adult traits.

By the time a toddler reaches three years of age he has begun to acquire the characteristics of an adult. He has rudimentary cognitive skills, social relations, a sex role, and a tendency to be aggressive or submissive in his interactions with others. In addition the toddler increases his motor and perceptual skills and has acquired a powerful tool for interacting with his world: language. Between three and six years of age the child matures and becomes independent enough to leave home for several hours a day, and finally he takes a huge step to maturity by beginning first grade in school. The path from toddlerhood to school is the preschool period.

The Preschool Child

Six years of age marks an important change in children's abilities.

Several important things happen between three and six years of age. During this interval we see a transition from the egocentric toddler into a practical six-year-old who is ready to begin reading, writing, and computing in the classroom. For many theorists of child development, six years of age marks a shift from primitive modes of thinking to more sophisticated cognitive processes. Piaget believes that the child shifts at about six years of age from prelogical to a logical understanding of relationships, which Piaget calls concrete operational thinking, and that this new, more powerful system of thinking allows the school-age child to comprehend problems which were beyond the abilities of his earlier years. Let us consider first how this cognitive transition happens, and then follow the preschool child's social, personal, and motor development through the nursery school years.

Intuitive Thought

The preschool period is characterized by intuition.

Piaget calls the period between three and six years of age the intuitive period of thought. He believes the preschool child is characterized by centration, attention to static states, and irreversibility of thinking. Specifically, centration is the tendency of a preschool child to concentrate his attention on one aspect of a problem and neglect other relevant parts. For example, suppose the preschool child is asked to make a comparison between the volume of water in a tall thin glass versus the volume of water in a short fat glass. He will center his attention on either the thinness of one container or the fatness of the other and will make his judgment on that basis, and be misled. Because he centers on only one aspect of the problem the child cannot see that the height and width of containers are interchangeable and compensate for each other.

Intuitive children are easily confused.

An example of attention to static states occurs when the child is confronted with two rows of five pennies. When these two rows are set up so that each penny in the first row is directly above a penny in the second row the mathematical process of transformation is operating. The intuitive child will be confused if the experimenter spreads one row of pennies so that it takes up a longer space than the other row. Even though he knew before the change that the two rows contained the same number of pennies, the preschool child will now be misled. He pays attention to the end state of increase in row length and remains unaware that the transformation of spreading does not change the number of pennies.

Preschool children cannot reverse their thoughts.

An example of irreversibility of thought occurs when the preschool child, confronted with a long thin container of water and a short fat container, cannot see that the water in the new, fat container could be poured back into the original container and would be the same amount. This inability to reverse his logic and reconstruct an original state hinders the preschool child's problem-solving ability. When he is able to decenter by taking in all parts of a problem, pay attention to states or transformations by judging with actual numbers, and is able to reverse his logical processes the child is ready for school and for concrete thinking rather than merely exhibiting intuition. In addition to developing more sophisticated cognitive abilities, the preschool child becomes better able to perceive, begins to acquire interpersonal skills, and increases his ability to communicate during these years.

We turn next to the development of perception, and then to social relations and personality development during the preschool years.

Development of Perception

Piaget believes that mental images begin at 3.

Piaget believes that children cannot form mental images of objects until the beginning of the third year of life. Because they lack mental imagery, Piaget has theorized that young children live in the perceptual present, without images from the past or conceptions about the future. However, when the preschool child acquires mental images, he begins to separate the past, the present, and the future into discrete stages, and thus becomes capable of more complex behavior.

Piaget studies children's thinking.

Piaget and his colleagues have studied the preschool child's abilities to use mental images in thinking. In one series of studies the researchers asked children to observe semicircular pieces of wire while the wire straightened and then asked the children to draw the wires as they would look in successive positions between semicircular and straight. The researchers found that children underestimated the length of a straight wire and were unable to draw successive stages of the transformation from curved to straight wire. To test whether this inability was related to motor skills or to perceptual understanding, Piaget then asked the children to select successive stages from curved to straight wires from among professionally drawn sketches. Most preschool children in the study could not select the correct sequence of the curved wire being transformed into a straight wire. Piaget believes this inability is due to concentration on static end states of the bent wires (centration).

Perception improves rapidly during preschool years.

The child's perceptual system rapidly improves during the preschool years. For example, he can form perceptual wholes from familiar items which are used to make up the whole. Specifically, suppose children are shown a tricycle which is composed of candy pieces in various shapes. The four-year-old child will recognize the tricycle, but will fail to note that the tricycle is constructed of candy pieces which are themselves objects. The older school-age child can easily recognize both the whole and its various parts.

The preschool child is empathetic.

In addition to increasing perceptual and cognitive abilities, the preschool child is also more sensitive to the needs and realities of other children. In particular, his ability to share the feelings of others, his conversations, and his personal perceptions of peers are more sophisticated and accurate than before. The toddler is egocentric and unable to see either the needs or wishes of others when he is confronted with them in social situations. However, during the preschool period children develop this empathy for the needs and desires of others and are able to hold reasonable conversations with other preschoolers.

Three-year-old children cannot empathize fear.

For example, Professor H. Borke read children of varying ages stories in which characters in the book were happy, frightened, or sad; then she asked the children to select pictured faces which would show how they thought the person in each story felt about what happened in the story. Her results showed that children's ability to correctly feel the emotions of others increased with age. Most three-year-old children in Borke's study could not choose correctly fearful or sad faces to fit the stories, although all children were able to choose happy faces appropriately. By the age of four years Borke found that a majority of children could correctly choose the happy, sad, or fearful face for each story. Thus, the preschool child is more complicated and social than the toddler, and his relations with his peers and parents reflect that increased complexity.

Most nursery-school programs begin when the child is 4 years of age.

Until around the age of four most children are guided and controlled by their parents or adults in the home, and have little chance to interact with peers or other adults outside of the home. But at four years of age many children begin to attend nursery school, and spend more time in the neighborhood playing with children or visiting important places like the fire station and the police station or water-treatment plants in the community.

Changes in Social Relations

Preschool children are social.

The outstanding social change during these preschool years is an increased interest in peers and playmates. The years from three to six produce changes in the child's social relations, play, and the social structure of the group. Numerous studies show that social relations increase in frequency and complexity as age increases. Specifically, the kinds of play in which children participate changes. The toddler engages in solitary or parallel play, where the child is by himself or plays next to but not with his peers. By contrast, the three-to-six-year-old begins cooperative and interactive play, in which he becomes an active member of a group and shares in group goals.

Peer groups are structured.

During these formative years a child becomes able to take the role of another and can fit into larger social relations. Because of this social development, peer groups change from loose, unstructured mobs into fairly rigid gangs. During the preschool years the role of leader and follower appear, and after four years of age, social hierarchies are evident in the social groups. Dominance-submission hierarchies happen in all human groups; they make their appearance during the preschool years all over the world. Boys establish a dominance hierarchy on the basis of strength by asking who is strongest or who is toughest? Most four-year-old boys are still fairly sure that each of them is the strongest member of the group, but by the time they are six years of age, boys pretty well agree on the dominance hierarchy of the whole group, and the egocentrism of the four-year-old is gone. There are several ways of determining dominance among children, but the surest sign of high status is the amount of time that lower members in a group spend watching higher-status members. Boys have been more interested in power and group hierarchies than girls.

Peer groups control children.

After about four years of age the peer group begins to exert powerful socializing influences on the preschool child, because to enjoy social relations a child must adjust his behavior to the group's expectations. To be a successful member of the group, a child must learn to share, to fend off aggression from other members of the group, and to compromise his own wishes. Peers reward those behaviors which they find good, and punish or reject those behaviors which they find bad by their standards. The peer group serves as a model of acceptable and unacceptable behaviors for the child to copy. Many children are introduced to peers in the nursery school.

Nursery schools teach social skills.

NURSERY SCHOOL An increasing number of preschool children attend nursery school. Most nursery schools are really social groups in which the preschool child had a chance to learn social relations and personal habits that will help him adjust to elementary school later on. In many cases the nursery school is the first introduction to a social group, and thus has a strong influence on his social and personal development. The modern nursery school has positive and negative effects on preschool children. On the positive side are:

1. The child becomes socially responsive, self-reliant, and independent of his parents.
2. The child grows more curious about the world and other people.
3. Nursery school gives the child a chance to develop language and social skills.

However, attendance at nursery school also has some undesirable effects, such as:

1. The child can imitate the aggression of other members in the group.
2. Emotional problems like neurosis, nightmares, or sleep disturbances may be called forth.

FIGURE 1.9 A nursery school provides social groups in which a preschool child can learn about social relationships.
(Featherkill Studio)

Personality Development

Teachers strongly affect children.

The effect of attending nursery school on a child depends primarily on the teacher. A sensitive, well-trained teacher can help an emotionally disturbed child overcome his problems and find a way into the group;

while an authoritarian teacher may have the opposite effect on a shy, sensitive preschooler. The teacher sets the stage for socialization in a peer group; and she has a significant effect on the group's aggressiveness. Also, the nursery school group can affect the child's self-concept. During his preschool years, the child is continuing to construct a self-image by becoming increasingly aware of his own feelings and abilities. One way the child learns to handle many of his emotions is through games. The game of "Run and Chase" is a universal scheme for childhood games. Many theorists of children's games argue that the child plays because he has a conflict about interpersonal relations and is trying to resolve his conflicts or emotional problems by playing them out. Pscyhologist Brian Sutton-Smith argues that there are sex differences in games. For example, he believes that females are more interested in games whose central theme is acceptance or rejection and he cites the "Farmer in the Dell" as an example. He also argues that boys play "Cops and Robbers" or similar games in which courage and skill are the main themes.

FIGURE 1.10 Some games, like "Farmer in the Dell," have acceptance and rejection as their central theme.
(Featherkill Studio)

Childhood fears help survival.

Childhood fears are essential to survival, but this emotion can interfere with adaptation if it is severe. Moderate fear keeps children away from automobiles, harmful situations, and dangerous animals. And as children mature, the intensity of their fear declines. Most preschool children also shift as they mature from a fear of objective things to a fear of imaginary things, like witches, the dark, and devils. Preschool children fear strange objects or people; they are afraid of falling and of loud noises; while near the end of the preschool period they are afraid of the dark, robbers, death, imaginary creatures, and being abandoned.

The School Child

Schools are competitive.

The overriding concerns of the school years are related to how a child adjusts to the competitive school situation, enforced peer interactions, and his own personal and moral needs. There is increasing uneasiness in the United States that the large, urban school system is not giving children a good education. To combat this problem, many educators have turned to the social sciences for procedures relating to cognitive skills, learning capacities, and the social and personal variables that apply to school achievement or adjustment.

The school child is able to think.

Some important work in cognitive development has been done by Piaget, who argues that several things happen to a child when he shifts from the intuitive to the concrete operational stage of thought, as we have seen. One new skill is the ability to consider more than one aspect of a situation at the same time. Another is the ability to ignore the perceptual aspects of a problem and concentrate on symbolic thinking. A third major skill of the school-age child is the ability to categorize information in several different ways. Finally, the school-age child is able to differentiate information better than his younger peers. Consider how these skills change the cognitive abilities of the school-age child.

School children understand conservation.

The mind of a school-age child is much more sophisticated and flexible than the cognitive system of the preschool child. For example, the school child can now decenter his attention and comprehend how the parts of a problem are interrelated. The school child can also see how one change may compensate for another and thus leave the total system unchanged. He now understands conservation of weight, matter, number, and size in the face of perceptual changes in shape, distribution, and arrangement of materials.

School-age children can reverse their thinking.

In addition, the school-age child is able to reverse his logical operations, so he can see that pouring something into one container can be reversed; thus he perceives that the change in shape does not change the amount of liquid. As another example, the school-age child understands that changing the arrangement of five pennies from a short to a long row does not alter the number of pennies. Generally, children master the conservation of quantity by seven years of age, conservation of weight by nine years of age, and conservation of volume by eleven years.

One effect of the child's increased cognitive ability is his shift from simple moral arguments to more sophisticated rules of ethics. This change has been studied most thoroughly by Lawrence Kohlberg in his experiments on the moral development of boys in several countries.

Moral Development

Moral development occurs in three stages.

Kohlberg argues that moral development occurs in three major stages, which he calls preconventional morality, conventional morality, and postconventional morality. He believes that during the preconventional stage children are guided by pleasure, pain, and the satisfaction of their own needs. However, in the next level of moral development, conventional morality, Kohlberg believes that children judge their actions in terms of being good and respecting authority. During the third level of moral development, postconventional morality, Kohlberg argues that the child is trying to find general principles which will govern his own actions and the actions of others. Kohlberg characterizes this stage as a legalistic period of development. Parallel with his moral and personal development, there is increased social sophistication and emotional development taking place in the school child.

Children change their rules of play with age.

During the school years a major change occurs in the child's attitude toward rules. During the earlier time of preschool play, the child was individualistic in his play rules. However, during the school years he becomes very rule-oriented and believes that all rules come from outside authorities. Finally, the child comes to recognize that rules can be made by the people who play the game; and that rules can be mutually agreed on and then used as the basis of interaction. His new understanding of the origin of rules is a major cognitive shift for the school-age child and reflects his increasing sophistication and his understanding of the world. These new cognitive abilities also affect his social relations.

During school, peer groups are segregated by sex.

In the school-age peer group boys play with other boys and girls play with girls. Boys tend to play strenuous games, which they see as masculine, and girls tend to play quieter, more feminine games. In addition to sex, social class and age determine the make up of the peer group in school. These groups exert several pressures on the school child, such as the dominance hierarchy, the group goals, and the group atmosphere. Mem-

FIGURE 1.11 The school child must adapt to dominance hierarchies in the group and become either a leader or a follower.
(Featherkill Studio)

bers must respect the dominance hierarchy within a group and either become leaders or followers. In addition, group members must conform to the morals of the group and develop a cohesiveness with insiders and hostility toward outsiders. Finally, the groups' atmosphere determines the members' satisfaction. Democratic groups are most satisfying to members.

Personal Development

School years are a time for mastering technical skills.

Several psychologists have theorized about the personal development of children during their school years. Freud labeled this period the latent stage of personality development, because he believed that the school-age child is preoccupied with the challenges of school rather than with play or sex. Erik Erikson called this time the stage of industry versus inferiority, because he believes that during the school years the primary challenge of development is the child's concept of himself. Erikson argues that the child must either master the social and technical skills to succeed in school or face feelings of inferiority. Due to this emphasis on competence development during the school years, the study of intelligence and achievement motivation has been particularly important. For the first time, the child's intelligence can be accurately measured and the Intelligence Quotient (IQ) score he receives at the age of eight years is closely related to his adult intelligence. In addition to IQ, the school-age child's ranking on a scale of dominance/submissiveness can be accurately measured and remains stable in adult life. The leaders and followers of the future begin to emerge and stabilize their ranks during this period. Leaders are characterized by better health, greater physical activity, more aggression, higher IQ, and more achievement motivation as compared with followers. Teachers believe that leaders are better adjusted to school and the community than followers are.

Dominance and friendships develop in peer groups.

PEER GROUPS AND TEACHERS   In addition to dominance and competition during the school years, peer friendships also grow. They become more stable and friendships develop between those of the same sex and age. Friendliness, compliance with social rules, high self-esteem, moderate aggression, and good social status are also important in the forming of friendships. However, boys tend to like friends who are somewhat aggressive, while girls seem more interested in friends who comply with social rules and are emotionally sensitive.

Teachers strongly influence school children.

A significant factor—other than parents and peers—that affects the school-age child is his teacher. Several investigators have studied the personality characteristics of teachers and measured their influence on children's performance and happiness in school. Generally, teachers who are independent, impulsive, and cold toward children have adverse influences on the child's school performance and personal adjustment. By contrast, self-controlled teachers who are methodological, pragmatic, calm and sensitive call forth good academic performance from students and have happy classrooms. Most pupils grow and work better under the influence of a warm, reasonable teacher than a cold, authoritarian one. Children who are exposed to authoritarian or rejecting teachers find the school situation makes them very anxious. Generally, anxious children also score low on measures of achievement and intelligence. Whether this correlation is caused by the fact that such children are not really very bright, and thus they have difficulty in school, or whether their anxiety somehow results in lowered intelligence and achievement scores is a matter for debate.

Prejudice harms children.

PREJUDICE   A source of trouble for some children in school is the prejudice of their teachers and peers. Consider what we know about this destructive attitude and its effect on children.

Prejudice means prejudgment.

Prejudice is the formation of an opinion about another person without sufficient facts; literally it means prejudgment. In the United States, prejudice has come to mean the rejection of certain minority group members simply because they have certain characteristics—like a different skin color or a different linguistic history. Generally, Black Americans, Mexican-Americans, and immigrants from Puerto Rico are most strongly affected by prejudice in the U.S. Since prejudice may have a detrimental effect on the development of minority children, several psychologists have studied its causes. They find that prejudice is present in most children when they reach kindergarten, and by the time these same children are in junior high school their attitudes are very similar to those of their parents. One study conducted in England measured the skin-color preference of children in middle childhood and found that black children's preferences for dark or light skin were equal, while white children's preferences were for light skin.

Prejudiced children have strong beliefs.

A recent study by Reed Tuddenham showed that both black and white children conform more to group decisions when the majority of the children in the group are white compared with groups in which the majority of children were black. Early investigators of prejudice measured the personal behaviors of prejudiced and nonprejudiced people, and found that prejudiced children have stronger beliefs about sex-role differences, more doubts about their own abilities, and a more rigid personality structure than children who are judged to be less prejudiced. In addition, the parents of prejudiced children are more likely to use harsh punishment and show less affection for their children compared with parents who are not prejudiced.

Prejudice is difficult to change.

How can prejudice be changed—for surely it must be? Recent measurements of children in integrated and segregated summer camps give some clues. For example, Paul Mussen found that prejudice increased in some children, but decreased in others, following experiences with minority-group children. When the counselor of the group actively encouraged all the children to be more friendly and get along with each other, the children actually became friendlier. Thus, it is possible to decrease prejudice if children are given a chance to interact and are taught less-prejudiced attitudes about minority children.

Adolescence means change.

The next stage of human development with which we are concerned is adolescence, the years from twelve to seventeen. We turn now to the average American teenager, with his physical and sexual maturity, his choices of careers, and his problems of competition, of dropping out, and of drugs.

The Adolescent

Adolescence is a time of challenge.

During the period of adolescence, begun by puberty and ended by adulthood, there are marked social, personal, and physical changes. The challenges of this stage are many: the adolescent must accept a more mature personal role, be able to think logically, develop a masculine or feminine sex role, and establish good relations with members of the group. Some social scientists believe that adolescence is universally a time of stress and strife. However, this stress seems not to be a necessary result of physical and emotional maturation. Probably the strain comes from the long interval during which the adolescent feels personally ready to accept independence and social responsibility, but actually remains financially dependent on his parents. There is a prolonged educational or training period generally accepted in the U.S. as a prelude for good jobs or professions. This waiting period, Erikson believes, brings a crisis of identity, during which the young person must struggle to establish his own self-concept in the face of social, physical, and emotional changes which challenge him. Erikson believes that some persons succumb to the stresses of adolescence and become neurotic or even psychotic, but he also believes that the vast majority will meet this challenge and develop into healthy and productive adults. The most outstanding changes which occur during adolescence are the growth spurt and sexual maturity.

The Growth Spurt

Girls mature earlier than boys.

Professor J.M. Tanner has studied the physical maturation of many adolescents and reports that females begin their adolescent growth spurt about two years earlier than do males. Girls generally reach their peak growth rate during the twelfth year, while boys reach theirs during the fourteenth year on the average. Growth includes larger muscles, longer bones, and the loss of fat.

Sexual development accompanies physical growth.

Associated with this rapid physical growth is the maturation of sexual characteristics. Again, girls begin their sexual development earlier than boys. The maturation of sexual characteristics for girls is fairly uniform, although the particular ages at which each stage is reached varies from female to female. The first sign of female sexual maturation is the appearance of breast buds at around eleven years of age. Next comes pubic hair, then an enlargement of the uterus and vagina, and finally the onset of menstruation, called the menarche. Menarche usually occurs during the thirteenth year, but can happen as early as ten or as late as seventeen. It is a sign that the uterus is mature, although the young female is usually not fertile for another year or so after the beginning of menstruation.

Adolescent boys also show a standard sequence of maturation. Generally, males begin to mature sexually with a rapid growth of the testes and scrotum; then comes an enlargement of the prostate gland and an increase in the secretion of male sex hormones, like testosterone. In addition to primary sexual characteristics like the development of the testes and penis, secondary sexual characteristics like a beard, pubic hair, and a deeper voice also occur during adolescent sexual maturation. Boys also vary in the age of maturation, and the effects of early or late sexual growth are different for boys and girls. Generally, boys who mature *early* are considered sociable, dominant, conforming, and secure in their vocational choices, compared with males who mature later. By contrast, girls who mature *late* are considered more feminine and socially well-adjusted than their early maturing peers.

The Development of Abstract Thinking

Besides physical changes the adolescent also experiences some remarkable cognitive changes during this period. Outstanding among these is the development of abstract thinking.

Piaget has proposed that the final stage of human intellectual development is the ability to think abstractly and logically. He calls this the stage of formal thinking, and believes it is characterized by an ability to understand the method of experimentation, the implications of various tests, and the meaning of experimental results. For example, Piaget and Barbel Inhelder performed this experiment on groups of children aged seven, eleven, and fifteen years. The task for all children was to determine which of four factors or their combinations exerted an influence on the frequency of a pendulum's swing. The four choices were:

1. The length of the string holding a weight.
2. The weight of an object.
3. The height from which the object on the end of a string was released.
4. The force with which the weight on the end of the string was pushed on the first swing.

As all physicists since Galileo know, only the length of the string has an effect on the frequency of a pendulum's swing. The children's answers were recorded by the experimenters. Piaget and Inhelder found that chil-

Sexual maturity follows a standard sequence.

Adolescents can think abstractly.

Piaget calls the final stage formal thinking.

A pendulum's swing changes with length.

dren of seven years of age were not able to understand the problem and could not perform the experiments necessary to decide whether length, weight, height, or force of the pendulum affected the frequency of oscillation of the pendulum. By the time these children had reached the age of eleven years, they performed a little better. Older children were able to do some simple experiments—like varying the length of the string to see if it had an effect—but they did not *independently* vary length, weight, height, and force, so their conclusions were almost always wrong. As you might guess, sometimes scientists also make this mistake with an untested hypothesis. By contrast, many children in the formal operations stage were able to perform several experiments, and one fifteen-year-old girl did all the experiments independently to show that only the length of the string was an important factor in determining the frequency of oscillation of a pendulum.

Most adolescents do not understand the scientific method.

Thus, even by the age of fifteen years most adolescents do not completely understand the relation between experimental facts and theoretical expectations. Yet increased cognitive abilities affect the adolescent's self-concept, because he is forced to re-examine many of his beliefs and values and change them in the light of his now more powerful cognitive abilities. The result of this mental re-evaluation is a more consistent cognitive system and an increased ability to plan for the future and profit from the past.

Social Change

Maturation brings increased responsibilities.

The most important social changes during adolescence are increased personal responsibility, preoccupation with education and vocational planning; stronger awareness of political processes; and a growing sophistication about friendships, peer-group interactions, dating, sexual behaviors, and marriage. This period usually brings the beginning of dating, and possibility of sexual relations with its accompanying joys and responsibilities and eventual marriage. Adolescence marks the end of single-sex social groups and the beginning of sexual exploration between males and females. There is some indication that the dating game is being replaced by more serious interpersonal relations between modern couples.

Maturity leads to sexual experimentation.

Generally, dating begins at about twelve years of age and at first is socially oriented. Later, sexual experimentation becomes part of the dating situation. Because most males have experienced stronger sexual urges than females, the constraints on sexual behavior are generally placed on young females in American society, although this, too, may be changing. The way young males and females adjust to their increased sexual awareness is regulated by several personal, social, and biological factors. The main biological factor is the sex of the individual; the main sociological factor is social class; while the foremost personal factor seems to be the acceptance of a personal sex role and the success with which the adolescent can meet an individual need within the constraints of a social/sexual role.

Kinsey says that males attain maximum sexual activity when they mature.

Young males reach sexual maturity about two years later than females, but they reach their sexual peak much earlier than young females seem to do. For example, Alfred Kinsey, the sex researcher, reported in 1948 that boys attain maximum sexual activity just a few years after sexual maturity, while females in the U.S. do not reach their maximum sexual activity until around thirty years of age. Whether this reflects social constraint or different biological processes in the two sexes is not yet known. Possibly both, because young females in this society are subjected to stronger sexual constraints during their early years and thus they may need more time to reach full sexual activity.

Social class affects sexuality.

There are also social class differences in premarital sexual activities of males and females. For example, young middle-class males most often masturbate or pet to orgasm, but engage in premarital sexual intercourse less often than lower-class males.

Premarital sexuality is increasing.

However, the sexual values of adolescents seem to be changing. Recent surveys suggest that over 40 percent of unmarried American women have engaged in premarital sexual intercourse before the age of nineteen. Also, although many of them know about birth-control methods, only a small percentage of these young women used birth control to prevent pregnancy. These statistics indicate a need for better access to birth-control information and equipment among young unmarried American females.

Adolescents want honesty.

When American adolescents are asked if they believe there has been a shift in sexual morals over the last generation, they often say no, that they are only more honest about what has been happening all along.

Adolescent Values

Many believe that Americans are hypocritical.

Adolescence is a time to question one's self-concept and values. Numerous studies find there has been a shift from authoritarian to more democratic approaches to social and political questions among adolescents. In addition, many surveys find that modern youth is cynical about a number of the traditional values of the U.S. culture. A good many young people believe that those who control this country are often corrupt and hypocritical. This might suggest that adolescents favor radical change in the values and institutions of our society, but that is apparently not the case. Most surveys suggest that the modern teenager is interested in personal, material rewards and that they value moral virtues like honesty, sincerity, and loyalty to country and friends. Most adolescents also claim a fundamental faith in U.S. institutions, but have little faith in political parties, the press, television, and organized labor.

Problem youths receive most attention.

However, there are some adolescents who receive a good deal of attention because they are much more radical and vocal than the majority. Some of the dissident youths are political activists; some are school dropouts; others are delinquents and drug-users. Consider what we know about these four divergent groups.

FIGURE 1.12 Most studies show that only a few students are political activists. Most students are passive and uninvolved, more concerned about their social relations, grades, and future careers than about active political protest. (Wide World Photos)

Only a few students are political activists.

Most studies of political activism show that only a few students participate, while a good deal of the student body remains passive. Less than 10 percent of the students have been involved in protests, and most protests have occurred on only a few campuses. The main characteristics of student activists are their commitment to high moral values, their liberalism, and their social consciences. The majority of students are not involved in active political protests, and are concerned about their career, grades, and social relations.

Some students just drop out.

A small proportion of students do not stay in the campus community at all; they drop out of high school or college. This dropout rate is highest among urban minority slum-dwellers. The cultural, social, familial, and intellectual environment, added to the economic condition in which they live, often causes an adolescent from the slums to reject education as a way to get ahead. Typically, the dropout has a long history of failure in school and difficulty on the playground. He is often not accepted in his peer group and tends to associate with other potential dropouts. The result is a gang of academically unqualified and unpopular adolescents who encourage each other to leave school. Once the adolescent drops out, he is also more likely to become delinquent.

To understand the magnitude of our juvenile delinquency problem,

Half of all those arrested are juveniles.

consider that half of all the arrests in the United States for theft were of adolescents between eleven and seventeen years of age. Crimes like murder, rape, and aggravated assault are rarely committed by young teenagers, and the frequency of these more serious crimes increases with age.

Urban minority males are most often delinquent.

An urban, minority male is often a delinquent. In addition to lower economic conditions, some psychologists argue that poor paternal identification accounts for a significant amount of delinquency.

Drugs vary C.N.S. excitation.

Drug abuse is also often associated with adolescence. Some authorities point out that a large percentage of young people say they have used drugs, and that this same statement can be made about their parents who set the stage for the abuse of drugs by using caffeine, cigarettes, alcohol, and sleeping pills. Some drugs raise the level of excitation in the central nervous system, while others depress activity in the C.N.S. Most campaigns to control drugs have used scare tactics to frighten children away from marijuana. But there has been little success in such campaigns.

Adolescence can be a positive period.

Perhaps the economic dependence of adolescents in the U.S. will be used by them as a period in which to evaluate their futures and the future of the society in which they live. There are signs of health and of positive change from the Victorian repressiveness of the post-World War II years among our youth. Perhaps the rebellion—active or merely thoughtfully passive—will make for more well-adjusted young adults in the future.

SUMMARY

Chapter 1 viewed human development as a sequence of discrete stages. During each stage the child is busy practicing and consolidating his skills and preparing to move on to the next plateau of human maturation. The particular stages of human development are somewhat arbitrary; the chapter presented one outline of human maturation. The first stage begins with conception and covers the period of prenatal growth. The second stage occurs at birth and is followed by infancy, toddlerhood, and the preschool experiences of nursery school. A major transition occurs around age six when the child enters school and comes under the influence of teachers and peers. The last stage of human development covered in this book —but by no means the final period of human maturation—is adolescence. This time of storm and stress in American society brings problems of sex-role development, physical growth, and the acquisition of abstract thinking skills and vocational choices. These stages should be used as a framework for the next several topical chapters.

SUGGESTED ADDITIONAL READINGS

Douvan, E., and J. Adelson. *The Adolescent Experience.* New York: Wiley, 1966.
Erikson, E.H. *Childhood and Society,* 2nd ed. New York: Norton, 1963.
Freud, S. *Civilization and Its Discontents.* New York: Norton, 1930.

2 The Biological Bases of Development

The Mechanisms of Evolution
The Evolution and Development of the
      Human Nervous System
   Vertebrate Evolution
   Development of the Human Central
      Nervous System (CNS)
Conception
Genetics and Behavior
   Genotype and Phenotype
   Genetic Mechanisms
      Single and Multiple Gene In-
         heritance
   Behavior Genetics
      Human Behavior Genetics
      Twins and Genetics
Stages of Prenatal Development
   The Germinal Phase
   The Embryonic Phase
   The Fetal Phase
Prenatal Influences
   Maternal Emotions

Maternal Nutrition
Drugs
   Smoking
Maternal Infections
Maternal Sensitization: Rh
   Factors
Maternal Age
Timing of Prenatal Influences
Birth
   Premature Birth
   Multiple Births
The Newborn
   Physiological Changes
      Circulation
      Digestion
      Immunity
   Newborn Behavior
      The Birth Cry
      Sleep
   The Newborn Brain
Summary

PREVIEW

Since today's humans are the product of a long evolutionary history many stages of our development now seem useless until they are placed within a biological context that highlights their evolutionary function (Darwin, 1859). For example, while the baby is growing in its mother's womb it first develops gill slits and then transforms these slits into ribs. Later, the human newborn can swim and support his entire weight by a grasp reflex of the arms and hands. These amazing inborn abilities serve no purpose in the present day, but their appearance during early human growth is easily understood when we recall that all life probably originated in the sea and that our evolutionary ancestors spent millions of years roaming the savannah in small uncivilized groups. Infant survival in a small mobile group would require that the baby be able to cling to its mother while she fed or fled. Thus, one way to begin the study of human development is through evolution and the biological bases of behavior.

An important question that any student of behavior might ask about our development is: How much human potential is controlled by our *biological* history, and what is the range of *environmental* influence on these biological processes? This complex and controversial question has appeared again and again in the history of developmental psychology. Chapter 2 provides some evolutionary background, a little behavior genetics (hereditary actions), and discusses some physiological or normal processes that are important for early growth. Later chapters will examine the interaction of biological constraints and environmental influences in other areas of development.

Man's biological
nature is important.

No matter what theoretical orientation a student of behavior prefers he should not ignore the biological nature of human development. Humans evolved through a long and difficult process of natural selection and they survive today precisely because their biological mechanisms meet the challenge of living and growing. Thus, all students of human development can profit from a survey of the evolution and present status of human physiological processes.

Chapter 2 covers
evolution and devel-
opment.

This chapter traces the evolution and development of the human central nervous system, the effects of genetics (our physical inheritance) on human behavior, the stages and influences of development before birth, the birth process and the characteristics of a human newborn.

The Mechanisms of Evolution

Evolution is based on
genetic variation and
selection.

Evolution requires two things: genetic variation from generation to generation and a mechanism of *selection*. Most human genetic variation is produced by sexual recombination of genes, meaning characteristics inherited from both a mother and a father. During conception, genes, which carry our hereditary characteristics, come from two parents and combine to produce a single new individual who is both similar to his parents and a unique person as well. Other genetic variation is generated by mutations which are random accidents in the reproduction of genetic material. Unhappily, most mutations are lethal, but occasionally a useful new trait can result. Scientists believe that mutation is primarily responsible for the development of new traits. Variability is produced by sexual recombination and mutation; but not all organisms survive and multiply. Those organisms which reproduce pass their *genotypic* characteristics (those traits inherited from each parent) to the following generation, and this competition for survival determines the course of natural selection.

The Evolution and Development of the Human Nervous System

Man has kept his
older control systems.

The complexities and contradictions of human perception, emotion, and thought result from man's competing control systems. Rather than discarding older control centers during the course of evolution, vertebrates such as humans have simply added more and more complex information-processing packages on top of earlier ones. The first animal control system was chemical, and chemical control is still the main mechanism used by multicellular organisms like the sponge. Even man uses chemical information transmission in his glandular system (such as growth hormones from the pituitary gland). The next step up the evolutionary ladder was a nerve net with specialized cells that transmitted information in all directions (*see* Figure 2.1). In fact, man's gut contains this kind of a primitive nerve net. The third stage of evolution produced a ladder-shaped nervous system with fibers that are collected in two cords and cell bodies

FIGURE 2.1
The Portuguese Man-o-War has an extremely primitive neuron arrangement.
(National Audubon Society, Robert Hermes)

that are concentrated toward the organism's head (*see* Figure 2.2). As an added feature, the ladder-shaped nervous system contains polarized nerve cells that transfer signals only one way. This one-way circuitry makes increasingly complex behavior possible. Beyond the ladder network evolution divides into invertebrate external skeletons and vertebrates' internal skeletons. Since humans have an internal skeleton, vertebrate evolution and development is more relevant to human development. There has been a gradual increase in the brain/body weight ratio of animals as they have evolved and an enormously rapid increase occurred during man's late evolutionary history.

Vertebrate Evolution

The vertebrate CNS contains three parts.

The nervous system of a primitive vertebrate, the dogfish shark, has a brain containing three parts: forebrain, midbrain, and hindbrain. The shark's forebrain controls digestive and muscle functions and acts as a sensory relay which transmits information from receptors to higher centers of the brain. Its midbrain processes visual information; while the hindbrain is concerned with balance, coordination, movement and the control of breathing, swallowing, and heartbeat. The vertebrate spinal cord is a sensory-motor cable that relays information to and from other parts of the body. Three further stages of vertebrate evolution beyond

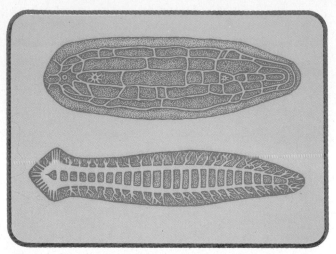

FIGURE 2.2
A simple nerve net and two laddlerlike cords, with some concentration of neural cell bodies in the head region, make up the nervous system of flatworms.
(After Simpson *et al.,* 1957)

Nerve Net and Ladder Nervous System in Flatworm

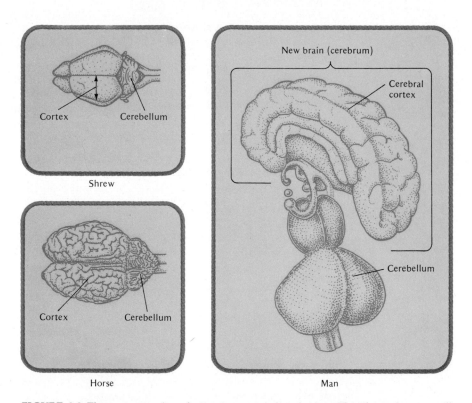

Shrew

Horse

Man

FIGURE 2.3 Three stages of evolution in mammalian brains. The shrew has a small cortex, while the horse cortex is larger but still small compared to man's massive cortical brain.
(After Simpson and Beck, 1965)

this shark are represented by the brains of a shrew, a horse, and a human as shown in Figure 2.3.

Nervous systems
operate differently.

Vertebrate central nervous systems operate differently at various stages of evolution. For example, visual processing is located in the midbrain among fish, while most human visual processing occurs in the cortex, the outer layer of the cerebrum and cerebellum. Between lower vertebrates and humans there is a gradual shift of sensory processing to higher centers of the brain. This shift in perceptual processing is easy to demonstrate by removing areas of the brain in various animals. For example, the

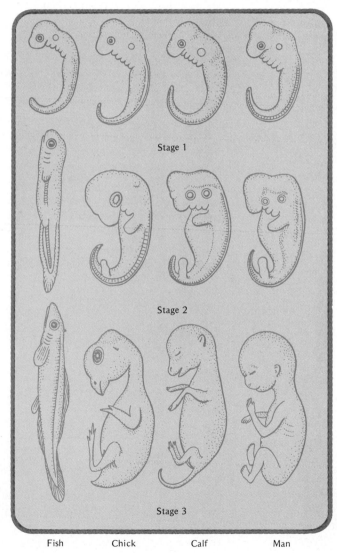

Stage 1

Stage 2

Stage 3

Fish   Chick   Calf   Man

FIGURE 2.4
Similarities in the structure of various embryos of the fish, chick, calf, and the human being at three stages of development.
(After Romanes, 1896)

removal of all cortical tissue from a fish has no effect on its vision. However, among reptiles and birds, removal of the cortex disrupts pattern vision; but leaves position, distance, and brightness perception unaffected. Further up the vertebrate branch of evolution, cats and dogs without a visual cortex can discriminate only brightness. And, if a human's visual cortical areas are removed, only the pupillary reflex remains. Human beings are completely blind without a cortex.

Development of the Human Central Nervous System (CNS)

Human development recapitulates evolution.

In the course of human development a baby's brain recapitulates, in abbreviated form, the evolution of the vertebrate nervous system. Some stages are short, while others are skipped; but the human evolutionary heritage reappears roughly in the stages of human brain development (*see* Figure 2.4). The main sources of information about early development of the embryo (the first two to eight weeks after conception) are therapeutic abortions and natural accidents. Observations under natural and sometimes controlled conditions have given us a rough understanding of early development of the central nervous system.

The early human brain is only a tube.

Figure 2.5 shows three stages of development in the human embryonic brain. Note the clear parallels between vertebrate evolution and the embryonic development of man's brain. During early stages of human central nervous system development the brain is in the shape of a long tube with bunches of neural or nerve cells. Later in the course of development the cerebral cortex begins to dominate the central nervous system of the human and starts its growth back over the lower brains. By the fourth fetal month (the next stage after the embryo) the cortex of the new brain completely dominates the other lower control centers of the human CNS.

Human development skips some evolutionary stages.

So we see that human development roughly parallels the course of vertebrate evolution. Many false starts were lost and some shortcuts taken in the course of modern human development. Nevertheless, there are clear parallels between the various stages of vertebrate evolution and the course of human development, and these parallels explain some of the complications of our development and add to the puzzle of Man.

Conception begins life.

Now that you know something about man's evolutionary heritage and early development, consider how the whole process starts. Human development begins the moment a single male sperm fertilizes a female ovum.

Conception

An ovum is released every 28 days.

Figure 2.6 shows a schematic diagram of the human female reproductive system. Once approximately every 28 days, usually in the middle of the female menstrual cycle, one or occasionally more ova or eggs reach maturity and are released from an ovary into a Fallopian tube and begin

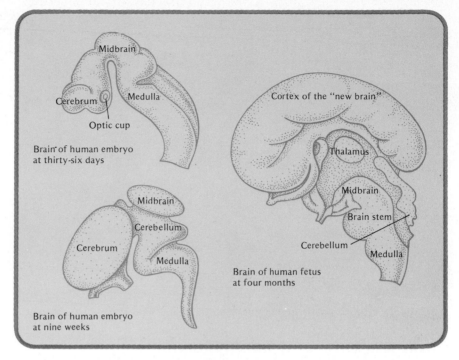

FIGURE 2.5 Three stages of human embryonic brain development. Note that this development parallels vertebrate brain evolution.

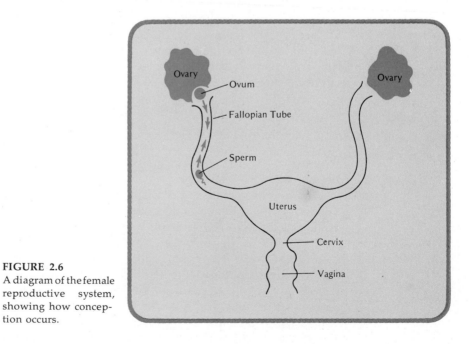

FIGURE 2.6
A diagram of the female reproductive system, showing how conception occurs.

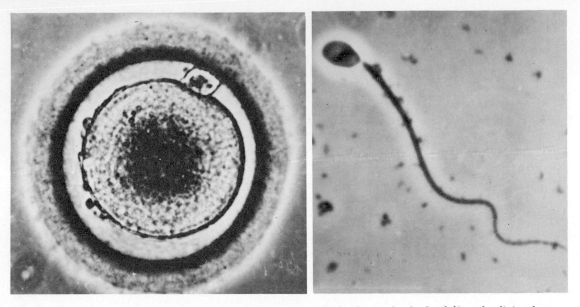

FIGURE 2.7 A living human ovum with the first polar body (*left*) and a living human sperm (*right*).
(Courtesy Landrum B. Shettles, M.D., F.A.C.S., F.A.C.O.G.)

to move toward the uterus or womb. Generally, it takes about five days for a released ovum to reach the uterus. During its descent down the Fallopian tube the mature egg may encounter a male sperm if the female has been sexually active (*see* Figure 2.7). If the ovum is fertilized it will continue into the uterus and attach to the uterine wall. If the egg is not fertilized, it will disintegrate in the uterus and be discharged during the next menstruation. At conception, male-producing sperm are more likely to penetrate an egg than female-producing sperm (1.3 to 1). However, male babies are aborted more frequently, so there are only 107 male births for every 100 females. This more rapid male loss continues throughout human life.

An ovum is about 1/200th of an inch.

The mature female egg is the largest cell in the human body, but it is still only about 1/200th of an inch in diameter. Once fertilized, the ovum starts to grow and cell division begins within twenty-four hours.

Prenatal development contains three stages.

The period of development from conception to birth is usually divided into three stages: The first is called the germinal; the second embryonic; and the third is called the fetal phase. The germinal phase covers the period from conception until the zygote (fertilized egg) is firmly implanted in the wall of the uterus. Implantation typically occurs about two weeks following conception. A second phase, the embryonic, covers from two to eight weeks and is the period when differentiation of the major

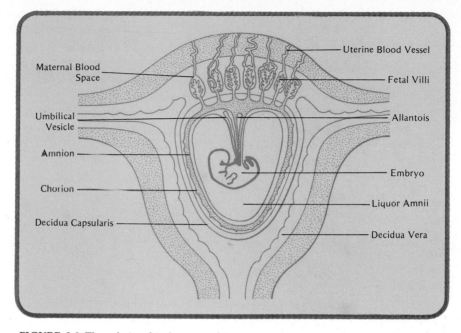

FIGURE 2.8 The relationship between the uterus, membrane, and embryo during early pregnancy.
(After Carmichael, 1933)

organs takes place (*see* Figure 2.8). The third phase, from eight weeks until birth, is for the growth and finer differentiation of the organism.

Early ovists believed the egg contained a small man.

Prior to the nineteenth century there were many notions about how human life begins. Medieval artists showed the human germ cell as simply a small man with all his human features intact. In the late seventeenth and early eighteenth centuries biologists proposed two hypotheses. One group believed that the mother's egg contained a prefabricated baby. They were called the ovists. Another group said that the sperm contained a preformed man, and they were called homunculists. In 1759 the German embryologist Caspar Wolff proposed that both the egg *and* the sperm were necessary for life (Needham, 1959). By the beginning of the nineteenth century Carl von Baer viewed a fertilized egg under his microscope; and later on conception itself was photographed.

Once conception occurs, a complex series of events determined by our genes begins. Consider what we know about human genetics.

Genetics and Behavior

Darwin sparked interest in heredity.

Two important events in the nineteenth century sparked our interest in the genetic determinants of behavior. One was Charles Darwin's publication of his books *On the Origin of Species (1859)* and *The Descent of*

Man (1871), which proposed that more complex forms of life emerged through mutation, genetic variation, and natural selection (see the opening pages of this chapter). Darwin's theory of evolution solved the mystery of man's origin, but created another problem. How do parental characteristics get passed on to their offspring? Darwin spent the last years of his life trying to answer this question.

Many thought that genes blend.

A common belief in Darwin's time was that the genes of parents blend. Darwin recognized that a mixing process would very quickly dilute all individual variation, but he did not suggest an alternative genetic mechanism.

Mendel studied sweet peas.

At almost the same time that Darwin was publishing his famous books, an obscure Austrian monk named Gregor Mendel began some studies of the garden pea. His results, which were reported to the Brunn Society for the Study of Natural Science in 1865, constituted the second great genetic advance of the last century.

Mendel's work was rediscovered.

The mechanism of heredity was essential to the theory of evolution, so scientists were becoming increasingly interested in it. Finally, in the year 1900 Mendel's work was rediscovered and presented to the scientific world. He had discovered the basic laws of heredity.

Mendel inferred the existence of genes.

Mendel never saw a gene; instead he inferred his laws on the basis of some simple experiments with garden peas. He began with peas that were either smooth or wrinkled. He found one variety that would produce only smooth peas when self-fertilized; and another variety that produced only wrinkled peas when self-fertilized. He then cross-fertilized the two varieties by taking pollen from the smooth pea and depositing it in the stamin of the wrinkled peas, and vice-versa. On this first crossing he opened the mature pods and found only smooth peas. The wrinkled characteristic had completely disappeared, so he called the surviving smooth characteristic *dominant* and the one that did not survive *recessive*. The following year Mendel planted his first-generation smooth peas and let them self-fertilize. During the late summer both smooth and wrinkled peas appeared in the same pod. After carefully counting the number of each, Mendel found about three smooth peas for every wrinkled one. He repeated this experiment using a variety of characteristics, and in every case self-fertilization of first-generation hybrid offspring—that is the offspring of mixed parents—always produced a 3 to 1 ratio. He found that one characteristic disappeared in the hybrid first-generation offspring and then reappeared later in the 3:1 ratio. On the basis of these simple experiments Mendel compiled a set of assumptions which would account for his results.

Genotype and Phenotype

Genes make up the genotype.

Mendel assumed that a full set of genes comes from each parent as part of the fertilized egg (the *zygote*). This double set of genes is the *genotype*, the hereditary make up of the new individual. A homozygous person (one whose inheritance from both parents is the same for a given characteristic) shows a one-to-one relation between his genotypic inheritance and the observable phenotypic characteristics. The *phenotype* reflects sets of genes from both parents plus the action on this inheritance by the environment. For example, an infant who inherits genes for genius, but is undernourished in the womb and in its early years, may be duller than its genes would predict.

A heterozygous person (one whose inheritance from the two parents is different for a given characteristic) has both dominant and recessive genes. A *dominant* characteristic, as we have seen, is one that can be transmitted to the child by the gene of a single parent; a *recessive* trait must be transmitted to the child's phenotype by similar genes from both parents. If a dominant and a recessive gene are both transmitted to the child, he will show the dominant trait. Thus, since recessive characteristics may not show in the phenotype, such a person may not perfectly mirror his genotype.

Humans breed unsystematically so a one-to-one correspondence between phenotype and genotype rarely exists. Genotypic characteristics in humans can be inferred when one has followed a phenotypic characteristic for several generations (*see* Figure 2.9).

Dominant genes always show in the phenotype.

Genotype and phenotype are rarely identical.

Genetic Mechanisms

Mendel established the laws of genetics.

Modern genetics began when Gregor Mendel published a small paper in 1866 describing his work on heritability in the sweet pea. His brilliant work, unrecognized for over half a century, contained several important principles: (1) inherited characteristics are produced by genes; (2) genes are passed along unchanged from one generation to another; (3) genes occur in pairs on chromosomes (carried in every cell); (4) members of a pair differ in their effects; (5) one gene of a pair dominates the other (*see* Table 2.1); (6) during egg or sperm formation, members of each pair of chromosomes recombine independently; and (7) one member of the offspring's chromosome pair comes from each parent.

All these assumptions are still believed to be correct. However, our

TABLE 2.1 Some dominant and recessive human genetic traits

Dominant Characters	Recessive Characters
Curly hair	Straight hair
Dark hair	Light or red hair
Brown eyes	Blue eyes
Normal sight	Night blindness
Normal hair	Baldness
Normal color vision	Color blindness

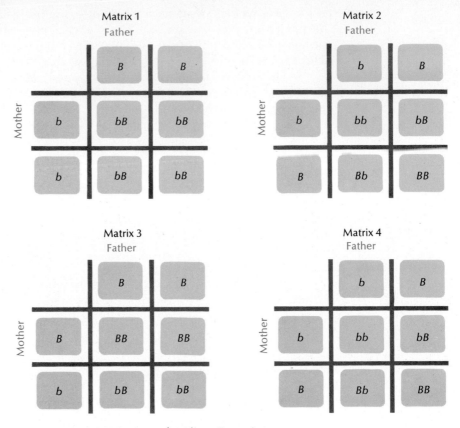

B = Brown = Dominant   b = Blue = Recessive

FIGURE 2.9 Possible combinations of brown- and blue-eyed parents. Note that two parents (BB and bb) who are purebred produce mixed (bB) brown-eyed children (Matrix 1); while mixed (bB) parents produce purebred (BB and bb) and mixed children (bB) (Matrix 2). Matrix 3 show the results of combining mixed parents, who produce both purebred (BB) and mixed children (Bb)—all brown-eyed. Matrix 4 shows the same result as Matrix 2, but the mother and father are reversed. The principle of this illustration is that only purebred recessive traits show in the phenotype.

understanding of the gene's structure has increased dramatically since Mendel assumed its existence a century ago. We now know that deoxyribonucleic acid (the genetic chemical DNA, which is the blueprint for inherited characteristics) comprises about 40 percent of a cell nucleus, yet is not present in other parts of the cell (*see* Figure 2.10). Since genetic material is contained in the nucleus, DNA must be the basis of inheritance. DNA is a long chain of compounds that may occur in many sequences; their ordering constitutes the code by which genetic information is stored.

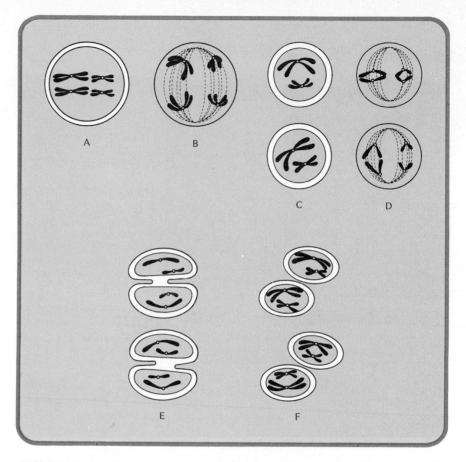

FIGURE 2.10 Meiosis, or cell division, begins with the pairing of chromosomes. The pairs move toward opposite ends and two spindles form. When the chromosomes split into two, leaving four in all, they again move to opposite ends, and cell walls form to separate the four pairs.

DNA is modeled
as a double helix.

A model of DNA's molecular structure won a Nobel prize for Watson and Crick in 1953. They postulated a double-helix (spiral) structure for DNA and assumed two basic activities—self-reproduction and control of protein production. Since the ingredients for new DNA are available to a cell, Watson and Crick hypothesized that the DNA double helix separates and duplicates itself by adding complementary compounds to the free bonds to form new DNA molecules.

Two rules govern genetic transmission: segregation and independent assortment. To understand these notions consider a simple example. If genes acted like liquids, mixing at conception would change their structure (*see* Figure 2.11). On the other hand, if genes behave like marbles,

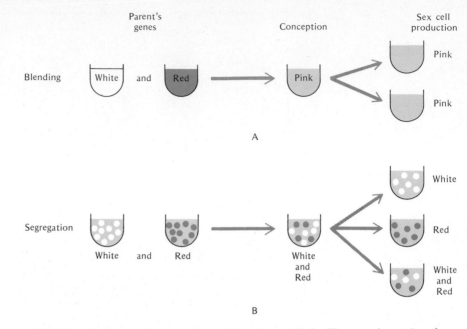

FIGURE 2.11 Genes behave as the marbles in part B do. They can be retrieved unchanged to generate new organisms after conception.

they can be poured into a single container at conception and retrieved intact at maturity for new sex cell production. The theory of *segregation* says that each gene acts like a marble and that it can be retrieved unchanged from the parent in producing new offspring. The theory of *independent assortment* means one marble is not connected to others and can be used independently of other marbles. In human genetics, independent assortment is limited because genes are linked into chains on chromosomes. Only during crossing, when parts of chromosome pairs are interchanged, is this linkage broken. A crossover does not usually disrupt the genetic code, but it does change the composition of a particular chromosome because genes are switched from one chromosome member to the other. Thus, independent assortment happens at the level of the chromosome, not the gene.

Each human receives 23 chromosome pairs.

An individual's *genotype* is, as we have seen, the genetic potential he received from his parents and transmits to his offspring; while his *phenotype* is the embodiment of that genotype in particular measurable characteristics. Each human baby has 46 chromosomes, 23 from the father's sperm and 23 from the mother's ova (*see* Figure 2.12). We don't know how many genes occur on a single chromosome, but geneticists think the number is very large and because of this, the number of possible combinations is astronomical. Thus it's unlikely that two unrelated human beings could ever be genetically identical. Occasionally, nature does

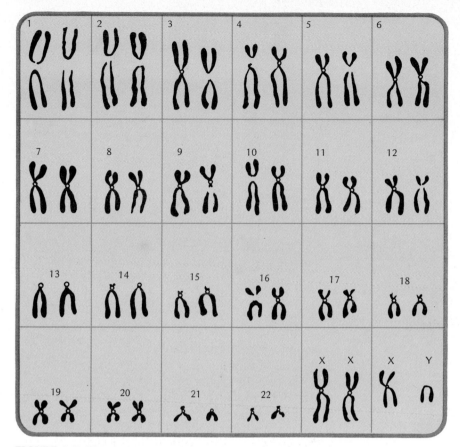

FIGURE 2.12 The chromosomes of a normal human female. The last area shows the X and Y chromosomes of a normal male.

produce identical twins by splitting a single fertilized egg. But before we explore this possibility let us consider how genes are related to the measurable characteristics of the individual.

Many genes may affect one trait.

SINGLE AND MULTIPLE GENE INHERITANCE   It is easy to see that distinct characteristics like eye color or sex can be described by a theory of genes that act like marbles where traits are passed on as a whole from parent to child. But how can we explain continuous characteristics like height, weight, or intelligence by recourse to separate and distinct genes? The answer is *multiple-gene theory,* which assumes that continuously varying traits are influenced by many genes which each make a small contribution to the total characteristic in question. By this logic, as the number of genes influencing a particular trait increases, the size of the distinct differences between various gene combinations becomes smaller, until the trait in

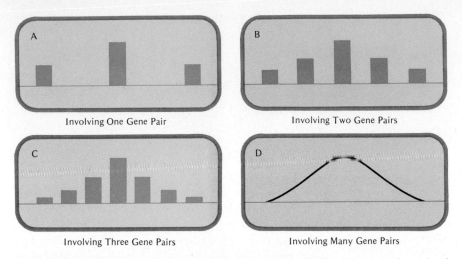

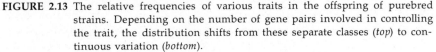

FIGURE 2.13 The relative frequencies of various traits in the offspring of purebred strains. Depending on the number of gene pairs involved in controlling the trait, the distribution shifts from these separate classes (*top*) to continuous variation (*bottom*).

question appears continuous. Figure 2.13 illustrates this statistical progression. Continuous characteristics are described by averages, variations, and correlations of the many contributing genes. Single gene effects are either dominant or recessive, but polygene (meaning many) characteristics vary from complete recessivity to complete dominance. This varying polygenetic dominance is called *penetrance* by geneticists. A trait with high penetrance makes for high agreement between the heredity of the individual (genotype) and the actual appearance (phenotype) under a variety of conditions. On the other hand, when penetrance is low, there may be little correspondence between genotype and phenotype. Low penetrant traits appear in the phenotype only when they are genetically the same, and therefore always breed true to type. Also, to complicate the picture even more, the relative dominance of traits can change with age. Some examples are eye and hair color that change as the person matures.

We are sure that genes control many bodily structures, but do they also affect behavior?

Behavior Genetics

Behavior genetics applies genetic methods to human abilities.

Earlier, geneticists had been primarily concerned with hereditary differences in body structure. But recently a new branch of inquiry has developed which applies the methods of genetics directly to behavior. Three questions dominate this field: (1) What proportion of the variation among individuals' behavior may be attributed to genetics, what portion to environment, and what part to the interaction of these elements? (2) What are the mechanisms responsible for inheritance of behavior? (3) How much difference can environmental variation make in heritable behavior (Falconer, 1960)?

Animal behavior geneticists use inbreeding and selective breeding methods.

There are two methods scientists use to study behavior genetics in animals: *inbreeding* and *selective breeding*. The logic of inbreeding is simple. By strict mating within a group of animals for several generations genetic variation approaches zero and there is little likelihood that two inbred strains from two animal groups will approach the same genetic endowment. Thus, any behavior difference between two such inbred strains under identical environmental conditions must be the result of genetic variation or interactions between genetic endowment and the environment. Fuller and Thompson (1960) report that inbred strains of animals have been found to differ on a wide variety of traits, including aggressiveness, activity, sex drive, maternal behavior, and learning abilities.

Selective breeding can produce genetic differences in behavior.

In a second technique, animals are selectively bred by assortive mating of extremes. This means, for example, that maze-bright parents are mated to produce maze-bright offspring, while maze-dull parents are mated to produce maze-dull offspring. Animals have been selectively bred for many behaviors—including maze learning (*see* Figure 2.14), emotionality, and alcohol preference. We know that genes affect animal behavior, but what can we say about the effect of genetics on human abilities?

The pedigree is one human genetic method.

HUMAN BEHAVIOR GENETICS   Studies of genetic constraint on human behavior are of three types—pedigree studies, the effect of environmental changes on hereditary behavior, and twin studies. Research with *pedigree* show that lines of famous men and lines of degenerates run in separate families. However, there is one major problem with all pedigree studies: genetic endowment and environmental influence are not separated. This means that desirable genes occur most often in desirable environments and deficient genes are often found in deficient environments. This does not mean pedigrees are useless; it simply means they are inconclusive when considered as a research source by themselves.

Twins and offspring are used to study human behavior genetics.

To decide whether genetics or environment controls intellectual or personal development we must find twins or offspring who were *not* reared in the same families and compare their intellectual development. Let us consider adopted children first, and then twins. If adopted children's abilities are more closely related to their biological parents than to their foster parents, even though the children have not lived with their biological parents, then genetic factors must control their development more than environmental events do. On the other hand, if adopted children more closely resemble their foster parents, then environment must control the children's behavior to a greater degree than their genetic inheritance.

Adopted children resemble their biological parents.

Consider some evidence about genetics and intelligence. Figure 2.15 shows the correlations between adopted children and their adopting and

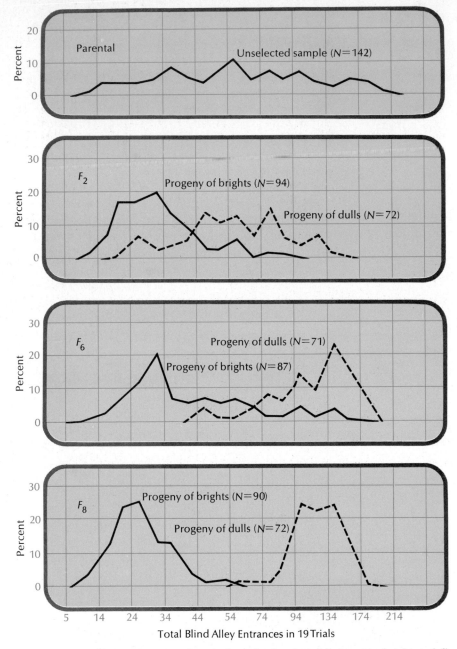

FIGURE 2.14 The distributions of errors for animals selected to be maze bright or dull. After eight generations there is practically no overlap in their error scores. This indicates that maze-learning is heritable.
(After Tyron, 1940)

biological parents. The correlations of adopted children with adopted parents are near zero, while the correlations of adopted children with their biological parents are about as high as one finds when children are reared with their biological parents. These data suggest that genetic endowment from the parent most strongly influences intellectual development. Taken together, pedigree and adopted parent-child studies imply that genetic endowment constrains human intellect, while the environment has relatively little effect. However, before accepting that conclusion, consider some twin data.

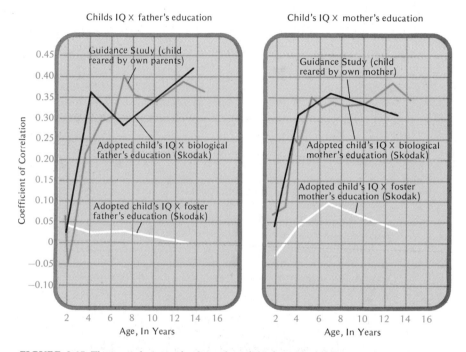

FIGURE 2.15 The correlation of adopted and biological children with adopted and biological parents. Foster parent-child correlations are near zero, while biological parent-child correlations are high, whether the family lives together or not. These results suggest that family environment has little effect on children's intellects.
(After Honzik, 1957)

There are two types of twins.

TWINS AND GENETICS   Some women produce several ova at the same time. Two or more of these eggs may be fertilized by different sperm. The resulting offspring are genetically like brothers or sisters. *Fraternal twins* (two eggs fertilized by two sperms at the same time) occur about once in sixty births; they run in families and are more frequent among some races than others. Also, fathers and mothers in their thirties produce more fraternal twins than younger parents do.

Portrait

Francis Galton was born in 1822 near Birmingham, England. His father was an extremely successful banker who thought that Francis should study to become a physician in case he should ever have to earn his own living.

Francis Galton is thought to be one of the most intelligent men in history; psychologists have estimated his IQ at around 200. He entered medical studies as a House Pupil at Birmingham General Hospital and spent a year enduring the horrors of amputations and disease on hospital rounds. He entered Kings College, London, where he attended medical lectures, and then moved on to Trinity College, Cambridge, where he studied mathematics. Following his graduation from Cambridge, he toured Egypt and Syria and wrote a book about his adventures which won him a medal from the Royal Geographic Society.

The turning point in his life came when he read a book by his cousin Charles Darwin entitled *On the Origin of Species*. Francis Galton become fascinated with the social implications of Darwin's genetic notions. Galton wrote: "I object to pretensions of natural equality." It seemed obvious to him that people were different and that the human strain could be improved by "proper breeding." To accomplish this improvement in human genetics Galton proposed a eugenics program, and published books to support his notions. The first, *Hereditary Genius,* argued that eminence occurs far too often within families simply to be the result of environmental advantage. His second book, *Inquiries into Human Faculty and Its Development,* was the beginning of mental measurement. Galton tried to develop a set of psychological measurements which would characterize all people. During the course of his investigations into psychological traits he invented the notion of correlation. But Galton's most important contribution was his application of hereditary notions to behavior.

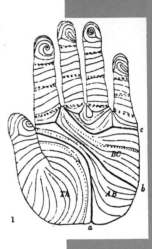

Sir Francis Galton pioneered the study of twins, developed statistics to describe human populations, and believed that genes strongly influence human behavior. In his studies of great men he found that their sons, brothers, and fathers are often great themselves and, although the next lower level of kinship—grandfathers, uncles, nephews, and grandsons—is less likely to accomplish great things, they are still much more prominent than the population at large. The third kinship level, cousins, was lower in achievement than the second, but still far above average. Galton found that this pattern of kinship and achievement was identical over several professions. He reported that genius ran in families, and then wondered if familial eminence results from genes or opportunity. Galton presented several facts that supported a genetic explanation: (1) Twins are more similar than siblings. (2) Adopted sons of Popes (who certainly don't want for advantage) rarely achieve greatness. (3) Great men can emerge from poor environments.

The following excerpt from his work, *Hereditary Genius,* outlines Galton's position and his experimental logic.

Sir Francis Galton, a photograph made in 1895. (The Granger Collection).

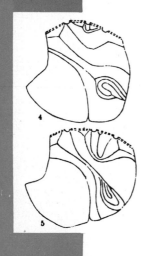

A plate from Galton's book, *Finger Prints*, published in 1892. (The Granger Collection)

I propose to show in this book that a man's natural abilities are derived by inheritance, under exactly the same limitations as are the form and physical features of the whole organic world. Consequently, as it is easy, notwithstanding those limitations, to obtain by careful selection a permanent breed of dogs or horses gifted with peculiar powers of running, or of doing anything else, so it would be quite practicable to produce a highly-gifted race of men by judicious marriages during several consecutive generations. I shall show that social agencies of an ordinary character, whose influences are little suspected, are at this moment working towards the degradation of human nature, and that others are working towards its improvement. I conclude that each generation has enormous power over the natural gifts of those that follow, and maintain that it is a duty we owe to humanity to investigate the range of that power, and to exercise it in a way that, without being unwise towards ourselves, shall be most advantageous to future inhabitants of the earth.

I am aware that my views, which were first published four years ago in *Macmillan's Magazine* (in June and August 1865), are in contradiction to general opinion; but the arguments I then used have been since accepted, to my great gratification, by many of the highest authorities on heredity. In reproducing them, as I now do, in a much more elaborate form, and on a greatly enlarged basis of induction, I feel assured that, inasmuch as what I then wrote was sufficient to earn the acceptance of Mr. Darwin (*Domestication of Plants and Animals,* ii. 7), the increased amount of evidence submitted in the present volume is not likely to be gainsaid.

The general plan of my argument is to show that high reputation is a pretty accurate test of high ability; next to discuss the relationships of a large body of fairly eminent men—namely, the Judges of England from 1660 to 1868, the Statesmen of the time of George III, and the Premiers during the last 100 years—and to obtain from these a general survey of the laws of heredity in respect to genius. Then I shall examine, in order, the kindred of the most illustrious Commanders, men of Literature and of Science, Poets, Painters, and Musicians, of whom history speaks. I shall also discuss the kindred of a certain selection of Divines and of modern Scholars. Then will follow a short chapter, by way of comparison, on the hereditary transmission of physical gifts, as deduced from the relationships of certain classes of Oarsmen and Wrestlers. Lastly, I shall collate my results, and draw conclusions.

It will be observed that I deal with more than one grade of ability. Those upon whom the greater part of my volume is occupied, and on whose kinships my argument is most securely based, have been generally reputed as endowed by nature with extraordinary genius. There are so few of these men that, although they are scattered throughout the whole historical period of human existence, their number does not amount to more than 400, and yet a considerable proportion of them will be found to be interrelated.

Another grade of ability with which I deal is that which includes numerous, highly eminent, and all the illustrious names of modern

English history, whose immediate descendants are living among us, whose histories are popularly known, and whose relationships may readily be traced by the help of biographical dictionaries, peerages, and similar books of reference.

I trust the reader will make allowance for a large and somewhat important class of omissions I have felt myself compelled to make when treating of the eminent men of modern days. I am prevented by a sense of decorum from quoting names of their relations in contemporary life who are not recognised as public characters, although their abilities may be highly appreciated in private life. Still less consistent with decorum would it have been, to introduce the names of female relatives that stand in the same category. My case is so overpoweringly strong, that I am perfectly able to prove my point without having recourse to this class of evidence. Nevertheless, the reader should bear in mind that it exists; and I beg he will do me the justice of allowing that I have not overlooked the whole of the evidence that does not appear in my pages. I am deeply conscious of the imperfection of my work, but my sins are those of omission, not of commission. Such errors as I may and must have made, which give a fictitious support to my arguments, are, I am confident, out of all proportion fewer than such omissions of facts as would have helped to establish them.

I have taken little notice in this book of modern men of eminence who are not English, or at least well known to Englishmen. I feared, if I included large classes of foreigners, that I should make glaring errors. It requires a very great deal of labour to hunt out relationships, even with the facilities afforded to a countryman having access to persons acquainted with the various families; much more would it have been difficult to hunt out the kindred of foreigners. I should have especially liked to investigate the biographies of Italians and Jews, both of whom appear to be rich in families of high intellectual breeds. Germany and America are also full of interest. It is a little less so with respect to France, where the Revolution and the guillotine made sad havoc among the progeny of her abler races.

There is one advantage to a candid critic in my having left so large a field untouched; it enables me to propose a test that any well-informed reader may easily adopt who doubts the fairness of my examples. He may most reasonably suspect that I have been unconsciously influenced by my theories to select men whose kindred were most favourable to their support. If so, I beg he will test my impartiality as follows:—Let him take a dozen names of his own selection, as the most eminent in whatever profession and in whatever country he knows most about, and let him trace out for himself their relations. It is necessary, as I find by experience, to take some pains to be sure that none, even of the immediate relatives, on either the male or female side, have been overlooked. If he does what I propose, I am confident he will be astonished at the completeness with which the results will confirm my theory. I venture to speak with assurance, because it has often occurred to me to propose this very test to incredulous friends, and invariably, so far as my memory serves me, as large a proportion of the men who were named were discovered to have eminent relations, as the nature of my views on heredity would have led us to expect.

Let us now bring our scattered results side to side, for the purpose of comparison, and judge of the extent to which they corroborate one another—how far they confirm the provisional calculations made in the chapter on JUDGES from more scanty data, and where and why they contrast.

The number of cases of hereditary genius analysed in the several chapters of my book, amounts to a large total. I have dealt with no less than 300 families containing between them nearly 1,000 eminent men, of whom 415 are illustrious, or, at all events, of such note as to deserve being printed in small capitals at the head of a paragraph. If there be such a thing as a decided law of distribution of genius in families, it is sure to become manifest when we deal statistically with so large a body of examples.

In contrasting the different groups, the first notable peculiarity that catches the eye is the small number of the sons of Commanders; they being 31, while the average of all the groups is 48. There is nothing anomalous in this irregularity. I have already shown, when speaking of the Commanders, that they usually begin their active careers in youth, and therefore, if married at all, they are mostly away from their wives on military service. It is also worth while to point out a few particular cases where exceptional circumstances stood in the way of the Commanders leaving male issue, because the total number of those included in my lists is so small, being only 32, as to make them of appreciable importance in affecting the results. Thus, Alexander the Great was continually engaged in distant wars, and died in early manhood: he had one posthumous son, but that son was murdered for political reasons when still a boy. Julius Caesar, an exceedingly profligate man, left one illegitimate son, by Cleopatra, but that son was also murdered for political reasons when still a boy. Nelson married a widow who had no children by her former husband, and therefore was probably more or less infertile by nature. Napoleon I was entirely separated from Marie Louise after she had borne him one son.

Though the great Commanders have but few immediate descendants, yet the number of their eminent grandsons is as great as any other groups. I ascribe this to the superiority of their breed, which ensures eminence to an unusually large proportion of their kinsmen.

As an alternative to Galton's position on genetics, behaviorism has dominated American psychology for most of this century. Behaviorists announced that they believed proper training could make any healthy baby into any type of man or woman, and this notion had enormous appeal for American science. One implication of behaviorism is that if you can control behavior by environmental events, there must be an environment which will wipe out ignorance, hostility and fear. Environmentalism is optimistic about human nature and education. The goal of behaviorism is the prediction and control of behavior, rather than an understanding of how the system functions.

The founder of American behaviorism, John S. Watson, wrote the following selection in 1930. It was a "Plan for Psychology," rather than a review of scientific knowledge. His call for healthy infants to be reared for various professions struck a responsive chord in the minds of many.

differences in structure and differences in early training will account for all differences in later behavior

JOHN S. WATSON

We have already asserted that even though there is individual variation in structure we can find no real proof that man's unlearned repertoire of acts has differed widely through the ages or that he has ever been either more or less capable of putting on complex training than he is now.

The fact that there are marked individual variations in structure among men has been known since biology began. But we have never sufficiently utilized it in analyzing man's behavior. I want to utilize another fact only recently brought out by the behaviorists and other students of animal psychology. Namely, that *habit formation starts in all probability in embryonic life and that even in the human young, environment shapes behavior so quickly that all of the older ideas about what types of behavior are inherited and what are learned break down.* Grant variations in structure at birth and rapid habit formation from birth, and you have a basis for explaining many of the so-called facts of inheritance of "mental" characteristics.

Such factors, especially those on the training side, have been wholly neglected in the study of inheritance. We have not the facts to build up statistics on the inheritance of special types of behavior, and until the facts have been brought out by the study of the human young, all data on the evolution of different forms of human behavior and eugenics must be accepted with the greatest possible caution.

Our conclusion, then, is that we have no real evidence of the inheritance of traits. I would feel perfectly confident in the ultimately favorable outcome of careful upbringing of a *healthy, well-formed baby* born of a long line of crooks, murderers and thieves, and prostitutes. Who has any evidence to the contrary? Many, many thousands of children yearly, born from moral households and steadfast parents become wayward, steal, become prostitutes, through one mishap or another of nurture. Many more thousands of sons and daughters of the wicked grow up to be wicked because they couldn't grow up any other way in such surroundings. But let one adopted child who has a bad ancestry go wrong and it is used as incontestable evidence for the inheritance of moral turpitude and criminal tendencies. As a matter of fact, there has not been a double handful of cases in the whole of our civilization of which records have been carefully enough kept for us to draw any such conclusions—mental testers, Lombroso, and all other students of criminality to the contrary notwithstanding. As a matter of fact adopted children are never brought up as one's own. One cannot use statistics gained from observations in charitable institutions and orphan asylums. All one needs to do to discount such statistics is to go there and work for a while, and I say this without trying to belittle the work of such organizations.

I should like to go one step further now and say, "Give me a dozen healthy infants, well-formed, and my own specified world to bring them up in and I'll guarantee to take any one at random and train him to become any type of specialist I might select—doctor, lawyer, artist, merchant-chief and, yes, even beggar-man and thief, regardless of his talents, penchants, tendencies, abilities, vocations, and race of his ancestors." I am going beyond my facts and I admit it, but so have the advocates of the contrary and they have been doing it for many thousands of years. Please note that when this experiment is made I am to be allowed to specify the way the children are to be brought up and the type of world they have to live in.

Identical twins are genetically the same.

There is another kind of twin pair which is much more alike in appearance than brothers and sisters usually are. These *identical twins* result from a single egg fertilized by a single sperm. This egg divides completely during its early development (*see* Figure 2.16) to form two new individuals with identical genetic endowment. They are thus of great interest to behavior geneticists. The splitting of the primitive fertilized cell mass to produce two identical genotypes, the identical twins, is a natural experiment. As a result, any correlations between twins reared apart must be the result of genetics, while any differences must be the result of environment. These correlations are often used as estimates of heritability. In those rare instances when identical twins were separated at birth or early in life and reared in different families, an almost perfect genetic experiment results.

There are tests to determine twin types.

How can you tell whether multiple births result from two eggs or one? It's easy if they are of different sexes because there must have been two ova and sperm in that case (fraternal twins). However, when the sex is the same, there are several clues to twinning. The most reliable tests are similar blood type, eye color, hair color, fingerprints, and blood-serum

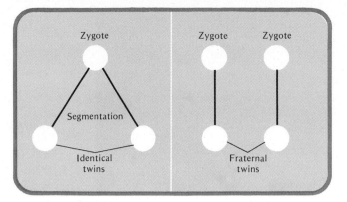

FIGURE 2.16
The origins of identical and fraternal twins. Identical twins result from one fertilized egg; fraternal twins originate from two different fertilized eggs.

proteins. A foolproof indicator of identical twinning is to transplant a piece of skin from one twin member to the other. If the graft survives, they are identical twins. This test is so strenuous it is rarely used; besides, the other tests are almost foolproof.

Genetic resemblance and IQ similarity are strongly associated.

What do we know about genetic endowment and behavior? Consider intelligence first. Figures 2.17 and 2.18 show how correlations of intelligence quotients (IQs) are associated with familial relationships. Note that as the genetic resemblance of individuals increases, so does the similarity of their IQs. However, differing environments systematically lower the similarity in IQ. Erlenmeyer-Kimling and Jarvik (1963) reported data from groups of unrelated people, siblings, and fraternal and identical twins reared together and apart. Notice first that there is a systematic increase in correlation of IQ as a function of familial similarity. Note also that if the family members are reared in different environments, the correlation drops about .15 over all categories of genetic relationship. These data suggest there is a strong genetic constraint on intelligence and that the environment can modify that control to some extent. Even in the case of identical twins, those reared apart show a lower average IQ correlation than those reared together. Varying environmental influences can differentiate even identical genetic endowments.

The environment can change IQ.

Thus, intellectual level is not unalterably fixed by genetic constitution; rather, its expression in the phenotype results from the fulfillment of patterns laid down by the genotype under certain environmental conditions.

Genetic control of IQ seems strong.

How flexible is genetic endowment? At the present time estimates of environmental effects on intellectual variation average about 25 percent, compared with 75 percent genetic control. Environmental influences like age of the mother, frequent births, prematurity, difficult labor, and poisonous substances in the mother's bloodstream can affect the child's intellect. Extreme prematurity (birth weight below three pounds) or severe malnutrition before the child is three years of age may be associated with

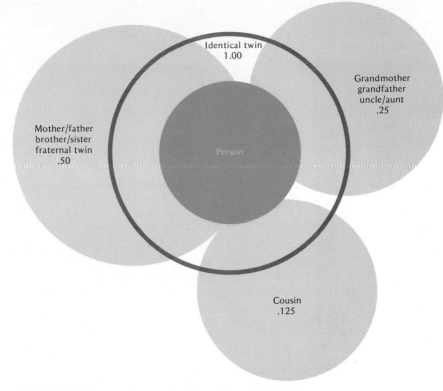

FIGURE 2.17 The genetic overlap of various family relations.

lower intelligence in the adult. In addition, twins generally average about 5 IQ points lower than only children, or singletons; identical twins score slightly lower than fraternal twins on IQ tests, and the identical twin with the lower birth weight usually has a lower IQ at maturity.

Chromosomal abnormalities can be detected.

Recent advances have been made in the detection of chromosomal abnormalities, so it is now possible, through a process called *amniocentesis,* to determine whether an unborn baby (the fetus) will have genetic defects. To perform an amniocentesis, a needle is inserted into the uterus of the mother and fluid which contains some of the baby's cells is extracted for later examination in a laboratory. If the chromosomal analysis shows that the baby is seriously defective, the parents may decide to terminate that particular pregnancy. Currently, amniocentesis is only performed when there is a serious genetic risk of chromosomal abnormality, because inserting a needle into the uterus holds some danger for the fetus, whether it is abnormal or not.

Genetic counseling can improve offspring.

It is also now possible to predict in some cases whether a particular couple runs a high risk of producing an abnormal child. The procedure, known as *genetic counseling,* traces the family history of both husband and wife to determine whether there are any genetic abnormalities which are likely to appear in their particular offspring. Genetic counseling can warn a couple against the dangers of abnormal babies; it can also reassure other couples who may be uncertain about their genetic risk. Combined with chromosomal analysis, genetic counseling has proved very helpful in handling many genetic abnormalities.

Correlations and averages suggest different theories.

The dispute over the influence of heredity versus environment still flourishes. One source of disagreement is over which data are appropriate to test the theories. Those who support an hereditary position point to high *correlations* between identical twins, biological parents and their children, and siblings to support their position. Environmentalists point to differences in the *average* performance of groups reared under deprived or normal conditions as evidence to support their view. Correlational data generally support a genetic view of development; while data based on group differences show that environmental deprivation retards development, and a normal or enriched environment will substantially raise the abilities of deprived children. Once conception occurs, a complex set of developmental stages follows. Consider how a baby grows before its birth.

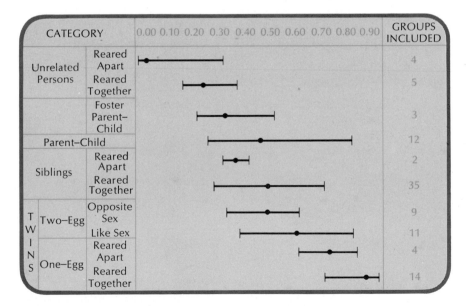

FIGURE 2.18 The relationship between genetic overlap and the correlation of intelligence for pairs of individuals reared together and apart are shown on this graph.
(After Erlenmeyer-Kimling and Jarvis, 1963)

Stages of Prenatal Development

Behavior begins in
the uterus.

Behavioral embryology covers the stages of human prenatal growth in the uterus, the effects of various factors on this development, and how the offspring (the embryo) behaves during this early period. It is a science with ancient beginnings. However, much of what we know about prenatal development and behavior has been discovered during the past few decades. The following material discusses intrauterine growth, which may be separated into three phases: germinal, embryonic, and fetal.

The Germinal Phase

The germinal phase
lasts two weeks.

During the first two weeks of the organism's life the fertilized egg (zygote) multiplies rapidly. Growth consists largely of cell division and differentiation into embryonic and life-support tissue.

The Embryonic Phase

The embryonic phase
brings major organ
development.

During the next six weeks all the basic structures of the human body are begun. In the course of early cell multiplication of the embryo, three layers are formed. The outer layer (*ectoderm*) produces human sense organs and the nervous system; the intermediate layer (*mesoderm*) becomes the skeleton, muscular structures, and circulatory system; while the inner layer (*endoderm*) gives rise to the digestive organs. Cell differentiation and multiplication continue, so that by the third week, the embryo is 1/10 inch long, its "heart" tubes begin to pulse, its brain has two lobes, and the spinal cord is formed. Growth is extremely rapid. By the end of the fourth week the embryo is nearly 10,000 times larger than the fertilized egg.

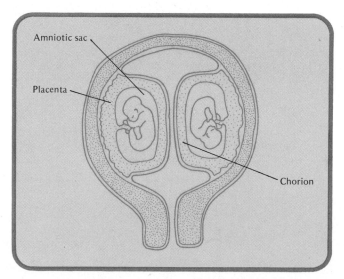

FIGURE 2.19
The protective membrane of the amniotic sac filled with fluid grows around the embryo within the first month after conception.

The amniotic sac
protects the baby.

Within the first month an envelope forms around the embryo, the amniotic sac, and amniotic fluid fills the bag. The sac grows with the organism, forming a protective membrane around the baby (*see* Figure 2.19). Inside this amniotic sac the embryo is warm, protected, and moist; it has enough room for movement without unduly disturbing its mother. At first the outside of the amniotic sac is covered with hundreds of rootlike fingers, called villi, which collect food from the uterine wall of the mother and deliver it to the fetus through a primitive tube or stalk. Later in the embryonic period most of these villi degenerate and the few remaining ones develop into the placenta. The placenta provides nourishment and oxygenated blood to the growing baby, and carries away its waste products. The placental membrane also serves as a barrier (which however can be partially penetrated) to prevent some harmful substances from reaching the embryo and fetus. The primitive stalk becomes an umbilical cord through which two arteries carry blood from the infant to the placenta and a vein carries oxygenated blood back to the infant.

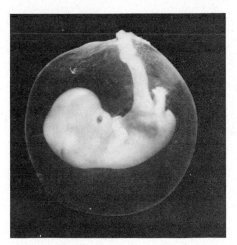

FIGURE 2.20
The human fetus at six weeks.
(Courtesy Landrum B. Shettles, M.D. F.A.C.S., F.A.C.O.G.)

The eight-week
embryo looks human.

By the eighth week the growing embryo has developed a reasonably human appearance (*see* Figure 2.20). Now it possesses most internal organs, arms, legs, muscles, and hands and feet with recognizable fingers and toes. It is ugly and only about an inch long, but it lives. The heart beats; it secretes some digestive juices; and the arms and legs move. The remaining changes during the fetal period are primarily in size, proportion, and the complexity of the baby.

The Fetal Phase

The fetal baby grows
rapidly.

Between the third month and birth the baby's size increases from seven or eight millimeters at conception to fifty centimeters, from about the size of a printed . to three times the width of this book. However, the

TABLE 2.2   Timetable of **Prenatal Development**

First Month
Fertilization; descent of ovum from the Fallopian tube into the uterus.
Early cell division and formation of embryonic mass.
Formation of the three embryonic layers—ectoderm, endoderm, and mesoderm.
A special layer forms in the uterus which becomes the placenta.
Another layer of cells forms the amnionic sac around the embryo.
The heart tube forms and begins to pulse; blood circulates about the embryo.
The nervous system begins to develop—the early neural tube forms.
The intestinal tract, lungs, liver, and kidneys begin to develop.

Second Month
The embryo increases from ¼ inch to about 1½ inch in length.
Bones and muscles begin to form.
The face and neck begin to take on human form.
The brain develops very rapidly.
Limb buds form and grow. Sex organs begin to appear.

Third Month
The fetus continues sexual differentiation; male sex organs show rapid development.
Buds of the temporary teeth are formed.
The digestive system becomes active and the stomach secretes fluids.
The liver and kidneys begin to function.
Spontaneous movement of the arms and legs and fingers occurs.

Fourth Month
Lower parts of the body show accelerated growth.
Hands and feet become well formed; the skin appears dark red.
Finger closure is possible.
Reflexes become more active.
Fetus begins to stir, and move its arms and legs.

---

most dramatic changes are in its proportions. At two months the fetus' head is half its length, but at birth the infant's head is only a quarter of its length (*see* Figure 2.21).

Movement begins at three months.

At around three months the fetus begins to move though its actions won't be felt by the mother for another month. Hooker (1952) obtained a generalized body response from a surgically removed fetus as early as seven weeks. More specific movements appear during the fourth month, and the response to touch becomes more coordinated.

The four-month fetus reaches half its birth weight.

By four months the fetus displays most of the actions of a newborn baby. However, the four-month-old fetus cannot breathe or cry. It also reaches half its birth height and increases its weight dramatically during the fourth month.

Strong movements begin at five months.

The fifth month of prenatal life brings a marked increase in activity. Movements become vigorous so the mother can now feel the baby when it kicks or turns. In addition, the five-month fetus shows periods of sleep and activity. Hair, eyelashes, and nails develop and its skeleton begins to

Table 2.2 (Continued)

Fifth Month

Skin structures begin to attain final form.
Sweat and sebaceous glands are formed and begin to function.
Finger and toenails appear.
Fetus is now about 1 foot long.
It weighs about 1 pound.
If aborted, it would breathe for a short time and then die; neural maturation is inadequate for pro-
longed life.

Sixth Month

Eyelids, which have been fused, now open.
The eyes are completely formed.
Taste buds appear on the tongue and in the mouth.
If born, the 6-month fetus would live somewhat longer than the 5-month fetus before death.

Seventh Month

The fetus is now capable of extrauterine life.
Cerebral hemispheres cover almost the entire brain.
It can emit a variety of reflex responses (startle, grasp, swimming).
The fetus is generally about 16 inches long and weighs about 3 pounds.
If born, it can breathe, cry, swallow, and live.
It is very prone to infections, however.

Eighth and Ninth Months

Final preparations for birth and life are made during these months.
Fat is deposited for later use.
Activity is greater; it can change position and usually is head down.
Periods of activity alternate with periods of quiet.
Its organs step up their activity.
Fetal heart rate increases to become quite rapid.
Digestive system continues to work.
Finally, uterine contractions expel the fetus into the world.

Source: M.S. Gilbert, *Biography of The Newborn* (Baltimore: Williams & Wilkins, 1938).

calcify or harden. It is easier to bring forth reflexes, and the five-month-old fetus moves its lips in a manner resembling sucking.

The six-month fetus breathes.

During the sixth month the baby begins to "breathe." It takes amniotic fluid into its lungs, but does not drown because it receives adequate oxygen through the umbilical cord. During the sixth month the fetus grows to around fourteen inches, and weighs about a pound and a quarter. Buds for its permanent teeth form; its eyelids may open and the eyes rotate. The grasp reflex becomes strong enough to support its weight. The baby could not survive birth at this stage because its nervous system is not mature enough to sustain life.

Between seven months and birth the fetus grows in size and its functions mature. A baby born in its seventh month has a fair chance of sur-

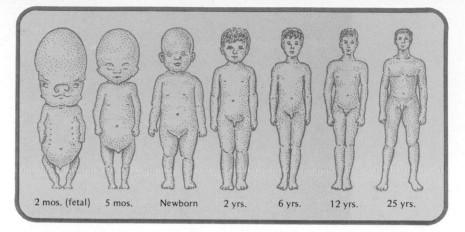

FIGURE 2.21 The changes in head/body proportion with maturation.

Seven-month-old
fetuses may live.

vival if good medical facilities are available. If it survives, this premature infant will not catch up with the normal-term, nine-month baby for many months. Its physical growth and behavior will be immature, but comparable to a baby of the same age from conception (Lubchenco, et al, 1963).

Many prenatal factors can affect the development of a baby. Consider some of the most important ones.

Prenatal Influences

The fetus is a parasite.

An unborn baby depends on its mother for nutrition, warmth, protection, and oxygen. At the same time it is an independent biological system. The fetus is a parasite who removes food and oxygen from the mother's body and returns its own waste products to her system through the placenta, as we have seen. The interrelation between mother and child profoundly affects the growing baby.

Specific factors may
harm the fetus.

Prenatal life is fairly safe for the baby, but specific damage and indirect effects from environmental deficiencies can harm a developing fetus. It is difficult to know precisely the cause of many congenital defects, because genetic factors and prenatal influences are often related. Some congenital or innate malformations are not apparent until a time following birth. For example, among the infants who survived from a large sample of 6,000 pregnancies, over 7 percent developed malformations by the time they were one year of age. Yet, less than half these problems were apparent at birth (McIntosh, 1954). In particular, the functioning of a child's higher central nervous system can't be assessed until several years following birth.

Maternal Emotions

Maternal emotions
may affect the un-
born baby.

There has been a long controversy among students of development concerning the influence of maternal emotions on the unborn baby. Some argue that since there are no connections between the mother's nerves and her baby's, the emotional state of the mother cannot affect the infant's development. Others point out that although there are no such neural connections gross chemical changes in the mother's circulatory system can still be transmitted through the placental barrier to the fetus. These chemicals might affect the emotional state of the baby and its subsequent development (Montagu, 1962).

Active mothers pro-
duce active babies.

Mothers with active autonomic (involuntary) indicators — like high heart rate, high respiratory rate, and/or variability in heart and breathing rate — produce active infants. Infants of mothers who are emotionally disturbed exhibit hyperactive autonomic nervous functions at birth. Taken alone these data suggest that the mother can transmit emotional states to the fetus. Remember, however, that infants of emotionally disturbed mothers with hyperactive autonomic nervous systems may well inherit that hyperactivity. Fetal emotionality is probably the joint result of genetic factors and maternal emotions.

Maternal Nutrition

Maternal nutrition is
important for infant
health.

The mother's nutrition is also important during pregnancy. In fact, some medical authorities argue that nutritional deficiency is the single most important factor contributing to below average prenatal development in infants. Since the mother must maintain herself and also supply the growing fetus, these authorities are concerned with both the quantity and quality of maternal nutrition and have studied it in depth. Low birth weight, prematurity, lowered vitality, rickets (a disease resulting from vitamin D deficiency), and high infant death rate have been attributed to inadequate maternal diets. Usually, the mother has endured a poor diet long before her pregnancy, and the combination of undernourishment while pregnant and a long history of malnutrition compounds the problem for her developing infant. These same authorities argue that the incidence of brain malformation and other mental difficulties is greater in the lower classes, where diet is often poor, than in the higher, richer classes. They agree that this class difference is confused with genetic factors, but many argue that most mental deficiencies can be attributed to nutritional problems.

Iodine deficiency
causes cretinism.

Cretinism, a mental and physical deficiency, is caused by lack of iodine during pregnancy. Happily, iodine deficiency is now rare because of the general use of iodized salt. However, in less medically sophisticated societies and in geographically isolated areas the incidence of cretinism can still be high.

A Dutch study
showed that maternal
malnutrition does not
affect adult male IQ.

Arguing from these data, many authorities have proposed that prenatal maternal nutrition has a profound effect on the later mental abilities of children (for example, Montagu, Hunt). However, a recent study by Stein, Susser, Salinger, and Marolla (1972) presents strong evidence that serious prenatal malnutrition has little or no effect on the mental performance of human beings when they become adults. The investigators used the Dutch famine of 1944–1945 as a "natural experiment" to discover the effects of prenatal malutrition on the adult mental abilities of 125,000 nineteen-year-old males. The investigators matched prenatally malnourished males with control subjects (those from the non-affected general population) on the basis of sex, date of birth, birth weight, fertility of mother, and social class. They measured the IQ of all subjects on the Dutch version of the Raven progressive matrices, a non-verbal intelligence test which requires the person to match patterns. Results (*see* Figure 2.22) showed that severe prenatal malnutrition had no effect on the IQ of adult males. The authors list some reservations about their data: (1) They only measured males; (2) the nutritional deprivation occurred among previously well-nourished mothers; and (3) the famine group produced many more spontaneous abortions and miscarriages than the control group did. Taking all these reservations into account, the authors conclude that "starvation during pregnancy has no detectable effects on the adult mental performance of surviving male offspring." In addition, Stein and his colleagues found no relationship between mental performance and birth weight among their subjects.

These data strongly suggest that prenatal malnutrition is *not* the major source of mental deficiencies.

Drugs

Americans consume
many drugs.

Members of our society consume many drugs, most of them to relieve minor pain or nervous tension, for example, aspirin, bicarbonate of soda, vallium. Many of the drugs are safe for adults, but their effect on the fetus is often unknown. As a result, we have seen outbreaks of neonatal abnormalities, which later are traced to a specific drug taken by pregnant mothers. The thalidomide disaster is probably the best known of several such instances. In that case, great numbers of deformed infants were born to mothers who had taken an apparently harmless tranquilizing drug during pregnancy. This tragedy stimulated public interest and led to increased governmental attempts at drug control, but there may be other dangers to come.

Pregnant women
consume many drugs.

The only effective safeguard against drug side effects during pregnancy is the elimination of all drugs which are not necessary to sustain life. A recent study found that 82 percent of pregnant women receive prescribed medication, and that 65 percent also take self-medicated drugs (Marx, 1973).

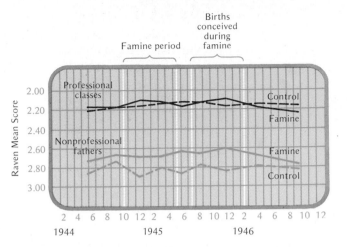

FIGURE 2.22

Mean grouped scores on the Raven progressive matrices test given to men in the Netherlands after enduring famine and classed by manual and nonmanual classes according to the father's occupation; compared with cities in which there was no famine.

Drugs may cross the placental barrier.

Drugs given to a mother will not affect her unborn baby unless they cross the placental barrier. In addition, drug transfer is faster with increased blood flow and the age of the placenta.

Not all drugs are dangerous to unborn babies.

The toxic effects of drugs depend partly on the unborn child's ability to break down the drug. The unborn of most other species cannot metabolize (break down and use) drugs; however, the human fetus can metabolize some. Happily, not all drugs are dangerous to the unborn child. Some are helpful, as for example, the administration of gluco-corticoids to the mother can correct respiratory distress symptoms among some premature infants.

Quinine may cause deafness.

There are a number of drugs known to affect the development of the fetus. Deafness may be traced to the mother's use of quinine in the treatment of malaria. Also, addiction to morphine can occur in the newborn of morphine-addicted mothers, suggesting that the placenta is not a barrier to opiates.

Smoking seems to produce premature infants.

SMOKING   Over 57 percent of pregnant women in the U.S. smoke. Tobacco smoke contains nicotine, carbon monoxide, collidine, pyridine, and various tar products. A number of studies have found large differences between the babies of smoking and nonsmoking mothers. Whether the differences are genetic or caused by smoking is not yet known. Smoking mothers are twice as likely to have premature infants compared to nonsmoking mothers. The full-term offspring of smoking mothers have a lower birth weight. Also, maternal smoking during pregnancy increases the heart rate of unborn babies.

Maternal Infections

Infections may cross the placental barrier.

Many parents used to expose their young daughters to viruses to immunize them against infection later in life, for viruses can affect the development of an unborn baby at critical periods by crossing the placental barrier. For example, during the first three months after conception, German measles can produce cataracts, deafness, and other sensory defects in the baby. In some instances, smallpox, chicken pox, measles, and mumps can be transmitted to the fetus with detrimental effects. The solution is to vaccinate females before they become pregnant. If a pregnant woman is still susceptible to these viruses, strict care must be taken to isolate her from potential infection.

Maternal Sensitization: Rh Factors

Rh negative mothers may be sensitized to Rh positive babies.

There are genetically determined differences in blood types. Occasionally a mother and child will have incompatible blood factors. For example, if the child's blood contains a substance which makes it clump in response to certain serums, and the mother's blood lacks that substance, the child is called Rh positive and the mother Rh negative. An Rh positive baby produces substances called *antigens,* which may pass into the mother's circulatory system during birth when the placenta is detached from the mother's uterus. If the Rh-negative mother is sensitized by her Rh-positive baby at birth in this way, the resulting antibodies can do serious damage to the next fetus if it is Rh positive. Damage occurs because the antibodies built up in reaction to the antigens destroy blood cells and prevent the baby from having enough red blood cells. Rh sensitization can have tragic consequence—miscarriage, abortion, stillbirth, or death of the baby shortly after birth. If the baby survives, it may be defective due to brain damage from inadequate oxygen supply. Rh incompatibility may occur if the mother is Rh negative and the father Rh positive. Even then consequences to the baby will happen only about half the time since Rh factors are genetically determined, and so not all children of Rh-positive men are Rh positive. In any case, the firstborn of an Rh-incompatible couple is not in danger if the placenta is whole. If, however, the antigens pass the placental barrier, a problem can result. It is generally after maternal sensitization during the birth of an Rh-positive baby to an Rh-negative mother that there is danger to subsequent Rh-positive babies. And this probability of damage is substantial. Happily, a new drug is available which can be given to Rh-negative mothers immediately after delivery to counteract the serious problems likely to occur during later pregnancies. The drug is advised for all Rh-incompatible couples. The only other method available is a complete blood exchange for an affected Rh-positive baby immediately after birth, a difficult and dangerous process.

Rh incompatibility is rare.

The incidence of Rh incompatibility between mother and infant in the total population is approximately 1 in 200. However, the rate is much higher among Rh-incompatible couples. Those planning to have children should be aware of their blood types so that they can avoid the possible dangers to their offspring from Rh incompatibility.

Maternal Age

Between 20 and 30 years of age is the optimum child-bearing interval.

Advances in medical care have made pregnancy and childbirth much safer for both mother and child. However, mothers under 20 and over 30 years of age experience more difficulties and produce more abnormal children (especially the firstborn infants) than do women between 20 and 30. Early pregnancies are often complicated by maternal immaturity. By contrast, middle age produces degeneration of the muscles and the reproductive apparatus, and changes that take place in the middle-aged woman's hormonal system complicate pregnancy (Montagu, 1962). Mongolism (called Down's syndrome) occurs much more frequently among infants of mothers over 40 years of age than among the children of younger women. The mongoloid child is mentally retarded and has a skin fold over the eye, as well as other physical symptoms. Penrose (1954) has reported that the incidence of mongoloid children among mothers under 30 is less than one in 2,000. Unhappily, after this age, every five years triples the risk of giving birth to a mongoloid child. Research has led to the belief that mongolism is caused by defective ova or abnormal early development. The defective ovum usually contains an extra chromosome on the number 21 pair.

Young or older mothers produce more abnormal babies.

Very young or middle-aged mothers are also more likely to produce children with anencephaly (lack of cortex), hydrocephalus (dilation of cerebral vesicles, leading to an enlarged brain, mental deficiency, and frequently an early death), congenital dislocation of the hip, miscarriage, and stillbirth. Neonatal death is also more frequent among the babies of very young and of older mothers.

Timing of Prenatal Influences

The timing of trauma affects its influence on the baby.

The timing of a trauma or injury is often equal in importance to *what* the particular trauma happens to be. During the embryonic period all the major structures of the baby are formed. If trauma occurs during this period it will have far-reaching effects on the organism. By contrast, if the same influence occurs later, it will have a more specific effect. For example, the effect of German measles is very different if contracted by the mother during the fifth or sixth week (when primary fibers of the optic lens are developing in the embryo) as opposed to the eighth or ninth week of fetal life (when the organ of Corti in the inner ear is undergoing differentiation). In the first case blindness results, while the second infant will be deaf.

Early trauma produces massive damage.

Ingalls (1960) reported many cases of congenital abnormality which resulted from specific factors at specific times. He inferred from clinical and laboratory evidence that trauma during the fourth week may result in loss of limbs, while trauma in the sixth week may cause heart defects to develop. More research remains to be done, but many defects which are labeled "cause unknown" may result from maternal trauma or deficiency at a specific time in development.

Birth

The newborn cries to breathe.

When a newborn child emerges from its mother's womb, the doctor or midwife picks it up by the feet, turns it upside down to drain fluid from the nose and mouth, and then gives the infant a smart slap on the buttocks. Following this rather crude welcome, the baby breathes, cries, and changes from a parasite into an independent human being. The placenta is still attached to the child and the umbilical cord connects the baby and mother at this point. However, the umbilical cord is already reflexively clamped off and ceases to function. The newborn is on his own.

Newborn babies are not beautiful.

What is a newborn like? Many people have never seen a newborn baby. Most advertisements for baby products show infants 2 to 3 months old. The newborn is tiny, wet, red, and wrinkled. A newborn's nose has been flattened and its head squeezed by the passage through the birth canal. These signs of stress disappear in a few weeks. The newborn may have dark, coarse hair over much of its body, which falls out and is replaced by finer strands. A newborn baby is covered with amniotic fluid and its skin is coated with a protective substance which dries to give the baby's skin a chalky look. Eye and skin pigments are not always developed at birth, so many babies have blue eyes and a light complexion. The average newborn infant weighs seven pounds and is twenty inches long. A quarter of its length is the head. Its limbs are almost totally useless. A newborn's skull has six soft spots that are not yet covered with bone. The large soft spot on top of its head will not close until the baby is about eighteen months of age.

Birth can be traumatic.

Some authorities have argued that birth is an event of enormous psychological significance. They point out that the infant is thrust from a calm, quiet, peaceful environment into a stimulating, threatening world. These speculative notions about the psychological impact of birth are not testable, but there are measurable consequences of birth injury. Birth trauma may seriously affect the child's later physical and intellectual development. Difficult labor, delivery with instruments, and anoxia (deprivation of oxygen) may produce central nervous system damage with consequent motor and mental defect. Cerebral palsy, a motor defect caused by disease-induced abnormalities in the brain, sometimes results from injury at birth.

Babies need oxygen.

Every baby requires a continuous oxygen supply. If breathing is delayed for several minutes, the baby may develop deterioration in the brain with subsequent mental retardation. Infants traumatized at birth are less sensitive to painful stimulation, less mature in their motor integration, and respond inadequately to visual stimulation (Graham, et al., 1956).

Traumatized infants are hyperactive, more irritable, and muscularly tense.

Premature Birth

Premature babies are vulnerable.

The premature infant is extremely vulnerable because it is not fully prepared for life out of the womb. Usually human infants can survive if they are seven months or older and receive proper care for the early weeks of life. Premature births are often very short or unduly long, and subject the infant to additional stress. Comparisons of the early development of premature and full-term babies suggest that extremely small babies have a greater chance of developing neurological or behavioral defects (Lubchenco, et al., 1963). At forty weeks of age, 8 percent of premature infants show neurological defects, primarily in motor functioning. This compares with only 1.6 percent of normal children. The long-term consequences of prematurity are not found in physical growth. Rather, the premature infant is more likely to show sensory defects and a lower IQ than its full-term brother or sister. The premature infant is also more likely to have speech difficulties and poor motor coordination than the full-term infant. The premature baby tends to be either hyperactive or quiet, and to be more shy and dependent on his mother.

There are two kinds of premature infants.

Tanner (1963) believes there are two different kinds of "premature" infants, and that much of the confusion about prematurity and later intellectual or physical development results from not separating these two types. Tanner argues that some infants who are labeled "premature" because they have a small birth weight are in fact full term. These babies have not developed normally during their full nine months of intrauterine existence. By contrast, other low-birth-weight babies are small because they have *not* spent a full nine months in their mother's womb. Tanner finds that the *small* full-term baby who is called premature because of his low birth weight is likely to have developmental defects later in life. These defects are the result of genetic problems or early environmental insults which have somehow arrested its normal growth pattern. Tanner also points out that the "true" premature infant, who is small because it was born before completing nine months within its mother's womb, develops quite normally once it is beyond these first critical weeks of life.

Multiple Births

Multiple births can cause problems.

If two or more babies share a common womb or the interval between two births is short, the offspring may suffer. Multiple births can be of two kinds: identical twins, who are produced when a single fertilized egg divides completely and produces two identical infants, or fraternal twins, who result from the simultaneous fertilization of two or more different eggs by different sperm, as we have already learned. Multiple births may be all identical, all fraternal, or some combination of these two types.

Multiple births are dangerous.

Babies from multiple births suffer some deficits. They may be born prematurely simply from lack of uterine space. In those cases where both infants share one placenta, one baby may occupy a much more favorable position and thus receive more nutrients. Multiple births often miscarry or produce premature infants. These infants frequently show slow motor development and average 5 points lower in IQ compared with singleton births. Triplets suffer more deficits than twins, quadruplets more than triplets, and so on.

Firstborn children are less viable.

Birth order and timing of pregnancies also may affect child growth in later life. Firstborn children have more malformations and are less viable than later born babies. Babies who are born less than one year after a previous pregnancy are less likely to be healthy than babies who are spaced several years apart.

The Newborn

Physiological Changes

Many changes happen at birth.

Immediately after birth the baby must shift to a new pattern of blood circulation, begin its own respiration, fight infections, and control its body temperature. Within a few days the newborn must begin the digestive process. Happily, almost any kind of stimulation will start the child breathing. Massaging, slapping, dropping it into water, mouth to mouth breathing, or simply turning the newborn upside down will begin respiration. The newborn baby's breathing tends to be poorly coordinated, irregular, shallow, and noisy for the first few weeks. Then it settles down to a more mature pattern.

The newborn's circulation shift.

CIRCULATION   The baby's circulatory system must shift from pumping large quantities of blood toward the placenta to circulating blood toward its own lungs and digestive system. The first step is constriction of a small circular muscle around the umbilical cord, cutting off or slowing down the circulation toward the placenta. The constriction is accomplished reflexively in many babies, but is also done by the physician to insure its happening. Following constriction of the cord, pressure on the left atrium or upper chamber of the heart closes a flap and begins a new blood route. Constricting the umbilical arteries and closing the left-right ventricle opening of the heart forces the baby's blood to his lungs, which now begin taking in oxygen and removing carbon dioxide, a job that was previously done by the placenta. The opening in the baby's heart closes permanently in a few weeks under normal circumstances.

Digestion begins soon after birth.

DIGESTION   A few days following birth the baby must begin to take in food, digest it, and eliminate its own waste. The newborn's digestive tract contains most of the enzymes necessary to digest simple foods, and it gets the necessary bacteria to complete digestion in just a few days by breathing and swallowing the atmosphere or touching things with its mouth. Most babies in the U.S. are not fed for a day or two following birth. But in some primitive societies newborns are breast fed by wet nurses almost immediately after they are born. Babies in American hospitals usually lose weight over the first few days of life and then begin to gain new tissue and fat.

Newborn temperature regulation is crude.

The body temperature regulation of the newborn is primitive, so it can be chilled or overheated easily. In addition, babies don't sweat until about a month after they are born, so the best indicator of body temperature is to feel the infant's hands or feet.

Babies gain immunity from maternal antibodies.

IMMUNITY   Within the womb a baby absorbs a variety of antibodies from its mother through the placental barrier. These immune factors give it several months of safety from most infections. The maternal immunity only lasts six months, so many of the infections traditionally associated with early teething probably result from loss of immunity rather than exposure to new dangers.

Later the infant builds his own immunity.

Following the loss of immunity from its mother, it takes the infant years to construct its own immunological defenses against disease. Modern vaccination methods and normal contagion expose the infant and child to polio, smallpox, diptheria, and tetanus in the course of development.

Newborn Behavior

The birth cry is reflexive.

THE BIRTH CRY   The first act of a newborn baby is usually a loud cry. The birth cry has captured the interests of poets, novelists, and philosophers who have described it as "a cry of wrath" or "the newborn's first feeling of inferiority when faced with reality" (Otto Rank). However, physiologists believe that the birth cry is only a reflexive response to the newborn's first breath. It is a sound produced by respiration and simply marks the onset of breathing when the newborn first secures its own oxygen through its lungs.

Emotions are very difficult to label.

Early students of behavior felt that the birth cry might reflect an emotional state, but types of infant crying cannot be reliably differentiated. For example, Sherman and Sherman (1929) asked nurses, psychology students, and medical students to judge the emotional content of infants' crying when the situation which produced the crying could not be seen. There was almost no agreement among the judges about what the infants' crying signified. Apparently, most people judge the emotional behavior of an infant in terms of the situation which produced the reaction, rather than on the basis of the sound of the cry itself. There are abundant data on the characteristics of newborn infants' crying. Babies usually cry about two hours out of every twenty four. The greatest amounts of crying occur when the baby's caretaker is too busy to attend the infant or right before mealtime. Surprisingly, the crying of one infant does not trigger crying among other babies around it.

Newborns sleep a great deal.

SLEEP   It is difficult to give a good definition of sleep without resorting to notions of attention and consciousness; and it is particularly difficult to define sleep in the newborn. The newborn's activity is lowest between its various nursing periods. There is a sharp drop in activity after nursing, followed by a general increase in bodily activity as the next feeding period approaches. With increasing age the periods of sleep increase in length. However, the total number of sleeping hours in a day decreases as the infant grows older (*see* Figure 2.23). In addition, the proportion of *REM* (rapid-eye-movement) sleep decreases with age. We know REM sleep is associated with dreaming because if you wake a sleeping person during that stage he will almost always report a dream. No one is sure why REM sleep decreases with age.

The newborn shows a variety of responses (*see* Table 2.3). Are these cortical or lower-level acts? Consider the newborn infant's central nervous system.

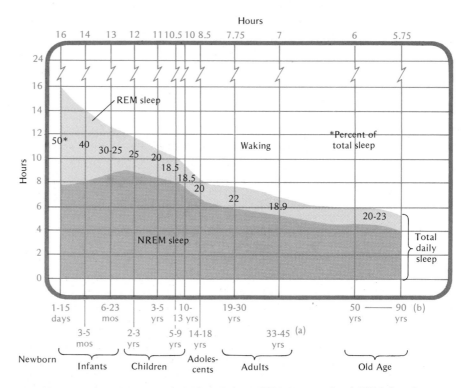

FIGURE 2.23 Changes in amounts of total sleep, REM sleep, and non-REM sleep by age. (After Roffwarg, Muzio, Dement, 1966)

TABLE 2.3 Responses Available to the Neonate and Young Infant

Eye Responses

1. *Opening and closing of eyelids*—spontaneously and in response to a variety of external stimuli. The closing of the eyes is usually a bilateral response, but more pronounced on the stimulated side.

2. *Pupillary response* (widening or narrowing of the pupils in response to light)—narrowing upon going to sleep and widening upon awaking. The pupillary response of the second eye is coordinated with the reactions of the stimulated eye.

3. *Pursuit* (following a visual stimulus) and *saccadic* (quick, jerky fixations as those which occur in adult reading) movements occur in the very young infant.

4. *Nystagmus* (rapid, restricted-in-scope eye-movement oscillations) may appear spontaneously or be evoked by thermal stimulation or rotation in the neonate.

5. *Coordinate, compensatory eye movements* occur spontaneously; when the newborn's head is moved quickly in one direction, eye movements in the opposite direction are elicited.

6. *Coordination of eyes*—eyes often move together, but not in well-coordinated movements.

7. *Convergence* of two eyes occurs in some infants; some indication of *accommodation* varying with convergence of the eyes. The newborn does not accommodate or converge his eyes.

8. *Eye position in sleep* is most frequently the upward and divergent position found in adults.

9. *Tear secretion* has been observed during crying and upon irritation of the nasal membranes; tear secretion is unusual in the newborn.

Facial and Mouth Responses

1. *Opening and closing mouth*—closed during sleep, opened after quinine application and as a part of yawning and coughing.

2. *Lip movements*—licking, compressing lips, pursing lips in response to tactual stimulation.

3. *Sucking* occurs spontaneously (possibly caused by stomach contractions) or in response to tactual and taste stimuli.

4. *Smiling* occurs spontaneously after feeding or in response to tickling under chin.

5. *Pushing objects from mouth*—strong solutions of salt and quinine are rejected.

6. *Yawning* has been observed some five minutes after birth; it is a common response.

7. *Grimaces* (including twisting the mouth; wrinkling the forehead) have been observed as spontaneous behavior and in response to noxious stimuli.

Oral Responses

1. *Crying,* usually accompanied by activity of the arms and legs, seen spontaneously and in response to stomach contractions, cold, pain, bright lights, loud noises, holding the nose, and hampering the neonate's movements. These stimuli do not invariably evoke crying.

2. *Swallowing* occurs in all normal newborn infants. *Gagging* may be elicited by noxious smells or tastes and by touching the back of the tongue or the tonsils. *Vomiting* have been observed.

3. *Coughing* occurs within the first hour of life. *Sneezing* may occur spontaneously or in response to noxious olfactory stimuli.

4. *Cooing* and *holding the breath* have been reported.

Head Movements

1. *Upward and downward movements*—upward head movements can be evoked by placing the newborn on its stomach, holding its nose, or flashing a bright light before its eyes. Downward or ventral movements occur less frequently than upward movements.

2. *Turning face to side* appears in response to tactual stimuli (such as nose cleaning), a touch on cheek, a dim light, the source of sound (in a few infants). *Turning face from side to side* occurs during hunger or crying periods, or when the infant is placed on its stomach.

3. *Head shudder* in response to "bitter" stimuli.

4. *Balancing head* in response to changes of bodily position (even when subjects are blindfolded); reported as early as two days of age.

Table 2.3 *(Continued)*

Head and Arm Responses

1. *Closing hand*—in response to tactual stimulation of fingers and palm. Many neonates are able to support their own weight momentarily by *reflex grasping* (discussed in some detail later in this chapter).

2. *Arm flexion* can be evoked by a prick with a pointed instrument or by a sudden slight "tap" against the hand.

3. *Rubbing face*—in response to noxious stimuli on nasal membranes—also appears spontaneously.

4. *Startle response of arms*—in response to almost any type of intense, sudden stimulation. Hands are thrown outward with an associated tremor of the arms.

Trunk Reactions

1. *Arching the back* frequently follows pinching the nose.

2. *Twisting of the trunk* accompanies squirming. When the head is rotated, the shoulders and pelvis twist in the same direction.

3. *Abdominal reflex*—in response to a needle as a stimulus.

Reproductive Organ Response in Males

1. *Cremasteric reflex* (raising of the testes) occurs in response to irritation of the inner thigh.

2. *Penis erection*—noted by several investigators shortly after birth.

Foot and Leg Responses

1. *Knee jerk* and *Achilles tendon reflex* present in most newborn infants.

2. *Flexion of the leg*—elicited by stimulating the foot or leg tactually or with a noxious stimulus.

3. *Extension of the leg* in response to a gentle push. This extension thrust is strong enough to support some infants' weight on the first day. Extension of the leg accompanied by dorsal flexion of the foot, the reverse of usual adult coordination.

4. *Protective reflex*—when one stimulates one foot or leg the free foot almost invariably comes up and pushes against the source of stimulation.

5. *Kicking* consists of pedaling and simultaneous extension of flexion of both legs; usually occurs during crying.

6. *Stepping movements* occur when the newborn is held upright with the feet touching some surface.

Coordinate Responses of Many Body Parts

1. *Resting and sleeping position*—the legs are flexed; the fists closed; the upper arms are out straight from the shoulders with the forearms flexed at right angles so they lie parallel to the head. The fists may lie below the chin, however, as in fetal life.

2. *Backbone reflex* consists of the concave bending of a side that is stroked or tickled; the leg of the concave side is extended while the leg of the convex side is flexed. This same response occurs when the newborn is held in the air by a hand under one side.

3. *Lifting the head and rear quarters* simultaneously appears in older infants; tendency toward such behavior in the newborn.

4. *"Fencing position"* is observed when the newborn's head is rotated; the arm toward which the face is rotated extends; the other flexes; the legs do likewise.

5. *"Springing position"*—when the infant is held upright and inclined forward, the arms extend forward and the legs are brought up.

6. *Startle response*, often called the Moro reflex or "fear reaction," consists of throwing the arms apart, spreading the fingers, extending the legs, and throwing back the head; may be followed by crying, depending on the intensity and duration of the stimulus. This response may be evoked

Table 2.3 *(Continued)*

by loud noises, falling, hot or cold stimuli, and other sudden and intense types of stimulation; has also been observed in the absence of any type of external stimulation, being similar in these cases to the startle pattern demonstrated by adults in dropping off to sleep.

7. *Creeping* movements have been observed when the newborn is placed in a prone position. The legs and arms are drawn under the body and the head is lifted; each pair of extremities alternates in movement.

8. *Bodily jerk* appears in response to loud noises; the arms and legs flex strongly and jerk upward.

From this summary it can be seen that the newborn's repertoire of motor responses is considerable and that the behavior patterns demonstrated are sometimes quite complex. The naïve observer does a grave injustice to the newborn by reporting its motor responses as limited to crying, sucking, and waving of the arms and legs. Some of the motor responses summarized above have been extensively studied or have an interesting history of theoretical conjecture; a more detailed discussion of these behavior patterns is presented in the following sections. *See* Graham, Materazzo, and Caldwell (1956) for a battery of test procedures especially designed to differentiate normal and traumatized infants. These procedures include tests and ratings of vision, muscular tension, general irritability, pain thresholds, and overall maturation.

Source: Adapted from a classification by Dennis (1934), based on a survey of eighty scientific reports.

The Newborn Brain

The newborn brain is immature.

Figure 2.24 shows a composite human newborn/infant brain. Darker sections represent areas of the baby's brain which mature earlier. The newborn brain contains mature motor and sensory areas, and parts of its primary auditory areas also function at birth. The rest of its cortex is very immature.

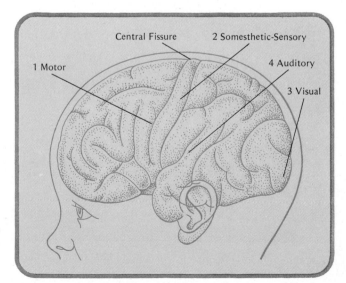

FIGURE 2.24
A human baby's cortex shows the various levels of maturity reached at birth. Dark areas represent mature brain functions; light areas are immature. The motor and primary sensory cortical areas are completely mature at birth.

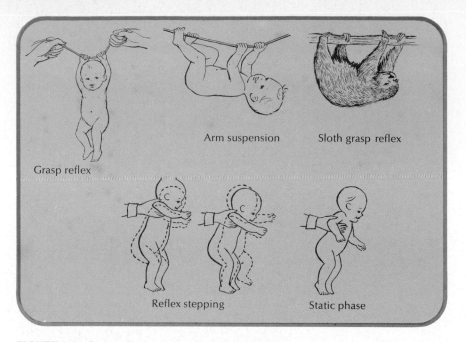

Grasp reflex

Arm suspension

Sloth grasp reflex

Reflex stepping

Static phase

FIGURE 2.25 Early reflexive behaviors of human babies.

Newborn babies show many reflexes.

The newborn's behavior consists primarily of reflexes. Figure 2.25 shows grasping and stepping reflexes typical of the newborn human baby. By the third month after birth a baby's brain shows rapid development in three areas: motor, primary sensory, and association. The baby's motor areas develop most rapidly, producing various stages of motor development. Although there is individual variation in the particular age each act is begun, most babies follow the same sequence of rolling, sitting, crawling, pulling up, walking when led, standing alone, and then walking alone. These functions closely follow physiological maturation of the baby's motor areas in its central nervous system.

The nervous system matures in a specific sequence.

The human baby's nervous system matures in a specific order. For example, the human embryo brain physically resembles that of primitive animals, but the fetal brain looks structurally like that of more advanced mammals. Functionally, however, the maturing baby's brain resembles an adult with less and less brain damage as it matures, rather than being similar to lower and then higher animals. This is because lower levels of the human nervous system cannot sustain such complex behavior as swimming in the fish. Basic life functions are performed by a baby's immature brainstem, while the brainstem of a fish performs many complex functions. The human baby must await development of his cortex before his responses become human. The baby is an immature man, not a reptile.

When does the human cortex first begin to function? A complete

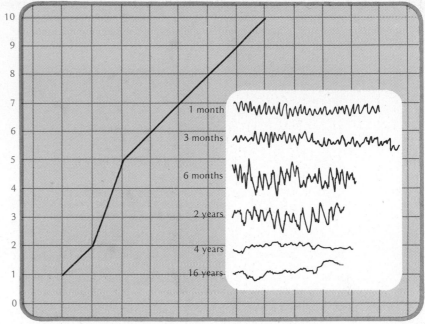

1 mo. 3 mos. 6 mos. 1 yr. 2 yrs. 4 yrs. 8 yrs. 16 yrs.

FIGURE 2.26 The development of the alpha rhythm in one boy from birth to maturity. By sixteen years of age his alpha rhythm has reached the adult level of ten cycles per second.
(After Lindsley, 1951)

answer is difficult, but Figure 2.26 shows the development of brain waves recorded from a developing human brain. These data were collected from one boy over the first several years of his life. Note that the frequency of brain waves increases very quickly from birth to six months, and then more slowly until the adult frequency of 10 cycles per second is reached at around fourteen years of age.

The brain contains three functional levels.

Lower brain functions are available to human babies at birth. With maturity these lower functions often disappear or are suppressed by higher-center control. Physiological psychologists often group brain functions into three levels: reflex, sensory, and cortical (*see* Figure 2.27). Examples of *level one* functions are: sucking, rooting, pupillary reflexes, bilateral coordination of eyes or trunk and the orienting response. The human orienting response includes turning the head, eyes, and ears; and an increase in muscular tone. The orienting reflex is typically followed by exploration.

Level one responses are all or none.

Another characteristic brainstem pattern is the defensive reflex that follows intense stimulation or pain. Level one responses either happen or not, and they do not interpret incoming stimuli. Instead, level one

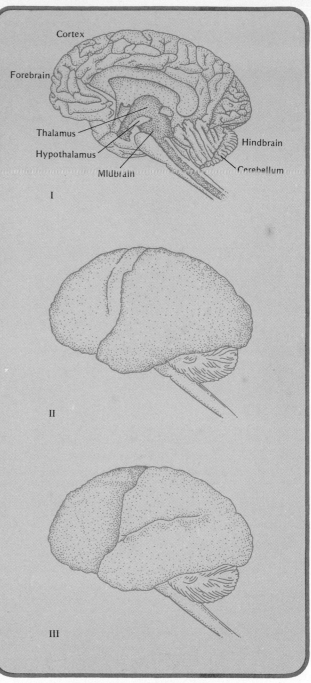

FIGURE 2.27
Three levels of the human nervous system. Level I is concerned with wakefulness, emotions, and arousal. Level II is concerned with processing sensory information; and Level III with planning and long-term goals.

A Functional Map of the Brain

responses alert other parts of the nervous system that something has happened; they are like a primitive alarm system. *Level two* of the human central nervous system is concerned with more specific stimuli. The second-level system provides a focused, rapid processing of sensory information. At the *highest level* the human cortex defines which events attract attention.

The cortex controls other levels.

A person's goals are the joint result of all three systems. The cortex defines long-term goals; the sensory system controls processing specific stimuli; and the brainstem modulates internal body states and alerts the other levels to novel events. As the baby matures, his cortex exerts more control over the level-one and -two systems. Finally, it develops into a functioning human adult.

Summary

The major theme of this book is that human development is controlled jointly by genetic and environmental factors. Chapter 2 traced the evolutionary history of man's central nervous system, the early biological maturation of the human brain, and the effects of genetic and environmental events on human abilities. The combination of evolution, development, and heredity form the biological bases of human behavior. In addition, the chapter outlined the stages of prenatal growth and the early environmental influences which can effect behavior. The main early influences are prenatal factors like drugs, malnutrition, and emotional upset or trauma as a result of a difficult birth. The final section outlined the biological changes and behavioral abilities of the human newborn.

SUGGESTED ADDITIONAL READINGS

Fuller, J.L., and W.R. Thompson. *Behavior Genetics.* New York: Wiley, 1960.

Hooker, D. *The Prenatal Origin of Behavior.* Lawrence: University of Kansas Press, 1952.

Kallman, F.J. *The Genetics of Schizophrenia.* New York: Augustin, 1938.

Lenneberg, E.H. *The Biological Foundations of Language.* New York: Wiley, 1967.

Newman, H.H., F.N. Freeman, and K.J. Holzinger. *Twins: A Study of Heredity and Environment.* Chicago: University of Chicago Press, 1937.

Sinnott, E.W., L.C. Dunn, and T. Dobzhansky. *Principles of Genetics,* 5th ed. New York: McGraw-Hill, 1958.

3 Sensory-motor Growth

Physical Growth
  Growth Norms
  Some Principles of Motor Development
  Motor Abilities
    Walking
    Left-right Preference
    Grasping
    Interrelations among Motor Abilities
  Problems in Physical Growth
    Overweight and Underweight
    The Tired Child
    Childhood Illness
Sensory-motor Integration

Stages of Sensory-motor Development
    Reflex Acts
    Primary Circular Reactions
    Secondary Circular Reactions
    Sensory-motor Coordination
    Tertiary Circular Reactions
    Insight
The Infant's Conception of the World
  Play
  Space
  Time
  Imitation
  Cause and Effect
  Object Permanence
Heinz Werner
Summary

PREVIEW

Most students of human behavior assume that the early years during which an infant grows quickly, develops motor skills, and begins to integrate *sensory-motor abilities* are particularly important for later development. Jean Piaget, the Swiss psychologist who has done many childhood studies, believes these early sensory-motor coordinations form the basis for all later development of understanding and knowledge. Psychologists who investigate how people act—their behavior rather than thoughts or feelings—believe that habits acquired during these early years affect how a child will later connect stimuli with responses. That is why it is important to know about normal human growth, the acquisition of motor skills, and the integration of sensory-motor abilities. Studies of growth show at least two distinct stages in human physical development: rapid early growth between birth and about six years of age; and a second spurt during adolescence, when the person is reaching physical and sexual maturity.

More than anyone else, Piaget has studied the sensory-motor development of children. He has devised ingenious tests of sensory-motor abilities and made fundamental observations on his own three children during their early years. Piaget believes that early sensory-motor development can be separated into six distinct stages and that each of these stages represents a fundamentally different way in which the child interacts with his world. Piaget points out, for example, that during the course of an infant's first two years the child progresses from rigid, reflexive reactions to insight, the ability to understand a situation or event in its context.

It is these early childhood years and their developmental stages that we will discuss in Chapter 3.

Early years are very important.

Almost all theorists of development agree that the first few years of a baby's life leave permanent imprints on his perceptions, thoughts, and personality. In Chapter 3 the baby's early physical and motor development, his attempts at coordinating sensory inputs with motor acts, and the infant's first ideas about his world will be outlined. The ideas of Jean Piaget and Heinz Werner, concerning the baby's early interactions with his world will be discussed later in the chapter. These investigations form the theoretical framework for this section.

Physical Growth

There are three measures of physical growth.

On the average, baby boys are 4 percent heavier and 2 percent longer than their female peers at birth. However, firstborn babies of either sex are generally smaller at birth than later siblings, although these early size differences fade with maturity. Three measures of physical growth are commonly used: weight, which is a three-dimensional measure; body area, which is a two-dimensional measure; and length, which is a one-dimensional measure. Figure 3.1 demonstrates that all three scores show similar growth trends with age.

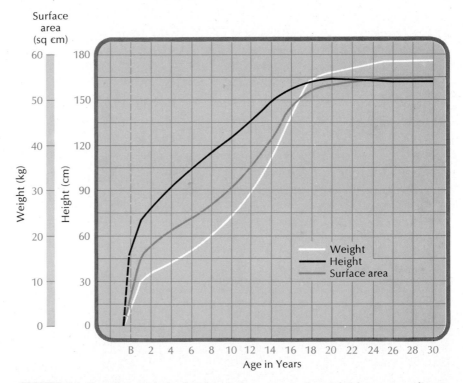

FIGURE 3.1 Growth curves for height, surface area, and weight drawn according to Quetelet's figures.
(From Boyd, 1935.)

Weight gain is seasonal.

Growth rate is not perfectly steady. There are no seasonal variations in the growth rate of length; but several investigators have found that preschool children are more likely to gain weight during the fall and summer months than in the spring and winter. These seasonal variations in weight gain are probably related to illnesses and the amount of outdoor exercise a child takes. In addition to collecting simple measures like height, weight, and surface area, students of human physical growth have tried to find more complex and subtle indicators of physical maturity. After trying several such indices, they have decided that the ratio of lower limb length to total body length is the best single indicator of physical maturity. This ratio shows that on the average girls are more mature than boys throughout their early lives, even at the age of eight weeks.

Height is related to general growth.

Body length is a good measure of general growth, while weight is a more sensitive measure of nutritional adequacy. Throughout childhood boys and girls gain weight faster than height. However, this changes rather abruptly at puberty.

Several growth patterns exist.

Various patterns of physical growth are shown in Figure 3.2. One is called the neural curve. It indicates growth trends for the brain, spinal cord, and eyes. Note that very rapid growth of the nervous system happens during infancy, while slower changes occur in childhood and maturity.

Sex organs mature during puberty.

A second pattern of growth characterizes primary and secondary sexual characteristics. For these organs little growth takes place during infancy and childhood, but there is a striking development during puberty.

Total body growth shows two stages.

Still another pattern of growth characterizes the total body. Total body growth is rapid during infancy, declines during middle childhood, and spurts into a rapid second growth during puberty (*see* Figure 3.2).

A child's total personal development can be affected by his body. If

FIGURE 3.2
Relative patterns of physical growth in the human body during postnatal life. The top curve demonstrates growth in the neural system; the middle curve illustrates body growth; and the lower curve shows development of sexual characteristics.
(After Scammon, in Jackson, 1928.)

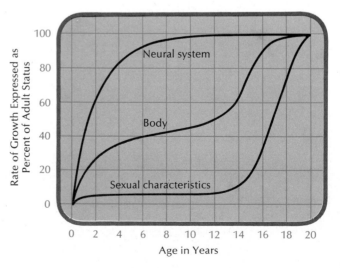

Body build affects
the self-concept.

the child is strong, healthy, and active, he will be capable in physical activities and socially attractive to others. However, if the growing child sees his body as weak, sickly, and undesirable, his social and personal adjustment may suffer. Thus, physical characteristics affect how we see another person, and color our self-concept as well.

Growth and motor
abilities are re-
lated.

To understand physical growth and development we must know something about the principles which govern body growth, the relationship among motor abilities, and the specific problems associated with physical growth.

Growth Norms

Growth norms chart
average development.

As a first step in the study of human growth, early investigators collected descriptions of so-called normal development. These norms were not intended to explain physical growth or early motor behavior but they were useful in locating extremes and charting the progress of both the average and the exceptional child. The normal child falls near the middle of a distribution of characteristics obtained from a representative sample of children. Some children mature more quickly than the average, while others may lag in their physical growth. Average growth does not mean "ideal" physical development. It simply shows how and to what extent a representative child grows and how a child acts.

Early norms were
collected by Gesell.

Development norms were collected by investigators who believed that most growth and early behavior results from genetic programing. This early genetic view of human development stressed the maturational "readiness" of children to perform particular motor acts. The investigators felt that the best way to study physical and motor development was to outline maturational sequences as they occurred in the general population. Arnold Gesell (1954) established norms for the development of early motor and sensory-motor behavior. He photographed infants under ordinary conditions and outlined the "typical behaviors" characteristic of children at various ages. These developmental norms were an attempt to chart the course of human growth according to significant landmarks, which would signal normal, accelerated, or retarded development in the individual child.

Environmental
theories stress en-
richment rather than
maturation.

By contrast, an environmental view of human growth was concerned about how to produce "readiness" in children who were not yet performing a particular motor act. Growth norms give little indication of what to do with children who are developing outside of the "normal" range. While there is no problem for the child who is maturing in the normal way and who seems average or better in his motor development, there is a problem of how to help the slow child. The environmentalists argued that once we understand the mechanisms which control growth (for example, nutrition or hormones) we can begin to accelerate physical development when it is too slow. Thus, norms are helpful in measuring who is slow and by how much. However, when we move beyond physical growth into areas of sensory and motor behavior, the problem becomes more complex. Let us consider early motor abilities.

Some Principles of Motor Development

Motor development is cephalocaudal.

There are several principles that emerge from research on motor development. First is the *cephalocaudal* progression of behavior. This means that growth and motor development proceed from the head toward the legs and feet. At birth the infant's head most closely approximates its adult size and his lower extremities least approximate their adult size. Also, the infant's first motor control occurs in the muscles that move the head. Only later do shoulder, arm, abdominal, and finally leg muscles come under control. Figure 3.3 illustrates this principle by showing the relative proportions of the child from fifteen months to maturity.

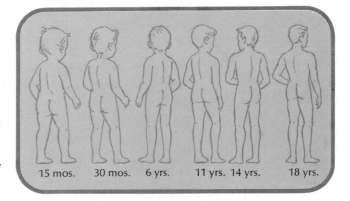

FIGURE 3.3
Changes in body proportions with growth, from fifteen months to eighteen years. The drawings are of the same boy at six ages, all adjusted to the same height.
(From Bayley, 1956.)

15 mos.   30 mos.   6 yrs.   11 yrs. 14 yrs.   18 yrs.

Motor development is also proximodistal.

A second principle of motor-development research is the *proximodistal* growth and development of behavior. This means that growth proceeds from the central axis of the body outward. Examples of this principle are the baby's early movements, which are gross body actions from the shoulder but without separate arm, hand, or finger movements. It requires about one year for the infant to make independent finger

Early motor responses are gross.

movements or oppose his thumb and forefinger, as in grasping an object.

Finally, early growth and development proceeds from general to more specific response patterns, and from gross to more refined control of the child's body.

Motor Abilities

The baby gradually overcomes gravity.

There are various physical and motor landmarks which occur in the course of growth (*see* Table 3.1 and Figure 3.4). These stages occur as the baby becomes more and more independent of gravity. At first a newborn baby can move only his arms and legs against gravity; many newborns

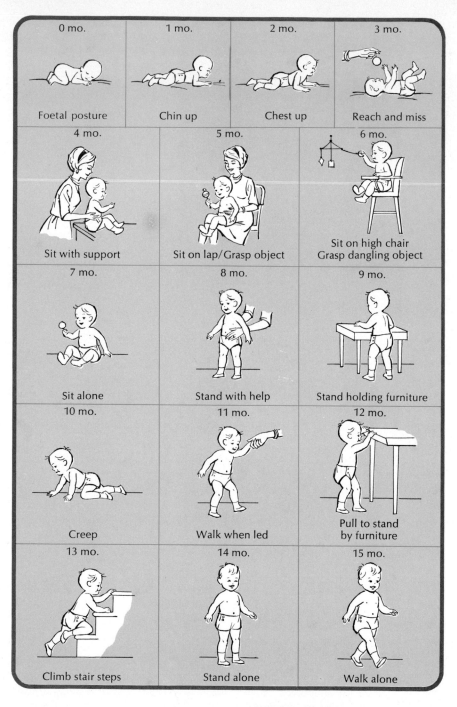

FIGURE 3.4 The motor sequence.
(Adapted from Shirley, 1933.)

cannot lift the head or trunk. During the first month some control over gravity occurs when most babies begin to lift their chins. The next step comes at around two months when the average baby begins to push his chest off the floor with his back, stomach muscles, and arms. At this stage the world the infant sees becomes much more varied because he can lift his head and turn it in order to look at various parts of his environment. Next, the baby matures enough to turn from his back to his belly and over again.

The average baby sits by age seven months.

At about seven months the average baby can maintain a sitting position, which gives him another new visual perspective. At around ten months of age creeping and crawling begin, and by one year the average infant can pull himself into a standing position. Almost immediately he starts moving around his crib or playpen holding onto its edge. Usually by fifteen months he walks independently.

TABLE 3.1   Second-year Items in Bayley's
Scales of Infant Development

Item	Age placement (Months)
Walks alone	11.7
Throws a ball	13.3
Walks sideways	14.1
Walks backward	14.6
Walks upstairs with help	16.1
Walks downstairs with help	16.4
Tries to stand on walking board	17.8
Walks with one foot on walking board	20.6
Walks upstairs alone; marks time	25.1

Source: N. Bayley, Bayley Scales of Infant Development (New York: The Psychological Corporation, 1969). Reproduced by permission. Copyright © 1969 by The Psychological Corporation, New York, N. Y. All rights reserved.

Babies show wide individual development differences.

Table 3.1 is useful for parents or those who want to know whether a particular child is showing average, accelerated, or slow motor development. However, it must be remembered that there are wide differences in the ages at which particular behaviors appear in individual children and that this variation is perfectly normal. For example, some children "walk alone" before the end of the first year, while others may not walk until they are eighteen months of age. Also, the average performance among groups of children varies from one study to another due to variations in the samples. For these reasons, parents should not be alarmed if their children are not growing at the so-called norms of motor-development. Only when there is a very great retardation from the average should a parent pay particular attention to the motor development of children.

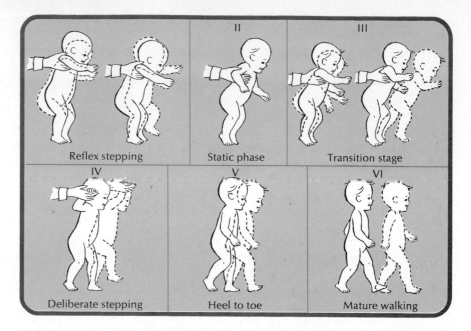

FIGURE 3.5 Six stages of walking. In the first stage the newborn child makes reflex stepping movements which occur quite often during the first three weeks of life. Stage II is the static, or inhibition, phase. This is characterized especially by better head control and by the loss of the reflex stepping actions from Stage I. Stage III, the transition phase, is noted for up-and-down movements of the body and stepping motions that are noticeably different from those of Stage I. Stage IV shows deliberate stepping while being supported. Stage V brings about heel-toe progression. And the final, more mature stage shows well-integrated walking.
(From McGraw, 1943.)

Walking follows six stages.

WALKING   There are six stages in the development of walking in the child (*see* Figure 3.5):

1. Reflex stepping in the newborn.
2. A static phase when this activity is inhibited.
3. A transition stage.
4. Deliberate stepping movements.
5. Foot movements from heel to toe.
6. Mature walking standing up.

The infant uses a broad base for walking.

The stability of an infant when he is standing depends on his body weight, the center of gravity, and the area enclosed by his feet. Most infants take their first steps from a broad base. They flex their knees to lower the center of gravity and raise their arms to facilitate balancing, and they reach for handholds to steady them. As the child improves his walking, his knees become straighter; his feet are placed closer together; and his arms no longer serve for balance and reaching. By this stage walking is smooth, coordinated, and automatic.

Left-right preference develops by 2 years of age.

LEFT-RIGHT PREFERENCE   Most children do not show hand or foot preference until about two years of age. Thus, during their first two years babies are ambidextrous, using both right and left hands and feet without partiality. By the end of the second year a majority of infants prefer to use their right hands. Most five-year-old children have established a consistent choice of one hand or the other, although this preference varies somewhat: A child may eat and write with his right hand, but bat or throw a ball left-handed. Right-handedness does not necessarily imply dominance of the right eye or right foot.

Cerebral dominance may explain handedness.

A *lateral cerebral dominance* theory was once widely accepted as an explanation for handedness. This theory assumes that if the left side of the brain is dominant, then the individual will be right-handed; and if the right hemisphere is dominant, he will be left-handed. Many thought that changing the preferred hand would damage the child, and several authors attributed stuttering and reading difficulties to changes in handedness. There is little evidence to support the notion that a change of handedness causes stuttering, for example. Problems are much more likely to be due to *how* the child is directed to change than to the change itself. Today the notion of brain dominance is considered to be only valid speculation.

Prehistoric tools exist for both hands.

Anthropologists have found large deposits of early prehistoric tools designed for both left-handed and right-handed people. Only later in history did right-handed implements predominate. Heredity may have something to do with handedness, although the evidence for determination by social learning is also strong. Further genetic evidence comes from pedigree studies, which show that handedness runs in families and that it follows Mendelian ratios (*see* Chapter 2) rather closely in frequency. However, hand preferences show cultural variation; they develop gradually and differ from task to task; and they are remarkably susceptible to training. All these characteristics suggest that early genetic hand preferences can be modified.

Grasping changes systematically with age.

GRASPING   At birth human babies possess a reflex grasp with two patterns: hand closure upon stimulation of the palm; and contraction of the hand, arm, and shoulder in response to strain. Between birth and twenty-four weeks of age many infants can support their weight with this grasp reflex (*see* Figure 3.6). After six months of age the reflex gradually disappears. In the human infant the grasp reflex is not very useful, but among lower primates the young infant must cling to its mother's back while she uses her hands to eat, run, or swing through the trees to escape a predator.

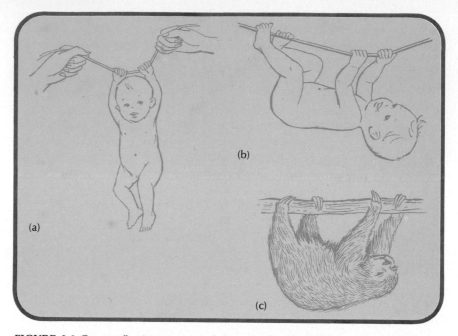

FIGURE 3.6 Grasp reflex in a prematurely born four-week-old twin (weight 6.7 pounds). Arm suspension from the palmar grasp reflex is shown in (a). Arm suspension with simultaneous leg suspension from palmar and plantar grasp reflexes is shown in (b). The grasp reflex in a human infant is similar to that of the sloth (*Choloepus didactylus*) as is shown in (c).

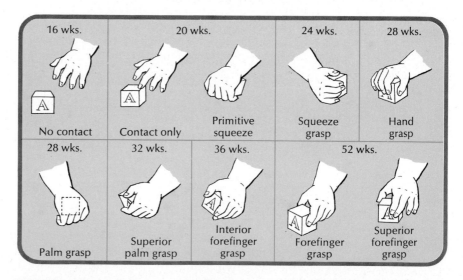

FIGURE 3.7 Types of grasping behavior in the human infant in the first year of life from primitive squeezing through crude palming to the development of fingertip and forefinger grasping.
(From Halverson, 1931.)

Grasping gradually becomes systematic.

The systematic changes in how infants grasp small objects are shown in Figure 3.7. Earliest attempts to grasp small things are made with gross shoulder and elbow movements. With further maturity the infant shows a crude palming pattern while trying to grasp. However, his thumb is still inactive. Next comes a period during which fingertip-and-forefinger grasping develops, and this is followed at around one year of age by the maturation of normal grasping with the thumb and forefinger in opposition.

Children increase their response speed with age.

INTERRELATIONS AMONG MOTOR ABILITIES There are three basic factors that contribute to the development of motor behavior in childhood: an increase in speed, an increase in strength, and a specific factor associated with throwing small objects. The rate of the signals sent along the nerve system increases until about age ten (*see* Figure 3.8). It is this factor which certainly accounts for some increase of speed in reaction time. However, some of the change is probably also due to practice. On the average, boys are slightly faster than girls in reaction time. Both coordination and strength increase with age, and until puberty most boys are stronger than girls. However, around eleven to thirteen years of age, strength (on the average) is temporarily equal, because girls mature earlier. In later years most boys will again become stronger.

Motor abilities are mostly independent.

Is a strong child also faster and does he have more endurance than his weaker peers? Does a child who handles a ball less ably also do badly at broadjumping, riding, and other sports? The general answer is yes for young children and no for older ones. The connections among motor

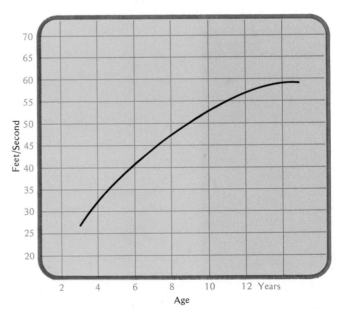

FIGURE 3.8
Rate of neural firing as a function of age; with increasing maturity the rate of impulse movement along the nerves increases. This result probably explains some of the decrease in reaction time and increase in speed of movement as the child grows older. However, increased speed and flexibility is in part due to better coordination of perceptual and motor functions.

abilities are much higher during infancy than in late childhood. These low relationships in later childhood suggest that:

1. Older children do not practice various skills equally.
2. There is no general motor achievement factor.
Or 3. The interests of the child lead him to perform particular skills exceptionally well.

The development of motor skills depends on several interrelated processes: neuromuscular maturity, opportunity to observe and imitate other children, availability of equipment, and the opportunity to experiment with various skills. If a child lacks the opportunity to explore or practice, or if he is inhibited in his movements, his motor abilities will be poor.

Gutteridge observed motor development.

Gutteridge (1930) observed motor development among 1,973 children between two and and seven years of age. She made observations of a number of activities: climbing, jumping, sliding, tricycling, hopping, galloping, skipping, throwing, bouncing, and catching balls. Her norms are shown in Table 3.2.

TABLE 3.2   The Course of Development of Four "Typical" Skills in Childhood

Climbing   An activity already well established for 50 percent of three-year-olds, with gradual increments in skill, until 92 percent of six-year-olds are proficient. Early in the fourth year most of the children had climbed as high as opportunity permitted.
Jumping   A motor skill well-developed in 42 percent of the three-year-olds, in 72 percent of the children at four and one-half years, and in 81 percent of the five-year-olds.
Tricycling   An accomplished skill among 17 percent of the two-year-olds and 63 percent of the three-year-olds. At four years of age almost 100 percent are skillful, stunting and using the tricycle for all kinds of imaginative variations.
Ball-throwing   At two and three years of age there is relatively no skill. At four years about 20 percent rated as throwing well. Between five and five-and-one-half years 74 percent can throw well. The earliest method of throwing a ball includes mass movements of the whole body. Gradually the movements become more specialized and the use of two hands gives place to the use of one hand in a "clean throw." The latter illustrates both the mass to specific and the bilateral to unilateral trends in motor development.

There are two kinds of motor skills.

There are two classes of motor skills: *phylogenetic skills* developed by all normal children (for example, walking); and special skills only acquired through *training* (for example, skiing). Phylogenetic skills (meaning those skills that came about in the course of evolution) develop in their own good time as a result of growth. Intensive early training or lack of experience have only minor effects on their development (*see* Figure 3.9). On the other hand, those special skills which are acquired only through training are greatly influenced by early practice. If training in these special skills is started early, the quality of the training and the abilities of the child and his motivation can have enormous influence on the final level of skill reached. For example, McGraw (1935) studied the effect of maturation and learning on several skills. She trained one fraternal twin in a variety of motor skills from the age of twenty-one days to twenty-two months, while the other (control) fraternal twin received no special training except for regular tests of motor ability. McGraw found that the trained twin was greatly advanced at some skills compared to his untrained sibling. For example, the trained twin was an accomplished roller skater before he was two. His superiority occurred in the area of uncommon skills. He showed no superiority in phylogenetic skills like walking, which all children acquire in their own good time.

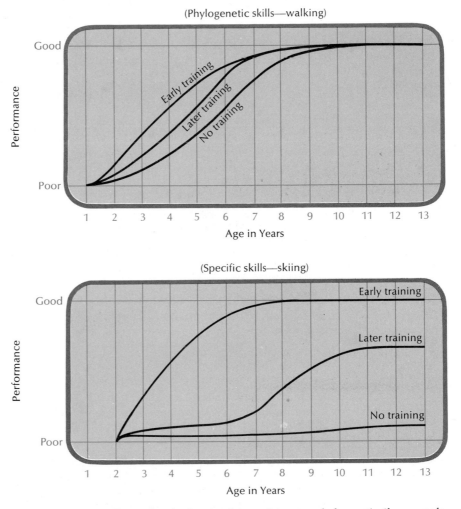

FIGURE 3.9 The effects of early, late, and no training on phylogenetic (for example, walking) and special (for example, skiing) skills of the child. Notice that little or no training produces relatively minor and short effects on phylogenetic skills, but long-lasting effects on special skills.

Swaddling does not affect walking.

Lack of early training seems to have little effect on skills requiring growth. Wrapping an infant with narrow bands of cloth attached to a board is an accepted cultural practice in the Near East, the Balkans, Poland, Russia and among some American Indians. Armenian children who have been swaddled—securely bound on a wood cradle in the darkest corner of the room—for a year show retarded coordination when they are first released, but they rapidly improve and suffer no permanent effects from such early restriction. Their social responsiveness and general motor behavior soon equal the behavior of unswaddled children at a similar age. The use of cradle boards during the first year of life, with the resultant lack of bodily contact and loss of opportunity for practicing movement, makes little or no difference in the age of which a child walks.

Dennis and Dennis studied Hopi Indians.

Dennis and Dennis (1940) studied various groups of Hopi Indians noting that in some villages infants were placed on a cradle board shortly after birth and kept there for the first several months of their lives, while other Hopi infants were reared in a similar environment but without a cradle board. The researchers found no significant differences in the ages at which the two groups of children walked.

Problems in Physical Growth

Physical growth is delicately controlled by hormones.

There are several factors which can upset the delicate balance of physical development. This equilibrium of blood sugar, water balance, and amount of oxygen is regulated by the autonomic nervous system. Together with man's endocrine system, the autonomic mechanism maintains basic bodily functions that take place automatically—like breathing and digestion. The equilibrium of human growth may be broken in a variety of ways. For example, either too much or too little secretion of a hormone or the lack of a particular food can cause trouble. A deficiency of the growth hormone produced by men's pituitary gland can cause dwarfism; and an excess of growth hormone can produce a giant.

Over- or underweight can be a serious problem.

OVERWEIGHT AND UNDERWEIGHT   A more recent problem concerns the weight gain by Caucasian males in the last hundred years—almost 15 percent on the average. This is a serious problem since overweight is associated with heart trouble and circulatory problems in later life. In addition to having a health problem, an overweight child has a variety of difficulties, the most serious of which is the scorn of his peers. "Fatty," "Two-by-four," or "Whale" are hard on a growing child's positive self-concept. The two causes of overweight are constitutional and environmental. The tendency to become overweight runs in families and may reflect either a genetic tendency to be overweight or habits of excess eating or—most often—both. The problem of overweight can be handled most effectively by a well-balanced program which includes an adequate diet prescribed by a physician, hormonal treatment if necessary, and possibly psychological consultation to see whether the eating problem is associated with anxiety or tension.

Growth is self-stabilizing.

Underweight can also be a serious problem. Children may be underweight from inadequate or unappetizing meals, too much tension, or a rejecting attitude toward food. Sometimes rejection of food may be a way of striking back at a parent. Happily, if a severely malnourished child is given an adequate diet, his growth will return to normal, because the physical maturation of a child is self-stabilizing. There is a strong tendency for a child's growth pattern to return to its natural rate after being slowed by disease or starvation. Tanner (1963) suggested that the regularity of growth of children's heights in the face of variations in the environment must be caused by a self-stabilizing mechanism which regulates physical growth. He proposed a genetic mechanism in the central nervous system which "knows" the expected size of the person. He also suggested that the actual size of the body is monitored by a substance produced in proportion to the increase in body size, and that the rate of growth is adjusted to the relationship between this substance and the genetic mechanism. A simple feedback system like this can explain both the normal growth curve and the catch-up of growth after starvation or disease. Tanner showed that during severe disease or acute malnutrition there is a slowing of the growth rate, but that later the affected child's body grows faster for a few months to catch up. During the catch-up period the child's growth may reach two or three times its normal rate.

"Catch-up" happens soon after birth.

The phenomenon of "catch up" can also be seen about a week after birth. For example, suppose the child is genetically destined to be large, but his prebirth environment is restricted by a small mother. The newborn will be smaller than normal at birth, but his rate of growth will increase substantially thereafter and will continue at the higher rate until he catches up to his genetically programed rate.

Human growth is stabilized internally.

The self-stabilized rate of human growth seems to be regulated by internal neural mechanisms which keep track of the rate of normal growth and also the difference between this normal pattern and the actual size of the individual. If the discrepancy between the expected growth pattern and the actual pattern becomes large, the rate of growth is increased to make up the difference. Then, as the gap between expected and actual growth patterns narrows, the rate of growth is correspondingly slowed.

Malnutrition can affect human development.

In a recent review of the relation between malnutrition and mental deficiency, Bonnie Kaplan (1972) concluded: "Inadequate nutrition can affect both physiological and psychological development in humans. The nine months of gestation and the first few years of life are most critical in the growth of brain tissue and are the periods of greatest vulnerability to malnutrition." She cited animal experiments with malnutrition which show fairly conclusively that malnutrition retards mental development. No definitive study on humans had yet been done. Kaplan also pointed out some of the problems associated with generalizing from animal studies, and the ethical and practical difficulties involved in studying malnutrition in human children. She concluded that one of the major factors associated with increased risk of mental retardation among off-spring of malnourished mothers is the smaller stature and resulting narrow pelvis of the mothers, which could cause damage to the newborn child's brain during delivery.

Tired children are often cranky.

THE TIRED CHILD   Improper nutrition, poor genetic constitution, or pro-longed tension can produce a tired child, who often acts unreasonable and cranky but denies feeling tired. Early signs of fatigue are an increase in activity and excitability. Later, the tired child may simply become listless. Such a child needs a balanced program of sleep, rest, and recrea-tion. Some guidelines are that most young children need about eleven hours of sleep, although the amount of sleep needed varies with indivi-duals and age. The best way to program sleep is to produce a quiet re-laxing interval right before bedtime. A secure place to sleep and a warm emotional climate will help a child relax and go to sleep easily.

Childhood illnesses can produce maternal overprotection.

CHILDHOOD ILLNESS   Between the ages of three and eight years children are subjected to a variety of contagious diseases like mumps, measles, and chickenpox. Many of these illnesses are caused by bacterial or viral infections. However, the child's genetic constitution and his overall physical and emotional condition can make him more or less vulnerable to infection. In addition, the total effect of an illness varies with parent-child interactions, for the psychological effects of an illness depend primarily on how the parents handle it. If they are worried and anxious the child will be worried and anxious. Prolonged illnesses often bring on maternal overprotection, and the child may then come to view himself as chronically ill. As a specific example, asthmatic children are often controlled by overprotective parents, and some children with heart disease are overanxious, dependent, and show behavior problems.

Accidents are of pri-mary danger to children.

Although every parent worries about illness and disease, accidents are the number one danger to young children. Most fatal accidents happen to children before the ninth birthday, and boys are much more accident prone than girls. The most common accidents are getting burned, bitten by a dog, breaking an arm, or being poisoned. The most common causes of the death of a child are motor vehicles, guns, and drowning. Accidents happen because children are curious and immature, or because they lack proper supervision. A few children are very accident prone. They become involved in a very large number of accidents. These accident-prone chil-dren break arms, get cut by glass, eat too many aspirin, or drink cleaning fluid. Some accident-prone children are overactive; others are nervous; and a few are simply preoccupied. Serious illness or accident can produce a permanent handicap.

Physical handicaps produce maladjustment.

About 5 percent of all children in the United States suffer from some sort of chronic physical impairment. Handicapped children often cannot compete with their peers. For example, deaf children have difficulty learning to speak, and blind children have difficulty learning to walk about or even to dress themselves. A visually handicapped child who is not blind may be unable to see the blackboard and this causes trouble with his schoolwork. Physical handicaps can also produce social maladjustment because children are brutally frank about the physical problems of others. Some handicapped children develop a healthy attitude toward their problems, but many simply try to ignore the fact that they are different. Handicapped children generally have a more positive attitude toward themselves if they attend special schools.

The severity of the handicap determines adjustment.

The age at which a child becomes handicapped is important. Congenital defects—those existing at birth—seem easier to accept than abnormalities which occur later. However, the psychological effect of any handicap increases with age—at least through adolescence. The severity of the disability is also a factor in the child's adjustment. As you might expect, more serious handicaps are more difficult to deal with. Some physical defects can be corrected by surgery, but many must simply be accepted.

There are several stages to sensory-motor development.

As the child matures physically, his ability to coordinate sensory inputs and motor acts also increases. The stages of sensory-motor integration and some possible reasons for the child's early mental growth are covered next, along with two theories about how children coordinate their sensory and motor abilities.

Sensory-motor Integration

Two theories of development exist.

There is no single accepted theory of how infants come to understand the world, but there are two main approaches. *Behaviorists* assume that principles of association, generalization, and reinforcement can explain all human intellectual development. We will discuss these principles later. Jean Piaget believes that growth carries the child from early sensory-motor stages to logical operations. Piaget's theory of early cognitive development is based on observations of his own three children. He argues that maturation and active interaction with the environment are required for cognitive growth. Piaget's assumption of an active, searching child stands in sharp contrast to the passive memorizer pictured by behaviorists. Who is correct? The final answer awaits further research.

Let us first consider the early cognitive changes and maturational theories of Jean Piaget and Heinz Werner.

Portrait

Jean Piaget, one of the world's most famous psychologists, came to the study of children through an interest in Genetic Epistemology, the science of how man can know his world. He believes that how children know their world has profound implications for any theory of knowledge. In his writings Piaget distinguishes *structures, functions,* and the *contents* of a child's mind. Structures include cognitive abilities, ideas, or habits of the infant which change through the passing of time and the gaining of experience. Functions are unchanging innate processes, present from birth, which are responsible for modifications of structure. Finally, content is the particular set of data the child is working with at the moment. For example, the rules of adding would be a structure; the acquisition of the ability to add is a function; and the numbers in a math problem would be content.

Piaget believes that newborns possess two functions which help to organize their world. One is called *assimilation,* the other *accommodation.* In assimilation new environmental events are placed into already existing structures. Assimilation produces no new cognitive structure, no matter how inappropriate the classification may happen to be, for the structures already exist. Accommodation, on the other hand, forces the infant to develop new cognitive structures. When the infant is presented with a novel sensory input, recognizes that it *is* novel, and then tries to produce a new category in order to understand the novel information, accommodation occurs.

To illustrate, the first time an infant contacts a ring or nipple he will make a series of innate assimilations. He will move his mouth toward the object and suck on it, because a ring or nipple or almost anything else is categorized under the class of things to be sucked by babies. Later the infant will begin to develop new ways of responding to things, but in the beginning he approaches most new objects with the structure "things to be mouthed." Only gradually can he accommodate different behaviors to encompass a ring or nipple.

A third notion of Piaget's is *schema.* Schemata (the plural of schema) may be cognitive structures, classes of similar actions, or thoughts. A schema can be all the means by which one can take a cookie from a jar or it may be the class of dogs. Schemata are developed through both experience and growth. Piaget stresses over and over that early sensory-motor abilities are the foundations for later intellect. This does not mean he is particularly interested in motor skills; he is concerned with the coordination of information from various senses into a common picture of the child's world. Piaget uses the label sensory-motor to mean the coordination of visual and positional information into a coherent whole.

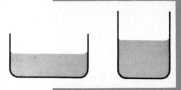

The amount of water in both glasses is the same, but for the pre-operational child, the tall, thin glass has more water in it than the wide, short glass.

Jean Piaget, one of the most respected theorists in the field of child development.

The preoperational child has difficulty seeing that the stick at the top and the three sticks at the bottom are the same length.

Piaget's discoveries of children's implicit philosophies, the construction of reality by the infant and the stages of mental development have altered our ways of thinking about human intelligence.

The man behind these discoveries is an arresting figure. He is tall and somewhat portly, and his stooped walk, bulky suits and crown of long white hair give him the appearance of a thrice-magnified Einstein. (When he was at the Institute for Advanced Study at Princeton in 1953, a friend of his wife rushed to a window one day and exclaimed, "Look, Einstein!" Madame Piaget looked and replied, "No, just my Piaget.") Piaget's personal trademarks are his meerschaum pipes (now burned deep amber), his navy blue beret and his bicycle.

Although Piaget . . . (has published more than 30 books and hundreds of articles), it is only within the past decade that his writings have come to be fully appreciated in America. This was due, in part, to the fact that until fairly recently only a few of his books had been translated into English. In addition, American psychology and education were simply not ready for Piaget until the fifties. Now the ideas that Piaget has been advocating for more than 30 years are regarded as exceedingly innovative and even as avant-garde.

His work falls into three more or less distinct periods within each of which he covered an enormous amount of psychological territory and developed a multitude of insights. . . .

During the first period (roughly 1922-29), Piaget explored the extent and depth of children's spontaneous ideas about the physical world and about their own mental processes. He happened upon this line of inquiry while working in Alfred Binet's laboratory school in Paris where he arrived, still seeking a direction for his talents, a year after receiving his doctorate in biological science at the University of Lausanne. It was in the course of some routine intelligence testing that Piaget became interested in what lay behind children's correct, and particularly their incorrect, answers. To clarify the origins of these answers he began to interview the children in the open-ended manner he had learned while serving a brief internship at Bleuler's psychiatric clinic in Zurich. This semiclinical interview procedure, aimed at revealing the processes by which a child arrives at a particular reply to a test question, has become a trademark of Piagetian research investigation.

What Piaget found with this method of inquiry was that children not only reasoned differently from adults but also that they had quite different world-views, literally different philosophies. This led Piaget to attend to those childish remarks and questions which most adults find amusing or nonsensical. Just as Freud used seemingly accidental slips of the tongue and pen as evidence for unconscious motivations, so Piaget has employed the "cute" sayings of children to demonstrate the existence of ideas quite foreign to the adult mind.

The second period of Piaget's investigations began when, in 1929, he sought to trace the origins of the child's spontaneous mental

From David Elkind, "Giant in the Nursery—Jean Piaget," The New York Times Magazine, May 26, 1969.

growth to the behavior of infants; in this case, his own three children, Jaqueline, Lucienne and Laurent. Piaget kept very detailed records of their behavior and of their performance on a series of ingenious tasks which he invented and presented to them. The books resulting from these investigations, "The Origins of Intelligence in Children," "Play, Dreams and Imitation in Children" and "The Construction of Reality in the Child" are now generally regarded as classics in the field and have been one of the major forces behind the scurry of research activity in the area of infant behavior now current both in America and abroad. . . .

The third and major phase of Piaget's endeavors began about 1940 and continues until the present day. During this period Piaget has studied the development in children and adolescents of those mental abilities which gradually enable the child to construct a world-view which is in conformance with reality as seen by adults. He has, at the same time, been concerned with how children acquire the adult versions of various concepts such as number, quantity and speed. Piaget and his colleagues have amassed, in the last 28 years, an astounding amount of information about the thinking of children and adolescents which is only now beginning to be used by psychologists and educators.

In the course of these many years of research into children's thinking, Piaget has elaborated a general theory of intellectual development which, in its scope and comprehensiveness, rivals Freud's theory of personality development. Piaget proposes that intelligence—adaptive thinking and action—develops in a sequence of stages that is related to age. Each stage sees the elaboration of new mental abilities which set the limits and determine the character of what can be learned during that period. (Piaget finds incomprehensible Harvard psychologist Jerome Bruner's famous hypothesis to the effect that "any subject can be taught effectively in some intellectually honest form to any child at any stage of development.") Although Piaget believes that the order in which the stages appear holds true for all children, he also believes that the ages at which the stages evolve will depend upon the native endowment of the child and upon the quality of the physical and social environment in which he is reared. In a very real sense, then, Piaget's is both a nature *and* a nurture theory.

Piaget would probably agree with those who are critical about premature applications of his work to education. He finds particularly disturbing the efforts by some American educators to accelerate children intellectually. When he was giving his 1967 lectures, in New York, he remarked:

"If we accept the fact that there are stages of development, another question arises which I call 'the American question,' and I am asked it every time I come here. If there are stages that children reach at given norms of ages can we accelerate the stages? Do we have to go through each one of these stages, or can't we speed it up a bit? Well, surely, the answer is yes . . . but how far can we speed them up? . . . I have a hypothesis which I am so far incapable of proving: probably the organization of operations has an optimal time . . . For example, we know that it takes 9 to 12 months before babies develop the notion that an object is still there even when a screen is placed in front of it. Now kittens go through the same sub-stages but they do it in three months— so they're six months ahead of the babies. Is this an advantage or isn't it?

"We can certainly see our answer in one sense. The kitten is not going to go much further. The child has taken longer, but he is capable of going further so it seems to me that the nine months were not for nothing . . . It is probably possible to accelerate, but maximal acceleration is not desirable. There seems to be an optimal time. What this optimal time is will surely depend upon each individual and on the subject matter. We still need a great deal of research to know what the optimal time would be."

Piaget's stance against using his findings as a justification for accelerating children intellectually recalls a remark made by Freud when he was asked whatever became of those bright, aggressive shoe-shine boys one encounters in city streets. Freud's reply was, "They become cobblers."

Despite some premature and erroneous applications of his thinking to education, Piaget has had an over-all effect much more positive than negative. His findings about children's understanding of scientific and mathematical concepts are being used as guidelines for new curricula in these subjects. And his tests are being more and more widely used to evaluate educational outcomes. Perhaps the most significant and widespread positive effect that Piaget has had upon education is in the changed attitudes on the part of teachers who have been exposed to his thinking. After becoming acquainted with Piaget's work, teachers can never again see children in quite the same way as they had before. Once teachers begin to look at children from the Piagetian perspective they can also appreciate his views with regard to the aims of education.

"The principal goal of education," he once said, "is to create men who are capable of doing new things, not simply of repeating what other generations have done—men who are creative, inventive and discoverers. The second goal of education is to form minds which can be critical, can verify, and not accept everything they are offered. The great danger today is of slogans, collective opinions, ready-made trends of thought. We have to be able to resist individually, to criticize, to distinguish between what is proven and what is not. So we need pupils who are active, who learn early to find out by themselves, partly by their own spontaneous activity and partly through materials we set up for them; who learn early to tell what is verifiable and what is simply the first idea to come to them."

Early sensory-motor experiences may affect later intelligence.

Piaget's early observations make it clear that children grow from reflexive reactions to symbolic thinking in about two years. It's a long way from the thought processes of children to the well-reasoned logic of a gifted adult. There is no well-articulated model of how the child acquires thinking. But Jean Piaget has some fascinating yet tentative notions of how the child builds simple sensory-motor units into complex systems of behavior and thought, based on his observations of children. Piaget believes early *sensory-motor* experiences have lasting effects on later intellect. He thinks infants start with a few innate reflexes and construct sensory-motor functions and sophisticated cognitive operations from these simple beginnings. He also argues that simple sensory inputs and responses are combined to allow the use of symbols. Once symbols are available, the child can actively search, manipulate, and test his environment to produce new solutions to old problems. This active searching stands in sharp contrast to the very young infant's passive registration of events. Piaget believes the young child becomes like a scientist inquiring into the secrets of the universe. The child uses simple tools with which to understand his world, then tests his model by experimentation and observation.

Stages of sensory-motor Development

Piaget separates sensory-motor growth into six stages.

Piaget organizes the sensory-motor period into six stages. He does not have a rigid age schedule for these stages, and he expects variations. But he does believe that every child must pass through all the earlier stages before he can achieve a later one. Previous stages determine the child's ability, because current thought is based on earlier schemata. For example, Piaget points out that the child cannot throw a ball unless he has first learned to grasp it and to move his arm—both activities which occur in earlier stages. Let us now consider the sensory-motor period in more detail.

Reflex acts character-
ize Stage One.

REFLEX ACTS   *Stage 1—Birth to One Month.*   A newborn's behavior is limited. He sucks, cries, swallows, thrashes about and moves his eyes, although he cannot focus them. These early behaviors are very primitive, but Piaget believes they form the base for all subsequent intellectual development. Further, the baby's simple reflexes show orderly changes through growth and contact with the environment.

The primary circular
reaction is centered
about the baby's own
body.

PRIMARY CIRCULAR REACTIONS   *Stage 2—One to Four Months.*   During this second stage the baby's reflexes are modified as a function of experience; simple habits are acquired; and elementary sensory-motor coordinations occur. Piaget lists three types of *circular reactions*—primary, secondary, and tertiary. They are classified on the basis of what the response accomplishes and how it is repeated. Primary circular reactions are centered on and around the infant's own body, and are not directed toward manipulating his surroundings. In contrast, secondary circular reactions reflect the relation between a child's body and outside events. Finally, tertiary circular reactions combine existing acts and goals in new ways. Observation of the infant's own body is an example of a Stage-Two primary circular reaction (*see* Figure 3.10). By observing, the baby begins to integrate input from his various senses and begins to know that what he feels and what he sees are somehow related.

FIGURE 3.10
Hand-watching by a Stage-Two infant (age about three months).

SECONDARY CIRCULAR REACTIONS   *Stage 3—Four to Eight Months.*   The Stage-Three child shifts from external stimulus control of his activities to more voluntary acts. Piaget believes this child begins to develop motor representations of external events, although these motor symbols are very crude. Instead of being simply governed by stimulation, the Stage-Three child's behavior is directed toward new goals. His behavior is controlled by the result it produces. Two things are important about secondary circular reactions. First, the infant's developing awareness of external events (*see* Figure 3.11) produces sensory-motor acts which are specific to certain objects. For example, a rattle is seen as something to shake, but a doll is something to hold. Second, Piaget believes the secondary circular reaction is fundamental to all further intellectual development throughout life. He suggests that when an adult faces a new situation he may resort to secondary circular reactions. The adult will push this or pull that and only continue acts that bring interesting consequences. There are enormous differences between infant and adult behavior. The secondary circular reaction represents the upper limit of an infant's abilities, while the adult possesses many other exploratory and experimental techniques. Moreover, the adult is systematically trying to make new adaptations, but the Stage-Three infant is not.

Secondary circular reactions are of fundamental importance for Piaget's theory, since they represent a landmark in the development of intentional thinking. For Piaget, the intentional pursuit of a goal by means of instrumental behavior is the distinguishing characteristic of intelligence.

How can intention be distinguished from passive response? Piaget points out that the assessment of intention is not difficult when we look at a newborn or a two-year-old child, but the case of a six- or eight-month-old is less clear. He suggests several interrelated criteria:

The secondary circular reaction reflects interactions of the child with his environment.

Intention is a landmark of Stage Three.

Intention is difficult to measure.

FIGURE 3.11
A Stage-Three infant (age about six months) attending to an external object.

1. Is an act oriented toward a goal rather than being sheer exercise for exercise's sake? Only acts concerned with goals are eligible for the label "intention."
2. The complexity of the intermediate links between the stimulus for an action and the action itself may be a second criterion. Piaget considers longer chains of links to be more intentional.
3. Finally, an intentional act should show adaptation to a new situation rather than simple repetition.

The infant uses signs during Stage Four

SENSORY-MOTOR COORDINATION *Stage 4—Eight to Twelve Months.* Near the end of the first year the average infant shows several new accomplishments. Earlier secondary circular reactions are now coordinated to form new patterns and these new reactions show more intention. Simultaneously, the infant begins to use signs to anticipate events. The infant's early circular reactions showed only a primitive intention. This may be illustrated by his attempt to bring a long narrow toy through the bars of a playpen (*see* Figure 3.12). Since the toy is long, the child must learn

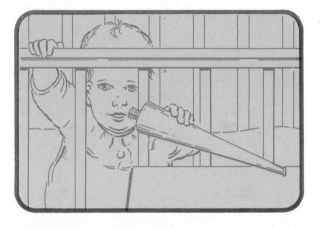

FIGURE 3.12
A Stage-Four infant's approach to space, showing the child's ability to rotate the toy and pull it between the narrow bars of his playpen.

FIGURE 3.13
A Stage-Four child can push aside a barrier and obtain an unseen object.

to rotate it so he can pull it through the vertical bars. His actions gradually change from a series of trials and errors to a pattern which succeeds smoothly in getting the toy into the playpen. During Stage Four these previously independent response systems become coordinated into a superordinate schema which is both more efficient and more flexible. Also, during the fourth stage new goals are established, and means are called forth to reach these goals. For example, the child will now push aside one object to reach a more desirable goal (*see* Figure 3.13), where younger infants followed an out-of-sight-out-of-mind pattern. For the young child overcoming an obstruction to reach a goal is a complex accomplishment. Infants simply forget the goal if a barrier intervenes. Later on, babies invent irrelevant habits that might help in reaching the absent goal. Piaget observed that the infant may hit the intervening barrier and by this means produce a successful way of pushing the barrier aside. During Stage Four some part of the infant's goal must be visible behind an obstacle before he will seek it. However, in subsequent stages (twelve to eighteen months of age) this visibility requirement disappears. The more mature child has symbolic ability, and he can now pursue a goal that is completely out of sight.

Tertiary circular reactions combine goals and acts in new ways.

TERTIARY CIRCULAR REACTIONS   *Stage 5—Twelve to Eighteen Months.* During this stage of tertiary circular reactions the infant first approaches a new object with an old, familiar response pattern, but then develops variations of these patterns to fit the new situation. For example, dropping or letting something go becomes throwing by a series of variations on the original act. The Stage-Five baby develops new behaviors through active experimentation.

FIGURE 3.14
A Stage-Five child finding an object which was hidden when he was not looking. The diagram shows how a fifteen-month-old will predict where an object will be and how he can go around a barrier to find it.

Object permanence develops in Stage Five.

Another basic characteristic of Stage Five, according to Piaget, is the permanence of objects for the infant. By this time the child will follow the movements of a hidden object. When an object disappears, he does not go back to the original spot where he first saw it, as he would have done in earlier stages, but he can now imagine or guess where the object is likely to be next (*see* Figure 3.14). For example, a Stage-Five infant who sees a ball roll under a couch will immediately go behind the couch to retrieve it because he can predict the future course of the unseen ball. The Stage-Five infant is an active, deliberate experimenter rather than simply a random explorer.

Stage Six brings insight.

INSIGHT   *Stage 6—Eighteen months to Two Years.* During this stage a child produces elements of what will later be called creative thinking. This major new pattern of behavior can be illustrated as follows. Suppose the child has a goal but no habitual act for obtaining it. The beginning of the solution is similar to Stage-Five behavior. No available means exist, so they must be discovered. However, instead of fumbling randomly for a solution through a series of trial-and-error actions, the Stage-Six child can produce new means through mental combinations—*he can think!* As an example, suppose an infant is in a playpen. He has a stick in the pen and he wants a toy duck that is outside the pen beyond the reach of his short stick. Piaget's first child, Lucienne, learned to use the shorter stick to pull in the longer stick, which could then be used to acquire the toy outside the playpen by trial-and-error groping. At eighteen-and-a-half months another of Piaget's children learned the same trick by thinking. Laurent was in a playpen and wanted the duck, which was outside of his reach. A longer stick was between him and the duck. He looked at the situation, immediately grasped the short stick and directed it to the longer one. Then he used the longer stick to pull the toy within his reach. This is called *insight*.

The Infant's Conception of the World

Development is caused by genes and interaction with the world.

Piaget believes development occurs by genetic maturation and the child's active interaction with his world, as we have seen. In addition to the six stages of sensory-motor period, Piaget has noted six special kinds of interactions which occur during the early stages of an infant's development. It should be kept in mind that achievement by the child in one area is partly dependent on developments in the other five. The six special areas are:

1. Play
2. Conception of space
3. Conception of time
4. Imitation
5. Causality
6. Object concept.

Early stages of play are amorphous.

PLAY   The early stages of an infant's play are hard to differentiate; and it is only possible later to classify them when more well-formed characteristics appear. Piaget believes that assimilation for assimilation's sake is the primary characteristic of play.

Little play happens before Stage Three.

All that can be said about the baby's play during Stage One is that he sometimes produces sucking movements without having either a breast or bottle presented, that he looks around when there are no unusual stimuli in the environment, and that he kicks and moves his arms with no apparent purpose. Even in Stage Two there is little behavior that unambiguously represents play rather than adaptation. The most characteristic pattern at this stage is that primary circular reactions are pursued first to gain competence and then for sheer pleasure. As an example, the two-month-old child will throw his head back to look at familiar things from a new perspective. At first the head movement is serious. However, Piaget feels that after a few repetitions head movement itself is performed

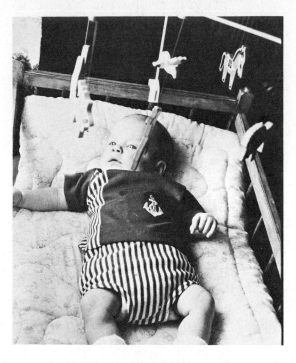

FIGURE 3.15
The baby tests his visual motor coordination when he plays with a mobile hanging over his crib. (Fishkill Studios.)

with increasing enjoyment and the child's interest in the external view is lost. He now brings his head to an upright position and jerks it back time and again, laughing loudly and enjoying what he is doing.

By four months the baby shows joy.

By the time an infant reaches Stage Three the differentiation between assimilative play and serious learning becomes much easier. For example, at about three months of age infants begin to study any object that is swinging over the top of their cribs. At first the baby has a look of intense interest, as though he were studying the swinging object. At about four months of age this same infant will watch a swinging toy with a great show of joy. Piaget speculates that the infant's attention is no longer an effort at comprehension. There was assimilation of the activity itself— use of the phenomenon simply for pleasure. This is play.

Play is not accommodation.

By the beginning of Piaget's Stage Four the distinction between play and adaptation or accommodation becomes clearer. By this stage an infant will abandon a goal in favor of playing with a particular means of attaining his goal. For example, at seven months a child first begins to remove a barrier that blocks his objective. After the child has learned to remove the barrier, he may begin to play with it and ignore the goal. In an experiment Piaget put his hand or a piece of cardboard between the child and the toy. The child reached the stage of momentarily forgetting the toy, pushing aside the obstacle, and then bursting into laughter at the sheer exercise of a function as he performed the pushing action. Once accommodation is achieved, actions are used for pleasure.

Stage Six children
have imaginations.

During the last stage of the sensory-motor period the child turns every new adaptation into a ritual of play as soon as it is discovered. By this time the child plays with each new behavior as soon as it is acquired. Finally, as the child grows older, symbolization emerges and the child can pretend or make-believe. Instead of having stimuli presented, which then produces an act, and using this behavior for play, the Stage-Six child can produce an independent action pattern. He can also treat an act as a symbol of another act. For example, the eighteen-month-old can say, ''soap,'' and rub her hands together, pretending to wash them. She may also pretend she is eating a piece of paper or a rock, saying, ''very nice.''

The infant's first con-
ceptions of space
are many.

SPACE   Piaget theorizes that the Stage-One and Stage-Two infant's early ideas about space are a collection of many separate spaces, each entirely centered about an activity with few interconnections among them. There is a space around the mouth, a visual space, an auditory space, and a touching space, for example. During Stage Three, with the infants' growing coordination between vision and grasping, the infant begins to collect these many spaces into one. This is the meaning of sensory-motor integration. Near the end of the sensory-motor period, Piaget believes that the infant comes to generate a single space concept within which all objects, including himself, are contained and interrelated. The psychologist proposes that the infant's development of a single space involves first a separation of things and self.

White studied
visually-directed
reaching.

Consider an example of sensory-motor coordination in the young infant. Burton White and his associates (1970) have studied in detail the development of visually-directed reaching. They report that this response is typically mature at about five months of age and that it has a definite growth sequence. They found that the one-month-old will look at an object but make no attempt to reach for it, even if it is very close. By two and one-half months he swipes at it, but may or may not hit his target. A significant change in strategy occurs at around four months of age. By then the infant puts his hand in the vicinity of the object, looks at his hand and the object, and then gradually moves the two together. He is using vision to direct his grasping. By five-and-one-half months he can reach and grasp an object in one smooth coordinated motion. This growth sequence can be accelerated a few weeks by giving the baby an enriched visual environment and attractive objects to touch. But the infant must be maturationally ready to reach before any visual-motor enrichment will be effective. Providing such stimulation before the baby is ready has little effect on the development of reaching (*see* Figure 3.15).

Spatial integration
begins with looking
and touching.

Piaget supposes that the integration of sensory spaces begins with the simultaneous visual search for and handling of objects. Beginning with Stage Four and continuing into Stage Five the infant explores relationships among sensations and movements and begins to discover the interrelations among objects. Near the end of the sensory-motor period the infant puts together into a single system different spaces in which an object appears and the different senses from which he receives information. By this time the Stage-Six infant can keep a running account of his own movements in space. He can represent his own movements in relation to other bodies and keep track of these other objects at the same time. As an example, let us look at the behavior of a typical eighteen-month-old. Suppose he throws a toy under a chair. Instead of bending over and searching for it on the floor at the base of the chair, as a younger infant would have done, he will realize the ball must have crossed under the chair. The eighteen-month-old will therefore go behind it to retrieve his toy, a clear example of a complex system of spatial representation at work.

Adjustment to distorting lenses requires active movement.

Recent experiments suggest that our ability to understand changing perceptual information requires feedback from the muscles and from our central nervous system (Held, 1965). For example, if a subject wears distorting lenses that displace or invert his vision and walks freely, he gradually makes adjustments to the distortions. However, another subject who is wearing the same lenses but is moved around in a wheelchair does not adjust to the distortions. Both people see the same visual stimuli, but only the subject who actively moves about in the environment receives feedback and can therefore adjust.

Passive observation is inadequate for sensory-motor coordination.

Held has performed experiments to support these speculations about the necessity of active participation in sensory-motor adjustment. Kittens raised in the dark with their mother and littermates were given visual stimulation for three hours each day in the apparatus shown in Figure 3.16. One kitten could move more-or-less normally; his gross movements were transmitted by a system of gears and pulleys to a second kitten inside the apparatus who was moved about in a basket. Both kittens received essentially the same visual stimulation because the pattern on the walls and the center post of the apparatus were the same. Eight pairs of

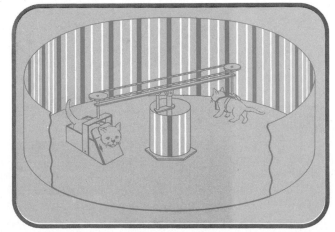

FIGURE 3.16
Apparatus for determining the effect of active versive passive movements on spatial orientation. The gross movements of the "active" kitten, who moves about more or less freely, are transmitted by means of the chain and bar to the "passive" kitten, who is conveyed in a gondola. Both kittens are raised in the dark, except for their daily experience in the apparatus, and are subsequently tested for visual-motor coordination.

kittens were raised and tested in the apparatus in this manner. After an average of thirty hours in the apparatus the active member of each pair showed normal behavior in a series of visual tests. It blinked at an approaching object and put up its paws to avoid collision when carried toward a surface. The passive kittens, on the other hand, failed to show this normal behavior. They developed appropriate behavior, however, after being allowed to run freely for several days. The sensory feedback accompanying active movement seems to be a requirement for the normal development of sensory-motor coordination and perception.

Time begins as a sequence of percepts.

TIME   Little material in Piaget is devoted to how the child's concept of time develops, probably because that information is difficult to gather. In his discussion Piaget draws heavily on analogies to the development of other concepts, such as causality and object perception. The area of time perception seems to be particularly ambiguous. However, Piaget seems willing to tolerate this ambiguity in order to gain some simple information about how time is understood by the infant. All Piaget says about the very young infant's conceptions of time is that sequences of perceptions do occur, which he belives, are the raw material from which a concept of time develops. At some point the infant does in fact perceive events as moving in a sequence. Piaget argues that the first example of a before and-after sequence for the child probably comes in the form of an action-result or means-end relation. He believes that a series of events is understood by the Stage-Three infant only if the child's own action intervenes at some point. By Stage Four, Piaget thinks an infant begins to relate an object which occurs first in time to another object or behavior which occurs later in time. The first object is conceived as the means, the second as the goal; this is a clear example of sequence.

The Stage six infant can conceptualize time.

During Stage Five the child's ability to order events that are independent of his own behavior becomes much stronger. For example, when a toy is hidden in a box and the box is hidden under a pillow, the Stage-Five infant can follow its path. He is able to arrange the events in an order, without the necessity of acting on those events himself. At Stage Six the child is able to represent events outside his immediate perception and to recall past events which did not occur in his own behavior. Piaget believes that at this stage the child is finally beginning to conceptualize time as a generalized medium, much like space, and to locate self and objects in relation to one another within the time medium.

Imitation is the opposite of play.

IMITATION   Imitation is the opposite of play because, for Piaget, imitation is accommodation (the constructing of new categories for novel information) while play is assimilation (information placed into existing structures). During Stage One the child is unable to imitate. Some researchers claim that an infant may be stimulated to cry by hearing the crying of other babies, but for the most part an infant seems sensitive only to his own internal states. During Stage Two there are weak, isolated instances when the baby may copy a particular act he has seen someone else perform. For example, infants may imitate adults when they utter a sound. The baby can produce some sounds, but during this stage the infant cannot imitate new sounds. The sequence is that the baby first produces a sound, then a model must reproduce it, and finally he can imitate the model's sound.

Stage three infants imitate a model.

Stage-Three infants have made substantial progress toward developing imitation. By now the infant will systematically imitate sounds and movements made by a model. Piaget describes an experiment he performed on his four-month-old daughter. First he put his hand in front of the child, opening and closing it slowly. He noted that the child did the same thing, opening and closing her hand whenever her father moved his. To test whether the infant might merely be trying to grasp his hand, Piaget put a carrot in front of her. Instead of opening and closing her hand, as she had done with Piaget's model, she immediately reached out and grasped the carrot.

Stage four infants can imitate new acts.

The Stage-Four infant coordinates information from seeing, hearing, touching, and moving. He can imitate new behaviors, and this becomes a special skill for the acquisition of new acts. During Stage Five the infant imitates much more frequently and purposefully. For example, Piaget swung a watch on a chain in front of his one-year-old daughter and then put the watch in front of her. The child picked it up, but she held the chain too close to the watch to allow it to swing properly. She immediately put the watch down and picked up the chain again, this time taking care to increase the distance between her fingers and the watch so that it would swing—a clear case of imitation.

The Stage six infant can pretend.

By Stage Six the child has developed primitive symbolic representation. He is now able to imitate behavior without having to perform it first. This child begins to imitate the actions of objects as well as of persons, and he begins to show imitation of an absent model. It is this deferred imitation, Piaget argues, that develops conscience. The ability to imitate a model who is not present suggests that the infant has an internal representation of the model, a notion quite similar to conscience.

The infant thinks all events are caused by his own actions.

CAUSE AND EFFECT   During the first three stages of the sensory-motor period cause and effect are undifferentiated for the infant. Piaget believes that for the young infant any continuity of time between two events means that the one which occurred first caused the other. Piaget also thinks that the infant believes his own actions during these early stages are the actual causes of most events, even if in fact there is no connection between them at all. For example, one of Piaget's children placed his hand on his father's hand to make it close. By Stage Four the infant still believes, according to Piaget, that external sources can be a cause only when the infant's own actions intervene. This means the infant must push the adult's hand to make it close. During Stage Five, when the infant actively experiments, he seems to acquire a clear notion of cause and effect. For the first time an infant will place an object in a position which will cause it to move, when that is what he desires. For example, he may put a ball on a slight incline and watch it roll. During this stage people and objects are seen as causes bringing about events that can be completely independent of the child's own action. The child's world has become less self-centered.

Stage six children can deduce causes.

By Stage Six the child not only understands causality but can begin to deduce a cause from its effect and predict an effect if he knows its cause. For example, Piaget's son Laurent was seated in his carriage with Piaget in a chair beside him. While reading, and without looking at the child, Piaget put his foot on the carriage and moved it slowly. Without hesitation Laurent leaned over the edge of the carriage and looked in the direction of the wheels. After seeing that his father had his foot on the carriage wheel, Laurent smiled.

Object permanence implies the existence of a separate entity.

OBJECT PERMANENCE   To understand the child's acquisition of an *object concept,* we must first appreciate an adult's conception of an object. For Piaget, a mature conception of objects demands that a group of sensations be seen as separate whole, an entity. Further, this entity must exist and move in a space common to it and the person perceiving the object. Finally, the existence of an object must be seen as separate from and independent of activities which the person applies to the object. Thus, the adult object concept includes knowing that the object has an independent existence even when the person is no longer acting on it or looking at it.

Piaget thinks young infants have no object concept.

Piaget believes that during the first two stages of the infant's sensory-motor development the infant has no conception of an object. At most, the child might try to prolong a pleasing situation by continuing to look or listen or grasp. The psychologist points out that during Stage Three the infant first tries to maintain or recapture sensory-motor relations. Now that the infant can begin to predict movement, he can anticipate where an object will appear next, as we have seen. The Stage-Three infant who leans over to look for an object he has seen drop to the floor is an example. Younger babies simply stare at the place where the object was. The Stage-Three infant can maintain sight of an object by removing an obstructing blanket resting on his face. However, he cannot uncover an object by removing an obstruction, for he apparently has no notion of an object as something that exists when he cannot see it. If a blanket is put over an object, therefore, the infant will not remove it. Because he wants to see, he will remove any obstruction over his own eyes.

Bower showed that young infants have a primitive object concept.

When do infants first assume that an object still exists even when they can no longer see it? Piaget's early studies indicated that young babies lose interest in objects they cannot see. However, a simple study by T. G. R. Bower (1971) indicates that infants around six weeks of age will continue to look for an object even when it is out of sight. Infants were placed in front of a barrier behind which a ball was rolled from left to right (*see* Figure 3 17) On some trials the ball was stopped behind the barrier, and on these occasions the infant continued to move his eyes toward the other side apparently searching the place where he expected the ball to reappear. In another, related study Bower moved a ball in a circle before the child's eyes. After the ball was stopped, the baby looked at the stationary object for a moment and then began searching in a circular path for the moving ball. Apparently he treated the moving and stationary balls as different objects.

Stage six infants have object permanence.

Piaget writes that by Stage Four the infant has developed a clear object concept. To support this belief, Piaget points out that by this time the baby begins to search actively for hidden objects, with one interesting restriction. The infant will search behind a screen for a hidden object *only* if he has been reaching for the object at the moment it was hidden. During later stages of development the infant will search for an object, if he knows it exists.

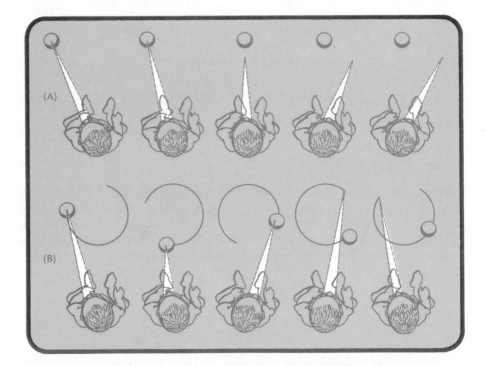

FIGURE 3.17 The top series shows Bower's experiment in object constancy. When a ball is rolled behind a screen and stopped, the infant continues to look toward the point where he expects the ball to reappear. This suggests the object still exists for the baby. In the bottom series the baby is shown a ball moving in a circle. When the ball is stopped, the baby looks at it a second then continues his following circular motion.
(After Bower, 1971.)

Stage five babies will search for hidden objects.

During Stage Five the infant overcomes his dependence on active searching and on external stimuli. By this stage the infant will now search in a place where the object was last seen, but if the object's journey to the hiding place was not visible to the Stage-Five infant, he will fail to search. Only during Stage Six is the infant capable of symbolic representation so that he can follow the invisible path of an object through the environment.

Piaget believes the method should be fitted to the idea and not vice-versa.

Little is known about how the child comes to develop object perceptions, conceptions of time and space, or other cognitive abilities. Some argue for genetics as a basis for such development, others for experience, and a third group believes that both act in combination. The observations of Piaget on his own children represent a promising body of insights and intuitions about very early intellectual growth. Without exception, Piaget is interested in applying techniques and models that are appropriate to our state of knowledge about an area of childhood development and he is firmly convinced that too quick an application of sophisticated methods will lead to rigid thinking and unproductive model building. His advice is to suit the tool to the task.

Another theorist who believes that growth is very important for the coordination of sensory-motor abilities is Heinz Werner.

Heinz Werner

There are two views of human development.

Throughout the history of developmental psychology there has been a persistent disagreement between learning and maturational views of human nature. On the one hand, behaviorists believe that babies are born with a blank mind and that processes like conditioning fill the child's mind with reactions as he grows. On the other hand are theories which assume that heredity guides the course and direction of human growth.

Werner believes that maturation governs development.

Heinz Werner, an early developmental psychologist, insisted that a child's hereditary tendencies affect the course of his growth. Werner argued that social-learning theories are wrong on two counts: They ignore the biological nature of human development; and they deal with isolated associations rather than the total organis n. He believed that notions of association ignore what determines behavior and concentrate on separate events.

Werner studied biology.

To understand Werner's emphasis on genetics and the growth of the whole organism we must know something of his background. He was educated in Austria and taught embryology and neurology in Germany. When Hitler rose to power he emigrated to the United States. Because of his strong interest in biology Werner constantly looked for parallels between human physiology and behavior. He felt that the correspondence between healthy physical growth and the appearance of more and more complex behavior was important. Werner also studied anthropology and human diseases so that he could place human development within a wide framework.

FIGURE 3.18 Heinz Werner.
(Courtesy the Granger Collection.)

Werner thinks development is complex.

Werner believed strongly that human development is made up of many factors, that it is not a simple process of accumulating habits. For example, he pointed out that the growth of a coral reef or a bank account is not a matter of development but merely the collection of more and more skeletons or dollars. He wanted to restrict the notion of development to systems which change in structure and complexity as they mature. Werner believed that the child proceeds from an undifferentiated, spread out, rigid, unstable organization to a differentiated, connected, flexible, ordered structure. Consider some examples (*see* Figure 3.18).

Werner believes that early thought is confused.

He argued that children begin in a diffused state, which Werner called *syncretic,* meaning that a child's sensations or concepts were somehow fused or confused. When the child hears sounds and at the same time experiences colors and smells he would be in a syncretic state; or when the child is unable to tell the difference between an actor and his actions he is in this state also. Werner gave examples of diffusion in the drawings of children, their early speech patterns, and their primitive logic. The psychologist believed that as the child matures, his sensations and conceptions of objects and actions become separated and differentiated.

The child becomes more articulate with age.

Werner's second principle of development was a gradual shift from conceptual diffusion to what he called *articulation.* From the diffused state the child grows and later is able to articulate various elements of speech, reading, or thought into a smooth, coherent pattern.

Young children are literal.

Not only does the structure of the child's mind change with development for Werner but the functioning of the mind changes as well. He argued that as a child matures, he becomes more flexible and at the same time more stable in his mental processes. Figure 3.19 shows that a common characteristic of the behavior of very young children is concreteness, but this changes with age. Very young children may make the same mistake many times in trying to solve a problem; and they enjoy hearing the same story or seeing the same set of pictures over and over. Several species of lower animals show this same behavioral rigidity, and lower animals are behaviorally stable in an unchanging environment. Werner argued that young children are somewhat like lower animals in that both are governed by habitual processes that are simple when compared to the more powerful cognitive abilities of a mature mind. He believed that maturation brings not only flexibility but also behavioral stability in the face of a changing environment. However, when the requirements for survival change because of rapid alterations in the environment, only a sophisticated, complex mind can develop the necessary new adaptations. Werner believed that growth in cognitive thinking requires the emergence of more and more sophisticated structures which gradually overshadow the functioning of more primitive mental processes.

Werner studied the development of word meanings.

Werner tested many of his developmental principles by studying the child's acquisition of word meaning. He developed a technique in which children were shown several sentences all containing the same nonsense word. The sentences were uncovered one at a time, and after the child

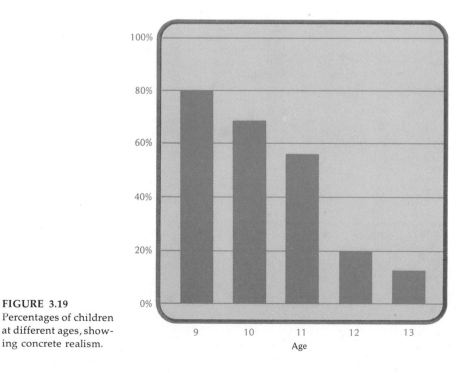

FIGURE 3.19
Percentages of children at different ages, showing concrete realism.

had seen each he was asked to tell the experimenter what he thought the meaning of the nonsense word was in each of the sentences. Here are examples of a nonsense word used in five sentences:

1. Several people will *corpum* in the park.
2. The man saw the horse *corpuming* down the road.
3. The woman *corpumed* into the room.
4. The policeman *corpumed* his beat.
5. Jimmy may never *corpum* again because of his accident.

Sentences like these were presented by Werner to five groups of children who varied in age from nine to thirteen years. The researcher grouped responses that were rigid, concrete, and disorganized into one set; and those responses which were abstract, flexible, and ordered into a hierarchy into a second set. Figure 3.20 shows the relative frequency of primitive and complex cognitive processes for these children in relation to their ages. Werner believed these data supported his notion that development involves shifting from one cognitive process to another, and that it is not simply an accumulation of associations.

Werner found that perceptions can be inaccurate.

Another area where Werner applied his theory of development concerned the influence of motives, attitudes, and beliefs on perception. Several studies have found that human perception is accurate under some circumstances and not under others. Illusions are an example of a perceptual error. Werner developed a problem concerning vertical and horizontal perceptions which called forth another error. He called his task the rod-and-frame test, which included a subject, a dark room, and a chair that could be tilted. The subject's task was to adjust a rod inside a frame until he felt that the rod was horizontal (or vertical) to the earth. Figure 3.21 illustrates the test situation. Werner found that when a sub-

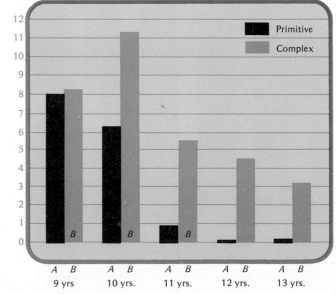

FIGURE 3.20
Age changes in different kinds of cognitive processes. The frequency with which more primitive (yellow) and more complex (white) responses appear is given.

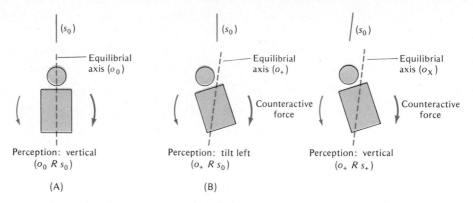

FIGURE 3.21 Werner's rod-and-frame test of balance and the perception of verticality. At (a) the body is erect and the rod is vertical. At (b) the body is tilted left and the rod tilts left as well. At (c) the body is tilted left and the rod is adjusted to the apparent vertical.
(From Werner and Wapner, 1956.)

ject was seated upright his estimates of vertical and horizontal were very accurate. However, if the chair and the subject were tilted to the left, the subject would make a compensatory adjustment of the rod by rotating it past the vertical toward the right to balance his feelings. Any kind of extraneous stimulation—like electrical stimulation of the left neck muscle, auditory stimulation of the left ear, or even rotation of the frame to the left—produced a compensatory rotation of the rod to the right, and vice-versa.

Werner studied the whole child.

Because he believed that many changes affect the child as he matures into an adult, Heinz Werner also felt that it would not do simply to study a single isolated human habit, but that it was essential to think about the total child.

Summary

The main topics in Chapter 3 were physical growth; sensory-motor coordination; and the child's conception of space, time, causality, and object permanence. The main conclusion about physical growth is that while maturation is most important, some problems can be overcome by sensible environmental intervention. Piaget's six stages of sensory-motor development form the framework for understanding the infant's early attempts at coordinating senses and motor abilities. The discussions of Piaget and Werner presented an interactionist and a nativist view of human development.

SUGGESTED ADDITIONAL READINGS

Baldwin, A. *Theories of Child Development.* New York: Wiley, 1967.

Bayley, N. *Bayley Scales of Infant Development.* New York: The Psychological Corporation, 1969.

Flavell, J. *The Developmental Psychology of Jean Piaget.* Princeton, N.J.: Van Nostrand, 1963.

Piaget, J. *Construction of Reality in the Child.* New York: Basic Books, 1954.

4 Perceptual Development

Vision
    The Eye
    Color Vision
    Color Mixing
Audition
    The Physical Stimulus
    Auditory Pathology
The Chemical Senses
    Taste
    Smell
Kinesthesis and Balance
The Skin Senses
    Touch
    Temperature
    Pain
Attention
    Perceptual Set
    Selective Listening
Theories of Perception

Nativism
Empiricism
Nativism and Empiricism
The Perception of Space
    Is There Innate Depth Perception?
    Monocular Cues to Depth
    Binocular Cues to Depth
Object Perception
    The Development of Object
        Perception
    Whole/Part Perception
    Eidetic Imagery
Perceptual Constancy
    Size Constancy
    Shape Constancy
Errors of Perception
    Illusions
    Perceptual Distortion
Summary

PREVIEW

The Greeks believed that human senses generate ether waves which travel to objects and return with information about the identity of these objects. Today, scientists think that human senses use chemical, mechanical, electrical, and other types of energy emitted from objects to stimulate perception of what goes on around them. Most people think seeing is believing; but is it? Does perception give an accurate picture of reality? The answer is not always. For example, eyes respond to light, but a person can also "see" brightness when touched in the corner of the eye. Both stimuli produce a sensation of brightness, but in the second case the effect is caused by physical pressure on the retina, which is interpreted in the brain as brightness. Because distortions of human sensory systems occur, humans do not always receive an infallible picture of reality. Rather, sensory systems transform physical or chemical energy into information transmitted to the nerves and the resulting impulses are in turn transmitted to higher centers for perceptual analysis and interpretation in the brain. Sensations are the raw materials from which higher centers construct perceptions. The reliability of sensation and perception is affected by expectations, the type of stimulation, experience, attention, and, above all, maturation.

Human beings have
nine senses.

Tradition and the English language suggest that human beings have five senses: vision, audition, taste, smell, and touch. But psychologists apply four criteria to distinguish sensory systems: a separate end organ, like the eye; an appropriate physical energy, for example, light; a unique sensory experience, like color; and a separate central area of the brain associated with processing, like the visual cortex. If these four categories are applied to the newborn human infant, nine senses can be differentiated. The sensory abilities above the five traditional senses derive from the body sense which becomes touch, pain, temperature, kinesthesis, and balance (*see* Table 4.1).

TABLE 4.1   Aspects of Sensory Experience

Sensory experience	Physical stimulus	Sense organ	Central-processing area	Sensation
Vision	Light	Eyes: rods and cones in retina	Occipital lobe	Hue, brightness, saturation
Audition	Sound	Ears: hair cells in Organ of Corti	Temporal lobe	Pitch, loudness, complexity
Smell	Volatile substance	Nose: hair cells in olfactory epithelium	Lower brain centers	—
Taste	Soluble substance	Tongue: taste cells in taste buds	Parietal lobe	Salt, sour, sweet, bitter
Touch	Mechanical stimulation	Skin: free nerve endings	Parietal lobe	Pressure
Temperature	Thermal stimulation	Skin: free nerve endings	Parietal lobe	Warmth, cold
Kinesthesis	Movement of body parts	Muscles, tendons, and joints: nerve endings	Parietal lobe	Movements of body parts
Balance	Change in movement	Ear: semi-circular canals	—	Acceleration, deceleration; upright, tilted
Pain	Tissue damage	Free nerve endings	Parietal lobe	Pain, hurt

Vision

The Eye

Vision begins with
light.

An understanding of the infant's response to light begins with some knowledge of light, a basic conception of the structure of the human eye, and the child's appreciation of brightness and color. Visible light is a narrow band of electromagnetic radiation sandwiched between ultra-

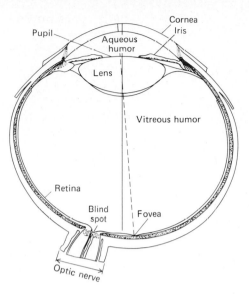

FIGURE 4.1
Drawing of the human eye. Important parts include the cornea and lens, the retina and the optic nerve.

violet and infrared emissions. The main characteristics of light are its wavelength, which is related primarily to color, and its intensity, which is related primarily to perceptual brightness. Light enters the visual system through the cornea and lens of the eye, where it is focused on the retina at the back of the eye (*see* Figure 4.1). Visual focusing is accomplished by thickening the lens to accommodate near objects, and flattening it to focus on objects beyond about twenty-five feet. Abnormality or immaturity in the shape of the eye or in the functioning of the lens system can produce seeing problems. Nearsightedness is the inability to distinguish objects clearly when they are far away. This happens because the retina is placed too far beyond the lens and cornea (*see* Figure 4.2). Farsightedness, on the other hand, is an inability to see close objects

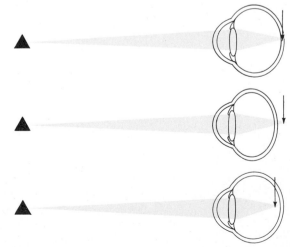

FIGURE 4.2
These three diagrams illustrate nearsightedness, farsightedness, and normal vision.

clearly because the retina is too near the lens. Normal distance vision is produced by a relatively flat lens, while normal close vision is produced by a round lens. Newborn babies are unable to accommodate the lens of their eyes until about six weeks of age (Haynes, White, and Held, 1965).

Color Vision

Color vision is very important.

One of the most astounding and exciting parts of vision is the ability to see color. The infant's retina seems to be most sensitive to three different wavelengths: blue, green, and yellow (Munsinger and Banks, 1974). The different wavelengths feed neural information to a higher center for decoding. Next the firing rate—which either increases, decreases, or maintains its current speed—is stimulated by a colored light. Any change in neural activity signals color.

Most psychological studies are performed with pure colors; but typical everyday color reception involves mixing and matching colors.

Color Mixing

Colored lights and paint pigments mix differently.

Colored lights and paint pigments mix colors in very different ways. For example, red, green, and blue lights produce white (*see* Color plate 1). Red and green lights add to produce yellow. Blue and green lights add to yield blue-green; while blue and red lights add to form pink. However, paint pigments or filters *absorb* wavelengths, and thus their mixing effects differ from those of light mixing, as we have said. For example, a mixture of three primary filters absorbs all colors and appears black (*see* Color plate 1). A mixture of yellow and purple filters or pigments produces red; and a mixture of blue-green and yellow filters or pigments produces green. It should be kept in mind that when mixing pigments or filters the outcome is not always predictable.

Human vision is based on three color processes.

Two fundamental observations have produced most of our information about color vision:

1. Humans can reliably name many different wavelengths of the visual spectrum.
2. It is possible to select three primary monochromatic stimuli which will produce all other colors in the spectrum for a normal adult.

These findings have produced several theories of color vision, all of which assume there are at least three types of color receptors. Not all people can see color, however. Some lack part of the color vision mechanism and that makes them colorblind to some degree (*see* Appendix).

Audition

Man is a visual animal.

Man is primarily a visual animal because more of his cortex is devoted to seeing than to any other sense. Fully one-quarter of human brain energy is devoted to visual processing. Taste, touch, and balance are called lower senses, because they are less important to humans. Other animals emphasize different senses. For example, dogs smell and fish taste. Children find that different senses become important at various times during their development. Man sees, but hearing is his second sense. Touch is important to infants; hearing is important to the child when he learns a language and vision when he learns to read.

The Physical Stimulus

Hearing is based on air vibrations.

Energy for hearing is represented by two independent physical components: frequency and amplitude. These two physical dimensions are related to psychological phenomena—frequency to pitch and amplitude to loudness. When a drum vibrates it first expands, pressing against air particles to create a condensed field; then the vibration causes contraction, which releases the pressure to form an adjacent area of rarefaction.

Two ears are better than one.

Man hears better with both ears than with only one, and previous exposure to sound affects his hearing sensitivity. Loud sounds cause the ear to adapt; very loud sounds can damage the human ear; and two or more simultaneous sounds can interfere with each other. Low frequency sounds mask high tones much more than the other way around. Also, louder noise covers a softer sound within its frequency and above; while soft frequencies below the loud noise are hardly affected.

The noise used in most psychological experiments is called *"white*

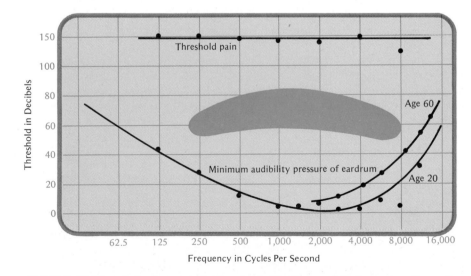

FIGURE 4.3 The relation between the threshold of hearing and the frequency of sounds. Note that frequencies between 500 and 8,000 cycles per second are easiest to detect. The hearing thresholds for age twenty and age sixty are plotted. Most speech sounds occur in the yellow area.

noise.'' It contains a random sample of most frequencies and amplitudes of sounds. A good example of white noise is the sound produced by a waterfall. Hearing is affected by both the physical stimulus and the structure of the human ear. Children are most sensitive in the frequency range of 400 to 8,000 cycles per second (*see* Figure 4.3).

White noise contains many different sounds.

Auditory Pathology

There are two kinds of deafness.

There are two distinct kinds of auditory defects: *Conductive impairment,* which involves some mechanical problem in the external or middle ear; and *neural impairment,* which results from damage to the cochlea, the auditory nerve, or the auditory cortex. A common form of conductive impairment is called *otosclerosis.* This results from extra calcium deposits around the bones of the middle ear. About one percent of the population of the United States suffers from such calcium deposits, which are more likely to occur with increasing age. Perforation of the ear drum is another common cause of conductive impairment.

Neural damage is most serious.

Neural damage can occur in several ways: The most common is from exposure to intense sound, such as that in a boiler factory, from a jet engine, or at a rock concert. Large doses of antibiotics like dihydrostreptomycin can also destroy auditory neural tissue. Tumors or circulatory trauma may produce cortical damage, which can lead to hearing loss.

Newborn humans respond to pitch, intensity, and duration of sounds.

We do know that newborns respond differently to three kinds of sounds: pitch, intensity, and duration (Stubbs, 1934). The movements of newborn babies increase with increases in sound intensities; they also respond with progressively more activity to tones of higher pitch within the frequency range of 128 to 4,096 cycles per second. Babies' responses also increase as the duration of a stimulus is lengthened. However, we know little about hearing sensitivity in relation to age. Keen, Chase and Graham (1965) tested babies under thirteen days of age by sounding two tones of the same pitch; one lasted two seconds, the other ten seconds. Recordings of the infants' heart rates showed that they responded more to the ten-second than to the shorter tone of the same pitch and intensity.

The Chemical Senses

Taste

Taste and smell are intimately related. However, special precautions in an experimental situation can separate their effects.

There are four basic tastes.

Chemical changes around a taste pore produce neural activity, although scientists are not sure how this happens. There are four primary taste qualities: sweet, sour, salt and bitter. Although people differ in their absolute threshold for taste, generally bitter is most easy to detect even at very modest concentrations. But differences in the intensity of bitter substances are difficult to distinguish. By contrast, the intensity of sour stimuli is very easy to differentiate, and salt or sweet stimuli are intermediate in intensity differences. Most females have lower thresholds for sweet and salt, while males are more sensitive to sour. Even very young infants prefer sweets; sour and salt are next most acceptable, and bitter is often aversive. Although taste can be analyzed into these four components, which represent different areas of the tongue, there is evidence that man's taste code is quite complex. For example, if a scientist measured the rate of firing from a single nerve fiber in the tongue, he would find that different concentrations of salt dissolved in water, water alone, and many other soluable substances all stimulate this single nerve fiber. Thus, a pattern of nerve-fiber activity must constitute man's neural information about taste.

Smell

Smell is a primitive sense.

From an evolutionary view smell is man's most primitive sense. In fact, the sense of smell has the most direct route to the central nervous system. Lower vertebrates—like fish and even some mammals like dogs—have large parts of their brain specialized for smell. In man, smell is a secondary sense.

There are six kinds of odors.

Odors can be classified into six primary groups based on their molecular structures. However, this does not account for all odors and we lack any evidence for six different smell receptors. One of the problems is that the physical properties of smell stimuli are difficult to control, so little is known about the sense. Smell is many times more sensitive than taste, but it adapts very quickly.

Let us now turn to a consideration of the five body senses—kinesthesis, balance, touch, pain, and temperature.

Kinesthesis and Balance

Detection of body movement is called kinesthesis and balance.

Body movement is detected by sense organs in the joints and muscles and by balance organs in the inner ear. For example, if a leg is moved, the stretching and contraction of muscle and tendon fibers is relayed to the central nervous system so movement can be recorded and planned. Information about body movement comes from nerve endings located in more than a hundred body joints. These sensors within the muscles and joints respond to movement with a burst of neural firing, and their discharge rate is associated with the speed and direction of the movement.

Balance is sensed by the semicircular canals.

Man's sense of balance comes from three receptors located on each side of the brain near the inner ear. These receptors are called the superior, lateral, and posterior semicircular canals (see Figure 4.4). The balance organs work as follows: If the head is moved in any particular direction, the liquid inside the canal moves in the opposite direction through inertia.

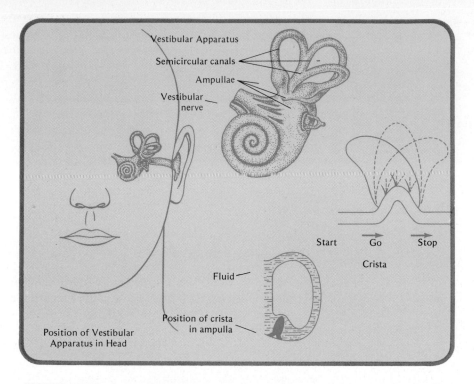

Vestibular Apparatus
Semicircular canals
Ampullae
Vestibular nerve
Start   Go   Stop
Crista
Fluid
Position of crista in ampulla
Position of Vestibular Apparatus in Head

FIGURE 4.4 The human balance apparatus located above the inner ear, showing three semicircular canals. Each canal contains a crista which is bent when the head undergoes acceleration or deceleration.

As a result sensory cells within the canal are stimulated by the movement of liquid and this movement is translated into information about acceleration or deceleration of the head. Frequent stops and starts or changes in direction will produce nausea or dizziness.

Dropping frightens babies.

Relatively little research work has been done on the effect of children's movements. Watson (1925) maintained that suddenly dropping an infant produces fear, and he concluded that fear of falling is innate in babies. Probably an infant's response to movement is a joint function of automatic reaction, personal security, and prior experience with falling.

The Skin Senses

Touch

The skin is sensitive to many stimuli.

Receptors in the skin are sensitive to warm, cold, touch, and pain. A cross-section of the human skin contains several receptor organs. Meissner corpuscles, free nerve endings, basket nerves, and nerve fibers all occur near the base of a hair. Psychologists believe these different receptor organs are associated with the various senses of touch, pain, warm, and cold. However, all that is known for certain is that nerve fibers at the base of hair follicles are sensitive to modest pressure; and that free nerve endings must be involved in pain reception. The specific function of other receptors is uncertain.

Temperature

The temperature sense registers warm and cold stimuli.

Although the temperature scale on a thermometer is continuous, the human body divides heat into cold and warm with a neutral zone in between. The experience of cold or warm depends on the difference between skin temperature and the object that is touched. For example, suppose you put one hand in warm water and the other in cold water for five minutes. If both hands are then placed in water at room temperature the hand that was in cold water will feel warm and the one that was in warm water will feel cool. Thus sensed temperature is related to both the temperature of the object touched and the temperature of the human body. There are no "hot" receptors in the human skin. Hot is actually a sensation constructed from simultaneous stimulation of warm and cold receptors. This can be shown easily by an experiment. Suppose both warm and cold liquids are flowing through parallel coils of tubing at the same time. When the coils are touched with the hand they will feel hot, although only warm and cold stimulation is available.

Babies become quiet in warm temperatures.

The newborn baby responds to temperature changes by increased general activity. It tends to be quiet if the air temperature is around 75° F, and to increase metabolic (processes going on inside the body) and general muscular activity if the temperature falls several degrees below that level. Babies also show a preference for milk warmed to a temperature of around 130° F (Jensen, 1932). Finally, newborn babies withdraw their legs or arms when touched with a cold cylinder of 50° F (Pratt, Nelson and Sun, 1930).

Pain

Pain is caused by tissue damage.

The final skin sense we will discuss is pain. It can be sharp and localized or deep, dull, and generalized. Injury to bodily tissue or overstimulation of a sense organ can generate pain. Injury to a free nerve ending produces pain, while puncture of the skin by a fine needle is not in itself painful unless a free nerve ending is hit. We know free nerve endings are associated with pain because they are the only sensory receptors in the cornea and gum pulp, and these areas both feel pain (see Figure 4.5).

Adaptation to pain is small.

Adaptation to pain is generally slow and only to a small degree. Insensitivity to pain may happen genetically, as a result of neurotic reaction (when it is called hysteria), by hypnosis, or with anesthetic. A person without sensitivity to pain constantly damages his body by cutting or burning himself or breaking his limbs. A person under hypnosis may

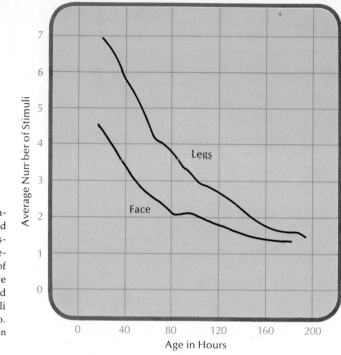

FIGURE 4.5
Number of pain stim-
uli applied to face and
leg which are neces-
sary to produce a re-
sponse from infants of
different ages. Note
that newborns need
many more stimuli
than older babies do.
(Adapted from Sherman
and Sherman, 1929.)

report that he feels no pain if he is given the suggestion that he will not
feel pain. However, non-hypnotized observers can withstand about the
same amount of pain if they are very highly motivated to do so.

Adults are percep-
tually more mature
than children.

Scientists believe that a newborn baby is sensitive to many of the
same physical stimuli as the average adult. However, there are wide
differences between infants and most adults in their ability to attend to,
process, and comprehend these sensations. While infants and adults
receive many of the same basic sensory inputs, the adult is much more
able to select relevant cues from a complex environment and attach meanings to these sensations (*see* Figure 4.6).

Let us consider next how the child and the adult perceive their environments.

Attention

Humans must select
stimuli.

Children and adults are constantly surrounded by more information
than they can process. Without some way to select important events and
suppress the rest, people would constantly be confused.

What does attract attention? In the classroom, teachers restrict distractions, often punish a pupil if he does not pay attention, and reward
him when he concentrates on the lesson. But what about the everyday

What attracts
attention?

world? What attracts a buyer's attention in an ad? How do people attract each other? How can a lecturer, for example, hold the attention of the class? Many experts agree that one of the most effective ways to attract attention is by change. An increase in sound volume, a shift in the type of stimulation, or a change from shouting to a whisper will attract attention.

Larger items attract
attention.

Advertisers have found that in general larger items attract more attention than smaller ones; and bright or strong stimuli, like a sharp poke in the ribs, get better attention than a light touch. Particularly for a child with a short attention span, change can create interest and at least momentary attention. Repetition may also at first attract and then can repel a potential buyer.

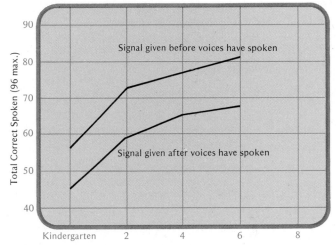

FIGURE 4.6
Differences in how much of a message is reproduced by the child when he is told to attend to the voice before and after he hears the voice.
(From Maccoby, 1967.)

Biological stimuli
attract attention.

One sure way to attract attention is to associate a product with a powerful biological need like hunger, thirst, or sexuality. Important goals, attitudes, and events with personal meaning also attract attention. A good example is your own name. If one is alerted before an auditory message is presented, one's perception and recall of the message is enhanced.

The orienting re-
sponse accompanies
attending.

Major behavioral changes accompany attending. When a child attends, he involuntarily adjusts his sensory organs, shifts his posture and muscular tension, and increases his pupil size. Collectively, these changes are called the "orienting response." Physiological processes— like the amount of electricity conducted by the skin, the heart rate, and brain-wave patterns—change when attention is given. Eye movements and pupil size are good clues for determining attention. Figure 4.7 shows

FIGURE 4.7 A good measure of attention is the location, duration, and sequence of eye fixation and size of pupil during fixation. These pictures show the attention given by females and males to a farm scene. Size of the circles indicates pupil size while viewing various parts of the picture. Enlargement of the pupil indicates interest, and constriction represents dislike.
(After Hess, 1965.)

Expectations affect seeing.

the sequence and duration of eye movements made by male and female participants looking at a picture.

Finally, the goals and expectations of the person aware of his surroundings influence his search for and interpretation of information. This process is called the "perceptual set."

Perceptual Set

Perceptual sets exist in children.

If someone is shown a systematic sequence of pictures, a perceptual expectation can be established, and this perceptual set will help determine how the person interprets ambiguous pictures. For example, suppose young children aged four to twelve years old were shown the two series of six drawings of human faces or animals illustrated in Figure 4.8. In an experiment some groups of children looked first at a series of human faces and then at an ambiguous picture which could have been interpreted as either a mouse or a man. Other groups of children saw an

FIGURE 4.8
The effect of expectation on the perception of ambiguous figures. Do you see a young woman or an old lady in the top picture? What is the last picture you see in the next two rows?

animal series of pictures followed by the same ambiguous picture. Following the first training session all the children were asked to sort the cards into sets of animals or people. Almost every child of six years and over sorted the ambiguous picture into the set he had seen. If the set was of people, for example, the ambiguous picture was put into that pile and not in the animal one.

Selective Listening

Maccoby studied dis-
traction and recall.

Eleanor Maccoby (1965) studied the effects of distraction on children's selective attention and recall. She measured children from the first through seventh grades. Half of her subjects saw pictures on colored backgrounds and listened to notes of music played at random intervals. The remaining children saw only the pictures on colored backgrounds. All the children were to remember the pictures and colors.

Older children can
listen selectively.

Maccoby's results showed that recall of relevant information increased regularly with age, while recall of irrelevant items showed no such change. Older children were also better able to separate relevant from irrelevant information. By contrast, Maccoby reported that the younger children paid attention to the total input, and as a result they had more trouble remembering relevant pictures or colors.

What facilitates selec-
tive attention?

The ability to select what one will notice, called the "cocktail party phenomenon," has fascinated psychologists as well as partygoers for a long time. The question is: How can a person follow one conversation in a noisy crowded room without being confused by all the other noises? One answer is that you cannot always. But when selectivity occurs, what is it about language that enables a listener to sort out some stimuli and suppress others?

Broadbent believes
that each ear is a
separate processing
channel.

David Broadbent (1963) theorized that each human ear is a separate processing channel and that information coming into one ear can be processed while data from the other is stored in short-term memory to be considered later. In a typical selective-attending experiment, a listener is given earphones over which different messages are presented to each ear at the same time. The messages are often lists of digits; for example, 3, 7, 5 to the left ear, and 2, 8, 6 to the right. The listener's task is to repeat these digits. One finding is that the listeners typically report all digits from one ear first and then those from the other. Since there are two hemispheres in the brain, Broadbent proposed that the left hemisphere serves the right ear and the right hemisphere processes input to the left ear. He further argues that for most people, better language processing occurs for input to the right ear because the left hemisphere usually contains the dominant speech center of humans. For this reason Broadbent believes that the left hemisphere of the brain is best equipped to process speech information, while the right hemisphere is better able to handle nonhearing signals. Is there a relationship between speech processing, localization of brain functions, and the personal or intellectual characteristics of humans?

Brain dominance and eye movements are related.

Paul Bakan (1971) found that people who move their eyes most often to the left when thinking or remembering, are suggestible, produce more alpha waves, show an interest in language, and are dominated by their right hemispheres much of the time. He also found that people who move their eyes to the right are resistant to suggestion, show more interest in mathematics, and are dominated more of the time by their left brain hemispheres. To explain these data he proposes that left or right hemisphere dominance is not a permanent occurrence. Rather, one hemisphere has primary responsibility for some tasks, while the other hemisphere is most involved in carrying out other activities. This flexible theory of *brain dominance* suggests that man's central nervous system is even more complex than scientists had previously believed. The central nervous system's sophistication implied by this theory is impressive.

How are objects perceived?

One consideration for the organization of man's central nervous system is how meaning is attached to objects. The construction and understanding of objects by children is just beginning to be investigated. Only recently have psychologists come to realize the torturous steps involved in the perception of objects. Consider what we know of this important topic.

Newborns have few perceptual abilities.

The human newborn's perceptual abilities are few. He is sensitive to variations in brightness, texture, and complexity of visual stimuli (Fantz, 1961). The young baby's perceptual systems are immature. Unlike human adults, infants cannot comprehend what they see. The primary difference between infants and adults is not in their sensations but in the ability of adults to add meaning to their impressions. Current research suggests that babies' perceptual systems are genetically programed to select some features from their environment (Hubel and Wiesel, 1963). But biological maturation and learning experiences are required before the automatic processing and comprehension of the adult is achieved. There are several theories about how this perceptual development happens.

Theories of Perception

Three theories of perceptual development exist.

Explanations of perception vary between evolution and experience. Those who believe that perception is innate and that there are genetically determined perceptual abilities are called nativists. They also think that even the human newborn is programed to see order in his universe from the moment of birth. The empiricist on the other hand maintains that the human newborn learns to understand and order what he sees through experience. A third theoretical school assumes that both primitive innate mechanisms *and* learning are required to explain perceptual development.

Portrait

George A. Miller was born in 1920, grew up in the South, and received his bachelor's degree in speech from the University of Alabama in 1940. Following his graduation, he began to work on voice-communication systems for the U.S. War Department during World War II. After the war he enrolled in the Psychology Department at Harvard University and earned his doctorate in 1946. He joined the teaching faculty of Harvard College in 1948; moved to the Massachusetts Institute of Technology where he taught from 1951 to 1954; and then rejoined Harvard University. By 1958 he was promoted to full professor and served as chairman of the Harvard Psychology Department between 1964 and 1968. In 1969 he left Harvard to teach in the psychology program at Rockefeller University in New York.

George Miller's early career in psychology came ". . . from the engineering-mathematical side." He became very involved and interested in the linguistic theories of Noam Chomsky while at M.I.T. The collaboration between Chomsky and Miller produced three chapters concerning the mathematical analyses of language and psychology in the *Handbook of Mathematical Psychology*. Miller worked for several years to show the psychological reality of the grammars that he and Chomsky postulated in their joint papers. Miller was concerned with describing the implications of their language theory for the way people see, remember, make choices, and construct meaningful sentences.

A highlight of Miller's career came in 1963, when the American Psychological Association gave him its distinguished scientific contribution award for that year. He was also named president of the American Psychological Association in 1969. Past presidents had used the APA convention to summarize their research activities, but Miller startled his colleagues by breaking this tradition. He decided instead to bring a pressing problem to the attention of his assembled colleagues. He argued persuasively that psychology should pay more attention to the social implications of discoveries about human behavior, and he suggested that more time should be spent in solving social problems and less time worrying about the advantages or disadvantages of particular approaches to behavior. While Miller was president of the APA he spent a good deal of his time working with Charles Thomas, leader of the Association of Black Psychologists, trying to establish better opportunities for blacks in the field.

George Miller has published many articles and a number of books. Probably his most famous article was "The Magical Number 7, Plus or Minus 2." In it he argued that there are several limitations on the ability of human beings to process and remember information. At the time he was the 77th president of the APA.

Professor George P. Miller of Rockefeller University. (Photo from Eugene H. Kone, Rockefeller University)

the magical number seven, plus or minus two: some limits on our capacity for processing information

GEORGE A. MILLER

My problem is that I have been persecuted by an integer. For seven years this number has followed me around, has intruded in my most private data, and has assaulted me from the pages of our most public journals. This number assumes a variety of diguises, being sometimes a little larger and sometimes a little smaller than usual, but never changing so much as to be unrecognizable. The persistence with which this number plagues me is far more than a random accident. There is, to quote a famous senator, a design behind it, some pattern governing its appearances. Either there really is something unusual about the number or else I am suffering from delusions of persecution.

I shall begin my case history by telling you about some experiments that tested how accurately people can assign numbers to the magnitudes of various aspects of a stimulus. In the traditional language of psychology these would be called experiments in absolute judgment. Historical accident, however, has decreed that they should have another name. We now call them experiments on the capacity of people to transmit information. Since these experiments would not have been done without the appearance of information theory on the psychological scene, and since the results are analyzed in terms of the concepts of information theory, I shall have to preface my discussion with a few remarks about this theory.

Information Measurement

The "amount of information" is exactly the same concept that we have talked about for years under the name of "variance." The equations are different, but if we hold tight to the idea that anything that increases the variability also increases the amount of information, we cannot go far astray.

The similarity of variance and amount of information might be explained this way: When we have a large variance, we are very ignorant about what is going to happen. If we are very ignorant, then when we make the observation it gives us a lot of information. On the other hand, if the variance is very small, we know in advance how our observation must come out, so we get little information from making the observation.

From *Psychological Review*, 1956, 63, 81–97.

The situation can be described graphically by two partially overlapping circles. Then the left circle can be taken to represent the variance of the input, the right circle the variance of the output, and the overlap the covariance of input and output. I shall speak of the left circle as the amount of input information, the right circle as the amount of output information, and the overlap as the amount of transmitted information.

There are two ways we might increase the amount of input information. We could increase the rate at which we give information to the observer, so that the amount of information per unit time would increase. Or we could ignore the time variable completely and increase the amount of input information by increasing the number of alternative stimuli. In the absolute judgment experiment we are interested in the second alternative. We give the observer as much time as he wants to make his response; we simply increase the number of alternative stimuli among which he must discriminate and look to see where confusions begin to occur. Confusions will appear near the point that we are calling his "channel capacity."

The Span of Immediate Memory

Let me summarize the situation in this way. There is a clear and definite limit to the accuracy with which we can identify absolutely the magnitude of a unidimensional stimulus variable. I would propose to call this limit the *span of absolute judgment,* and I maintain that for unidimensional judgments this span is usually somewhere in the neighborhood of seven. We are not completely at the mercy of this limited span, however, because we have a variety of techniques for getting around it and increasing the accuracy of our judgments. The three most important of these devices are (*a*) to make relative rather than absolute judgments; or, if that is not possible, (*b*) to increase the number of dimensions along which the stimuli can differ; or (*c*) to arrange the task in such a way that we make a sequence of several absolute judgments in a row.

Recoding

. . . we must recognize the importance of grouping or organizing the input sequence into units or chunks. Since the memory span is a fixed number of chunks, we can increase the number of bits of information that it contains simply by building larger and larger chunks, each chunk containing more information than before.

A man just beginning to learn radio-telegraphic code hears each *dit* and *dah* as a separate chunk. Soon he is able to organize these sounds into letters and then he can deal with the letters as chunks. Then the letters organize themselves as words, which are still larger chunks, and he begins to hear whole phrases. I do not mean that each step is a discrete process, or that plateaus must appear in his learning curve, for surely the levels of organization are achieved at different rates and overlap each other during the learning process. I am simply pointing to the obvious fact that the dits and dahs are organized by learning into patterns and that as these larger chunks emerge, the amount of message that the operator can remember increases correspondingly. In the terms I am proposing to use, the operator learns to increase the bits per chunk.

In the jargon of communication theory, this process would be called *recoding*. The input is given in a code that contains many chunks with few bits per chunk. The operator recodes the input into another code that contains fewer chunks with more bits per chunk. There are many ways to do this recoding, but probably the simplest is to group the input events, apply a new name to the group, and then remember the new name rather than the original input events.

In my opinion the most customary kind of recoding that we do all the time is to translate into a verbal code. When there is a story or an argument or an idea that we want to remember, we usually try to rephrase it "in our own words." When we witness some event we want to remember, we make a verbal description of the event and then remember our verbalization. Upon recall we recreate by secondary elaboration the details that seem consistent with the particular verbal recoding we happen to have made. . . .

The inaccuracy of the testimony of eyewitnesses is well known in legal psychology, but the distortions of testimony are not random—they follow naturally from the particular recoding that the witness used, and the particular recoding he used depends upon his whole life history. Our language is tremendously useful for repackaging material into a few chunks rich in information. I suspect that imagery is a form of recoding, too, but images seem much harder to get at operationally and to study experimentally than the more symbolic kinds of recoding.

I have come to the end of the data that I wanted to present, so I would like now to make some summarizing remarks.

First, the span of absolute judgment and the span of immediate memory impose severe limitations on the amount of information that we are able to receive, process, and remember. By organizing the stimulus input simultaneously into several dimensions and successively into a sequence of chunks, we manage to break (or at least stretch) this informational bottleneck.

Second, the process of recoding is a very important one in human psychology and deserves much more explicit attention than it has received. In particular, the kind of linguistic recoding that people do seems to me to be the very lifeblood of the thought processes. Recoding procedures are a constant concern to clinicians, social psychologists, linguists, and anthropologists; and yet, probably because recoding is less accessible to experimental manipulation than nonsense syllables or T mazes, the traditional experimental psychologist has contributed little or nothing to their analysis. Nevertheless, experimental techniques can be used, methods of recoding can be specified, behavioral indicants can be found.

And I anticipate that we will find a very orderly set of relations describing what now seems an uncharted wilderness of individual differences.

Third, the concepts and measures provided by the theory of information provide a quantitative way of getting at some of these questions. The theory provides us with a yardstick for calibrating our stimulus materials and for measuring the performance of our subjects. In the interests of communication I have suppressed the technical details of information measurement and have tried to express the ideas in more familiar terms; I hope this paraphrase will not lead you to think they are not useful in research. Informational concepts have already proved valuable in the study of discrimination and of language; they promise a great deal in the study of learning and memory; and it has even been proposed that they can be useful in the study of concept formation. A lot of questions that seemed fruitless twenty or thirty years ago may now be worth another look. In fact, I feel that my story here must stop just as it begins to get really interesting.

And finally, what about the magical number seven? What about the seven wonders of the world, the seven seas, the seven deadly sins, the seven daughters of Atlas in the Pleiades, the seven ages of man, the seven levels of hell, the seven primary colors, the seven notes of the musical scale, and the seven days of the week? What about the seven-point rating scale, the seven categories for absolute judgment, the seven objects in the span of attention, and the seven digits in the span of immediate memory? For the present I propose to withhold judgment. Perhaps there is something deep and profound behind all these sevens, something just calling out for us to discover it. But I suspect that it is only a pernicious, Pythagorean coincidence.

Nativism

Mueller proposed a nativistic theory of perception.

Johannes Mueller (1838) proposed a nativistic theory of perception when he noted that the mind can have direct contact only with the states of nerves and not with external bodies. Mueller believed that because spatial relations are preserved in the optic nerve fibers arrangement,

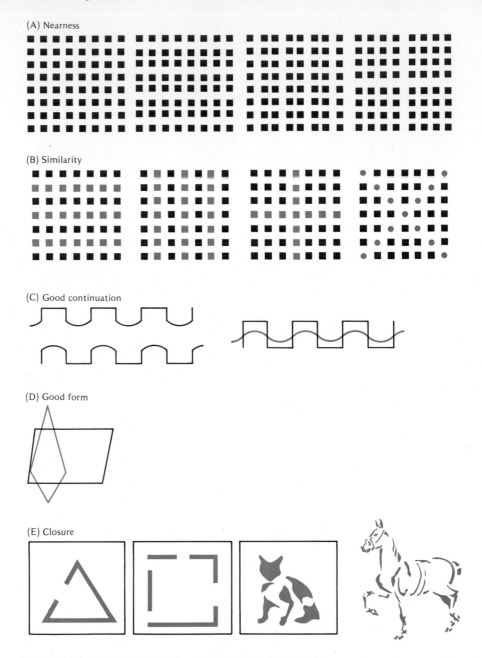

FIGURE 4.9 Six Gestalt principles of perception. *A* shows that *near* things are grouped; while *B* demonstrates that *similar* items are seen together. *C* illustrates that a *continuing* line is seen as a whole; while *D* shows the perceptual strength of simple forms like squares or diamonds. *E* demonstrates the ability to *close* broken lines to form a whole; while *F* illustrates the *figure-ground* phenomenon. Can you see faces or the globet in *F* at the top of page 143?

(F)

FIGURE 4.10 Examples of four principles of perceptual organization proposed by the Gestalt school of perception.

the mind directly perceives the retinal image. He believed there is a precise inborn harmony among retinal cells, nerve fibers, perceptual processes, and stimuli from the external world and that this harmony directed the process of perception.

The Gestalt school supported nativism.

A nativist view of perceptual development was also supported by the Gestalt school, whose members theorized that things are seen as whole units rather than as bits and pieces. They believed that perceptual organization is controlled by the structure of man's nervous system, and articulated several rules of perception to illustrate their thinking (*see* Figures 4.9 and 4.10):

1. *Nearness*—things close together in the perceptual field are seen as a unit.
2. *Similarity*—identical items are grouped into one perceptual unit.
3. *Good continuation*—lines that continue in a straight line or project a smooth curve become a single unit.
4. *Good form*—shapes like squares, circles, and triangles are "good" perceptual objects and resist disruption.
5. *Closure*—man's perceptual system fills in blanks to form a good percept.
6. *Figure-ground*—some parts of an array are seen as figures and the rest become background.

Gestalt psychologists assumed that these rules result from innate structures in the central nervous system, not from experience and learning.

Empiricism

John Locke first proposed empiricism.

Early British empiricists like John Locke (1690) pointed out that the eye is aligned with any object that comes under attention, so that each retinal point can be associated with an intensity and a particular sensation. They argued that man learns to see B between A and C because, as he moves his eyes, he experiences items in the order A, B, C. An empirical view of perceptual development says man must *learn* how to group sensations into perceptual objects. The empiricist claims man *learns* that four equal straight lines connected at right angles make up a square.

Learning theories assume that stimuli need enrichment.

Theories of learning assume that perceptual abilities develop through enrichment of the stimulus by associations. There are several versions of the perceptual enrichment theory. Some are based on thinking, while others are more response-oriented. Cognitive theories assume that perception is unconscious problem-solving; while response-oriented theories claim that perception reflects the world by making a motor copy of it.

One theory of perception is called "acquired distinctiveness of cues."

The most popular response theory of perceptual learning is called *acquired distinctiveness of cues*. This theory says two similar stimuli become unique by acquiring separate and distinctive associations. For example, two similar sensations of color may be seen as different by associating one with a dress and the other with a house. These differential associations are assumed to make each color more unique. Theories of perceptual learning assume that man's sensory environment is meager and the only way he can differentiate stimuli is to add associations to these sparse sensations. However, human sensory systems often collect too much information, and then perception requires the reduction of sensory data rather than its enrichment. In many instances the perceiver's task is to separate important information from irrelevant stimuli. A good example of perceptual selection occurred in a study by Eleanor Gibson (1962). She explored children's sensitivity to distinctive and irrelevant features of letters. She found that older children could differentiate and attend to the correct features of letters and at the same time ignore irrelevant features like size or color changes. Gibson defined relevant features of letters as those characteristics that do not change under minor transformations of the stimulus. For example, a C is curved in a particular direction whether it is red, blue, written, typed, small or large. Young children were not able to ignore the irrelevant changes in the letters. One feature of mature perception must be the ability to select from available sensations.

Nativism and Empiricism

Innate perceptual mechanisms exist.

Recent work by two physiologists, Hubel and Wiesel (1963), suggests that innate mechanisms for form and movement detection exist in the perceptual systems of newborn kittens. They also found that these innate mechanisms require postnatal stimulation to continue their functioning. The work showed that newborn kittens who were raised with their eyes closed for two months lose the functioning of cortical cells which normally detect simple form and movement. Thus, innate perceptual processes are lost if they are not used. How much stimulation is required to maintain innate perceptual mechanisms is not known, but some minimal patterning of light certainly is needed.

Both nativism and empiricism are necessary for perception.

Both Donald Hebb (1949) and Jean Piaget (1947) have proposed theories of perception which integrate these extreme positions. They assume the infant has a primitive innate mechanism which separates the figure from its background; and that the infant uses this basic mechanism to define distinguishing qualities. In addition, the infant is assumed to learn the *orders* of those qualities which enter into the perception of objects. Thus, through the interaction of an innate figure-ground mechanism, learning, and eye movements the infant constructs his perceptual world through sensory experience and active interaction with the environment.

The Perception of Space

How do we see space?

One of the most important products of perception is three-dimensional space. The human retina is only two-dimensional, but in spite of that limitation children can easily see depth. How is that possible?

Is There Innate Depth Perception?

Is depth perception innate?

Adult human beings automatically perceive three dimensions. Do we learn that the world is three-dimensional or has the process of evolution selected for survival only creatures who are automatically sensitive to three dimensions and aware of the potential consequences of falling? To answer that question for human infants, Walk and Gibson (1961) designed an apparatus to study depth perception. Gibson constructed a table with a center board that is one foot wide and is elevated one inch from a glass surface (*see* Figure 4.11). Tiles were placed directly under the glass on one side of the center board to match a pattern of floor tile forty inches below the glass on the other side. Raised boards around the outside of the table kept the infant from accidentally falling off the edge. This construction of a *visual cliff* offers the baby a choice between a very small apparent drop on one side of the center board and a much larger drop on the other side. A strong sheet of glass actually covered both sides of the "cliff" to control non-visual cues and to catch adventurous babies. During the experiment the baby's mother stands alternately at the deep and shallow sides of the table, attempting to persuade the baby to come her way. Infants who are old enough to crawl consistently refused to cross the deep side, although they almost always crossed the shallow side to their mothers.

The visual cliff test requires locomotion.

Gibson's visual cliff test of depth perception depends on a baby's ability to crawl, so the question of whether babies see depth before they achieve this stage cannot be answered by this device. However, these data do show that human infants possess depth perception by the age of six months, because they refuse to approach the deep side of a visual cliff. Even cues from one eye are enough to determine depth in a six-month-old infant, since the researchers tested a one-eyed baby and he would not cross to the deep side of the visual cliff even when coaxed by his mother. This shows that having good vision in two eyes is not necessary for depth perception among young infants, although cues from both eyes contribute to more precise depth perception among older children and adults. Tests with the visual cliff suggest that space perception may be innate, or that it requires only a minimum of experience. To be sure, you would have to isolate babies from visual space experience for their first six months, or find a way to test for depth perception in newborn human babies. Even if depth perception is innate, psychologists are still interested in the cues people use to compute depth. There are two major kinds.

Monocular Cues to Depth

There are two kinds of cues to depth.

A retinal image registers only *two* dimensions yet almost everyone is aware of three. How do people translate the two retinal dimensions of height and width into three, adding depth? There are many cues. Some are called *monocular* because only one eye is necessary to detect the cue; others are called *binocular* because it takes both eyes to identify the cue. One important monocular cue is the size of a retinal image, since larger images are produced by near objects and smaller ones by distant objects. Another monocular cue to depth is *interposition,* referring to perception of an object that is placed between the viewer and another object. Thus, one object partially covers another, because it is in front of the other and obscures it. Another monocular cue is *linear perspective.* Lines converging toward an horizon—like telephone poles, trees, or train tracks—seem to decrease systematically in size and suggest increasing distance from the observer.

Binocular Cues to Depth

Convergence is a binocular cue.

There are two important binocular cues to depth: convergence and retinal disparity. *Convergence* means that when the eyes focus on a near object they must turn inward; when they focus on an object that is further away they move outward from the nasal point. However, convergence of the eyes has little value as a cue to depth except for close objects.

A more reliable binocular depth cue is *retinal disparity.* Since human eyes are located at two slightly different points in the head, they enable the viewer to obtain two views of the same object. For example, the right

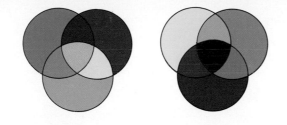

WHITE

9/

8/

7/

6/

5/

4/   /2   /4   /6   /8   /10 /12 /14

3/

2/

1/

BLACK

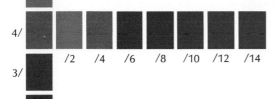

Plate 1

Color mixtures. Additive mixtures *(top left)* occur when the three primary colors are blended (overlap); they can produce all the colors seen by a human observer. Subtractive mixtures *(top right)* can produce primary colors from a combination of other hues (canceling).

(Left) Brightness ranges from black to white are shown on the vertical scale. Steps are numbered according to a standard (Munsell) system of notation. The saturation range from a hue approaching gray to a "pure" red is shown on the horizontal range.

Plate 2

A color circle, which consists of spectral and nonspectral hues. The diameters of the circle connect complementary hues which, when mixed, produce gray.

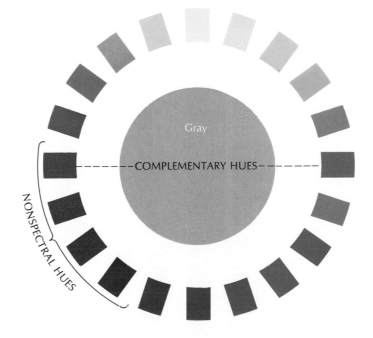

Gray

COMPLEMENTARY HUES

NONSPECTRAL HUES

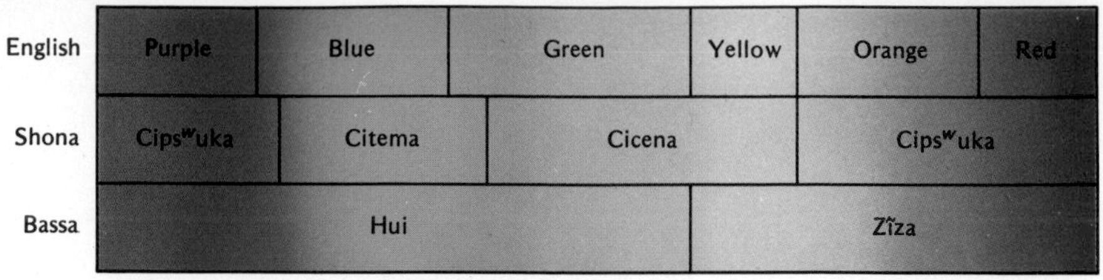

English	Purple	Blue	Green	Yellow	Orange	Red
Shona	Cips^wuka	Citema	Cicena		Cips^wuka	
Bassa	Hui			Ziza		

Plate 3

How three linguistic communities partition the visible spectrum of color.
(After Gleason, 1961.)

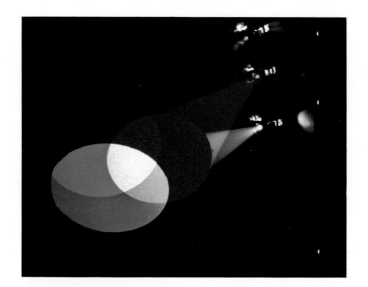

Plate 4

Additive and subtractive color mixtures. Additive color mixture occurs when color lights are combined. Red and green lights produce yellow, green and purple give blue, and all three produce white. Subtractive color mixture happens when filters or pigments are mixed. Usually yellow and blue subtract to give green, and blue and red subtract to produce purple. The three subtract to yield black. (Fritz Goro, LIFE Magazine © Time Inc.)

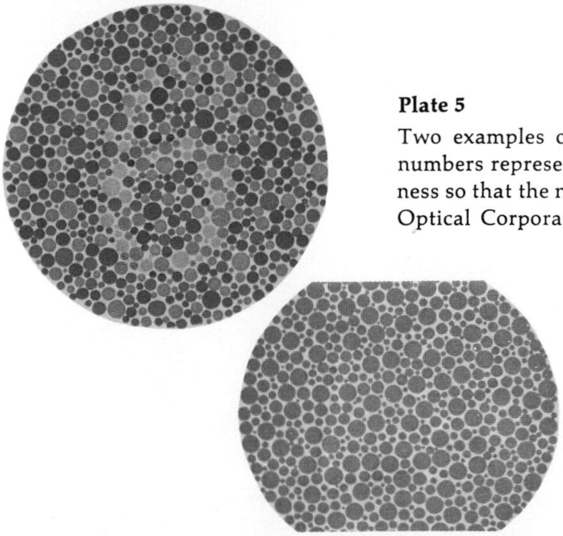

Plate 5

Two examples of a colorblindness test. The ability to see the colored numbers represents normal color vision. The dots are equated for brightness so that the numbers are invisible to colorblind individuals. (American Optical Corporation from their AO Pseudo-Osochromatic Color Tests.)

These reproductions of color recognition tests cannot be used for actual testing. The examples are only representative of the total of 15 charts necessary for a complete color recognition examination.

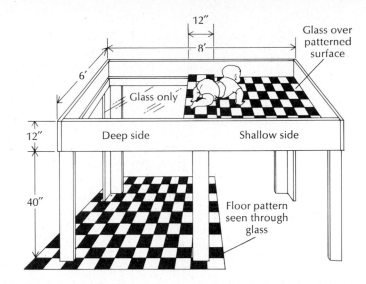

FIGURE 4.11 The "visual cliff," which allows psychologists to test human infants for depth perception. Few babies who crawl are willing to venture onto the "deep" side of the cliff.
(After Walk and Gibson, 1961.)

Retinal disparity is the best depth cue.

eye sees a little more of the right side of an object, while the left eye sees a little more of the left side. This difference in view allows one to locate the position of an object in space. An easy way to demonstrate retinal disparity is to hold your finger about six to eight inches in front of your face and alternately close one eye and then the other.

Object Perception

The Development of Object Perception

Newborn perception is difficult to measure.

Speculation and debate on the origins of object perception is an old hobby. Psychology's early sources of information were armchair speculation or experimental observation of adults. More recently, these data have been supplanted by direct observation of the newborn and young infant. The measurement of object perception in a newborn is complicated because he has very limited response abilities. The traditional psychophysical methods, requiring verbal instructions and responses, won't work with babies, so alternate techniques had to be developed which make use of the baby's restricted abilities. For example, changes in sucking rate, eye orientation, heart rate, skin conductance, conditioned responses, and total body movement are all used as indicators of infant perception.

Fantz first studied in-
fant perception.

Robert Fantz (1961) pioneered the study of infant perception when he used looking time to explore newborn perception. In one study he presented babies with three black-and-white patterns: horizontal stripes, a bull's-eye, and a checkerboard. Each black-and-white stimulus was presented simultaneously with a standard gray field while Fantz measured the amount of time a reflected image of the stimulus appeared in the center of the baby's eye. If the baby looked more at one stimulus than at others, Fantz assumed the baby could discriminate between the patterns. He observed thirty babies weekly from one to fifteen weeks of age. Fantz' data showed that infants respond differentially to these visual stimuli by the age of eight or ten weeks.

Fantz found that
human babies prefer
complex patterns.

In another study forty-nine babies, aged four days to six months, were presented with three flat stimuli painted black on a pink background (*see* Figure 4.12). One stimulus was a face; a second stimulus contained the facial features in a scrambled position; the third stimulus was a brightness control, which included an oval with a solid patch of black equal in area to that covered by the features on each of the other two stimuli. All possible pairs were presented to the infants. For all age levels, the infants looked most at the real and scrambled patterns and infrequently at the black patch. These data do not show that babies up to six months of age prefer human faces to other complex patterned stimuli, but they do sug-

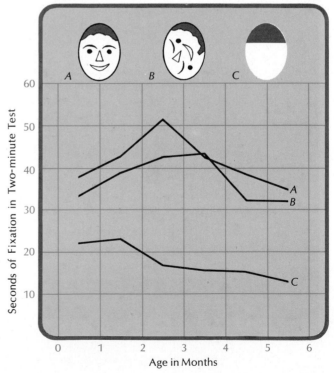

FIGURE 4.12
These three stimuli were shown to babies from two weeks to six months of age. All babies preferred to look at the face and scrambled features rather than the black-patched oval.
(After Fantz, 1961.)

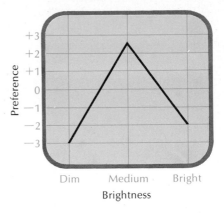

FIGURE 4.13
Relation between newborn's preference and
the brightness of lights.
(From Hershenson, 1964.)

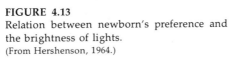

gest that even young babies can differentiate between simple and complex
stimuli.

Hershenson studied
newborn perception.

Maurice Hershenson (1964) studied the visual preferences of thirty-
six newborn babies between the ages of two and four days. Using an
elegant photographic technique and film sensitive to infrared light, he
he examined each infant under semi-dark conditions. The stimulus materials were projected onto two viewing screens above the baby's face.
Hershenson recorded the total proportion of time spent by each baby
looking at each stimulus. Hershenson's stimuli included brightness and
the human face. He presented three levels of brightness in increasing
logarithmic steps and found significant differences for all three pairs of
brightness levels. To test the newborn baby's preference for facial organization, Hershenson used first a photograph of a female face, next
the same face with the features moved into different positions, and finally
the same face with all features randomly arranged. The light-dark ratio
was the same for all faces and the degrees of complexity were matched
for two of the faces. Hershenson found no systematic preference over the
entire set, suggesting that newborn babies are not sensitive to "facial"
organization (*see* Figure 4.13).

We know little about
what newborn infants
see.

The results from these early studies of infant perception suggest that
babies do see something, but that the nature and extent of their preprogramed perceptions is complicated in a way we do not yet understand.
More work is needed to comprehend how infants and children become
able to perceive objects and their component parts.

Whole/Part Perception

Children can perceive
a whole and its sepa-
rate parts.

Young children usually react to an entire stimulus rather than to its
separate parts. This is particularly true of unfamiliar forms. Yet older
children can attend to both a whole figure and to its component parts,
particularly if the parts are familiar (*see* Figure 4.14). Not only do young

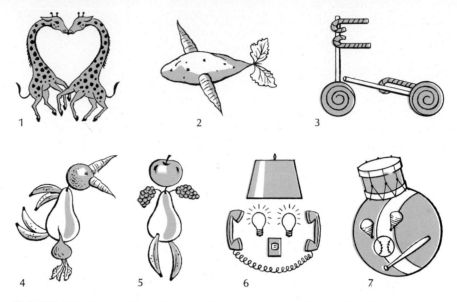

FIGURE 4.14 These pictures show whole images composed of small parts.

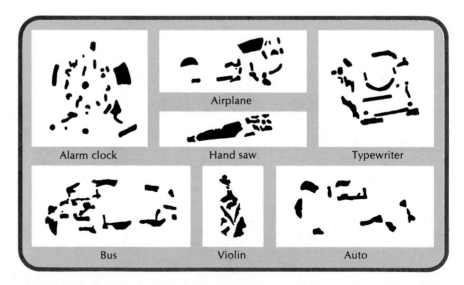

FIGURE 4.15 These incomplete figures are much more difficult for children to identify compared with adult performance. Children need more redundant perceptual cues for recognition.

children have difficulty in analyzing a stimulus but they also need many clues in order to recognize an object. For example, if adults are shown the series of pictures in Figure 4.15 they are likely to perceive them correctly as a clock, saw, bus, and so on. Young children need many hints before they can recognize any of these incomplete patterns. With increasing age, less stimulus completeness is necessary for object perception. However, in one unique way, the perceptual systems of some children are more efficient than are adult's perceptions. This process is called eidetic imagery.

Eidetic Imagery

Eidetic ability enables a child to evoke an extremely clear image of an absent object or event. Individuals who possess eidetic imagery can report with remarkable accuracy even minor details of a visual event from their pasts, for they see a clear mental image of what they are trying to recall. Eidetic imagery is rare in the general population. It declines after nine years of age and is less frequent in Western countries than in African populations.

Ralph Haber (1964) reported that among 151 children tested in an elementary school in Connecticut, 12 showed some eidetic imagery. These children were far more able to reproduce images and to report them accurately than were their peers. After the image faded, the recall of the eidetic children was little better than others. Haber added that children with eidetic memory produced some interpolations and transformations on their images, which suggests that the children were coding and storing images and not just reporting a visual picture from their retinas. The eidetic children also reported that they could move their eyes, and that this movement did not erase the images, again suggesting more than simple retinal storage. Eidetic children are more likely than most to have difficulty with reading, although no one is quite sure why.

Perceptual Constancy

One of the startling features about perception is that the perceived size and shape of objects remains fairly constant even though man's retinal image varies with distance and the viewing angle. Perception of an object does not change as it moves away from you, and although the viewing angle of an object and its corresponding retinal image change, the object still appears to be the same shape. How is that possible?

Size Constancy

The problem of *size constancy* is in understanding how man's perceptual system combines the distance of the object and retinal size to produce an impression of unchanged size. Retinal projection of an object

Eidetic imagery is like photographic memory.

Haber found that some children have eidetic abilities.

Perceived size and shape remain fairly constant.

Size constancy exists.

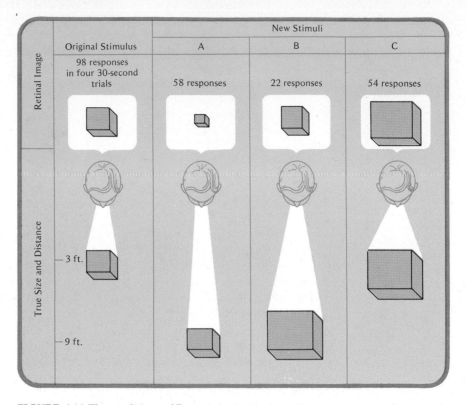

FIGURE 4.16 The conditions of Bower's interesting experiment on perceptual constancy. Six-week-old babies were trained to respond when shown an original stimulus three feet away. The original stimulus was then moved to nine feet and another stimulus, a square three times as large as the first, was presented at both three and nine feet. The results show that six-week-old infants respond on the basis of object rather than retinal size.

varies with its distance from the observer, so distant objects have a smaller retinal image. If the perceiver uses only retinal size to construct an impression, people would appear to shrink as they move away and would grow as they move closer. Somehow the human perceptual system allows for distance and corrects the retinal projection to give an unchanged size representation of the world. Scientists don't understand how this happens.

Bower showed that infants possess size constancy.

However, the ability to correct for retinal size changes seems to develop rather quickly in children. T.G.R. Bower (1966) performed an intriguing experiment in which babies aged six weeks were conditioned so they would respond to an original stimulus three feet from their eyes. They were then tested in three new stimulus situations (*see* Figure 4.16). One of the test situations presented the original stimulus at a new distance of nine feet (*see* Figure 4.16A). A second test presented the baby with a

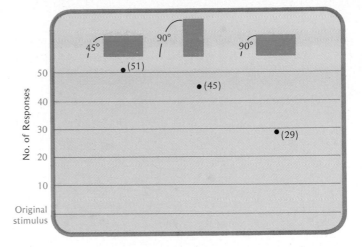

FIGURE 4.17
Eight-week-old babies were trained to respond to a square at 45 degrees as an original stimulus. When shown the same stimulus at 90 degrees, they responded almost as much as they had earlier at 45 degrees. A rectangle which projects a similar retinal pattern to the original stimulus did not elicit very many responses.
(After Bower, 1966)

square three times larger also at nine feet (*see* Figure 4.16B). The final test situation showed the larger square three feet from the baby's face (*see* Figure 4.16C). If the baby were responding to retinal size he should believe the second test situation (large square at nine feet) is the same as the original situation (smaller square at three feet). If he is able to correct for distance changes, he should think that the first test situation (smaller square at nine feet) is most similar to the original stimulus (smaller square at three feet). The results show that babies do correct for distance, since they responded more often in the condition where the original square had been moved to a distance of nine feet from their faces. Thus, at six weeks of age human babies have attained size constancy.

Another puzzle we will discuss now is how children and adults correct their perceptions for variation in the shape of objects viewed from varying angles.

Shape Constancy

Bower also studied shape constancy.

T.G.R. Bower also studied *shape constancy* in human infants between fifty and sixty days old. The babies were reinforced for moving their heads to the left following presentation of a square turned 45 degrees from the infant's frontal plane. Following conditioning to the initial stimulus, the infants were shown either:

1. The original stimulus in its original position.
2. The original stimulus in a position parallel to the infant's plane.
3. A trapezoid in the frontal plane whose retinal projection was equivalent to the original stimulus at a 45-degree plane.
4. The trapezoid at an angle of 45 degrees (*see* Figure 4.17).

The mean number of responses elicited by the four different presentations was: 51 to the original stimulus, 45 to the same stimulus in a different

Even children see illusions.

The simplest illusion is of movement.

Illusions change with age.

orientation, 29 to the stimulus that projected a retinal shape identical with the original, and 26 to the trapezoid at 45 degrees. Apparently, eight-week-old babies possess a well-developed mechanism of shape constancy because these infants were able to recognize a familiar shape in a new orientation and to see the difference between that familiar shape and other similar retinal images. This is a remarkable achievement and points to the possibility of an innate mechanism.

Babies make errors in seeing, but their perceptual systems are remarkable. However, even the sophisticated perceptual processes of an adult are error-prone at times. Countless visual illusions exist in which adult perception seems unable to discover reality. There are illusions of movement, size, and shape. Let us consider some of the well known perceptual errors.

Errors of Perception

Illusions

A motion picture does not really move. Rather, it is a series of still pictures flashed rapidly on a screen at the rate of around sixteen frames per second. The human perceptual system somehow fuses the gaps between each still picture into continuous motion. A simple form of illusory movement is called the "phi" phenomenon. If four lights are flashed in rapid succession around the circumference of a circle an observer in a dark room will see the four lights as a moving circle of light.

No one fully understands why such illusions occur. Even more puzzling are the age changes linked to the perception of illusions. For ex-

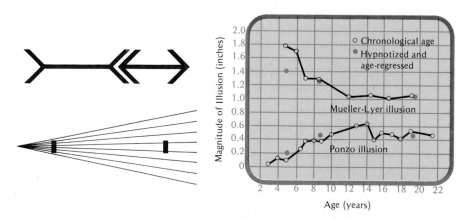

FIGURE 4.18 The age changes found in the Mueller-Lyer (*top*) and the Ponzo illusion (*bottom*). The dots are data collected from hypnotized adults who were instructed to see in the same way as children do. The correspondence is remarkable.

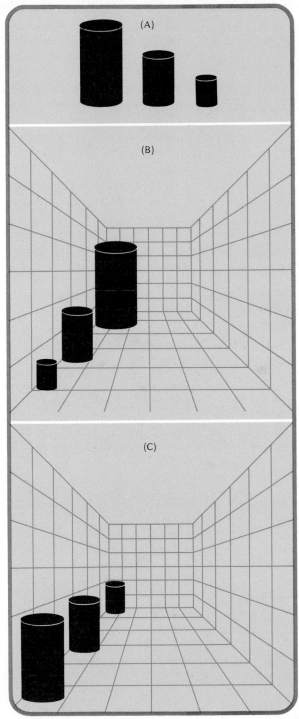

FIGURE 4.19
Rules of perception may produce illusions. The barrels in *A* are of different sizes. If they are placed in the context of *B* they appear even more different. In *C*, however, the depth produces an illusion of equivalence in size.

ample, the Mueller-Lyer illusion *decreases* with age, while the Ponzo illusion increases as children mature (*see* Figure 4.18). Further, if adults are hypnotized and told to imagine they are young children the hypnotized adults show the same illusory trends as young subjects—a surprising finding (Parrish, 1968).

There are several theories about illusions.

There are several theories about why illusions occur. One assumes that the viewer has either too little or too much information and in the process of completing a degraded image or selecting from a surplus of data he produces distortions or perceptual errors. Another theory proposes that the observer has expectations about how sensory data should look and he distorts his sensations to fit these expectations. Unhappily, most illusions are not explained by either of these theories. Illusions most often occur when sensory information stimulates two or more incompatible perceptual processing rules at the same time. Sensory evidence must be interpreted by rules because reality is not a direct perception. The many rules of perception may also be incompatible. So if two rules are activated at the same time and they are in disagreement, there is a resulting uncertainty which produces a visual illusion. The human perceptual system strives for a consistent picture of the world. When this consistency is *not* easily obtained, as in the case of ambiguous or conflicting perceptual rules, then some compromise is achieved. The result is usually an illusion (*see* Figure 4.19).

Perceptual Distortion

Adult perception can adjust to distortions.

Conflicting sensory experiences can influence the well-developed perceptual processes of adults, as we have seen. A study by Ivo Kohler showed that a mature adult will adapt his perceptual rules following several weeks of wearing lenses that distort his visual field. Suppose

FIGURE 4.20
What it may be like to wear inverting prisms. Ivo Kohler was able to ride a bicycle successfully after wearing inverted prisms continuously for several weeks.
(Photo courtesy de Villeneuve)

the distorting lenses invert his sensory world so everything appears to be upside down (*see* Figure 4.20). After a few weeks of wearing the lenses the person begins to notice that the world close to him appears right side up, although distant objects still seem to be inverted. The distorting lens wearer is finally able to move about in his inverted world with little trouble. When the inverting lenses were removed, sensations appeared wrong and the subjects had to relearn movements through space. It is not clear whether the change occurs in visual or in sensory-motor coordination; but, there is a change.

Kohler studied adult perceptual adaptations.

Kohler also studied adult subjects who adjusted their perceptual rules to compensate for blue on the left and yellow on the right side of a pair of glasses. His subjects reported that in a few weeks the world appeared to be in normal colors again. Apparently when they looked to the right their perceptual system added a complement of blue; when they looked to the left it added a complement of yellow. When the colored lenses were removed, the subject's perceptual world was temporarily distorted toward the complementary color of the original lens — now blue was on the right and yellow was on the left.

Adult perceptions are quite flexible.

The human being has great flexibility built into his perceptual/sensory system, and this flexibility allows for change as a function of sensory-motor coordination and experience, especially in children. Sensory-motor changes may occur even among adults, if their experience is extensive. Thus, perceptual development is a continuing compromise between various sensory inputs, past experiences, and the innate structure of the human central nervous system.

Summary

Perception begins with the transformation of physical energy collected from the environment into neural impulses. This important function is carried out by numerous sensory systems scattered about the body — the eyes, ears, taste buds, and semicircular canals. Each sensory system is tuned to a particular physical energy and translates that energy — or any other type of accidental stimulation — into a specific type of sensory information appropriate for that system. Thus, the eyes see brightness, no matter what particular energy produced the stimulation. The sensations that are generated by these sensory systems are selectively attended on the basis of expectations, past experiences, and the total current situation. Once a sensation is attended, higher centers of the Central Nervous System process the information and construct a perception of depth, of objects, and occasionally of illusions.

SUGGESTED ADDITIONAL READINGS

Geldard, F.A. *The Human Senses.* New York: Wiley, 1953.

Gibson, J.J. *The Senses Considered as Perceptual Systems.* Boston: Houghton Mifflin, 1966.

Riesen, A.H. Receptor Functions. In P.H. Mussen, ed., *Handbook of Research Methods in Child Development.* New York: Wiley, 1960.

part II

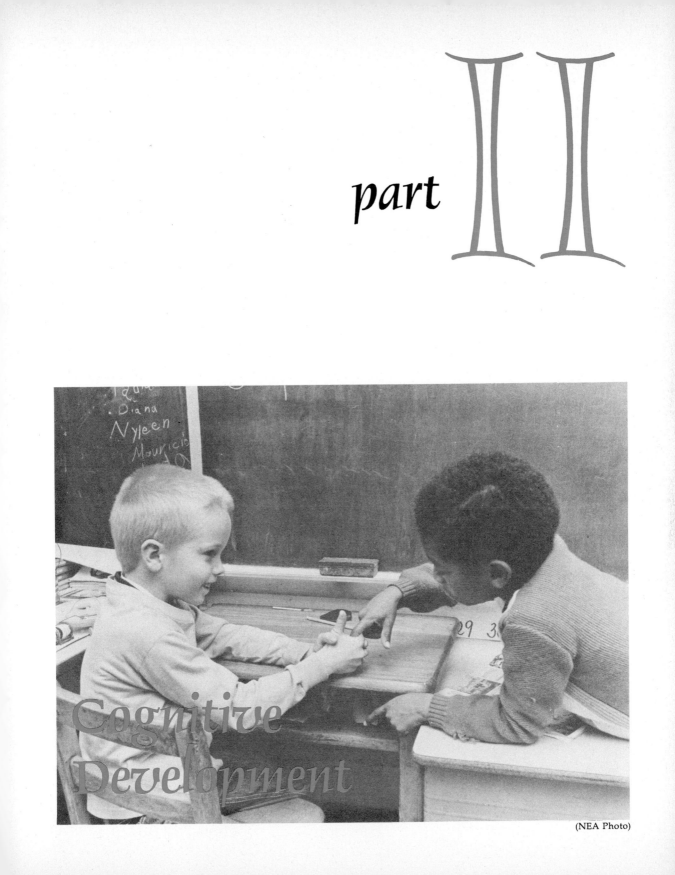

Cognitive Development

(NEA Photo)

5 Learning and Remembering

Behaviorism
  The Reflex
  Habituation
  Classical Conditioning
    Classical Conditioning of Infants
    Generalization
    Classical Conditioning in Everyday
      Life
  Operant Behavior and Reinforcement
    Reinforcement
    Nonreinforcement and Punishment
    The Shaping of Behavior
    Operant Conditioning of
      Involuntary Acts
    Schedules of Reinforcement

Operant Conditioning and
  Superstitious Behavior
Latent Learning

Human Memory
  Sensory Information Storage (SIS)
  Short-term Memory (SIM)
    Individual Factors in Memory
    Situational Variables in Memory
    Organization of Memory
    Consolidation of Learning

Long-term Memory (LTM)
  Rote Learning and Memory
  Mnemonics and Memory
  Rule Learning
Summary

PREVIEW

How flexible is behavior? The answer depends on the particular organism you happen to be studying. For example, chickens, spiders, and trout act pretty much the same throughout their lives because the behavior of birds, insects, and fish is primarily regulated by innate patterns of action called instincts. Robins build nests automatically; spiders weave their own characteristic webs; and salmon must return to their own birthplace to spawn. Higher organisms, like monkeys and men, begin life with innate behaviors, but quickly modify these with experience. Primate babies show mainly instinctive patterns of reacting, but as they mature human children come to modify their behavior through learning and intellect. In this chapter we will be concerned with what psychologists know about the effects of learning and memory on children's behavior.

Human behavior is controlled by genetics and environment.

Apparently human behavior can be changed, adpated, and reshaped, but only at some cost. This is true even though humans are subject to the same innate instincts as animals. The double influence of experience and learning, on the one hand, and of biological inheritance, on the other, has led to a heated argument among scientists called the "nature-nurture controversy." How much human behavior is determined by our biology and how much it can be modified by experience is at the heart of this discussion. *Environmentalists* have assumed that a baby's mind is blank when he is born, and that experience will develop his intelligence and behavior. This view of human development assumes an optimistic attitude about humans, and has been very attractive to many American psychologists. Environmentalists feel that human evils like stupidity, crime, and war are simply the effects on people of bad early experiences rather than of their inborn human nature. Thus, they look for new environments that will eliminate these social ills. On the other side of the controversy, *Nativists* argue that human babies have inherited tendencies which must be taken into consideration when studying human development. They point out the similarity between twins and other family members even when they have matured in different families.

Most American psychologists believe in environmentalism.

A majority of American psychologists believe that inherited traits are relatively less important than the modification of human behavior by learning and memory. Most also agree that human behavior begins with a few innate reflexes, and that these are modified by habits which are reinforced by conditioning.

Let us first consider some behaviorists (behaviorism is an early form of environmentalism) and what they proposed concerning the principles of human development.

Behaviorism

Ivan Pavlov first observed and described the conditioned response.

Ivan Pavlov's observance and notation of the *conditioned response* was welcomed by many American psychologists, who wanted only to work with behavior that could be seen and measured. Pavlov noticed the conditioned reflex while studying the process of the digestion of food. During the course of his physiological studies Pavlov observed the workings of a dog's stomach through a "surgical window." He noticed that the dogs came to secrete gastric juices *before* they were actually fed, and he concluded that the sight of food or even of a laboratory attendant would become an automatic signal for digestive reflexes in the animals. Thus, previously neutral stimuli like attendants or food dishes were automatically associated in the dogs with reflexive processes in their stomachs.

John B. Watson argued for the study of behavior.

The existence of these automatic associations led another psychologist, John Watson, to reject conscious mental process (thinking) and establish a psychology that would deal only with observable behavior. Watson argued that since physicists study only objective events, psychologists should follow their lead and be as scientific. He declared that mental life cannot be observed directly; therefore it cannot be studied scientifically and so it should not be studied at all. This notion led some to say that Watsonian behaviorism caused psychology to lose its mind!

Watson believed he could make any baby into any type of person.

Watson was an environmentalist who doubted the existence of innate knowledge, and believed that training could make any normal baby into a doctor, lawyer, beggar, or thief. Watson's strong statements about behaviorism burst on the psychological world when there was much dissatisfaction with the available methods of studying mental processes. The methods of psychology were being questioned, and many jumped on the behaviorist bandwagon, seeing it as *the* way to make psychology respectable. The Watson tradition of stimulus-response behaviorism is carried on today by B.F. Skinner, who studies how reinforcement affects behavior.

B.F. Skinner is the leading modern behaviorist.

This school of psychology has contributed much to our understanding of how reward and punishment control both human and animal performance. Skinner thinks that environmental events, like rewards and punishments, completely determine what a person does, and he argues that the notions of self and personal freedom are outmoded and romantic. Indeed, modern behavior theorists believe they can predict and control human behavior without the concept of self. The accompanying reading gives some background on Skinner and outlines his position that man is controlled only by the environment. Some of the problems with this idea are also reviewed.

Behaviorism assumes that babies learn everything.

Behaviorism assumes that a baby begins life with a few simple reflexive acts and that all other abilities are acquired by experience. The mechanisms that are assumed to modify human development are habituation, classical conditioning, reinforcement, generalization, and extinction. Let us consider first the basic reflexes and then how these mechanisms may be modified by experience.

The Reflex

Newborn babies have many innate reflexes.

All normal human babies are endowed with innate behaviors (*see* Figure 5.1). For example, a touch on the lips will cause sucking motions, a stroke on the cheek will produce head-turning, a tickle on the foot will make the baby flex his toes, and a loud noise will startle him. These are inborn *reflexes* which help the baby survive. Human babies' instincts are not as elaborate as the nest building instincts of birds, for example, but these human reflexes bridge the transition from birth to walking.

A reflex has three parts.

What is a reflex and how does it work? There are three parts: a stimulus, a connection, and a response. The reflex acts like a prewired telephone switchboard. To illustrate with the example of a sucking response stimulated by touching the baby's lips. The sensors in the lips, which detect the touch, are connected through the lower brain centers directly to effector muscles, which produce the sucking motions. A reflex begins at the

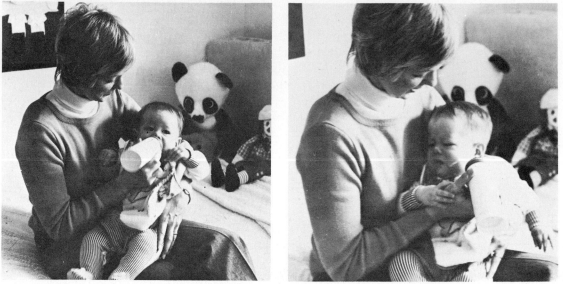

(Fishkill Studios)

FIGURE 5.1 Human infants come into the world with several preprogramed behaviors—such as sucking and crying—and other forms of human reflexes.

sensory system (touch). The connections in the lower brain centers transfer the stimulus to the correct muscles to produce the same reflex each time. Reflexes can be modified by stopping them and by connecting new stimuli to old responses. By presenting a stimulus over and over, the response will stop. This is called *habituation*.

Beyond reflexes comes conditioning.

In addition to stopping the reflex, previously neutral stimuli can be associated with a reflex through *classical conditioning*. Consider these two simple types of learning.

Habituation

Habituation means the baby is inhibiting a reflex.

Habituation happens when a baby stops responding reflexively to a familiar stimulus. For example, a baby will automatically turn his head toward a stroke of his cheek. However, suppose a blanket keeps accidentally touching his cheek. At first the baby will reflexively turn toward the touch, expecting a nipple and milk. After several repetitions of this unfruitful exercise he will begin inhibiting his reflexive acts and will no longer respond to the blanket's touch. If the other cheek is touched, or another stimulus occurs, his head turning reflex will reappear.

The formal characteristics of habituation are:

1. Repeated application of a reflexive stimulus decreases the reflex-response, as we have just seen.
2. If the stimulus is withheld, the reflex recovers spontaneously.

3. Repeated alternation of habituation training and spontaneous recovery strengthens both processes.
4. Frequent stimulation produces stronger habituation.
5. Weak stimuli produce rapid habituation, while very strong stimuli may never habituate.
6. Habituation generalizes or spreads from the original stimulus to other, similar cues.
7. Presentation of a second strong stimulus may block habituation (Thompson, 1966).

Habituation is the baby's first adaptation.

Habituation of a reflex is often a baby's first adaptation to his environment. Most infants stop producing a response following repeated stimulation. Thus, habituation is adaptive. If he did not come to ignore frequent signals, the baby would soon exhaust himself by responding to every stimulation that came along. Instead, he quickly comes to respond only when new or infrequent stimuli occur. In addition to learning not to respond, babies soon begin associating new stimuli with old reflexes. This automatic process of association is called classical conditioning (Hilgard and Marquis, 1940).

Classical Conditioning

Classical conditioning has four components.

Classical conditioning is a primitive type of learning which has four parts:

The unconditioned stimulus (*US*)—a biologically important event which calls forth a reflexive response.
The conditioned stimulus (*CS*)—any neutral event which can be associated with the unconditioned stimulus.
The unconditioned response (*UR*)—a reflex produced by the unconditioned stimulus.
The conditioned response (*CR*)—a reaction which is similar to the *UR* but anticipates it (*see* Figure 5.2). The most efficient conditioning pro-

FIGURE 5.2
A diagram of classical conditioning. The association between the unconditioned stimulus (*US*) and the unconditioned response (*UR*) exists at the start of the experiment; it does not have to be learned. The association between the conditioned stimulus (*CS*) and the unconditioned stimulus-conditioned response (*US-CR*) is learned. It arises through the pairing of the conditioned and unconditioned stimuli. The conditioned response resembles the unconditioned one, though they need not be identical.

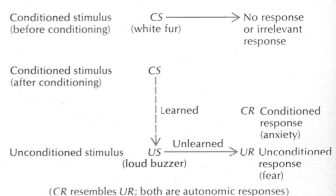

FIGURE 5.3

The optimum ordering of events to obtain classical conditioning. The conditioned stimulus (*CS*) should precede the unconditioned stimulus (*US*) by one-half second. The *US* will elicit an unconditioned response (*UR*). Repeated pairings of the *CS* and *US* will produce an association between them. To test for conditioning, eliminate the *US* on some trials; if the *CR* appears in response to the *CS* alone, classical conditioning exists.

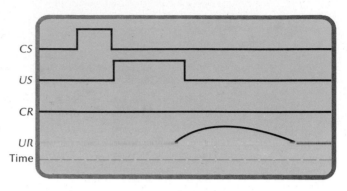

cedure involves presenting the conditioned stimulus one-half second before the unconditioned stimulus (*see* Figure 5.3).

Many emotions are classically conditioned.

An example of classical conditioning may help you to understand the events. Suppose a psychologist wanted to teach a child to fear a rat (*see* Figure 5.4). In the formal language of classical conditioning he could use a very loud sound as the unconditioned stimulus (*US*), since young chil-

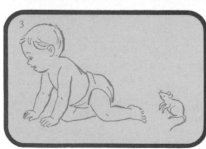

FIGURE 5.4 Three steps in the classical conditioning of fear. The baby is not afraid of the rat (conditioned stimulus) until the rat is associated with a loud noise (unconditioned stimulus) which frightens him. Conditioning is tested and the fear is generalized.

dren are afraid of loud noises and will react to them by showing fear, the unconditioned response (*UR*). In an early study of conditioning, Watson used a white rat as his conditioned stimulus (*CS*), since children are neutral about white rats. Anxiety and crying was the conditioned response (*CR*). How events are ordered in classical conditioning is very important. The best way to bring about classical conditioning is to present the *CS* (white rat) first, then follow it one-half second later with the *US* (loud sound). Conditioning often occurs in just a few trials. The experimenter tests for conditioning by eliminating the *US* (noise) and observing whether the *CR* (crying) occurs after presenting only the *CS* (white rat). By pairing the white rat with a loud bell, Watson found that fear of the loud noise became automatically associated with the animal. Thus, simple classical conditioning procedures can make a previously neutral stimulus positive or negative. Many emotional reactions in the child probably result from early accidental classical conditioning of neutral stimuli and reflex responses.

Even newborns show some classical conditioning.

CLASSICAL CONDITIONING OF INFANTS   When is learning first possible in the human infant? To answer this question, a scientist must expose a minimum of two groups of babies to various conditions: an experimental group who receive the conditioned stimulus paired with the unconditioned stimulus in a typical classical conditioning situation and a control group of infants who receive the unconditioned stimulus and conditioned stimulus in random associations. If the experimental group (which receives the conditioned stimulus followed immediately by the unconditioned stimulus) shows learning, while the control group (which receives only random presentations of *CS* and *US*) shows no learning, then the scientist has properly tested for conditioning. Lewis Lipsitt (1964) used a tone as a conditioned stimulus and the insertion of a nipple into the baby's mouth after one second as the unconditioned stimulus to test for classical conditioning in young babies. A control group of infants received both the conditioned stimulus (tone) and the unconditioned stimulus (nipple), separated by at least thirty seconds. This was to control for possible increases in general responsiveness and to make sure the conditioned stimulus was neutral. All infants received five trials with the conditioned stimulus alone, followed by twenty-four training trials on the same day. On every fifth training trial only the conditioned stimulus was presented to test for learning. Sucking in response to the tone increased systematically with training for the experimental group, while responsiveness increased initially and then leveled off in the control group. Thus, simple classical conditioning may occur in the first days of baby's life.

Conditioning improves with maturity.

Until about four years of age, human infants and children acquire classical conditioned associations faster and faster as they grow older. However, after about four years, the speed of acquisition of classical-conditioned responses stabilizes at the adult level (Mateer, 1918).

Portrait

B.F. Skinner was born in 1907 and grew up wanting to be a writer. He majored in English at Hamilton College, graduated Phi Beta Kappa, and then went to Greenwich Village in New York to write. When he entered Harvard University in 1930 to work on his Ph.D. in psychology, he also gave up writing. After graduation, Skinner taught at Harvard College and then at the University of Minnesota. He next moved to the University of Indiana and was head of the Psychology Department at Bloomington, Indiana, for several years before returning to Harvard University as Edgar Pierce Professor of Psychology.

Professor Skinner leads two lives—One as a serious academic, a scholar who publishes scientific books and articles about his work on operant conditioning and the control of behavior; the second as a popular writer who has successfully published important books on the social implications of behavior control. His earliest novel, *Walden Two*, published in 1948, was set in a behaviorist Utopia, a place without frustrations, where everyone was controlled by positive reinforcement. The book has gained popularity with the years. On the scientific side he has published such books as *Science and Human Behavior*, *The Behavior of Organisms*, *Verbal Behavior*, and *Schedules of Reinforcement*.

Skinner is probably best known for the "Skinner Box," or to give it the name he prefers, the "Operant Conditioning Apparatus." This device is a small, soundproof container in which an animal can be maintained, stimulated, reinforced, and measured automatically. Skinner's scientific contribution—and it is considerable—is based on the ideas of operant conditioning, the control of behavior through schedules of reward and punishment.

Skinner taught pigeons to bowl by using a shaping technique involving a system of rewards.

Skinner has invented other apparatus as well. When his younger daughter, Deborah, was born, he decided that diapers and blankets and all the other paraphernalia parents use to care for their babies are hopelessly outmoded, so he designed a modern baby care system. Called the "air crib," Skinner's system is a large box with control of temperature and humidity, an easy to change floor, and a clear safety glass door for baby and parent to interact through. The air crib has not become popular with parents, but Skinner believes it is a vast improvement over conventional baby clothes.

More recently, Skinner has left the laboratory to concentrate his talents on the social and moral implications of behavior control. In particular, a recent book, *Beyond Freedom and Dignity*, argues that notions of individual freedom and dignity are outmoded fictions that may have been useful in an earlier age but can now be rejected in favor of more efficient methods of behavior control. He argues that the sooner we accept behavior control and stop rationalizing freedom and dignity, the sooner man and his society will begin to function well. As you might guess, this thesis has caused considerable controversy. When asked recently whether there was anything in his life that he would change, Skinner answered: "Yes, I would never teach those pigeons to play ping-pong." If you want to know what he meant, see the reading in the Profile. Skinner's most recent book, *About Behaviorism*, is an answer to his critics, but it has not lessened the controversy about his beliefs.

Harvard psychologist and teacher
B. F. Skinner. (Rick Stafford photo)

"I've had only one idea in my life—a true idée fixe. To put it as bluntly as possible—the idea of having my own way. 'Control' expresses it. The control of human behavior. In my early experimental days it was a frenzied, selfish desire to dominate. I remember the rage I used to feel when a prediction went awry. I could have shouted at the subjects of my experiments, 'Behave, damn you! Behave as you ought!'"

—B.F. Skinner's *Walden Two*. 1948.

The speaker is T.E. Frazier, a character in *Walden Two* and the fictional founder of the utopian community described in that novel. He is also an alter ego of the author, Burrhus Frederic Skinner, who is both a psychology professor and an institution at Harvard. Skinner is the most influential of living American psychologists, and the most controversial contemporary figure in the science of human behavior, adored as a messiah and abhorred as a menace. As leader of the "behavioristic" psychologists who liken man to a machine, Skinner is vigorously opposed both by humanists and by Freudian psychoanalysts.

Like the utopians who preceded him, Skinner hopes for a society in which men of good will can work, love and live in security and in harmony. For mankind he wants enough to eat, a clean environment, and safety from nuclear cataclysm. He longs for a worldwide culture based on the principles of his famous didactic novel, *Walden Two*. Those principles include: communal ownership of land and buildings, egalitarian relationships between men and women, devotion to art, music and literature, liberal rewards for constructive behavior, freedom from jealousy, gossip, and—astonishingly—from the ideal of freedom.

Disastrous Results

Skinner acknowledges that the concept of freedom played a vital role in man's successful efforts to overthrow the tyrants who oppressed him, bolstering his courage and spurring him to nearly superhuman effort. But the same ideal, Skinner maintains, now threatens 20th century man's continued existence. "My book," says Skinner, "is an effort to demonstrate how things go bad when you make a fetish out of individual freedom and dignity. If you insist that individual rights are the *summum bonum,* then the whole structure of society falls down." In fact, Skinner believes that Western culture may die and be replaced, perhaps, with the more disciplined culture of the Soviet Union or of China. If that happens, Western man will have lost the only form of immortality he can hope for—the survival of his way of life.

Skinner's reasoning is that freedom and free will are no more than illusions; like it or not, man is already controlled by external influences. Some are haphazard; some are arranged by careless or evil men whose goals are selfish instead of humanitarian. The problem, then, is to design a culture that can, theoretically, survive; to decide how men must behave to ensure its survival in reality; and to plan en-

Having responded "correctly" — as the experimenter wanted it to do — this rat in a "Skinner box" is being rewarded with food pellets. (Pfizer, Inc.)

From "Skinner's Utopia: Panacea, or Pass to Hell," *Time* magazine (September 20, 1971).

vironmental influences that will guarantee the desired behavior. Thus, in the Skinnerian world, man will refrain from polluting, from over-populating, from rioting, and from making war, not because he knows that the results will be diastrous, but because he has been conditioned to want what serves group interests.

Is such a world really possible? Skinner believes that it is; he is certain that human behavior can be predicted and shaped exactly as if it were a chemical reaction. The way to do it, he thinks, is through "behavioral technology," a developing science of control that aims to change the environment rather than people, that seeks to alter actions rather than feelings, and that shifts the customary psychological emphasis on the world inside men to the world outside them. Central to Skinner's approach is a method of conditioning that has been used with uniform success on laboratory animals; giving rewards to mold the subject to the experimenter's will. According to Skinner and his followers, the same technique can be made to work equally well with human beings.

Underlying the method is the Skinnerian conviction that behavior is determined not from within but from without. "Unable to understand how or why the person we see behaves as he does, we attribute his behavior to a person inside," Skinner explains. Mistakenly, we believe that man "initiates, originates and creates, and in doing so he remains, as he was for the Greeks, divine. We say that he is autonomous." But Skinner insists that autonomy is a myth, and that belief in an "inner man" is a superstition that originated, like belief in God, in man's inability to understand his world. With the rise of behavioral science, understanding has grown, and man no longer needs such fictions as "something going on inside the individual, states of mind, feelings, purposes, expectancies and all of that." The fact is, Skinner insists, that actions are determined by the environment; behavior "is shaped and maintained by its consequences."

Avoiding Punishment

To Skinner, this means that there is nothing wrong, emotionally or morally, with people who behave badly. For example, youths who drop out of school or refuse to get jobs behave as they do not because they are neurotic or because they feel alienated, but "because of defective social environments in homes, schools, factories and elsewhere." As Skinner sees it, environments are defective when they fail to make desirable behavior pay off and when they resort to punishment as a means of stopping undesirable behavior.

In short, it is punishment or reward that determines whether a particular kind of behavior becomes habitual. But Skinner believes that punishment is generally an ineffective means of control. "A person who has been punished," he writes in his new book, "is not less inclined to behave in a given way; at best, he learns how to avoid punishment. Our task is not to encourage moral struggle or to build or demonstrate inner virtues. It is to make life less punishing, and in doing so to release for more reinforcing activities the time and energy consumed in the avoidance of punishment." The way to release that time and energy is "to build a world in which people are naturally good," in which they are rewarded for wanting what is good for their culture.

But arranging effective rewards, complicated enough in the laboratory, is even more complex in the real world. Why not solve society's problems by using the much simpler physical and biological technologies we already have? Because, Skinner says, that will not work. "Better contraceptives will control population only if people use them. A nuclear holocaust can be prevented only if the conditions under which nations make war can be changed. The environment will continue to deteriorate until pollution practices are abandoned. We need to make vast changes in human behavior."

Early Christian thinkers pondering the mystery of man believed that it was the "soul" that set human beings apart from animals. To them, the essence of man was his God-given spirit, immaterial, impalpable, otherworldly, something quite outside the natural world. But with the decline of religion and the rise of materialism, 17th and 18th century philosophers like Thomas Hobbes and Julien de La Mettrie increasingly viewed the soul as an aspect of the body, man as an animal, both men and animals as machines.

It was this kind of thinking that influenced

Watson. Drawing, too, on the work of Pavlov, he repudiated the subjective concepts of mind and emotion and described human behavior as a succession of physical reflex responses to stimuli coming from the environment. It was the environment alone, he felt, that determined what a man is: "Give me a dozen healthy infants," he wrote in 1925, "and I'll guarantee to take any one at random and train him to become any type of specialist I might select—doctor, lawyer, even beggarman and thief, regardless of his talents, penchants, tendencies, abilities." The goal of this Watsonian behaviorism was the prediction and control of behavior—which suited Skinner to perfection.

The process as explained by Skinner: "I watch a hungry pigeon carefully. When he makes a slight clockwise turn, he's instantly rewarded for it. After he eats, he immediately tries it again. Then I wait for more of a turn and reinforce again. Within two or three minutes, I can get any pigeon to make a full circle. Next I reinforce only when he moves in the other direction. Then I wait until he does both, and reinforce him again and again until it becomes a kind of drill. Within ten to 15 minutes, the pigeon will be doing a perfect figure eight."

By a similar process, Skinner has taught pigeons to dance with each other, and even to play Ping Pong. During World War II, he conceived the idea of using pigeons in guided-missile control; three birds were conditioned to peck continuously for four or five minutes at the image of a target on a screen. Then they were placed in harness in the nose of a missile, facing a screen on which the target would appear when the missile was in flight. By pecking at the image moving on the screen, the pigeons would send corrective signals that moved the missile's fins and kept it on target. The missile, called the Pelican, was never used in warfare; the pigeon-aided equipment was so complex and bulky that the missile could carry little high explosive. Furthermore, Skinner mourns, "our problem was no one would take us seriously."

All of these conditioning feats were accomplished with the now-famous Skinner box. It is a soundproof enclosure with a food dispenser that a rat can operate by pressing a lever, and a pigeon by pecking a key. The dispenser does not work unless the animal has first performed according to a specially designed "schedule of reinforcement."

Explains Skinner: "One of the most powerful schedules, the variable-ratio schedule, is characteristic of all gambling systems. The gambler cannot be sure the next play will win, but a certain mean ratio of plays to wins is maintained. This is the way a dishonest gambler hooks his victim. At first the victim is permitted to win fairly often. Eventually he continues to play when he is not winning at all. With this technique, it is possible to create a pathological gambler out of a simple bird like a pigeon."

Venture in Self-therapy

For a while, that beguiling possibility and others suggested by Skinner left the academic world pretty cold, as did his first book, *The Behavior of Organisms*, published in 1938. "People didn't reinforce me, but my rats did," Skinner says regretfully, remembering how rewarded he felt every time his command to "Behave, damn you!" was obeyed.

Pigeons Aren't People

Unlike Burris, the numerous and articulate anti-Skinnerians remain skeptical, if not downright hostile toward him and his followers. Yet they feel that his long, patient campaign against freedom must be studied and understood. Their criticism is directed not at Skinner the scientific technician (the soundness of his laboratory work is seldom questioned) but at Skinner the philosopher and political thinker; his proposal for a controlled society, they say, is both unworkable and evil.

Giving as an example the failure of the North Koreans to brainwash many of their G.I. war prisoners, Stanford Psychologist Albert Bandura asserts that control of human behavior on the scale advocated by Skinner is impossible. Psychologist Ernest Hilgard, also of Stanford, thinks control of mass behavior is theoretically possible but realistically improbable, because there are too many bright people who would never go along.

Skinner himself admits that "pigeons aren't people," but points out that his ideas have already been put to practical use in schools, mental hospitals, penal institutions and business firms. Skinner-inspired teaching machines have begun to produce what amounts to an educational revolution. It was after a visit to his daughter's fourth-grade arithmetic class that he invented the first device for programmed instruction in 1954. Having seen "minds being destroyed," he concluded that youngsters should learn math, spelling and other subjects in the same way that pigeons learn Ping Pong. Accordingly, machines now in use in scores of cities across the country present pupils with a succession of easy learning steps. At each one, a correct answer to a question brings instant reinforcement, not with the grain of corn that rewarded the pigeon, but with a printed statement—supposedly just as satisfying—that the answer is right.

Juvenile Offenders

Some critics, loyal Skinnerians among them, argue that this teaching process bores all but the dullest students, and that there is little solid evidence as to how well programmed instruction sticks. But Skinner insists that his devices teach faster than other methods and free teachers to give personal attention to students who are trying to master complex subjects.

In some mental hospitals, reinforcement therapy inspired by Skinner is helping apathetic or rebellious patients to behave more like healthy human beings. The staffers of one institution, for instance, were troubled by patients who insisted on trailing into the dining room long after the dinner bell sounded. Attendants tried closing the doors 20 minutes after the bell rang, refusing admittance to those who showed up any later. Gradually, the interval between bell and door closing was shortened to only five minutes, and most patients were arriving promptly. "You shift from one kind of reinforcement—annoying the guards and getting attention—to another, eating when you're hungry," says Skinner. To charges that this kind of conditioning is sadism, he replies

that "the patients are going in quickly because they want to." That is strange logic; he seems to ignore the fact that the patients are compelled to "want to" unless they care to go hungry.

In yet another practical example of Skinnerism in operation, a point system for good behavior was set up for juvenile offenders—armed robbers, rapists and murderers—in the Robert F. Kennedy Youth Center in West Virginia. Though no requirements were imposed on the delinquents, they earned points if they voluntarily picked up books, or went to lectures and managed to learn something from them. With the points, they could then buy such rewards as better food, a private room, or time in front of the TV set.

Mothers who practice Skinnerism—knowingly or by instinct—have an easier time with their youngsters when they reward good behavior instead of punishing bad. Explains Skinner: "If a mother goes to her baby only when he yells, she reinforces fussing. But when she goes to him while he's happy and perhaps saying 'Mama' softly, the baby will always speak to her that way."

Uncompromising View

Though such apparent successes persuade Skinnerians that reinforcement is eminently practical, critics find the technique philosophically distasteful and morally wrong.

Many of their objections center around the ancient, crucial argument over free will v. determinism: is man in charge of himself and his destiny, or is he not? Skinner argues that belief in free will comes only from man's need to be given credit for his "good" behavior and achievements. "Consider a woman who has a baby. It cost her a lot of pain and trouble to have it. But she didn't design that baby; it was all settled at the moment of conception what the baby was going to be like. The same thing is true when a man writes books, invents things, manages a business. He didn't initiate anything. It's all the effect of past history on him. That's the truth, and we have to get used to it." Theologians, humanists and conventional psychologists, including Freudians, cannot accept this uncompromising view. "The chief source of man's dignity." Reinhold Niebuhr wrote, "is man's essential freedom and capacity for self-determination." Carl Rogers has asserted that "over and above the circumstances which control all of us, there exists an inner experience of choice which is very important. This is the kind of thing Skinner has never been willing to recognize."

Skinner's detractors attack the whole concept of behaviorism, which Novelist Arthur Koestler, who has high amateur standing in psychology and other sciences, maintains is nothing but pseudoscience, "a monumental triviality that has sent psychology into a modern version of the Dark Ages." In ignoring consciousness, mind, imagination and purpose, Koestler says, Behaviorist Skinner and his admirers have abandoned what is most important. Similarly, Historian Peter Gay speaks of "the innate naiveté, intellectual brankruptcy and half-deliberate cruelty of behaviorism."

The gravest menace from Skinner is his authoritarianism in the view of his critics. They reject the notion that man can no longer afford freedom and believe in fact that he cannot afford the opposite. Says Harvard Social Psychologist Herbert C. Kelman: "For those of us who hold the enhancement of man's freedom of choice as a fundamental value, any manipulation of the behavior of others constitutes a violation of their essential humanity, regardless of the 'goodness' of the cause that this manipulation is designed to serve." To Kelman, the "ethical ambiguity" of behavioral manipulation is the same whether the limitation on choice comes "through punishment or reward or even through so perfect an arrangement of society that people do not care to choose."

Existential Psychoanalyst Rollo May believes that Skinner is a totalitarian without fully knowing it. "I have never found any place in Skinner's system for the rebel," he says. "Yet the capacity to rebel is of the essence in a constructive society." Richard Rubenstein, Professor of Religion at

Florida State University, wonders what might happen to would-be rebels in a Skinnerian society: "Suppose some future controller told dissenting groups to 'behave, damn you!' What would prevent the controller from employing his own final solution?"

The ultimate logical dilemma in Skinner's thinking is this: What are the sources of the standards of good and evil in his ideal society? Indeed, who decides even what constitutes pleasure or pain, reward or punishment, when man and his environment can be limitlessly manipulated? Skinner himself believes in Judeo-Christian ethics combined with the scientific tradition. But he fails to answer how it is possible to accept those ethics without also accepting something like the "inner person" with an autonomous conscience.

Skinner has never responded fully to any of his critics, despite their number and stature. Often he has failed to understand them. Sometimes he has even branded them as neurotic or even psychotic. Occasionally he has seemed to imply that he himself is beyond criticism. "When I met him, he was convinced he was a genius," Yvonne Skinner remembers. And in *Walden Two,* Skinner's alter ego Frazier, assuming the posture of Christ on the cross, says that there is "a curious similarity" between himself and God—adding, however, that "perhaps I must yield to God in point of seniority."

In another *Walden Two* passage, Skinner sketches a more realistic self-portrait. With some bitterness, his alter ego Frazier addresses Burris: "You think I'm conceited, aggressive, tactless, selfish. You're convinced that I'm completely insensitive to my effect upon others, except when the effect is calculated. You can't see in me any personal warmth. You're sure that I'm one who couldn't possibly be a genuine member of any community . . . Shall we say that as a person I'm a complete failure and have done with it?"

The first phase of conditioning is acquisition.

Figure 5.5 shows the course of acquisition, extinction, and spontaneous recovery for a conditioned response. *Acquisition* occurs when a neutral conditioned stimulus is repeatedly paired with an innate unconditioned stimulus. For example, a light being lit as the baby's foot is tickled causing

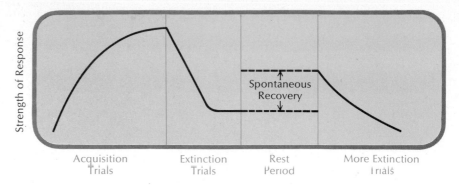

FIGURE 5.5 A schematic diagram of the course of acquisition, extinction, and spontaneous recovery of a conditioned response. Within limits, the longer the rest period, the greater the degree of spontaneous recovery. A rest period occurs when the child is removed from the experimental situation for an interval (from a few minutes to several days).

him to flex his toes. The gradual disappearance of a conditioned response, called *extinction*, occurs when the conditioned stimulus is presented several times without the innate unconditioned stimulus.

Recovery occurs after rest.

Spontaneous recovery of a conditioned response following extinction often occurs because the learner recovers from fatigue and his drive level (to respond to the stimulus) increases during a rest period.

Animals generalize a response to similar stimuli.

GENERALIZATION   Pavlov found quite early in his work that if an animal was conditioned to one kind of stimulus it would also respond to other, similar stimuli. (*See* Figure 5.6 for a diagram of Pavlov's original apparatus.) He called this effect stimulus *generalization,* and established a rough rule of thumb that stimuli that were very similar produced a stronger generalization of a conditioned response than less similar stimuli.

FIGURE 5.6
The original apparatus Ivan Pavlov used to study classical conditioning. The dog was restrained and his saliva collected through a tube. Pavlov used food as his unconditioned stimulus and many different signals — such as bells or tones — for his conditioned stimuli.

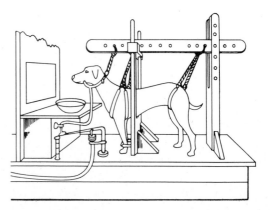

CLASSICAL CONDITIONING IN EVERYDAY LIFE   Classical conditioning is more than a laboratory phenomenon. In fact, early emotional conditioning probably accounts for many children's fears, as we have seen. Emotional conditioning happens automatically when unconditioned stimuli produce pain and that pain becomes associated with neutral stimuli. Here is an example: Most children like dogs and show little fear of them. But if a large dog bites the child, the pain becomes conditioned to the dog automatically. The child will now fear not only the dog that bit him but generalization will make him fear any other animal of the same general size or color. Children can learn even to fear their parents if parents and pain are often associated. Children can unlearn conditioned fears by experiencing the conditioned stimulus many times without the accompanying unconditioned stimulus.

Children acquire emotions by classical conditioning.

While much emotional learning is based on simple classical conditioning, other types of learning—how to ride a bicycle or solve a maze—are based on instrumental or operant conditioning. In the case of operant learning the animal or child performs an act, which produces a reward. There are several differences between classical and operant conditioning.

Operant conditioning is about actions.

Operant Behavior and Reinforcement

Operant conditioning is distinguished from classical conditioning by these four differences:

Classical and operant conditioning are quite different.

1. Classically conditioned responses are automatically brought forth, or *elicited,* by the unconditioned stimulus; while operant responses are produced, or *emitted,* by the animal in a free responding situation.
2. Classically conditioned responses are reflexive; but operant responses are under the voluntary control of the animal.
3. In classical conditioning, the pairing of conditioned stimulus and unconditioned stimulus is automatic; but in operant conditioning, reinforcement is dependent on the subject's behavior.
4. Classical conditioning is a stimulus-stimulus association; while operant conditioning is a response-reinforcement association (Skinner, 1938).

An example may help to make this clearer. Figure 5.7 shows a typical operant learning situation. Its main components are a small area isolating the animal from distraction, a response bar, lights which indicate when the bar will bring a reward, and some way to dispense reinforcement automatically. If an animal is placed in this area, it will sit around for a while, then begin to explore. Eventually it will somehow move the response bar. If the bar mechanism is activated, a reward like food or drink will appear in the reinforcement tray. After eating its reward the animal may wander around, and then accidentally activate the response bar a second time. Reward is given again, and the animal will eat it. After several of these accidental incidents, the animal will tend to stay near the response bar, and as a result it will activate the bar more often. Finally,

In operant conditioning the outcome is contingent on the subject's response.

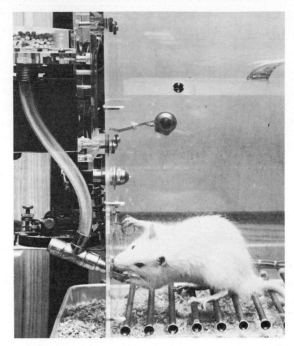

FIGURE 5.7

The essential parts of a Skinner box, with its plain enclosure, an animal, a discrimination light, a response bar, and a tray for reinforcement. This simple environment produces maximum control of behavior.

the animal will do little else but respond and be rewarded. Each response is tallied and recorded on a "cumulative recorder," the animal's response causing a recording pen to move along a roll of paper. This gives a record of the behavior, with high rates of response producing steep slopes and low rates producing shallow slopes (*see* Figure 5.8). No response produces a flat cumulative record.

One of the main factors affecting operant behavior is the reinforcement a subject receives.

There are many reinforcements.

REINFORCEMENT There are four kinds of *reinforcement:* primary or secondary, and positive or negative. *Primary reinforcers* are innate positive

FIGURE 5.8

The cumulative response tracings of children working at four different rates. Note that the fastest rate (50 responses per minute) produces the steepest slope; while no responding produces a flat line.

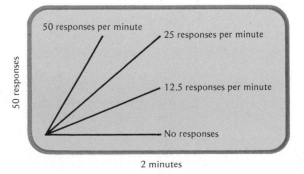

50 responses per minute

25 responses per minute

12.5 responses per minute

No responses

50 responses

2 minutes

or negative events like food and pain, while *secondary reinforcers* are stimuli associated with innate rewards. For example, food is a primary reward, but money is a secondary reinforcement. Psychologists usually measure the effectiveness of reinforcement by how much work a child will perform after a reward has stopped, or his speed of responding during the rewarding session. More work following reward or faster responding during reward is considered an indication of stronger reinforcement effectiveness. The amount of work a child will perform following reward is called *resistance to extinction.* This persistence is greater following more reinforcement, larger reinforcements, or when rewards are only intermittent rather than following every response (*see* Figure 5.9).

Children are rewarded by many things.

Food, toys, money, and social approval—all influence human performance. The effectiveness of particular reinforcers depends on the social class, age, and sex of the child being examined. Lower-class children prefer tangible rewards, like toys or candy, while middle-class children will work equally well for toys or social approval. Older children and most adults perform for social approval and the opportunity to be correct, but younger children prefer tangible rewards.

No one is sure why reinforcement works.

Why does reinforcement work? No one is sure, but early theories assumed that primary reinforcers reduce biological drives—food for hunger or water for thirst. Yet there are events that are innately reinforcing but do not reduce primary drives. Examples include stimulation of certain parts of the brain and sexual excitement without climax. Apparently, during the course of evolution man has developed centers in his brain which react positively to sexual stimuli or to direct stimulation. The main effect of these particular reinforcing events is to arouse the organism and to attract his attention, rather than to reduce his drives. Most psychologists now define reinforcers as any event which systematically changes performance.

FIGURE 5.9
Cumulative curves during extinction. Curves of extinction of operant responses in the rat are plotted following a single reinforcement and following 250 reinforcements. The response is that of bar-pressing to obtain food. The plot shows the cumulative number of responses; every response raises the height of the curve, and the curve levels off when responses cease. (After Skinner, 1938.)

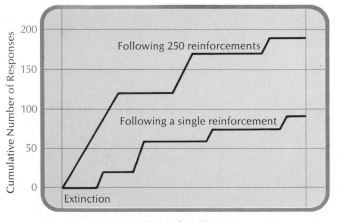

NONREINFORCEMENT AND PUNISHMENT   Behavior may be modified by reinforcement, nonreinforcement, or punishment. The consequences of these widely used controls are quite different. Positive reinforcement increases the likelihood of the response it follows, and acts are eliminated if they do not bring rewards. Yet if a response is suppressed by punishment, it will reappear again when the threat of punishment is removed (Estes, 1944).

In a classic study William Estes first taught animals to respond for reinforcement and then punished some animals while doing nothing to others. He found that the punished animals responded slower for a short interval, then resumed their regular rate of response and ultimately produced as many responses as the nonpunished group (*see* Figure 5.10).

Behavior can be modified by nonreinforcement or punishment.

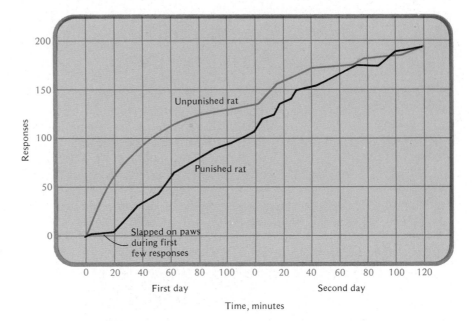

FIGURE 5.10 The effect of punishment on response production during extinction. Note that punishment suppresses responding for a few minutes, but the total number of responses until extinction are the same for punished and unpunished animals. This means that punishment suppresses a habit, but does not eliminate it.

Estes showed that punishment suppresses a response.

Suppression of a response by punishment has a short-term influence on behavior, but it produces undesirable side effects like increased arousal, heightened activity, and lower sensitivity to external cues. In addition, punishment limits a child's learning and abilities to pay attention, and it may bring about counterhostility from the child. The most effective control of behavior probably comes from simultaneously punishing unwanted responses and rewarding desirable ones.

Shaping means approximating a finished response and rewarding the animal for examples closer to the final behavior.

THE SHAPING OF BEHAVIOR   Skinner and his students have shown how to string several pieces of behavior into a complex act by using successive approximations to the final behavior desired. The successive approximations are any response that builds toward the final goal. This technique is called *shaping*. Suppose you want your dog to bring the newspaper to you at night. You should start by rewarding the dog for grasping things in his mouth. Once he learns that, reward him only for grasping newspapers, and then reinforce him for bringing the newspaper to you anywhere out in the yard. Finally, reward him only for bringing the newspaper to your chair in the living room. By a series of such approximations you can produce a complicated sequence of behavior that ends in your dog bringing the newspaper to you at night. Animal trainers teach bears to play musical instruments, rabbits to put coins in piggybanks, and tigers to jump through hoops by shaping their behavior (*see* Figure 5.11).

Miller believes that involuntary functions can be conditioned by reward.

OPERANT CONDITIONING OF INVOLUNTARY ACTS   For a long time psychologists thought that involuntary body functions could not be manipulated by operant conditioning. However, Neal Miller of Rockefeller University (1968) reported that blood pressure, heart rate, contraction of the stomach muscles, and glandular activities can be influenced by reinforcement. It has been known for some time that classical conditioning can change autonomic nervous activity (which is involuntary). But Miller thinks that operant conditioning of autonomic *processes* is also possible.

(Wide World Photos)

FIGURE 5.11 The results of shaping by an animal trainer.

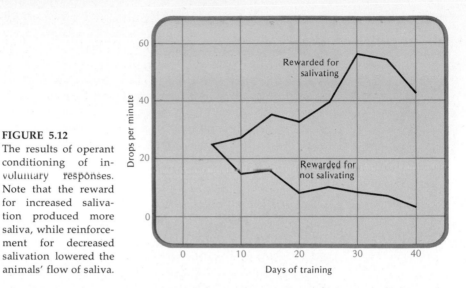

FIGURE 5.12
The results of operant conditioning of involuntary responses. Note that the reward for increased salivation produced more saliva, while reinforcement for decreased salivation lowered the animals' flow of saliva.

Figure 5.12 shows the results of rewarding salivation or no salivation in animals. Note the changed amounts of saliva that were secreted.

Miller taught rats to regulate their heart rates.

Miller also changed the heart rate in rats by operant conditioning techniques. All the voluntary muscles in his rats were paralyzed with a drug called curare, and the animals were kept alive by artificial respiration. Miller then used reinforcing stimulation of the hypothalamus in the brain to reward increases in heart rate. The rats showed a 20 percent change in their heart rate following operant conditioning. This discovery has fascinating possibilities if it is stable and the learning remains. If human subjects can learn to increase or decrease their blood pressures by operant conditioning, they might live longer. Miller suggests that many psychosomatic problems (physical disorders influenced by the emotions) might be relieved in this way. For example, those who suffer from nervous stomachs might learn to relax and "cure" the problem. Miller also suggested that psychosomatic symptoms are produced by operant conditioning in the first place. Suppose a child has to go to school but is not prepared for a test. He will be anxious and a variety of autonomic symptoms will occur—he will get pale and look sick and perhaps vomit. If his mother keeps him home because he is sick, he finds he doesn't have to take the test. He has been rewarded for producing a gastric upset. The next time he is put in a similar situation, the same autonomic responses may appear and be reinforced again. If this happens, he is well on his way to psychosomatic illness by operant conditioning. The effect of reinforcement is complex, because not only reward and punishment but the pattern of reinforcement also influences human behavior.

SCHEDULES OF REINFORCEMENT   If a response is followed by reinforcement, it will increase in frequency. But what happens if the response is

Reward schedules
affect behavior.

only reinforced occasionally? Does partial reinforcement produce weaker
or stronger learning than 100 percent reinforcement? The answer depends
on whether you are interested in quick learning or persistent performance.
Reward on every trial often leads to faster acquisition of a response, but
reward on only some trials produces more persistent responding following
the stopping of the reward. Occasional rewards make the person or animal
work longer without reinforcement.

Partial reinforcement schedules can come in many forms because
delivery of reinforcement can be made dependent on:

1. Number of responses.
2. Rate of responding.
3. The pattern of responses over time.

On a fixed-ratio schedule (*FR*), reinforcement is determined by the *number*
of responses; for example, every third (ratio of 3/1) or every hundredth
response (ratio of 100/1).

There are various
schedules of reward.

Figure 5.13 shows the cumulative response curve of a child receiving
various schedules. Consider first the fixed-ratio schedule. This pattern

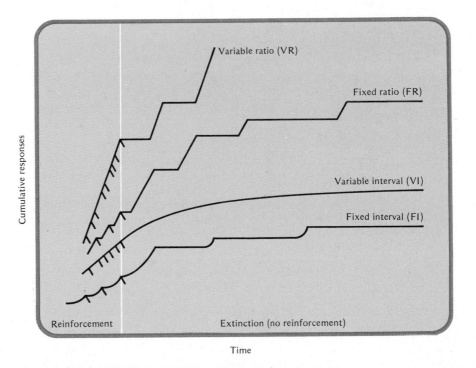

FIGURE 5.13 Cumulative response tracings following four patterns of reinforcement.
Variable-ratio reinforcement produces the most rapid response rate; fixed
ratio is next; while variable and fixed interval reinforcement produces
much slower response rates.

Variable ratio schedules produce rapid responding.

of reinforcement is similar to piecework pay scales. It produces high rates of response. A second pattern of reinforcement is a fixed-interval schedule (*FI*), in which reinforcements are given after a certain *interval* of time no matter what the child does during that interval. No matter how slow or fast he responds between reinforcements, his reward is available after a given interval of time. Under this schedule subjects slow their responding immediately after reinforcement, and then increase their rate of response toward the end of the interval. The result is the scalloped cumulative curve shown in the figure. Partial reinforcement can also be delivered at varying ratios or intervals. These schedules are called variable-ratio or variable-interval reinforcements. Under variable-ratio schedules (*VR*) subjects are rewarded after a changing number of responses. For example, reinforcement might come after six, after twenty, or after three responses. Variable-ratio schedules are specified by the average number of responses needed for reinforcement and the distribution of these ratios. On a variable-interval schedule (*VI*) the child is reinforced after changing intervals. Sometimes there is a long interval between reinforcement, and at other times a short one. These schedules are specified by the average interval and their distribution. Variable-ratio and interval scales produce faster and more consistent response rates than their fixed ratio or interval counterparts.

Accidental reward can produce superstition.

OPERANT CONDITIONING AND SUPERSTITIOUS BEHAVIOR   Sometimes subjects will produce irrelevant behaviors immediately before a reward. These chance associations of a particular response and reinforcement can produce superstitious behaviors; they are accidental acts which *seem* to produce reinforcement. For example, if you are hungry or thirsty and you find food or water right after you scratch your ear, you may come to scratch your ear a lot.

Animals can learn without reinforcement.

LATENT LEARNING   Is reinforcement necessary for learning? Apparently not — because learning can occur without external rewards (Tolman, 1932). Consider an experiment in which three groups of rats were put in a maze. One group received a reward after every trial in the maze; a second group never found food in the maze; and a third group found food only after eleven days of wandering around in the maze. The results are shown in Figure 5.14. The group that was reinforced on every trial showed learning immediately; their performance was superior to the other two groups during the first ten days of practice. However, when the second group of rats was reinforced on the eleventh day, their performance was the same as that of the animals that had been reinforced all along. Apparently, reward changes what the organism *does,* not what he *knows.*

Similar effects have been found with children by other researchers, where children often performed according to the reward schedule offered;

but when asked about other, nonrewarded parts of the experimental situation were perfectly able to produce those acts as well (Bandura, 1961).

Children can be conditioned.

Skinner's operant conditioning procedures have been used many times with children. Standardized laboratories for the study of operant conditioning have been developed, which use trinkets, cookies, and candy as rewards and lever pressing as the response. These laboratories have replicated, or repeated, many of the original studies using various schedules of reinforcement. It was found that the acquisition, retention, and extinction of operant responses in children are similar to results from animals.

Can the fetus be conditioned?

A number of investigators have asked when classical or operant conditioning first occurs. Can the fetus be conditioned? How about the newborn or the young infant? The answer to these questions depends pri-

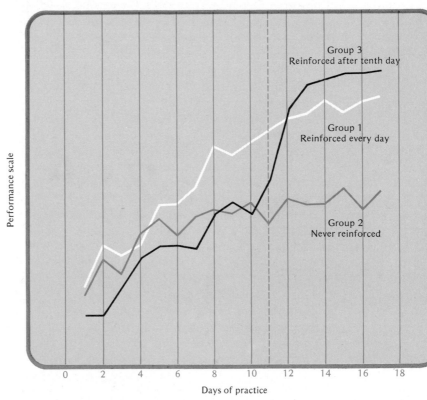

FIGURE 5.14 The performance of three groups of rats in a maze. Group 1 was rewarded every day for running the maze. Group 2 was never reinforced; Group 3 was reinforced only after ten days of wandering through the maze. These results show that animals learn without external reward, but need reinforcement to maximize their performances.

marily on the type of learning involved. Arnold Samaroff (1968) has reported much more difficulty demonstrating classical, as opposed to operant conditioning, in the newborn. He writes that several investigators have tried to obtain classical conditioning in the human newborn using such unconditioned responses as sucking, blinking, general activity, and breathing. Most of them met with failure. Some investigators have established classical conditioning with some newborn infants, but it is difficult to obtain.

Operant conditioning of the newborn human baby is fairly easy to demonstrate. In fact, babies are so sophisticated about operant conditioning that Samaroff could reinforce a single element of sucking behavior independently of another. This is possible because human babies get their milk in two ways: by squeezing the nipple and by creating a vacuum within the oral cavity which draws milk through the nipple. Samaroff reinforced either squeezing of the nipple or production of a vacuum independently in groups of normal bottle-fed babies ranging in age from two-six days. Reinforcement was with their normal formula and was made dependent on squeezing the nipple in one group of babies or generating a vacuum in another group. Samaroff found that babies reinforced for squeezing came to do that almost exclusively, and those reinforced for creating a vacuum did that most of the time. Newborn human babies, it seems, are remarkably subtle about operant conditioning and reinforcements.

The primary functions of reward, and the primary aim of scientists who study conditioning and reinforcement, is to control human behavior, not to govern what is learned. The prediction and control of human behavior raises serious practical and ethical problems. Who will control? Who decides what the allowable behavior will be? What safeguards can be built into society to guard mankind from the effects of behavior control? These and other questions are difficult to answer, but must ultimately be faced as psychology becomes more and more successful at predicting and controlling human acts.

Not only are children influenced by conditioning and reinforcement but they come to actively impose organization and structure on their learning. How this organization helps in the storage and retrieval of memories is the subject of the next section.

Human information-processing involves the selection, short-term storage, long-term retention, and retrieval of verbal and visual information. Investigators have discovered that vast amounts of information stream into the central nervous system from many sensory channels. Human short-term information storage is severely limited, so persons must select only a few important events for processing and retention. A major concern of developmental psychologists is the structure and organization of human memory and how children come to acquire the ability to do this.

Marginal notes: Newborn babies acquire operant conditioning quickly. / Behaviorism's goal is the prediction and control of human behavior. / Children structure their learning. / Human information-processing is a complicated affair.

Human Memory

There are three types
of human memory.

Information processing uses past experience, current input expectations, and environmental cues to put together meanings. One unfortunate
by-product of this system is error, since humans often see and hear what
they expect rather than what really happened. Distortions of perception
and memory can occur without the person being aware of them. A common example is the recalled phone number that gets scrambled between
the brain and the fingertips. During the course of information processing
the human nervous system uses several storage devices to hold information until it can be acted on and moved to another location. For example,
the visual system holds environmental signals for a short time in a device
called the Sensory Information Storage (SIS). Sensory Information Storage
retains enormous amounts of visual information for very short intervals
(Norman, 1970).

Sensory Information Storage

Sensory-information
storage is short but
rich in information.

The Sensory Information Storage device was first studied by George
Sperling (1959). In the beginning, Sperling assumed that SIS holds signals
and is scanned for processing during a short interval immediately after
stimulus presentation. If this is true, he reasoned, a second stimulus
(mask) presented during the processing interval should disrupt the
stored visual image of the first stimulus and prevent further scanning
of it. To test this notion he presented subjects with a 3 × 3 matrix of
letters and followed this stimulus with a visual mask in the form of black-
and-white squares. Figure 5.15 shows a sample stimulus array, a typical
mask, and the effects of visual erasure by the mask. Sperling found that
longer delays between presentation of the stimulus and the visual mask
produced better performance. More letters were recognized after 100
milliseconds of processing than after 50 or 0 milliseconds. Yet delays
longer than 100 milliseconds produced no significant improvement in
performance. These results are important for two reasons. They suggest
that the processing of visual information occurs in about 100 milliseconds,
and that only about five items can be transferred from SIS to the next
level of memeory.

Sensory-information
storage decays in 300
milliseconds.

In another, related experiment Sperling used a matrix composed of
letters in three rows of three each, followed shortly by either a high-,
medium-, or a low-pitched tone to tell his subjects whether to report
the top, middle, or bottom row of letters. The remarkable result was that
the subjects could report all three letters from any indicated row. Taken
together, these results suggest that SIS is a large-capacity memory device
which decays in about 300 milliseconds.

Marshall Haith (1970) has repeated some of Sperling's studies with
children, and found that below five years of age the storage capacity is

Stimulus

Mask

Letters correctly reported

0 50 100 150 200
Time between stimulus and mask

FIGURE 5.15
The stimulus (A) and erasure mask (B) used by Sperling to study Sensory Information Storage. The results (C) show that most information processing from SIS is complete by 100 milliseconds.
(After Sperling, 1963.)

limited to only three items rather than the five or six items of the human adult.

Short-term Memory (STM)

Short-term memory contains about seven items.

The first stage of human memory involves processing and labeling stimuli. Once verbal labels have been attached to stimuli, they are transferred into a second holding device called the "short-term memory," which is a temporary storage system for verbal information. Short-term memory is an intermediate station between Sensory Information Storage and long-term memory. SIS can hold vast quantities of information for only part of a second, while short-term memory has a more limited capacity but is able to retain information for several seconds. Recall of unrehearsed information from short-term memory begins at about seven items; by the end of fifteen seconds all seven pieces of information have disappeared (Peterson and Peterson, 1959).

Rehearsal helps memory.

Many psychologists believe rehearsal of the items in short-term memory is a crucial step in their transfer to long-term storage. Rehearsal involves saying something over to yourself. During the course of rehearsal errors may happen. The typical confusions which occur in short-term memory are auditory sound confusions (d with t), or sound substitutions, rather than visual-spatial confusions (v with u). Several things determine whether information is transferred or lost: the individual, the situation, and the organization of the material before it is learned.

Memory is affected by age.

INDIVIDUAL FACTORS IN MEMORY   Human learning is affected by the person's age. Figure 5.16 shows that learning ability increases from age five to eighteen, remains constant until around age fifty, and then verbal memory begins to decline (Thorndike, 1928). The kinds of skills, responses, and associations a person brings to a new learning situation partially determine how he acquires new memories. Past experiences can either help or interfere with new learning, depending on whether or not current material and older memories are similar. Specifically, new *responses*, which are similar to old ones, are easy to acquire; while new stimuli, which are similar to old stimuli, interfere with the formation of new associations.

Memory is also affected by intelligence.

A child's intelligence affects some types of learning. In particular, bright people learn complex material more quickly than their duller peers, especially when the new material lends itself to organization. The ability to acquire simple rote associations, as we have seen earlier, seems not to depend on general intelligence. Intention to learn is important. Although humans often learn things incidentally, acquisition and storage is usually more efficient if one sets out to remember.

Feedback helps learning.

SITUATIONAL VARIABLES IN MEMORY   Many studies show that feedback about performance produces more rapid learning and more stable storage. Feedback gives the child information about previous responses so he can eliminate future errors. It has three functions:

1. To provide information about errors.
2. To dispense positive or negative reinforcement.
3. To provide motivation for continued effort.

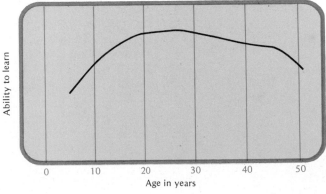

FIGURE 5.16
The general form of the curve of ability to learn in relation to age. (After Thorndike, 1928.)

Feedback can be intrinsic or external.

Specific feedback about individual responses is more effective than over-all information about total performance. Informational feedback can be of two kinds, *intrinsic* or *external*. When a child moves an arm or counts to 100 his intrinsic sensory processes provide information about what he did. But external feedback can help control other responses of the body. Under most circumstances a person is not aware of his own brain waves. By using an EEG (electroencephalogram) device to pick up electrical activity from the brain, and displaying these waves directly on a tele-vision screen, a person can view his own cortical functioning. By think-ing about different things and viewing his brain waves at the same time, the person can learn to alter their frequency. A short delay of information feedback disrupts this behavior. For example, if speech is picked up by a microphone, played through a tape recorder, delayed one-half second, and then fed back through earphones to the speaker he will have great diffi-culty continuing to talk. The delayed auditory feedback will make him stutter, hesitate, misspeak, and experience grave difficulty enunciating words.

Organization helps memory.

ORGANIZATION OF MEMORY   The organization of material introduced into long-term memory affects the child's ability to recall that informa-tion at a later time. The use of strategies like grouping of materials into meaningful categories, reviewing the information from time to time during learning, systematic search of memory, and attempts to recall an item all help later retrieval of information from long-term storage. Most children show a sharp increase in the number of items they can recall at around seven years of age. John Flavell (1970) believes that this improved memory is due to the seven-year-old's ability to automatically organize his memory, when children begin to group strings of items into triplets rather than trying to recall all the items in a single string. These memory organizational tricks, Flavell argues, help increase the child's memory ability.

Children increase their memories with age.

By contrast, Professor Pascual-Leone believes that the increase in children's memory ability at around seven years of age is due to a real increase in memory capacity rather than the use of tricks. He argues that there is an increase in the absolute number of items that the child can manipulate at one time and not just an increase in the child's ability to group unrelated items into manageable categories. The information needed to decide the correctness of these two theories of the child's in-crease in memory between six and eight does not yet exist.

Poorly organized memories are gen-erally forgotten.

Poorly organized information is difficult to store and almost impos-sible to retrieve. To store new information a child should pay attention when it is presented; extract those features which are most meaningful; work on rote practice; rehearse material in short-term memory; and or-ganize it into whole, meaningful units for long-term storage. In the case of complex information it helps to organize material before it is learned.

One good strategy a child can use in school is to work through a lesson quickly, find out what's required, organize the new information in terms of previous conceptual structures, decide on an overall plan, and then begin serious recitation. A limitation on learning new material is the small capacity of short-term memory. Most people can retain about seven items in short-term memory at any one time, as we have seen. To sidestep this problem it helps to impose an organization that groups five or six related items into each classes of an overall framework of five or six categories.

Children recall better by category.

Consider an experiment which illustrates the effect of organization on recall. George Mandler (1965) asked children to arrange as many as fifty items into five or six categories during an initial sorting task, and then required his subjects to recall the items at a later time. The remarkable result of this study was that many of the children were able to retrieve almost all the items because of the grouping into five or six sets of six or seven items each. The pattern of recall called for retrieving the items in one category, and then going on to the next. The memorizer's task was effectively reduced to retrieving six sets of seven items rather than forty-two disconnected pieces of information. There is little doubt that organizing information into chunks helps to better recall enormously.

Long-term memory requires an interval for consolidation.

CONSOLIDATION OF LEARNING   Another aid to memory is to sleep after learning. Why do teachers urge their students to study and then sleep on it? Jim McGaugh (1970) believes the technique works because there is a consolidation period immediately after learning when the human brain reorganizes and stores new materials. This consolidation works best during sleep. To test the notion, McGaugh used four groups of subjects in an experiment. Group 1 learned a lesson, slept for eight hours, and then relearned it. They retained 82 percent and had to relearn 18 percent. Group 2 learned the lesson, slept for eight hours, participated in eight hours of waking activity, and then relearned the original material. They retained 86 percent and had to relearn 14 percent. Group 3 learned the lesson, experienced eight hours of waking activity, and relearned the material. They retained only 64 percent of the material and had to relearn 36 percent. Group 4 learned the material, had eight hours of waking following by eight hours of sleep, and then tried to relearn the material. They retained only 59 percent and had to relearn 41 percent. Sleep immediately after learning produced much better retention than a period of wakefulness immediately after learning. McGaugh believes his results show that the human brain needs time to consolidate new material without interference before the information is stored in long-term memory.

Long-term Memory (LTM)

Children remember better if they use rules.

Jerome Bruner believes that children learn best when they are taught how to organize, to discover patterns, to use rules, and to seek information rather than approval. He admits that not all children are able to organize their information inputs and that we don't know how to teach this kind of thinking. However, Bruner is surely correct when he argues that information organized by the student on his own terms is more likely to be available for later use than information fed to him in another's language. In the light of this discussion, what does psychology know about the factors affecting long-term memory storage?

Ebbinghaus studied rote memory.

ROTE LEARNING AND MEMORY   *Rote learning* produces new associations while *rule learning* generates new categories or concepts for handling information. The first systematic study of rote learning and memory was carried out in the late 1800s by Ebbinghaus with himself as a subject. He had two problems: how to produce completely new material for learning and how to measure retention of the material at some later time. Nonsense syllable lists were his answer to the new materials problem. To avoid the contaminating effects of past experience, Ebbinghaus (1913) constructed meaningless combinations of a consonant, vowel, and another consonant. He could pronounce these syllables, but they had few associations and so were better as rote-learning materials. Ebbinghaus measured retention by learning a list to a criterion (a standard of how many items were learned correctly), then waiting some interval of time, and relearning the list. The number of trials required to relearn the original material to a fixed level of performance was his measure of recollection. Retention of the nonsense syllables dropped rapidly during the first day and then stabilized at a low level.

Mnemonics are aids to remembering.

MNEMONICS AND MEMORY   One way to help rote memory is to employ *mnemonic* aids to learning and recall. The artificial organization of rote memory by mnemonics has changed from an area that was once neglected to an interesting psychological subject. Once considered simply a trick used by nightclub entertainers, mnemonic organization has been rediscovered by psychology. Mnemonics work by associating a well-memorized ordered sequence to an unorganized list. Simple mnemonics are often rhymed. For example, "Thirty days has September. . ." This kind of organizational structure imposes proper sequence on the total list by associating individual items to a known order. One problem with any ordered mnemonic is that a person must retrieve the whole sequence in order to remember any part of it.

The Greeks used mnemonics.

Mnemonics have been used for centuries as aids to memory. History tells us that the Greeks spoke for hours without notes by means of mnemonic aids. One popular mnemonic scheme is the key-word system, illustrated by an adjective list where there is a rhyme between numbers and key words. For example, One is a bun; two is a shoe; three is a tree; four is a door; and five is a hive. The list itself is easy to learn and the words are concrete, short, and easy to visualize. The key-word mnemonic can work in either direction. If you want to learn a list in sequence, you

FIGURE 5.17 A possible set of mnemonic images related to the sequence: 1—bun, 2—shoe, 3—tree, 4—door, and 5—hive.

associate the first item with a bun (*see* Figure 5.17). Suppose the first item you need to recall is a chicken. Imagine a bizarre image of a chicken baked in a bun. Next, associate a shoe made into a boat, a horse sitting in a tree, a pig opening a door, a horse sitting on a hive. Then, when you want to retrieve the sequence, say to yourself: "One is a bun," and think of the chicken cooked into a bun; two is a shoe, and think of a shoe made into a boat; three is a tree, and think of a tree with a horse on top of it; four is a door, and think of a pig opening a door; five is a hive, and think of the horse sitting on a hive. If you want to remember numbers—such as 5, 2, 1—think of a hive, shoe, and bun. A hive with honey pouring over a shoe in a bun. It may seem silly, but it works!

Rule learning
facilitates learning
of similar tasks.

RULE LEARNING   A number of experiments show that children and adults can learn rules which facilitate their performance on similar tasks. Learning to learn requires extensive practice with the same set of problems. In particular, children must learn basic skills before proceeding to more complex tasks. Learning to learn requires intelligence, and brighter children transfer past experience to new situations much more easily than their duller peers. Positive transfer occurs when general principles, or rules, are learned in one situation which can be applied to another.

Judd taught boys
about the refractive
index.

A classic study of principle learning and transfer was performed by Judd (1902). Two groups of boys shot air rifles at a target under water. One group was told about refraction, so they understood the visual displacement and distortion of objects under water; the other group had no such explanation. Both groups of boys learned to hit the original target with about the same amount of practice. After the water level was changed, the group that understood about refraction showed much greater positive transfer in ability to hit the target than the uninformed group. Knowledge of a principle let the first group master the new task in just a few trials, while the other group required further trials to find the new target.

Human beings learn.   Human learning begins with the modification of innate reflexes, and rapidly develops into a complex set of conditioned associations, reinforcements, and strategies for remembering. The child's progress from simple reflex to rule learning is a remarkable achievement.

Summary

Two of the child's most remarkable traits are an ability to learn new behaviors and to recall past events. Many psychologists believe that the basis of most later learning is the innate reflex, and that the earliest and simplist adaptations of the child involve inhibition of reflexive acts by a process called habituation. Beyond the reflex and habituation are two more complicated kinds of learning called classical conditioning (which primarily involves children's emotional learning) and operant conditioning (which is concerned more with the effect of reward and punishment schedules on children's performance of various acts). Once behavior is acquired or an idea grasped, these must be stored so as to be available at a later time. The storage and retrieval of information is the province of human memory. There are three kinds of memory: sensory-information storage, short-term memory, and long-term memory.

SUGGESTED ADDITIONAL READINGS

Hilgard, R. *Theories of Learning.* New York: Appleton-Century-Crofts, 1956.

Miller, N.E., and J. Dollard. *Social Learning and Imitation.* New Haven, Conn.: Yale University Press, 1941.

Spiker, C.C. Research Methods in Children's Learning. In P.H. Mussen, ed., *Handbook of Research Methods in Child Development.* New York: Wiley, 1960.

6 Language Acquisition

The Biological Bases of Language
  Is There Animal Language?
  Critical Periods
  Brain Damage and Language
Early Vocalizations
  Babbling
  The Development of Morphemes
Grammar Acquisition
  Imitation
  A First Grammar

Differences in Language Acquisition
  Nonstandard English
  Studies of Grammar Acquisition
Speech
  Stuttering
The Development of Meaning
  Language and Thought
  Language Universals
Nonverbal Communication
Summary

PREVIEW

Many social scientists believe that the ability to use language is our most human ability. They believe that this complex, flexible communication system enables people to form organized social groups, evolve solutions to problems, pass on insights to later generations, and, most important of all, use a powerful tool which can inform and direct human thought. One amazing thing about human language is the apparent ease with which three-year-old children acquire their native tongue without obvious and systematic instruction. Only in those rare cases where babies are born deaf, lose their hearing early in life, or have their language centers damaged do language difficulties occur. This tremendous ease of language acquisition in the face of such complexity has led many psychologists, who are biologically oriented, to propose that children are born with an innate device for language learning. The notion of a biological basis for language has stirred opposition from most environmentally-oriented psychologists and support from many psycholinguists. No matter which side of the nature-nurture controversy one supports, it is clear that most children pass through very similar stages on their way to mature language development, even when they are confronted with the different sounds and symbols of language.

The Biological Bases of Language

All animals communicate.

All animals communicate about food, sex, fear, and anger. These signals are transmitted chemically by the honeybee, through song among birds, and by words between humans. By far, humans possess the most complex and flexible communication system (Bronowski, 1970), although some scientists speculate that other animals may possess complex signal systems of which we are as yet unaware. "Talking" birds, like the parrot, do not use language; they merely reproduce sequences of sounds which can be interpreted by human listeners. The development of bird songs does display some of the characteristics of speech acquisition among human children:

1. There is a tendency to learn some sound patterns rather than others.
2. The young bird or human must hear feedback from his own voice in order to produce precise songs or sentences.
3. Both children and birds at first produce simple sounds followed by more and more complex sequences.
4. Specific dialects are characteristic of limited regions.
5. Dialects promote inbreeding within local populations when birds and children are older.

Do animals have language?

Among human children, a few basic sounds are built into words and these words are combined into a very large number of grammatical strings called sentences. There is no question that man possesses a language. But, what about animal communication? Can animals acquire a complex language?

Is There Animal Language?

Psychologists have tried to teach English to chimps.

Several psychologists had tried to teach human language to chimpanzees during the early part of this century (Hayes, 1951). The psychologists, often a man and wife team, raised chimps in their homes to see if such bright animals could acquire human language. The chimps adapted readily to a human environment and became strongly attached to their caretakers, but they did not learn to speak. A chimp named Viki learned to utter four sounds which resembled the human words "momma, poppa, cup, and up." But her language was very primitive. What was the problem? Possibly chimps are not able to produce human sounds.

Gardner taught American Sign Language to a chimp.

To get around this problem, two recent attempts to teach chimps a language have substituted sign systems for human vocalizations. Allen and Beatrice Gardner (1969) used *American Sign Language* to communicate with a chimp named Washoe (after the Nevada county in which they live). In the first twenty-two months they taught Washoe about thirty signs, which she used in appropriate situations. In addition, the Gardners report that their chimp is beginning to combine signs into short strings and to use old signs in new situations. They believe Washoe is using language.

In another, related experiment David Premack (1970) has devised symbols cut from plastic to enable Sarah, an eleven-year-old female chimp, to write sentences. After some experience Sarah learned that a blue triangle meant an apple, a red square a banana. In time she came to know the symbols for her teachers, for colors, a pail, a cup, and a dish. There is nothing remarkable about this part of Sarah's performance since any primate can master simple rote associations between symbols and objects. However, Premack next introduced the preposition *on,* and then began presenting Sarah with sentences like green goes *on* red. In just a few sessions Sarah was following the commands. Figure 6.1 shows some sample vocabulary and three simple sentences used with Sarah. Even the understanding of sentences is not so remarkable as her ability to use the symbols in novel situations and to make up simple sentences of her own. When Premack asked Sarah to recognize the concept "color of" in a totally new situation she was able to do it. Sarah could generalize the concept red from an apple to a persimmon. In addition, she learned the meaning of verbs and questions. Premack does not claim that Sarah understands all the functions of human language, or that she will ever be able to do all the things a human being can do with language, but he adds, "We have only been working with her for a relatively short while." Unhappily, Sarah has stopped cooperating with her tutors at this point so there is no way of knowing how much human language she might have mastered.

Historically, there have been three approaches to language acquisition. The *Associationists* assume that children possess simple processing mechanisms like learning or generalization, and that all knowledge is acquired by the application of these simple mechanisms to elementary sensory

Premack taught Sarah an artificial language.

Some psychologists believe that language is learned.

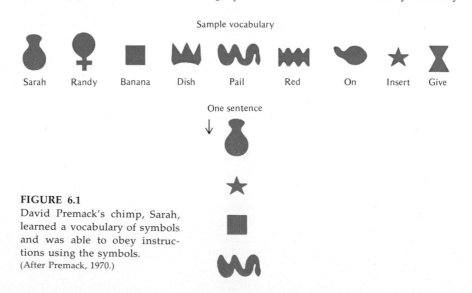

FIGURE 6.1
David Premack's chimp, Sarah, learned a vocabulary of symbols and was able to obey instructions using the symbols.
(After Premack, 1970.)

data (Skinner, 1957). *Psycholinguists* believe that in addition to sensory processing mechanisms the infant has innate grammatical structures which determine the form of his language. These innate grammar rules are assumed to remain dormant until stimulated by appropriate experience or maturation (McNeill, 1970). Finally, *Cognitive* theorists argue that language acquisition is simply another example of children's general intellectual ability. They believe that human language is acquired by the same mechanisms as addition or multiplication, for example (Piaget, 1947).

Many linguists believe grammar is innate.

Many modern linguists disagree with the association theory. They point out that simple rote learning—within the time, memory, and attention capabilities of the child—is incapable of generating the sentences any three-year-old child can produce, or the learning of such a complex structures as human grammar. Also, young children produce words and phrases they have never heard before, like sheeps, goed, and runned (McNeill, 1970).

Both learning and innate theories may be partially correct.

The rational approach, represented by recent developments in the theory of grammar, can more easily explain grammar acquisition. Some argue that association theory is more appropriate for explaining the acquisition of meaning, while rationalists are more correct about the acquisition of grammar.

Children learn to speak by 3 years of age.

The cognitive theory of language might explain both grammar and semantics, but there is one difficulty: Almost all children learn to speak by three years of age but most cannot learn to add until they are five or six. Is addition that difficult, or is the child's acquisition of language innately programed?

Piaget believes children learn language just as they do any other cognition.

Learning theorists claim that even chimps can acquire simple communications by experience and behavior modification (Rumbaugh, 1973). Linguists argue that human language is very complex and that there is no evidence that mothers reinforce their children during the course of language acquisition (Brown, 1970). A current theory, proposed by Jean Piaget (1947), assumes that children have a general cognitive ability which is reflected by their acquisition of both language and logic. The data necessary to decide among these three theories do not exist, although such data are beginning to be accumulated. The most likely explanation seems to be that words and grammar are preprogramed, but get connected to ideas and objects through experience. There is increasing evidence that children show biological tendencies toward language acquisition. Let us consider some data.

Critical Periods

Young children are adept at language learning.

A number of investigators have theorized about a critical period during a child's early life when he is particularly adept at acquiring language. They assume that if disruption occurs during this sensitive period of development, the effects on later language learning may be serious and irreversible. One way to test this idea of an early critical period for language acquisition is to study the effect of acquired deafness on the development of children's language. Becoming deaf affects speech fluency throughout childhood, and becoming deaf before six years of age seriously affects a child's learning of grammatical rules. Until he is about four years of age, deafness will cause a child to lose his speech ability completely unless he is given special training. For this reason congenitally deaf children (those who are born deaf) and children who become deaf before four years of age require special classes in which to learn speech and reading. Children who can hear speech for even one year have fewer problems in these special classes than do congenitally deaf children. Apparently, even minimal exposure to sound aids language learning among children, and until about six years of age additional exposure to sound aids later language development.

Most children begin speaking in their second year.

Average children begin to speak between one and two years of age. Is this because parents initiate language training during the second year? Probably not, because there is little evidence of serious language training by adults at all. Rather, the important influences seem to originate within the child as he matures (Lenneberg, 1967). The hallmarks of behavior controlled by growing are:

1. Abilities appear in a regular sequence that is related with age.
2. Environmental stimulation is available throughout development, but the child makes different uses of the stimulation as he matures.
3. Behavior emerges before it is useful to the individual.
4. Early abilities are not goal-directed.

Language growth follows a maturational sequence.

Language development satisfies all these criteria (*see* Figure 6.2). Speech acquisition shows little relation to other motor development, like crawling or walking. Muscular disease or early muscular atrophy (weakness and wasting away) does not retard speech acquisition. Thus, language acquisition is fairly independent of other motor development. If the speech center of a baby's brain is damaged, his language production will lag, while other aspects of his development proceed normally.

Deaf and hearing children show similar early language development.

Children who are deaf and born of deaf parents pass through the same early language stages as other children do. They coo at about three months of age and babble spontaneously at around six months. However, later language acquisition is impaired by deafness. There is little doubt that audition (hearing) is necessary for normal speech development. The effects of becoming deaf and of brain damage are complementary. Specifically, brain damage in babyhood produces a difficult recovery of language learning; while early deafness is most destructive of later language skills. These data suggest the existence of a critical period between two and ten years of age in which language is particularly easy for children to acquire.

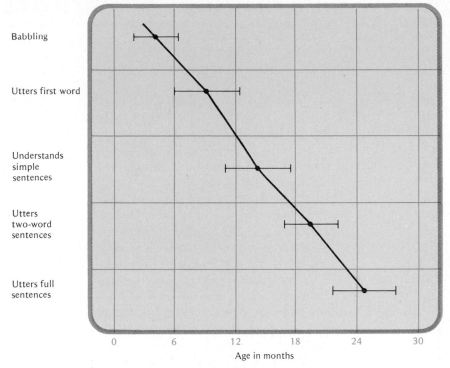

FIGURE 6.2 The range and average age for several landmarks of verbal behavior. Note that most children begin to speak simple sentences before they are two years of age.

Disruption of language learning during this critical period has serious consequences for language growth.

After puberty, language learning is more difficult.

Eric Lenneberg argues that early in life exposure to a language is enough to insure acquisition, but this natural language-learning stage ends at puberty. He points out that language acquisition after puberty is much more tedious, compared to the ease with which three-year-olds master their native tongue.

Studies have shown that the course of language development among identical twins is much more similar than among fraternal twins (Lenneberg, 1967). This result suggests that language development is genetically programmed to some extent.

Brain Damage and Language

Brain damage affects children and adults differently.

If an adult's speech or language comprehension center is damaged, he either recovers his functions within a few weeks or never regains his lost language skills at all. Babies react very differently following brain damage. If an infant suffers damage to his speech or language comprehension center, he may recover in a few weeks *or* he will begin again the normal developmental stages of acquiring language. Unhappily, this ability of the human brain to reacquire skills that have been interrupted is apparently lost by the beginning of adolescence.

Early Vocalizations

The smallest unit of language is the phoneme.

Human language probably evolved so that people, with their limited memories, could transmit and receive large amounts of information in the midst of distractions. One way to generate a communication system is to assign a unique sound to each message. This is an easy system to produce and learn, but it would exhaust all human sounds long before we had a reasonable set of meanings. Instead, man evolved a system which combines a few sounds in many ways to produce speech. These individual sounds are called *phonemes.* Figure 6.3 shows some phonemes and their approximate age of utterance among U.S. children. Phonemes have no meaning by themselves, and only a few exist in any language. English uses forty-five phonemes; the range of phonemes in all languages is from ten to seventy (Greenberg, 1966). The forty-five phonemes of English combine to produce all the words of the language without making any word very long. Since only about half the possible combinations of phonemes are used to generate words, the listener can correct errors in transmission without distorting the message. For example, most users of English can correctly interpret the following message: *Thw girh signallxed thar whe wis abailable,* even though it contains several phonological errors.

Morphemes are the smallest meaningful language unit.

Phonemes are the raw material of speech; *morphemes* represent a higher level of language construction—the smallest meaningful unit of language. Following the development of phonemes and morphemes (sounds and words), the child learns to group words on the basis of grammatical structure. He begins to use simple sentences. The production of words is

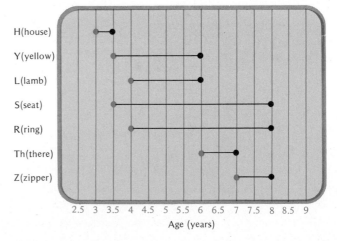

FIGURE 6.3
The ages at which some English phonemes are acquired. Yellow dots indicate that 75 percent of the children can pronounce the phoneme; black dots show that 95 percent have mastered it.
(After Templin, 1957.)

a problem in morphological analysis; the generation of sentences is a problem in grammatical analysis; semantics is the study of meaning. Let us consider how human sounds begin.

Babbling

Babies produce most sounds from all languages.

Babies produce similar sound patterns across different language groups, cultures, and races. All the basic phonemes of language are present in these early babblings. Systematic repetition of sounds occurs early in the life of a child, and has aroused interest among some theoreticians who speculated that babbling is the raw material from which speech is shaped. Before four months of age babbling has no relationship to either later language development or the cognitive growth of the child. But after four months it has been found that girls who had babbled a great deal as babies score higher than their peers on measures of attentiveness, vocabulary, and intelligence when they are older (McCall and Kagan, 1967; Cameron, Livson, and Bayley, 1967). There has been no such relationship with later growth discovered for boys who had babbled a lot. No one is sure why such sex differences occur. One theory assumes that infant girls mature earlier than boys; therefore, their early vocal behavior is a greater predictor of later cognitive abilities. Another theory, proposed by Howard Moss (1967), suggests that the amount of conversation between mothers and daughters is significantly higher than between mothers and sons, and that this increased social interaction produces the sex difference. No definitive data has yet been found to make one theory more acceptable than the other.

Vowels outnumber consonants in early speech.

Most early work on the development of speech sounds concentrated on the frequencies of several vowels and consonants produced by children at various ages. One study of phonemic development, the appearance of meaningful speech forms, was carried out by Velten on his daughter. Velten (1943) considered a form meaningful if it was used with consistency of reference. He concluded that "ba," "da," and "za" were meaningful forms for "bottle," "down," and "that." Unhappily, this kind of analysis is not definitive.

Phonemes contain distinctive features.

To help decide the question, psycholinguists might try to teach babies to differentiate among several phonemes not already available in their repertoires. Procedures for training and the limitations of the child would be of particular interest in such a study. Several investigators have found that vowels appear early in the child's speech, while consonant production catches up later (*see* Figure 6.4).

Roman Jacobson (1952) has proposed that all English phonemes are made up by combining only eleven *distinctive two-valued features*. Examples of such features are:

1. Whether a sound is nasal or not.
2. Whether the pitch goes up or down.

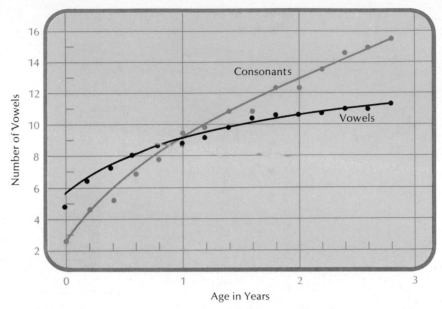

FIGURE 6.4 The increase in mean number of different vowels and consonants with age. Note the greater number of vowels learned during the first year of life. (After Chen and Irwin, 1946.)

3. Whether the cutoff of a sound is sharp or gradual.

Table 6.1 lists Jacobson's distinctive features under positive and negative characteristics. Once the baby masters phonemes he begins to blend them into groups to form words (morphemes).

TABLE 6.1 Eleven proposed two-valued distinctive features from which all human speech is produced.

Feature	Positive +	Negative −
Vocalic	Single haromonic structure	Noise
Consonantal	Occlusion of vocal tract	Open vocal tract
Tenseness	Long, high energy sound	Short, low energy
Voiced	Strong low frequency	No low frequency sounds
Nasal	Nasal added to sound	Oral cavity only used
Continuant	Gradual onset	Abrupt onset
Mellowness	Irregular	Patterned waves
Checked	Abrupt decay	Gradual decay
Grave	Lower frequencies	High frequencies
Flat	Downward shift of sounds	No down shift
Sharp	Rise to higher pitch	No rise

Source: (After Jacobson, 1952.)

The Development of Morphemes

There are three kinds
of morphemes.

Roughly, morphemes are the minimal meaningful signs of a language, as we have seen. Example, include "the," "man," and "bought." Morphemes come in three types: free, bound, and combined. *Free morphemes* may stand alone; but *bound morphemes* must accompany free morpheme. "Cat" is a free morpheme; "cats" is a combination of the free morpheme "cat" and a bound one "s." Other bound morphemes include prefixes, suffixes, and tense endings.

Word use and sen-
tence size mature
with age.

The correct use of words in sentences and the size of the child's vocabulary grow together, but this does not necessarily mean they reflect the same process (*see* Figure 6.5). By the age of two an average child can spontaneously use about forty different words combined into about 2,000 utterances (Brown, 1970). He can understand many more words than he uses. The average two-year-old understands around 250 words.

Children and adults
structure language
differently.

An experiment on the joint development of word associations and grammar was performed by Brown and Berko (1969). They presented words to children and adults and asked for a primary association. Their results showed that children produce associations on the basis of meaning, while adults generate associations on the basis of grammatical class. If the stimulus was "table," the children said "eat," but adults said "chair," a word of the same grammatical class. In response to the word "man," children gave a verb like "works," while adults used another noun like "woman."

Children form words
by rules.

At an early age children use rules that transform words to fit different language functions. An interesting illustration was provided by Brown when he presented totally strange words to three- and five-year-olds— a single noun or verb, for example. The children were asked to point to a

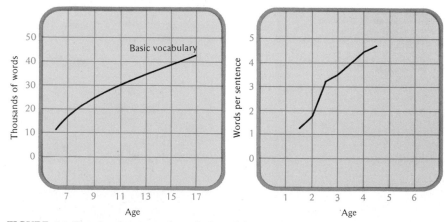

FIGURE 6.5 The development of vocabulary (*left*), and length of sentence as a function of age (*right*). Although both processes increase with age, there is good reason to believe that they reflect different linguistic mechanisms.

This is a wug.

Now there is another one.
There are two of them.
There are two——.

FIGURE 6.6 Berko's method for eliciting inflections. (After Brown, 1965.)

picture of the same functional category as the word presented. Even at age three, children were able to select the correct picture reliably. Given a strange "thing" word, children could point to a "thing" picture rather than an "action" picture. They were not able to define the adult category of "noun," but they were aware of the functional nature of words.

Berko tested for trans-
formations.

Figure 6.6 shows how Jean Berko tested young children's knowledge of other word-forming rules (Brown, 1965). She showed young children one "wug" and then two, asking them to form plurals. They did, although they had never seen the word "wug" before.

Transformations
change words into
new forms.

These kinds of word rules are called *transformations* by linguists. Most English verbs form the past tense by adding an ending like -d, -t, -ed. A few English verbs are irregular. Their number is small, but they are very frequent in ordinary speech and writing. If a child were learning word forms by rote he should pick up these irregular verbs first, because they are used so often. However, the child begins to generate rules from less frequent regular verbs, and then overgeneralizes these rules to cover the irregular verbs. He will say "goed, comed, doed." Such overgeneralizations are strong evidence that the child is using rules rather than rote memory. Only later can he differentiate between regular and irregular verbs and use rules or rote correctly.

After the child learns to form some words, he begins to string these words together into sentences. Grammar is beginning.

Grammar Acquisition

Psycholinguists began
the study of grammar.

Until recently grammar acquisition was ignored by psychologists. Most theories of verbal learning gave grammar a passing glance or completely ignored it. Early work on children's language most often counted the frequency of nouns, adjectives, prepositions, tense, and so forth. Although this approach produced interesting data, it is not a useful way of forming an idea of how *grammar* is learned. With the birth of *psycholinguistics,* theoretical and experimental interest in children's grammar has grown. Psycholinguistics combines the theoretical strengths of linguistics, the science of language, and the experimental methods of psychology. Its goal is to understand the acquisition of language by children and its use by adults.

Psycholinguists write grammars about children's utterances.

A favorite technique of psycholinguists is to record the utterances of a few children and then write a grammar about these sentences. Roger Brown (1965) followed the language development of three children in this way. Every second week he visited them for two hours to record their utterances. In addition to tape recordings, important events were noted. Brown found that dialogue between mother and child is quite unlike that between two adults. An example may be seen in Table 6.2. The mother's speech is short and simple and models what her child will produce a year later. The mother's sentences are grammatical and maintain the order and sense of the child's utterances. Brown also noted a degree of imitation.

Imitation

Children's sentences maintain word order.

When a child imitates his parents' speech, the child's utterance preserves the word order from the original sentence. Several words of the parents' sentences may be missing in the child's imitation, but those words that are repeated are usually ordered correctly. Why is the order preserved? Perhaps the child understands the sentence and wants to communicate with the parent, or maybe his brain preserves word order.

When the parent's sentences grow longer, there is no corresponding increase in the length of the young child's repetitions. His imitations still contain only two or three morphemes. The limitation is not caused by the

TABLE 6.2   A Section from Adam's First Record

Adam	Mother
See truck, Mommy.	
See truck.	
	Did you see the truck?
No I see truck.	
	No, you didn't see it.
	There goes one.
There go one.	
	Yes, there goes one.
See a truck.	
See truck, Mommy.	
See truck.	
Truck.	
Put truck, Mommy.	
	Put the truck where?
Put truck window.	
	I think that one's too large to go in the window.

Source: From Brown, 1965.

number of words the child knows but by the number he can plan or program at one time. The words he is most likely to retain are nouns and
verbs which have semantic meaning and, less often, adjectives. Omitted
words are less meaningful inflections, auxiliary verbs, articles, prepositions, and conjunctions. Why should the young child omit connectors like
"and," "the," and others, and yet keep nouns and verbs? Probably because nouns and verbs refer to something concrete. If adults must speak
while limiting the number of words they can use—when writing a tele-
gram, for example—their language becomes more childlike. Telegrams
tend to contain verbs, nouns, and adjectives; yet a telegraphic message
communicates because it retains the highly meaningful words in a language and leaves out the connectives which any reader can replace from
his knowledge of English grammar. There is another possible explanation
of how children select words. If you say a sentence aloud, you stress those
words which the child tends to retain. However, McNeill showed that in
foreign languages, where the stress is on other parts of the sentence,
young children still produce telegraphic speech unrelated to stress, suggesting that meaning and communication are more important for language
acquisition than vocal stress.

Another feature of parent-child language is imitation with *expansion*.
In the course of a brief conversation the child may say, "There go one";
to which the parent may reply, "Yes, there goes one." The parent extends
the sentence to a more correct grammatical form but preserves the order
of the child's words. From the parent's view expansion is a communication check ("Is this what you mean?"). The parent expands sentences by
adding auxiliary verbs, prepositions, articles, and pronouns—the words
a child omits. The verbal interaction between parent and child is often a
continuous cycle of reduction by the child and expansion by the parent.

Extending the mean-
ing of a sentence
helps children's
learning.

How does the parent choose the correct expansion of a child's simple
utterance? Primarily from the context in which it is said. For example, if
the child is holding a ball and says, "John ball," it is likely that he means
"John has the ball." Does expansion of the child's utterances help him to
learn language? Courtney Cazden (1965) compared the effectiveness of
expanding the utterances of disadvantaged children (repeating what they
say in a more grammatical way) with *extending* their utterances (answering
the child without repeating his words). To expand a sentence an adult
would take the child's sentence, "Baby hungry," and answer, "The baby
is hungry." The extension group would be answered by: "Yes, the baby
wants to eat." The adult tested children before and after three months
of grammatical expansion or semantic extension. The results showed that
grammatical expansion helped language acquisition very little, while
semantic extension helped much more. Apparently, improved grammar is
not so helpful as is extension of the child's own sentence.

What sort of grammar does the very young child use in producing his
utterances? To answer this question data is needed about the simple
sentences young children use.

A First Grammar

Braine studied children's early grammar.

Martin Braine (1963) published a biographical account of grammar development among three small children. Although the study touched briefly on the sequential appearance of speech types (vowels, vowel-consonant pairs, morphemes, and word combinations), Braine was primarily interested in examining the development of children's early grammar. Within the limitations of his sample size, Braine noted consistent evidence for a position pattern in sentences (*see* Table 6.3). He believes that young children begin to learn grammar with two classes of words: *pivot* and *open.* As the vocabulary of the child develops, he begins on some unknown basis to select certain morphemes as pivot words and anchor them in a fixed position relative to all other words, which are his open vocabulary. In these early stages Braine's subjects combined no more than two words to make up semi-sentences. During this two-word stage the position of pivot words were always the same. If placed first in the child's two-word grammar, the pivot word remained there in later utterances and combinations. Braine says children also experimentally manipulate various combinations of words to test correct language usage. In addition, children develop an active process of making up and testing new grammars. Having accepted or rejected various combinations of words, the child's vocabulary continues to build. Now, the child tests each new word within the context of this primitive grammar. Next, he moves on to three-word utterances, and these combine open and pivot words in more complex ways (*see* Figure 6.7).

TABLE 6.3   Examples of two-word sentences. Those in the first column contain a pivot word in a two-word sentence, while those in the right column contain a word plus the pivot.

Pivot-Open Constructions	Open-Pivot Constructions
That truck	Hat off
That blue	Blanket off
That chicken	Pants off
Here goes	Pants on
Here Mum	Sweater on
Here is	That on
See boy	Do it
See eye	Push it
See Mummy	Close it
Two girl	Kitty allgone
Two men	Microphone allgone
Two reel	Reel allgone

(After Meynek, 1970.)

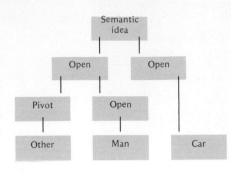

FIGURE 6.7
Tree diagrams showing some possible derivations which emerge when a pivot construction begins to govern a child's utterances. (After Slobin, 1969.)

Differences in Language Acquisition

There are large indi-
vidual differences in
language use.

Theories about language acquisition describe the course of development for the typical or average child. In reality, there are large differences in the acquisition and use of language for children. For example, girls acquire language sooner than boys, as we have seen; family size also affects language performance; children who speak two languages show a different pattern of language growth than children who speak only one; and children from low socioeconomic classes acquire language more slowly than their peers from higher socioeconomic classes.

Let us consider what we know about the differences in language acquisition and use.

Girls develop lan-
guage use earlier than
boys.

We already know that girls develop language skills earlier than boys, probably because females mature more rapidly and seem to have greater interest and abilities in language use. Most studies show that females develop larger vocabularies, better articulation, and longer sentences up through about age ten, and they generally average slightly higher on verbal tests when compared to males. The only child is superior in verbal ability to children with siblings. Twins are slightly retarded in language development compared with single-birth children. There are at least two possible explanations for these differences. One group of researchers argues that the amount of interaction between parent and child causes the difference. Single children seem to interact more with adults, who possess a larger vocabulary; thus the single child has a better chance of picking up words. There is also a genetic view which points out that only children usually have brighter parents than do children from larger families. Again, no one is sure which theory is correct, but both seem plausible.

Children can easily
acquire two languages
simultaneously.

Many children grow up speaking two languages. Early studies suggested that these children, particularly if they learned a simplified form of English, were linguistically handicapped compared to children who learn only English. However, recent studies show that learning two or more languages does not necessarily have a negative effect on the child. There are several factors associated with the successful acquisition of two languages. First, both languages must be presented in all their complexity rather than in a simplified form. Second, each language should be heard from a different source. One parent might communicate in German or French or Spanish, and the other in English. Also, the languages should be used at different times or in different situations. Finally, the child must use both languages. If the parent uses only one language or responds to the child in only one, he will lose interest in acquiring a second language.

Upper-class children use more correct grammar.

There are large social class differences in children's language skills. Upper-class children are generally ahead of their lower-class age mates in language development. Lower-class children score less well on all measures of language—including articulation, sound discrimination, size of vocabulary, and length of sentence—and some of these differences appear as early as the second year of the child's life.

Nonstandard English

There are several dialects of English.

Language often serves as a communication link between people, but it can also be a barrier because we do not all speak the same way. These variations within a language are called *dialects,* and they differ depending on education, age, geographic region, social class, and race. The most important single determinant of your dialect is the particular area in which you are born. The largest language differences are on the East coast; dialects gradually diminish as you move westward. A second major factor in dialect development is social class. Because of this, people tend to judge social status on the basis of language skills.

Communications may be formal and standard.

Linguists classify communications into formal and informal sets, and language usage into standard and nonstandard grammars. This means we have four classes of utterances in English:

Formal standard English
Informal standard English
Formal nonstandard English
Informal nonstandard English.

Non-standard English contains different rules and meanings.

The major difference between formal and informal English usage is the carefulness or casualness of the communication. Ordinary conversation is informal, while a lecture before an audience is formal.

The main differences between standard and nonstandard English are the rules, permissible transformations (which is the process by which rules are applied to sentence structure), and sometimes the meanings of words. There are several nonstandard English dialects in the U.S. In the southwest and in New York City a nonstandard dialect has developed from a blend of Spanish and English. In some areas of the West the interaction of English and American Indian languages has produced other nonstandard English dialects. However, the most widespread nonstandard English dialect in the U.S. is black English.

Portrait

Avram Noam Chomsky was born in Philadelphia, Pennsylvania, in 1928. He received his early education at Oak Lane Country Day School and Central High School. At the University of Pennsylvania, where he earned both his A.B. and Ph.D., he studied linguistics, mathematics, and philosophy. He actually completed his dissertation research while he was a Junior Fellow of the Society of Fellows at Harvard University, between 1951 and 1955. Chomsky has taught at the Massachusetts Institute of Technology since 1955, and he now holds the Farrari P. Ward Chair of Modern Languages and Linguistics at M.I.T.

Chomsky's early work was concerned with historical linguistics, and his M.A. thesis discussed modern spoken Hebrew. His most important work, the development of a grammar which will generate correct sentences of any language without producing incorrect ones, grew from his interest in modern logic and mathematics. Chomsky began his work with an analysis of the foundations of logic and mathematics, and only later applied this analysis to natural languages. His results have revolutionized linguistics and psycholinguistics. Because of Chomsky, linguists now study the structure of language. The psychological reality of Chomsky's grammar has been tested and verified in studies concerning the acquisition, use, and understanding of languages by children and adults.

Chomsky is the author of several important books and many articles. Perhaps his most influential book is *Syntactic Structures*, which was published in 1957. This is a relatively nontechnical account of an earlier, unpublished work, ''The Logical Structure of Linguistic Theory.'' The publication of *Syntactic Structures* changed the thinking of almost everyone interested in language and linguistic analysis.

Another famous publication is Chomsky's 1959 review of B.F. Skinner's book, *Verbal Behavior,* in which Chomsky argues that Skinner's theory of operant conditioning cannot fully account for the complexities of grammar acquisition by young children. Recently, Chomsky has become interested in the political situation in the United States, and a recent book deals with the American involvement in Indochina.

A thoughtful Noam Chomsky at M.I.T. (Christopher S. Johnson)

I would like to focus attention on the question, What contribution can the study of language make to our understanding of human nature? In one or another manifestation, this question threads its way through modern Western thought. In an age that was less self-conscious and less compartmentalized than ours, the nature of language, the respects in which language mirrors human mental processes or shapes the flow and character of thought—these were topics for study and speculation by scholars and gifted amateurs with a wide variety of interests, points of view, and intellectual backgrounds. And in the nineteenth and twentieth centuries, as linguistics, philosophy, and psychology have uneasily tried to go their separate ways, the classical problems of language and mind have inevitably reappeared and have served to link these diverging fields and to give direction and significance to their efforts. There have been signs in the past decade that the rather artificial separation of disciplines may be coming to an end. It is no longer a point of honor for each to demonstrate its absolute independence of the others, and new interests have emerged that permit the classical problems to be formulated in novel and occasionally suggestive ways. All of this is highly encouraging. I think there is more of a healthy ferment in cognitive psychology—and in the particular branch of cognitive psychology known as linguistics—than there has been for many years. And one of the most encouraging signs is that skepticism with regard to the orthodoxies of the recent past is coupled with an awareness of the temptations and the dangers of premature orthodoxy, an awareness that, if it can persist, may prevent the rise of new and stultifying dogma.

I remember quite clearly my own feeling of uneasiness as a student at the fact that, so it seemed, the basic problems of the field were solved, and that what remained was to sharpen and improve techniques of linguistic analysis that were reasonably well understood and to apply them to a wider range of linguistic materials. In the postwar years, this was a dominant attitude in most active centers of research. I recall being told by a distinguished anthropological linguist, in 1953, that he had no intention of working through a vast collection of materials that he had assembled because within a few years it would surely be possible to program a computer to construct a grammar from a large corpus of data by the use of techniques that were already fairly well formalized. At the time, this did not seem an unreasonable attitude, though the prospect was saddening for anyone who felt, or at least hoped, that the resources of human intelligence were somewhat deeper than these procedures and techniques might reveal. Correspondingly, there was a striking decline in studies of linguistic method in the early 1950's as the most active theoretical minds turned to the problem of how an essentially closed body of technique could be applied to some new domain—say, to analysis of connected discourse,

From Noam Chomsky. *Language and Mind,* enlarged ed. (New York: Harcourt Brace Jovanovich (1972).

or to other cultural phenomena beyond language. I arrived at Harvard as a graduate student shortly after B.F. Skinner had delivered his William James Lectures, later to be published in his book *Verbal Behavior*. Among those active in research in philosophy or psychology of language, there was then little doubt that although details were missing, and although matters could not really be quite that simple, nevertheless a behavioristic framework of the sort Skinner had outlined would prove quite adequate to accommodate the full range of language use. There was now little reason to question the conviction of Leonard Bloomfield, Bertrand Russell, and positivistic linguists, psychologists, and philosophers in general that the framework of stimulus-response psychology would soon be extended to the point where it would provide a satisfying explanation for the most mysterious of human abilities. The most radical souls felt that perhaps, in order to do full justice to these abilities, one must postulate little *s*'s and *r*'s inside the brain alongside the capital *S*'s and *R*'s that were open to immediate inspection, but this extension was not inconsistent with the general picture.

Critical voices, even those that commanded considerable prestige, were simply unheard. For example, Karl Lashley gave a brilliant critique of the prevailing framework of ideas in 1948, arguing that underlying language use—and all organized behavior—there must be abstract mechanisms of some sort that are not analyzable in terms of association and that could not have developed by any such simple means. But his arguments and proposals, though sound and perceptive, had absolutely no effect on the development of the field and went by unnoticed even at his own university (Harvard), then the leading center of psycholinguistic research. Ten years later Lashley's contribution began to be appreciated, but only after his insights had been independently achieved in another context.

The technological advances of the 1940's simply reinforced the general euphoria. Computers were on the horizon, and their imminent availability reinforced the belief that it would suffice to gain a theoretical understanding of only the simplest and most superficially obvious of phenomena—everything else would merely prove to be "more of the same," an apparent complexity that would be disentangled by the electronic marvels.

In the United States at least, there is little trace today of the illusions of the early postwar years. If we consider the current status of structural linguistic methodology or stimulus-response psycholinguistics . . . a careful analysis shows that insofar as the system of concepts and principles that was advanced can be made precise, it can be demonstrated to be inadequate in a fundamental way. The kinds of structures that are realizable in terms of these theories are simply not those that must be postulated to underlie the use of language, if empirical conditions of adequacy are to be satisfied. What is more, the character of the failure and inadequacy is such as to give little reason to believe that these approaches are on the right track. That is, in each case it has been argued— quite persuasively, in my opinion—that the approach is not only inadequate but misguided in basic and important ways. It has, I believe, become quite clear that if we are ever to understand how language is used or acquired, then we must abstract for separate and independent study a cognitive system, a system of knowledge and belief, that develops in early childhood and that interacts with many other factors to determine the kinds of behavior that we observe; to introduce a technical term, we must isolate and study the system of *linguistic competence* that underlies behavior but that is not realized in any direct or simple way in behavior. And this system of linguistic competence is qualitatively different from anything that can be described in terms of the taxonomic methods of structural linguistics, the concepts of S-R psychology, or the notions developed within the mathematical theory of communication or the theory of simple automata. The theories and models that were developed to describe simple and immediately given phenomena cannot incorporate the real system of linguistic competence; "extrapolation" from simple descriptions cannot approach the reality of linguistic competence; mental structures are not simply "more of the same" but are qualitatively different from the complex networks and structures that can be developed by elaboration of the concepts that seemed so promising to many scientists just a few years ago. What is involved is not a matter of degree of complexity but rather of quality of complexity. Correspondingly, there is no reason to expect that the available technology can provide significant insight or understanding or useful achievements; it has noticeably failed to do so, and, in fact, an appreciable investment of time, energy, and money in the use of computers for linguistic research—appreciable by the standards of a small field like linguistics—has not provided any significant advance in our understanding of the use or nature of language. These judgments are harsh, but I think they are defensible. They are, furthermore, hardly debated by active linguistic or psycholinguistic researchers.

At the same time there have been significant advances, I believe, in our understanding of the nature of linguistic competence and some of the ways in which it is put to use, but these advances, such as they are, have proceeded from assumptions very different from those that were so enthusiastically put forth in the period I have been discussing. What is more, these advances have not narrowed the gap between what is known and what can be seen to lie beyond the scope of present understanding and technique; rather, each advance has made it clear that these intellectual horizons are far more remote than was heretofore imagined. Finally, it has become fairly clear, it seems to me, that the assumptions and approaches that appear to be productive today have a distinctly traditional flavor to them; in general, a much despised tradition has been largely revitalized in recent years and its contributions given some serious and, I believe, well-deserved attention. From the recognition of these facts flows the general and quite healthy attitude of skepticism that I spoke of earlier.

. . . The rationalist theory of language, which was to prove extremely rich in insight and achievement, developed in part out of a concern with the problem of other minds. A fair amount of effort was devoted to a consideration of the ability of animals to follow spoken commands, to express their emotional states, to communicate with one another, and even apparently to cooperate for a common goal; all of this, it was argued, could be accounted for on "mechanical grounds," as this notion was then understood—that is, through the functioning of physiological mechanisms in terms of which one could formulate the properties of reflexes, conditioning and reinforcement, association, and so on. Animals do not lack appropriate organs of communication, nor are they simply lower along some scale of "general intelligence."

In fact, as Descartes himself quite correctly observed, language is a species-specific human possession, and even at low levels of intelligence, at pathological levels, we find a command of language that is totally unattainable by an ape that may, in other respects, surpass a human imbecile in problem-solving ability and other adaptive behavior. I will return later to the status of this observation, in the light of what is now known about animal communication. There is a basic element lacking in animals, Descartes argued, as it is lacking in even the most complex automation that develops its "intellectual structures" completely in terms of conditioning and association . . .

It is important to understand just what properties of language were most striking to Descartes and his followers. The discussion of what I have been calling "the creative aspect of language use" turns on three important observations. The first is that the normal use of language is innovative, in the sense that much of what we say in the course of normal language use is entirely new, not a repetition of anything that we have heard before and not even similar in pattern—in any useful sense of the terms "similar" and "pattern"—to sentences or discourse that we have heard in the past. This is a truism, but an important one, often overlooked and not infrequently denied in the behaviorist period of linguistics to which I referred earlier, when it was almost universally claimed that a person's knowledge of language is representable as a stored set of patterns, overlearned through constant repetition and detailed training, with innovation being at most a matter of "analogy." The fact surely is, however, that the number of sentences in one's native language that one will immediately understand with no feeling of difficulty or strangeness is astronomical; and that the number of patterns underlying our normal use of language and corresponding to meaningful and easily comprehensible sentences in our language is orders of magnitude greater than the number of seconds in a lifetime. It is in this sense that the normal use of language is innovative.

Thus, the study of language had arrived at a situation in which there was, on the one hand, a set of simple concepts that provided the basis for some startling successes and, on the other, some deep but rather vague ideas that did not seem to lead to any further productive research. The outcome was inevitable and not at all to be deplored. There developed a professionalization of the field, a shift of interest away from the classical problems of general interest to intellectuals like Arnauld and Humboldt, for example, toward a new domain largely defined by the techniques that the profession itself has forged in the solution of certain problems. Such a development is natural and quite proper, but not without its dangers. Without wishing to exalt the cult of gentlemanly amateurism, one must nevertheless recognize that the classical issues have a liveliness and significance that may be lacking in an area of investigation that is determined by the applicability of certain tools and methods, rather than by problems that are of intrinsic interest in themselves.

The moral is not to abandon useful tools; rather, it is, first, that one should maintain enough perspective to be able to detect the arrival of that inevitable day when the research that can be conducted with these tools is no longer important; and, second, that one should value ideas and insights that are to the point, though perhaps premature and vague and not productive of research at a particular stage of technique and understanding. With the benefits of hindsight, I think we can now see clearly that the disparagement and neglect of a rich tradition proved in the long run to be quite harmful to the study of language. Furthermore, this disparagement and neglect were surely unnecessary. Perhaps it would have been psychologically difficult, but there is no reason in principle why the successful exploitation of the structuralist approach in historical and descriptive study could not have been coupled with a clear recognition of its essential limitations and its ultimate inadequacy, in comparison with the tradition it temporarily, and quite justifiably, displaced. Here, I think, lies a lesson that may be valuable for the future study of language and mind.

Most dialects are quite similar in structure.

From a linguistic point of view the differences between standard English and black English are small. The basic structure of sentences and the formal representations of utterances are very similar, as are most of the transformation rules and sound systems. However, there are some differences. A transformation rule may be present in black English and not in standard English, or the conditions for the use of a transformation rule may be different. Specifically, agreement between a subject and verb in person and number is not necessary in black English. This can produce sentences of the form: *"She have a cake."* Or *"He were coming."* There are also cases in which black English makes distinctions that are not present in standard English. For example, use of the verb *be* indicates an habitual state rather than a transitory one: *"He be working"* indicates that the person has a steady job; while *he works* means that occasionally the person works, but he is not regularly employed.

Some assume that dialects produce academic problems.

The differences between black and standard English have led some authorities to theorize that academic failure among some black children is due to impoverished or retarded language development. This verbal deficit hypothesis assumes that black Americans do not know the names of many common objects, cannot formulate complete sentences, and therefore are handicapped with a standard school curriculum. There *is* evidence that children who learn Spanish or a non-English language as their first language have difficulty comprehending a standard school curriculum presented in English. Some children who learn standard English as a second language are helped in school when their lessons are presented in their first language (Coleman, 1966).

Black Americans emphasize verbal fluency.

The hypothesis that black children's academic difficulties are due to language-learning problems rests on problematic evidence (Dale, 1972). First, it is assumed that language is basic to thinking, but this is a controversial issue in cognitive psychology at the present time. The language deficit hypothesis is also contradicted by several pieces of experimental evidence. First, there is great emphasis within the black community on verbal ability, and verbal fluency is a mark of distinction. In fact, Stodolsky and Lesser (1967) found that the verbal ability of black Americans is their greatest strength. Although black English is a nonstandard dialect, these language differences probably do not account for the academic difficulties of some black-American students.

Studies of Grammar Acquisition

Chomsky's theory has generated several studies.

Noam Chomsky's theory that grammar (*see* the Advanced Topics Appendix) includes two kinds of elements has suggested a number of experiments. The two elements are phrase structure, which enables the speaker to form simple sentences, and transformations, which allows the speaker to convert simple sentences into more complex ones. In one early study Dan I. Slobin (1963) used several interesting notions derived from Chomsky's transformational grammar to study the acquisition of grammar. Children were presented with a number of sentence-picture pairs, one at a time. Their task was to say whether the sentence was true or false about the picture. Errors and the time required to decide about each picture were recorded. The sentences were of four grammatical types— *declarative, passive, negative,* and *negative-passive.* The pictures were of two kinds— *reversible* and *nonreversible.* The former permitted reversibility of subject and object (a dog chasing a cat; a cat chasing a dog). The second kind of picture did not permit reversibility (a boy raking grass).

Passive sentences are more difficult to comprehend.

For the most part a transformational theory of grammar predicts the results. Slobin found that passive sentences took longer than declarative sentences to comprehend, and that passive negatives took more time than simple negatives. In addition, passives were more often correct. Most of these results would be expected. But, on the basis of transformational grammar alone, it is difficult to understand why negative sentences require more time than passive ones. They *should* take about equal time, since both are single transformations. However, as we know from several other sources, negative information is difficult for children to process.

Thus, psychological processes must be added to linguistic theory to make a complete picture. Noam Chomsky writes about how and why he developed modern linguistic theory in the following excerpt.

Transformational grammar explains some language uses.

A hint of this process is contained in the results from the reversible and nonreversible picture study. With irreversible pictures, there was no difference in evaluation time between passive and declarative sentences, and passive-negatives were no more difficult than negative sentences. Slobin also found that skill in dealing with the complexity of sentence structure increases with age, and that some transformations are not available at six years and younger. Finally, the results show that passive transformations are easier to handle than negatives. Although transformational grammar does not easily produce a complete psychological theory of language acquisition, it does give many clues about the processes involved.

Linguists study competence and performance.

There are two levels of interest in language:

1. *Competence*—the knowledge an idealized individual has about a language without considering memory limitations, shifts in attention, false starts, and so on.
2. *Performance*—the actual ability of the language user to produce strings of words (Chomsky, 1965).

Only when we are dealing with the ideal language user, who has human limitations, do these two levels directly correspond. Most linguists take the ideal user as their starting point, because they want to understand the structure and underlying grammar used by this ideal speaker. Only recently have psycholinguists begun to make statements about how the speaker comes to produce sentences. There are two sets of criteria by which sentences are judged:

1. *Grammaticalness*—does the sentence follow the rules?
2. *Acceptability*—can it be understood by real people?

Competence concerns the understanding of grammatical rules.

Linguists measure the grammaticalness of sentences when they study language competence, and their acceptability when studying human speech performance. Grammaticalness reflects keeping to the theoretical rules of grammar; while acceptability concerns whether sentences can be pronounced and understood. These characteristics interact with the native speaker's memory, age, and attention limitations. A successful theory of language should call forth all the grammatical sequences of a language and none of the ungrammatical ones. A way to test the adequacy of a theory is to determine whether or not the sequences it calls forth seem grammatical to a native speaker. Linguists do this by asking such native speakers to judge various sentences.

Grammar is unrelated to meaning.

How do linguists decide on grammatical rules? Grammar must be unrelated to meaning, and is not related directly to the particular body of sentences used in its construction or in testing grammar. Sentences can be nonsensical, but grammatical—"Colorless green ideas sleep furiously," is a grammatically correct, nonsensical sentence. "Furious sleep ideas green colorless" is both nonsensical and ungrammatical. Currently, the acceptability, or grammaticalness, of utterances is based on the judgment of native speakers, as we have seen. This leads to relatively few problems, since the judgment is usually easy to make.

Adults can make judgments about the grammaticalness of sentences, but how can you test for children's competence? Parents often believe their children understand much more than they really do. For example, a parent may ask a child to go over to the chair and bring the glasses. If the child follows instructions, the parent is impressed. Yet the child need only understand the words chair and glasses to do what is asked. At an even lower level of sophistication, the parent may have pointed in the direction of the glasses, and then the child need understand only the one word, chair.

To test whether a child understands a particular linguistic utterance the parent must control many things. If glasses are wanted, the parent should put his hand in his lap and say, "Bring me my glasses." If that works, he might return the glasses to the table and then say, "Me glasses bring." Young children often hear simple declarative sentences which have an actor, an action, and an object; so they may interpret all sentences in this simple three-way manner. Thus, if he rearranges the sentence, a parent can produce strange results; for example, "The truck was broken by John may become: "Truck broke John." Adults recognize some English sentences that are reversible: "The boy feeds the girl." "The girl feeds the boy." It is also possible to produce correct English sentences in which the actor is before the verb and the object follows. These are called passive sentences. "The truck was broken by John" is the passive form of "John broke the truck." These two sentences mean the same thing to adults, even though the order of the elements is reversed. One

Children's grammar is difficult to measure.

Children's grammar is assessed by non-verbal means.

FIGURE 6.8 A three-year-old can correctly act on the sentence, "The boy washes the girl." When he is told, "The girl is washed by the boy," he will perform the opposite action.

of the ways to test for children's understanding of active and passive is to say the same sentence in two different ways (*see* Figure 6.8): "The boy is washed by the girl." "The girl is washed by the boy." When three-year-old children are asked to react to passive sentences of these sort, they usually perform exactly the opposite action. When they hear the boy is washed by the girl, they make the boy wash the girl and vice-versa. These errors are so systematic that it seems as if age-three children process passive sentences as active sentences with some extra nonsense thrown in.

Speech

Speech perception is reliable.

Not only do children acquire the ability to form sentences, they are also able to understand the speech of others, even though it is distorted, clipped, or transformed. Remarkably, speech perception is very resistant to disruption. The perception of speech has been extensively studied by engineers at the Bell Telephone Laboratories to help improve telephone communication (Neisser, 1967). Their main speech perception findings can be summarized in three statements:

1. Beyond a minimal level, large increases in the intensity of speech have trivial effects on understanding.
2. Large shifts in overall level of pitch produce trivial problems. Male voices range from about 120 to 8,000 cycles per second and around 20 to 115 decibels. If this spectrum is transformed into a female voice, there is no loss of understanding for the average listener. Also, restriction of the frequency range of speech has no effect on its perception. Finally, if we turn speech off and on very quickly (on for $1/10$ of a second and then off for $1/10$ of a second, so that in twenty minutes we have only ten minutes of actual sound), the loss of half the sound will have no effect on speech understanding. As long as the pattern, or organization, of the sounds is maintained, particular frequencies make trivial contributions to understanding. These data suggest that speech is a very robust communication system.

However, some children have grave difficulties producing speech patterns. They stutter.

Stuttering

Some children stutter.

Children are said to stutter if they cannot say a structured sentence correctly. Many speech problems, like sound substitution for example, disappear with growth, but stuttering can be a persistent problem. Several explanations of stuttering have been proposed by theorists. One explanation assumes that right-handed people's motor responses are dominated by the left hemispheres of their brains; in left-handed people the right hemisphere is supposed to dominate. The theory further assumes that when a left-handed child is made to use his right hand, confusion about hemisphere dominance results and might produce stuttering.

A second explanation supposes that stuttering is caused by parent-child relations, where parents reinforce their children for stuttering. All children show a certain amount of stammering and stuttering in their early speech development. This social reinforcement theory of stuttering states that if parents pay particular attention to early stuttering, the child may continue to make more and more mistakes until it becomes a habit. The parent may then say to the child, "You are beginning to stutter"; this will make the child anxious. Since anxiety produces more stammering and stuttering, the result is a vicious feedback system. Finally, the theory suggests that once negative feedback begins, a child's speech will deteriorate because of built-up anxiety, and the parent will become increasingly concerned, thus producing even more anxiety.

Some parents make their children anxious.

A third theory of stuttering suggests a defective speech center because of brain damage or a birth defect. Perhaps the answer is that different causes are probably involved in various cases of stuttering. Immaturity, damage to the language centers in the human brain, parental pressures, and anxiety can all cause the problem. Primary physiological stuttering seems to be due to brain disfunction, and it is particularly difficult to remedy. In contrast, secondary stuttering caused by anxiety and reinforcement can be helped by psychological therapy.

Stuttering may be caused by brain disfunction.

The Development of Meaning

Semantics is about meaning.

The structure of words and sentences is the concern of *grammar;* the meaning of sentences and words is the concern of *semantics.* Many combinations of words can be made into grammatical sentences that have no meaning. Children need a grammar, but they also need rules to tell them whether a word may be used meaningfully in a particular way. Grammatical development is fairly advanced by the time a child is five, but his semantic ability lags. Young children do not find the sentence, "The chair is unhappy," strange at all; most adults do.

Word meaning is learned.

Children probably learn the meaning of many words by associating them with objects (*see* Figure 6.9). Roger Brown suggested that parents reinforce their children for meaningful, correct utterances but ignore the grammaticalness of their sentences (Brown, 1970).

Language and Thought

Are language and thought the same?

A persistent problem in the study of language is its relation to thought and perception. Are language and thought the same? The behaviorist, John Watson (1912) believed that thought is nothing but motor movement of the larynx, so his answer was yes. Early German psychologists argued that thought can occur without images or speech. The Russians assert that language and thinking are intimately related in childhood, but are separated by the adult. The Swiss psychologist Jean Piaget thinks cognition and language follow separate rules of development.

Whorf believed that language affects thinking.

Benjamin Whorf (1956), an American, experienced considerable difficulty in translating English into other languages, particularly American-

FIGURE 6.9 One way an infant might learn the connection between a sound and the object it signifies is shown here.

Indian dialects. He suspected this difficulty arose because the thought processes underlying various languages are different. There is little evidence to support Whorf's claim, although differences among languages certainly exist. Some languages contain categories which others do not, and one language may have a term for which another language must use compound (two or more) words. There is no clear English equivalent for the German word, "*Gestalt,*" meaning a whole, organized perception. American psychologists had to borrow this term from German.

Language structures vary among cultures.

In other languages some superordinate (overall ranking) may be missing. For example, English has the superordinate, "animal" for birds, reptiles, and mammals; but it does not have a superordinate word for fruits and nuts as a group. Chinese does. Another difference occurs in the way people differentiate their perceptual world. Consider how colors are named (see color Plate 3). Compare the division of colors by Englishmen, Rhodesians, and Liberians. If people are shown a color which lies on a boundary between two colors, some languages will have a single word for it—say "green" as English does—but in Shona in Rhodesia people would have to put two words together to name the boundary color. These differences in words show only that labels vary, not that thought or perceptual processes are different. Anyone who is not colorblind can discriminate most colors. Another classic language difference is the single word for snow in English; Eskimoes have several. English speakers can learn to connect many words with different kinds of snow. Skiers routinely speak of corn, powder, and slush.

Language and cognition may be independent.

Words that are frequently used in a culture may simply indicate those concepts which are important to that group. Only by showing that a child who developed within one language system cannot understand an idea expressed in another language would you have conclusive evidence of the inseparability of language and thought. Such data do not exist, possibly because language does not seem to confine children's thought that completely, and also because linguists are beginning to believe that universal characteristics exist which all languages share.

Language Universals

Linguists are search ing for language universals.

Currently, linguists are concerned with language universals which are common to *all* languages rather than with cultural differences. The linguist argues that Whorf was concerned with the surface structure of language only, while at more basic levels all languages are very similar. They all have phonemes, morphemes, a grammar, and semantics. Yet Vygotsky (1962), who thinks that intelligence derives from inner speech, partly agrees with Whorf. Vygotsky believes thought and speech have different genetic origins and develop independently for a while. He assumes there is a prelinguistic phase of thought and a preintellectual phase of speech. Then, the child discovers that speech has a symbolic function and begins to connect it with intelligence. Vygotsky distinguishes several phases of language and thought development. First comes primitive, preintellectual thought, where speech and cognition are parallel but independent. A second stage occurs during which the child accumulates intellectual structures and grammatically correct sentences. The third stage begins when he comes to use self-centered speech to aid his thinking. In a final stage the child begins to connect inner speech and thought into a coordinated system.

Deaf and hearing children show similar cognitive development.

There is evidence that language and cognition are not so parallel. Furth (1970) has studied deaf children in the U.S. and says that they don't learn reading, writing, and speaking until fairly late. In fact, most U.S. deaf children never learn to use proper English. In terms of cognitive development, however, Furth argues that deaf children are *not* different from children who hear. Both develop similar cognitive sequences at similar rates. Furth concludes that language has only an indirect effect on cognitive development. He believes language accelerates cognitive development, but that it is not necessary for thought.

Nonverbal Communication

People communicate nonverbally.

An important set of communications between people other than spoken language has been neglected until recently. These are the signs we transmit by inflection, gesture, and body position. In fact, nonverbal language may or may not agree with a person's speech. One important body sign is pupil dilation to pleasant or interesting experiences. Touching is the ultimate nonverbal communication. Charles Darwin argued that animals and man have preprogrammed signals about hostility, sexuality, or territory.

Body language is an important form of communication.

Nonverbal communications include eye movements, posture, facial expressions, and almost every other possible signal from the human body. The purpose of nonverbal communications is to reinforce what the person is saying, or to signal a message which cannot be sent verbally. Nonverbal signals deal primarily with emotions—dominance, territory, sexuality, anger, and fear. Because of its subtle importance, body language deserves more attention from scientists and others as well. Some examples of human nonverbal communication include: Looking at your watch to indicate that you want a conversation to end; nodding and saying "hmm" when you are listening and agreeing with a speaker; moving about and diverting your gaze if you are disinterested in a conversation. People sometimes signal their sexual interest in each other by smiling, glancing shyly, and then looking away. Moving close to another person, touching an arm, and brushing lightly are indications of special interest.

Children learn body language by imitation.

How do children learn body language? Probably the same way they learn any other language, by imitating the behavior of those around them. Little boys imitate their fathers and respected males; little girls try to be like their mothers and admired women. There are regional, class, and ethnic differences in body language. In the U.S., for example, a woman will stand with her thighs together, walk with her pelvis tipped forward, and hold her upper arms close to her body. When she sits, a woman in the U.S. will cross her legs at the knee; if she is older she may cross her ankles. Men in the U.S. by contrast, hold their arms away from their bodies, swing them when they walk, and stand with their legs apart. How one sits reflects such important signals as status, respect for others, and one's own perceived social situation.

Both language and nonverbal systems are important, and they need to be taken into account in any attempt at understanding the human child or adult.

Summary

There are two competing theories about how children come to string single word utterances into complicated sentences. The environmental theory assumes children are taught language by their parents pretty much the same way they are taught other skills—by imitation, rewards for correct responding, and non-rewards or punishment for incorrect utterances. The nativist theory holds that children have innate tendencies to babble, form words, and string these words into grammatically meaningful sentences.

SUGGESTED ADDITIONAL READINGS

Bellugi, U., and R. Brown, eds. *The Acquisition of Language*. Chicago: University of Chicago Press, 1970.

Bloom, Lois M. *Language Development: Form and Function in Emerging Grammars*. Cambridge, Mass.: MIT Press, 1970.

Brown, R. *Words and Things*. Glencoe, Ill.: Free Press, 1958.

Ervin-Tripp, S. "Language Development." In M. Hoffman and L. Hoffman, eds., *Advances in Child Development Research*, Vol. II. New York: Russell Sage Foundation, 1966.

Jakobson, R. *Child Language, Aphasia and Phonological Universals*. The Hague: Mouton, 1968.

Lenneberg, E.H. *Biological Foundations of Language*. New York: Wiley, 1967.

7 Cognitive Development

Cognitive Processes
  Symbols and Meaning
  Logic
  Illogical Thinking
  Children's Thoughts—Jean Piaget
Stages of Children's Thought
  Sensory-motor Period
  Preoperational Period
  Concrete Operational Period
  Formal Operations
The Nature of Preoperational
  Thought

Egocentricsm
Centration
States and Transformations
Reversibility
Concrete Operational Thought
  The Primary Addition of Classes
  Multiplication of Classes
  Combination of Asymmetrical
    Relations
  Multiplication of Relations
Logical Thinking
Summary

PREVIEW

Possibly the most amazing transformation of a child is his change from a reflexive, rigidly responding newborn into an active, symbol-manipulating thinker. The method by which children turn their confused world into a coherent representation of reality is a source of controversy. Two major theories exist about how children change from reflex to thought. One argues that the child's mind is a blank tablet on which experiences are recorded. This passive view of development is opposed by the theory of Jean Piaget, who argues that children actively construct a representation of the world by developing categories and operations and then testing these ideas through experimentation. Piaget derived his view of cognitive development by studying his own three children during their early years. He developed a sensitive method of observation and posed some fundamental problems for any theory of cognition. These problems include how children develop symbols, how language and thought get connected, and what the mechanism of cognitive development is. We will discuss these problems in Chapter 7, as well as how children become able to manipulate symbols in a directed and deliberate way.

Children's and adult's minds work differently.

Most people appreciate how vast the differences are between a child's mind and an adult's. But no one is really sure how the illogical infant becomes a mature, reasoning adult. Several theories of cognitive development exist. Some researchers argue that the simple accumulation of associations accounts for the development of thought. Opponents of this habit view of mind believe that the child possesses a few innate functions which let him construct a knowledge of the world through a process of hypothesis testing. The leading advocate of this second view is the Swiss psychologist Jean Piaget, who is fast becoming one of the world's most influential social scientists (Flavell, 1963). Until recently, little attention was given to Piaget's work because he wrote in French, proposed unorthodox ideas, used unusual methodology, and studied children's thinking when most everyone else was interested in habits. Currently, there is keen interest in Piaget's work because psychologists are again becoming interested in the human mind. Chapter 7 will cover Piaget's methods, evidence, and theory of the child's cognitive development with particular attention given to the later stages through which children pass on their way to logical thinking.

Cognition is about the manipulation of symbols.

Cognition has been defined by many as the manipulation of symbols during the course of solving a problem. Thus, one of the first things to consider is the development of signs and how they get attached to objects. Cognition concerns the manipulation of symbols which represent current objects, events from the past, or imaginary things. There are at least four kinds of symbol manipulations:

1. *Directed* — where the manipulation of symbols is for a particular purpose.
2. *Free* — as in wishful thinking, revery, dreams, or free association on a psychoanalytic couch.
3. *Critical* — as when a person evaluates the products of his thinking.
4. *Creative* — which is an attempt to produce new solutions or ideas.

Cognitive Processes

Symbols and Meaning

Symbols have two kinds of meaning.

Two of the most important symbol systems for humans are language and logic. The most important characteristic of symbols is their meaning. Symbols have two kinds of meaning: *denotative,* which connects symbols to specific events or objects; and *connotative,* which concerns suggestive meaning or feelings about a symbol. The interactions and inconsistencies of denotative and connotative meaning can cause confusion. Many believe denotative meanings are acquired by association.

Connotative meaning has been studied most extensively by Charles

FIGURE 7.1
How many people rate the word "father" on three characteristics. The rating scale is taken from Osgood's Semantic Differential test.

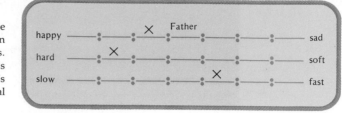

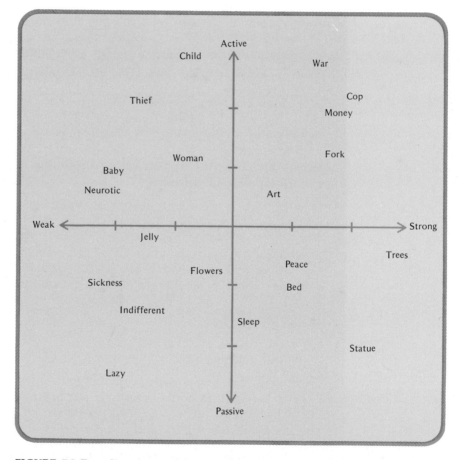

FIGURE 7.2 Two dimensions of connotative meaning described by Osgood. One factor is weak-strong; the other is active-passive. Note that "war" is active and strong; a "statue" is passive and strong; a "baby" is active and weak; and a "lazy" person is passive and weak.

Osgood developed the semantic differential.

Osgood (1957), with his Semantic Differential test. It is called semantic because it has to do with meaning; and differential because Osgood found three characteristics labeled evaluation, strength, and activity which describe words. To obtain a measure of meaning with the Semantic Differential test, subjects are asked to rate a word on several characteristics like happy-sad, hard-soft, or slow-fast. Figure 7.1 shows part of a rating profile from both the semantic differential and the connotative meaning of "father," which is moderately happy, fairly hard, and moderately fast. Osgood derived his scale by analyzing responses from hundreds of people to thousands of words. He found that people rate words most often in terms of good or bad feelings, and after that in terms of how strong or active the word seems to them to be. Figure 7.2 shows the ratings of several words on the active and strong dimensions of the Semantic Differential test.

Children differentiate symbols and objects.

We know that adults use symbols, but how do children come to represent events by signs? To develop symbolic representation a child must differentiate signs (words, symbols) from what they stand for (objects, relations). Although the one-year-old is capable of very primitive sign-representation relationships through action, only much later can he easily evoke an image or a word to stand for an absent event. Because of this developing symbolic ability, children's thinking differs dramatically from infant behavior. Infants with simple sensory-motor skills can only deal with actions or perceptual states. After the development of symbolic abilities the child can grasp separate events at the same time. He can symbolically recall the past, represent the present and anticipate the future simultaneously. The ability to differentiate between signs and what they signify, and to develop relations among those signs, gives the child a more powerful and flexible cognitive structure than anything available to the more undeveloped sensory-motor infant.

Bruner believes that there are three kinds of symbols.

Jerome Bruner (1965, 1968) suggests that the infant and child use three modes of symbolization during the course of development:

1. *Enactive representation* — the use of motor responses to stand for objects or relations.
2. *Iconic representation* — the use of images to signify events.
3. *Symbolic representation* — the use of arbitrary signs — for example, language — to represent things.

Bruner believes there is a progression through these stages of representation as the child matures, although adults may use any of the stages at varying times. He also believes that language is not essential to thought, but that it does amplify thinking by systematizing and symbolizing. Beyond symbols are the rules which govern mature thought. These rules have been organized into what philosophers call logic.

Portrait

Jerome Bruner was born in 1915 and grew up in Lawrence, Long Island, as something of a "water rat" — according to his own description. He sailed, waded, fished, and read a lot during his childhood. His father, a German-Jewish watch manufacturer, died when Bruner was still in high school. After graduation, Bruner earned a B.A. from Duke University and then a Ph.D. in psychology from Harvard University in 1941. He served in the Office of War Information during World War II, and then returned to Harvard College, where he taught and studied psychology until he recently accepted a professorship at the University of Oxford.

Bruner helped reintroduce cognition, the study of thinking, to American psychology. During the late 1950s he and others at Cambridge, Massachusetts, began studying how people think and talk. He proposed, along with Noam Chomsky and George Miller, that language acquisition is just another example of the child's remarkable ability to reconstruct logical rules which govern any system on the basis of sample evidence. It is difficult to characterize Bruner's area of psychology because he has studied everything from animal learning to perception, child development to innate behavior. However, the theme of all his work is to reorganize and revitalize neglected areas of psychology.

Bruner first became interested in education during the early 1960s. He made it fashionable for psychologists to write and think about teaching children. His most controversial statement about education is still repeated: "Any subject can be taught effectively in some intellectually honest form to any child at any stage of development." Although a number of prominent psychologists have challenged this statement, Bruner still believes there is no evidence to refute it.

At the same time that he was becoming interested in education, Bruner helped found the Center for Cognitive Studies at Harvard University. During these early years he and his colleagues revolutionized American psychology's conception of man by arguing that not only learning but also perception, thinking, and language are important human abilities. It was at about this time that Bruner published his most important book, *A Study of Thinking*.

In recent years, the Center for Cognitive Studies has concentrated on infancy. Its members argue that babies are much brighter than anyone had previously thought. Bruner and his colleagues believe that the infant is an active experimenter rather than simply a creature of habit. They discovered that young babies have expectations about what should happen in the world, and if these expectations are somehow violated, the infant will react by crying.

Professor Jerome Bruner of Harvard's Center for Cognitive Studies. (Fogg Art Museum, Harvard)

A good many psychological experiments are being performed on very young children nowadays in efforts to lift the amnesic veil that divides us from our infancy. The purpose is to answer a question that has tantalized science and philosophy for hundreds of years, the question of whether such a thing as the mind can be said to exist. Initially, psychology had been established to explore the mind, but in time many psychologists abandoned that aim. The concept of the mind involves a host of intangibles and non-observables, including thought, emotions, imagination, and will. In their efforts to get a grip upon what was at best a slippery discipline anyway, most American psychologists subscribed to the "behavioral" view that since the mind could not be studied scientifically, psychology should ignore it.

Within the last decade or so, however, a great deal of evidence has accumulated that suggests the behaviorists may have been too hasty. Some of this evidence comes from psychological experiments . . . But much of it comes from other fields such as ethology, anthropology, linguistics, information processing, and neurophysiology.

The last of the sciences to break free from their common origins in philosophy, psychology has always been subject to the shifting winds of philosophical doctrine. Philosophers debated the mind's nature for thousands of years, their speculations reaching their sharpest focus in the great ideological split between the rationalists and the empiricists. The rationalists, notably René Descartes and Immanuel Kant, maintained that humans were born with mental organizing principles. The mind took raw material furnished by the senses and shaped and organized it into thought in accordance with its own built-in structure. On the other hand, the empiricists, notably John Locke, contended that the newborn child had no such capacity. What mind he possessed was, in Locke's phrase, a *tabula rasa* — a blank slate — upon which experience wrote not only the contents of knowledge but the form as well.

The Writing on the Slate

Psychology attained its majority as a separate scientific discipline only about a century ago, at a time when empiricism was beginning its climb to dominance. The father of experimental psychology was the German physiologist Wilhelm Wundt, who set about analyzing the mind and perceptions, mainly through the technique of careful self-observation, or introspection. But by the early 1920's most American psychologists were following behaviorist John Watson in proclaiming that the scientific way to discover what had been written upon Locke's blank slate was by applying a stimulus of some kind to the organism — man or lower animal — and recording the ensuing response. From this, it was only a step to more radical forms of behaviorism, in which the stimulus-response paradigm is more than a produc-

Source: Tom Alexander. "Psychologists Are Rediscovering the Mind," *Fortune* (November 1970).

tive experimental method; it is regarded as the very basis for all behavior, of man or beast. In the view of the radical behaviorists, it was the organism's response to drives and stimuli (such as hunger) and to rewards and punishments (such as food or electric shocks) that ultimately would be found adequate to account for all learning, all emotions, all desires.

Among the implications of this view is that terms such as *mind, emotion, thought,* and *intention* are scientifically unproductive ways of talking about a mechanism basically akin in principle to a telephone switchboard or dialing system. Such a system would have incoming wires from the senses and outgoing wires to signal muscles to contract. At the birth of the organism, most of the circuits would be open, but with experience—i.e., conditioning or learning—connections would become more or less permanent. All behavior, therefore, is a proliferation of results of past history and present circumstances, but hardly different in kind from the human knee-jerk reflex or the automatic scratching motions of a dog whose back is rubbed.

In very recent years, however, behaviorism has been giving way to an entirely different school, called "cognitive" psychology. This school holds that the stimulus-response model is simplistic when it comes to actually describing why people do what they do. It suggests that psychologists have been arrogant, or perhaps naive, in dismissing the innate wellsprings of behavior. . . .

Still, the revisionism has by now proceeded to the point where even many former behaviorists have changed their beliefs or at least modified their position. Indeed, the most influential of modern behaviorists, Harvard's B. F. Skinner, has recently published a book, *Contingencies of Reinforcement,* in which he says that the simple stimulus-response model falls short as an explanation for behavior. To repair behaviorism, Skinner now emphasizes the mediation of what he calls "contingencies," which are complicating circumstances that determine when reward or punishment will or won't work in eliciting the associated response. And while still refusing adamantly to acknowledge the term "mind," Skinner does acknowledge that genetic endowment—shaped to be sure by ancestral environment—is an important determinant of variations in behavior.

The debate about the mind is far more than a mere squabble over terminology. It has implications for such crucial activities as child rearing, education, psychiatry, and perhaps the designing of society itself and the shaping of its goals and expectations. At the simple pedagogical level, the likelihood that humans have innate mental structures suggests that there might be better ways to design educational approaches suitable to these structures than the step-by-step programmed-learning techniques pioneered by disciples of Skinner. Much more encompassing is the sensitive question of "nature versus nurture." Even many of the cognitive psychologists still sidestep the question of whether differences in human intellectual achievement could have genetic as well as environmental origins. Their primary fear is that what they say could be used to buttress racism.

In even larger terms, the nativist viewpoint carries within itself both pessimistic and optimistic implications for the long-term fate of man. On the one hand, it raises the possibility that there are dark and ineradicable human traits, molded over millions of years of primal history, that are inimical to utopian hopes for mankind. On the other hand, the existence of an innately creative, nonmanipulable component in the mind implies that mankind cannot be permanently programmed by either circumstances or design—men may always have the latent capability to invent their way out of messes.

Substitutes for Mother Goose

A powerful source of evidence against the behaviorist point of view is the comparatively new field of ethology—the study of the natural behavior of animals. The most influential of the ethologists have been the Dutchman Niko Tinbergen and the Austrian Konrad Lorenz, whose animal studies focused attention on instinctive behavior, a topic absent from the concerns of the behaviorists. Ethological research suggests that far from being simple or incidental, instinct—defined as heritable patterns of behavior—actually dominates the lives of most creatures most of the time. The instincts can be extremely specific and well developed as in the case of newly hatched cuttlefish, which very expertly catches the first passing shrimp it sees. Or it can be less specific and imperfectly developed. A newly hatched gosling follows the first moving thing it spots—whether mother goose, rolling basketball, or passing ethologist—and after this initial "imprinting" the gosling can never be dissuaded from its chosen mother figure. But most of the instincts of the higher animals take the form of capacities and tendencies that require considerable practice to express. Examples of this are the birds' urge to song and perhaps the human urge to speech or thought.

The ethologists have also found highly evolved patterns of social behavior, including some that seem ceremonial. Most of these appear designed to express or deal with other instinctive urges, such as sex and aggression. Many of the social arrangements in primate troops resemble those in human cultures. In the case of nonhuman primates, at least, the design of these arrangements may be genetically determined, for even animals raised in captivity develop them. All this has naturally raised questions in the minds of the ethologists—and more recently in the minds of students of human behavior as well—as to just how much of human behavior has similar innate origins, developed during a long, evolutionary history as an ancient, tribal hunter-primate.

Of late, a number of young anthropologists—notably Lionel Tiger and Robin Fox—have been laying stress upon the large number of traits that most human cultures have in common. These include such practices as incest taboos, religious propensities, marriage, and the clubby fellowship of men in groups. The suspicion is gathering strength—though also amidst controversy—that far more human individual and cultural behavior than had ever been realized has its roots in our genes, not in chance or choice and certainly not in stimulus-response conditioning. The anthropologists have been issuing warnings that if we disregard such genetic roots in arranging our lives and societies, we may do so at our peril.

The sharpest frontal attack upon the radical behaviorists has come from, of all places, the department of linguistics at M.I.T., specifically from language scholar Noam Chomsky. Better known outside his field as a radical of another sort, a hero of the New Left, Chomsky is also at once a soft-spoken scholar and an outspoken intellectual gut fighter. Skinner incurred Chomsky's wrath in 1957 by publishing *Verbal Behavior,* a book that purported to extend stimulus-response conditioning as the explanation for the acquisition of language. As it happened, Chomsky himself was then beginning to revolutionize the stodgy field of linguistics by proposing some theories about innate language-generating faculties in human beings. In a long review of Skinner's book, Chomsky contended that Skinner's explanation was empty. First attracted to Chomsky's ideas by this attack upon their idol, many behaviorist psychologists have actually been swayed from behaviorism largely by the impact of those ideas.

The heart of Chomsky's thesis is a question at once obvious and subtle: if a child learns language only through the stimulus of hearing sentences spoken around him and through rewards for correct imitation, how is it that he can ever speak a sentence he has never heard? The force of the question is a little hard to appreciate at first, probably because of the trouble most of us have in attaining what Chomsky calls "psychic distance" from such familiar activities as language. Behavioral psychology seems unable to deal with the question. Moreover, the question expands into the larger question: how can we ever do *anything* we have not explicitly learned? In other words, how is creativity—whether in conversation, in art, in science, or in simple manual actions—possible in a mere stimulus-response mechanism?

Chomsky's suggested answer from the standpoint of the linguist is that every human child, far from being merely a stimulus-response switchboard, must be born with some elaborate kind of language-generating propensity and capacity. Thus equipped, a child is able to pick from the babble around him certain unconscious and extraordinarily complicated logical rules of "deep grammar" that apply to all human languages in common. These rules give human language its unique communicative flexibility—as opposed, say, to the primitive vocal signals of other creatures, which have fixed and narrow meanings — and they may be major components as well of that capacity called *thought*. In a sense, they would be akin to rules of mathematics that permit not only mathematical communication but also mathematical creativity as well. In any event, these rules of deep grammar appear far too complicated for a child to acquire during its brief language-learning period unless basic outlines of some kind are already present. Something else shapes our actions, it seems, besides simple switchboard connections accumulated through experience. Some psychologists are now prepared to call this something by the ancient designation *mind*.

Another major source of revisionism in psychology has been computer theory. In crude terms the digital computer resembles the telephone switchboard, being largely an agglomeration of electric switches. But the computer has two additional properties that make all the difference. One is the way the switches are wired together into a multiplicity of discrete circuits that can actually perform the function known as *logic*. The other ingredient is the "stored program" — the array of instructions that enables the machine to carry out complicated computing assignments automatically. Though programs take the physical form of, say, holes in punched cards or magnetized regions on a tape or other material, the real substance of any program, and the real product of the computing machine as well, is something intangible but undeniably "real" — information.

All of a sudden, the precedent of the computer gave psychologists new justification for talking about the very kinds of internal mental processes the behaviorists had shunned. Many psychologists who talk this way would agree with Cornell's Neisser: "The task of a psychologist trying to understand human cognition is analogous to that of a man trying to discover how a computer has been programmed."

There has been a special stimulative value in the various efforts to devise computer hardware and software that could stimulate what men do when they think or when they recognize visual or auditory patterns, e.g., speech, or handwriting, or objects in photographs. Some of Chomsky's

early research, for example, was performed in the course of government-sponsored efforts to achieve a special kind of pattern recognition, namely language translation. The potential value of such "artificial intelligence" and pattern-recognizing principles is at once obvious and incalculable. At the very least they would make possible devices such as typewriters that could transcribe spoken dictation and even robot slaves.

A Need for an Inner Pattern

But after years of effort on many fronts, employing the largest computers, the problems of pattern recognition — not to mention artificial intelligence — have eluded all but the simplest and narrowest applications. Time after time, the theorists of pattern recognition found themselves returning to a single underlying principle: any machine for recognizing patterns must employ some means of matching the outside pattern with an inner counterpart — a template or a set of expected features. The lesson is summed up by a leading cognitive psychologist, Jerome Bruner of Harvard: "People had been saying that the essential mechanism of the brain was the simple stimulus-response reflex, though even the digital computer doesn't work that way. But the moment they comprehended what it would take to set up a simple pattern-recognition program, they finally realized what they were talking about: brains had to be *this* complicated, at least!"

Confusion in the Cards

Harvard's Bruner, perhaps the most widely known name among U.S. cognitive psychologists, suggests that the mind employs two basic rules in perceiving and putting order into the cocktail-party confusion of ordinary existence. Both aim at the larger principle of economy in information processing. The first rule is "minimization of surprise." In general, people expect things to stay the same. Bruner and his colleagues have carried out amusing experiments that demonstrate the extent to which people prefer their expectations to contradictory evidence from their senses. In one, the experimenters used specially printed decks of playing cards, with some of the cards of the red suits printed in black ink. When one of the anomalous cards, say a black four of diamonds, was flashed upon the screen and subjects were asked what they had seen, they might at first identify it as a four of diamonds but then hedge when asked to try again. Most subjects began mixing the real image with the image of expectation; they would report after some hesitation that the projected image was "shadowy" or "purplish," or that they were not sure of the shape.

The second of Bruner's principles of information economy can be called "maximization of attention": at different times and circumstances, the mind can deploy its resources differently, depending upon purposes of the moment. A hungry motorist is aware of little on the highway but restaurant signs; a guest at a cocktail party is able to reconstruct one voice in the din.

Growth through Trouble

Though cognitive psychologists tend to stress the inner, order-forming capacities of the mind, most agree that these capacities get developed only through involvement with the outer world. The basic theoretical framework for the new outlook is one that the Swiss genius, Jean Piaget, has been elaborating in Geneva since the 1930's. Piaget's theories are a tight synthesis of Kantian rationalism and Lockean empiricism. He originally arrived at the synthesis in the course of observing the development of his own three children. (One reason these theories were long in taking hold in America was that his choice of methods and experimental subjects offended the sensibilities of many psychologists.)

Bruner, who has done a great deal to push Piaget's views here and test them experimentally, calls them the "trouble" theory of development. A child's intellectual growth, according to Piaget, proceeds through a succession of stages. In some respects these stages resemble the progress of any scientific discipline. The child, in effect, invents increasingly better intellectual models or theories about the world as he grows up. Each new version gets tested against reality through experience and experiment. The child stretches the current model as far as possible to accommodate new ob-

servations, but he ultimately abandons it after he has trouble reconciling it with the inescapable facts of life.

In general, the child's progress consists of going from a period in which the mind is dominated by actions the child can take upon objects in the outer world, through an intermediate period in which the actions and objects can be internally represented within the mind, to a final stage in which actions can be represented symbolically, in the form of words or even mathematical concepts. Piaget identifies five or more separate stages through virtually every child passes. Each stage, in effect, represents the mobilization of a new intellectual capability.

While most American cognitive psychologists accept the general outlines of Piaget's "trouble" theory, there are sharp differences over specifics. Bruner and some of his colleagues at Harvard's Center for Cognitive Studies disagree with Piaget over the number, and even the existence, of distinct developmental stages. They also disagree with Chomsky and others about whether there are, for example, separate mental faculties responsible for language. The Bruner group believes that human beings have a nonspecific order-generating propensity that develops into all the human faculties, including language, thought, and manual dexterity. But Piaget, Bruner, and most of the rest of the cognitive psychologists seem to agree on at least one thing: that even a very young child possesses an active, alert, intellectual capacity, plus drives to use and perfect it; comparable in their insistence, to the biological drives that are so basic a part of conventional stimulus-response psychology.

The Competence of the Infant

One way of assessing the extent to which the faculties of the mind are innate rather than acquired is to study the behavior of very young children. Recognizing that an infant has only limited means of expression and action, Bruner and his colleagues have been finding experimental ways to enable children to maximize what means they do possess. One device consists of a familiar pacifier that has been fitted with tiny sensors; these measure both the pressure of the child's lips and the vacuum caused by his sucking. These indications are then fed into a computer system that can be programmed to respond in various ways. For example, the child can exercise his sucking to change patterns in an array of colored lights or to operate a slide or movie projector.

By sucking, he can call up a picture on a screen, bring it into focus, and hold it there for study. The experimenters have found that the infant is eager and able to achieve clearer definition of the picture and effect other changes he prefers. One of the problems faced by the infant is that he cannot concentrate on his sucking and on the picture at the same time, and if he stops sucking the picture goes out of focus. It doesn't take long for the average baby to arrive at a solution to this dilemma: he simply averts his gaze while he sucks the picture into focus, then stops sucking long enough to sneak a quick peek before it slides out of focus again.

"All the evidence," says Bruner, "is going against the notion that a child is a passive organism being acted upon by the environment." Psychologists have traditionally overlooked the competence of the infant, and attributed all his performance to biological urges or environmental conditioning. Now the cognitive psychologists, working with younger and younger children, are finding that even at a very early age the infant will regulate his actions in the pursuit of goals shaped by his own mind. "So far," Bruner adds, "we haven't found an age at which this wasn't present."

Logic

One kind of reasoning is the syllogism.

Philosophers and mathematicians have been trying for a long time to develop formal rules of reasoning to describe how conclusions may be drawn from assumptions (Whitehead, 1925). Reasoning which conforms to these rules is called logical, while reasoning that does not conform is illogical. Children do not begin life using the rules of logic. They come to understand rules and fit their thinking into the pattern of rules as they grow and learn. By the time most young people reach college they have learned a form of reasoning called the *syllogism* (Copi, 1954). A syllogism contains three main parts:

1. A *premise*—which is a statement that may be proven as true or false through experiment or observation.
2. An *argument*—which is valid or not depending on whether it follows logical rules.
3. A *conclusion*—which can be true only if the premise is true and the logic is valid.

Simple syllogisms are diagrammed in Figure 7.3. There are two ways to evaluate a syllogism: by looking at its internal consistency for *validity* and at its premise for *truth*. If the conclusions are correctly drawn, the logic is said to be valid. However, the premise must be true and the logic must be valid for a conclusion to be true. Figure 7.3A—"All *A* is *B,* all women are mortal; all *C* is *A,* all housewives are women; therefore, all *C* is *B,* all housewives are mortal"—the syllogism is valid. *C* is contained within *A,* and *A* is contained within *B,* so the conclusion that all *C* is *B* is valid; as is shown in the figure, the outer circles surround the inner ones. The syllogism is correctly reasoned and the premise is true, so the con-

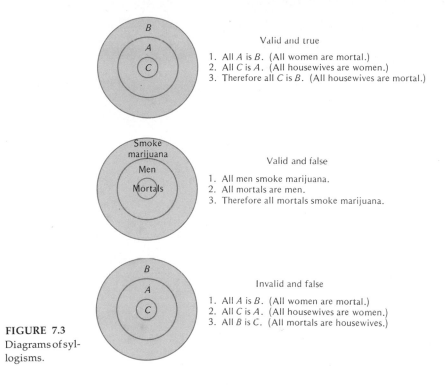

Valid and true

1. All *A* is *B*. (All women are mortal.)
2. All *C* is *A*. (All housewives are women.)
3. Therefore all *C* is *B*. (All housewives are mortal.)

Valid and false

1. All men smoke marijuana.
2. All mortals are men.
3. Therefore all mortals smoke marijuana.

Invalid and false

1. All *A* is *B*. (All women are mortal.)
2. All *C* is *A*. (All housewives are women.)
3. All *B* is *C*. (All mortals are housewives.)

FIGURE 7.3
Diagrams of syl-
logisms.

clusion is also true. The second syllogism (*see* Figure 7.3B) reads — "All men smoke marijuana; all mortals are men; therefore all mortals smoke marijuana." The statement follows logically from the premise, so the conclusion is valid. However, the premise is false at the present time so the syllogism is valid but false. Figure 7.3C makes the statement — "All *A* is *B* — All women are mortal," which is a true premise. Next, it takes an argument — "All *C* is *A* — All housewives are women" — and makes the conclusion that — "All *B* is *C* — All mortals are housewives." The conclusion does not follow the rules of logic and so must be invalid and false even though the premise is true.

Illogical Thinking

Children think
illogically.

One major problem with trying to think logically is that language and perceptions may disagree with a logical thought process. All of us use language to persuade and stimulate others; but parents sometimes teach their children not to think logically.

Children's opinions
affect their thinking.

The form of a statement affects whether a child will agree or disagree with it. If the premises of a syllogism are presented affirmatively, children tend to accept the conclusions, even if they are false. If one premise is positive and the other negative, children will usually accept the negative conclusions. Another important factor in reasoning is the child's opinions,

FIGURE 7.4
Jean Piaget.

(Black Star, Yves de Brau)

prejudices, and beliefs associated with a subject. We all tend to accept as valid those arguments which agree with our beliefs, even if the argument is false or invalid.

Children's Thoughts—Jean Piaget

Piaget has a theory of cognition.

To recapitulate, it's a long way from the thought processes of children to well-reasoned logic, and there is no well-articulated model of how the child acquires thinking. However, Piaget has some fascinating but tentative notions of how the child builds simple sensory-motor units into complex systems of behavior and thought. His observations about children are theoretical landmarks of cognitive development. Piaget (1950) believes that early sensory-motor experiences have lasting effects on later intellect. He thinks infants start with a few innate reflexes and construct sensory-motor functions and sophisticated cognitive operations from them. He also argues that such simple sensory inputs and responses are combined to produce symbolic processes. Once symbols are available the child can actively search, manipulate, and test his environment to produce new solutions to old problems. This active searching stands in sharp contrast to the very young infant's passive registration of events. Piaget believes the young child is similar to an inquiring scientist, who has elementary tools with which to understand the world. The child tests his model of the world by experimentation and observation, Piaget assumes.

Through an interest in genetic epistemology, the science of how man can know his world, Piaget began to study children's minds. He believes that how children know has profound implications for any theory of knowledge. Piaget distinguishes structures, functions, and the contents of a child's mind. *Structures* include cognitive abilities, ideas, or habits of the infant which change through time and experience. *Functions* are unchanging innate processes present from birth which are responsible for modifications of structure. *Content* is the particular set of input data the child is working on at the moment. The rules of adding would be a structure; the acquisition of the ability to add would be a function; and the numbers in a math problem would be content (*see* Figure 7.5).

In Chapter 3 we learned that Piaget believes the newborn possesses two functions which help him organize his world. One is called *assimilation* — new environmental events are placed into already existing structures — the other is accommodation — the infant is forced to develop new cognitive structures.

A third notion of Piaget's is *schema.* Schemata (plural of schema) may be cognitive structures, classes of similar actions or thoughts. A schema can be all the means by which one takes a cookie from a jar, or it may be the class of dogs. Schemata are developed through both experience and

Piaget assumes that there are structures, functions, and content to the mind.

Children acquire new structures.

Schema are mental operations.

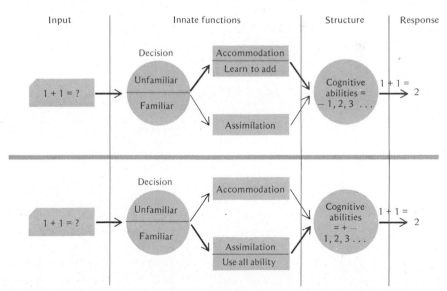

FIGURE 7.5 The elements in a child's mind that Jean Piaget believes lead him to learn to think about a math problem.

growth. Piaget stresses over and over that early sensory-motor abilities are the foundations for later intellect. This does not mean he is particularly interested in motor skills; rather he is concerned with the coordination of information from various senses into a common picture of the world. He uses the label sensory-motor to mean the coordination of visual and kinesthetic (the position of the body in space) information into a coherent whole.

On the basis of his extensive observations and experiments with children, Piaget has proposed several stages through which children's thought processes pass on the way to mature logic.

Stages of Children's Thought

Children think many objects are alive.

Piaget believes two intellectual traits characterize children's early thought: realism and animism. These tendencies occur because children can neither differentiate themselves from the world nor discriminate clearly between psychological and physical events. For a child, human experiences like thoughts, feelings, or wishes are constantly confused with objective reality. The child tends to see psychological events like thoughts, dreams, and names as physical entities. Piaget calls this *realism*. Another part of such self-centeredness is the tendency to give physical objects and events psychological attributes, to endow them with life or consciousness. This he calls *animism*.

Children believe that names are part of the object itself.

Young children are inclined to identify thought with the act of speaking and assume that a name is an essential part of an object. In one study Piaget asked children a series of questions about dreams, taking care whenever possible to avoid suggestion. He asked questions like: "Do you know what a dream is? Do you dream sometimes at night? Tell me where the dreams come from. While you dream, where is the dream? What do you dream with?" And so on. Here is part of his resulting record from the first stage:

> *Meter* (5:9):
> "Where does the dream come from?"
> "I think you sleep so well that you dream."
> "Does it come from us or from outside?"
> "From outside."
> "What do we dream with?"
> "I don't know."
> "With the hands . . . ? With nothing?"
> "Yes, with nothing."
> "When you are in bed and you dream, where is the dream?"
> "In my bed, under the blanket. I don't really know. If it was in my stomach (!) the bones would be in the way and I shouldn't see it."
> "Is the dream there when you sleep?"
> "Yes, it is in the bed beside me."

We tried suggestion:

"Is the dream in your head?"

"It is I that am in the dream: it isn't in my head (!) When you dream, you don't know you are in the bed. You know you are walking. You are in the dream. You are in bed, but you don't know you are."

"Can two people have the same dream?"

"There are never two dreams (alike)."

"Where do dreams come from?"

"I don't know. They happen."

"Where?"

"In the room and then afterward they come up to the children. They come by themselves."

"You see the dream when you are in the room, but if I were in the room too, should I see it?"

"No grownups (*les Messieurs*) don't ever dream."

"Can two people ever have the same dream?"

"No, never."

"When the dream is in the room, is it near you?"

"Yes, there!" (pointing to 30 cms. in front of his eyes)

(Piaget, 1929, pp. 97–98).

Children gradually restrict animism.

Another study by Piaget concerned the types of objects a child will classify as alive. Piaget discovered a gradual restriction of the objects a child is willing to believe live. A similar investigation was devoted to the child's classification of consciousness—thought, feeling, intention, and so on—to various types of objects. The questions were: "If I pull off this button, will it feel it? Does the sun know it gives light? Would a table feel it if I were to prick it?"

Piaget suggested four stages of classification of consciousness:

1. Almost any object is potentially conscious, given the right conditions. For example, a stone may normally be considered nonfeeling, but it will "feel it" when moved. Piaget appears to have found no children willing to assert that all objects are at all times conscious.
2. Later, the potential for consciousness is generally attributed only to objects that regularly possess some kind of movement or whose special function is movement. A bicycle and the wind may feel, but a stone cannot.
3. In the third stage only objects capable of spontaneous motion are believed to be conscious. The sun and wind are aware, but a bicycle no longer is.
4. Finally, the child attributes consciousness only to people and animals.

Here is an interesting example of spontaneously expressed animism:

We hung a metal box from a double string and placed it in front of Vel, in such a way that, on letting go of the box, the string unwound making the box turn round and round. "Why does it turn?"

"Because the string is twisted."
"Why does the string turn?"
"Why?"
"Because it wants to be unwound (it wants to resume its original position, in which the string was unwound)."
"Does the string know it is twisted?"
"Yes."
"Why?"
"Because it wants to untwist itself, it knows it's twisted!"
"Does it really know it is twisted?"
"Yes, I am not sure."
"How do you think it knows?"
"Because it feels it is all twisted."
(Piaget, 1929, pp. 175–176.)

Piaget organizes the growth of a child's mind into four periods—the sensory-motor, the pre-operational, the concrete operational, and the period of formal operations.

The sensory-motor period is about coordination.

SENSORY-MOTOR PERIOD—BIRTH TO 2 YEARS   Piaget believes the newborn baby does not differentiate himself from the environment but simply uses his reflexes. Over the first twenty-four months the baby begins to use thought and imagination, shows the beginning of foresight, and gains the ability to predict the consequences of his actions.

The preoperational period is about perception.

PREOPERATIONAL PERIOD—2 TO 6 YEARS   During the second period the child shifts from complete self-centeredness, or egocentrism, to a modest appreciation of other points of view. However, he is constantly misled by appearances, static states, and the rush of his own undisciplined illogic. The result is at best confusion and at worst total illogic.

The concrete-operational period concerns intuition.

CONCRETE OPERATIONAL PERIOD—7 TO 11 YEARS   During this third period Piaget believes the child overcomes his illogic by growing less self-centered, learning to handle changes as well as static conditions, and breaking loose from reliance on appearances. The result of this maturing is the development of a rudimentary logical mind.

Formal operations are logical.

FORMAL OPERATIONS—12 YEARS PLUS   In this final period children begin to use formal rules of thought. They can now formulate and test hypotheses and follow systems of deductive logic to their conclusion. Not all people reach this stage of development.

Cognition is cumulative.

Piaget's theory of thought assumes that earlier stages are incorporated into later ones and that this incorporation produces intelligence where one stage builds into the next higher stage and so on to the limits of the person's intelligence. A dominant feature of the sensory-motor period is the child's integration of various sensory inputs into one coherent set.

During the sensory-motor period an infant develops the concepts of time and space, objects, and some notion of causality (*see* Chapter 3 on sensory-motor growth). In the next period Piaget believes the child builds on these simple abilities in an attempt to understand his world.

The Nature of Preoperational Thought—2 to 6 Years

Young children are egocentric.

EGOCENTRISM   Preoperational thought is primitive, confused, and rigid because it is the infant's first real attempt at thinking. What sort of primitive characteristics does preoperational thought possess? They are first of all egocentric, as were the sensory-motor actions of the infant. This *egocentrism* is shown dramatically when the child must at the same time look at a three-dimensional display from one position and draw the way it would look from another angle. A common response of the preoperational child is to describe his own perspective, no matter what the task calls for.

Young children cannot take another's view.

Suppose a preoperational child is shown the three-dimensional display of mountains pictured in Figure 7.6 and is asked to draw it from an imagined position. He will always draw the view he sees in front of him. He cannot take another position or imagine that his current view might change if his position varies. The preoperational child feels no need to apply logic or to look for internal consistency in his thoughts. Only through a long series of social and environmental experiences, coupled with growth, does he emerge as a primitive logician who can take another's view.

(a)   X

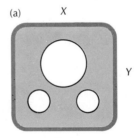

Y

Top
View

FIGURE 7.6
If a preoperational child is shown the three-dimensional display in (a) from the top view, and is asked to draw it from his position at X, he will draw the view shown in (b). If he is asked to draw the same display (still standing at X) from the imagined position Y, he will not produce (c) but will again draw the view from X.

(b)

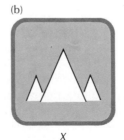

X

Child's
View

(c)

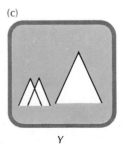

Y

Children center on
one aspect of a
problem.

CENTRATION   A second characteristic of preoperational children is that they concentrate on one feature while neglecting other important aspects of a problem. This is called *centering*. The preoperational child is often wrong because he cannot consider other aspects of a situation that may compensate for the distorting effect of a single dominant perceptual factor. For example, while admitting that two identical containers (*see* Figure 7.7 *A* and *D* have the same quantity of liquid, the child will deny their equality if he watches the contents of *A* being poured into the tall thin container, *B*, or into a short broad container, *C*. The preoperational child will almost always insist that the content of *B* is now greater than that of *A* because he is centering on the height of *B*, to him this glass contains more liquid because it is tall. Alternately, he may center on the width of *B* and say it contains less liquid because it is thin. The preoperational child fails to consider both height and width, and does not see that change in height may be compensated for by a simultaneous change in width. He cannot process information from two sources at the same time; as a result he does not understand that quantity or weight will not change simply because of the changes in the shape of the container.

FIGURE 7.7
Preoperational children (before about seven years of age) concentrate (*center*) on one aspect of the tall jar or the short, wide jar; they either say the glass (*B* or *C*) contains less, if they are centered on thinness or shortness; or that it contains more, if they are centered on tallness or wideness, than the original jar. The inability to consider two factors at the same time characterizes the preoperational child.

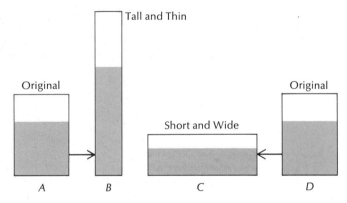

Young children attend
only to static states.

STATES AND TRANSFORMATIONS   A third characteristic of preoperational thought is the child's attention to states rather than transformations. He responds to successive patterns rather than to the alterations by which one state gradually changes into another. The experiments in which liquids are poured from one container to another may be used to illustrate this process. There is an initial state, *A*; some transformation; and a final state, *B*. The transformation of pouring *A* into *B* is lost to the preoperational child, so he can only base his judgment on the initial and final states. Preoperational thought attends to static conditions, but cannot link successive states into a coherent sequence. This process reflects a limitation on the ability of the young child to handle complex information-processing. Because of this limitation, he selects a few simple events to code, and the result is particular attention to end states rather than changes. Later, the child develops more complex information-processing rules, and then he can include both the initial state and a transformation into a single thought. With these more advanced processing rules comes a gradual understanding of logically coherent systems and the notion of conservation (retaining the same amount of liquid, for example, even though the shape of the container changes).

Young children cannot reverse their thought processes.

REVERSIBILITY   Another characteristic of preoperational thought is its nonreversibility. For Piaget, a cognitive organization is reversible if the child can come up with a train of thought, and then return through the same steps to his original premise. If a thought process is not reversible, the child cannot regain the beginning state of the logical process once he has carried out part of the chain. One limitation of the preoperational child is his inability to see that one change may compensate for another, and thus produce an underlying lack of real change. The more mature concrete operational child's thought sequence is flexible and can consider several characteristics of the situation at the same time. As we have learned, the perceptually-oriented processes of early preoperational thought are not *reversible*, because the preoperational child centers on single states. For example, the preoperational child cannot understand that conservation of a quantity of liquid is insured because a reverse transformation is possible which will reproduce the original state. He could pour the liquid from a short wide jar back into a tall, thin one; these two transformations exactly cancel each other, showing that the quantity of liquid has remained the same.

Concrete Operational Thought — 7 to 12 Years

The concrete-operational child is more mature mentally.

The preoperational child is more sophisticated than the sensory-motor infant, and the concrete-operational child represents still another advance. His thought processes become even more stable and integrated than is true of less mature children. Concrete operations are flexible, consistent cognitive structures, which are not full of the perplexing contradictions that plague preoperational children. Let us consider an example of how concrete operations might influence a child's understanding of liquids poured into different-shaped vessels. As we have seen, the preoperational child believed that appearance is reality. He was centered on the last state of a transformation and erred according to the perceptual dominance of a single characteristic. The concrete-operational child devotes more attention to transformations; and he can coordinate and reverse his thoughts. These new abilities help him to see that the liquid is unchanged in different vessels. The same improvement in thinking is visible in other cases. The concrete-operational child's thoughts are decentered, reversible, coordinated schema. The final step is to produce logical systems which are general in nature. Consider some studies in concrete operations.

THE PRIMARY ADDITION OF CLASSES   Considerable evidence is available concerning addition of sets or classes. Piaget and Barbel Inhelder have shown that the ability to add single sets or classes is present in the late concrete-operational child, but not in the preoperational child. The child with mature concrete operations can develop rough classifications, combine elementary classes into superordinate classes in a hierarchy, and reverse this process by decomposing higher-order sets into their parts. As an example, suppose a ten-year-old child is given twenty wooden beads (*see* Figure 7.8), seventeen brown and three white ones. He is asked: "Can you make a longer necklace with the brown beads or with the *wooden* beads?" The younger child would insist that the *brown* beads make a longer necklace, because there are only three *white* ones. Piaget interprets this to mean that the young child has no reversible system of classes. The evidence is that although Piaget previously established that the child knows *all* the beads are wooden, the child has forgotten this fact. When his attention is directed toward the brown beads, he forgets about wooden beads as a class because he is working at the perceptual level, and only brown and white beads remain for his comparison. He cannot reconstitute the perceptually absent class "wooden."

Older children can classify on the basis of verbal cues.

FIGURE 7.8
This experimental situation is presented to a child to test for primary addition of classes. The preoperational child says that there are more brown beads than white ones. The correct answer to the question is that there are more *wooden* beads, since all beads are wooden.

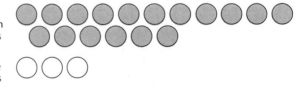

1. There are 20 wooden beads here.

17 brown beads

3 white beads

2. The child is asked whether there are more brown beads or more wooden beads.

MULTIPLICATION OF CLASSES   Classes can be multiplied and divided as well as added and subtracted. Suppose we take a group of people and divide it into subclasses according to skin color (white, black, yellow). We can take the *same* group of people and subdivide them according to where they live (urban, suburban, rural) or by sex (male, female). Once these classes are made up, one can logically multiply a member of one class by a member of the other (*see* Figure 7.9). The result of this multiplication is the logical product of intersection (the largest class where two or more characteristics appear in common). Thus, one can perform operations like determining the class of people who are white, male, and live in a city; or people who are yellow, female, and live in the suburbs.

Concrete-operational children can perform logical intersections.

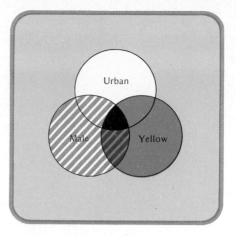

FIGURE 7.9
A set of Venn diagrams which illustrate the multiplication of classes. In this case the intersection of urban, yellow, and male is colored black.

Children can classify by two attributes.

A number of experiments have looked at class multiplication. Piaget studied the simple operation of one-to-one correspondence, the most fundamental class multiplication. He has also performed a series of experiments in which a child is presented with a horizontal row of forms that meet at right angles with a vertical column of differing colors (*see* Figure 7.10). The child's task is to determine which picture should be placed at the intersections. Since the picture in question will be in both a row and a column, it must contain both class attributes—form and color. In this example the correct intersection is a yellow square. The mastery of this simple matrix problem comes at around eight years of age, but complex class multiplications come a few years later.

Transitivity occurs about 8 years of age.

COMBINATION OF ASYMMETRICAL RELATIONS Operations can be performed upon the *asymmetrical relations* between two or more classes; for example *A* is smaller than *B*, higher than *B*, and so on. The operation

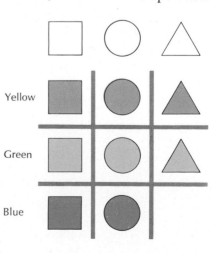

FIGURE 7.10
The diagram shows multiplication of classes. The child's task is to construct the intersections of form and color. For example, the first intersection should produce a yellow square, the second a yellow circle, and so on. If the child can combine the characteristics of a row and a column into a single class, he understands simple multiplication of classes.

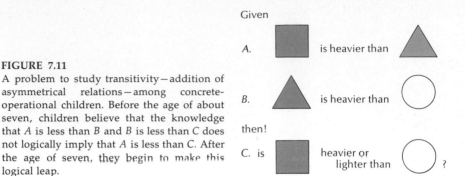

FIGURE 7.11
A problem to study transitivity—addition of asymmetrical relations—among concrete-operational children. Before the age of about seven, children believe that the knowledge that *A* is less than *B* and *B* is less than *C* does not logically imply that *A* is less than *C*. After the age of seven, they begin to make this logical leap.

requires some understanding of transitivity. *Transitivity* implies that if *A* is smaller than *B*, and *B* is smaller than *C*, then *A* must be smaller than *C*. Asymmetrical relations illustrate ordered differences between terms— differences because smaller than *C* indicates a way in which *B* differs from *C*, ordered because the differences go in a special direction (*A* is smaller than *B*).

Younger children cannot comprehend transitivity.

Piaget and Inhelder have studied this problem extensively. Usually the subject is presented with three objects of different shapes and is allowed to compare only two at a time (*see* Figure 7.11). The younger child does two unusual things with this task. First, for a set of three objects *A*, *B*, and *C*, he is willing to believe they are a complete ordered set after having established only that *A* is smaller than *B* and *A* is smaller than *C*. Younger children apparently worry about the ends of a sequence but not the middle. The younger child is also unsure that *A* is smaller than *C* can be shown from the knowledge of only *A* is smaller than *B* and *B* is smaller than *C*.

Classification of ordered series is very difficult.

MULTIPLICATION OF RELATIONS   Suppose a child is shown eight dolls of differing size and eight boxes of differing lengths and is then asked to arrange the dolls and boxes so that each doll finds its own home (*see* Figure 7.12). The task involves one-to-one multiplication of two series. If the dolls grow larger from *A* to *H* and the boxes from 1 to 8, the correct one-to-one correspondence between toys and boxes would be *A*1, *B*2, . . . , *H*8. The ability to form such a correspondence is achieved late in the con- crete-operational period.

Logical Thinking—12 Years Plus

Logic is the goal of cognitive growth.

Piaget believes that the adolescent mind can be described as a logical computing machine that manipulates abstract structures. He argues that logical structures make up the ideal patterns toward which all living systems grow. He belives also that logic provides a useful test of how

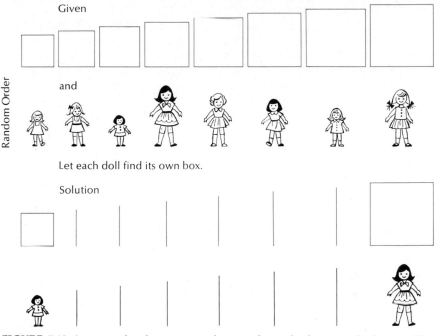

FIGURE 7.12 An example of a game used to test for multiplication of relations. The child's task is to match the dolls to their own homes.

mature thought is organized. However, logic is not a totally accurate model of the adult mind. The formal operational adolescent still has some irrational or illogical moments. Piaget simply argues that logic is an ideal toward which the mind develops rather than a description of all its operations.

Piaget's writings are diverse.

At the moment Piaget's model of the mind is more a frame of reference than a precise theory. The data necessary to support his logical system as a theory of cognition exist only in fragments, but the theory has suggested some interesting experiments. Consider first the formal properties of the theory and then some evidence.

Piaget's theory has four properties.

The basic properties of Piaget's logical theory resemble algebraic rules. They are:

1. *Composition*—the product resulting from the combination of any elements is itself an element which can enter into other logical operations. In the equation $a + b = c$ the c can also be a part of the equation $c + d = e$.
2. *Associativity*—the sum of a series of elements is independent of the way in which they are grouped. $a + (b + c) = (a + b) + c$.
3. *General Identity*—there is one and only one element (the identity element) that, when added to any other element whatsoever, leaves the

other element unchanged. Piaget defines this element somewhat arbitrarily as the equation $0 + 0 = 0$ (the sum of two null, or zero, classes).

4. *Reversibility* — for each and every element there is one and only one element, called its inverse, which yields the identity element when added to the element. $a + (-a) = 0$.

Adolescents can solve some logical problems.

There is evidence from adolescents concerning only some of these processes (*see* Advanced Topics at the end of the book under "Cognition"). One logical problem is the yellow-liquid puzzle pictured in Figure 7.13.

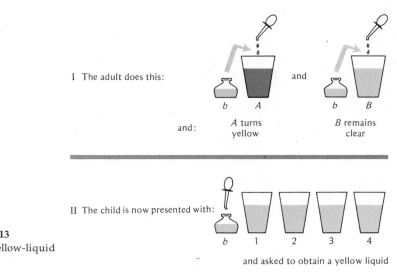

I The adult does this: and

b   A   b   B

and: A turns   B remains
yellow   clear

II The child is now presented with:

b   1   2   3   4

FIGURE 7.13
Piaget's yellow-liquid
problem.

and asked to obtain a yellow liquid

The experimenter shows the adolescent that $A + b$ turns yellow, but $B + b$ remains clear. The adolescent's task is to find A among the four pails of liquid presented in the bottom part of the figure. This particular problem is relatively easy, but later problems in the series require the mixing of two or more unknown liquids to produce a specific effect. For these more complex problems only those adolescents who systematically mix liquids are successful.

Is logic innate?

How do children gain logic? Is it maturation of innate ideas or the accumulation of habits? No one is sure.

Cognitive psychology studies rule learning.

Psychology is moving away from emphasis on stimulus-response associations toward a theory of mind. This new school of psychology is concerned with cognitive processes like grammar, perception, thinking, and competence rather than simple habit. Cognitive psychology is interested in innate organization, complex rule learning, and forceful interaction between the child and his environment; it puts less emphasis on learning, simple habits, and passive acceptance of environmental forces. The conflict between innate organization and learned behaviors and between active or passive relations with the environment will probably not be settled for some time. It is clear that children enter the world with much written on their minds and not with the blank tablet assumed by early behaviorists. There is also good evidence that these early innate structures can be modified by experience. The important question to ask is how much early organization is there and what are the limits and consequences of environmental influences on these innate structures?

Summary

A compelling theory of cognitive development has been outlined over past decades by one of the world's most influential psychologists, Jean Piaget. He argues that children develop sequentially through four major stages of mental functioning by a process that he calls equilibrium. This is a balance between existing cognitive structures to understand a problem and acquiring new mental operations to help solve the difficulty. According to Piaget's theory, the four major periods of cognitive functioning are: the sensory-motor period, during which the child is preoccupied with coordinating his sensory and motor abilities; the preoperational stage, during which perception and language are dominant forces; the concrete-operational period, during which the child acquires the ability to think intuitively; and the period of formal operations, during which adolescents acquire the ability to think logically and understand the scientific method.

SUGGESTED ADDITIONAL READINGS

Kohlberg, L., and E. Turiel. *Research in Moral Development: The Cognitive-Developmental Approach.* New York: Holt, Rinehart and Winston, 1971.

Piaget, J. *Logic and Psychology.* New York: Basic Books, 1957.

————. *The Origins of Intelligence in Children.* New York: International Universities Press, 1952.

————. *Play, Dreams and Imitation in Childhood.* C. Gattegno and F.M. Hodgson, trs. New York: Norton, 1951.

8 Intelligence and Creativity

The Intelligence Test
Test Characteristics
  Reliability
  Validity
  Standardization
Tests of Ability
  Infant Tests
  Preschool Tests
  School-age Tests
  Adult Tests

Group Differences in IQ
  Mental Retardation
  The Mentally Gifted
  IQ and Age
  IQ and Social Class
The IQ Debate
  Environmental Debate
  Learning Ability and Intelligence
IQ and Learning
Creativity
Summary

PREVIEW

Alfred Binet laid the foundations of intelligence testing when he began measuring mental abilities by asking questions. Instead of simply recording sensory processes, such as the thresholds for hearing or seeing, and then trying to reconstruct intelligence from these, Binet directly tested memory, imagery, comprehension, and esthetic appreciation. The result was a mental test which can quite accurately predict which children should be placed in special classes for slow learners, and which can profit from accelerated programs. Currently, intelligence testing is a major concern of schools, employers, and many psychologists. Why is it important to measure IQ? Primarily the answer is that schools must decide whether a particular child will profit most from one course of instruction or another, and that employers want to hire workers who can successfully perform their jobs.

There is considerable controversy about exactly what IQ tests really measure, but there is almost total agreement that objective tests are the most valid way known to predict success in school or on the job. Scores on standard tests of intelligence significantly increase the precision with which administrators can match human talents and human opportunities. The alternative to mental testing is an open-admission system and in too many cases failure for those students and workers who cannot achieve a minimal standard of excellence.

Intelligence testing is
controversial.

Recently, intelligence testing has created heated controversy. The difficulties stem from what psychologists and statisticians call individual and group differences and the question of whether intelligence tests are fair and accurate. Figure 8.1 shows that in the total population of the United States some people make much higher scores on tests of intelligence than others do. These variations within the total population are called individual differences, which simply means that all people are not the same. In addition, this figure shows that various subgroups of the total population are also unequal. For example, accountants score almost fifty IQ points higher on tests of intelligence as compared with farm hands and teamsters. Group differences in tested IQ abound. Do these differences reflect true variation in ability, or are they simply testing errors? The answers are complex and controversial, but they are beginning to emerge as research continues.

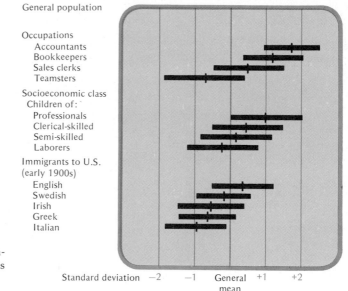

FIGURE 8.1
Averages and distributions of intelligence test scores for various groups.

The Intelligence Test

The debate is about
economic and social
rewards.

The disagreements about IQ tests reflect concern with economic, social, and educational goals—economic, because people who score higher on IQ tests often earn more money or have more prestige in our society; social, because the upper class generally makes higher scores than the lower class; and educational, because adults who complete more years of school score higher on tests of intelligence than less-educated people do. Some critics of IQ testing claim that all tests are culturally or racially biased, and are therefore unreliable and irrelevant to real life.

Richard Herrnstein outlines the history of IQ testing in the reading that accompanies the "Profile." Herrnstein considers the problems of current measures and argues for continued development and use of the intelligence test.

Intelligence is not a single factor.

Two types of evidence argue against a single factor comprising intelligence. One is that several different and often independent kinds of intelligence can be found (*see* Table 8.1). The other is the existence of feeble-minded persons who have one highly-developed talent. To illustrate: A six-year-old boy could give days of the week for dates from 1880 to 1950, could add ten or twelve two-digit numbers as quickly as they were spoken, and could spell words forward *and* backward. However, he failed in a regular school curriculum and earned an IQ of only 50 on the Stanford-Binet Intelligence Test.

TABLE 8.1   Seven kinds of intelligence found among adults

1.	Number	The ability to add, subtract, multiply, and divide. This ability is not the same as arithmetic-reasoning ability, because it involves only the four fundamental arithmetic processes.
2.	Word fluency	The ability to write and speak with ease. This ability is not the same as verbal meaning (the next primary ability) because a person who knows very few words may be able to use them fluently, whereas a person who knows many words may be halting in his speech.
3.	Verbal meaning	The understanding of ideas in word form.
4.	Memory	The ability to retain and revive impressions or to recall and recognize past experiences.
5.	Reasoning	The ability to solve complex problems, profit from experience, and plan new activities based on past experience.
6.	Spatial perception	The ability to perceive size and spatial relationships correctly.
7.	Perceptual speed	The ability to identify stimulus objects quickly. In developing reading skill, for example, it is necessary to identify entire words without carefully examining each letter in the word.

(After Thurstone, 1938)

One theory of intelligence proposes both a general and several specific factors.

A number of researchers believe that the theoretical structure of intelligence can be diagrammed as overlapping circles. This model assumes that there is both a general component to intelligence and several more specific mental abilities (Butcher, 1968). Some developmental psychologists also argue that intellect begins as a general ability and becomes more specific with maturity. There is no conclusive evidence for this notion, but analyses of correlation of intelligence with age make it plausible. If there are several special abilities in addition to general intelligence, then a single IQ score will not tell the complete story of a child's abilities.

Portrait

Alfred Binet was born in Nice, France, in 1857. While he was still a small boy his mother moved him to Paris, where he later studied law. However, Binet found he was more interested in the natural sciences and medicine, since his father and grandfather had both been physicians. Gradually Binet's interests shifted more and more toward the study of psychological problems. His early interest in associationism and hypnotism combined with his training in biology and medicine to produce great originality in his work. Many of Binet's early publications were about abnormal behavior, but his major contribution to psychology was the mental test. In a single stroke he broke with the empirical tradition of measuring sensory keenness and attempted to assess higher mental functions directly. Rather than starting with simple elements and adding them together, Binet drew on his experience as a clinician and tried to measure the human mind.

In 1904 the Minister of Public Instruction in Paris appointed a commission to deal with the problem of subnormal children. The commission's task was to find a way of identifying these intellectually subnormal children so that they could be placed in special classes. Binet was a member of the commission and he became distressed about the vagueness of their discussions concerning mental abilities. He decided, therefore, to develop a scientific measure of intellect. In 1905 Binet and a fellow researcher named Theophile Simon published the first battery of tests they had written. The instruments were so successful that by 1911, when Binet died, the Binet-Simon scale was used all over the world with one exception. It was not until the 1920's that France rediscovered the intelligence test.

The French psychologist Alfred Binet was photographed by C. H. Stoelting Co. of Chicago, Illinois. (The Bettmann Archive, Inc.)

The measurement of intelligence forced its way into America's public consciousness during World War I, when almost two million soldiers were tested by the Army and categorized as "alpha" and "beta," for literates and illiterates respectively. The lasting effect of that innovation has not been the surprise at learning that the average American soldier had an intelligence equal to that of a thirteen year old, or that artillery officers were substantially brighter than medical officers, or any of the myriad other statistical curiosities. Even if those facts are still as true as they were in 1918, the lasting effect has been the mere use of the tests and their serious consideration by responsible people. For intelligence tests, and the related aptitude tests, have more and more become society's instrument for the selection of human resources. Not only for the military, but for schools from secondary to professional, for industry, and for civil service, objective tests have cut away the traditional grounds for selection—family, social class, and, most important, money. The traditional grounds are, of course, not entirely gone, and some social critics wonder if they do not lurk surreptitiously behind the scenes in our definition of mental ability.

But at least on the face of it there is a powerful trend toward "meritocracy"—the advancement of people on the basis of ability, either potential or fulfilled, measured objectively.

Lately though, the trend has been deplored, often by the very people most likely to reap the benefits of measured intellectual superiority. More than a few college professors and admissions boards and even professional testers have publicly condemned mental testing as the basis for selection of people for schools or jobs. The IQ test, it is said with fervor, is used by the establishment to promote its own goals and to hold down the downtrodden—those nonestablishment races and cultures whose interest and talents are not fairly credited by intelligence tests. These dissenting professors and testers are naturally joined by spokesmen for the disadvantaged groups. We should, these voices say, broaden the range of humanity in our colleges (to pick the most frequent target) by admitting students whose low college entrance examination scores might otherwise have barred the way. For if the examinations merely fortify an arbitrarily privileged elite in its conflict with outsiders, we must relinquish them. The ideals of equality and fraternity must, according to this view, take precedence over the self-interest of the American-Western European middle class.

The issue is intensely emotional. It is almost impossible for people to disagree about the pros and cons of intelligence testing and long avoid the swapping of oaths and anathema. Yet should not the pros and cons be drawn from facts and reason rather than labels and insults? For example, is it true that intelligence tests embody only the crass interests of Middle America, or do they draw on deeper human qualities? Is the IQ a measure of inborn ability, or is it the outcome of experience and learning? Can we tell if there are ethnic and racial differences in intelligence, and if so, whether they depend upon nature or nurture? Is there only one kind of intelligence, or are there many, and if more than one, what are the relations among them? If the tests are inadequate—let us say, because they overlook certain abilities or because they embody arbitrary cultural values—how can they be improved? For those who have lately gotten their information about testing from the popular press, it may come as a surprise that these hard questions are neither unanswerable nor, in some cases, unanswered. The measurement of intelligence is psychology's most telling accomplishment to date. Without intending to belittle other psychological ventures, it may be fairly said that nowhere else—not in psychotherapy, educational reform, or consumer research—has there arisen so potent an instrument as the objective measure of intelligence. No doubt intelligence testing is imperfect, and may even be in some sense imperfectible, but there has already been too much success for it to be repudiated on technical grounds alone. If intelligence testing is to change, it must change in light of what is known, and more is known than most might think.

Mental testing was one of many responses within psychology to Darwin's theory of evolution. In fact, the connection here is intimate and direct, for the idea of measuring mental ability objectively was first set forth by Francis Galton, the younger cousin of Charles Darwin. Far more versatile (perhaps smarter) than his great cousin, Galton was a geographer, explorer, journalist, mathematician, eugenicist (he coined the term), and articulate essayist. In 1869, just a decade after Darwin launched modern biology with the *Origin of Species,* Galton published *Hereditary Genius,* which applied evolutionary thinking to the question of intellect. Galton noted, first, that men varied greatly in their intellectual capacity and, second, that various kinds of excellence run in families, suggesting that the basis of intelligence may be inherited. Going back through British history, Galton found that judges, statesmen, prime ministers, scientists, poets, even outstanding wrestlers and oarsmen tended, for

each kind of endeavor, to be related by blood. The eminent families of Great Britain were taken as evidence of superior human strains, comparable to the natural biological variations that figure so prominently in the doctrine of evolution. Today, our sensitivity to the role of the environment (not to mention such mundane complications as money and family connections) make us skeptical of his evidence. Nevertheless, in the first flush of Darwinian social theorizing, Galton called for constructive change. The inheritance of human capacity implied "the practicability of supplanting inefficient human stock by better strains," and led him "to consider whether it might not be our duty to do so by such efforts as may be reasonable, thus exerting ourselves to further the ends of evolution more rapidly and with less distress than if events were left to their own course."

Galton was not much more content with the genealogical approach to mental ability than are we today. Within a few years, he was trying to test mental ability directly, but the problem was how to do it. In 1882, Galton set up a small laboratory in a London museum where people could, for a fee, have their hearing, vision, and other senses tested. Galton knew that mental defectives—idiots and imbeciles—often lacked sensory acuity, and he guessed that there might be a reasonably consistent relation between intelligence and sensory keenness in general. As it turned out, his hunch was wrong, or at least not right enough to be useful as a way of testing on a large scale.

Galton was soon just one of many scientists searching for a practical intelligence test, with no one much worried at this point about the ultimate definition of intelligence. Intuition and common sense set the standards as the few simple measures of sensory acuity gave way to a host of tests, some sensory and others drawing on other psychological processes. An American psychologist named James McK. Cattell coined the phrase "mental test" in 1890 in an article recounting his studies at the University of Pennsylvania on the mental abilities of students. In addition to simple sensory function, Cattell measured color discrimination, time perception, accuracy of hand movement, and memory; and he collected descriptions of imagery. People no doubt differed, but it was hard to know what to make of the differences. By the mid-1890s, testing had attracted so much attention that professional organizations began taking note of it. The newly founded American Psychological Association formed a committee in 1895 "to consider the feasibility of cooperation among the various psychological laboratories in the collection of mental and physical statistics"; in 1896 the American Association for the Advancement of Science instructed a committee of its own "to organize an ethnographic survey of the white race in the United States." The quotations in both cases are Professor Cattell's words; he was a member of both committees and was determined that the ethnographic survey for AAAS include some of APA's mental (and physical) tests.

For all of the ferment, it was not yet certain that anything useful was brewing. There was spirit and energy in abundance, but there were as yet no indisputably good tests. It took the work of a French psychologist named Alfred Binet to make intelligence testing practical. In a key article written in 1895, Binet and his junior collaborator, Victor Henri, argued for mental testing based not on sensory or motor functions but on the psychological processes thought to be involved in intelligence. Instead of supposing that being smart is the outcome of having keen senses or speedy reactions, Binet argued that intelligence operates at its own level and that, therefore, a proper test must engage the person at that very level. As for what such tests might be, Binet, like everyone else in 1895, was just guessing. The article suggested a variety: tests of memory, mental imagery, imagination, attentiveness, mechanical and verbal comprehension, suggestibility, aesthetic appreciation, moral sensibility, the capacity to sustain muscular effort, and visual judgment of distance.

Binet criticized his contemporaries for their preoccupation with sensory and other simple processes, which, although fulfilling their desire for exactitude in measurement, had sacrificed the still more salient need for relevance. For Binet, exactitude was secondary. His pragmatism directed him to tests that sorted people out—for, whatever intelligence is, it varies from person to person. The sensory data did not distinguish among people as sharply as intuition required for a test of intelligence. Binet committed himself to seeking the tests that would do so, which was an undertaking that occupied the rest of his life. In the following ten years, Binet and his collaborators worked on mental testing at the psychology laboratory of the Sorbonne, using as their subjects mainly children from the schools of Paris and its suburbs.

The use of children was a happy accident, for it focused attention on the chronology of intelligence. Of all the countless ways one may want to distinguish between smarter and duller people, it may not seem especially insightful to choose the simple fact that during the first fifteen or so years of life, age confers intelligence (on the average). Thus, if an intellectual task sorted children according to their age, then it might properly be included in an intelligence test. In one experiment, for example, Binet tested over five hundred schoolchildren by reading them a sentence and then asking them to write down as much of the sentence as they could remember. Between the ages of nine and twelve (the ages tested), each successive grade of student did better, albeit slightly, than the grade younger. From this, Binet knew that the "sentence-reproduction test" could be taken as one measure of mental capacity. And knowing that, he could say that if two children of equal age differed in their sentence-reproduction scores, they were to some degree different in intelligence. One such test was, however, far from a usable measure of general intelligence, as Binet well knew.

As the years passed, Binet and others stocked a rich store of norms and measures of mental ability, based on many tests of many children. Even Binet's own two daughters were the subject of intensive study, culminating in a book called *The Experimental Study of Intelligence* (1902), in which the vital psychological facts about the teen-age girls were expressed as scores on their father's tests of word-writing speed, mental imagery, sentence completion, and so on. It was to Binet, therefore, that the Minister of Public Instruction turned in the fall of 1904 when he wanted a better way to spot subnormal children in the Parisian schools. The children were to be put into special schools where they could be helped, but the first problem was to find them. If mental tests were any use at all, here was a task to prove it. Binet and his psychiatrist collaborator, [Theophile] Simon, decided to use a series of tests graded in difficulty, first standardized on normal children of various ages.

The idea of using equivalent age as the measure of intelligence was obvious only after Binet, not before him, for it was one of those rare and elegant turns that make for historic innovation. Here were some tests that distinguished between children of different ages, on the average. However, at each age some children did better than their exact chronological peers. Those children, he had found, were judged by teachers to be bright or gifted. Conversely, other children did worse than their peers and were judged to be dull. Hence, if all one knows about a child is that he outperforms his age peers, he can still be assumed to be bright. If his performance matches his age, he is probably an average child in intelligence. And if he underperforms, he is probably dull. As Binet well knew, the chronological approach to intelligence finessed the weighty problem of defining intelligence itself. He had measured it without having said what it was. It took a while to know whether the sleight of hand had in fact yielded a real intelligence test or just an illusion of one.

For their first practical venture, Binet and Simon drew up a progression of thirty tests covering the range of mental capacity. At the very bottom, the examiner simply noted eye-head coordination as a lighted match was moved across the field of vision; thence he observed the making of grasping movements, imitating gestures, the following of instructions to touch various parts of the body, the naming of familiar objects, repeating sentences, arranging identical-looking objects in order of weight, constructing sentences to include three given words ("Paris," "gutter," "fortune"); and finally the ability to distinguish between abstract words such as "liking" and "respecting." After some preliminary trials, Binet and Simon gave their test to about fifty normal children between the ages of three and eleven, thereby establishing the

cutoffs for each age. Finally, using children already diagnosed by standard clinical procedures to be idiots, imbeciles, and morons, they found the corresponding criteria for mental disability in their series of tests.

Is a retarded child really the equal of a normal child at a younger age? For example, the average five year old passed the first fourteen tests, while the upper limit for an imbecile was to pass the first fifteen tests whatever age he was. Anyone who passed more was not an imbecile. Was Binet saying that a twelve-year-old imbecile precisely equals a slightly brighter-than-average five year old? The answer is no, for Binet specifically denied the charge. The imbecile, he said, is "*infirme*," the five year old is healthy, and their mental processes are in some respects different, even if the difference is not captured by his test. Nevertheless, the test did its job, for a twelve year old who tested at the five-year-old level was, indeed, retarded, while a five year old who did so was not (or at least did not seem to be at that time). As always, Binet's approach was doggedly pragmatic and empirical. He was picking out the retardates with his test more quickly, cheaply, and for all anyone knew, more accurately than ever before. The social benefits were self-evident.

The Binet-Simon test was put into use immediately and was criticized as quickly for this or that item. But criticism was corrective, for in showing that some item was not, for example, distinguishing between three and four year olds, the critic was opening the test to improvement. An ineffective item could be dropped, a useful one added, without in the least altering the kernel idea, which was to measure intelligence by a graded series of tasks ("stunts," Binet often called them). The tests and the criticisms were rooted in actual experience with ever-growing numbers of children, adding greater and greater empirical stability to the results. In America, Great Britain, Belgium, Italy, Germany, and elsewhere, the tests were being used and perfected. In a cheering counterexample to Gresham's gloomy law, good test items tended to drive out bad ones, and the better the test in sorting out children, the more it was used and improved. In 1908 Binet and Simon published a much-revised series of tests, to be used for rating children in general, not just retarded children. In 1911 the final Binet-Simon scale came out; it was Binet's last work, for he died that year at the age of fifty-four. But the evolution of testing continued unabated and still does.

In the 1911 version, there were five problems which the average child of each age could or could not solve. Here, for example, are the five items for the six-year level:

1. Distinguish between morning and afternoon.
2. Define familiar objects in terms of use.
3. Copy a diamond shape.
4. Count thirteen pennies.
5. Distinguish between ugly and pretty faces.

And here are the five problems for the average ten year old:

1. Arrange five blocks in order of weight.
2. Draw two designs from memory.
3. Criticize absurd statements.
4. Answer comprehension questions.
5. Use three words in not more than two sentences.

A child who passes all the tests up to and including those for six year olds and none beyond has a "mental age" of six, whatever his actual chronological age. Suppose, however, that he passes all the tests up to but not including the six-year level, and then passes only three at the six-year level and one at the seven-year level. His mental age is credited with .2 additional years for every item he passes beyond the level where he has passed them all. The child's mental age would be $5 + .6 + .2$, or 5.8 years of mental age. If his chronological age were six years, he would be slightly below average; if five years, somewhat above.

Binet did not come up with the "intelligence quotient" (IQ) itself; this fell to the German psychologist William Stern to do soon thereafter. Stern saw that a child who is one year behind at the age of six is more retarded than a child who is one year behind at the age of thirteen. It is the *relation* between mental and chronological age that matters, not just their *difference*, and this relation is best expressed by the ratio

of the two numbers. To get the IQ divide mental age by chronological age and multiply by 100 to get rid of the decimals. Thus, a six-year-old child who comes through with a mental age of nine is in these terms as bright as an eight year old with a mental age of twelve, both having the impressive IQ of 150.

The IQ of 100 divides the population into two roughly equal groups. This is not a fact of nature but an outcome of how the tests were made. Binet and his successors picked and chose until they found items that the average child at each age could just pass, thus assuring that the average child's mental age equals his chronological age and his IQ 100. The idea of a mental age assumes that mental growth is accumulative and consecutive, so that a child who has mastered the items at a given age level one year will (barring disease or trauma) continue to do at least that well as he ages. In this case nature, not the test-makers, meets the condition. At each age during childhood we can do intellectually what we have done before, adding competence rather than replacing it. Binet's idea for mental testing would not have worked for grubs and caterpillars, which appear to lose their grasp of burrowing and cocoon spinning as they become competent at flight. In other respects too, Binet was fruitfully combining nature and artful design in his tests. Items on the test were included only if some children were ahead of their age in solving them, some behind, but the largest number were neither. Overall, the spread of performance conformed to the bell-shaped curve that statisticians call "normal," with about as many superior children as inferior, but with most crowding around the average.

Binet's ideas took hold powerfully and quickly. It was not only in France that the average eight-year-old child could just barely repeat accurately five digits read to him, for the Binet scale was readily exported to Belgium, Great Britain, America, Italy, and so on. The remarkable exportability of the tests was probably the first convincing argument for their soundness. Items that drew on bits of specific, seemingly arbitrary knowledge crossed national and linguistic boundaries as easily as the fundamental tests of memory and reasoning. It could be relied upon, for example, that the average nine year old would be able to name in order the months of the year. What does this say about the IQ? Would we downgrade a Papuan child, raised in New Guinea, if he could not name the months? Clearly not, if his language had no such names or had some different scheme for cutting up the year. Some of the items on a test are specific to a culture, but that does not make them poor items. A given test is only for people drawn from the same general population that the test was standardized on. Even if it is hard to locate the precise boundaries of this general population, a useful intelligence test should incorporate at least some of the material of a culture, or it may miss gauging the child's ability to assimilate his surroundings. Virtually every child grows up in some culture or another, and his intelligence score (if that concept is to retain its ordinary meaning) must reflect his sensitivity to it. The Papuan child cannot sensibly be tested on a Western intelligence test. He would do poorly, but he would also do poorly in most other contacts with Western society. It would not mean that he was not intelligent. It would mean only that he was not meeting the underlying conditions of the test, which assume that he has been drawn from the standardizing population. Analogously, a child who gets a very high IQ after being drilled by parents or teachers on test items is probably not all that bright, and for the same reason. Like any other instrument of measurement, the IQ test must be used according to the directions. One does not use an oral thermometer after eating hot soup or sucking on ice cubes—not if one wants to know one's temperature. One may have a fever with a cool mouth, but the thermometer will not reveal it. So, the Papuan child may be bright or dull or average, but only a test standardized in his cultural environment can show which. It is not that "intelligence" itself is peculiarly European or North American, even if the instrument for gauging it is.

A person's IQ is a different sort of fact about him than his height or his weight or his speed in the hundred-yard dash, and not because of the difference between physical and mental attributes. Unlike inches, pounds, or seconds, the IQ is entirely a measure of relative standing in a given group. No such relativism is tolerated for the conventional measures. Gulliver may have looked like a giant in Lilliput and a mite in Brobdingnag, but he was just about 70 inches tall wherever he went. Relativism is tolerated for the IQ because, first of all, we have nothing better. If the testers came up with something like a platinum yardstick for mental capacity, it would quickly displace the IQ. But more than this can be said for the IQ. Because the group with which a child is implicitly compared is effectively the entire population of Western society, there is great stability to the comparison. The IQ gives one's standing among the people with whom one will live. And if it can be assumed that so large a sample of mankind is reasonably representative of the whole, then a relative measure is quite informative. An IQ of 100 would then indicate average intelligence, compared to people in general and not some small group; an IQ of 150 would denote high intelligence, and so on.

At around adolescence, people seem to stop acquiring new intellectual powers, as distinguished from new information or interests. For example, immediate memory span grows until the age of fifteen, but not thereafter. The average person can repeat seven digits at fifteen or at fifty. Other items in the Binet scale similarly level off at about the same age. Thus, if one were to continue calculating IQ in the same way, dividing a fixed mental age by a growing chronological age, one's score would plummet, reaching (for the average person) IQ 50 at about the age of thirty and IQ 25 at the age of sixty (assuming that the mental age is stuck at fifteen). To avoid such nonsense, some other measure of relative standing is often used for adults. Thus, instead of saying that a man has an IQ of 130, say instead that he tests higher than 96 percent of his peers, and then define the peer group. It can be all American adults, or Caucasians, or college graduates, or members of the United Auto Workers or the League of Women Voters. In fact, since the IQ is itself standardized on groups of peers (usually children), it and the percentile score are directly and simply translated one into the other.

Binet invented the modern intelligence test without saying what intelligence is. At first he was trying to sort out the mental defectives; later he was trying to rate all the children—defective, average, or superior. Some rough-and-ready notion of intelligence lurked in the background—having to do with mental alertness, comprehension, speed, and so on—but he was not forced to defend an abstract definition in order to sell the idea of his test to the world. Instead, he could point to how well the test worked. Rarely did a bright child, as judged by the adults around him, score poorly, and rarely did a poor scorer seem otherwise bright. Occasionally a child would do worse than expected on the test because a teacher had confused obedience with brightness, or better than expected when rebelliousness had been mistaken for stupidity, but in general most children ended up about where they were expected to. The value of the test was that it gave an objective assessment about a child in an hour or so, and any trained technician could administer it. With the test as a yardstick, children who knew no one in common could be directly compared, for whatever purpose.

But is intelligence really an attribute, like height, that can be expressed in a single number? Even granting that IQ is a measure only of relative standing, can relative standing be given in a single number? Is Jimmy really altogether brighter than Johnny if his IQ is higher? Perhaps Jimmy is brighter as regards A, B, C, and D, but Johnny has him beaten on E, F, and G. Even Binet admitted that intelligence was not just one thing; otherwise his labors in creating a test would have been far easier. Once, when he was speculating about the nature of intelligence, Binet mentioned the attributes of directedness, comprehension, inventiveness, and critical capacity, which he thought may vary somewhat independently from person to person. Usually, however, he was too busy with his practical goals to dwell on hypotheses.

Even as Binet was developing the first intelligence scale, others were grappling with the conceptually tougher problem of the structure of intelligence. The story of the key mathematical discoveries would be out of place here, but the highlights may be worth noting. An Englishman named Charles Spearman resigned a commission in the British Army after serving in the

Boer War and set to work on the problem. Taking the intercorrelations between scores on simple mental tests as his basis, he concluded that there was a "universal" intellectual capacity—which he labelled "g" for "general"—plus a host of minor, unrelated capacities of no great scope. The universal factor, he said, permeated all intellectual activity, while the others were variously absent or present in any given task. To be smart, for Spearman, mainly meant having lots of g. Although he had some evidence for this theory, it did not endure even for Spearman, who revised it after a decade or so. Nevertheless, his mathematical procedures were an essential link between Francis Galton's formulas for assessing correlation and the vastly more complex methods of "multiple factor analysis," which is the contemporary term.

Following Spearman, the next big step was taken by L.L. Thurstone, an American electrical engineer who left a job in Edison's laboratory in East Orange, New Jersey, to work on psychological measurement. A long and illustrious career, covering the measurement not only of intelligence but also of attitudes, personality, sensory capacity, motivation, and the learning process was the result. For intelligence, Thurstone subdivided Spearman's general factor, g, into a set of Primary Mental Abilities (PMA): spatial visualization, perceptual ability, verbal comprehension, numerical ability, memory, word fluency, and reasoning (inductive and deductive). These are just verbal labels tagged on at the end of a mathematical procedure that really has no verbal labels in it. It would be more precise (if less informative) to say that Thurstone found evidence for seven or eight separate factors or aspects of intelligence, and to leave it at that. With more powerful mathematics and more abundant data, Thurstone's successors have teased out new factors. Like nuclear physics with its proliferation of elementary particles, the study of intelligence has suffered from its riches. Now there are experts who find evidence of over one hundred components in intelligence, and there is no sign of a limit.

Thurstone noted some intercorrelations among the Primary Mental Abilities. People who excelled, for example, in verbal comprehension

were often high in word fluency. Other constel-
lations also kept turning up. Such correlations
among the factors themselves could signify that
mental abilities are hierarchical, arranged in
layers. At the very top, there may be a general
intellectual power, like Spearman's g, pervading
all mental activity. To be smart means having
the power in abundance, to be stupid means
having a shortage, so that all of Thurstone's
PMA's will be to some degree correlated. At the
next level down, the PMA's break into clusters
involving either verbal abilities or numerical or
logical abilities. Then there are the separate
PMA's themselves, which vary somewhat independently despite their intercorrelations. In
addition to being generally bright or stupid or
average, people are verbal, numerical, imaginative, and so on. People can be so strong in one
factor or another that they excel in some areas
without any special abundance of g. And, in-
versely, some people may be so poorly endowed
in one or the other factors that they appear occasionally incompetent, notwithstanding substantial g. Although the hierarchy seems like a
plausible theory of intelligence, it will remain
hypothetical until the experts agree on its specific
features—which has yet to happen.

Even at best, however, data and analysis can
take us only so far in saying what intelligence is.
At some point, it becomes a matter of definition.
For example, we would reject any intelligence
test that discounted verbal ability or logical
power, but how about athletic prowess or manual
dexterity or the ability to carry a tune or qualities
of heart and character? More data are not the
final answer, for at bottom, subjective judgment
must decide what we want the measure of intelligence to measure. So it is for all scales of measurement—physical as well as psychological. The
idea of measuring length, weight, or time comes
first; the instrument comes thereafter. And the
instrument must satisfy common expectations as
well as be reliable and practical. In the case of
intelligence, common expectations center around
the common purposes of intelligence testing—
predicting success in school, suitability for
various occupations, intellectual achievement in
life. By this standard, the conventional IQ test
does fairly well. The more complex measures,
such as Thurstone's PMA's, add predictive power
that is sometimes essential. As for what intelligence "really" is, the concept still has ragged
edges where convenience and sheer intuition set
boundaries that will no doubt change from time
to time. The undisputed territory has, however,
become formidable.

A total IQ score can be earned in many ways.

Figure 8.2 shows that identical total IQ scores can be derived in different ways. In the particular examples given one child is strong in verbal
fluency; another is strong in general information; and the third child
scored well in problem-solving ability. When considering alternate
school programs or occupations it may be important to know both the
total IQ score of the child or adult and his particular pattern of strengths
and weaknesses in special abilities. Before a psychologist uses a particular
test, he asks three questions about how the test was constructed. For any
test to be useful, it must be reliable, valid, and properly standardized.
Consider these test construction requirements in more detail.

Test Characteristics

There are three important methodological problems every test-maker
must solve: *reliability, validity* and *standardization*. A test is said to be reliable if it produces the same score for the same individual over different

A test-maker must solve three problems.

testing sessions; it is valid if it measures what it is supposed to measure; and it is well standardized if the sample used as a basic comparison group for the instrument was representative of the general population. Reliability is the first requirement we will consider.

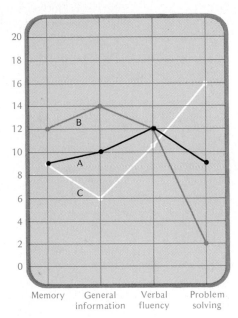

FIGURE 8.2
Three people who earned about the same total intelligence scores and yet were very different in abilities. Note that the first person is highest in verbal fluency; the next in general intelligence; while the last is strongest at solving problems.

Reliability

Reliability is estimated in three ways.

The reliability of a test can be estimated in at least three different ways: by giving the same test twice, by relating and comparing various parts of the same test, or by producing two similar forms of the test and administering both forms to the same subjects. If the scores received with retesting, or on the two parts of the test, or from equivalent forms are highly correlated, the test is said to be reliable. Modern individual intelligence tests generally show test-retest reliability correlations of around .95 (1.0 is perfect reliability; Cronbach, 1963).

Split-half reliability is most often used.

However, there are some restrictions on how reliability can be estimated. For example, estimating reliability by correlating the person's score on one half of the test with his score on the other half, called "split-half" reliability, is legitimate only if the test is measuring just one kind of intelligence or if the different subtest items are distributed equally within each half of the test. Another restriction occurs when you use the same test and administer it to children two times. They may recall some answers from the first session, and this recall may produce a higher score on the second test. However, since the examiner is interested primarily in the test's reliability, this may not be a serious problem. In measuring reliability, the children's relative *rank* is important, not the average score of the group. If each child remembers a comparable amount (either the same for all test-takers or, more likely, some amount proportional to their IQ), relative ranks will not be changed and the correlation between sessions one and two will reflect reliability of the test basically unaffected by memory.

Once a test is proved reliable, one must know if it measures the right things. This is the problem of validity.

Validity

One must have a criterion to estimate validity.

To measure validity you must select a separate criterion that is known to be a part of intelligence and then correlate your test with that external criterion. Any item on the test that correlates with the intelligence criterion is a good candidate for the test, while items that do not correlate with the criterion should be rejected as not valid measures of intelligence.

Most theorists believe that mental age increases until adolescence.

All theories of intelligence assume that mental ability increases with age, so Binet and Simon selected age as their external criterion of intelligence. Specifically, their criterion was the number of children passing an item at various ages up to fifteen years. Since older children were assumed to possess more mental ability than younger ones, more older children should have passed a test item compared with their younger peers. In addition, Binet and Simon used three other characteristics in evaluating test items—the items had to be positively related to one another, they had to be easy to administer, and they had to be reliable to score.

There are four kinds of validity.

Modern test-makers are concerned about four kinds of validity: *face, predictive, theoretical,* and *content*. Face validity is important because if the test obviously seems to be a good measure of an ability, it will be easier to convince the test-taker to do his best on the examination. On the other hand, if the test has no face validity, it will not be taken seriously.

Predictive validity means the test predicts other behavior.

Predictive validity concerns the test's usefulness in predicting other kinds of performance. For example, if scores on the intelligence test are highly correlated with success in school, the instrument has predictive validity. Theoretical validity concerns whether the test is consistent with known facts and theories of intelligence. Specifically, if a researcher believes there is only one kind of intelligence and the test items all correlate with each other, that gives him a theoretically valid general intelligence test.

Content validity is about the representativeness of the test.

Finally, content validity is concerned with whether the test contains a representative sample of the types of items which measure what the researcher wants to assess. For example, if you want to measure perceptual ability, does the test contain perceptual items or only math and verbal tasks? Once a researcher is satisfied with the reliability and validity of the test, it is time to standardize it on a representative sample of the total population.

Standardization

A test is standardized against a large representative sample.

Intelligence tests measure the relative ability of individuals as compared with a standard group. The group used as a comparison must be selected carefully so it will adequately represent the population. Generally, a standardization group is formed by stratifying the population into various sets—for example, by geographical region, sex, age, race, social class, and urban-rural residence—and then selecting from these various sets on the basis of their frequency in the general population. If the stratification is carried out carefully and the sampling is accurate, the standardization sample will faithfully reflect the total population, and the scores obtained from the sample will represent a good yardstick for comparison. Once an intelligence test is standardized, particular scores take on meaning. Generally, a score of 100 is assigned to the average performance of the standardization group, and scores higher than 100 reflect more intelligence while scores below 100 reflect lower intelligence than the average. At least one other important requirement must be satisfied before a test can reflect a person's ability accurately—it must be of appropriate difficulty. There is enormous variation in the type and complexity of intelligent behavior generated by infants, children, and adults. Because of this large variation, and the independence of early sensory-motor measurements and later IQ scores (McCall, 1972), psychologists have produced four main categories of ability tests: the infant sensory-motor test, the preschool developmental test, the school-age intelligence test, and the several tests of adult abilities. Consider the types of behavior each of these tests measure and the relation between them.

Tests of Ability

There are four tests of ability.

The four general types of ability tests are related to the behavior each age group exhibits. For example, infants are predominantly sensory-motor; young children are more perceptual; school-age children are concrete and literal in their intellectual abilities; and adults are more abstract and complex in their intellectual abilities.

Infant tests do not correlate with later IQ scores.

Generally, tests given at later ages are more valid. Below the age of five years tests measure mainly sensory-motor and perceptual skills rather than problem-solving or thinking. Babies are usually tested lying down or on their mother's laps; while older children can sit alone, use their hands to manipulate objects, and communicate with language. These early tests of sensory-motor abilities do not predict adult intelligence accurately. School-age tests measure memory, arithmetic, and information; and they are more valid. Finally, adult tests measure complex intellectual abilities like memory, information integration, perceptual completion, and vocabulary. We will discuss these tests in more detail later in this chapter.

School-age and adult tests are most valid.

While adult and school-age tests are most reliable and valid, preschool and infant tests are primarily useful as developmental indicators. Some adult tests differentiate among very bright candidates applying for advanced training in graduate or professional schools. They are designed to differentiate among people who score at the upper limits of regular adult intelligence tests.

Infant Tests

Bayley and Gesell developed infant tests.

The most widely used *developmental* scale for infants is one designed by Arnold Gesell, although a recent instrument developed by Nancy Bayley is gaining in popularity among professionals who use such instruments. Finding test items which tap the problem-solving or intellectual ability of an infant has been impossible so far, because a problem involves a goal, and the infant must be tested on his ability to obtain that goal. The goals of young infants are primitive and impermanent, since they mainly want to be well fed, warm, and dry. The infant has few direct means of reaching goals. He is by nature dependent on adults.

Infant tests contain sensory-motor items.

Because of these difficulties, infant-ability tests have concentrated on such sensory-motor tasks as turning the head and eyes in the direction of a bell or light, picking up one of two cubes, or looking at his hands. A baby who is advanced in sensory-motor coordination earns a high score on the infant scale. However, scores on infant sensory-motor scales are *not* related to later measures of intelligence (McCall, 1972).

Gesell developed the first infant scale.

Gesell (1940) developed an extensive series of measures at the Yale Clinic of Child Development. He obtained data on 107 normal infants selected from parents whose socioeconomic status was about average for the population. He examined the children at four, six, and eight weeks of age, and then every month through their first year. Follow-up measures were made at eighteen months; and at two, three, four, five and six years of age, with a reexamination every ten years thereafter. The studies were designed to determine the children's level of development in four areas: motor, adaptative, language, and social.

The Bayley scale has been well standardized.

The newest infant sensory-motor scale is the *Bayley scales of infant development: birth to two years,* which is standardized on a representative sample of 1,262 children drawn cross-sectionally from the United States (Bayley, 1969). Many of the items on the Bayley scale are similar to those found on other infant tests. Bayley sensory-motor items include attending to visual stimuli, grasping, manipulating or combining objects, shaking a rattle, ringing a bell, smiling at the examiner, cooing, babbling, imitating, following simple directions, putting a cube into a cup, banging spoons together, and showing memory for a fallen or hidden toy. The scale also contains some simple goal-directed tasks like placing pegs in a pegboard, completing simple puzzles, using correct names for common objects, and understanding the notion of an object. The Bayley motor scale includes abilities like holding up the head, turning over, sitting, creeping, standing, walking, going up and down stairs, grasping small objects, and throwing a ball.

Infants are difficult to test.

The Bayley scale measures most of the behaviors which a normal infant should exhibit, and since her samples used in standardization are larger and more representative than previous ones, these sensory-motor scales should give an accurate picture of an average young baby's development during his first two years of life. However, it is difficult to test infants because their interests and attention spans are so narrow. An examiner must set the stage so that a response occurs. The only means to motivate a baby are an intrinsic interest in the test and interaction with the experimenter. The baby is hardly concerned with doing his best. Also, scoring of items is difficult because there is no objective record of the infant's pattern of responses.

Infant tests are reliable but not valid measures of intelligence.

Infant sensory-motor tests have respectable reliabilities, but their validity is questionable. As we have said, infant sensory-motor tests *do not* correlate with measures of adult intellect. There is little theoretical reason to expect that infant sensory-motor development should correlate with later adult intelligence, since adult sensory abilities are not related to adult intelligence. The validity of infant tests is based on two criteria: age differentiation and prediction of adult IQ. By the first criterion, infant tests are valid because they do show increases in developmental abilities with age (*see* Figure 8.3). Intelligence quotients do not begin to accurately differentiate between children until eight to ten years of age (*see* Figure 8.3). Even school-age tests of concrete intelligence do not predict adult intelligence very well until around eight years of age. In fact, before around five years of age the best early predictor of adult intelligence is the average IQ score of both biological parents.

IQ tests are most valid after 8 years of age.

Infant tests are useful.

However, infant tests are useful. In the hands of a sensitive, well-trained tester infant tests can detect gross sensory or motor disabilities, and they produce a moderately accurate picture of a baby's current sensory-motor functioning.

Preschool Tests

Preschool tests are more verbal than infant scales.

The best-known preschool tests are the Merrill-Palmer and Minnesota Scales (Anastasi, 1968). The Merrill-Palmer was standardized on 631 children between the ages of eighteen and seventy-seven months. Its items are arranged in order of difficulty. Although a few items deal with simple questions like: "What is this? or What is it for?" most items on these scales measure sensory-motor coordinations like throwing a ball, pulling a string, standing on one foot, cutting with scissors, buttoning,

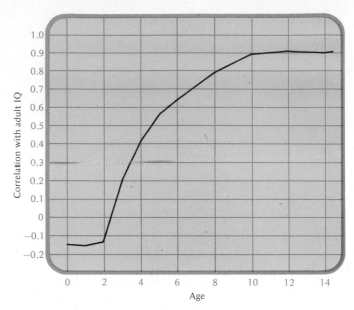

FIGURE 8.3
The correlation between intelligence scores collected at various ages and adult IQs of the same individuals. Children's intelligence is not highly correlated until about eight or ten years of age.

building with blocks, or forming several cubes into a solid. Testing is begun at a level near the child's chronological age. He is presented with simpler items until he passes all of them, and then is given more difficult items until he fails five out of ten. The child's score is determined by crediting one point for each item passed, including all test items below a *base mental level* where he passed all test questions. Test validity was determined by selecting items passed more often by older children.

The Merrill-Palmer test is not valid.

The major problem with the Merrill-Palmer scale is its lack of correlation with tests of intellect for older children. Its principal asset is the undoubted appeal of many of the items to young children.

The Minnesota Preschool test is mostly verbal.

The Minnesota Preschool Scale contains almost no motor items. The test is not timed. The scale is part verbal and part nonverbal, and each section yields a separate score. Verbal items include pointing at parts of the body, pointing to objects, naming things, telling what a picture is about, following directions, and answering simple questions like: "What should you do if you're hungry?" There are items about naming objects from memory, naming colors, identifying incomplete pictures, using vocabulary, and the number of words in the child's longest sentence. The nonverbal items include drawing a circle, a triangle, and a diamond; drawing vertical and horizontal cross strokes, block building, discriminating forms, recognizing forms, tracing, rearranging cutout puzzles, paper folding and indicating the missing parts of pictures. The child's score for the verbal and nonverbal scales is found by adding the number of points earned in each task. Validity of the Minnesota Preschool Scale was determined by the criteria of age differentiation, internal consistency of items, and correlation of test scores with the father's occupational level.

The problems encountered in administering infant tests are still

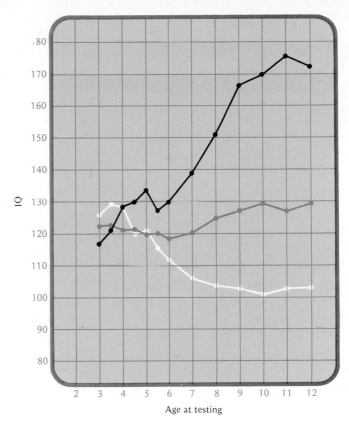

FIGURE 8.4
The longitudinal intelligence scores of three children. Note that differences in intelligence begin to appear and stabilize at around eight to ten years of age. This is the same age when children's intelligence tests begin to correlate highly with adult IQ.

Preschool children are also difficult to test.

present at the preschool level. Verbal directions can be used, but the problems of motivation, short attention span, and susceptibility to fatigue still exist. Subjectivity of scoring still occurs, and shy children have trouble scoring well with these preschool tests. It helps if the child's mother remains in the examination room or holds the child to reassure him. Standardization is more adequate for the preschool than for the infant tests, but the preschool test total scores are still *not* correlated to any significant extent with adult intelligence. Interestingly, those subtests which use incomplete pictures, block building, discrimination of color and form, definitions, detection of verbal absurdities, and vocabulary are modestly related to mature intelligence, probably because these skills are also measured more fully at a later stage. Truly valid tests of intelligence exist only for school-age children and adults. Let us consider a well-known school-age test (*see* Figure 8.4).

School-age Tests

The WISC has two parts.

The Wechsler Intelligence Scale for Children (WISC) is an individually administered test divided into several parts. Within each subtest items are arranged in order of difficulty, and the total test contains an equal

TABLE 8.2   The Weschler Intelligence Scale for Children

	Verbal Scale	
1.	General information	The child may be asked 30 questions covering a wide variety of information which he has presumably had an opportunity to acquire in our culture. An effort was made to avoid specialized or academic knowledge. It might be added that questions of general information have been used for a long time in informal psychiatric examinations to establish the individual's intellectual level and his practical orientation.
2.	General comprehension	Designed to measure practical judgment and common sense, this test is similar to the Stanford-Binet comprehension items, but its specific content was chosen so as to be more consonant with the interests and activities of children. It consists of fourteen items, in which the child is requested to explain what should be done under certain circumstances or why certain practices are followed.
3.	Arithmetical reasoning	This test consists of sixteen arithmetic problems similar to those encountered in elementary school arithmetic. Each problem is orally presented and is to be solved without the use of paper and pencil. Speed and correctness of response determine the score.
4.	Similarities	In each of the sixteen items of this test the child is asked to state in what way the two things named are alike. The resemblance to certain Stanford-Binet items is again apparent.
5.	Vocabulary	A list of forty words, steeply graded in difficulty, is presented orally. The child is asked to state what each word means.
5a.	Digit span (optional)	This is a memory-span test for orally presented lists of digits, ranging from three to nine digits. In the second part of this test, the subject is instructed to reproduce each list (two to eight digits) in reverse order.

number of verbal and performance items. Separate verbal and performance IQs are computed along with a total intelligence score. A brief description of each subtest is included in Table 8.2 with some sample questions. The WISC contains twelve subtests, ten regular subparts, and two alternate or supplementary tests called digit span and mazes. Raw scores on each subtest are transformed into standard scores, which are then summed to give a verbal IQ, a performance IQ, and a full-scale IQ. Two hundred children at each age between five and fifteen years (a total of 2,200 children) were used in the standardization of the WISC. Split-half reliability of the test is between .92 and .94 (Anastasi, 1968). In general, the correlations between verbal and performance scores are quite high, although a few children show fairly large differences. The performance scores show

TABLE 8.2   *(Cont.)*

	Performance Scale	
6.	Picture completion	The child is shown twenty cards, each containing a picture from which a part is missing. He must state (or show) what is missing from each picture.
7.	Picture arrangement	Each item consists of a set of cards containing pictures that are to be rearranged in the proper temporal sequence so as to tell a story. One set of cards is used for preliminary demonstration only (a dog in three parts) and is followed by the seven sets in the test proper. Both time and accuracy are scored.
8.	Block design	In the Wechsler adaptation of the block design test, the patterns use only the red, white, and red-and-white sides of the cubes. Two simple demonstration items are followed by seven designs of increasing complexity requiring from four to sixteen cubes each. Both time and accuracy are scored.
9.	Object assembly	Modeled after the Pintner-Paterson Manikin and Feature Profile this test includes improved versions of both of these objects (a boy and a face) together with a horse and an auto (four in all). In each part the task is essentially similar to that in a jigsaw puzzle. Both time and accuracy are scored.
10.	Coding	This is a version of the familiar code-substitution test which dates back to the early Woodworth-Wells Association Tests and has often been included in non-language intelligence scales. There are two codes: the more difficult set contains nine symbols paired with the nine digits. The simpler code contains five figures (star, circle, triangle, cross, and square). The subject's score is the number of symbols correctly written in 1½ minutes.
10a.	Mazes (optional)	Five paper-and-pencil mazes are provided on a separate sheet to measure the child's ability to plan his moves in advance.

smaller differences between rural and urban groups and between different occupational groups than do the verbal scores. Several studies report correlations ranging from .60 to .90 between the WISC and the Stanford-Binet test of intelligence. Verbal parts of the WISC correlate more highly with the Stanford-Binet (*see* Table 8.3) than the performance parts. This is to be expected, since the Stanford-Binet is primarily a verbal test of IQ. The WISC is a well-standardized intelligence test and a model of test construction. The children's test is significantly correlated with adult intelligence and is also quite similar to adult IQ tests. Table 8.4 shows the percentage of people in the general population who earn various scores on tests of intelligence.

TABLE 8.3 Stanford-Binet tests of verbal abilities classified by age.

Three years

Show eyes, nose, mouth
Name objects in a picture
Repeat two figures
Repeat a sentence of six syllables
Give last name

Six years

Repeat a sentence of sixteen syllables
Compare two figures from an esthetic point of view
Define, by use only, some simple objects
Execute three simultaneous commissions
Give one's age
Distinguish morning and evening

Nine Years

Give the complete date (day, month, day of the month,
  year)
Name the days of the week
Give definitions superior to use
Retain six memories after reading
Make change
Arrange five weights in order

(From Binet & Simon, 1948)

Adult Tests

The WAIS is a valid IQ test.

The main difference between school-age and adult IQ tests is the increased difficulty of items on the adult tests. The Wechsler Adult Intelligence Scale (WAIS) is constructed like the children's version except that some adult items are more difficult. The standardization, reliability, and validity of the WAIS are excellent. The only problem with adult intelligence tests is that very high IQ's (over about 145) cannot be differentiated accurately, since high-intelligence adults score near the top of the scale. To solve this problem, special adult intelligence tests have been devised to differentiate between very bright people. Special adult tests include aptitude examinations in verbal and mathematical ability and advanced scales in such areas as Spanish, English, history, psychology and physics. Reliabilities for the special tests range from .85-.95. What are the characteristics of people who score near the top or bottom of intelligence-tests scales?

TABLE 8.4 Percentile values of various IQ scores. The percentage of people who fall below various intelligence scores is given. For example, 99.99 percent of the population have scores below 160, while 50 percent score below the average of 100.

The child whose IQ is	Equals or exceeds (percent)	The child whose IQ is	Equals or exceeds (percent)
160	99.99		
156	99.97		
152	99.92		
148	99.8		
144	99.6		
140	99.3		
136	99	99	48
135	98	98	45
134	98	97	43
133	98	96	40
132	97	95	38
131	97	94	36
130	97	93	34
129	96	92	31
128	96	91	29
127	95	90	27
126	94	89	25
125	94	88	23
124	93	87	21
123	92	86	20
122	91	85	18
121	90	84	16
120	89	83	15
119	88	82	14
118	86	81	12
117	85	80	11
116	84	79	10
115	82	78	9
114	80	77	8
113	79	76	8
112	77	75	6
111	75	74	6
110	73	73	5
109	71	72	4
108	69	71	4
107	66	70	3
106	64	69	3
105	62	68	3
104	60	67	2
103	57	66	2
102	55	65	2
101	52	64	1
Average: 100	50	63	1
		62	1

Group Differences in IQ

Mental Retardation

Most retarded children come from dis-advantaged homes.

A majority of retarded children are from disadvantaged homes, which are characterized by low income, limited education of the parents, and unskilled occupation (Coleman, 1968). These children begin school without adequate language skills and have great difficulty learning to read, write, and compute. Table 8.5 describes the levels of mental retardation and their accompanying age changes in social and personal abilities. Note that severe retardation produces dependent adults who cannot care for themselves, while moderate or mild retardates may be able to live independently if placed in unskilled jobs and given supervision. There may be different causes for mild and for very severe retardation. Mild retardation (IQ 40-70) seems genetically and environmentally determined, while severe retardation (IQ below 35) seems primarily caused by brain injury. The evidence for this difference is that the brothers and sisters of *moderately* retarded children are usually also retarded, while the siblings of *severely* retarded children have average intelligence scores. These results suggest that severe retardation is probably caused by brain injury to a particular child and not the result of genetic or postnatal environmental factors. The health of pregnant mothers is of particular importance in this regard. Some severely retarded children have suffered from poor prenatal and infant nutrition; others from maternal toxemia or infection. At present treatment for genetic retardation is usually not available, except in rare cases of phenylketonuria (PKU) where it is possible to moderate genetic defect by proper diet.

Early enrichment can help a severely de-prived child.

Can early enrichment reduce retardation? Yes, if there has been sensory or social deprivation of the child. However, if the child's family-social environment is within "normal" bounds, the results to date suggest that early education will not raise his intelligence (Jencks, 1972). Intensive early education enrichment has produced modest immediate gains in measured intelligence, and the magnitude of gain is related to the intensity of the educational program and how specific it is. Nursery school generates small gains, while specific training in verbal skills (teaching names for parts of the body and familiar objects) produces larger gains. However, these modest improvements in IQ disappear in a few months.

Head Start programs seem not to have eliminated mental retardation.

Has the preschool program failed? We can't really know yet. The crucial data to make that judgment are achievement and intelligence scores of adults who received preschool enrichment compared with adults who did not, but were from the same backgrounds. When Head Start children mature, we can measure the results. However, current evaluations of early enrichment programs show mostly that IQ gains fade quickly with age and that no effects of enrichment persist. A recent study

TABLE 8.5 The Preschool, School, and Adult Characteristics of Four Levels of Mental Retardation.

Degrees of mental retardation	Preschool age (0–5)	School age (6–20)	Adult (21 and over)
Profound (IQ below 20)	Gross retardation; needs nursing care.	Some motor development present; cannot profit from training; needs total care.	Some motor and speech development; totally incapable of self-maintenance.
Severe (IQ 20–35)	Poor motor development; speech is minimal; generally unable to profit from training.	Can talk or learn to communicate; can be trained in simple habits; cannot learn functional academic skills.	Can contribute partially to self-support under complete supervision.
Moderate (IQ 36–52)	Can talk or learn to communicate; poor social awareness; fair motor development; can be managed with moderate supervision.	Can learn functional academic skills to approximately fourth-grade level by late teens, if given special education.	Capable of maintaining himself in unskilled occupations.
Mild (IQ 53–69)	Can develop social and communication skills; minimal retardation in the sensorimotor areas; is rarely distinguished from normal until later age.	Can learn academic skills to approximately sixth-grade level by late teens. Cannot learn general high-school subjects; needs special education, particularly at secondary-school age levels.	Capable of social and vocational adequacy with proper education and training.

(After Kisker, 1964)

by Rick Heber suggests that intensive early intervention may overcome some of the child's intellectual deficits. Heber (1972) and his group report that the average IQ difference between their enriched and control groups was 30 points at three years, 31 points at four years and 26 points at five years of age.

What about the mentally gifted? What can be expected of a very bright individual?

The Mentally Gifted

Bright children become bright adults.

What sort of people do very bright children become? To explore the characteristics of people who were very bright as children, Lewis Terman (1947) studied several hundred gifted children. He found that children who scored over 145 points on the Stanford-Binet IQ Scale were also above average in physical health and appearance. Further, they were better adjusted, more socially adaptable, and more capable of leadership than their duller age peers. As adults, these bright children were much more likely to be listed in *Who's Who* and have managerial or academic positions than adults who scored lower on IQ tests. Over 150 of Terman's original 700 cases were highly successful adults. However, some of these very bright children were dismal failures as adults. Terman believed that the primary cause of failure was lack of motivation or poor personal adjustment. Thus, two factors are important for success: intellectual ability *and* proper motivation. Terman's data suggest that bright children grow into bright adults and they remain superior throughout their lives. Is that really the case, or does IQ decline with age?

IQ and Age

IQ scores are stable after 10 years of age.

In general, individual intelligence test scores are stable after about ten years of age. Figure 8.5 shows the relation between mental and chronological age for bright and average children from five through fourteen years. Note that the superior children grew in mental age faster than the average children did. If we test different people at various ages within a short interval (*cross-sectional measurement*) intelligence seems to increase with maturity until around age thirty-five, and then it begins to decline. On the other hand, if we measure the same people several times as they

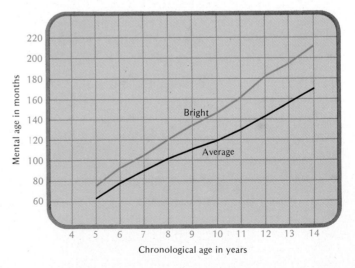

FIGURE 8.5
The relation between mental and chronological age for groups of bright and average children. Note that the bright children gained in mental age more quickly than their average peers.
(After Baldwin and Stecher, 1922.)

mature longitudinal then we find that IQ increases until about fifty years of age. The longitudinal data are probably more accurate, since they reflect comparable social, historical, and personal influences acting on the same people. In any case, intellect seems to increase early in life, reach a plateau, and then begin to decline with advancing age.

IQ and Social Class

Social-class differences in wealth, education, and intelligence do exist. Although there are certainly exceptions, the trend is for higher status to be connected with higher intellect. There seems to be a minimum amount of intelligence necessary for some occupations, and society pays more for those jobs that require brighter people, for the most part. In addition, intellectual ability is necessary for the successful completion of advanced education. Since sociologists use amount of education as one index of social class, there would have to be a correlation between IQ and social class.

Social-class differences exist.

Table 8.6 lists the intelligence of offspring from various occupational groups in the United States, England, and Russia. Note the remarkable similarity among various occupations in these three countries. Yet recent studies (Lesser, 1965) show that Americans of Jewish or Chinese origin earn higher intelligence scores than black or Mexican Americans (*see* Figure 8.6 and Table 8.7).

Children of various occupational groups differ in IQ.

Do these differences reflect real differences in intelligence or simply the cultural bias of the IQ test? This is a difficult question to resolve. Consider what we know about group differences in intellect.

The IQ Debate

According to some critics a major problem with today's intelligence tests is that they were developed by and are most appropriate for middle-class Western Europeans and people in the United States who come from

Critics say that IQ tests are biased.

TABLE 8.6

Occupational level of father	Children's IQ		
	U.S.	England	Russia
Professional	116	115	117
Semiprofessional and managerial	112	113	109
Clerical, skilled trades, retail business	107	106	105
Semiskilled, minor clerical, minor business	105	102	101
Slightly skilled	98	97	97
Day laborers, rural and urban	96	95	92

This table shows the average IQ of children from parents in various occupational groups for three different countries. Note the remarkable similarities.

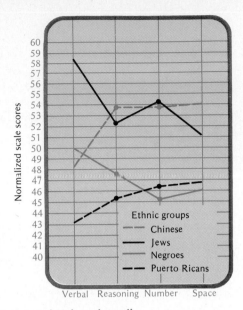

FIGURE 8.6
The pattern of mental abilities of middle- and lower-class children from two ethnic groups. Whether the differences reflect genetics, environment, or both is as yet unknown. The pattern is similar for class, but changes with ethnic background; which means that middle- and lower-class people of the same ethnic group have similar strengths and weaknesses.
(After Lesser, 1965.)

TABLE 8.7   Nationwide median test scores for 1st- and 12th-grade pupils, United States, fall 1965

	Racial or ethnic group					
Test	Puerto Ricans	Indian Americans	Mexican Americans	Oriental Americans	Black Americans	White Americans
1st Grade						
Nonverbal	45.8	53.0	50.1	56.6	43.4	54.1
Verbal	44.9	47.8	46.5	51.6	45.4	53.2
12th Grade						
Nonverbal	43.3	47.1	45.0	51.6	40.9	52.0
Verbal	43.1	43.7	43.8	49.6	40.9	52.1
Reading	42.6	44.3	44.2	48.8	42.2	51.9
Mathematics	43.7	45.9	45.5	51.3	41.8	51.8
General Information	41.7	44.7	43.3	49.0	40.6	52.2
Average of the 5 tests	43.1	45.1	44.4	50.1	41.1	52.0

Source: J. S. Coleman et al. *Equality of educational opportunity.* Washington, D.C.: U.S. Government Printing Office, 1966.

Note: This table presents the results of standard achievement tests of certain intellectual skills such as reading, writing, calculating, and problem-solving. The tests were designed to measure the skills which are the most important in our society for getting a good job and moving up to a better one, and for full participation in an increasingly technical world. The scores in each test were standardized so that the average over the national sample equaled 50 and the standard deviation equaled 10. This means that for all pupils in the nation, about 16 percent would score below 40 and about 16 percent would score above 60.

this background. These critics of IQ tests maintain that children from the lower socioeconomic classes and other cultures or ethnic groups are at a disadvantage with these tests because of cultural bias. The critics argue that the IQ tests abound in abstract verbal conventions which form part of the Western European middle-class culture, but are foreign to lower-class children and children from other ethnic groups. Figure 8.6 illustrates that the intellectual abilities of ethnic groups and social classes have been shown to be different according to one study. Do these findings reflect basic differences in intellectual ability, or are they the result of a culturally biased test? One way to answer that question is to develop a test which samples only items familiar to all social or ethnic groups. To do this, critics of standard intelligence tests developed "culture-fair" versions of IQ tests, in which conventional abstract items were rewritten in familiar, concrete language. A conventional item might read: "Cub is to bear as gosling is to _____," and the alternative choices would be fox, grouse, goose, rabbit, duck. The culture-fair item might be: "Puppy goes with dog like kitten goes with _____," with an answer choice among fox, goose, cat, rabbit, or duck. In a case where the conventional item reads: "*A* weighs less than *B; B* weighs less than *C;* therefore _____," with ending choices of "*B* weighs more than *C; A's* weight is equal to *B's* and *C's;* or *A* weighs less than *C.*" The analogous-culture fair item might be: "Jim can hit harder than Bill; Bill can hit harder than Ted; so _____," with choices: "Ted can hit harder than Bill; Bill can hit as hard as Ted and Jim; Jim can hit harder than Ted." It is possible that not having ever seen a gosling or not being motivated by interest in the subject matter of the test questions can account for some of the lower scoring among lower-class children.

Haggard found that culture-fair tests do not erase social-class differences in IQ.

Haggard measured 671 children aged ten to twelve years old to see how they performed on conventional and "culture-fair" forms of the same test. He expected that the lower-class children would improve their performances on the culture-fair test, but that there should be little change for the middle-class children. He argued that familiarity with and interest in the "culture-fair" test items should help the lower-class children compared with middle-class children. However, his results showed that both middle *and* lower-class children made large gains on the "culture-fair" intelligence tests, and that social class differences were just as marked on the "culture-fair" as on the conventional IQ test. In addition, he found that "culture-fair" intelligence tests do *not* predict school success as well as standard IQ test scores do. Thus, existing "culture-fair" tests do not seem to be valid predictors of achievement compared with the conventional tests of intelligence.

The IQ controversy still rages.

The controversy about cultural bias is by no means resolved. In some states the courts are restricting the use of IQ tests for school placement, a restriction based on the assumed bias of the tests. However, based on

Haggard's data, cultural bias seems not to be the sole cause of the difference between various groups. Two other explanations of this difference have been suggested: One assumes that children who score lower on tests of intelligence are environmentally deprived; the other assumes that some of the difference between group IQ scores is genetically determined. This is a complicated and explosive issue in contemporary psychology, and there is not enough space in this book to treat all the complex issues and disagreements in detail. However, the next section will try to present balanced and simplified views from both sides of the debate. First the environmental deprivation theory will be outlined; then the genetic theory of IQ differences will be presented.

Environmental Deprivation

Environmental deprivation may affect sensory-motor abilities.

There is little doubt that if animals are experimentally deprived of stimulation during early life, their sensory-motor coordinations will be adversely affected (Thompson, 1970). The data on human environmental deprivation generally confuse the effects of genetic endowment, environmental deprivation, and disease, so there are serious problems of interpretation. For example, in early studies on institutionalized infants, many of the lively, healthy babies were placed for adoption early and were removed from the study. Thus, the babies who remained may have been sickly and less bright. Thompson (1970) stated that: "A number of investigators have not discovered negative effects in all children raised in institutions, in spite of the fact that they had all suffered maternal deprivation."

Several observations have been made on deprived children.

There are three kinds of observations on human infants relevant to environmental deprivation, and these data vary in the care with which experimental controls were used. The least well-controlled data are simply IQ measurements of children who were isolated from normal environmental stimulation. Next are observations on nonrepresentative samples of infants or children who received different kinds of experience. Finally, there are a few observations on randomly selected children exposed to deprivation and to enrichment.

The earliest IQ studies used English canal-boat children.

Early observations about the environmental deprivation theory were taken from English canal-boat children. Measures of IQ from these children showed that most were mental defectives and that their mental deficiency increased with age since groups of older canal-boat children earned lower IQ scores than their younger peers. Three interpretations of these data are possible. Some argued that the decreasing IQ occurred because the children lived in an isolated environment. Critics of the environmental hypothesis argued that the brighter children simply moved from the canal boats into other environments as they matured, so that only the duller children remained on the boats as they grew older. These critics also pointed out that the canal children may have been genetically deficient in the beginning and that the gradual decline in IQ could have been the result of more valid IQ measurements with increasing age. These early observations have been repeated in the U.S. with similar results in various isolated parts of the country—and with the same varying interpretations. The data are essentially inconclusive because many times the brighter children among those tested migrated from the isolated community as they matured. Also the original sample of children in the isolated area may have been genetically inferior in the beginning.

Nursery-school children were also observed.

A second set of observations were carried out on self-selected, or volunteer, groups in the early 1940's and 1950's. Several studies claimed that attendance in nursery school raised children's IQ five points compared with control children who had not had this special early experience. However, these nursery-school studies contain a number of statistical problems. First of all, there was no relation between the number of days spent in nursery school and amount of IQ gain, although such a correlation might be expected if nursery school exposure were a critical factor in producing the IQ difference. Second, the nursery-school children were tested much more frequently than were the control children. Since practice in taking IQ tests produces small gains in scores, the IQ advantage of the nursery-school group may to some extent have been practice on the tests. Finally, a number of university nursery schools simply could not replicate, or repeat, the early results.

The most persuasive data come from adopted-family studies.

The most persuasive evidence for an environmental theory of group differences in intelligence was compiled by Maria Skodak and Howard Skeels (1949). They measured the intelligence of one hundred adopted children who were separated from their biological parents within the first weeks of life and were reared in environmentally enriched adopting families. The researchers reported that the final average intelligence of these adopted children was above average. They interpreted this result as evidence for the effectiveness of environmental enrichment. One paradoxical finding in their study was that the individual IQ scores of the adopted children were highly correlated with their biological parents, but were unrelated to the education of the adopting family in which they were reared. This result is contrary to an environmental hypothesis and suggests that some unfound factor may have confounded or influenced Skodak and Skeels' experiment. More recently, Munsinger (1974) suggested that the original intelligence estimates of the biological parents by Skodak and Skeels may have been too low, because the biological parents who gave their children for adoption were much younger than the adopting families and thus the biological families would not yet have reached their full educational potential. Since the intelligence of all the biological fathers and many mothers was estimated from educational data, Skodak and Skeels' expectations about the adopted children, based on what may have been the artifically low estimates of biological parents' intelligence, would also be too low. Thus, the apparent increase in in-

TABLE 8.8 Identical twin IQ studies

Study	Number of pairs	Mean IQ	Standard deviation	Intraclass correlation
Burt	53	97.7	14.8	.88
Shields	38	93.0	13.4	.78
Newman	19	95.7	13.0	.67
Juel-Nielsen	12	106.8	9.0	.68
TOTAL	122	(avg.) 96.8	14.2	.82

telligence among these adopted children may be the result of a poor initial estimate of their likely adult IQ. Munsinger replicated Skodak and Skeels' study using two ethnic groups and found a strong relation between the education of biological parents and the IQ's of their children in both groups. Yet he found no correlation between the education of the adopting parents and their adopted children's IQs. The pattern of average education for the three samples of biological parents was identical to the pattern of average intelligence among the children. By contrast, the pattern of average education for the three samples of adopting families was exactly opposite of the average IQ among their adopted children.

There are four studies of adopted identical twins.

Between 1937 and 1962 four studies were published on the intelligence of large samples of identical twins reared apart (Jensen, 1970). These four studies included 122 twin pairs. Table 8.8 shows some statistics on these twins. The average intelligence is slightly below the population mean of 100, which is a usual finding for all studies of twins. However, the IQ distribution is normal and representative of the general population. The most important statistic is the intraclass correlation of .82 between pairs of twins who were reared in different environments. In this case the IQ similarity is probably not due to the environments in which the twins were reared, for these differed. The results suggest that about 80 percent of the total IQ variance among twins can be accounted for by genetic factors.

Learning Ability and Intelligence

Simple learning is not related to IQ.

There is uncertainty about the effect of intelligence on learning ability. Some students of behavior suggest that IQ is independent of the ability to learn; while others believe learning skill is related to intelligence. Recent evidence suggests that certain types of learning are directly related to intelligence, but others are not. For example, simple discriminations or rote associations show little relation to intelligence. On the other hand, more complex learning tasks, in which the child must comprehend a rule or solve a problem, are directly related to IQ (Harter, 1965).

What effect does intelligence, family background, and education have on the economic success of an individual? In a recent book, *Inequality: A*

Reassessment of the Effect of Family and Schooling in America, Christopher Jencks asserts that schools do almost nothing to affect such success, while family, intelligence, and luck recreate economic and social inequality with each new generation.

closing the gap?*

It has been a traditional American belief that doing well in school can help even the poorest and most culturally disadvantaged child achieve economic success. But can it? Not according to Harvard Sociologist Christopher Jencks. Jencks asserts that schools do almost nothing to close the gap between rich and poor. Moreover, he argues, the quality of the education that public elementary and high school students receive has little effect on their future income.

That conclusion alone would provoke angry debate among educators, but in reaching it, Jencks makes many other astonishing assertions as well. His book seems destined to be the most controversial educational topic of the season, despite its jargon-laden prose and myriad detailed footnotes. "A fact for nearly every occasion," quips Jencks, and he adds cheerfully: "I think it's safe to assume that we will be decried on all sides."

Jencks draws part of his data from the survey of 4,000 public schools and 645,000 students directed by Johns Hopkins Sociologist James Coleman, who concluded in 1966 that the quality of a school has little to do with how well its students learn. Jencks agrees. "The character of a school's output depends largely on a single input, namely the characteristics of the entering children," he writes. "Everything else—the school budget, its policies, the characteristics of the teachers—is either secondary or completely irrelevant."

In fact, Jencks believes that schools "serve primarily as selection and certification agencies, whose job is to measure and label people, and only secondarily as socialization agencies, whose job is to change people." The reason, he says, is that schools cannot control the factors that most

* *Time* magazine

determine test scores: heredity and home environment. Jencks believes that genes play a significant role in determining IQ, though he does not assign to them the overwhelming importance found by Berkeley Psychologist Arthur Jensen. Just how do genes influence the IQ? Only partly by predetermining the ability to learn, says Jencks. Genes also affect the environment in which a child develops, a factor ignored by traditional methods of estimating genetic influences. "If, for example, a nation refuses to send children with red hair to school, the genes that cause red hair can be said to lower reading scores. This does not tell us that children with red hair cannot learn to read."

Jencks' book particularly challenges all of the nostrums that have been tried over the past decade in an effort to make educational opportunity equal in America. He finds no reason to believe that spending more money will greatly improve the quality of schooling. As evidence, he reports that children who attend elementary schools with high budgets probably gain no more than a five-point advantage on standard tests over those enrolled in low-budget schools. Differences among public high schools affect their students even less. "Almost every high school has some dropouts, some students who take a diploma but do not attend college, and some students who enter college." With surprisingly little variation between schools, the ratio of those groups to one another is now about 1 to 2 to 2, according to Jencks.

Income

Jencks doubts the value of school integration when judged purely by academic achievement. The average white child scores about 15 points higher on both IQ and achievement tests than the average black child. Desegregation helps the black children raise their scores, but only if they go to school with white children from better backgrounds than theirs. In that case the gain might be 20% or 30%, according to Jencks' calculations. One major shortcoming in his book, however, is that there are no large-scale studies on the effects of school desegregation in the South. Therefore Jencks' conclusions are at best tentative.

"There is a general trend in the country to ask what went wrong in the '60s," says Jencks, "and this book is part of that." Specifically, the federal strategy "to try to give everyone entering the job market or any other competitive arena comparable skills" had to fail. Even if all children could be made to score equally well on tests, the result would do little to erase economic inequality. For example, two people with equal schooling, IQ and family background often have widely differing incomes. At least 75% of the variation, Jencks believes, "must be due either to luck or to subtle, unmeasured differences in personality and on-the-job competence." Thus, he says, "instead of accepting the myth that test scores are synonymous with 'intelligence' and that 'intelligence' is the key to economic success, we would do better to recognize that economic success depends largely on other factors."

Jencks wants to tackle economic inequality directly. He suggests that the Government might force employers to make the wages of their best- and worst-paid workers more equal, pay income supplements to the poor or even provide them with more free public services. Congress is unlikely to adopt this approach. "But that does not mean it [is] the wrong strategy," Jencks writes. "It simply means that until we change the premises on which most Americans now operate, poverty and inequality of opportunity will persist at pretty much their present level."

Equations

Critics have already raised serious questions about Jencks' methods and conclusions. Most telling is the argument that his way of analyzing data is faulty. Financed by $750,000 in grants, primarily from the Carnegie Corporation of New York, Jencks worked for three years with seven collaborators at Harvard's Center for Educational Policy Research. The team gathered almost no new data, depending instead on hundreds of existing studies that vary widely in scope and method.

To weave together the scattered data and reach his conclusions, Jencks employed a sophisticated statistical technique called "path" analysis, which has long been used by researchers in genetics and biology but only recently in sociology. For this book it involved programming a computer with a chain of mathematical equations embodying the variables that Jencks assumed influence economic success — among them family background and education. The computer then gave back estimates of the relative importance of each variable. If any one of the assumptions were wrong or if a factor were missing, it could throw off at least some of the conclusions. Admits Jencks: "It's beguiling to assume that because you've fitted a very complicated world into your assumptions that they are right. In fact, path analysis tells you nothing about how good they are."

Jencks, of course, believes that both his assumptions and his conclusions are correct. Other scholars, however, have doubts. Says Berkeley Education Professor James Guthrie: "We are just beginning to learn what questions to ask in education, let alone coming to any conclusions. Moreover, the data on which Jencks bases his conclusions are so frail, so faulty, as not to justify any public position." Adds Stanford Education Professor Henry Levin: "We have only the crudest understanding of the actual forces creating differences in people's abilities. It's like analyzing what is beauty. You can study fingernails and knuckles, but this would have nothing to do with the overall concept of beauty."

In addition, critics like Guthrie see Jencks' findings as "political dynamite" that is likely to be misused by politicians as an excuse for giving up on the schools. Jencks agrees. "It's a message a lot of people want to hear pieces of," he says, and adds with a trace of bitterness: "If, as we argue in this book, intellectual and moral experiments on children have little effect on adult life, many people are likely to lose interest in schools. Children per se do not interest them very much."

The book also has its strong defenders, for example Harvard Urbanologist Daniel Patrick Moynihan. "All new information is thought to be threatening at first," he says. Harvard Sociologist Daniel Bell calls *Inequality* "an argument both against stilted American myths and vulgarized Marxism," and Yale Psychologist Edward Zigler, former director of the U.S. Office of Child Development, agrees that "we've been sold a bill of goods. School people keep saying we should do more, whereas the real wave of the future is for schools to do less and let other social institutions play a larger role."

It is ironic that Jencks, who strongly favors integration and school reform, should author a book that is likely to be misinterpreted as an argument against both. Jencks fervently wants schools to be stimulating, inviting and open to any students who want to attend them. His reason is not, however, that such schools may reduce inequality among their alumni in later years. Promising this leads, in the long run, to disillusionment. Good schools can be more than justified, Jencks says, on the grounds that they make life better for children and teachers right now.

There are many critics of IQ tests.

There have been many public attacks on intelligence testing in recent years. Some argue that all testing is an invasion of privacy. Others claim that tests are prejudicial against some cultural or ethnic groups. To prevent bias psychologists prefer to obtain two or more test scores before making any decision about the abilities of a person. They use social and cultural factors along with test scores in making their recommendations about future schooling, for example.

Current tests are probably the most objective way of making decisions about ability.

At the moment there is more heat than light associated with the achievement and intelligence testing of minority groups. The question is very complex. However, current intelligence and achievement tests are probably the best and most objective way of assessing ability among people. A fair and objective test may be the best long-term hope of overcoming discrimination, so that sex and race no longer influence teachers and others.

Many psychologists argue that there is another type of intellect called creativity. Consider how this trait might be measured and how it is related to IQ.

Creativity

Creativity requires a novel idea.

For most scientists the essence of creativity is novelty *and* inventiveness; many claim that creativity is neglected by standard tests of intelligence. They conclude that a minimum level of intelligence is required before one can be creative. Above that minimum level there is some reason to believe that creativity is independent of IQ as it is traditionally measured (Wallach & Kogan, 1965).

Guilford argued for three factors of intelligence.

Professor J.P. Guilford (1967) proposed that there are three aspects to intelligence. The first he called *content*—the particular medium in which the child happens to be operating at the moment. The content may be symbolic, graphic, semantic, or physical. The second aspect of intelligence Guilford labeled *operations*—this refers to the particular cognitive process

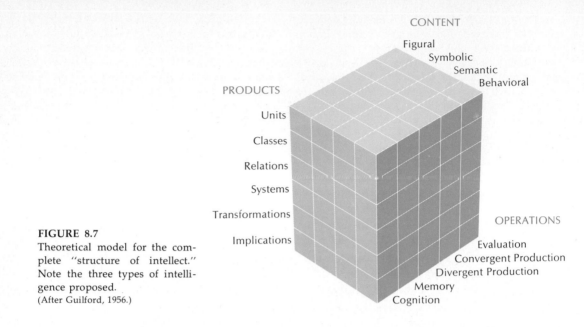

CONTENT

Figural
Symbolic
Semantic
Behavioral

PRODUCTS

Units

Classes

Relations

Systems

Transformations

Implications

OPERATIONS

Evaluation
Convergent Production
Divergent Production
Memory
Cognition

FIGURE 8.7
Theoretical model for the complete "structure of intellect." Note the three types of intelligence proposed.
(After Guilford, 1956.)

which the child is using. Examples of operations are cognition, memory, and the divergent or convergent production of ideas. The final aspect of intellect according to Guilford is *products*—which are the output of operations and content. Examples of products are classes, relations, transformations, or evaluations. (The connections among Guilford's three aspects of intellect are shown in Figure 8.7.)

Creativity involves four steps.

Many famous men of science have thought about how an idea is created. They uniformly report at least four steps in the thinking process (*see* Table 8.9). First comes a stage of *intense preparation* when the scientist learns all he can about a subject. Following this intense period of study, most scientists report a period of *incubation,* when little or nothing seems to be happening. However, during this incubation period there probably is intense activity at the unconscious level, because after an interval of incubation a new way of looking at the problem will be found. Often a final solution, the third stage, results from this insight. The last stage of creative thought is to evaluate the insight by testing its implications in the laboratory or the field.

The first step in creativity is hard work.

The first period requires intense dedication and long hours of work. Few great discoveries have been made by ignorant men. Tedious work seems necessary for later creation. The second period can be most frustrating, because during that interval there is little apparent progress and the solution may appear to slip further and further from the inquiring grasp. However, the creative person will often experience an insight soon after he has given up thinking about the problem for a while. Incubation at times produces a new approach to an old problem. Usually an insight

TABLE 8.9   Different Stages of the Creative Process

Stages of the creative process	Expected form	Predominant thinking operation	Personality factor or attitude required
Preparation	Neat Well organized Well stated	Cognitive memory	Studiousness Sustained attention
Incubation	Sloppy Often confused		Intellectual freedom Risk-taking
Insight	Incoherent	Divergent thinking	Tolerance of failure and ambiguity
Verification	Neat Well organized Clearly stated	Convergent thinking Evaluative thinking	Intellectual discipline Following logical sequence

Source: From Gallagher, 1964.

comes in a flash, and only the details remain to be elaborated. The process of verification may require days and days of painstaking work, but it is something of an anticlimax if the idea is valid.

Several personal factors affect creativity.

Several factors affect a person's creativity. Chief among these are personality and family relations. Let us consider personality first. Generally, the creative scientist is less sociable than his peers. He seeks less social interaction and is more interested in ideas and things than in people. In addition, creative people are more self-assured than others. Terman and his colleagues studied several very bright children who scored about 145 on the Stanford-Binet Intelligence Test. They found that the outstanding characteristic of successful children in this creative rank was their self-assurance. They showed perseverance and generally lacked feelings of inferiority. The successful adults of Terman's group of creative children showed these characteristics during early adolescence. They also reported a more integrated set of goals than their less successful but equally bright peers. Finally, creative people report that they are less repressed and less neurotic than individuals who are not as creative.

Families of creative people are supportive.

The family of a highly creative individual tends to support his divergent ideas, to respect his individuality, and to allow for risks in his everyday life. They tolerate the ambiguities and frustrations of new ideas. However, the creative child's peer group is seldom so supportive. For example, ratings by members of a peer group suggest that the child who contributes the most novel ideas in a group problem-solving situation receives little social credit or reinforcement for his efforts. In fact, his group peers rate the creative child as low in producing ideas, not producing many good ideas, and being silly or scatterbrained. The creative child's teacher often prefers a less-innovative high IQ child to the equally bright but creative child.

FIGURE 8.8
Examples of abstract visual designs used by Wallach and Kogan to measure creativity in young children.

Pattern meanings

Are IQ and creativity related?

A continuing controversy in the field of intelligence testing concerns the similarity or difference between intelligence and creativity. Some investigators argue that there is little difference between these two concepts, because two researchers, Getzels and Jackson (1962), found that the correlation between tests of creativity and tests of intelligence are as high (.30) as the agreements among tests of creativity alone. Many scientists interpret these results to mean that there is no difference between creativity tests and more conventional tests of intelligence. Other studies have found results similar to Getzels' and Jackson's. For example, Cline, Richards, and Needham (1963) reported higher correlations between tests of creativity and intelligence than among various tests of creativity, supporting the notion that intelligence and creativity are two names for one process.

Wallach and Kogan say IQ and creativity are independent.

However, Michael Wallach and Nathan Kogan (1965) argued that IQ and creativity are different. They believe that creativity is both a free flow of ideas during certain periods and an abundance of associations during these periods of creativity. They argue that a good measure of creativity is the number and uniqueness of relevant associations which a child can come up with in an open situation. Wallach and Kogan further argue that earlier measures of creativity were taken under test conditions in which the time constraints and group atmosphere of the situation stifled creativity. They particularly tried to generate an atmosphere in which time pressures and test-taking anxieties were at a minimum. They began their experiments on creativity with 151 children in the fifth grade of a suburban public school in a middle-class neighborhood. To offset test anxiety they introduced two young women experimenters into the classrooms as people interested in children's games rather than as testers. These experimenters gathered measures of children's abilities to produce unique associations in five general areas: One task was to generate verbal instances of round things; another task required the child to think of as many unique uses as possible for something; a third was finding similarities between pairs of items like train and tractor. Two other procedures required the children to think of possible meanings for various abstract visual pictures like those shown in Figure 8.8. In addition, the experimenters measured the children's intelligence by several standardized IQ tests. They found an average correlation among the various creativity measures of .40; an average correlation among the indicators of intelligence of .50; but an intercorrelation between all intelligence and creativity measures of .10. They believe this is evidence that under special conditions creativity can be differentiated from general intelligence.

There are high-IQ, low-creativity children.

Wallach and Kogan found a number of psychological differences between creative and noncreative children in their sample of 151 fifth-grade children. Table 8.10 lists some traits characteristic of the four types of children the researchers named. These were children high in both intelligence and creativity, those high in creativity and low in intelligence, those low in creativity and high in intelligence, and those low both in creativity and intelligence.

TABLE 8.10

	Low creativity	High creativity
High IQ	Confident Self-assured Not disruptive of class Cool-aloof socially Not attention-seeking	Very confident Highly sociable High achievement Long attention span Disruptive Attention-seeking
Low IQ	Confident Self-assured Sociable Not disruptive Not attention-seeking	Cautious Hesitant Lacking in self-confidence Shy and unsociable Low ability to concentrate Attention-seeking

High creativity is associated with attention-seeking.

Wallach and Kogan concluded that high intelligence seems related to confidence and achievement, while high creativity seems to produce attention-seeking and disruptive behavior among both the high and low intelligence children. By contrast, low IQ, high-creative children in this study were particularly troubled by the school situation, because they were seeking attention, had low ability to concentrate, and could not handle the academic tasks required of them in school. The low IQ, low-creative children compensated for their lack of academic ability by becoming more sociable. Thus, for a more complete picture of a child's mental abilities, his total IQ score, his pattern of strengths and weaknesses on special abilities, and his creativity need to be taken into account. Mental testing can be both a complex and important function, making our schools a better place for children and giving them greater opportunities to fulfill their potential.

Summary

Intelligence testing has come under increasing attack in recent years as both an invasion of privacy and a way of discriminating against minorities. The arguments relating to intelligence tests have been heated, and the controversy promises to continue for some time to come. On one side are proponents of IQ tests who argue that the scales are reliable, valid, well standardized, and the most objective way now known of measuring ability. On the other side of this debate are psychologists who believe that IQ tests are too often used to make personal decisions that should be based on other criteria. To understand this important and complicated controversy, it is essential that the student know something of how tests are constructed, how they are used, their predictive validities, their limitations, and the social costs and advantages of utilizing objective measures of ability.

SUGGESTED ADDITIONAL READINGS

Anastasi, A. *Psychological Testing*, 2nd ed. New York: Macmillan, 1968.
Kogan, N., and M. Wallach. *Risk Taking: A Study in Cognition and Personality*. New York: Holt, Rinehart and Winston, 1964.

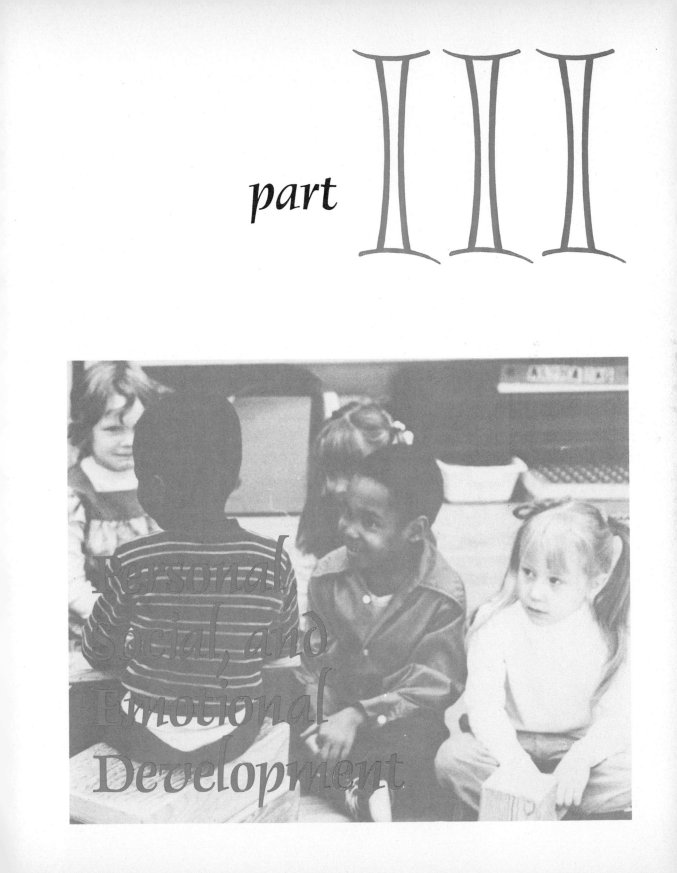

part III

Personal,
Social, and
Emotional
Development

9 Motivation and Emotions

Innate Behavior Patterns
  Taxis and Reflex
  Instincts
Biological Drives
  Thirst
  Hunger
    Overeating
    Innate Feeding Patterns
Sex
  Human Sexuality
  Sexual Maturity
Aggression
  Field Observations
Fear
Human Motives
  Early Attachments

Imprinting
  Maternal Care and Attachment
  Human Sex Role
Cognitive Motivation
  Curiosity
  Achievement
  Fear of Failure and Risk-taking
Emotions
  Indicators of Emotions
    Pupil Size and Emotions
    Facial Expressions
  Changes in Awareness
    Sleep
    Dreams
    Meditation
    Isolation
Summary

PREVIEW

Newborn babies are motivated by biological drives, but children have complex goals like achievement and curiosity. A full appreciation of human motivation requires both an understanding of a baby's basic drives and instincts and how these primitive biological processes are integrated and controlled by more complicated motives and feelings as the child grows. Motives are internal states of children and adults which psychologists use to explain why people do different things under the same conditions. Emotions concern the child's awareness of his internal physiological states. They are expressed by facial or behavioral means.

The history of human motives and emotions is complex. Early theologians believed the human soul initiates all actions, so no specific theory of motivation was required by them to explain human behavior. Later, psychologists substituted notions like will, instincts, and learned needs for the idea of man's soul. A famous American psychologist and philosopher, William James, thought there were many powerful human instincts including mother love, love between people, jealousy, cleanliness, secretiveness, shyness, sociability, curiosity, play, constructiveness, inquisitiveness, fear, hunting, sympathy, pugnacity, rivalry, and imitation.

This chapter will discuss the primitive biological processes of the young baby and the more complex goals of children and adolescents.

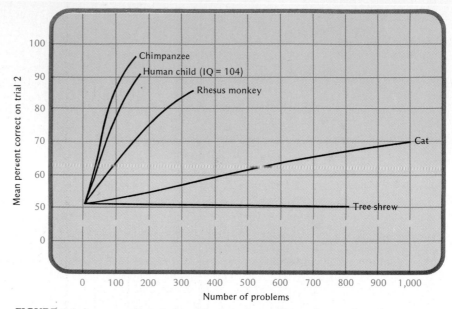

FIGURE 9.1 A comparative study of the learning abilities of a number of primates.

Darwin began the study of evolution.

Early religious doctrine taught that man and animals are different because man has an immortal soul. But Charles Darwin's theory of evolution displaced man from this superior position and installed him as just another animal with a long biological heritage. As a result of Darwin's revolutionary ideas, scientists now explore the similarities and differences between children and the lower animals in order to gain a more complete picture of development.

Ethologists study animal behaviors.

The study of man's biological nature has two distinct branches: ethology and comparative psychology. *Ethologists* study the behavior of animals in their native habitats, while *comparative psychologists* explore innate and acquired behaviors in the laboratory. The ethologist's first step is to gather detailed observations of an animal's behavior in its natural setting. This includes patterns of mating, dominance, affiliation, maternity, feeding, and migration. Next the ethologist performs simple experiments to point up the stimuli which control behavior. The ethologist's goal is to understand how innate behaviors, physiological states, and specific stimuli interact under various environmental conditions to produce complex actions.

Comparative psychologists study animal learning.

Comparative psychologists explore animal learning across several species. Figure 9.1 shows a typical comparative study in which the learning abilities of several primates is compared with the cat's ability to learn. The ethologist emphasizes innate instincts, while the comparative psychologist is concerned more with learning. This difference in theoretical orientation has caused many arguments about innate versus acquired patterns of behavior.

Whether sensory-motor connections are innate is being debated.

There has long been a heated controversy over whether sensory, motor, and neural patterns are innately organized or are learned. Early behaviorists argued against instincts by claiming such connections result from experience. However, Roger Sperry (1951) showed that if sensory-motor neural connections in frog and salamander embryos are surgically rearranged, and the connections are allowed to regenerate, the animals show reversed behavior. Specifically, Sperry rotated reptile's eyes in one study so that the top was now below, and in another case he exchanged left and right eye buds. The regenerated connections produced reverse behavior so that the animals which had been operated on moved in an opposite direction when they searched for food. The salamander which had its left and right eyes exchanged always moved left when a fly was on its right and vice-versa. This sort of behavior is consistent with the notion that the "right" eye in the salamander is innately connected to right-turning effectors, and when it is reversed, the animal still operates in terms of the original circuits. Sperry's work is strong evidence for innate sensory-motor organization in lower animals. But, what about man?

Innate Behavior Patterns

Taxis and Reflex

Taxes and reflexes are primitive behaviors.

Man's and other animal's remarkable biological structures and behaviors have developed through eons of evolutionary pressure. Under this relentless selection, structures and activities that were useful persisted, while those that were not disappeared. Evolutionary pressure has created many innate acts in animals and man. There are three main classes of innate behavior patterns: taxis, reflex, and instinct. A *taxis* is the primitive tendency to orient an organism's body toward specific stimulation. For example, flowers turn toward the sun, and the moth circles a light. A taxis is produced by a very simple mechanism: Each receptor is connected to the opposite effector; stimulation of the right receptor will cause activity in the left effector muscles and the animal will turn toward the stimulation. A second, more complex innate behavior pattern is the *reflex*. These are usually defensive or approach responses to restricted stimuli which affect specific receptors. Infant sucking in response to stimulation around the mouth is a good example of a human reflex.

Instincts

Instincts are complicated innate patterns of acting.

The third class of unlearned acts is *instincts*, and they are more complex. They are complicated, species-specific behaviors that appear despite isolation of the individual from other members of his group. For example, young wolves pounce in a characteristic way even when raised as pets away from other wolves. Instinctive behaviors follow a prescribed sequence: A *fixed action pattern* (FAP) is triggered by an *innate releasing stimulus* (IRS) when specific internal states are achieved. For example, lower animals usually react to courting stimuli only during specific cyclic intervals. The releasing stimuli are not effective in producing fixed acts except when the animal's sexual hormone balance is appropriate. For a process to be instinctive it must satisfy several criteria:

1. It must be characteristic of all members of the species.
2. It should be found in modified form among closely related species.
3. The behavior must be released only by certain patterns of stimuli called innate releasing stimuli (IRS).
4. The instinct, when it appears, must be organized without prior practice.
5. The behavior should not appear without this releasing stimulus.

Animals' reliance on instincts varies.

The relative importance of learning and instinct vary with different animal species. Figure 9.2 shows the relative importance of instincts, learning, and intellect among several species of animals. Note that simple animals rely primarily on taxis; while more complex organisms use reflexes, instincts, and learning. In humans, reasoning is prominent. However, reflexes and instincts are not absent from humans, but have simply been supplanted by more complex processes in the adult. Taxis, reflexes, and instincts are still prominent in the human infant.

Instincts are innate patterns.

Dictionaries describe instinct as the innate tendency to produce specific acts without conscious design. In everyday speech we use "instinct" to describe any automatic behavior regardless of its origin. The ethologist restricts the word to innately determined classes of behavior.

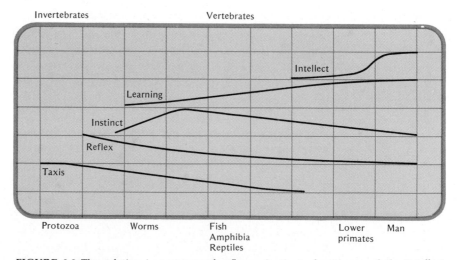

FIGURE 9.2 The relative importance of reflexes, instincts, learning, and the intellect for various species. Notice that higher organisms simply add more complex processes and do not only discard primitive behavior patterns.

Lorenz believes that humans have instincts.

How about humans? Do they inherit stereotyped behavior which is released by specific stimuli? The noted ethologist, Konrad Lorenz (1966) thinks so. He also believes man accumulates a specific energy which makes him sensitive to certain appropriate releasing stimuli. Lorenz argues that many human sexual and aggressive behaviors are instinctive. In the same tradition, Sigmund Freud felt that instincts form the basis of much human behavior.

Biological Drives

Biological drives are measured in four ways.

A precise definition of motivation is difficult. However, the notion of *biological drives* is used to explain why one animal seeks food, another water, and a third to mate under similar environmental conditions. For drives concern the fundamental needs of life. Varying acts under similar conditions suggest that internal physiological states of the organism can influence behavior. Drives are measured in four ways:

1. How quickly an organism performs a particular act.
2. How active the organism is.
3. What his choice of goals is.
4. How much punishment the subject will endure to reach a goal.

By all these measures, animal and human behaviors show strong variations as a function of physiological state. What are the mechanisms which signal an animal's physiological needs? A long controversy has existed in physiological psychology about whether these cues are central or peripheral. Peripheral determinants are cues from areas such as the mouth or stomach, while central determinants are cues from within the central nervous system. In fact, both central and peripheral information are often used to signal drive states, the condition of being without something needed for life. Consider some examples.

Thirst

Animals must retain water or die.

Animals and men must retain an optimum amount of water in their bodies because too much or too little will kill them. Living organisms use a number of cues to signal thirst. Dryness of the mouth and throat is one, while the fluid/solid balance of the blood and bodily fluids is another. The blood of most animals contains about 0.9 percent salt, but as the body loses water the percentage of salt increases. Animals and men drink water to offset this loss and restore their blood balances. If a saline solution (one containing salt) with more than 0.9 percent salt is injected into the body, a person will drink more water, even though his thirst was satisfied before the injection. Apparently, the injected salt solution activates monitors in the brain which regulate water balance in the blood, and these central monitors signal the person to drink more water.

Hunger

Eating is controlled by internal and external cues.

Children must eat enough to repair their body needs and grow, but if they eat too much, they will become fat and may die early. All animals have mechanisms for regulating both the amount and the specific types of food intake. In the average human being, overeating by only six ounces a day will produce a weight gain of a hundred pounds in one year. Undereating by the same amount would cause a person to lose a hundred pounds in one year. The amount a person eats is controlled by both internal needs and, for some people, external cues. As every dieter knows, the amount a person eats is difficult to reduce. What signals hunger?

Nisbitt found that fat people are controlled by external stimuli.

OVEREATING　R.E. Nisbitt (1968) performed several interesting experiments to discover why children and adults may overeat. He left fat and lean subjects alone in a room with food. Some were given plates with very little food on them, while others were given plates which contained a great deal of food. All the subjects were told, "There is more food in the refrigerator." Slim and fat people responded very differently to the situation. Slim people ate about the same amount regardless of how much food was on their plates. If there was little food on the plate they went to the refrigerator for more; if there was too much food they left some. In contrast, fat people ate what was put before them. If there was too little they went hungry; if there was too much they ate it all. This study suggests there is a basic difference between what controls lean and fat people's eating. Apparently, slim persons are more internally controlled, and fat people are influenced to a greater extent by external factors.

Human babies show instincts.

INNATE FEEDING PATTERNS　In addition to specific hungers, animals and human babies possess innate action patterns associated with many drives. This is particularly true of the young. Very young children possess an instinct associated with hunger in the form of a fixed action pattern of head-turning and sucking in response to a touch on the cheek. When any object touches the human infant's cheek, his head turns in the direction of the contact; and when his lips are stimulated, he begins to suck. Figure 9.3 shows some of the parts of this fixed action pattern. The first sequence of the action pattern produces head movements which cause the infant to brush his cheeks against the stimulating object and orient his mouth toward it, the nipple. Once the baby's lips touch the object, finer movements orient the mouth onto it and once the object is in his mouth, sucking begins. This is a very adaptive pattern and one which is quickly fitted to the particular feeding style of his mother.

A mated female tick is sensitive to butyric acid.

Another example of a specific instinctive response to hunger is illustrated by the mated female tick. This ingenious little creature climbs into the branches of a tree and waits there for days or weeks until a mammal passes beneath her. She remains unresponsive to the many sights, sounds, and smells that float up to her. Only when the specific mammalian smell of butyric acid signals that there is a meal approaching will she let go of her perch and drop onto the host. This extreme selectivity of the mated female tick to butyric acid is instinctive, since she need not mature around other ticks nor have experience with mammals before the pattern becomes effective. As another example, young herring gulls are innately programed to peck at a red spot. The female herring gull possesses a red spot on the bottom of her beak. This is so the young gull can get food from the mother's beak.

Babies change from liquid to solid food by 1 year of age.

How and when do human babies satisfy their primary needs? The process changes rapidly during the first several months of an infant's life. Eating, sleeping, and control of elimination are all important for the baby's health. Human babies eat six or seven times a day during the first few weeks of life, but they usually reduce their feedings to five by the age of four months. Most children eat three solid meals a day by the time they are a year old, yet may continue to take liquids by bottle until they are two. There is a gradual progression from liquid to solid food beginning around five months of age.

Infant-feeding schedules are flexible.

Babies are adaptable to various feeding schedules, so some mothers feed their babies any time they cry, while others feed an infant by a clock. Most try to establish a three- or four-hour schedule with some flexibility in it. The change from liquid to solid food is called weaning,

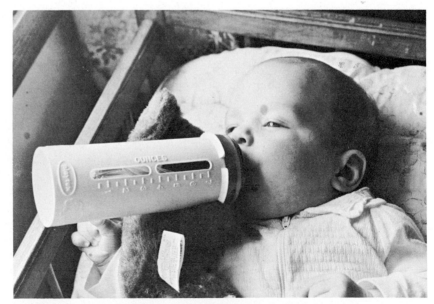

FIGURE 9.3 The fixed action pattern of head-turning, nipple location, and sucking in a baby. Head-turning is caused by stimulation of the baby's cheek, while nipple location and sucking are controlled by stimulation of the lips.
(Featherkill Studios)

and is a complicated process. The baby must learn to eat solid foods. He must have teeth and he must acquire the skills of biting, chewing, and drinking. Early baby foods, such as cereals and apple sauce, are semi-solid. Most parents begin weaning at about one year, and it is usually completed in about six months. The best process seems to be a gradual introduction of solid food so that there is no discontinuity in the baby's diet.

Sex

Most animals show seasonal variation in sexual activity.

The drives discussed so far are necessary for individual survival. Sexual needs are necessary for the survival of the species. Although it may be uncomfortable, most animals can live without sex. Among mammals, the male is usually sexually active throughout the year, although a few like the Virginia deer are sexually active only in the fall. In contrast, sexual activity in many female mammals follows an estrous cycle (a period of fertility) to some extent. The length of a cycle varies with the species. It is four or five days in the female rat and around twenty-eight days in the human female. Many animals, like the female rat, are only sexually receptive at the height of the estrous cycle; at other times they are uninterested in male sexual advances. Human females show monthly variation in temperament, although this change is not dramatic.

Human sexuality is defined four ways.

HUMAN SEXUALITY   Sex may be defined in several ways—chromosomal, hormonal, genital, and social; and inconsistencies may occur between these levels. Genetic information is probably most basic, and sex assignment is usually consistent with the baby's chromosomes. However, hormonal or social abnormalities can produce sex change. How these happen can shed important light on the biological and social control of sex roles.

Human castration may produce moderate or no change in sexual activity.

Castration or hormone injections modify the sexual behavior of rats, while castration of adult male dogs does not change their sexual drive.

Human castration was common until the nineteenth century. Eunuchs, employed as guards in Oriental harems, and castrati, boys whose testes were removed to preserve their beautiful soprano voices, are two examples of this practice. Early removal of the testes depresses sexual drive, but human male sexuality can survive castration; the effects depend on the individual. Older human males who have been castrated experience modest changes in sexual interest, while prepubertal (before about thirteen years) human castrates do not develop active sexual interests without being injected with male hormones.

Female sexual interest is not affected by removal of ovaries.

Removal of the ovaries in the female has little effect on the woman's sex drive. This suggests that female sexual interest is controlled by something other than ovarian secretions. Congenital (or inborn) lack of ovaries, testes, or adrenal glands will inhibit a baby's sexual differentiation.

Experience will also affect sex role, particularly the objects of sexual interest.

Early levels of sex hormones apparently influence male/female characteristics of the human brain during its development, and later experiences modify male or female brains to produce the adult man or woman. Sexual abnormalities can come from too low or too high a hormone level. Levels of androgen (a male sex hormone) are low in human beings until about eight years of age, when all children begin to produce some of this hormone, although boys generate about twice as much as girls. Estrogen (a female sex hormone) makes its appearance around nine years of age in girls. The female estrogen cycle begins about eighteen months before menarche (the onset of menstruation). Many women experience mild distress and lowered intellectual performance during *premenstrual* and *postpartum* (after childbirth) periods. Probably their varying *estrogen* level affects female emotions. Boys produce a trivial amount of estrogen and its level is not determined on any time cycle.

Further, synthetic hormones given to pregnant women for the prevention of abortion or miscarriage sometimes produce masculinized baby girls. Mothers show few signs of masculinization while taking the hormone, and only some female babies are affected, so there is probably a critical period and dose for these effects.

Studies of guinea pigs and rats suggest that sex hormones act in two ways: They control early sexual differentiation of the brain, and in the adult they release or inhibit patterns of sexual behavior. If rats are castrated at birth they develop both male and female brain stem mechanisms. If castration is delayed just a few days after birth, male rats do not retain female central nervous mechanisms.

The administration of testosterone to pregnant monkeys produces *pseudohermaphrodite* female offspring—infants with both male and female sex organs—and these animals interact with normal females in a masculine way. The pseudohermaphrodite monkey threatens, initiates play, engages in rough and tumble action, and mounts other females. The masculine behavior persists throughout her life. In addition to its effect on behavior, sex hormones sensitize animals to specific sexual stimuli.

Lower animals react to many sexual stimuli specific to their species. The male stickleback fish is interested in the swollen belly of a female; the female ring dove reacts to specific dancing patterns of courtship by the male dove; and the male monkey reacts to signs of vaginal swelling among females of his group. Most sexual signs are innate among lower animals. Does man have similar innate releasing stimuli programed into his animal heritage? Possibly, although there is serious disagreement about what is innate and what acquired.

There are several possible examples of innate sexual stimuli among human beings. Civilized men and women hide direct sexual stimuli, although clothes are used to display or enhance some sexual characteris-

Early sex hormone levels influence brain development.

Synthetic hormones may masculinize female babies.

Sex hormones act two ways.

Testosterone injections produce pseudo-hermaphroditic monkeys.

Animals possess specific sexual stimuli.

Civilized people hide most sexual stimuli.

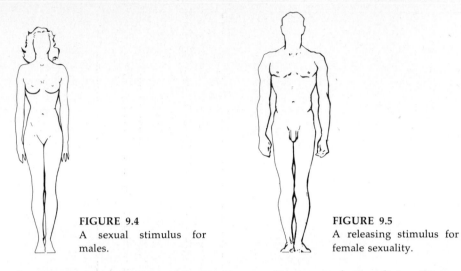

FIGURE 9.4
A sexual stimulus for males.

FIGURE 9.5
A releasing stimulus for female sexuality.

tics. For males, breasts and buttocks are salient sexual stimuli (*see* Figure 9.4.) Female fashions have capitalized on these male preferences despite occasional sexless styles like the chemise. The nineteenth century bustle gave great emphasis to the female posterior and today's pants for females are doing the same. The tight breeches and conspicuous *cod piece* of eighteenth-century male fashion, with its exaggerated padding of calves and crotch, probably excited Victorian females (*see* Figure 9.5). Western jeans serve the same function. A current rage among some magazines aimed at a female audience is the nude male centerfold.

Sexual maturity is occurring earlier.

SEXUAL MATURITY Maturity itself is coming earlier and earlier (Tanner, 1970). Puberty now occurs at around thirteen years for girls (*see* Figure 9.6). Some scientists suspect that better nutrition is causing this early maturity, but no one really knows why it is happening.

Aggression

Is human aggression innate?

A long-standing controversy exists about the relative flexibility or rigidity of human nature. We know that human babies possess several prewired patterns of behavior—such as sucking, clinging, and looking—which support their transition from womb to walking. The human adult does not display instinctive fixed patterns of behavior. Instead, ethologists argue that man inherits the capacity and inclination to learn those behaviors, like language and logic, that are essential for humanity. Is there evidence for biological constraint on animal and human behavior? Ethologists claim there is.

Field observations help scientists understand behavior.

FIELD OBSERVATIONS One way to explore man's biological past is by field observation of related primates. These natural observations can point up similarities and differences between man and the other primates.

Animals in the wild are assumed to lack a cultural polish, so biological constraints are revealed more clearly among them. Also, free animals are more representative of natural behavior than are animals who live in cages, where an animal's competence to survive is degraded.

Field studies help clarify the function of behavior. Seeing a human newborn reflexively cling gives no hint of how important this grasping reflex can be for primate survival in the wild. The primate baby must cling to his mother so that she is free to move about and feed, or both will die. The infant's clinging serves several needs—survival, comfort, and safety.

Many physiological psychologists (Milner, 1970) believe primate aggression is released by man's primitive midbrain, and that hormones or habits determine the strength and frequency of the hostility. They point out that man's higher centers are concerned with the inhibition of aggression and are highly developed compared with the lower primates. Thus, primate aggression is biologically programed, enhanced by play and social reinforcement, and inhibited by cognitive controls. The perpetual struggle between biological impulse and rational restraint reflects man's evolution. Killing and fighting are easy for man to learn and difficult for him to inhibit. A crucial question for civilization is how hostility may be inhibited and its energy channeled into constructive activities. Can man learn to control his dangerous biological impulses? Possibly. It is unrealistic to argue that man is completely controlled by his environment, and it is incorrect to say he is biologically bound and unable to modify his behavior with experiences. The fact is, man has an evolutionary heri-

Most behaviors have a purpose.

Man's midbrain controls aggression.

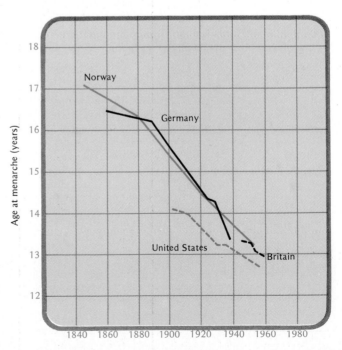

FIGURE 9.6
The decline in age of first menstruation among various Western European countries and the United States over the last hundred years. No one is sure of the cause for earlier menarche. (After Tanner, 1968.)

tage which restrains and directs his behavior *and* he is endowed with adaptive abilities. The important questions to ask are: What are the biological constraints on behavior; how may they be modified by experience; and what is the cost of that modification for human happiness?

Ethologists believe human aggression is innate.

A number of ethologists and popular writers like Konrad Lorenz and Robert Ardrey argue that man has a strong legacy of innate aggression and hostility, and that the cost of modification can be high. Current evidence suggests that man has a long history of aggression, that he possesses innate tendencies to dominate, that men are more aggressive than women, and that uncontrolled violence results from disruption and crowding rather than from an innate drive to kill. These results are open to modification by further research.

Man and animals are innately fearful.

In addition to aggression and sexuality, man and animals exhibit biologically-based fears. Such innate anxieties range from fear of falling, among human babies, to flight from hawklike objects, among young turkeys. No experience or social modeling is necessary to elicit these fears. How important innate fears are for human adults is an unanswered question. But there is little doubt of their existence and possible importance in the motives of children. Let us consider some specific examples.

Fear

Young turkeys are afraid of a hawklike shadow.

Innate control of fear can be demonstrated easily by an experiment with young turkeys. Suppose the object shown in Figure 9.7 is moved to the right. It will cast a hawklike shadow, and young turkeys who have never seen a hawk will withdraw. If the same figure is moved to the left, it casts a gooselike shadow and produces no fear. The young turkeys need no experience with a hawk or a goose to show their innate fear of the visual object.

Dogs show innate expressions.

As another example of innate fear reactions, Figure 9.8 shows hostile and fearful expressions in the domesticated dog. These expressions appear even when the animal has been raised in isolation from other dogs.

Innate mechanisms of fear exist even among primates. Gene Sackett (1965) raised rhesus monkeys in isolation where their only visual experi-

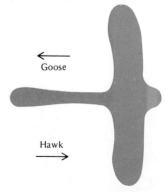

FIGURE 9.7
This stimulus elicits fear from young turkeys if moved above them from the right so that it resembles a hawk. The same stimulus resembles a goose if it is moved to the left, when it fails to frighten young turkeys.
(After Tinbergen, 1951.)

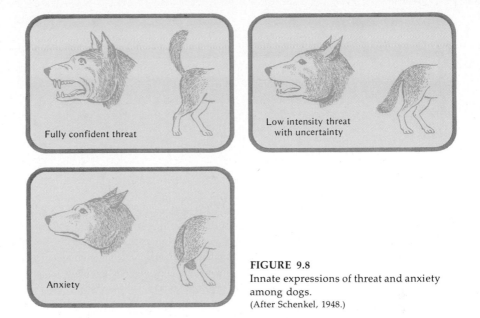

Fully confident threat

Low intensity threat with uncertainty

Anxiety

FIGURE 9.8
Innate expressions of threat and anxiety among dogs.
(After Schenkel, 1948.)

Infant primates understand threat.

ence was with colored slides projected onto a screen in their cage. Sackett presented pictures randomly and allowed the monkeys to choose whether to look at the picture again or go on to another. By the second and third month his baby monkeys rarely chose to look at a picture of another monkey in a threatening position although they looked at pictures of monkeys involved in other acts. When the threatening picture appeared, the isolated baby monkeys showed innate fear.

Many persons fear snakes.

Do human beings have innate fears? Konrad Lorenz (1966) believes about half the adult human population is innately afraid of snakes. He suggests there are two separate things about a snake which are frightening

FIGURE 9.9
A stimulus which many people find frightening, even without prior painful experience.
(Courtesy Russ Kinne.)

FIGURE 9.10
Many find a steady gaze from a stranger
disconcerting.
(Courtesy Dick Owen.)

—legless movement and winding motion (*see* Figure 9.9). People differ
in their response to these two activities. Lorenz argues that people who
are afraid of mice also fear legless movement in the snake.

Eye-to-eye contact
can be frightening.

Another fearful stimulus may be eye-to-eye contact with a strange
man. Most people find a steady gaze like that shown in Figure 9.10 to be
threatening. Eye-to-eye contact between a mother and her child is attractive.

Human Motives

One early human
motive is mother-
child attachment.

The earliest and perhaps most important source of human motives
is the bond between mother and child. Many psychologists believe the
flavor and stability of all mature social interactions derive from this
early relationship. Sigmund Freud (1916), Donald Hebb (1949), and Jean
Piaget (1960) all believe early experiences dominate human development.
Because the infant has few well-established reactions, and only limited
intellectual abilities, they argue that early environmental events exert
strong influences on later growth. They think that since the young infant
lacks the capacity to use symbols and knowledge gained from previous
experience, he has no easy way of handling early encounters. As a result,
early periods in the life of many infants can have decisive effects on their
later behavior.

Early Attachments

Many animals im-
print on the first
object they see.

IMPRINTING   The most striking example of early experience determining
later behavior is imprinting. The first clear demonstration of imprinting
by Niko Tinbergen (1951) showed that newly hatched ducks or geese will
become permanently attached to any moving object they see during a
critical early period (*see* Figure 9.11). The objects these young birds
learned to follow were not particularly good models of their species. The
main characteristics Tinbergen identified as facilitating imprinting were
movement and sound. Species-specific imprinting stimuli exist, but these

can be overcome by experience during a critical period. Yet the imprints are almost impossible to break once they have been formed. When Tinbergen's experimental animals matured, they became sexually attracted to the species on which they imprinted — no matter how inappropriate mating might have been.

Imprinting follows a typical sequence.

Imprinting follows characteristic stages. During the early period an animal begins to see or to move. Shortly after the development of sight or locomotion, the animal is most likely to imprint. Later, he develops fear of new objects or animals and becomes less likely to imprint. The critical period for imprinting usually comes between the beginning of movement and of fear. If an animal is exposed to no object or is drugged during this critical period, it will not imprint. Instead, it will simply fear everything. The domestication of mammals by man often takes advantage of early imprinting. For example, if a wolf is raised by a human from the time the wolf is born until it is six or eight weeks of age, it will come to accept and seek human companionship. This is because a wolf cub forms strong social attachments to objects he sees or smells during his first several weeks of life. Many mammals show this early critical period of socialization. Charles Darwin pointed this out over a hundred years ago in his chronicle of the voyage of the *Beagle*.

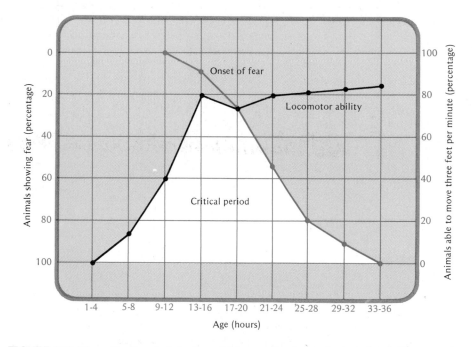

FIGURE 9.11 The critical period during which an animal may be imprinted. The period falls between the developing ability to move and a growing fear of strangers. (After Hess, 1959.)

Portrait

Niko Tinbergen was born in 1907 and spent his early years watching birds and collecting fish near his father's home in the Netherlands. The elder Tinbergen encouraged his son, but wondered privately how anyone who spent his time watching birds could earn a living.

As an adolescent, Tinbergen was interested in biology, physical education, photography, and farming. A casual remark to Niko's father by a physicist acquaintance that the young Tinbergen was a born biologist led him to spend several months at a bird-banding observatory in East Prussia in Germany. After several weeks of watching beautiful birds, Tinbergen was inspired to apply for graduate training at the University of Leiden. After finishing his thesis, Tinbergen and his new bride departed almost immediately for Greenland to study a small finch, the snow bunting, and husky dogs. He also spent time with the Eskimos.

At the beginning of World War II, Tinbergen was involved in a clash with the Nazi Occupation Forces. He protested when three Jewish professors were dismissed from the University of Leiden and for his resistance was interned in a concentration camp for two years. While in this camp he wrote an early draft of his book, *Social Behavior in Animals*. Near the end of the war he was released from the camp and immediately made his way to the Dutch Underground.

After the war he completed several lecture tours of the United States and Great Britain, but found that most English-speaking psychologists were not interested or impressed by the work of ethologists. Then and there he decided that an ethologist who looks at instinctive behaviors among animals and men should teach at an English or American school, so he accepted a lectureship at the University of Oxford.

Now, when he is not lecturing or writing, Tinbergen may be found in his eighteenth-century hideaway in the far north of England. The house was abandoned when Tinbergen found it, and he has nearly restored it to its former grace and charm.

The highlight of Tinbergen's life may have been when he, Konrad Lorenz, and Karl von Frisch became the first behavioral scientists to win a Nobel Prize in 1974. He was also awarded the Swammerdam medal for scientific achievement by the Dutch government in his last year before retirement from Oxford. His modesty is evident in the following statement: "I agree with what my brother, Jan, said when he received the Nobel Prize in economics: Such distinctions should be given to fields of research rather than individuals."

Probably the most influential aspect of Tinbergen's life was the fight between European ethologists and American behaviorists concerning instinctive or learned aspects of behavior. During the early days of ethology there were aggressive attacks from both sides favoring instincts or learning. Now much of the rancor has died, and the two branches of animal behavior are more-or-less on speaking terms. There is still some distrust and misunderstanding, but even ardent behaviorists agree that biological differences have some effect on the behavior of animals.

In 1973 Niko Tinbergen shared the Nobel Prize in Medicine. Here he accepts his award from King Carl Gustaf. (Wide World Photo)

I nstinctive behaviour is dependent on external and internal causal factors. The external factors, or sensory stimuli, are of a much simpler nature than our knowledge of the potential capacities of the sense organs would make us expect. Yet they are not so simple as the word 'stimulus' would suggest, for the 'sign stimuli' have *gestalt* character, that is to say, they release configurational receptive processes. . . . These facts led us to the postulation of Innate Releasing Mechanisms, one of which is possessed by each separate reaction. Apart from releasing stimuli, directing stimuli play a part, enabling or forcing the animal to orient itself in relation to the environment. The internal causal factors controlling . . . the motivation of the animal may be of three kinds: hormones, internal sensory stimuli, and, perhaps, intrinsic or automatic nervous impulses generated by the central nervous system itself. Instinctive 'reactions' are of varying degrees of complexity; even the simplest type, the 'fixed pattern', depends on a system of muscle contractions which is of a configurational character.

These results are incomplete in more than one respect. First, the evidence is still very fragmentary, and the generalizations are still of a very tentative nature. Second, the work done thus far has been mainly analytical, and no attempt has yet been made to combine the separate conclusions into a picture of the causal structure underlying instinctive behaviour as a whole. We have, however, gained one thing: we are realizing more and more clearly that the physiological mechanisms underlying instinctive behaviour are much more complicated than we were able to see at the start. Previous attempts at synthesis, such as Pavlov's reflex theory and Loeb's tropism theory, now appear to be grotesque simplifications.

While thus realizing both the relative paucity of analytical data and the complexity of the causal structure, we will nevertheless venture to sketch, in rough outline, a synthetic picture of the organization of the partial problems within the main problem as a whole.

Some Characteristics of the Objective Study of Instinct

Description

As in every field of science, the description of the observed phenomena, which has to precede their causal study, is not random but selective; that is to say, it is adapted to the problem under consideration. It is, therefore, necessary to point to some characteristics of the descriptions required for our study.

1. Because it is our task to analyse behaviour as co-ordinated muscle activity, the ultimate aim of our description must be an accurate picture of the patterns of muscle action. Except in some especially simple cases, this has never been done, probably because most workers are only dimly aware of the necessity.

From Niko Tinbergen, *The Study of Instinct* (Oxford: The Clarendon Press, 1951), pp. 7–9, 30, 32, 60–64, 102–103.

309

The preparation of such a description is an exacting task. It requires an objective recording of movements, in which the help of still and motion pictures is often indispensable, and a study of the muscles taking part in each movement.

2. For some purposes, however, the descriptions of behaviour need not be complete but merely sufficiently accurate to characterize the behaviour. An activity is described in this way when the causal factors responsible for a certain reaction as a whole are being studied. For instance, in an investigation of the external stimuli releasing the pecking response of a herring gull chick it is sufficient to characterize the pecking reaction by describing only some of its features. However, as soon as this reaction has to be broken down into its components, the description has to be much more detailed.

3. Whenever an activity of one animal causes a response in another, the description of this activity has to fulfill still different requirements: it will be concentrated on those peculiarities that influence the other animal's response.

Thus the descriptive part of an ethological study may vary with the purpose it is serving. However, this is still sadly neglected in many papers appearing at present. Too many descriptions are rather haphazard collections of fragmentary details.

'Spontaneous' and 'Reactive' Behaviour

One of the old controversies in the study of animal behaviour concerns the question of whether behaviour is 'spontaneous' or whether it could be explained as a combination of simple reactions to the environment. Most workers of physiological, objective temper have claimed that behaviour was all 'reaction'. This attitude was natural in so far as the discovery of the simple reflex movement made it possible for the first time to study, by physiological methods, a type of co-ordinated functioning of the three organ systems involved in behaviour. The early development of 'reflexology' and, later, the discovery of the 'conditioned reflex', caused a wave of optimism in physiological circles, and several prominent physiologists claimed that reflexes and conditioned reflexes were the only elements of behaviour. Pavlov simply identified 'instinct' with 'reflex' and stated, for instance, that the tendency to collect money in man is 'an Instinct or Reflex'. Science, according to Pavlov, is the result of the activation of the 'What-is-that-Reflex', and so on . . .

Spontaneity, on the other hand, has always been stressed by psychologists. Many of these psychologists were definitely superior to the reflexologists in their knowledge of animal behaviour as a whole. But, unfortunately, many of them had a certain disinclination to objective study, and this has created considerable confusion and delay in the development of our science, because it has helped to establish the opinion that spontaneity is not susceptible of objective study. Somehow it was assumed that, once it could be shown that a certain type of behaviour was 'spontaneous' (that is, independent of external stimulation), it would be futile to attack it with physiological methods.

We are at present in a position to say that both opinions contain part of the truth. Behaviour is reaction in so far as it is, to a certain extent, dependent on external stimulation. It is spontaneous in so far as it is also dependent on internal causal factors, or motivational factors, responsible for the activation of an urge or drive.

In the visual domain, motion may often be a powerful stimulus. One of the earliest studies of this type concerned the 'recognition' of prey by dragonflies . . . Mosquito-hunting species do not react to properties of shape, although their highly developed compound eyes certainly enable them to see even minor differences in shape. They react specially to the type of motion of flying mosquitoes. Mosquitoes are not hunted when walking on solid ground. Small scraps of paper of varying shape but of approximately the right size promptly release the hunting responses when they are thrown in the air. . . .

Striking examples of restriction to chemical stimuli are found in the reactions of the males of certain Noctuid moths to the sexual odours emanated by the females. In . . . many species, males in sexual condition are attracted by virgin females. Fabre was the first to suspect that this must be a reaction to smell. This has since been proven in several cases . . . The males react so vigorously and so exclusively to the odour that they may try to copulate with any object bearing the female scent and even with the object on which a female has just been sitting.

In every study of the releasing value of sensory stimuli one is faced by the phenomenon of a varying threshold. The very same stimulus that releases a maximal reaction at one time may have no effect at all or may elicit a weak response at another time. This variation of threshold could be due to either (1) a variation of the intensity of another external stimulus not controlled in the experiment, or (2) a variation of the intensity of internal factors, or (3) both. In this chapter we shall consider the internal factors. The effect of these internal factors determines the 'motivation' of an animal, the activation of its instincts.

The methods of collecting facts bearing on this problem are of different kinds. First there are indirect methods. These are of three types: (a) changes of intensity or frequency of a response are observed under constant conditions; (b) the minimum intensity of the stimulus necessary to release a response is determined at different times while the conditions are kept constant in every other possible respect; (c) the minimum intensity of a stimulus required to inhibit a reaction is measured and its variations in the course of time are observed (obstruction method) . . .

Secondly there is more direct evidence. This has been obtained by studying the effects of experimentally controlled changes within the animal. . . .

Hormones

Not long ago endocrinologists rarely studied the influence of hormones on behaviour; their interest was focused primarily on problems of growth. Only occasionally did they mention behaviour elements, and if so, they used them as more or less accidental indications supporting their primary evidence. In recent times, however, behaviour has been included in several studies and it is certain that some of the internal factors responsible for the fluctuations in responsiveness and for vacuum activities are hormones. This is especially obvious in reproductive activities. In others, like reactions to food or escape reactions, it is less probable that hormones are the internal factors responsible.

The evidence concerning the influence of sex hormones on behaviour, though sufficient to justify the conclusion that such influence is far-reaching, is still rather fragmentary. Of course, many indications are found in the fact that castrated animals do not show complete reproductive behaviour, but further analysis is only just beginning. . . .

In the American chameleon, the male sex hormone testosterone propionate, when implanted subcutaneously as pellets into gonadectomized and intact immature and adult males and females, induces several elements of male sexual behaviour, such as territorial fighting and copulation. However, in both sexes female behaviour was induced in the very same individuals, although it was very incomplete in the treated males.

Evans injected males of the same species in winter with pituitary extracts and found that their fighting and mating behaviour resembled that of normal males in spring and early summer, whereas the controls did not change their normal lethargic winter behaviour.

In birds most of the work has been done with the domestic fowl. Male chicks injected with testosterone propionate exhibited all the sexual behaviour patterns (crowing, complete copulatory behaviour) of the adult cock. A female chick, after receiving a pellet of testosterone propionate when 5 months old, copulated in the male fashion after 4½ months. On one occasion it crowed three times.

Differences in Degree of Complexity of 'Reactions'

So far I have been using the terms 'reaction', 'motor response', 'behaviour pattern', 'movement' for muscle contractions of very different degrees of complexity. This fact is of paramount importance, and I will emphasize it by presenting some more instances.

As we have seen, the swimming of an eel is a relatively simple movement. In every somite there is alternating contraction of the longitudinal muscles of the right and the left half of the trunk. In addition, the pendulum movements of successive somites are slightly out of step, each somite contracting a short time after its predecessor. The result is the propagation of the well-known sinusoid contraction waves along the body axis. . . .

The swimming movements of a fish like *Labrus* or *Sargus* . . . are more complex. The pectoral fins, moving back and forth in alternation, are also in step with the dorsal, caudal, and anal fins, each of which makes pendulum movements as well.

The movement of a male stickleback ventilating its eggs is of a similar type. The pectorals make pendulum movements alternately. This motion is directed forward, resulting in a water current from the fish to the nest. In order to counteract the backward push this exerts upon the fish, forward swimming movements of the tail are made in absolute synchronization with the rhythm of the pectorals.

Although locomotion might be considered merely an element of a 'reaction' in the sense in which I have been using this term, the stickleback's ventilating movement is a complete reaction, responding in part to a chemical stimulus emanating from the nest.

The reaction of a gallinaceous chick to a flying bird of prey is, again, somewhat more complicated. It may consist of merely crouching, but often it consists of running to shelter provided by the mother or by vegetation, crouching, and continuously watching the predator's movements.

Finally, a male stickleback in reproductive condition responds to visual and temperature stimuli of a rather simple type by behaviour of a very complicated pattern: it settles on a territory, fights other males, starts to build a nest, courts females, and so on.

Now, whereas both nest-building and fighting depend on activation of the reproductive drive as a whole, no observer can predict which one of the two patterns will be shown at any given moment. Fighting, for instance, has to be released by a specific stimulus, viz. 'red male intruding into the territory'. Building is not released by this stimulus situation but depends on other stimuli. Thus these two activities, though both depend on activation of the reproductive drive as a whole, are also dependent on additional (external) factors. The influence of these latter factors is, however, restricted; they act upon either fighting or building, not on the reproductive drive as a whole.

Now the stimulus situation 'red male intruding', while releasing the fighting drive, does not determine which one of the five types of fighting will be shown. This is determined by additional, still more specific stimuli. For instance, when the stranger bites, the owner of the territory will bite in return; when the stranger threatens, the owner will threaten back; when the stranger flees, the owner will chase it; and so on.

Thus the effect of a stimulus situation on the animal may be of different kinds. The visual stimulus 'suitable territory' activates both fighting and nest-building; the visual situation 'red male in territory' is specific in releasing fighting, but it merely causes a general readiness to fight and does not determine the type of fighting. Which one of the five motor responses belonging to the fighting pattern will be shown depends on sign stimuli that are still more restricted in effect. The tactile stimulus 'male biting' releases one type of fighting, the visual stimulus 'male threatening' another type. The stimulus situations are not of an essentially different order in all these cases, but the results are. They belong to different levels of integration and, moreover, they are organized in a hierarchical system, like the staff organization of an army or of other human organizations.

Do human babies imprint?

Do human babies imprint? They begin to smile at around forty-five days of age, most crawl at around six months; and by eight months they show fear (*see* Figure 9.12). Is there a critical period between the onset of smiling or crawling and the development of fear during which human babies form a close attachment with others? No one is sure, but the evi-

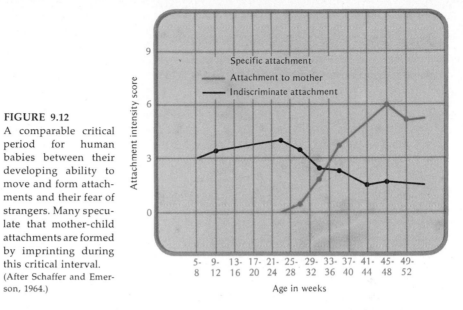

FIGURE 9.12
A comparable critical period for human babies between their developing ability to move and form attachments and their fear of strangers. Many speculate that mother-child attachments are formed by imprinting during this critical interval. (After Schaffer and Emerson, 1964.)

dence is certainly suggestive. While some psychologists believe imprinting is just another example of learning, there are differences between early imprinting and later learning. Learning is quicker and more stable when experimental trials are separated; but imprinting is more rapid when trials are massed together. The last thing that happened is maximally effective for learning, while with imprinting the first thing that happens is most effective (Hess, 1959). Punishment increases the strength of imprinting during a critical period, but punishment produces avoidance learning during later ages. Finally, chicks and ducks who are given a tranquilizing drug can learn color discriminations, but the tranquilizer reduces imprinting to zero. Early imprinting follows different rules than later learning. Therefore, imprinting should be considered a special kind of attachment formation.

Attachment deprivation is serious.

The effects of attachment deprivation are severe. Experimental studies with lower primates and "natural experiments" with human infants both strongly suggest that early mother-child attachments are crucial for later social-personal development.

Let us consider first experimental studies with animals and then natural observations of human infants deprived of their mothers.

Harlow studied monkey mother love.

MATERNAL CARE AND ATTACHMENT Harry Harlow's (1958) studies of emotional attachment among monkey mothers and their offspring grew out of efforts to produce and maintain a colony of sturdy, disease-free animals for research. He had hoped to produce a high rate of survival and to be able to remove the infant animals for testing without the problem of maternal protest. In Harlow's early efforts baby monkeys were housed each in a separate bare wire cage in a large room. Each baby monkey could see and hear others of his kind but could not make direct physical contact. Both mothers and baby monkeys became emotionally disturbed following separation (*see* Figure 9.13). However, the infants' disturbances were much more intense and enduring than were those of the mothers. Harlow observed many behavioral abnormalities among the separated infants as they matured. They stared into space, circled the cage in a stereotyped manner, or clasped their heads in their hands and arms and rocked for long periods. They often developed compulsive habits, like pinching the same patch of skin, and occasionally an animal would chew on his body until it bled. Also, all his isolated monkeys were sexually inept at maturity. The laboratory-born animals did not lack sexual drive, since the males approached females and the females displayed normal sexual presentation. However, they were unable to carry through. The isolated monkeys paid little attention to other animals when they were caged in pairs; they sat in opposite corners and did not interact. No complete heterosexual behavior ever occured between pairs of males and females who were raised in isolation, even though they were caged together for as long as seven years at maturity.

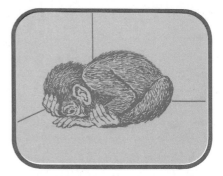

FIGURE 9.13
A depressed infant monkey who has been separated from his mother.
(After Harlow and Zimmerman, 1959.)

Harlow built a wire and a cloth mother surrogate.

Following these initial observations, Harlow studied mother-infant relations more systematically. He built two surrogate caretakers to raise other monkey babies: one covered with terrycloth, the other with wire mesh (*see* Figure 9.14). Bottle-holders were installed in each surrogate caretaker, and both provided the basic requirements for nursing, like a 45-degree-angle bottle and a place for the baby to grasp. The terrycloth surrogate also provided contact comfort and familiar smells, which the wire surrogate did not. Harlow's second experiment investigated the effect of nursing and touching on mother-infant attachment. A cloth mother and a wire mother were placed in each separate cubicle attached to eight infant monkey's living cages. Four baby monkeys were fed only by the wire surrogates and four only by the cloth surrogates. However, all the babies spent most of their time clinging to the terrycloth "mother" and ignored the wire surrogate. Those babies fed by the wire "mother" approached her only during mealtimes. Figure 9.15 shows the long-term effects of

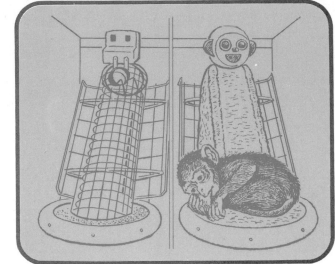

FIGURE 9.14
Wire and cloth mother
surrogates.
(After Harlow, 1958.)

contact comfort and nursing on mother-infant attachment. Apparently maternal-infant attachment is more affected by touch and smell than by feeding, because all the babies stayed near the terrycloth surrogate no matter where they were fed.

Cloth mothers are comforting.

The cloth mother surrogate also provided a safe base from which to explore new or fearful situations. Harlow experimented with the effect of fear on baby monkeys in contact with surrogates, compared to baby

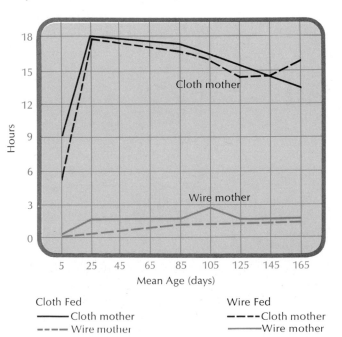

FIGURE 9.15
A comparison of time spent on cloth and wire mother surrogates. Long-term effects show that infant monkeys spend their time on the terrycloth mother surrogate no matter which surrogate feeds them—a clear rejection of the reinforcement-theory explanation of infant-mother attachment.
(After Harlow, 1958.)

Hours

18

15

Cloth mother

12

9

6

Wire mother

3

0

5   25   45   65   85   105   125   145   165

Mean Age (days)

Cloth Fed
———— Cloth mother
– – – – Wire mother

Wire Fed
– – – – Cloth mother
———— Wire mother

FIGURE 9.16
A typical fear stimulus.
(After Harlow, 1958.)

FIGURE 9.17
A typical exploratory
response by a baby
monkey with his cloth
surrogate mother.
(After Harlow and Zim-
merman, 1959.)

monkeys who were isolated. When shown a typical fearful stimulus, illustrated in Figure 9.16, infants in a room with a cloth mother rushed to their surrogates and clutched them tenaciously. Following several minutes of close contact, these infants relaxed and began to explore (*see* Figure 9.17). However, when the babies were alone in a strange room they huddled in the middle of the floor and did not move (*see* Figure 9.18).

Peer relations can
substitute for mother-
child attachment.

In a third set of experiments Harlow allowed infant monkeys to have contact with other infant monkeys during their early development. These primate infants developed more naturally; showed few abnormal tendencies; and matured into more normal, sexually-active adults. Apparently, *maternal* care is not absolutely necessary for normal lower-primate development. Rather, any type of social interaction during the early years seems adequate to produce healthy adult primates.

What about humans? Can they develop normally without maternal care? Can early social relations substitute for mothering?

Human babies are strongly affected by maternal care.

Human mothers may treat their babies in at least three important ways: by paying no attention to the infant (*maternal deprivation*), by forming a close attachment and then abandoning the child (*maternal separation*), or by forming a warm stable attachment with the baby (*maternal care*). Does the amount of maternal care affect the baby? Yes, since neglected babies are often indifferent and withdrawn. However, before about six months of age a human infant can't usually differentiate his own mother from other human beings, so any responsive caretaker can be substituted for the mother. Then, at around six months of age the baby begins to differentiate familiar people from strangers; and, following the onset of stranger anxiety, new social attachments are more difficult to establish. After the baby develops differentiation and fear, he may not accept a stranger as a caretaker. There seems to be a critical period between birth and eight months during which mother-child attachment develops (Schaefer, 1961). If maternal separation occurs when the infant is over eight months of age, he will protest and remain upset until his mother returns. Before eight months the baby's attitude seems to be "out of sight, out of mind." Separation effects are most marked between eight and twenty-four months of age.

Maternal separation produces child protest.

Maternal separation means there is a physical distance between mother and child, while maternal deprivation implies the relation is poor. Early separation need not produce deprivation if an adequate mother surrogate is available. The child living with his own mother can suffer maternal deprivation through the least possible interaction with the mother without actual separation.

As an alternative to maternal care, the Israeli kibbutz suggests that

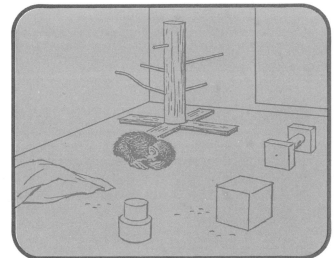

FIGURE 9.18
A typical fear response of a baby monkey placed in an open area without his cloth surrogate mother.
(After Harlow and Zimmerman, 1959.)

human infants can develop into healthy happy children and adults through interaction with their peers and a number of caretakers. In the kibbutz parents visit their children on a regular basis, but the children are managed in groups of fifteen to twenty by several professional caretakers.

Early attachments affect sex role.

HUMAN SEX ROLE   A universal conclusion from animal and human research is that early emotional attachments can affect later sex-role development. This is so whether the experimenter believes sexuality is biologically determined or is the result of social influences.

Sexual behavior is controlled at several levels.

The various human nervous systems are all involved in human sexuality (Maccoby, 1966). At the most primitive level hormones from the chemical system determine the strength of the sexual drive. At the next level the hypothalamus of the brain processes sexual stimuli. Early attachments determine the particular stimuli which arouse sexuality; and later learning determines how these sexual feelings get expressed. Hormones apparently don't determine sexual direction because injecting male homosexuals with androgen only increases their homosexual activity.

Some animals must learn sexuality.

Some primates are born with programmed sexual acts, while others must rely on learning. Male monkeys and chimpanzees need to be taught sexual behavior by their parents and others in the troop, while female monkeys perform perfectly well without prior experience. If a young male and female monkey are put together, the female instructs him.

Are there innate sex differences among people?

There is an important controversy in the U.S. about human sex-role development. Some proponents of Feminism have claimed that all sex-role differences are culturally determined and should be eliminated. Whether one argues for biology or experience as the ultimate sex-role determinant, there *are* differences between men and women on almost every measure imaginable (Maccoby, 1966). There is also considerable overlap in the abilities of both sexes. But some of the differences are striking. One must remember that these findings are general and that individuals may differ widely. Vocational aptitude tests show that many women are superior to men in skills which require rapid attention shifts, like number-crossing or symbol-checking, while many men are better at tasks that require analytical thinking. Females are aware of color earlier, and this advantage increases with age. Sex differences in reactivity are detectable by the first year of life. Boys prefer novel toys more than girls, suggesting either higher information processing or shorter attention span. There are even sexual differences in intelligence. IQ tests were constructed to eliminate sexual differences in the total score so any male/ female variation must be reflected in the pattern of subtest scores. These subtests show several differences: Most girls test somewhat higher in overall IQ during preschool years, probably because they mature faster; while most boys score better during high school and from then on. Correlations between parents' and daughters' IQ are significant by three years of age, but not until five years for sons. Young girls exceed boys in verbal abilities, but by the age of ten boys catch up with girls in reading ability. However, girls continue to excel in grammar, spelling, and word fluency. Boys possess greater reasoning ability by the time they reach high school, and even young boys do much better than most girls on tests of spatial relations. Some scientists argue that experience and expectation jointly determine these sex differences. Do little girls excel at reading because they may need the skill later or because at six years of age they are aware of sexual stereotypes? According to Eleanor Maccoby, sex differences in spatial ability are not easy to explain on the basis of opportunities to learn. It's true that little boys have played more with blocks while little girls tended to play with doll houses, but can these experiences produce differential spatial ability? These sex differences appear very early in life, and it is not at all clear that they result from experience alone. Current trends may change the behavior of children of both sexes.

Cultures define man and woman variously.

Different people define man and woman variously, but few cultures claim equivalence. Most have partitioned human characteristics, opposing stupidity-brillance, or beauty-ugliness, or friendliness-hostility in some way. Only maternity is exclusively female. This cultural diversity is used to challenge biological restraints. However, diversity may also reflect genetic variation. The basic question is: Are there genetic dispositions toward sex which may be masked by the culture or is the human being totally capable of being shaped by experience?

There are at least three possible answers:

1. Important biological sex differences exist and are difficult to ignore.
2. There are genetic constraints, but they can be modified without distress.
3. Sex differences are only a stylistic extravagance imposed on genetically equivalent organisms.

Few cultures claim there are no sex differences.

No one knows the answer, but the problem is pressing. There are many dimensions along which the sexes vary. If men and women are arranged along any single line, average differences in both directions appear, but there is considerable overlap no matter what characteristic is considered. To claim that *all* elements of a sex role are socially directed *or* are biologically constrained is surely wrong. What is needed in this area is reason, understanding, and an appreciation of biological diversity, coupled with sensitivity to people's legitimate needs.

Cognitive Motivation

Children have cognitive motives.

Children's behavior is neither a simple reaction to stimulation nor the direct result of physiological drives. In order to understand even the simplest human acts, stimuli, drives, *and* cognitive motives must be included. All three are important in governing behavior.

Most animals are curious.

CURIOSITY   Consider the case of curiosity. Harlow showed that a monkey, if given a relatively simple puzzle, will take it apart hour after hour with little or no rest and without external reward. Many psychologists argue that even young children have needs beyond food, water, and sleep. They point out that children can get bored. Consider a theory of cognitive curiosity that assumes four things:

1. Children are sensitive to the complexity of environmental events.
2. There is a limitation on their ability to process separate environmental events.
3. It is possible to escape this restriction on processing ability through rules derived from past experience.
4. Children prefer events that match their ability to process them—they do not want to be bored by simple events nor overcome by complex ones. They prefer an intermediate level of complexity.

Children prefer intermediate complexity.

A clear case of preference for increased complexity happens when children learn to read. They begin by processing *letters*. At this early stage each letter is a complex perception, and they concentrate on dealing with them one at a time. The next step is to learn groups of letters and put them together into *words*. The structuring of letters into words, words into sentences, and sentences into thought characterizes the development of rules and the shifting taste for more complexity. Obviously, the newborn can't read English, nor for that matter can the average five-year-old. The adult can easily process what the child cannot even understand. This analysis suggests that by structuring his world through rules and experience, the person becomes able to handle more complex events. As a result, what was complex before he learned the rules is now simple, and the person will constantly seek newer, more complex tasks. This interest in more complex events is called *curiosity*.

Consider some evidence for these notions. Suppose the predictability of sequences of letters is varied. The same letter repeated over and over is most simple. Next in complexity would be the same word repeated over and over, next a short passage of prose, then a passage that looks a bit like English but contains no grammar, and finally a series of random words and letters. These sequences of letters and words provide increasing unpredictability or complexity; they vary from simple to complex. The propositions discussed earlier (sensitivity to complexity, a limit on the ability to process environmental events, the sidestepping of this limit by the learning of rules, and preference for complexity at or near the child's ability to process) predict differences in children's and adults' preferences for these sequences of letters and words. Assume that as a child matures he develops more-and-more sophisticated processing rules. Young children should then prefer simple strings of letters and words, and as they mature should prefer more complex strings.

Harry Munsinger and William Kessen (1964) presented the stimuli shown in Table 9.1 to third-grade and sixth-grade children and college

TABLE 9.1 Varying levels of complexity from simple redundant letters through prose to complex random letters. Notice that the amount of processing required is much greater for random letters than for any other set.

Predictability of letters and words	*Set I*	*Set II*	
Redundant letters	DDDDD DDDDD DDDDD DDDDD DDDDD DDDDD	YYYYYY YYYYYY YYYYYY YYYYYY YYYYYY YYYYYY	(simple)
Redundant words	Current Current Current Current Current	Include Include Include Include Include	
Prose	A short time at Alexandria is fine	He made life long friends there	
Second-order phrases	Him and substance was a piano is	Is that game since he lives in school	(intermediate)
Random words	Obeisance cordial dip long bed hammer	Forget lethargy fluted watch attend	
Random letters	Ffjccyk cqagx ydalm bixz xmrfj	Sjoml rxklr jffjuj zip wofckeyj	(complex)

People prefer intermediate uncertainty.

adults for preference judgments. Their results are shown on the table. As expected, all participants preferred neither the very simple letters and words, nor the very complex strings. Instead, they liked an intermediate level of complexity. Adults, with their sophisticated reading rules, preferred more complex verbal stimuli than did third- and sixth-grade children. Thus, not only are children and adults curious but they also strive to meet a standard of excellence. This striving is called achievement motivation.

McClelland designed a test for achievement motivation.

ACHIEVEMENT   The original test of *achievement motivation* was developed by David McClelland (1953). He designed one situation in which students were relaxed and another in which they were motivated to try hard; then he gave his subjects a test of their imagination. The relaxed group was told they were taking the test to help in its development; while the aroused group was told that the test would determine their standing in school; and then all subjects were given false feedback which showed they had failed the tests. Both groups were presented with four pictures and asked to tell a story about each one. McClelland assumed that students who were trying to do well and thought they had failed tell stories about achievement; while students who were relaxed would say little about achievement. He was right.

High-achievement children have demanding parents.

As part of an overall study on achievement motivation, Winterbottom gathered achievement scores from twenty-nine boys aged eight to ten years. She asked the boys' mothers questions about how children should be reared, and what kind of independent action was expected of their children. Each mother was asked to tell when she expected her children to:

1. Know their way around the city.
2. Try new things for themselves.
3. Do well in competition.
4. Make their own friends.

As you might guess, mothers of high-achievement children expected more from their offspring than mothers of low-achievement children. The primary demand was for high-achievement children to do new things. The mother's expectations about routine tasks were similar. Early attempts at independence training are apparently successful, but if parents suddenly try to foster independence and achievement motivation among their adolescent children, they are doomed to failure. In addition to achievement and independence, the person's level of aspiration and the fear of failure affect the choice of goals and the amount of persistence.

Fear of failure is debilitating.

FEAR OF FAILURE AND RISK-TAKING   Every task is both a challenge to succeed and a chance to fail. How do achievement needs and fear of failure interact? Psychologists have studied the problem by manipulating risk and success in games. They find that most children choose tasks with some chance of success and yet enough challenge to let them feel personal accomplishment. Apparently completing easy tasks gives these children no feeling of achievement, while very difficult tasks offer little chance of success. Children who are plagued by *fear of failure* find very easy or very difficult tasks most attractive. The fearful child chooses a difficult task with no chance of success, or an easy task with no chance of failure. In this way he can't feel incompetent.

Fearful children choose easy or impossible tasks.

The relative strength of achievement motive and fear of failure determines whether a person will choose an easy, impossible, or reasonable task. If a child's achievement need is high and fear of failure low he will risk realistic tasks; but if he fears failure he will choose trivially easy or impossibly difficult jobs, as we have seen.

Emotions

Indicators of Emotion

There are many indices of emotion.

Strong emotions activate other parts of a child's body. Tremors occur; the teeth are clenched; the eyes blink more often; and the face may form a grimace. Strong emotions are also associated with internal physiological changes, such as increases in heart rate, shifts in the pattern of blood flow from internal organs to muscles, and a strong increase in available blood sugar. Salivation and digestion slow, while the body's metabolic rate increases. Breathing comes more quickly; and the pupils enlarge, causing a wide-eyed look.

Large pupils signal interest.

PUPIL SIZE AND EMOTIONS   If brightness is controlled, changes in the size of the pupil of the eye are good indicators of emotion. Pupil size increases with interest and decreases with disgust. Figure 9.19 shows what happened to the pupil of a male's eye when he looked at a mother and baby, a nude male, and a nude female. Note that males are interested in females, while female's pupils expand when they see pictures of a mother and child or a nude male. Not only does pupil size indicate interest but other people are attracted by increases in pupil size. Although this difference in pupil size is often not noticed consciously, most men find women with larger pupils more interesting. Is that because large pupils mean she is interested in the man? Pupil size also increases when people try to solve a problem or remember a number; harder problems produce larger pupils.

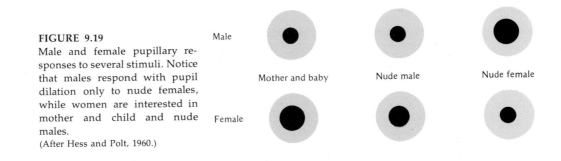

FIGURE 9.19
Male and female pupillary responses to several stimuli. Notice that males respond with pupil dilation only to nude females, while women are interested in mother and child and nude males.
(After Hess and Polt, 1960.)

Male

Mother and baby   Nude male   Nude female

Female

Facial expressions signal emotions.

FACIAL EXPRESSIONS   There are several stereotyped facial expressions and body postures typical of emotional states in man and animals. The facial expression and the tail display of dogs signal threat or submission. Human children have universal emotional expressions for happiness and anger. Unhappily, adult facial expressions often become separated from specific emotional states. The result is ambiguity at best and, sometimes, hypocrisy.

A few emotional signs are universal.

Some cultural differences in the interpretation of stereotyped facial expressions exist, although most cultures recognize the universal meaning of smiles, frowns, and tears. The ambiguity of adult emotional expressions probably occurs because they are more complex than children's. Adults have also learned to inhibit many emotional expressions.

Babies' activity levels vary.

Human infants are either active or quiet (*see* Figure 9.20). During their periods of activity infants can be distressed or happy. The physiological changes associated with distress are probably innately programed, but

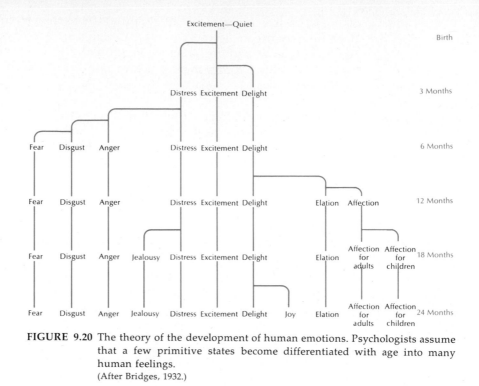

FIGURE 9.20 The theory of the development of human emotions. Psychologists assume that a few primitive states become differentiated with age into many human feelings.
(After Bridges, 1932.)

new stimuli become associated with distress through classical conditioning.

Boys have more angry outbursts than girls.

How frequent are outbursts of distress among children? Florence Goodenough explored the frequency of children's anger as a function of age and stimulus situation. She found a peak frequency at around eighteen months of age and then a gradual decline, with girls showing lower levels of angry outbursts than boys at most ages (*see* Figure 9.21). She discovered four causes of anger:

1. Conflicts about routine physical things like going to bed or having their faces washed.
2. Conflicts about discipline.
3. Rejection of parental authority.
4. Anger over social situations, such as competing with a sibling for a toy or for parent's attention.

Several factors determine anger.

Conflicts about physical care and discipline accounted for about 40 percent of the child's anger; another 30 percent was associated with social interaction. A variety of factors contribute to development of anger: the child's own particular needs, the amount of frustration in his world, and the child's state of fatigue. Most outbursts occur before meals and at bed-

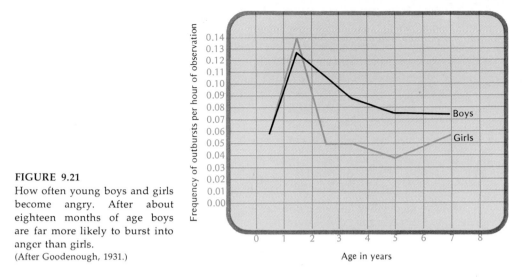

FIGURE 9.21
How often young boys and girls
become angry. After about
eighteen months of age boys
are far more likely to burst into
anger than girls.
(After Goodenough, 1931.)

time. A child's general physical health also affects his emotions, since
children become angry more easily if they are ill or tired.

Infants smile socially
by six months of age.

The expression of pleasant emotions is a neglected area of child development. Joy is not so dramatic as fear or anger, and there are few accompanying physiological changes. Smiling and laughing are the main
indicators of joy. Many investigators report that social smiling begins at
about six months of age among human infants, although they smile
spontaneously at an earlier age. Laughter can occur when a child is mildly
surprised, when there is perceptual incongruity, and when other people
are smiling at him (*see* Figure 9.22).

Laughing or smiling happens in a social situation and most often after

FIGURE 9.22 Stimuli that provoke smiles in young infants. As they grow older, more sophisticated stimuli are required to bring forth
the response.
(After Ahrens, 1954.)

the child has completed a task. The development and expression of emotions is intimately related to the child's personal adjustment. If emotions are denied, they can produce serious difficulties in body and mind, and may lead to personal maladjustment. Not only do physiological states affect the child's goals and needs but his state of awareness also influences behavior dramatically. Examples of changes in awareness are sleep and meditation.

Changes in Awareness

Psychologists believe that animals dream.

SLEEP   Recently, scientists have developed techniques for studying sleep and dreams. On the basis of these studies some psychologists believe even animals dream, and that there is a link between dreaming and some abnormal behaviors.

Sleep loss can produce serious behavior problems.

Everyone sleeps and most people dream, but until quite recently psychologists knew almost nothing about the function of sleep and dreaming. Children spend about half of their time asleep. During final examination time every student wishes he could spend fewer hours sleeping and more time studying. Is it possible to avoid sleep? The answer is yes, but only for a short interval and at the cost of reduced performance. There are recorded examples of physicians in hospitals, soldiers on the battlefield, or others under stress who avoided sleep for a day or so. What happens when someone stays awake for extended periods? The longest recorded

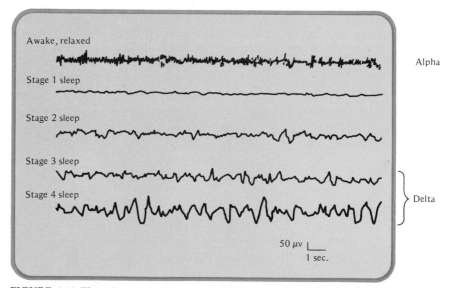

FIGURE 9.23 The relaxed, awake person's EEG is characterized by ten-cycle per second alpha rhythms. Stage 1 sleep is a low-amplitude, irregular pattern similar to the awake person's EEG. During Stage 2 the EEG shows sleep spindles; while Stages 3 and 4 show high-amplitude delta waves which indicate deep sleep.

period of wakefulness was achieved by a radio announcer in New York who stayed awake for 200 hours! Physicians examined and tested him throughout his period of wakefulness. By the end of 48 hours the radio announcer reported hallucinations and by 100 hours his memory was so poor he could not do simple tasks. Later, his hallucinations became paranoid. He saw people's clothes turn to animals and the walls burst into flames. At this point simple mathematical problems were impossible feats, and he could not remember the alphabet. After 160 hours without sleep he began losing his identity and measures of his electrical brain patterns resembled sleep (*see* Figure 9.23). He was so paranoid by then that he believed the doctors were trying to kill him. There were no permanent effects reported by him after he resumed a more normal sleep pattern.

How much sleep does the average person need? What can you do when you can't get to sleep or when you wake up too early? The accompanying interview with Dr. Julius Segal of the National Institute of Mental Health answers some of these questions.

sleep

JULIUS SEGAL, M.D.

Q. Dr. Segal, how much sleep does an average person need?

A. That's like asking, in effect, what size shoe the average person needs. That is, it is commonly assumed that there is a "normal" quota of sleep for all mankind. Eight hours often is cited as the generally accepted norm—a figure, incidentally, that goes far back, at least to Maimonides, the twelfth-century Jewish philosopher and physician.

The scientific study of sleep, however, shows a range of sleep requirement among us that is much broader than we have ever assumed in the past.

One survey, for example, showed that 8 per cent of a large sample in Scotland required only five hours as a maximum, and many of these got along with less than five hours. Fifteen per cent needed five to six hours of sleep. It is true, as the survey indicates, that the large bulk of the population usually takes between seven and eight hours of sleep. But 13 per cent required nine to 10 hours, and a few needed even more than 10 hours.

Q. Was this all continuous sleep—not counting cat naps?

A. It was continuous nighttime sleep. Even among infants, incidentally, there are already differences. It has been presumed that every newborn spends roughly 20 hours of the 24-hour day asleep, but laboratory studies show a much greater variability—from 10 to 23 hours. So, you see, sleep is a very individual matter.

Q. Do certain types of people need more sleep than others?

A. There have been few studies correlating personality types against need for sleep. Many years ago, William H. Sheldon, the physical anthropologist, suggested that body type was related to a number of aspects of human personality and behavior, including sleep. He held that the "endomorph"—the soft, fat, rotund type of person—slept easily and slept a lot, whereas the thin, sensitive, fragile "ectomorph" was prone to insomnia. But no rigorous studies support hypotheses of this sort. Yet, we shouldn't be surprised if there were a built-in, constitutional, genetically determined predisposition for sleep—as in many other areas of behavior.

I'm not discounting the importance of training and environment in shaping sleep habits or eating habits or any other bit of behavior. But the old phrase, "born that way," referring to genetic inheritance, seems increasingly relevant here. That is, the patterns of sleep that many people exhibit or complain about are apparent from earliest childhood. Many parents who are very upset about a child's sleep patterns ought best to make peace with the fact that those patterns came with the child and are not all that easy to change.

Q. Is it unusual for any child to have trouble going to sleep or awakening?

A. It is not at all unusual. Laboratory studies do show that deep sleep is much more apparent in the records of young children than in those of adolescents and, certainly, of adults. That is, the quality of sleep deteriorates with age, and scientifically, the phrase "slept like a baby" is not an idle one.

On the other hand, the emotional and psychological problems of which we're all victims at times can beset youngsters as well as adults. Anxiety, depression, excitement—such enemies of sleep are not absent in the lives of young children. Later, the stresses of adolescence can also cause a disruption of sleep habits—including, incidentally, a phenomenon called "hypersomnia," which is oversleeping, or sleeping more than the individual's norm.

Q. Why would that be?

A. Psychologically, sleep can sometimes be seen as a vehicle for retreating from reality. All of us have experienced the kinds of stresses in which the most comfortable thing to do upon awakening in the morning would be to duck under the covers and escape reality—sleep some more.

Q. Are there actually "day people" and "night people"?

A. There are, indeed—the "larks" and the "owls." There are notable differences in the time of our daily peaks and lows. For some of us, body temperature begins to rise early during sleep, and we wake up whistling, but hit our low point early in the evening. Others begin slowly, and don't hit their stride until afternoon. For them, sleep is not an attractive prospect until much later at night.

Q. How are "owls" going to get to school at 9 o'clock in the morning—or how do "larks" get used to working an overnight shift?

A. These are problems with enormous implications for our whole society—schools, industry, perhaps even hospital schedules for surgery. All of us—parents, teachers, bosses, doctors—should be more sensitive to differences in people.

Q. Can youngsters be trained to modify their sleep patterns to the necessary extent?

A. Not as easily as many parents expect. It is difficult to alter the rhythm built into each of us, and often we do no good by trying to impose on children a sleep schedule that is not part of their norm. Many parents expect their children to be entirely pliable where sleep is concerned. Remember, children not only have their own unique patterns of sleep, but their own emotional turmoil, disappointments and crises that can affect their attitudes toward sleep.

After a difficult day at work, you might come home distraught and upset and would want nothing more than to sit down with a bottle of beer and watch an innocuous program on television, maybe a football game, or read a magazine. The thought of sleep is something in the dim future. What if, at that moment, your mother-in-law or wife pokes a finger at you and says: "O.K., lights out and not a sound out of you"? I think you would feel violated. But we do this to our kids.

Q. Are there presleep habits for youngsters that should be encouraged, such as a period of quiet reading?

A. Absolutely. That is, reading, watching television, working at a hobby—I wouldn't discourage any of those things for my adolescent youngster for whom sleep is not appropriate at the hour it is for me.

I'm not suggesting social chaos in a household, in which everybody eats and sleeps at a different hour. But in one's own room without disturbing the rest of the household, I think individual differences should not be stifled.

Dangers in "Lost Sleep"

Q. Is it possible to make up for lost sleep?

A. Yes, but not as quickly or as easily for everyone.

Some young, stable people have endured 10 to 12 days of sleeplessness with no apparent ill effects. Others have suffered persistent symptoms. Many mothers date the onset of insomnia problems to the pregnancy and postnatal period, in which sleep becomes fragmented. Many doctors testify that their insomnia problems began in medical school or internship, when sleep schedules were upset or reversed for long periods of time. We still don't know whether prolonged sleep deprivation might cause irreversible damage to some persons. Therefore, a person should treat dramatic and prolonged changes in sleep schedules with caution.

Q. What about children's nightmares? Do they follow periods of dreamlessness?

A. Not typically. The dreams of children are more frequent, and often more vivid and terrifying, because they are difficult for the youngster to distinguish from reality. The child is being flooded with new experiences and sensations all the time.

The most terrifying nightmares of all, however, arise not out of the REM period, but from the periods of deepest sleep. During such episodes, a child may scream in terror but be difficult to awaken. Sleepwalking and bedwetting also appear to arise from these periods of deep, dreamless sleep.

Q. Do people tend to get trapped into using sleeping pills because of this fear of insomnia?

A. No question about it, and the use of sleep drugs must be a major issue in any discussion of drug abuse in this country today. Just a couple of statistics: We spend over half a billion dollars a year on sleeping pills. There are 800,000 pounds of barbiturates alone produced in this country each year. Now that's only one family of sleep drugs—enough, incidentally, to supply one capsule a week for each man, woman and child in the country. Multiply that figure by the more than

200 types of sleep potions available today and you get an idea of the problem.

Q. Are you talking of sleep potions available on prescription or available over the counter?

A. On prescription. And it's not only true in our own country. Ten per cent of all prescriptions by British general practitioners are for sleep drugs.

The spiraling use of drugs for sleep is clearly apparent, and neither patients nor many of their doctors are entirely aware of the potential dangers involved. That is why the insomniac should try to use avenues other than drugs in living through or overcoming sleep problems.

Q. Do sleeping pills affect only sleep adversely, or can they have more far-reaching effects?

A. Both are possible. It is now clear that many of the drugs we have been taking to capture sleep are capable of distorting the very sleep they induce. For example, the nightly rhythm of vivid dreaming—the apparently essential REM periods of the night—is dampened by heavy doses of most sleeping pills. When the drug is stopped abruptly, the results are often further sleep problems, including ugly and disturbing nightmares.

As to longer-range effects, we shouldn't assume when we take a sleeping pill that all we are going to affect is our sleep.

Long after the sedation has worn off, an impact on your mental and emotional state may remain. Barbiturates, for example, may intensify feelings of depression and reduce intellectual acuity. But most important, a person builds up a "tolerance" to a particular drug, and then needs ever higher doses to get the desired effect. That is where the really serious trouble begins—leading down the road to possible addiction.

Psychologists study dreams indirectly.

DREAMS Psychologists must study sleep indirectly, since sleeping subjects can't communicate in ordinary ways. Good information about sleep was difficult to obtain because there were no reliable measures of what happens to the person during sleep. A breakthrough came when scientists began putting electrodes onto the outside of the sleeping person's head to measure the brain's electrical activity. Such electrical activity is called the electroencephalogram (EEG). Early sleep scientists found that brain waves change with the onset of sleep and show four systematic stages throughout the sleep cycle:

Stage One Sleep is characterized by irregular EEG activity of low amplitude, much like the EEG collected from an awake, relaxed person.

Stage Two Sleep shows periods of activity on the EEG followed by pointed waves called "sleep spindles."

Stage Three and Stage Four Sleep produce high-amplitude, slow cycle "delta waves." A person in Stage Four Sleep is very difficult to arouse.

Dreaming happens during REM sleep.

Beyond these four stages of sleep is another called REM sleep, in which the person's electroencephalogram looks like Stage One Sleep but the brain pattern is accompanied by Rapid Eye Movements (REM) and inhibition of gross motor activity. A sleeper awakened from REM sleep almost always reports that he was experiencing a dream. The electroencephalogram during REM sleep resembles Stage One, but the sleeper is more difficult to awaken.

The sleeper drifts through various stages.

There is no regular sequence of sleep stages. The sleeper drifts from Stage One through Stage Four and back several times during a single period. Stage Four sleep occurs most often during the first half of a night's sleep, while REM sleep is most likely in the last Third Stage.

Why do people dream?

Why do people dream? One clue may be found in the amount of dreaming among infants, children, adolescents, and adults (see Figure 9.24). Dreaming happens about eight out of sixteen hours in the infant, but only around one out of six hours in the mature adult. Thus, REM sleep occurs during half a baby's sleeping hours, but only 20 percent of the time among mature adults. The major change in amount of sleep as a person matures is the time spent dreaming.

REM sleep decreases with age.

REM sleep decreases, though nondreaming sleep remains fairly constant with age. Why do babies dream so much? No one knows, but possibly their dreams promote development of the central nervous system or maybe dreaming is simply information processing and storage for them. Another possibility is that young children's emotional processes are less stable and they need more REM sleep to stabilize their feelings. In this theory children's frequent dreams may simply reflect an attempt to cope with a novel, frightening world. Alternately, children may be less inhibited about dreaming than adults are.

Meditation changes awareness.

MEDITATION   There has recently been increased interest in another state of altered awareness called meditation. With practice, many people can produce voluntary variations in awareness. The process is called *meditation,* when the person attends to one thing and restricts other sensory input. People say they meditate in order to experience the world in new ways, or to gain deeper personal understanding. During meditation a person's EEG is similar to the pattern of brain waves for a relaxed, awake subject. A similar subjective state and EEG pattern can be produced in some subjects by showing them a completely homogeneous perceptual field called the Ganzfield. Some scientists argue that meditation is a new form of consciousness, while others simply say it is a natural result of lowered motor and brain activity. No one is sure what meditation means to the person, but it certainly produces changes in awareness.

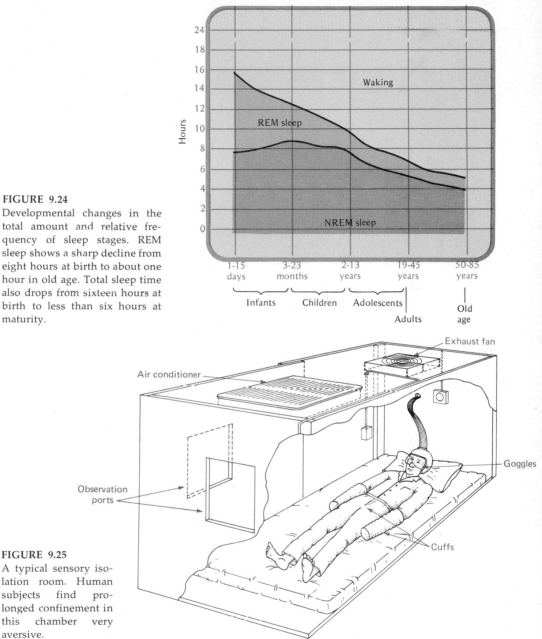

FIGURE 9.24
Developmental changes in the total amount and relative frequency of sleep stages. REM sleep shows a sharp decline from eight hours at birth to about one hour in old age. Total sleep time also drops from sixteen hours at birth to less than six hours at maturity.

FIGURE 9.25
A typical sensory isolation room. Human subjects find prolonged confinement in this chamber very aversive.

Biofeedback can facilitate control of involuntary processes.

Feedback from a person's EEG pattern has been used experimentally to alter his state of awareness. Called *biofeedback,* the technique entails measuring human EEG patterns and then immediately feeding them back to the person in the form of a tone or color. Biofeedback gives the person immediate information about the kind of brain waves he is producing. A person's EEG can be displayed on a TV screen or used to change the frequency or intensity of sound or light. This immediate feedback makes voluntary control of brain waves, blood pressure, heart rate, and other autonomic functions possible for many people, as we have seen. However, not all claims to such control are substantiated. Biofeedback is not the answer to all psychological problems. If children with heart and other serious diseases can be taught to use the biofeedback technique and it is workable for them much suffering could be relieved.

Isolation depresses brain activity.

ISOLATION   Solitary confinement is a serious punishment for prisoners, and even a few days' restriction in an isolated environment becomes aversive to most people. Many believe man's central nervous system requires external stimulation to maintain its normal functions. We know that the brain is buffered against short-term *sensory isolation* by the *recticular activation system* (RAS), which maintains central nervous system arousal during periods of sparse signals.

Long-term sensory isolation is aversive.

The human central nervous system slows its functions when sensory information is restricted for prolonged intervals. A person in an absolutely quiet environment (*see* Figure 9.25) sleeps for several hours, then becomes agitated or depressed; further isolation produces boredom. His brain-wave patterns change; his awareness of the outside world diminishes; and his judgment is impaired. Prolonged isolation produces visual and auditory hallucinations and finally disorganization of thinking, similar to the person who lacks sleep for a lengthy period of time. The human central nervous system apparently needs sensory stimulation, otherwise the person's awareness of the world is reduced. This is one reason why babies especially should be given opportunities for varied experiences with people, surroundings, and objects.

Summary

Human motivation is a complicated process based on many interconnected levels of the Central Nervous System. A baby's most basic behaviors are motivated by innate instincts and primary drives, like hunger and thirst. Beyond these primitive systems of motivation are more complicated processes, like aggression and sexuality, which seem to be governed by both innate factors and socially acquired attitudes. At the highest level of human motivation are human social attachments and cognitive motives, like curiosity or the need to achieve. In addition to having motives, human beings are also aware of their bodily states and goals; we call this awareness emotion.

SUGGESTED ADDITIONAL READINGS

Freud, S. *The Basic Writings of Sigmund Freud.* A.A. Brill, ed. New York: Modern Library, 1938.

Mowrer, O.H. *Learning Theory and Behavior.* New York: Wiley, 1960.

IO Parent-child Relations

How Parents Influence Their Children
  Genetic Predispositions
    Intelligence
    Personality and Abnormal Behavior
  Critical Periods in Childhood
    Birth
    Imprinting and Attachment
    Maternal Separation or
      Deprivation
  Discipline
    Imitation
    Rewards and Punishments
    Inconsistent Discipline
Parent-child Interaction
  Family Atmospheres
    Love/Hate
    Control/Autonomy
  Types of Offspring from Various
    Home Environments

Control and Love
  The Overprotected Child
Control and Hate
  The Rejected Child
Autonomy and Love
Autonomy and Hate
Parent-child Relations
Children's Views of Parents
Variation in Family Relations
  Variations within the Family
    Family Size and Composition
    The Working Mother
    The Single Parent
    Divorce
    Institutionalization
    Social Class Differences in
      Family Relations
Practical Child-training Suggestions
Summary

PREVIEW

Everyone agrees that parents affect their children's personal and emotional development, but how does this happen? What can parents do to make their offspring healthy and happy? Simple statements about good or bad parent-child relations ignore both the large variation in parental values and the individual differences in children. If parents want aggressive, self-sufficient children, whether consciously or unconsciously, they should not be warm and controlling. Aggressive children will develop most readily in an atmosphere of assertiveness, autonomy, and frustration. If parents want quiet, modest children, they should handle them with very little love and infinite control.

The main purpose of studying parent-child interactions is to generate predictions about what types of children result from different family atmospheres. But two things should be remembered: Children come into the world with strong genetic predispositions, and parents are affected by what their children do, just as children are influenced by their parents. The parents of a calm, loving, and happy child can afford to be democratic, warm, and charming in their discipline. By contrast, the parents of a hostile, irritable, and unruly child may experiment with many different ways to control him. Parent-child relations work both ways.

How Parents Influence Their Children

Parents influence children in three ways.

Three main factors determine parental influences on children. The first occurs at conception, when the mother and father each contribute unique genetic traits to their offspring. Next, the child passes through several critical stages of development, during which he is particularly susceptible to influences from his parents. Finally, the social model and schedules of reward or punishment that parents present to their children determine the course of their child's maturity. First, consider the genetic influences.

Genetic Predispositions

One factor is hereditary.

Numerous studies of family pedigree, twins, and adopted children show that many of the parents' genetic characteristics are passed along to their children, as we have seen earlier. Everyone agrees that physical traits — height, hair color, and nose length — are influenced by genes. Now, more and more evidence is accumulating which suggests that the parents' intelligence, emotions, and abnormalities are also passed along to their children through heredity. Let us review what we know about genes and behavior.

Intelligence is partially genetic.

INTELLIGENCE   Erlenmeyer-Kimling and Jarvik (1963) reported data from groups of unrelated people, siblings, and fraternal and identical twins reared together and apart. The researchers discovered that there is a systematic increase in the relationship of IQ to family connection. If the family members are reared in different environments, the correlation between them drops about .20 for all categories of genetic relation. These data suggest that there is a strong genetic constraint on intelligence, *and* that the environment can modify genetic control to some extent. This may also be the case with some personality traits.

Personal and abnormal behaviors are inherited.

PERSONALITY AND ABNORMAL BEHAVIOR   Controversy also surrounds the effects of genetics on personality and abnormal behavior. Some believe neurotic and psychotic behavior is primarily genetic (Eysenck, 1967), while others view abnormal reactions as being the result of early experiences. Schizophrenia, a major mental disorder, does run in families, and studies consistently show that the frequency of psychosis in family groups is far in excess of what can be expected in the general population. Estimates of the expected incidence of schizophrenia among siblings of schizophrenics is 5–10 percent, if both parents are free from schizophrenia; 8–18 percent, if one parent is schizophrenic; and 45–68 percent, if both parents are schizophrenic. These numbers are far higher than in the general population, where the incidence of psychosis is around 1 percent. Expectancies based on other categories of relationships (half-siblings, grandchildren, nephews, nieces, and first cousins) are all above the general population figure, and they increase systematically with closer familial relation, as we have seen. The high incidences of schizophrenia in certain families in the absence of any common environmental factor also suggests a genetic influence. Kallman's extensive study of nearly a thousand pairs of twins and several thousand of their close relatives showed that if one twin was schizophrenic, 86 percent of identical co-twins were also schizophrenic; the corresponding frequency of schizophrenia in fraternal twins was 15 percent (*see* Table 10.1). Happily, the total incidence of schizophrenia among twins is no higher than in the general population. The much higher percentages are for twins who have a co-twin who is already psychotic.

TABLE 10.1   The results of several studies comparing the similarity of identical twins, fraternal twins, and siblings. Note that in all cases identical twins are much more alike than fraternal twins or siblings.

Trait	Investigator	Intrapair concordance rate		Intrapair correlation coefficient		
		Identical twins (percent)	Fraternal twins (percent)	Identical twins	Fraternal twins	Siblings (percent)
Schizophrenia	Kallman (1953)	86	15	—	—	15
Manic-depressive psychosis	Kallman (1953)	93	24	—	—	23
Psychopathic personality	Slater (1953)	25	14	—	—	—
Alcoholism	Kaij (1957)	65	30	—	—	—
Male homosexuality	Kallman (1953)	98	12	—	—	—
Hysteria	Stumpfl (1937)	33	0	—	—	—
Suicide	Kallman (1953)	6	0	—	—	—
Extraversion-introversion	Gottesman (1963)	—	—	.55	.08	—
Depression	Gottesman (1963)	—	—	.47	.07	—
Neuroticism	Eysenck and Prell (1951)	—	—	.85	.22	—

Schizophrenia is partly genetic.

Slater, in a smaller study, reported similar results when he found that schizophrenia occurred in both identical twins for 70 percent of his study as compared with 14 percent for fraternal twins. Whatever the precise estimates may be, there is a strikingly higher risk of schizophrenia among identical than among fraternal twins when one member of the pair is psychotic. Recent studies by Hansen of adopted children of schizophrenic mothers show that these children can manifest schizophrenia even if separated from their mothers at birth. Thus, it appears that the family environment has much less to do with schizophrenia than was previously thought.

TABLE 10.2   Similarity in various types of criminal, antisocial, and asocial behavior among twins

| | Number of twin pairs | Identical twins | Fraternal twins | Proportion of similarity | |
				Identical twins	Fraternal twins
Adult crime	225	107	118	71	34
Juvenile delinquency	67	42	25	85	75
Childhood behavior disorder	107	47	60	87	43
Homosexuality	63	37	26	100	12
Alcoholism	82	26	56	65	30

Source: Adapted from H.J.Eysenck, *Crime and Personality* (Boston: Houghton Mifflin, 1964). Used by permission.

Neuroticism is influenced by genes.

Table 10.2, along with Table 10.1, indicates strong evidence that the child's tendency to be introverted, depressed, or neurotic is controlled to some extent by his genes. Both the personal and abnormal characteristics of parents seem to be passed along to their children by genetic factors. In fact, one study even suggests that the early emotional relation between mother and child is partly genetic.

Babies' social responsiveness seems innate.

Schaffer and Emerson (1964) studied two groups of babies whom their mothers described as cuddlers or noncuddlers between the ages of one and two years. The investigators tried to find an index of maternal care, social interaction, or parental attitude that was related to cuddling or noncuddling in these babies; but could not find a single social indication that would distinguish the two groups of infants. They did discover that noncuddlers were more restless, wakeful, walked earlier, disliked being physically confined in a car seat or playpen, and scored higher on developmental measures of sensory-motor abilities—like Gesell and Bayley measures of infant development—compared with cuddling infants. By contrast, cuddly babies liked soft toys, were less active, and slept more. Since these investigators could find no maternal or social factors related to cuddling, they concluded that the tendency is a congenital trait controlled by hereditary factors.

Critical Periods in Childhood

There are critical periods in childhood.

In addition to the genetic predispositions and limitations which a child receives from his parents, early development contains several critical periods during which the child is particularly sensitive to outside influences. The most important critical intervals are birth, primary social attachment, language acquisition, and puberty. At birth the infant's task is survival; during his first year he must form strong attachments to his family; in the second and third years he acquires a language;

and beyond those early challenges the child must accumulate a coherent sex role and self-concept. The child's parents play crucial roles in birth, early attachment formation, and sex-role development.

Important events happen at birth.

BIRTH   Birth is a major event in the life of every baby. Some authorities have claimed that birth is the most important event in a person's history. While it is true that birth injuries resulting from difficult labor, instrumental delivery, obstetrical mishandling, oxygen loss, or hemorrhaging may produce central nervous system damage and affect the child's later physical and intellectual status, speculation about "birth as an emotional experience for the infant" will probably not help us to understand a child's growing personality. There is evidence of critical periods during birth. For example, during and immediately after birth the infant is exposed to moderate oxygen deprivation. We know that complete lack of oxygen for five to seven minutes can produce degenerative changes in brain cells that would lead to mental retardation. Studies on the effect of oxygen loss and brain development show that infants who have been affected by injuries at birth are less sensitive to painful stimulation, less responsive, more irritable, less mature in motor integration, and exhibit more muscular tension and rigidity than their peers (Graham *et al.,* 1956). Birth presents problems even for the full-term infant, and these difficult adjustments can be more strenuous for the baby who is born prematurely.

Very small premature babies are at risk.

The premature infant is less able to cope with life than the normal, full-term newborn. Many premature babies cannot maintain their body temperature, and their lungs often do not function adequately. However, there is little relation between weight at birth and the later development of the infant. Very small birth weight is associated with later mental or neurological defects among infants who were not developing properly during their prenatal period, but birth weight among normally developing babies is not associated with later problems. The optimum interval for birth is between eight and nine months following conception.

Early family attachments influence later development.

The next critical interval in a baby's life is the development of early family attachments. The simplest notion of early effects suggests that events immediately after birth produce the strongest influence on a baby's later development. This theory produces a simple decreasing relation between amount of influence and time of occurrence. In addition to birth events there are later critical intervals in the development of human infants when they are particularly sensitive to injury or social events.

There are at least three kinds of critical periods:

1. In anatomical development there are periods during which the growth of organs like the brain is vastly accelerated. During these rapid growth periods any kind of injury can have massive consequences, and the destruction is most pronounced on those organs which are growing at the fastest rate.

FIGURE 10.1
Konrad Lorenz leading his gosling "children."
(Thomas McAvoy, *Life* magazine ©
1972 Time Inc.)

2. There are critical periods in the primary socialization of all young animals. Wild animals can be domesticated if their young are raised with human beings during a critical early interval.
3. Finally, there are critical periods in the development of skills like language.

Consider first the critical stages of attachment formation and then some possible critical periods for higher human learning like perception and language.

IMPRINTING AND ATTACHMENT   Imprinting results in a very strong *attachment* between the young of several animals like ducks, geese, or sheep and the first object they encounter which moves, makes noise, or looks like their natural mother, as we have already learned. Let us review some of our knowledge of imprinting. Young animals have genetic tendencies to prefer certain types of objects for imprinting, but these natural preferences can be overcome by strong experience during a critical period (Hess, 1959). Studies of wild mallards show that during a short period between eight and twenty-four hours following hatching they can be imprinted on a maternal duck or a man (*see* Figure 10.1). Before eight hours the young mallards are insensitive to stimuli, and after twenty-four hours they become afraid of new objects or sounds.

There are several important differences between imprinting and simple associations. Learning an association is quicker when practice trials are spaced, but imprinting is more rapid if the trials are bunched together. People tend to remember the last role association they formed, but with imprinting the first attachment is longer lasting. Punishment increases the attachment of a young animal to its mother, but punishment leads to avoidance learning. Once an attachment is formed, maternal deprivation or separation can cause problems for the infant.

Many animals imprint on the first object they see.

Imprinting and conditioning are different.

MATERNAL SEPARATION OR DEPRIVATION   Maternal separation means there is a physical distance between mother and child, while maternal deprivation means that the relation is somehow deficient. Separation need not produce deprivation if an adequate mother surrogate is provided. And deprivation does not necessarily mean separation, since the infant may be physically with his mother but experience only minimal interaction with her. To understand the varying effects of separation, consider a study by Schaffer and Callender (1959). They observed seventy-six children between three and fifty-one weeks of age who were hospitalized and thus separated from their mothers for an average of fifteen days. They recorded two distinct reactions by babies to the separation from their mothers. Infants over seven months of age protested and developed feeding difficulties following maternal separation, and were excessively dependent on their mothers when they were reunited. In contrast, babies below six months of age showed no upset following separation. Adjustment to a different feeding schedule and the absence of their mothers produced minor difficulty in the young infants. After hospitalization, the young babies returned to their homes with minimal fuss. Apparently the older babies realized that their mothers were gone, while the younger infants were unaware that anything had happened.

Spitz and Wolf (1946) also studied the effect of mother-child relations on the child's response to maternal deprivation or separation. They concluded that separation after a good mother-child relation produces mild or severe upset in the infant or child, while separation following a poor maternal relation may produce a better adjustment by the infant. These investigators suggested that a good mother-child relation generates a more severe separation reaction than a poor mother-child relation.

Two emotions govern the young baby's social interactions. One is a positive attachment to familiar figures; the other is fear of new or strange objects and people. The first is called *attachment*; the second *stranger anxiety*, which first appears at about six months of age. Stranger anxiety is strongest around eight months and usually diminishes by the time an infant is about one year old. An eight-month-old baby is less likely to show fear of strangers if it is close to or sitting on its mother's lap, because babies are most secure when being held by their mothers. Even lower animals show stranger anxiety. Kittens that have been handled by only one experimenter, or have not been handled at all, show more fear of strangers than kittens exposed to several different handlers. Thus, babies first form a close attachment to one or two people and then come to fear anyone different from the familiar person. This is one reason why fathers should handle their babies starting at an early age.

Another kind of anxiety begins to appear after the child's first year. It is called *separation anxiety*, and occurs when the one-year-old baby sees his mother leave the room. A seven-month-old infant who sees his mother leave will not cry, but the one-year-old infant does. What makes the

Maternal separation and deprivation are different.

Separation produces upset.

Infant attachment is regulated by love and fear.

Separation anxiety occurs at 1 year.

difference? There are several possible explanations. Separation anxiety seems related to three things:

1. The baby must have formed a clear concept of its mother as a familiar human being.
2. The baby must be aware of its mother's absence.
3. The baby must have no specific path for getting to its mother.

Rheingold studied
separation anxiety.

Harriet Rheingold (1969) studied the effects of maternal separation anxiety by placing ten-month-old babies in a strange room under one of four conditions: with their mothers, with a stranger, with toys, or alone. If their mothers were in the strange room with them, the babies were happy. However, all babies without their mothers cried in less than one minute, and neither toys nor the presence of a stranger could comfort them. In a second part of her experiment Rheingold placed ten-month-old babies with their mothers in a room that opened onto the same strange room where the infant had cried when left alone. Interestingly, these babies would often crawl away from their mothers into the empty room, wander around the previously fearful place, and then crawl back to their mothers. They did not cry when they were alone in the strange room. Apparently, anxiety can be dispelled if the baby knows how to get back to its mother.

Discipline

Discipline affects
children's behavior.

The final factor in how parents influence their children is the method of discipline that mothers and fathers use. Some parents discipline their children by setting an example and encouraging the children to follow. This method of discipline assumes that children will imitate the actions of others around them. A second manner of discipline is to reward or punish the child for desired or undesired actions. Finally, parents can combine these approaches by setting a good example for their children *and* rewarding or punishing them for various acts. Parents may agree on their manner of discipline, thus being consistent in the treatment of the child, or they may disagree and be inconsistent. Consider how these disciplinary factors might work in dealing with a child's behavior.

Children imitate
parents and peers.

IMITATION   Social learning theories suggest that if parents are aggressive toward the child they are simply providing a model for the child to imitate (*see* Figure 10.2). Several studies show that boys whose parents are punishing will be aggressive in school. By contrast, girls whose parents are low or high in the use of punishment are not aggressive, while those girls whose parents use a moderate amount of punishment are aggressive in school. Cross-cultural studies support the positive relation between parents' use of punishment and the amount of children's aggression. Harsh discipline is used in societies where the gods or the government are perceived as being aggressive, compared to societies where the gods are

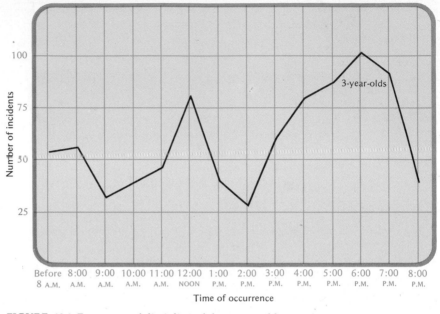

FIGURE 10.2 Frequency of discipline of three-year-olds.
(After Clifford, 1959.)

Harsh discipline
produces aggression.

seen as passive. The first society is an aggressive one; the second is not.

Harsh discipline is frustrating and the punishing parent is an effective model of aggression for the child. When the child is punished, his frustration is increased, and he imitates the model of effective aggression. Hostile parents not only serve as a model, they also reinforce aggression directed toward others outside the home. Sears, Maccoby, and Levin (1957) interviewed 379 mothers of five-year-old children concerning their child-rearing practices. One area the investigators explored was the relation between a child's aggressiveness and the pattern of control parents use. They found that punishing mothers expected their children to fight with other boys and girls, and that these mothers were quite permissive of children's hostility. The mothers used physical punishment and were more aggressive toward their children than other parents were.

Punishment can
produce dependency.

REWARDS AND PUNISHMENTS   Physical punishment tends to drive a child away from his environment and make him dependent on adults. In contrast, children who are encouraged to make their own mistakes and to learn from these mistakes possess more attractive personalities than those who are subjected to adult interference and punishment. Punitive parents produce dependent children who experience great difficulty adjusting to school and later life in the community. Punished children avoid nursery-school peers, are more inhibited, withdrawn, and are less popular in their classes.

Permissiveness produces popular children.

Permissive child-rearing produces boisterous children who are aggressive and popular. The punished child feels shame when he does something he knows he shouldn't, but the child trained with love and positive reinforcement feels guilty if he breaks a social rule. The child who receives punishment and negative reinforcement feels bad most of the time, no matter what he does. There are several reasons why love and guilt are connected. Withdrawal of love is more effective as a disciplinary measure where love exists; a loving parent provides a model of guilt for the child, where the child feels guilty about breaking a social rule, and permissive parents are more likely to use reason in their discipline, thus giving the child some understanding of what he did wrong. Explanations of wrong-doing provide a source for the child's evaluation of his own behavior, so he gains explicit training in moral judgments.

Love produces guilt in children.

The relation between guilt and love exists in other cultures. In a cross-cultural study, Whiting and Child asked groups of natives to list causes of illnesses. Attribution of such causes to the person rather than to external agents was assumed to reflect feelings of guilt or personal responsibility. Such personal responsibility for illness was more prominent in cultures using love-oriented techniques of training than in those other types of child-training practices.

Inconsistent discipline can confuse the child.

INCONSISTENT DISCIPLINE   Parents are inconsistent with their children for many reasons. At times parents may simply be too busy or too tired to exert control over their offspring. The child may do something which would normally earn him disciplinary action, and not have to suffer the consequences. This type of inconsistency is probably not harmful to the child's development, if it doesn't happen often. Two other kinds of inconsistency in parents can cause serious problems to growing children. If parents are often inconsistent in applying patterns of reward or punishment so as to confuse the child, or if they cannot agree about how to rear the child, then serious problems with authority may develop. Children who become delinquent have a history of inconsistent disciplinary action by their parents. Consistent discipline produces reasonable children. If one parent is strict and the other permissive, their children exhibit much more antisocial behavior than when both are either strict or permissive. Warm, consistent, supporting families produce friendly, healthy children; hostile, inconsistent parents rear frightened, angry offspring.

Parent-child Interaction

Genes and environment determine development.

A baby enters the world with genetic predispositions, primary drives, and a unique pattern of strength and weaknesses. Every family has a particular set of expectations about that baby, and they reward him when he conforms to these expectations and penalize him when he does not.

Thus, a baby's behavior is manipulated by the people who take care of him. *Socialization* is the name we give to this process of control. It is the complex interaction of a baby's genetic predisposition with the social and cultural expectations of parents.

Infants are primarily attached to mothers.

During the baby's early years his mother is the primary agent of socialization. Infants cannot feed themselves or even communicate, except in the most primitive language, so they are completely dependent on mothers or caretakers. Very young infants are in almost continuous contact with their caretaker, as they are fed, changed, talked to, and carried about. Later the mother or caretaker forms a safe home base from which to explore. There are many ways to study maternal influences on the child's development. One early way was to choose a specific maternal practice—like whether the child was breast or bottle fed, when he was toilet trained, or how weaning was handled. Later, psychologists studied general maternal attitudes to determine whether the caretaker was positive and permissive or hostile and rejecting. Now we are beginning to study the effects of complex maternal acts on the child.

Maternal attitude seems to affect the child's development.

First of all, results from countless studies on specific training practices like breast versus bottle feeding, demand versus schedule feeding, timing of toilet training, and a variety of other practices show that specific training has little relation to the child's later personal development. Once it became clear that what a mother does in specific instances is generally unrelated to later child development, psychologists began to explore the mother's total attitude toward her child. This newer approach would not ask whether mothers breast or bottle fed their babies, but would want to know how she felt about the baby. Today, the mother's general attitude toward her child is assumed to be more important for the child's later personal adjustment than the specific practices she uses for socialization.

The parent must tolerate a child's needs.

What are some characteristics of a good parent? Most psychologists agree that a parent must be able to relate emotionally to a child. The parent must be willing to tolerate the child's own unique needs and wishes. How do parents acquire this type of understanding? There is good evidence of maternal instinct in lower animals, and there is a connection between hormonal secretion and maternal feeling among human mothers (Maccoby, 1966). The unique abilities which determine how a human mother will handle her offspring do not seem to be instinctive. Human child-rearing attitudes seem to be influenced by fads and fashions. Some parents adopt their own parents' methods while others are controlled by the current child-rearing advice from experts.

Child-rearing practices run in families.

A variety of studies have looked at the similarity between parents and offspring in their handling of socialization. Most studies find that dominating parents were dominated by their own parents, while permissive parents were freer in their childhood. If a parent's mother exercised authority in the home, the parent will be an authoritarian mother. This can cause conflicts, because the authority in a family can be either vested in a mother, a father, or it can be shared. A particular husband/wife combination can either be from the same background or from various authority patterns. In families where the husband and wife had similar authority backgrounds, they usually reproduce the pattern of authority used by their parents. If they were reared in a father-dominated home, the husband will make most decisions; if they were both reared in a mother-dominated home the wife will wield the authority in the household. If the husband and wife were reared in homes with different kinds of family authority there may be conflict. If the husband was socialized in a family where his mother dominated the household, while the wife was reared in a father-dominated family, both the husband and the wife will expect the other to take the lead in making decisions. This type of misunderstanding is not nearly so disruptive as the couple who both expect to lead. Most serious quarrels about authority come between husbands and wives who were reared in homes where the same-sexed parent was dominant. In these unhappy cases either some compromise must be worked out or the family atmosphere will be a constant battleground. Literally hundreds of surveys about family atmosphere have been collected, and they show great variety in how parents treat children.

Family Atmospheres

Three main factors appear in most studies of family atmosphere:

1. Reward or punishment used in controlling the child.
2. Strictness or permissiveness used in child control.
3. Consistency in application of discipline.

Three factors affect family atmosphere.

Schaffer (1960) proposed a model to account for his argument that autonomy or control, and hostility or love are the basic characteristics of all parent-child interactions (*see* Figure 10.3). Schaffer believes that parents cannot give their child both autonomy and control, or love and hostility because these attitudes are incompatible. Consider some characteristics of these parent attitudes. Love and autonomy produces an atmosphere which is democratic and accepting of the child. In contrast hostility and autonomy produce a rejecting, indifferent, detached family atmosphere.

One factor is love or hate.

LOVE/HATE The warm, accepting, affectionate parent is approving, understanding, child-centered, uses frequent examples and explanations in discipline, gives a positive response to dependency, uses reason in discipline, is low in the use of physical punishment, and does not criticize the other parent. A hostile parent is rejecting, cold, disapproving, and self-centered. The hostile parent also uses negative reinforcement, little or no reasoning, physical punishment, and is critical of the mate.

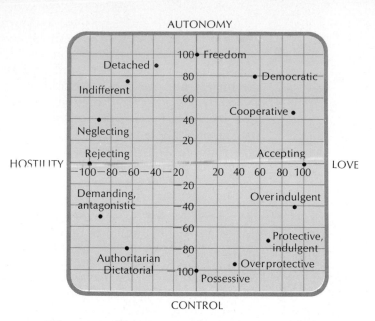

FIGURE 10.3

A two-dimensional model of parent-child interactions as proposed by Schaefer. The four combinations of love/hostility and autonomy/control produce very different children. The types of parental attitudes characteristic of the various combinations are outlined along the perimeter of the figure. (From Schaffer, 1968.)

Another factor is control.

CONTROL/AUTONOMY   The controlling parent places many restrictions on the child and strictly enforces them. Permissive parents place few restrictions on the child and do not enforce even these modest demands.

Types of Offspring from Various Home Environments

There are four family atmospheres.

There are four possible combinations of love or hate and control or autonomy: Love/control, love/autonomy, hostility/control, and hostility/autonomy. Using these four descriptive phrases, we can discuss various parent-child relations and their consequences for children (*see* Table 10.3).

TABLE 10.3   Children's personality traits resulting from love or hostility and control or autonomy in the home

		Control	*Autonomy*
Love		Submissive, dependent, polite, neat, obedient	Active, socially outgoing, creative, successfully aggressive
		Minimal aggression	Minimal rule enforcement, boys
		Dependent, not friendly, not creative	Facilitates adult role-taking
		Maximal compliance	Minimal self-aggression, boys
		Maximum rule enforcement, boys	Independent, friendly, creative, low projective hostility
Hostility		"Neurotic" problems	Delinquency
		More quarreling and shyness with peers	Noncompliance
		Socially withdrawn	Maximal aggression
		Low in adult role-taking	
		Maximal self-aggression, boys	

CONTROL AND LOVE   Parents who control and love their children produce submissive, polite, neat, and obedient children who are "seen and not heard." These children are considered ideal by parents, teachers, and little girls. However, boys tend to see these male children as sissies and are uninterested in the girls. Children of controlling and loving parents display little outward aggression. If they are boys, they insist on following the rules themselves, and they want others to follow rules too. Children of loving and controlling parents are dependent, unfriendly, show little creativity, and comply with the wishes and demands of almost everybody. They are the *overprotected* children who hover around their mothers' skirts long after others have gone off to explore the world.

The Overprotected Child   Overprotected children receive excessive parental care. They are treated like babies and are not allowed to grow up. Overprotection prevents the development of independence. Overprotective mothers spend an enormous amount of time with their children and give them prolonged nursing care. If the child is ill, the mother will fondle him excessively. She also will encourage the child to sleep in her bed long past infancy. She seeks and acts on medical advice often, and her children undergo three times as many operations as other children. The overprotected child is probably not less healthy than his peers, but is simply overexposed to preventative medicine. A sure sign of overprotection is prolonged breast feeding. Overprotected children average fourteen months of breast feeding compared with about four or five months for other children. Social maturation is blocked by limiting the child's social contacts, and any friendships that develop with other children are discouraged or destroyed.

There are two kinds of overprotective parents—indulgent and domineering. The indulgent, overprotective parent satisfies the child's every need and attends to his every whim. This overprotected child is rebellious, aggressive, disrespectful, and disobedient. He is a little tyrant who may hit or kick his mother, and throw food on the floor. He may even make mother sleep in a particular bed. The domineering mother, on the other hand, produces a submissive, dependent child. Typically, a dominated, overprotected child is timid and seclusive, clean, neat, obedient, and polite. He does not fight with other children, and is usually regarded as a sissy. The dominated child is as submissive in school as he is at home.

CONTROL AND HATE   This combination of parental characteristics produces children who become *neurotic*. Controlled and hated children are socially withdrawn, do not take on adult roles well, show little aggression toward others, and are self-aggressive. Children reared in an atmosphere of hostility and in the control of dominant parents tend to quarrel with and withdraw from their peers. Their self-image is low, and they feel guilty most of the time. These children are seen as quiet, shy, ideal chil-

Loving, controlling parents produce dependent children.

Overprotected children are mothered too much.

There are two types of overprotection.

Control and hate produce neuroticism.

dren by parents and teachers because they give so little trouble to adults. However, children raised in an atmosphere of hostility and control feel worthless. They become depressed easily, and tend to withdraw from frustrating situations instead of finding solutions to their problems. These children experience great difficulties adjusting to the adult world. They are not viewed as "problem" children and are frequently overlooked by teachers and others. Neurotic children may function quite well in a school situation, but they do so at a cost in happiness and well-being which can only lead to serious adjustment problems later in their lives.

Rejected children are hostile and anxious.

The Rejected Child   A *rejected child* is rather difficult to identify, and he may appear to be similar to the overprotected child. In our society parents are supposed to love their children. Parental rejection therefore exists only in disguised forms. The rejecting mother may dress her child very well, look after his physical comfort solicitously, and appear to be a very good parent. Yet, she may deny her child what he needs most—acceptance and affection from her. Maternal rejection is manifest in several ways— excessive physical or verbal punishment of the child may come from the parent's underlying hostility, for example. Some rejecting parents constantly expect too much of the child intellectually or developmentally, thus making him feel inadequate. The rejected child is never good enough for the rejecting parent—no matter how hard he tries. Since the healthy development of a child depends on parents accepting real accomplishments, the personality of the rejected child suffers severe damage. Often, rejected children refuse to grow up. They may become hostile and aggressive or withdraw into a shell of anxiety.

Autonomy and love produce a happy child.

AUTONOMY AND LOVE   The child reared by parents who fill their home with love and permissiveness becomes socially outgoing, creative, active, and successfully aggressive. Boys who grow up in this environment feel little need to enforce rules; they can easily take the role of adults in their environments, and then incorporate adult characteristics into their own personality structures. Children reared in a milieu of love and permissiveness develop minimal self-aggression. They become independent, friendly, and creative. These children are noisy, interested in others, and are well enough adjusted to tolerate some frustration. A successfully aggressive child, he is not hostile toward himself or others. He is *a happy child.*

Autonomy and hate produce delinquency.

AUTONOMY AND HATE   The family atmosphere which combines hostility and lack of control produces children who receive considerable attention from authorities: They become delinquent. This type of child is maximally aggressive to all except his parents. He has little respect for authority, is nonsubmissive in almost all situations, and is primarily interested in social interaction and freedom from authority. He is hostile and vents his hostility against all external authority. He lacks internal controls and feels the world is trying to keep him from expressing himself. There is little or no guilt associated with doing wrong among these children. They do have a feeling of shame when they are caught. Their moral code is force and power over others and freedom for themselves. They are constantly frustrated because society does not permit them to enjoy the autonomy they were allowed at home.

Parent-child Relations

Parents should be flexible.

The balance between parents' permissiveness and the child's demands for independence cannot be answered by a flat statement about how discipline should be applied. The situation is complex, because the treatment of an infant must be vastly different from the way one handles a five-year-old or an adolescent. The parent should be flexible enough to treat the child in a way that is appropriate to his developmental level. When the baby is very young he should be nurtured; as he develops, competence can be rewarded. The scheduling of weaning and the expectations of parents toward their children can be tempered by the child's level of growth.

Older children require less control than babies.

The optimum parent-child relation probably should include a subtle combination of indulgence and support during the early formative period when a baby is weak and dependent. Once a basic feeling of security is established, a schedule of independence training should be started. The older child can be shifted toward more and more independence, as he progresses toward competence in handling his own affairs. A simple prescription of permissiveness or restriction will not work. The balance between a child's competence and his parents' expectations is fragile. By proper scheduling of parental demands, the child can develop a feeling of competence.

The child's sex also influences personal development.

Not only does the child's age affect his needs, but the sex of the parent and sex of the child are important variables in parent-child relations. Mothers often reward aggressiveness in sons but not in daughters, and reward dependency in daughters but not in sons. Fathers are often more permissive toward daughters, and mothers are permissive toward sons. These data suggest that the optimum balance of affection and control is now different for boys and girls. But should it be? The effect parents have on their children depends on the child's age, sex, and how the parents discipline him. All these considerations should be kept in mind when rearing a child.

Children's Views of Parents

Children and parents disagree about discipline.

There is little correspondence between how parents and children view parental behavior. Almost three-fourths of preschool children say their mothers spank them, although parents say they rarely use spanking as a discipline. Also, 83 percent of these children say they feel spanking is a just punishment when they are naughty.

Young children prefer their mothers.

A consistent result of research on *young* children's attitudes is that they prefer their mothers to their fathers. However, as children mature, they come to prefer the same-sex parent. Then daughters see themselves as more similar to the mother, while sons identify with their fathers. Boys believe their parents are harsh disciplinarians compared to girls, probably because boys tend to be more active and aggressive than girls and are confronted with more situations in which they must be disciplined. Finally, well-adjusted children think their parents are happy, but children who are not well-adjusted believe their parents are unhappy. The type of discipline that parents impose on children affects the child's attitude toward his parents when he matures. College students who remember their discipline as positive are less critical of their parents than children who believed parental discipline was negative.

Discipline should begin early.

How can a parent begin a positive program of discipline? The first thing to remember is to start early. Next, both the child's needs and the parent's feelings should be considered when a program of discipline is formed. Most children find restrictions frustrating. A few simple rules are best, and they should be geared to the child's changing level of comprehension. The parents should also look into their own feelings. Are their demands reasonable? Parents have a definite advantage, since power and authority is with them. A child must obey or suffer the consequences. If parents take advantage of this relation they can breed resentment. On the other hand, parents must give their children guidelines to help them grow. A balanced set of restrictions and a generous helping of warmth and respect are probably the best prescription.

Variations in Family Relations

Family structures vary.

In this chapter family life has been treated within the context of a typical nuclear family containing a mother, father, and children. However, there is enormous variation in the structure of families. The number of children may be one or many; the family may have a mother who works; there may be one or two parents; and, in rare cases, the child may be in an institution. All these kinds of families exist in the United States. There are also differences in family relations among social classes, ethnic groups, and nations. Let us consider first the variations within a nuclear family and then the differences among various social and ethnic groups.

Variations Within the Family

Small families emphasize individuality.

FAMILY SIZE AND COMPOSITION   A small family emphasizes the individual child's development. The parents of an only child have a larger emotional and financial investment in the one child than the parents of ten children have in each member, simply because attention and income must be divided by ten. In small families the mother is usually a primary disciplinarian, while in large families there may be several levels of organization and control. Older siblings or grandparents may direct younger children in a large family.

Birth order affects development.

During the early part of this century developmental psychologists studied in detail the effects of birth order and family composition on a child's development. Early authorities in the field of child development believed that being an only child was harmful to human growth. More recent studies, which compared singletons with children from large families, found no differences on that aspect alone. "Only" children acquire language more rapidly than children with siblings, but this may be caused by the fact that brighter parents tend to have fewer children.

Firstborns develop superior language abilities.

Birth order and status within a family may or may not be related. The firstborn child may not be the most important member of the family, although there is some tendency for older children to dominate younger siblings. Alfred Adler (1939) argued that older children are dethroned by younger ones, and that sibling rivalry and a feeling of inferiority are dominant influences in early development. Consider some differences between first- and later-born children. Firstborn children identify more strongly with their parents, while later children identify more with their peer groups. Helen Koch studied 360 five- and six-year-olds from two-child families. She found the language development of firstborn children consistently superior to that of younger siblings. Boys with an older sister did not develop so masculine a sex role compared with firstborn boys or males with an older brother. Mothers reported that firstborn children are dependent, fearful, and anxious; but secondborn siblings are stubborn, happy, and aggressive. Firstborn children yield more often to social pressure than later children; they have a higher need for achievement; and they possess more demanding superegos—the part of the psyche that is self-critical. Koch reported that mothers tend to be cold and restrictive toward firstborn children, but tend to protect and be permissive with a second baby. The most consistent finding in all studies of birth order is that firstborn children are overrepresented among college populations (*see* Figure 10.4).

U.S. parents want fewer children.

Fewer U.S. citizens are in favor of four or more children than in the past. The birth rate in the U.S. has been declining since 1945. The trend toward favoring smaller families has been most pronounced among young adults, women, Catholics, and persons with higher education. Similar surveys from Western European countries show the same downward trend in large families.

A majority of women work.

THE WORKING MOTHER   More and more women are working in the U.S. Current estimates vary between 50 and 60 percent. What effect does this change in employment status have on children and the family? Two things seem most important when the effect on children is considered: the child's age and the type of substitute care provided. In some families the husband and wife share child-rearing tasks. They may arrange their work so one is home all the time. In this situation the father interacts with his child much more than is usual, and he may exert a positive influence on the child's adjustment. Many working mothers report that they return to child care with better attitudes after an absence from household routines. However, parents who both work and care for children often lack patience. In some cases the father's self-esteem may be challenged if he must do housework. He may feel inadequate as a male, and marital tension may result, causing severe emotional strain in the home.

Substitute child care can be hazardous.

Turning child care over to another person or an institution raises a different set of problems. In lower-class homes this substitute care can be haphazard. Children of working mothers may be left with a neighbor or someone who may be responsible for many children. Often, older children are left to roam the streets by themselves.

Children need security.

The success of any caretaking arrangement depends on the attitude of the substitute parent. Children need security and comfort. If the surrogate mother provides these, it may sometimes be beneficial to separate a mother and child. This is particularly true if the child's mother encourages

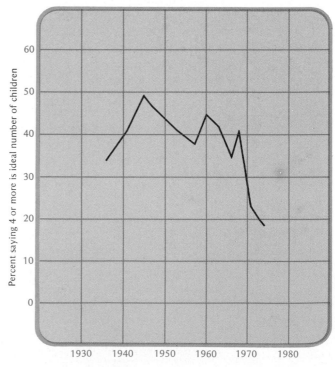

FIGURE 10.4
The shifting preferences of Americans for four children between 1930 and the present. (Data from the Gallup poll.)

dependency or is punishing or rejecting. The children of some working mothers benefit from a reliable, warm caretaker.

THE SINGLE PARENT   The typical U.S. family is nuclear. What happens if a parent is removed from the home by death, divorce, or separation? Loss of a mother is quite different from the effects of losing the father. A single father who is responsible for children most often continues his working role. He hires a caretaker to take over housekeeping duties and to supervise his children, and this new agent is a substitute mother. When the father is missing from a family, the single mother usually works, and she may or may not hire a substitute caretaker. The plight of single women with children seems most desperate, and is increasing in frequency.

The single parent has a difficult time.

How a mother regards an absent father significantly affects her child's feelings toward the missing parent. Studies of children in father-absent homes show that mothers who hate the children's father tend to foster similar feelings in their children.

Maternal attitudes affect children.

There are a number of severe problems associated with not having a father in the home. The children can become excessively dependent on the mother. They may be rebellious and difficult to control, and boys often become delinquent. Young boys from homes with no fathers tend to display less aggression than do those with a father. Researcher Robert Sears suggested that during the preschool years the father contributes to the sex typing of boys, and serves as a model for aggression. If he is absent, there would be less imitation and thus less aggression.

Father-absent homes create discipline problems.

What does a father mean to his family? Most young children see their fathers as a source of strength and security. To a growing boy the father is an important model of sex-appropriate behaviors. Boys learn how to be men by copying their fathers or other important older males. For a boy to develop sex-appropriate behavior, he needs to have a good relation with someone who has practical knowledge of such appropriate male behavior. Not all father-son relations are adequate in this area. A boy who is rejected by his father will have difficulty learning to be a man. If the father wanted a daughter, the boy may become feminine to win acceptance. Masculine mothers may inhibit their son's identification with his father. As a result, these boys may show feminine characteristics.

Fathers are a source of security for children.

A father can foster femininity in a growing girl. He can admire her clothes, comment on her hair, and treat her as a young woman. If he admires tomboys, a father may encourage his daughter to act like a boy, and this may make her task of becoming a woman more difficult.

Fathers encourage little girls' femininity.

The role of women is in the process of change and it is possible that what we consider masculine or feminine may no longer be so clearly differentiated as in the past.

Woman's role is changing.

DIVORCE   Divorce clearly affects a child's development. However, it is difficult to know how much influence may be attributed to divorce and

Divorce affects children.

how much to the conflict and tension prior to the divorce. Adolescents from broken homes report less psychosomatic illness, less delinquent behavior, and better adjustment than those from unhappy, unbroken homes. In some cases, separation or divorce is the best solution. A broken home can be more desirable than a family atmosphere of hate and conflict. Divorce does not have the same effect on all children. Adolescents who recall their family as happy before a divorce react quite differently to the event than those who feel their homes were unhappy. Children who believed their homes were happy feel divorce is a painful experience. These same children admit to little change in their feelings of security and personal happiness following divorce, strongly suggesting they are not honest with themselves about their own feelings. Children who believed their homes were unhappy tend to feel more secure and happy following a divorce.

Children must adjust to divorce.

In a divorce there are several unhappy events which must be accepted by the child. He must adjust to the fact that his parents are separating. Then he must adjust to the divorce itself. Before or after the divorce, one or both parents may use the child as a weapon, with painful effects for the child. The child must learn to establish new relations with his parents and make new adjustments in his peer group. Finally, there may be adjustment problems for the child if his parents remarry.

Children may feel guilty about divorce.

Divorced women report that following a divorce their children are difficult to manage. The child may feel guilty about his parents' separation. If the family must move, as many do, this adds to the problems facing the child, particularly if he must change schools. In approximately 90 percent of divorce cases, the mother receives custody of the child.

Divorce can be healthy.

If parents seek expert help during or following their separation, they may establish a warm relation with the children and help them grow into mature, productive adults. The effect of divorce depends on what both parents do in relation to the children. If they remain hateful and use the children as weapons in the battle over who is right, the divorce has accomplished nothing. If they achieve a new maturity through separation, the divorce has been the right surgery for a poor personal relation.

Father absence disrupts female sex-role interactions.

Recently, E. Mavis Hetherington (1973) has studied the effect of growing up without their fathers on adolescent girls. She found that among seventy-two adolescent girls, those who came from families in which the parents were divorced, exhibited uneasiness and assertive or seductive behavior with male peers and adults. Girls whose fathers had died showed strong sexual anxiety, shyness, and discomfort in the company of males. Hetherington interpreted these results to mean that the absence of a father makes it difficult for adolescent girls to develop emotional security and social skills in dealing with males. She found no disruptions in sex-role development among girls without fathers; the only effect seemed to be in their interaction with males.

INSTITUTIONALIZATION   Most children in the U.S. are associated with at least one adult who devotes a good deal of time to their care. Institutionalized children, however, are supervised by groups of caretakers who often can devote only minimal attention to individual children. As a result institutionalized infants are less likely to form attachments to a single person, show less stranger anxiety, are anxious and depressed, are less socially responsive, and smile less than children reared in a single-family atmosphere. Happily, few human babies grow up in total isolation. But, institutionalized children develop in different surroundings than do children in an average family. Institutionalized babies are usually physically separated from each other and enjoy little social interaction with adults while they are being fed. The average attendant in a typical institution is responsible for eight babies per eight-hour period. During the remaining sixteen hours of a day, no one enters the nursery except to feed and change the babies. Before four months of age these babies show the same kind of social-interaction patterns as infants reared in families. After four months of age differences begin to appear: Institutionalized babies now vocalize less, babble little, and cry infrequently. By eight months of age institutionalized babies are less interested in grasping objects and are generally less curious than those reared in a family. By ten months of age repetitive rocking is very common among institutionalized infants. They are not afraid of strangers, but seek little or no social interaction. In addition to social retardation, the institutionalized baby shows retarded motor development.

Several theorists have attempted to explain the development of the passive institutionalized child. Some argue that the lack of a single mother figure is the cause; while others blame their impoverished sensory environment, genetic defects, or even disease. We know that institutionalization alone does not always produce a passive baby, because residential nurseries in the Soviet Union care for babies who show normal social, physical, intellectual, and emotional development. Institutional babies in the U.S.S.R. receive large amounts of social interaction with a mother surrogate and have ample opportunities for learning verbal and motor skills. They experience a rich, stimulating sensory environment and abundant physical contact with their caretakers and peers.

Goldfarb investigated the consequences of institutionalization in the U.S. He compared infants reared in an institution for the first three years of their lives and then transferred to a foster home, with other babies who were placed in foster homes at an early age. He found that children who grew up in an institution for the first three years earned lower scores on tests of intelligence than foster-home children. Whether this difference reflects the effects of early institutionalization or biased selection is unknown. In addition to lower intelligence scores the institutionalized children were more aggressive, detached, dependent, and hyperactive

Institutionlization can be difficult for children.

Soviet institutional care is stimulating.

Goldfarb found that U.S. babies in institutions are retarded.

than the foster-home children. Goldfarb (1947) argued that the lack of a single caretaker during the early years of a baby's life produced abnormal social behavior and some retardation of language and cognitive development in institutionalized children.

Ribble felt mothering is necessary for normal infant development.

In another study of institutionalization Margaret Ribble (1965) observed six hundred infants in three different settings, and recorded their early development and later personality. She noted signs of withdrawal, regression, negativism, and exaggerated reactions to frustration among the institutionalized infants. Attempting to determine whether these abnormal reactions were inborn or had developed as a result of early infant deprivation, Ribble followed the six hundred children for several months, taking motion pictures and notes for case histories. She concluded that a good mother-child relation requires three types of stimulation — tactile (touching), kinesthetic (holding and moving) and auditory (hearing). She thought that human infants are particularly sensitive to touch around the head and face and show signs of satisfaction after vigorous sucking. Ribble also felt that the infant gets a sense of security from touch and movement, and receives pleasure from being held and fondled by its mother. Ribble also argued that the soft sound of a mother's voice is soothing and pleasurable to a baby. The researcher noted two main reactions to inadequate mothering: negativism and regression. *Negativism* meant such symptoms as refusal to suck, rigidity of body, shallow breathing, and constipation; while *regression* produced motionlessness, stuporous sleep, and gastrointestinal disturbances. In her conclusions she argued strongly that considerable handling during the first few months of a human infant's life contribute greatly to the positive development of the baby.

Rheingold found additional mothering had little effect on infant interactions.

Institutions have provided settings for many studies of maternal care. For example, Harriet Rheingold (1956) explored the effects of additional mothering on institutionalized infants during their first eight months of life. One group of babies was cared for by an experimenter alone for daily periods of seven-and-one-half hours, while a matched control group was cared for in the usual institutional manner. The single experimenter was able to perform many more caretaking acts than the busy institutional caretakers. Infants under the normal institution routine were often without a caretaker, and they spent much more time alone in their cribs than did the experimental babies. Both groups were given tests to measure their social responsiveness, postural development, motor abilities, and general development. The experimenters supposed that the group which received more maternal attention would become more socially responsive, and might improve more in other test scores than would the control infants. Results did show that infants who received more individual attention became more socially responsive. Rheingold's impression was that this responsiveness developed through day-by-day play between the experimenter and the babies outside of regular caretaking duties.

Additional mothering did not affect language.

The investigators continued their original experiment with a re-examination of all the children one year later. By the second testing the experimental infants were slightly more vocal than the control children, but were not more socially responsive. The main conclusion of the researchers was that additional maternal care can affect infants' social behavior immediately after intervention, but the extra care is not enough to maintain the difference unless such care is continued.

Institutionalization retards early sensory-motor coordinations.

Wayne Dennis (1957) studied the effects of institutionalization on infants in Lebanon. Because of inadequate financial support, the facility he examined was able to provide few caretakers for their infant wards. Dennis explored the development of Lebanese children between one and four-and-one-half years of age. For comparison he used children at the Well Baby Clinic of the American University at Beirut Hospital. Infants under one year were given the Cattell Infant Intelligence Tests, while those around four-and-a-half years were given the Goodenough Draw-a-Man Test. The results showed that at two months there was little difference between the various groups of children from the different institutions. However, by one year of age, children in the institution were retarded in comparison with children living at home. By the age of four-and-a-half years the groups were again comparable in measured abilities. The older children were apparently able to compensate for their early lack of experience by moving about the institution on their own, and they overcame their early developmental deficiency. The author speculated that further testing would show retardation of the institutionalized children in comparison with the control children, especially measures involving language comprehension.

Institutional babies need social interaction.

Institutional care is necessary for various reasons, but we now know some of its problems. Any sound program of child care should provide, in addition to the caretakers, people who are free to play with institutionalized babies. It is difficult to make other firm generalizations about institutionalization because the level of observation in studies that have been done is usually superficial, and few objective methods are available by which one can separate the effects of maternal separation and sensory deprivation. However, studies of lower animals show that some early social interaction is necessary to insure normal social and emotional development.

There are social class differences in child-rearing techniques.

SOCIAL CLASS DIFFERENCES IN FAMILY RELATIONS   Not only is there variation within the family structure but various groups show unique family characteristics as well. The most conspicuous group differences in parent-child relations are among various social classes. Beyond these obvious differences are variations in ethnic and national groups. Consider first the variation over social classes in child-training techniques; and then we will discuss some possible ethnic and national differences.

Even in an open society, like that of the United States, social-class differences exist. In the U.S. social class is defined by a combination of several factors. Most scientists follow the definition based on a composite score that includes the source and amount of a family's income, the parents' education, their place of residence, and the father's occupation. Specifically, larger income, more education, a comfortable home, and a profession characterize the upper classes; while low income, little education, day work, and shared homes characterize the lower class. This definition of social class balances the influence of education, money, and occupation, and forms a composite estimate of a person's social status. A person may climb in social rank by earning more money, inheriting money, getting more education, or entering a profession. He can fall in social standing by not earning money, dropping out of school, avoiding the professions, and squandering inherited wealth through gambling or bad investments.

Middle-class child-rearing varies more than lower-class techniques do.

There is a good deal of social mobility in the United States and other Western industrial nations. Many studies show that the child from a lower-class home differs in important ways from the middle-class child, and that social classes differ in child-training procedures. However, we have conflicting reports on what these differences really are. Davis and Havighurst (1946) reported that middle-class parents are stricter with their children, train them earlier, and cause them to suffer more frustration as compared to lower-class parental treatment of children. Robert Sears (1957) published a study of child-rearing practices which contradicted the Davis-Havighurst findings. Sears *et al.* claims that middle-class mothers are generally more permissive than lower-class mothers, although in the middle-class they are more severe in toilet training and sex education. Probably the conflicting results from these two studies reflect changing socialization practices in the family in the U.S. Havighurst and Davis' study was conducted prior to World War II, when lower-class mothers were probably in fact more permissive than middle-class mothers about feeding, weaning, and toilet training. However, a shift in child-training recommendations began in the early 1940's. Benjamin Spock (1946), among others, advocated permissive child-rearing after World War II. Since such practices change more quickly in those segments of society which have access to the literature, physicians, and counselors the shift was most noticeable in the middle class. Comparison of child-training techniques over a twenty-year period from 1940 to 1960 shows that before 1940 middle-class mothers were strict with their children. However, they entered a period of permissiveness during the 1950's when baby-care books began suggesting that permissiveness was the best method of rearing children. More recently, parents have shifted toward a middle ground in which they set limits on behavior, but are not so severe as in the 1940s. Lower-class mothers have maintained a stable pattern of childrearing practice throughout these shifting fashions.

Currently, lower-class children are disciplined with physical punishment, deprivation of privileges, and ridicule from their parents during

TABLE 10.4   The variation in child-rearing practices between middle- and lower-class families.

	Percentage of parents rated "high"	
	Middle class	Working class
Severity of toilet training	15	26
Use of physical punishment	17	33
Use of ridicule	31	47
Stress on child's doing well at school	35	50
Pressure for neatness and order	43	57
Father's insistence on immediate obedience	53	67
Permissiveness for aggression toward parents	19	7
Sex permissiveness	53	22

Lower-class discipline is physical.

socialization; while middle-class children are more likely to experience reason, praise, and rewards (see Table 10.4). Middle-class families allow their children to express mild aggression toward parents, while lower-class parents do not. Well-educated mothers are more likely to have approving attitudes toward child-rearing than are mothers from lower-class levels. The middle-class parent has high expectations for his child compared to the lower-class parent, and this is particularly true of academic achievement. Middle-class parents expect their children to attend and finish college, while lower-class parents hope their children will finish high school. Middle-class families permit more variation in child behavior, and they don't define appropriate sexual behavior nearly so rigidly as do lower-class families. Lower-class children become aware of sex-role patterns earlier than middle-class children. In addition, sex education occurs earlier among lower-class children, since lower-class parents are not as anxious about children's sexual curiosity. Lower-class children explore and learn more about sex, and they have less anxiety associated with sexual subjects.

Ethnic differences in child-rearing are slight.

Most child-rearing authorities argue that once social class is eliminated from the comparison there are few differences among various ethnic group in their methods of bringing up children. Some believe that Mexican-American families are a bit more paternalistic than white or black families, even if social class is not considered in the comparison.

Practical Child-training Suggestions

Children need controls.

Mothers universally find that once a baby begins to move he is into everything almost immediately. Once this happens even the most permissive parent begins trying to establish some control over the child.

Portrait

Benjamin McLane Spock was born in 1903 in New Haven, Connecticut, where his father was general counsel for the New Haven Railroad. Young Benjamin spent his early years in private schools around New Haven, and in 1919 enrolled in Andover Preparatory School. He entered Yale College in 1921, where he took a conventional liberal arts program. Following graduation from Yale in 1924, Spock entered Yale Medical School, about one mile from his home in New Haven. But after two years at medical school, he transferred to Columbia University's College of Physicians and Surgeons in New York to get away from home. Once in New York, he married his childhood sweetheart. Spock nearly failed psychiatry, but through application managed to graduate with the highest average in his class. His postdoctoral training included pediatrics at a hospital connected with Cornell Medical College, and a year's residency in psychiatry. He then tried to apply psychoanalytic practice to the prevention of mental illness in children. During his psychiatric residency, Spock was analyzed by Dr. Bertram Lewin, a student of Freud's.

In 1933 Spock began the private practice of pediatrics, and in the course of his work often gave advice to his patients' parents about the care and feeding of babies. During these early years the preference among most pediatricians was for rigid schedules and bottle feeding. Many young babies were poisoned by contaminated milk in the 1930's, but pediatricians thought the deaths were due to overfeeding, so a rigid schedule was advised. Only much later were pediatricians able to overcome their early beliefs about rigid schedules and adopt the more flexible system advocated in these early years by Spock. He also encouraged breast feeding at a time when it was unpopular among both pediatricians and mothers.

An editor for Pocket Books, one of the pioneer paperback publishers, asked him to do a small book about child care in 1943. Settled comfortably into the Adirondack League summer colony in upstate New York, Spock began to write *Baby and Child Care*. He has said that his mother's demand for two letters a week during his early years helped him learn to write. His first goal was to increase parents' confidence in their own abilities to handle child-care problems, so he tried to develop common-sense rules of how to handle children. Spock says that the entire book came out of his own head, and not from reviewing the medical literature or other books on child-rearing. Three years after publication *Baby and Child Care* had sold over one million copies, and the book is now an all-time bestseller at over twenty-five million copies.

Reactions to *Baby and Child Care* ranged from grateful acceptance by parents to almost total rejection by some pediatric authorities. They said that Spock was too permissive. Some pediatricians rejected his emphasis on lax schedules and his concern for emotional development. In fact, he has modified his views over the years. The later editions of *Baby and Child Care* reflect more concern with discipline, and the author has been careful to point out that children need limits in order to mature well. Spock no longer rejects physical punishment. Instead, he says that it should never be the main element of discipline. In spite of this controversy *Baby and Child Care* has become a vital part of growing up in the United States.

Common Nervous Symptoms

Child-care expert Benjamin Spock.

Babies Who Startle Easily

Newborn babies are startled by loud noises and by sudden changes in position. Some are much more sensitive than others. When you put a baby on a flat, hard surface and he jerks his arms and legs, it's likely to rock his body a little. This unexpected motion is enough to make a sensitive baby nearly jump out of his skin and cry with fright. He may hate his bath because he is held so loosely. He needs to be washed in his mother's lap and then rinsed in the tub, while held securely in both her hands. He should be held firmly and moved slowly at all times. He will gradually get over this uneasiness as he grows older. . . .

The Trembles

Some babies have trembly moments in the early months. The chin may quiver, or the arms and legs may tremble, especially when the baby is excited or when he is cool just after being undressed. This trembling is nothing to be disturbed about. It is just one of the signs that the baby's nervous system is still young. The tendency passes away in time.

Twitching

Some babies twitch occasionally in their sleep, and once in a while there is one who twitches frequently. This, too, usually disappears as the baby grows older.

Head-rolling, Head-banging, Jouncing

It's disturbing to a mother to have her baby take up the habit of banging his head. It seems so senseless and painful that it makes her doubt whether he's really bright, after all. She wonders if the repeated blows can injure his brain. Even if she doesn't have these worries, she finds it nerve-racking to sit in the next room and listen to the steady thud, thud, thud.

As one baby bangs his head against the bed, another rolls it from side to side. Still another gets up on his hands and knees and rhythmically jounces down against his heels. This moves the crib across the room until it bangs against the wall.

What is the meaning of these rhythmic movements? I don't think we know for sure, but here are some suggestions. In the first place, these motions usually appear in the second half of the first year, in

From Benjamin Spock, M.D. *The Common Sense Book of Baby and Child Care* (New York: Duell, Sloane & Pearce, 1945).

the age period when babies naturally begin to get a sense of rhythm and try to sway in time to music. But this is at best only a partial explanation. Jouncing and head-banging occur mostly when a baby is going to sleep or is partly awakened. We know that many babies when they are tired do not go directly and peacefully to sleep, but must go through a slightly tense period first. There are the 2- and 3-month-old infants who always scream for a few minutes before dropping off. Perhaps those older babies who suck their thumbs to go to sleep, and the others who bang their heads or jounce, are also trying to soothe away a tense feeling.

I think that the first baby is more likely to bang his head or jounce than his younger brothers and sisters, and the solemn, high-strung one more often than the jolly, easygoing one. Some doctors have the impression that these rhythmic movements are commoner in babies who don't get quite enough cuddling. Maybe these notions have some connection with each other. It's natural for parents with their first baby to be more serious. They forget at times to relax, to be natural and comfortable, to show physical affection for the baby. As a result, he may be less cuddly, less sociable, less easygoing.

This idea may give a useful clue to some parents of jouncing, head-rolling, or head-banging babies, but I certainly don't want to give you the impression that it applies to all the babies who do these things, or that it's a proved theory for even a few. These habits do not mean that a baby is lacking in intelligence. They do not injure his brain.

If a baby bangs his head, you can pad his crib to keep him from bruising himself. One father solved his baby's head-banging by sawing the headboard out of the crib and tacking a piece of canvas in its place. For the jouncing baby who rattles the whole house, you can put the crib on a carpet and tack the carpet to the floor, or tie some kind of homemade pads, preferably of rubber, onto the feet of the crib. Or you can put the crib against the wall, where it's going to end up anyway, and place a big wad of padding between the crib and the wall.

In any case, I would not scold the baby or try to restrain him physically. Either of these measures would only make him more tense.

Thumb-sucking

Thumb-sucking is a subject about which there is yet no final agreement. I'll give you an idea of what is known and my suggestions of what to do about it. It used to be thought of as just a bad habit. That's why, when a baby first started, the mother would try to prevent it before it became a "habit." But we now know that it isn't this kind of habit, at least in the beginning. The main reason that a young baby sucks his thumb seems to be that he hasn't had enough sucking at the breast or bottle to satisfy his sucking need. Dr. David Levy pointed out that babies who are fed every 3 hours don't suck their thumbs as much as babies fed every 4 hours, and that babies who have cut down on nursing time from 20 minutes to 10 minutes (because the nipples have become old and soft) are more likely to suck their thumbs than babies who still have to work for 20 minutes. Dr. Levy fed a litter of puppies with a medicine dropper so that they had no chance to suck during their feedings. They acted just the same as babies who don't get enough chance to suck at feeding time. They sucked their own and each other's paws and skin so hard that the fur came off.

If your baby begins to try to suck his thumb or finger or hand, I think it's preferable not to stop him directly but to try to give him more opportunity to suck at the breast or the bottle or the pacifier . . . There are two things to consider: the number of feedings, and how long each feeding takes.

The Time to Pay Attention to Thumb-sucking

The time to pay attention to thumb-sucking is when the baby first tries to do it, not when he finally succeeds. I make this point because there are lots of babies who, for the first few months of their lives, haven't much control over their arms. You see such a baby struggling to get his hands up, and searching around with his mouth. If by good luck he gets his fist to his mouth, he sucks it vigorously as long as it happens to stay there. This baby, just as much as the real thumb-sucker, is showing a need to suck longer at the breast or bottle.

The very young baby needs help most, because the sucking need is strongest in the first 3 or 4 months. From then on it tapers off gradually. One baby seems to have had enough sucking as early as 7 months, another not till he is over a year.

All babies aren't born with the same amount of instinct to suck. One baby never nurses more than 15 minutes at a time and yet never once has put his thumb in his mouth, and another whose bottles have always taken 20 minutes or more thumb-sucks excessively. A few begin to thumb-suck in the delivery room, and they keep at it. I suspect that a strong sucking instinct runs in some families.

You don't need to be concerned when a baby sucks his thumb for only a few minutes just before his feeding time. He is probably doing this only because he's hungry. It's when a baby tries to get his thumb just as soon as his feeding is over, or when he sucks a lot between feedings, that you have to think of ways to satisfy his sucking craving. Most babies who thumb-suck start before they are 3 months old.

I might add here there the thumb-, finger-, and hand-chewing that almost every baby does from the time he begins to teethe (commonly around 3 or 4 months) should not be confused with thumb-sucking. Naturally, the baby who is a thumb-sucker is sucking at one minute, chewing at another, during his teething periods.

The Effect on the Teeth

You may be worried about the effect of thumb-sucking on the baby's jaws and teeth. It is true that thumb-sucking often pushes the upper front baby teeth foward and the lower teeth back. How much the teeth are displaced depends on how much the child sucks his thumb and, even more, on what position he holds his thumb in. But dentists point out that this tilting of the baby teeth has no effect on the permanent teeth that begin coming in at about 6 years of age. In other

words, if the thumb-sucking is given up by 6 years of age — as it is in a great majority of cases — there is very little chance of its hurting the permanent teeth.

But whether thumb-sucking displaces the teeth or not, you naturally prefer to have your child give it up as soon as possible. The suggestions I have been making are the ones that I think will end thumb-sucking soonest.

Why Not Use Restraints?

Why not tie a baby's arms down or put aluminum mittens over his hands to keep him from thumb-sucking? This would frustrate him a great deal, which theoretically is not a good idea. Furthermore, it usually doesn't cure the baby who is thumb-sucking a lot. We have all heard of despairing mothers who use elbow splints or metal mitts or bad-tasting paints not just for days but for months. And the day they take off the restraint, the thumb pops back in the mouth. To be sure, there are some mothers who say they have had good results from using such restraints. But in most of these cases, the thumb-sucking was very mild. Many babies do a little thumb-sucking off and on. They get over it quickly, whether you do anything or not. I think, myself, that restraints only make the confirmed thumb-sucker do it more in the long run.

The Pacifier

A Pacifier Is Helpful for Colic and to Prevent Thumb-sucking

A pacifier is a 'blind" nipple (without a hole in it), attached to a plastic disk that rests against the baby's lips. He can suck vigorously on the nipple, and the disk keeps it from being pulled entirely into his mouth.

In former times pacifiers were used freely for colic and fretfulness. But in the first half of the twentieth century, when so much emphasis was put on cleanliness and proper habits, they came to be frowned on as unhygienic and disgusting. In the past few years they have returned to favor with some parents and some doctors for use in treating colic or preventing thumb-sucking. Other doctors and parents still disapprove quite strongly.

It has been observed by parents and doctors that very few babies who have used pacifiers in their early months ever turn to thumb-sucking. On the other hand, a fair proportion of the pacifier babies continue to want the pacifier until they are 1 to 2 years old and a few until 3 years old. Some parents feel this is as unattractive as thumb sucking, or even worse. I have a theory about why a baby or child is able to give up the pacifier earlier than the thumb. The greatest sucking need is in the first 3 or 4 months of life. Yet most babies can't get their thumbs into their mouth or keep them there until they are about 3 months old. So perhaps the longing for more sucking has added up to a greater total in the would-be thumb-sucker by the time he can finally manage to do it. He has a lot of missed sucking to make up. The baby whose mother gives him the pacifier freely after meals, from his earliest weeks, can suck as long as he wants and gets his craving well satisfied during those early months when it's greatest.

But if you are disgusted by the appearance of a pacifier in a baby's or child's mouth, you'd better not use one; it wouldn't be good for you or for your feelings for the child. If you feel that your baby needs a pacifier and are worried only about what the neighbors or relatives will say, tell the neighbors that this is a very modern practice (or tell them that this is your baby).

How to Use a Pacifier

If you are using a pacifier mainly for colic, you naturally use it most during the hours when the baby is suffering from the discomfort. In a great majority, the colic is over by 3 months of age.

How would you use the pacifier to prevent thumb-sucking? In the first place, many babies — perhaps 50% — never try to thumb-suck at all or do it only casually and for brief periods. In these, there is nothing to prevent and no need to get involved with the pacifier (unless there is colic). On the other hand, you have to decide, not on the basis of what a baby is actually accomplishing,

but from what he is *trying* to do. If he tries after meals to get his thumb in his mouth and sucks eagerly when he succeeds, then there is good reason to consider the pacifier.

What age to start? If a baby becomes used to his thumb over a period of weeks or months, the chances are that he will refuse the pacifier. He has learned to enjoy not only the sensations in his mouth but the sensations in his thumb. So if you are going to use a pacifier, start it in the first few weeks of life.

What times of day? The logical time to offer the pacifier is whenever the baby is searching around with his mouth and trying to suck on thumb, fingers, wrist, clothing, or anything else he can reach. In the early months, a baby is seldom awake except before and after feedings, so these are the usual times. But if he's awake between feedings, I'd give it to him then, too. The idea is to give it to him not as little as possible, but as much as he can use it in the first 3 months, so that he will be satisfied and give it up as soon as he can.

I think it is preferable to remove the pacifier when the baby begins to be drowsy, if he doesn't object too strongly, or just as soon as he is asleep. There are two reasons. A baby who is accustomed to having a pacifier in his mouth when asleep may, if it falls out, wake and cry unhappily until it is replaced. This can happen a dozen times a night — especially when a baby who has previously slept on his back learns to turn over on his abdomen — and it can be an awful nuisance. The other reason for not letting a baby form the habit of falling asleep with a pacifier (or bottle) in his mouth is that after a few months he may become utterly unable to fall asleep without it, no matter how tired he is. This problem can postpone the giving up of pacifier or bottle for many months.

Giving Up the Pacifier

When does the baby give up the pacifier? Many mothers who have tried pacifiers report that between 3 and 6 months of age their baby has shown a decreasing desire to suck the pacifier. Some of these infants have even come to the point of spitting out the pacifier and refusing to take it again. When the baby's interest has lessened a great deal, mothers report no difficulty or un-happiness when they remove the pacifier for good. I'd advise parents who see lack of interest at 3 or 4 or 5 months to take advantage of it and get rid of the pacifier if the baby is willing. I don't mean that I'd try to dispose of it the first day a baby cuts down his use of it. He couldn't outgrow his need that fast. But I'd follow his lead closely and begin omitting it gradually, first at one and then at another time of day when he sucks it least. If I found that I was going too fast for him or that he had off days when he was looking for it anxiously, I wouldn't be afraid to give in to him for a day or so. On the other hand, I wouldn't be so hesitant that I failed to take full advantage of his readiness.

Though the majority of babies seem willing to give up the pacifier in the 3-, 4-, 5-month-old stage, there are some who are unready until the last half of the first year, others who are not ready until some time in the second year, and a very few who cling to it beyond the age of 2. If your baby is clinging to the pacifier, should you insist that he give it up? I think it is unwise to take it away forcibly, to refuse to give it to him, or to pretend that it is lost when he's begging for it. I wouldn't nag and tease him about it. In other words, it's fine to help him outgrow it, a mistake to make him miserable by taking it away.

Precautions with the Pacifier

If, when he's older, it's going to embarrass you to take him out in public with a pacifier, you may be able to accustom him from the start to going without it when away from home.

If your baby has already become dependent on a pacifier through the night but keeps losing it in his sleep, you can probably help him over this hump by putting 2 or 3 in his crib so that he is more likely to find one by himself.

In any case, have several pacifiers in the house so that the baby and you won't be frantic if one gets lost or broken.

There is another precaution that you ought to take. When a baby has a few teeth, he can pull the nipple of an old, tired pacifier off the disk or chew pieces out of the nipple. These pieces may cause serious choking if swallowed the wrong way. So buy new pacifiers when the old ones become at all weak or crumbly.

Some pacifiers are too long in the nipple for a newborn baby. They hit against the back of his throat and gag him. If so, try to find shorter ones.

Socialization is learning to eat, speak, and play responsibly.

Socialization includes learning how to eat, speak, and dress, and what will break versus what can be used as a toy. Some parents find authority difficult. They apparently confuse the freedom of responsible adults with the imposition of control on a necessarily irresponsible infant. The first thing to remember is that a child is not an adult. He cannot exercise judgment on his own, and must have dangerous situations pointed out to him and controls placed on him if he is going to live safely and come to behave in a reasonable social manner. As a general rule, the best way to decide if a child is ready for a particular rule or a control is to try it. The timing of control training is important. Until a child is mature enough to handle the training the parent is simply wasting his time. The transition from freedom to complete control cannot be made overnight. A gradual change in the situation, so that the child can satisfy his needs and yet has the opportunity to learn new things, is the best plan.

Safety is important.

The most basic reason for socialization is the physical safety of a baby. If he is going to mature, he must survive. The growing child wants to try everything, and his curiosity far outstrips his judgment or ability to deal with potentially dangerous situations. Babies and young children are not knowledgeable about the consequences of their actions. They do not understand what is dangerous. Cars are attractive to them; water is fascinating; and they don't understand that there is electricity in a wall circuit, or that many chemicals are poison. A responsible adult must keep the child away from moving autos, out of deep water, and away from electrical outlets and poisons. The best way to stop a baby from reaching into a medicine chest is to say "no," and when necessary slap his hand. The general rule is to remove major hazards from the baby's path, and then train him not to touch those which cannot be removed. Then the parent must relax. Minor bumps and bruises are an inevitable part of growing up.

Children need toilet training.

All children must learn sooner or later to use a toilet. Before beginning toilet training an infant should be mature enough to be able to control his bladder and understand simple commands. Bowel and bladder training are two different processes. Bowel control is easier to accomplish, and can usually be established at around eighteen months of age. The most important ingredient of bowel training is to establish an advance warning system. Either the toddler should be asked to say when he must go to the toilet or some other standard signal should be established. Then, the child can be placed on his own toilet, not one that fits over the adult toilet, which is too high to let him be comfortable. Once a toddler is willing to try and can give a signal about his needs, the parent should proceed in a relaxed and cheerful manner. Bowel control is usually easier to establish among girls than boys. Bladder control comes next, and happens in two stages: first, control comes when the child is awake, and then night control develops automatically. Waking control usually happens at around two years of age in girls; boys often take longer. Bladder control is also a gradual process. If a child has been dry for several hours, he should be invited to use the toilet. Sometimes it helps to wake the child an hour after he goes to sleep if nighttime control is delayed longer than one year.

Summary

Parents influence their children both through the genes passed along to the offspring and through the family atmosphere in which the child grows. There is evidence that an offspring's intelligence, personal behavior, and tendency toward abnormality are all partly determined by genetic factors. The type of discipline applied, whether harsh or loving; the amount of control, whether little or too much; and the structure of the family, whether nuclear, extended, paternal, maternal, or singular also affect the child's development.

SUGGESTED ADDITIONAL READING

Baldwin, A.L. *Theories of Child Development.* New York: Wiley, 1967.

II Social Relations and the School

The Peer Group
  Children's Groups
  Peer Aggression
    Leadership
    Conformity and Obedience
    Friendship or Rejection
    Studies of Childrens Groups
    The Inner Child—Kurt Lewin
    Play
The Teacher
  Types of Teachers

Teacher Background
Teaching Methods
The School
  The Purpose of School
  Evaluating Pupil Performance
  School Achievement and Failure
Educational Problems
  Dropouts
  Competition and Cheating
  Television versus the Classroom
  Violence
Summary

PREVIEW

There are three major influences on a child's social development. The first important social interactions occur within the family, as we have seen, but after about six years of age two other groups come to exert more and more control over the child's social behavior. As the child matures he is influenced less by parental pressures and more by peers and teachers. This chapter reviews how classmates and educators influence the growing child and how education affects development. Some major problems in the classroom are also discussed.

The Peer Group

Children acquire
social attitudes within
the family.

As we have learned, a child's social relations begin with his mother and a little later include his father. By eight months of age the baby begins to show attachment and affiliation with his family and rejection of strangers. Ordinarily, children acquire their early social attitudes within the family. However, Jacob Gewirtz (1965) showed that early social relations are influenced by the social environment of the child (*see* Figure 11.1). During his first year of life the average child has only trivial social interaction with peers. If two children ten months of age are placed together, they will relate to objects in their surroundings rather than to each other. At one year of age other children continue to be ignored. If young children do accidently interact or make contact, they will do little more than look at,

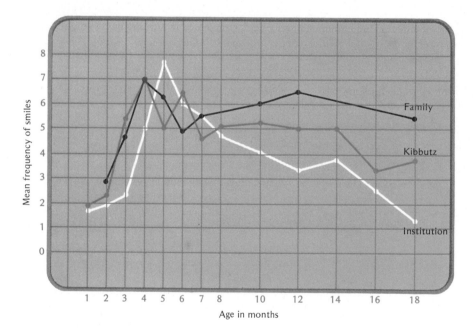

FIGURE 11.1 Smiling among infants reared in three different environments. (From J. L. Gewirtz, 1965.)

smile, or maybe touch each other. Conflict will occur only if both of them want the same object at the same time.

Competition begins
during the second
year.

Because of their interest in objects and insensitivity to the rights and needs of others, children fight and compete for toys during their second year. However, their main focus is on the toy, not on the playmate (*see* Table 11.1). By eighteen months the average baby's social needs outweigh his interest in objects and conflict begins to decline. At around two years of age children occasionally interact with peers and they begin to

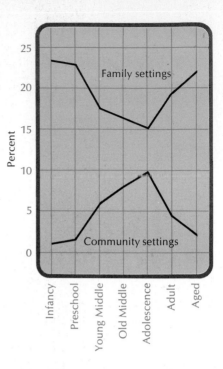

FIGURE 11.2
Average percent of time spent in family and community settings.
(From Wright, 1956.)

adjust their behavior to the action of others. This is where social interaction really begins (*see* Figure 11.2).

Children's Groups

Children spend more time interacting as they mature.

As children mature, they spend less time alone or passively watching other children, and more time interacting with their peers in games. Three-year-old children exchange social rewards of approval and affection. Children who give rewards to others are also more likely to receive rewards from their peers. By the time a child enters school he depends more on his contemporaries than on his parents for approval and social relations. Parents control the young child, but later on peer relations become more and more important to the individual. The child's social relations need not become a conflict between peers and adults. Often the mother, father, or another adult will supervise several children, and in schools in the U.S. there is a teacher who modifies the interactions of children. Only during adolescence are peers the most important social group.

Peer Aggression

Peer interactions affect aggression.

Children influence each other through their actions. Social approval or attention are reinforcing; and isolation, rejection, or aggression are unpleasant and negatively reinforcing for most children. A recent study by Gerry Patterson, Richard Lipman, and William Bricker (1967) showed that even at a nursery-school level peer interactions affect the amount of

TABLE 11.1   Indicators of social development, first three years

Behavior item	Age expected
	(Weeks)
Responds to smiling and talking	1
Knows mother	3
Withdraws from strangers	8
Responds to inhibitory words	12
Waves "bye-bye"	12
	(Months)
Is no longer shy toward strangers	15
Plays alone	18
Shows beginning of concept of private ownership	21
Has much interest in and watches other children	24
Is not sociable; lacks social interest	27
Begins to resist adult influence; wants to be independent	30
Is in conflict with children of own age	30
Begins to accept suggestions	36
Is independent of mother at nursery school	36

(Abridged from L.H. Stott, 1955.)

aggression that children direct toward each other. These investigators observed groups of children and recorded their reactions to aggression. They found that nursery-school children are passive, cry, tell the teacher, or retaliate in response to aggression from a peer. After the investigators had recorded the consequences of aggression and had followed the children for several more days, they discovered that when physical attack or aggression was followed by crying, defensiveness, or passivity, the attacker would aggress against the victim again. If retaliation or counter-aggression occurred, the agressor's behavior changed. He would either pick another victim, alter his interactions with his original victim, or both. Even in the nursery school, it seems, the outcome of aggression influences whether the attack is continued or transferred to someone else. Most relations with peers supplement the objectives of parents and teachers, and for this reason, parents and teachers may actively enlist peers to modify a child's behavior. This is particularly true in the Soviet Union and China, where formal peer influence is continued into adult life (Bronfenbrenner, 1970).

LEADERSHIP   Whenever two or more people come together in a group their actions influence each other. Most group interaction results in an ordering of members by dominance, attractiveness, influence, status, or responsibility. From the baboon herd to modern governments, almost all groups have leaders and followers. Figure 11.3 illustrates some typical roles that emerge in most small groups. These roles can be ordered along three independent dimensions of dominance/submission, positive/negative,

All groups have dominance hierarchies.

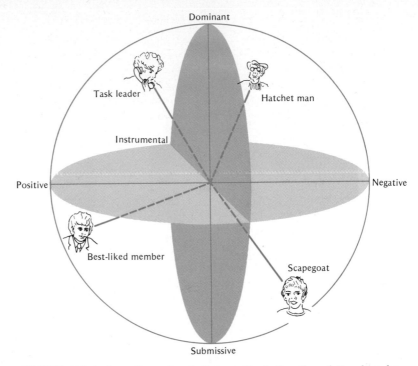

FIGURE 11.3 A three-dimensional diagram illustrating the relationships between members of most small groups. The three dimensions are dominance, approval, and task orientation.

and task-oriented/emotional. The *task leader* and *hatchet man* are dominant members of most groups. The task leader is liked, while the hatchet man is hated. At the other end of the power continuum are the *scapegoat* and the *silent member*. Both are submissive, but the scapegoat is disliked, while the silent member evokes more neutral feelings from his peers.

Dominance is established by threat among most animals.

Most groups form some kind of ranks, or dominance hierarchy. These were first studied systematically in the barnyard among chickens, because their pecking order is an easy measure of who dominates whom. Among chickens and children *dominance* is established by fighting. Once a hierarchy is stabilized, a simple threat from the dominant member can settle most squabbles without resort to further physical violence. Dominance hierarchies can be simple or complex and their importance varies with the species. Animal studies of dominance—among the free-roaming baboons of Africa, for example—have been far-reaching. Baboons are primates; they are ground-dwellers; they form groups; and some scientists believe they share many social characteristics with man's early ancestors. For all these reasons, plus the fact that baboons are inherently interesting, they have been extensively studied.

Baboon males are dominance-oriented.

Baboons have lived in Africa for over a million years. They are a successful species, highly male dominance-oriented, with striking sexual differentiation. Baboon leaders mate more often, dominate other males, are larger than others, and are aggressive in their ordinary relationships. When the group is attacked, dominant baboon males usually stand their ground, while other members of the group retreat. A male's dominance is determined by his own strength and the support he can muster from others. It is demonstrated in several ways—in competition for food and in many other areas of interaction such as:

1. Mating—dominant males mate more often with high-ranking fertile females of their choosing.
2. Aggression—dominant males attack others most often.
3. Protection—new mothers and young children cluster near dominant males.
4. Arbitration—dominant males break up squabbles among their subordinates.
5. Grooming—dominant males are groomed by everyone but fertile high-ranking females.
6. Personal space—dominant males maintain a larger area for their own personal use than other members of the group.

Many believe that man and baboons share social processes.

Many scientists believe there are similarities between baboon groups and human society, in spite of the fact that man's social systems are more complex and confusing than the simple baboon hierarchy. The accompanying excerpt from *The Human Zoo* by Desmond Morris outlines how baboons achieve and hold dominant status. Morris also suggests that children on the playground, adolescents in gangs, and adults running for political office can all profit from the techniques used by baboon males to attain and keep their status in the group hierarchy.

rules for rulers

DESMOND MORRIS

In any organized group of mammals, no matter how cooperative, there is always a struggle for social dominance. As he pursues this struggle, each adult individual acquires a particular social rank, giving him his position, or status, in the group hierarchy. The situation never remains stable for very long, largely because all the status strugglers are growing older. When the overlords, or 'top dogs', become senile, their seniority is challenged and they are overthrown by their immediate subordinates. There is then renewed dominance squabbling as everyone moves a little farther up the social ladder. At the other end of the scale, the younger members of the group are maturing rapidly, keeping up the pressure from below. In addition, certain members of the group may suddenly be struck down by disease or accidental death, leaving gaps in the hierarchy that have to be quickly filled.

If you are to rule your group and to be successful in holding your position of power, there are ten golden rules you must obey. They apply to all leaders, from baboons to modern presidents and prime ministers. The ten commandments of dominance are these:

1. *You must clearly display the trappings, postures and gestures of dominance.*

For the baboon this means a sleek, beautifully groomed, luxuriant coat of hair; a calm, relaxed posture when not engaged in disputes; a deliberate and purposeful gait when active. There must be no outward signs of anxiety, indecision or hesitancy. With a few superficial modifications, the same holds true for the human leader. The luxuriant coat of fur becomes the rich and elaborate costume of the ruler, dramatically excelling those of his subordinates. He assumes postures unique to his dominant role. When he is relaxing, he may recline or sit, while others must stand until given permission to follow suit. This is also typical of the dominant baboon, who may sprawl out lazily while his anxious subordinates hold themselves in more alert postures near by. The situation changes once the leader stirs into aggressive action and begins to assert himself. Then, be he baboon or prince, he must rise into a more impressive position than that of his followers. He must literally rise above them, matching his psychological status with his physical posture.

The ingenuity of our species permits the human leader to have it both ways. By sitting on a throne on a raised platform, he can enjoy both the relaxed position of the passive dominant *and* the heightened position of the active dominant at one and the same time, thus providing himself with a doubly powerful display posture.

2. *In moments of active rivalry you must threaten your subordinates aggressively.*

At the slightest sign of any challenge from a subordinate baboon, the group leader immediately responds with an impressive display of threatening behaviour. There is a whole range of threat displays available, varying from those motivated by a lot of aggression tinged with a little fear to those motivated by a lot of fear and only a little aggression. The latter—the 'scared threats' of weak-but-hostile individuals—are never shown by a dominant animal unless his leadership is tottering. When his position is secure he shows only the most aggressive threat displays. He can be so secure that all he needs to do is to indicate that he is about to threaten, without actually bothering to carry it through. A mere jerk of his massive head in the direction of

the unruly subordinate may be sufficient to subdue the inferior individual. These actions are called 'intention movements', and they operate in precisely the same way in the human species. A powerful human leader, irritated by the actions of a subordinate, need only jerk his head in the latter's direction and fix him with a hard stare, to assert his dominance successfully. If he has to raise his voice or repeat an order, his dominance is slightly less secure, and he will, on eventually regaining control, have to re-establish his status by administering a rebuke or a symbolic punishment of some kind.

3. *In moments of physical challenge you (or your delegates) must be able forcibly to overpower your subordinates.*

If a threat display fails, then a physical attack must follow. If you are a baboon boss this a dangerous step to take, for two reasons. Firstly, in a physical fight even the winner may be damaged, and injury is more serious for a dominant animal than for a subordinate. It makes him less daunting for a subsequent attacker. Secondly, he is always outnumbered by his subordinates, and if they are driven too far they may gang up on him and overpower him in a combined effort. It is these two facts that make threat rather than actual attack the preferred method for dominant individuals.

The human leader overcomes this to some extent by employing a special class of 'suppressors'. They, the military or police, are so specialized and professional at their task that only a general uprising of the whole populace would be strong enough to beat them.

4. *If a challenge involves brain rather than brawn you must be able to outwit your subordinates.*

The baboon boss must be cunning, quick and intelligent as well as strong and aggressive. This is obviously even more important for a human leader. In cases where there is a system of inherited leadership, the stupid individual is quickly deposed or becomes the mere figurehead and pawn of the true leaders.

Today the problems are so complex that the modern leader is forced to surround himself with intellectual specialists, but despite this he cannot escape the need for quickwittedness. It is he who must make the final decisions, and make them sharply and clearly, without faltering. This is such a vital quality in leadership that it is more important to make a firm, unhesitating decision than it is to make the 'right' one. Many a powerful leader has survived occasional wrong decisions, made with style and forcefulness, but few have survived hesitant indecisiveness. The golden rule of leadership here, which in a rational age is an unpleasant one to accept, is that it is the manner in which you do something that really counts, rather than what you do. It is a sad truth that a leader who does the wrong things in the right way will, up to a certain point, gain greater allegiance and enjoy more success than one who does the right things in the wrong way. The progress of civilization has repeatedly suffered as a result of this. Lucky indeed is the society whose leader does the right things and at the same time obeys the ten golden rules of dominance; lucky—and rare, too. There appears to be a sinister, more-than-chance relationship between great leadership and aberrant policies.

5. *You must suppress squabbles that break out between your subordinates.*

If a baboon leader sees an unruly squabble taking place he is likely to interfere and suppress it, even though it does not in any way constitute a direct threat to himself. It gives him another opportunity of displaying his dominance and at the same time helps to maintain order inside the group. Interference of this kind from the dominant animal is directed particularly at squabbling juveniles, and helps to instil in them, at an early age, the idea of a powerful leader in their midst.

The equivalent of this behaviour for the human leader is the control and administration of the laws of his group. The rulers of the earlier and smaller super-tribes were powerfully active in this respect, but there has been increasing delegation of these duties in modern times, due to the increasing weight of other burdens that relate more directly to the status of the leader. Nevertheless, a squabbling community is an inefficient one and some degree of control and influence has to be retained.

6. *You must reward your immediate subordinates by permitting them to enjoy the benefits of their high ranks.*

The sub-dominant baboons, although they are the leader's worst rivals, are also of great help to him in times of threat from outside the group. Further, if they are too strongly suppressed they may gang up on him and depose him. They therefore enjoy privileges which the weaker members of the group cannot share. They have more freedom of action and are permitted to stay closer to the dominant animal than are the junior males.

7. *You must protect the weaker members of the group from undue persecution.*

Females with young tend to cluster around the dominant male baboon. He meets any attack on these females or on unprotected infants with a savage onslaught. As a defender of the weak he is ensuring the survival of the future adults of the group. Human leaders have increasingly extended their protection of the weak to include also the old, the sick and the disabled. This is because efficient rulers not only need to defend the growing children, who will one day swell the ranks of their followers, but also need to reduce the anxieties of the active adults, all of whom are threatened with eventual senility, sudden sickness, or possible disability. With most people the urge to give aid in such cases is a natural development of their biologically co-operative nature. But for the leaders it is also a question of making people work more efficiently by taking a serious weight off their minds.

8. *You must make decisions concerning the social activities of your group.*

When the baboon leader decides to move, the whole group moves. When he rests, the group rests. When he feeds, the group feeds. Direct control of this kind is, of course, lost to the leader of a human super-tribe, but he can nevertheless play a vital role in encouraging the more abstract directions his group takes. He may foster the sciences or push towards a greater military emphasis. As with the other golden rules of leadership, it is important for him to exercise this one even when it does not appear to be strictly necessary. Even if a society is cruising happily along on a set and satisfactory course, it is vital for him to change that course in certain ways in order to make his impact felt. It is not enough simply to alter it as a reaction to something that is going wrong. He must spontaneously, of his own volition, insist on new lines of development, or he will be considered weak and colourless. If he has no ready-made preferences and enthusiasms, he must invent them. If he is seen to have what appear to be strong convictions on certain matters, he will be taken more seriously on *all* matters. Many modern leaders seem to overlook this and their political 'platforms' are desperately lacking in originality. If they win the battle for leadership it is not because they are more inspiring than their rivals but simply because they are less uninspiring.

9. *You must reassure your extreme subordinates from time to time.*

If a dominant baboon wishes to approach a subordinate peacefully, it may have difficulty doing so, because its close proximity is inevitably threatening. It can overcome this by performing a reassurance display. This consists of a very gentle approach, with no sudden or harsh movements, accompanied by facial expressions (called lip-smacking) which are typical of friendly subordinates. This helps to calm the fears of the weaker animal and the dominant one can then come near.

Human leaders, who may be characteristically tough and unsmiling with their immediate subordinates, frequently adopt an attitude of friendly submissiveness when coming into personal contact with their extreme subordinates. Towards them they offer a front of exaggerated courtesy, smiling, waving, shaking hands interminably and even fondling babies. But the smiles soon fade as they turn away and disappear back inside their ruthless world of power.

10. *You must take the initiative in repelling threats or attacks arising from outside your group.*

It is always the dominant baboon that is in the forefront of the defence against an attack from an external enemy. He plays the major role as the protector of the group. For the baboon, the enemy is usually a dangerous member of another species, but for the human leader it takes the form of a rival group of the same species. At such moments, his leadership is put to a severe test, but, in a sense, it is less severe than during times of

peace. The external threat . . . has such a powerful cohesive effect on the members of the threatened group that the leader's task is in many ways made easier. The more daring and reckless he is, the more fervently he seems to be protecting the group who, caught up in the emotional fray, never dare question his actions (as they would in peace-time), no matter how irrational these actions may be. Carried along on the grotesque tidal-wave of enthusiasm that war churns up, the strong leader comes into his own. With the greatest of ease he can persuade the members of his group, deeply conditioned as they are to consider the killing of another human being as the most hideous crime known, to commit this same action as an act of honour and heroism. He can hardly put a foot wrong, but if he does, the news of his blunder can always be suppressed as bad for national morale. Should it become public, it can still be put down to bad luck rather than bad judgment. Bearing all this in mind, it is little wonder that, in times of peace, leaders are prone to invent, or at least to magnify, threats from foreign powers that they can then cast in the role of potential enemies. A little added cohesion goes a long way.

These, then, are the patterns of power. I should make it clear that I am not implying that the dominant baboon/human ruler comparison should be taken as meaning that we evolved from baboons, or that our dominance behaviour evolved from theirs. It is true that we shared a common ancestor with baboons, way back in our evolutionary history, but that is not the point. The point is that baboons, like our early human forbears, have moved out of the lush forest environment into the tougher world of the open country, where tighter group control is necessary. Forest-living monkeys and apes have a much looser social system; their leaders are under less pressure. The dominant baboon has a more significant role to play and I selected him as an example for this reason. The value of the baboon/human comparison lies in the way it reveals the very basic nature of human dominance patterns. The striking parallels that exist enable us to view the human power game with a fresh eye and see it for what it is: a fundamental piece of animal behaviour.

FIGURE 11.4
Four different social networks. Members of each group are designated by circles. The lines between them represent interaction. The wheel, chain and Y are centralized; one position, C, has access to more information than any of the others. The circle is decentralized because all positions receive equivalent information. None of these networks accurately describes the typical peer group; children usually form more unstructured groups in the beginning, and only later, when they mature, do leaders, strict lines of communication, and chains develop.

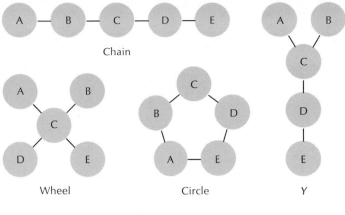

Ethologists argue that man and animal social structures are similar.

As you can see, Desmond Morris believes that human leaders often mimic the methods dominant baboon males use to control their herds. Whether the parallels are fundamental, as ethologists argue, or only accidental, as the behaviorists believe, there are clear similarities between the social relations of lower primates and man.

Three factors determine group leadership.

Laboratory studies of children's groups show that three factors are most important in determining who is viewed as the group's leader:

1. Control of communication within the group.
2. Personal competence.
3. Personal attractiveness.

Children without one or more of these assets do not become leaders. Figure 11.4 shows some possible communication networks in which a child can speak only to another if they are connected by the network. The member with the most arrows is usually seen as the group's leader.

Asch performed early studies on conformity.

CONFORMITY AND OBEDIENCE   Not only does a group produce leadership and responsibility, it also demands some comformity to its common goals and values. The first systematic laboratory study of *conformity* was begun by Solomon Asch (1956). He asked his subjects to sit around a table and told them they were taking part in an experiment on perceptual discrimination. However, all but one subject were really confederates of the experimenter, and they gave prescribed answers to the questions. The naïve subject was often presented with opinions by other members of the group that differed from his own. Under these conditions the naïve subject was often found to conform to the group answer, even when it was wrong. And, when he did not conform, his independence from the group produced various signs of conflict.

Asch discovered that several factors determined conformity:

1. *Unanimity within the group* — if everybody else agrees, it is more difficult for the naïve subject not to conform.
2. *Credibility* — if members of the group seem competent, the individual is more likely to conform; but if they make obviously stupid decisions, he will often not agree with them.
3. *The size of a group* — one other person produces little conformity; two others generate strong conformity; and three, four, or five add extra coercion.
4. *Sex and age* — in the Asch judgment task women and children conformed more than men (*see* Figure 11.5, Costanzo and Shaw, 1966).
5. *Task difficulty* — a naïve subject was more likely to conform if the judgment were difficult than if the decision were easy.
6. *Intelligence* — bright people were more independent than their less intelligent peers in judging tasks of this sort.

More recently another kind of comformity has been studied. It is called *obedience* and has some dark implications for society.

Obedience to authority concerns hurting others.

If an adult in authority ordered a child to hurt another person, would he do it? Most children and adults claim they would not. In fact, the Allied Nuremberg war crime trials after World War II rejected the defense, given by German officers, that they were simply obeying legal authority and were not individually responsible for their acts. The Allied war crime judges would not accept *obedience* to authority as a justification for violence. They attributed the Nazi atrocities to evils of individual personality.

Milgram found widespread obedience.

Experiments by Stanley Milgram (1965) show that in some social situations almost anyone will administer very strong electric shocks to a victim when ordered to do so by an authority. Milgram's experiment was simple. Volunteer adults came to his laboratory in the role of "teachers." Their job was to punish a "student" whenever the student made an error in order to make him learn.

Milgram found that five factors contribute to maximum obedience:

1. There must be a legitimate authority who is trusted and has a valid position in society.
2. The authority and the obedient person must be face to face.
3. A clear dominance-submission relation must exist between the authority and the subject.
4. The subordinate must feel he is *not* personally responsible for what is happening, since he is simply following orders.
5. The closer the punisher is to his victim, the less shock he will administer before disobeying the order to shock the student (*see* Figure 11.6). Punishment at a distance is apparently easier to administer than face-to-face pain.

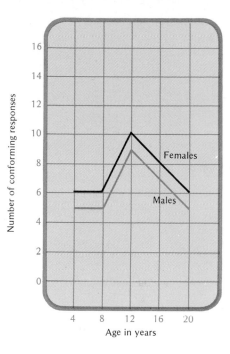

FIGURE 11.5
The relative number of conforming responses produced by males and females of varying ages. Note that females and adolescents produced more conforming responses than males and children or adults.

Most people are obedient most of the time.

The implications of Milgram's study are clear — most people are obedient most of the time, and society as we know it probably could not survive without some kind of obedience. But, blind obedience can have serious consequences. Milgram's experiment has caused much criticism among scientists, who, to simplify, feel the experimenter inflicted emotional pain to an uncalled for degree on his subjects. The important question for child development is what can be done to balance blind obedience to authority with some kind of moral sense of individual responsibility? It is certainly true that a complex social order requires obedience to authority. Can we somehow strike a better balance than currently exists between submission and individual initiative? Most social scientists hope so, but no one is quite sure at this time how to go about constructing that moral balance.

Children like similar others.

FRIENDSHIP OR REJECTION   The child's reaction to his peers is sometimes positive and on other occasions negative. What determines whether a social encounter will be happy or hostile? Children form general impressions of others and respond to these impressions with avoidance or attraction. The way other children are perceived depends primarily on two things — the viewer's attitudes and how the other child presents himself. Perceived similarity makes others attractive. In fact, the more similar two people appear to be, the more attractive they will be to each other (*see* Figure 11.6). The relation between similarity and attraction is so strong that children who like each other exaggerate their similarities.

Status is controlled by personality, intellect, and social class.

School friendships and status are determined by the child's personality, intellect, and social class during the elementary-school years. Bright children are generally more popular than their less intelligent peers, although very smart children are not popular. Retarded children are seldom accepted in social groups. If social class is equal, brighter children are more popular; when intelligence is held constant, children of higher social class are more popular than their lower-class peers. In addition to intelligence and social class, skills in sports and physical appearance affect friendship. Sports are most important for boys and physical appearance counts more for girls.

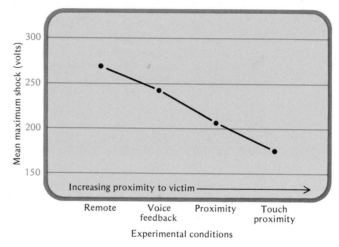

FIGURE 11.6
The relation between a "teacher's" proximity to the "student" and his willingness to punish. Note that close proximity produced less willingness to shock the victims.
(From Milgram, 1965.)

Families of popular children are permissive.

The family backgrounds of popular and unpopular children show several differences. The families of popular children make few demands and do not punish their children. Mothers of popular, likeable children seldom use deprivation of privileges when they discipline the children, and the fathers of popular children enjoy being with them. Popular boys come from families that discourage aggression, avoid frustration or punishment, and encourage social interaction.

Nursery school teaches social interaction.

Some studies report that children who attend nursery school can more easily relate to other children. However nursery school is not the only way to develop social skills. When children reach school age they are exposed to a teacher and several peers in a single classroom, who become increasingly important in the development of the child as he shifts from family to community control. School children must learn to handle hostility, dominance, friendship, competition, and many other complex social problems. The relative influence of parents and peer group varies. U.S. children are more concerned with peer approval and social conformity than children in either Mexican communities or Chinese living in Hawaii. The Soviet Union's early school programs make peer pressure a more important influence than either parents or teachers.

Children's groups are often segregated.

Children's peer groups are almost always segregated along racial, religious, ethnic, and class lines. However, there is some shift in group composition with age. At six years of age informal groups include both boys and girls, and they play both so-called masculine and feminine games. At around seven or eight years of age children usually associate with their own sexes. Boys chase girls away and do not play with them; and girls tend to stay in their own social groups. From eight years of age until adolescence, friendships are based primarily with the same sex. Late in this period formal, highly structured organizations with special membership requirements and rituals appear: Boy Scouts, Girl Scouts, Campfire Girls, Little League, and ballet classes are examples. Almost all societies separate their children by age and sex in order to teach them the skills of life.

Prejudice can be overcome by forced cooperation.

STUDIES OF CHILDREN'S GROUPS   Muzafer Sherif (1969) studied group ties and prejudice at a boys' summer camp. He and his colleagues waited until the boys knew each other and had formed temporary informal friendships before beginning their experiment. Then Sherif arbitrarily divided the boys so that new friends saw little of each other, except during competition. The friendships which had developed before the experiment soon deteriorated into rivalry and hostility during competition. But new friendships grew quickly within each experimental group. After several weeks of competition the two groups were on the verge of a fight. At this point the experimenters introduced a problem of great importance to both groups, which could only be solved by cooperation among all the boys. The forced cooperation decreased group rivalry, and early friendships reappeared. Sherif and his colleagues concluded that while reactions and feelings are important for friendships in groups, enforced cooperating can bridge the gap of rivalry and re-establish old ties.

Social climate affects group productivity.

Kurt Lewin and his students (1939) studied the effect of differing social climates on group productivity and satisfaction. The researchers organized democratic, authoritarian, and leaderless groups. The democratic process produced both high production and group satisfaction; the authoritarian system produced high group production, but less group satisfaction; while the leaderless group produced neither activities nor satisfaction for its members. The theoretical foundations for much of the early research into children's groups were laid by Lewin. Let us consider his notions of child development.

Portrait

Kurt Lewin was born in the city of Mogilno, a part of Prussian Germany, during 1890. He was the first son of a Jewish storekeeper. Early records show that young Lewin was an indifferent student until he entered high school and discovered philosophy. In those years psychology was still academically a part of philosophy, so Lewin's interest led him to enter the University of Berlin's Institute for Psychology, where the Gestalt School of Perception was beginning to expand. But Lewin became interested in the development of personality and motivation rather than perception, and began to create his own theories while he was still a graduate student. In 1933 Lewin left his native Germany to accept a visiting professorship at Stanford University in California. His first regular academic appointment in the U.S. was in the Department of Home Economics at Cornell University in upstate New York. While at Cornell he studied the effect of social pressure on the eating habits of nursery-school children. From Cornell he moved to the Iowa Research Station and began studying group interactions. When World War II began, Lewin and his colleagues at Iowa mobilized to study psychological warfare, military leadership, food consumption, and the rehabilitation of wounded soldiers. In 1942 Lewin founded the Society for the Psychological Study of Social Issues, which still functions as an organization.

Lewin moved to Newtonville, Massachusetts in 1944 to establish the Research Center for Group Dynamics. During his last years at the center he initiated a technique called leadership training, an early form of T-group, or sensitivity, training, which later became very popular in the United States. Lewin was one of the first academic psychologists to try changing society through social experimentation. He argued that social scientists should not approach society with idealistic aims and little practical notion of how to change its structure. Lewin wanted to experiment and find out what really worked.

He was also one of the first psychologists to study prejudice, but he died without ever developing a single theory. Instead, he advocated an approach which he believed would solve many problems.

environmental forces in child behavior and development

KURT LEWIN

Kurt Lewin, photographed early in 1947. (Wide World Photos)

It has long been recognized that the psychological influence of environment on the behavior and development of the child is extremely important. Actually, all aspects of the child's behavior, hence instinctive and voluntary behavior, play, emotion, speech, expression, are codetermined by the existing environment. Some . . . theories, notably those of Watson and Adler, assign to environment so predominant an influence upon development that hereditary factors are usually neglected. Stern's theory of convergence emphasizes, on the contrary, that a predisposition and an environmental influence must operate in the same direction in order to effect a particular mode of behavior.

Present-day investigation of the environment uses primarily statistical methods. The average of as many school records as were obtainable for only children is compared, for example, with that of eldest, middle, and youngest children in families of three. Particular environmental factors may be excluded to a certain degree, for example, in the investigation of the effect of size of family or of position in the series of siblings, by including only children of approximately the same economic status. These investigations have brought to light a wealth of interesting facts; for example, that in certain social levels in Germany the number of children optimal for school achievement is three or four, but that in proletarian families, on the contrary, only children display, on the average, the best records.

The psychological environment of the small child can be characterized neither as a real nor as an unreal world, but the two strata are still relatively undifferentiated. Jaensch and his students have shown for sensory psychology that the eidetic images . . . of children have the properties . . . of both the perceptions and the imaginings of adults. Piaget has shown that the child's conception of the world, especially his ideas of causation, is still essentially "magical" and "animistic," that name and thing, act and magic word, are not yet clearly separated.

These properties of the child's perceptions and intellectual view of the world are only an expression of the general fact that in the child's psychological environment the differentiation between the levels of reality and unreality is still slight. This fact is further displayed in the peculiar seriousness of the child's play. From it derives the relative lack of distinction between wish and reality that is expressed, for example, in the very tenuous distinction between "false-

From Kurt Lewin, *A Dynamic Theory of Personality* (New York: McGraw-Hill, 1935), pp. 66-70, 104-107.

hood" and "truth." The great "suggestibility" of children is related to the same fact. For not only are the child's psychical processes closely dependent upon his present physical condition (*e.g.*, illness), but, which is more often overlooked, the reverse also holds. Bodily condition may be very greatly influenced—especially in children—by the psychological. Thus it is that a small child's pain ceases when one blows on the spot and that the horse may be "gone" when someone "throws him out the window."

Closely related to the slighter differentiation of the child's psychological environment into real and less real or unreal planes is a second factor: for the child, the boundary between the self and the environment is less defined than for the adult. This circumstance is of critical significance to the operation of the environment upon the child.

In other words, the child, to a greater extent than the adult, is a dynamic unity. The infant, for example, acts first with its whole body and only gradually acquires the ability to execute part actions. The child learns only gradually to separate voluntarily certain parts of its environment, to concentrate.

Analogously to this relatively slight delimitation among the various inner psychological systems, the functional firmness of the boundary between his own person and the psychological environment is also in general less with the child than with the adult. This is expressed, for example, by the fact that the "I" or self is only gradually formed, perhaps in the second or third year. Not until then does the concept of property appear, of the belonging of a thing to his own person. The same relative indistinctness of the limits of the self is apparent in the fact that external impressions touch the central nucleus of the child's personality decidedly more readily than is the case with adults. Conversely, needs or other tensions of the inner psychological systems burst through very easily in the form of impulsive behavior and uncontrolled affective demonstrations.

It has been found in the course of psychopathological investigations that in certain circumstances children are more readily induced

to talk openly of personal matters when they are naked. Children also are usually inclined to talk more freely about experiences otherwise kept back when they are going to bed in the evening.

The same factors that are critical for the momentary situation are also characteristic of the *total milieu* of the child over longer periods of his life. Their effects upon the development of the child's personality and his whole behavior are similar to the effects of the forces described in the momentary situation upon his momentary behavior. Particular features of the environment are usually less important than its total character in determining its effect upon development and, more particularly, upon the rate and mode of differentiation of the child's personality. Overly harsh or severe surroundings may lead to the child's encapsulating or insulating himself from the environment. The child becomes stubborn and negativistic . . . Optimal environmental conditions, for example, optimal tension level, vary considerably with different individuals. . . .

It is already clear from the circumstances just discussed what great significance a change of environment may have for the child's development. The so-called difficulties of training are not infrequently related to the particular requirements of the parents, to their characters, and to the way they get along together. These difficulties disappear as soon as the child has been for some time in a suitable environment. To be sure, the difficulties usually begin all over again after a return to the old environment.

Quite analogous cumulative series due to this vicious circle may be seen in psychopathic children or in other children that have difficulties in social groups. The overexcitable or socially disagreeable child is not only less competent in his social situation, and thus makes his task harder, but also the other children reject him, drive him to a defensive attitude, etc. The child soon gets himself into a social situation, originating perhaps in some quite trivial conflicts, that would tax the capacities of a child of high social endowment. Similar developments of a circular causal relationship between capacity and environment are basic, for example, to stammering. Conversely, not the least advantage of the gifted child consists in the especially favorable environmental conditions that he usually creates for the future.

I consider it one of the fundamental tasks of pedagogy so to constitute the situation of chil-dren in difficulties that the severe injuries usually occasioned by the circular causal relation may be avoided or undone. For here at least lie genuine pedagogical possibilities which do not require changing the child's "abilities."

Lewin called the child's psychology a life space.

THE INNERCHILD—KURT LEWIN   Lewin's basic theoretical unit was the life space of a child, and a typical example is the approach and avoidance tendencies illustrated in Figure 11.7. The top diagram represents a child's conflict about two positive goals, while the bottom diagram concerns two negative alternatives. Lewin called the total area within his oval symbol the individual's *life space*. He believed that this space contains all the factors which determine a child's behavior.

Lewin tried to explain behavior as changes in the life space.

Lewin argued that the task of psychological theory is to describe the contents of the life space, show how the contents are related to each other, and then explain how the life space itself develops. He described the child's life space in terms of forces, combinations, and tensions between forces. Lewin argued that human behavior is determined not by the immediate environment but by an inner representation of that environment. He also pointed out that the child may reflect incomplete data, distortions, fantasies, and reality in his inner representation; but, never-

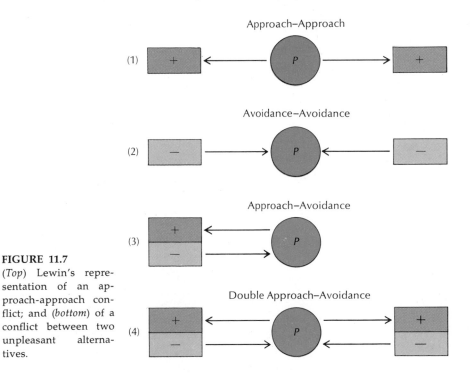

FIGURE 11.7
(*Top*) Lewin's representation of an approach-approach conflict; and (*bottom*) of a conflict between two unpleasant alternatives.

theless, all these factors determine a child's actions. Thus, Lewin rejected the notion that the human physical environment directly controls behavior. He assumed that only a psychological representation of the physical world is important in explaining behavior. He pointed out that if the environment ceased to exist, that fact itself would not change behavior until the child somehow represented the loss of the environment in his own life space.

Behavior is any change in the life space.

Another radical aspect of Lewin's theory was his definition of behavior, which he defined as any change in the child's life space. Thinking about a problem and coming to a conclusion, but doing nothing about that conclusion, is a kind of behavior according to Lewin.

He described the life space of a child by geometric maps in which he used regions to stand for physical areas of the environment, psychological barriers, or alternate ways of reaching a goal. Lewin applied three rules to these regions to predict the child's behavior. He assumed that any psychological force has:

1. A point of application.
2. A strength.
3. A direction.

The life space was represented by a map.

After formulating psychological forces, Lewin applied the laws of physical forces to solve an equation and determine where and how fast a child would respond in his life space. He also distinguished three kinds of forces—those generated by the individual, those induced by outside factors, and those produced by social relations. Lewin believed that a child's own forces are his goals, that induced forces are made up of pressures from the environment, and that interpersonal forces result from social interactions.

Conflict occurs when two forces are equal.

He defined the strength of a force in terms of life-space distance from a goal. Figure 11.8 shows the relation between a child's distance from his goal and the strength of positive and negative forces. Note that positive forces increase more slowly than negative ones, as a child approaches his goal.

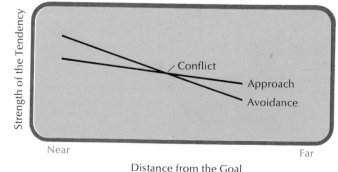

FIGURE 11.8
Forces in an approach-avoidance conflict.

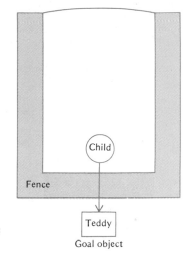

FIGURE 11.9
A detour problem. B = transparent U-shaped fence;
C = child; G = teddy bear.

Lewin studied chil-
dren's responses to a
detour.

A typical Lewinian problem was the *detour task*. A child was placed in a room, shown an attractive goal, and then a barrier was placed between the child and his goal (*see* Figure 11.9). Lewin believed that the barrier detour problem had to be solved in terms of the child's psychological space. He found that young children tried to approach the goal directly and often did not move away from the barrier directly opposite their goal, even though they could not reach the goal. Older or brighter children looked at the situation and detoured around the barrier, attaining their goal without frustration or delay.

As the child matures,
his life space becomes
more complex.

Features of development, according to Lewin, included the complexity and differentiation of the child's life space. He assumed that the child has quasi-needs in addition to basic biological drives like hunger or thirst, and Lewin dealt with these quasi-needs in the same way that others used the major drives. Lewin assumed that when a child intends to mail a letter he establishes a need or intention in his life space and then tries to satisfy that need whenever he has the opportunity. Lewin also felt that as the child matures, his life space becomes more and more differentiated (*see* Figure 11.10). Differentiation was defined by Lewin

FIGURE 11.10
(*Left*) The diagram of a young child's life space, illustrating its simplicity. (*Right*) The more mature child's life space becomes extremely complex.

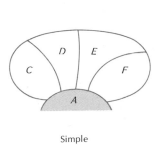

Simple

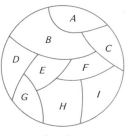

Complex

as an increase in the number of regions in a child's life space. He felt that these rules are characteristic of human development:

1. With maturity, the child produces more varied behavior.
2. Despite this greater variety, older children are better organized.
3. The life space of a child expands in area and time with age.
4. As the child matures, life regions become organized in a hierarchy.
5. With maturity, the child becomes better able to distinguish between reality and fantasy.

Play is the universal occupation of children.

PLAY   In addition to expanding his life space and social skills, another task for children is to play, which is the universal occupation of children and has a long history. Many modern games and childhood rituals can be traced back through the Middle Ages to Roman or even earlier times. Games and their rules have evolved through centuries of use. Bruegel, in the sixteenth century, painted "Children's Games" (see Figure 11.11).

FIGURE 11.11 An early painting by Bruegel illustrates many children's games.
(Courtesy Kunsthistorisches Museum, Vienna.)

Even older Chinese paintings also show children at play. The shape of modern jacks is derived from the animal vertebrae used as toys in Roman times.

Piaget studied children's games.

Where do game rules originate? Piaget (1962), in his studies of children's games, discovered three stages of childhood beliefs about rules. Young children believe rules are just given and cannot be broken. During the middle years children begin to think that rules are made by a rule-maker who sets down their final form. Finally, by junior high school children understand that rules can be agreed upon in many different ways and serve only to define the action in a particular game.

Groos initiated the study of play.

Children's play was a neglected area of study until Karl Groos (1915) published his book *The Play of Animals.* Groos proposed that play in man and animals provides early training for adult life, and this theory flourished for many years.

Freud and Piaget disagree about play.

How does play develop, and why do children choose their toys? Early theories relied on the notion of instinct, in which play simply discharged surplus energy and prepared the infant for later life. Theories were then proposed that fantasies are needed in order to handle anxiety (Sigmund Freud) or are the results of developing symbolic abilities (Piaget). Freud assumed that the early stages of life produce anxieties and deprivations which children deny, distort, or work through by means of play. He believed that children avoid objects with lots of anxiety, or play with them if the anxiety is tolerable. Thus, Freud assumed that children choose play materials which are related to mild fears and deprivations, and avoid toys associated with severe anxiety. He also believed there are four phases through which children's playing grows:

Freud felt play solves emotional problems for the child.

Phase 1. Freud thought that babies experience general anxiety because they are deficient and helpless. The toys used during this early period would be substitute or improved versions of the baby's own body.

Phase 2. During a second phase Freud believed that play is related to mother-child relations. The central theme of the child's play is: "I can do to you what mother did to me," or "I can leave you as she left me." Play becomes repetitive, serious, and sober.

Phase 3. During the third stage, beginning at around three years of age, Freud thought that play stems from attempts to solve the Oedipal/Electra conflict which occurs when children are attracted to the opposite-sexed parent. During this period, children become interested in tricks, jokes, riddles, and puns and play now includes another person. Freud felt that this social play would compensate the child for his painful disappointments about impossible family attachments.

Phase 4. In the post-Oedipal stage Freud felt a peer group would become important; strict rules would emerge and give the child a sense of independence from parents' authority. Children's games at this stage begin, follow a prescribed course, and end, suggesting to the child that problems have a solution.

For Freud, play was related to the child's emotions.

Piaget believes that play is a function of cognitive development.

In contrast, Piaget wrote that all development involves changes in cognitive structures. He believed that children choose toys which they can understand; they stay away from too simple or too complex playthings. Piaget sees play as a set of cognitive stages:

Stage 1—birth to 1 Month: Behavior during this stage is reflexive, so there is neither imitation nor play.

However, by *Stage 2—1 to 4 Months:* The infant has mastered simple circular reactions and his actions can become intentional. Once a baby has learned to throw his head back to look at familiar things from a new position, the infant will throw his head back and laugh without concern for what he can see; the action is simply play.

Stage 3—4 to 8 Months: Piaget believed that play remains essentially the same as in Stage 2, but it becomes easier to differentiate play and adaptation. One of Piaget's children found that she could make objects that were hanging from her crib swing. At three and one-half months she studied this phenomenon seriously, but by four months she performed the activity with great joy. Piaget pointed out that the eight-month-old infant pays more attention to his general environment than to peers or to specific play materials. Social interaction is ignored, as we have learned; and social contacts, when they occur, are limited to looking at, smiling, and grasping the other infant. Infant games are unsystematic and short. Fights are also equally short and impersonal. Usually they result when both babies try to grab the same toy at the same time.

Stage 4—8 to 12 Months: The distinction between play and adaptation becomes clearer. Piaget believes that when a child pursues a "means" for its own sake, he is obviously engaged in play. Early in Stage 4 the child will attack a barrier to reach an object beyond it. Later, the same child may ignore the goal and simply enjoy attacking the barrier itself. The Stage 4 child still prefers toys to playing with another child. However, if another child gets in the way, fighting will flare, and the conflicts are more personal than at earlier ages.

Stage 5—12 to 18 Months: Play becomes noted by its elaborate rituals. When a child's hand slips as he is tugging at the hair on his head and splashes into the bath water, he will repeat the entire sequence with great glee. He may vary the height of his hand, but he will always grasp his hair first, although this act has no effect whatever on the splash. If a child sets an orange peel to rocking on a table immediately after having looked at its convex side, he will look at its underside again before rocking it.

Stage 6—18 to 24 Months: The distinctive new characteristic here is symbolism. Earlier, the child could produce only simple motor games. Now he is capable of representing previous experiences in "make believe" games. One of Piaget's children accidentally fell backward while sitting on her cot. Seeing a pillow, she seized it and pressed it against her face

FIGURE 11.12 (*A*) Solitary play—the child is alone. (*B*) Parallel play—the children are beside each other but they do not interact. (*C*) Cooperative play—the children form a socially interacting group.

as though she were sleeping on it. Then after a moment she "sat up de-lightedly." This procedure was repeated many times during the day, even in places other than the cot and with no pillow available. Each time she would first smile, and then throw herself back and press her hands against her face as though the pillow were there. She was pretending to sleep.

There are many theories of play.

We have discussed the many theorists who think play is only instinct; those, like Piaget, who believe play is a means of learning about novel or complex objects and events; and Freud, who saw play as a way to handle emotions.

Gilmore tested Freud's and Piaget's theories.

Bernard Gilmore observed children about to undergo surgery and com-pared them with a matched group of schoolchildren. He found that both Freud's and Piaget's theories about play can be applied. Novelty *and* anxiety affect a child's preference for toys, but anxiety is not so powerful as novelty in determining the child's choice.

Parten studied chil-dren's play.

Mildred Parten studied group size and the nature of children's play by sampling interactions on a playground. She found that two-year-old children play in groups of two 30 percent of the time, but groups of five or more occur only 9 percent of the time (Parten, 1932). By contrast, she observed that four-and-a-half-year-olds spend 25 percent of their play time in groups of five or more. Parten also classified the play of children into six categories (*see* Figure 11.12):

1. Unoccupied.
2. Independent play.
3. Onlooker.
4. Parallel activity (playing alongside, but not with other children).
5. Associative activity (common activity with borrowing, lending, and taking turns).
6. Cooperative (working toward some common goal with different roles that supplement one another and taken by various members).

Older children co-operate.

Parten confirmed that very young children engage in either solitary or parallel play, while older children interact or cooperate to a much greater extent. Finally, she reported that the frequency of parallel play does not change with children's ages.

The Teacher

Teachers influence their pupils.

Schools are important socializing agents in U.S. society. They exert a strong influence on the developing child. Schools offer academic skills, varied cultural groups, an opportunity for achievement, and an ordered set of challenges toward maturity. With a few exceptions, the average U.S. school succeeds in carrying out most of these functions. One reason schools are so important in children's development is the teacher. When a child begins school, he shifts from parental control to peer and teacher influence. A child's first teacher sets the stage for all later teacher-pupil relations, and is often a mother substitute. For that reason, most children's first teacher is female. It is usual for nursery school, kindergarten, and early elementary-school teachers to be the same age, sex, and social class as the children's mothers. For this reason the transition from home to school is less painful for the average middle-class child. If all elementary teachers were men, there might well be more tension and anxiety during the early school years. Yet young boys might benefit from greater exposure to males in these early years. School-age boys are often just beginning to identify with their fathers, and starting to understand the relation between males and females, when they are confronted with a school situation where there are few males with whom to identify. Lower-class boys often react negatively to female power in the school, and as a result they are more often punished by the teacher. Since most elementary-school classes are supervised by females, many children come to believe that schoolwork is a feminine activity. Most children enter elementary school expecting to like it. Unhappily, by the time many of these children are in junior high school they dislike school. Why? Is the teacher, the school, the home environment, or the student responsible?

Types of Teachers

Children spend many hours in school.

The elementary teacher can have a strong effect on children because they spend many hours in the classroom she controls. She can make it pleasant or uncomfortable for the children. Her rules and the way she enforces them help determine a child's attitude toward himself, his schoolwork, and his future.

There are three main types of teachers.

A number of surveys (Travers, 1972) have separated elementary teachers into three main types: the impulsive teacher, the self-controlled teacher, and the fearful teacher. An *impulsive teacher's* feelings and thoughts about hostility and sexuality are close to consciousness all the time. This teacher is emotionally unpredictable, has little interest in orderliness, dislikes self-discipline, and is fairly uninhibited. In contrast, the *self-controlled teacher* is methodological, self-disciplined, well-organized, and becomes upset about making small changes in plans. This person is sensitive to the reactions of others, and authoritarian toward pupils. A *fearful teacher* is helpless, dependent, and offensive. She tries to enforce many rules, is irritated by children who do not obey, and is ineffective both in teaching and controlling her class. These three types of teachers have different effects on the academic growth of students as measured by the Stanford Achievement Tests and measures of social development. Children show greater gains on achievement tests in classes with self-controlled teachers and learn least under fearful teachers.

Elementary pupils may be divided into four main types: conformers,

Various teachers are differentially effective.

opposers, achievers, and the uncertain. As you might expect, different types of teachers have various effects on the four types of pupils. Self-controlled teachers are generally effective with all types of pupils. Children who oppose everything in the classroom make more academic progress under self-controlled teachers. Conforming children make more academic progress when their teachers are impulsive.

Teacher behavior influences student interest in elementary school.

Teachers are also differentially effective in teaching various subjects. Self-controlled teachers do their best in writing, reading, and spelling; while impulsive teachers are most effective in teaching arithmetic and science. Surprisingly, fearful instructors are best at teaching social studies.

In another study Ryans (1960) asked a group of trained observers to rate teachers on three dimensions:

1. Understanding versus objective.
2. Responsible versus planless.
3. Stimulating versus dull.

These same observers also rated pupils on seven dimensions of behavior:

1. Disinterested versus alert.
2. Obstructive versus constructive.
3. Restrained versus participating.
4. Rude versus self-controlled.
5. Apathetic versus initiating.
6. Dependent versus responsible.
7. Uncertain versus confident.

The observers' ratings of all seven student dimensions were very similar, so Ryans used a single score for the students' behavior and compared pupil interest with the three types of teacher behavior among elementary- and secondary-school classes. Ryans found that the teacher's behavior *is* related to student interest during elementary classes, but by the time students reach secondary school there is no relation between how a teacher behaves in the classroom and the students' reactions to her.

Responsible, stimulating teachers produce alert students.

In elementary-school classes, Ryans (1960) found that kind, responsible, stimulating teachers produce alert, constructive, participative students. However, by the time these students reach secondary schools the student-teacher relation is again more independent. The result may reflect either emotional maturity on the part of students or simply the fact that they spend less time in any single teacher's classroom than when they were younger. In any case, no matter what type of teacher happens to be in a classroom, girls receive significantly better grades than boys in elementary school, even though standard achievement scores between boys and girls are the same. In fact, boys perform slightly higher than girls on some standard achievement tests. Boys are also more often disciplined and disapproved of than girls (*see* Figure 11.13). Boys are more active, outgoing, and aggressive than girls, and most female teachers prefer quiet,

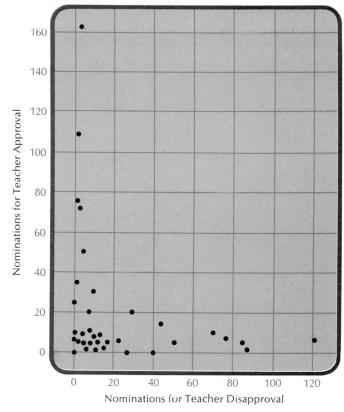

FIGURE 11.13
The distribution of teacher approval-disapproval in a sixth-grade classroom as indicated by pupils' responses to a "guess who?" inventory. The distribution is very similar to the one obtained by the recordings of an outside observer during thirty one-hour samples of teacher-pupil interactions. Note that one pupil received over 160 nominations for teacher approval, whereas another pupil received over 120 nominations for teacher disapproval. Is it any wonder that some children dislike school?
(From De Groat and Thompson, 1949.)

obedient pupils. As a result boys often acquire a negative attitude toward school.

While every teacher tries to maintain an atmosphere that is conducive to learning, the teacher's own needs often help determine what atmosphere they feel is most appropriate. What are teachers' attitudes toward children's behavior? A classic survey by Wickman (1928) found that there are large differences between the seriousness of children's behavior problems as rated by teachers and by psychologists (*see* Table 11.2). Psychologists feel that withdrawal and regressive behavior are serious problems; while teachers feel that sexual problems and rebellion against authority are the most serious problems they face in the classroom. There are several reasons for these differences between clinical psychologists' and teachers' judgments of children's behavior. First of all, a teacher's primary responsibility is to develop academic skills. The withdrawn child presents little interference to this goal, while antisocial behavior disrupts the class and makes effective teaching difficult. The clinical psychologist is more interested in emotional adjustment, so he sees withdrawal as a major problem. Table 11.2 shows that teacher attitudes are shifting toward

Teachers' needs affect their instruction techniques.

TABLE 11.2 Comparison of mean ratings* by teachers in 1955 and by teachers and mental hygienists in 1926 of the relative seriousness of fifty behavior problems

Behavior problems	Teachers (1955) N = 308	Teachers (1926) N = 511	Mental hygienists (1926) N = 30
1. Heterosexual activity	12.9	17.3	9.9
2. Stealing	14.9	17.0	12.5
3. Masturbation	10.7	16.7	6.4
4. Obscene notes, talk	11.5	16.6	8.8
5. Untruthfulness	13.3	15.8	10.3
6. Truancy	13.6	15.6	10.3
7. Impertinence, defiance	13.4	15.0	7.1
8. Cruelty, bullying	13.5	14.8	13.5
9. Cheating	11.9	14.7	10.3
10. Destroying school materials	13.7	14.3	5.1
11. Disobedience	13.0	14.1	6.4
12. Unreliableness	13.1	13.9	10.4
13. Temper tantrums	11.7	13.0	11.7
14. Lack of interest in work	12.1	12.8	9.6
15. Profanity	10.5	12.3	2.9
16. Impudence, rudeness	12.4	12.2	7.6
17. Laziness	11.6	12.2	7.2
18. Smoking	7.3	12.0	2.3
19. Enuresis	9.2	11.8	9.2
20. Nervousness	11.1	11.7	3.4
21. Disorderliness in class	11.5	11.7	3.4
22. Unhappy, depressed	13.4	11.5	16.2
23. Easily discouraged	11.9	11.5	13.4
24. Selfishness	11.6	11.3	11.8
25. Carelessness in work	11.8	11.3	7.1
26. Inattention	11.1	11.2	7.3
27. Quarrelsomeness	12.0	11.1	8.3
28. Suggestible	11.4	11.0	13.3
29. Resentfulness	12.5	10.8	14.1
30. Tardiness	9.7	10.5	5.6
31. Physical cowardice	9.8	10.4	12.0
32. Stubbornness	10.1	10.3	10.9
33. Domineering	11.2	10.3	13.0
34. Slovenly in appearance	9.7	10.1	7.2
35. Sullenness	10.2	9.9	12.6
36. Fearfulness	10.4	9.7	14.0
37. Suspiciousness	9.5	9.1	16.4
38. Thoughtlessness	9.7	8.7	6.8
39. Attracting attention	10.2	8.5	8.5
40. Unsocial, withdrawing	11.6	8.3	17.3
41. Dreaminess	8.8	8.3	11.3
42. Imaginative lying	8.0	8.1	7.5
43. Interrupting	9.0	8.0	2.8
44. Inquisitiveness	8.8	8.0	5.3
45. Overcritical of others	9.8	7.9	13.2
46. Tattling	8.1	7.5	8.8
47. Whispering	6.3	7.5	0.8
48. Sensitiveness	9.6	7.0	13.1
49. Restlessness	8.6	6.9	6.4
50. Shyness	9.5	5.4	12.5
Average	10.9	11.3	9.5

Rating chart: slight consequence, 5.0; considerable difficulty, 12.0; extremely grave problem, 20.0.

those of the clinical psychologist, which reflects an increased awareness and concern with emotional and personal development by educators. Teachers are now considered responsible for both the academic training and the social adjustment of their pupils.

Most teachers come from the middle class.

Teacher Background

One of the difficulties that teachers and some students face in the classroom is that they have different social-class backgrounds. Most teachers come from a middle-class family, while many pupils come from lower-class families (*see* Table 11.3). There are social-class differences in taste, income, intellect, and expectations. Children from higher social classes are more likely to attend college, earn higher incomes, and be professionals. Social class is based primarily on an index of status. The most important social trait is the father's occupation. In the table a rating of 1 is given to professional people; while a rating of 7 is given to domestic servants, migrant workers, and unskilled laborers. The family's source of income is also considered. A rating of 1 is given if half the income is derived from inherited investments, while a rating of 7 is assigned to income from public-welfare grants. Housing is also rated, with a family receiving a 1 if they live in a house with nine or more rooms in good condition, and being given a 7 if they live in an apartment in bad condition. A fourth social characteristic is the area in which the family lives and the educational level of the father. A 1 is given for a residential area in the best part of town, and a 7 is assigned to the slums. In the area of education, a 1 is assigned for one or more years of graduate work in a college or university, and a 7 is given to older fathers who left school below the third grade or for younger fathers who stopped before the eighth grade. Surveys of teachers show that they often come from middle-class families.

What happens to lower-class children in middle-class schools? They

TABLE 11.3 Socioeconomic status of fathers of 409 student teachers at San Diego State College

	Socioeconomic status	Percent
Upper	1	1
	2	11
	3	22
Middle	4	30
	5	26
Lower	6	6
	7	4

(Adapted from Groff, 1962.)

usually either disrupt the class or become passive, withdrawn, and disinterested in learning. What can the school system do to foster better academic achievement among lower-class children? One possible course is to hold preschool programs for the disadvantaged which will teach children those skills needed in later classes. In the past several years psychologists have devised various curricula for lower-class children during the preschool years. Unfortunately, after having tried several of these programs for from three to five years, the academic gains seem to be marginal. However, these programs do improve the lower-class child's attitude toward school.

Rosenthal originated Pygmalion in the Classroom.

In 1968 Robert Rosenthal published his controversial book *Pygmalion in the Classroom.* He described an experiment designed to test the notion that teacher's expectations about students cause the teacher to maintain an attitude that makes those expectations come true. The subjects in Rosenthal's experiment were three sets of teachers in each of six grades in a lower-class urban elementary school. Intelligence tests were given to all pupils in the classes at the beginning of the school year, and randomly selected pupils in each class were labeled "late bloomers" by the experimenters. The teachers were told that these students would make large achievement gains over the year, and the experimenters measured all the pupils' IQs again at the end of the school year. The result was a significant gain in IQ for girls in the first and second grades, but no gains in any of the other four grades.

Repetition of the Pygmalion study has failed.

This study captured the imagination of the popular press, but within professional education journals severe criticism of the study began to appear (Snow, 1969; Taylor, 1970; Thorndike, 1968). Attempted repetitions of the *Pygmalion* study have failed to find any significant effect of teacher's expectation on the IQ of children in classrooms (Claiborn, 1969). Jere Brophy and Thomas Good (1974) summarize this research by writing that; "The controversial findings of *Pygmalion in the Classroom* have yet to be replicated unambiguously, in that no other investigators have succeeded in showing significant expectancy effects on achievement tests or IQ tests." The notion that teacher expectation has a significant influence on pupils' achievement is controversial and not well supported. Apparently, other factors are contributing to the difficulties that lower-class children experience in schools.

Teaching Methods

Structured schools teach by traditional methods.

No matter what the attitude and background of a teacher, her classroom can either be structured or not. A *structured school* generally teaches reading by traditional methods that stress phonics, while an *unstructured school* might use the whole-word or look-and-say approach. Structured classrooms are more authoritarian and present a traditional academic curriculum, while unstructured classrooms are more permissive and are concerned with the emotional development of children. Grimes and Allinsmith (1961) studied the effect of structured versus unstructured school curricula on the academic achievement of children who differed in their degree of anxiety and responsibility toward school. The researchers found that structured schools produce significantly higher achievement among children compared with unstructured schools, and the difference was larger for anxious or very responsible children. The result was clear: A traditional teaching approach produces better academic achievement for all types of children.

Children's work-books are receiving increased attention.

Recently, a great deal of importance has been attached to the structure and content of children's workbooks and other materials used for reading instruction. A number of educators have proposed that the child's reaction to and interest in reading is influenced by the kinds of materials used to teach him reading. They believe that children will be more interested in reading material which is related to their everyday life experiences. Children's readers have been criticized because they are said to be biased toward white, Anglo-Saxon, Protestant, upper-middle class worlds that are friendly and without frustrations. Also, the readers are dominated by suburban themes, despite the fact that over 65 percent of the people in the U.S. live in urban areas. Recently, textbook publishers have focused more attention on working-class, mixed neighborhoods and on minority groups. A number of critics argue that the textbook writers have simply taken a minority family and established them in a nice, happy, stable suburban neighborhood.

Boys experience more difficulties with school.

Probably the most disturbing fact about early reading is that boys are three times more likely than girls to have difficulty learning to read. Some children never learn to read, even after years of intensive remedial instruction in the language arts.

The School

The main function of a school is teaching.

Every society must transfer its values, traditions, and social organization to succeeding generations. In the U.S. the school system is being given more and more responsibility for passing on knowledge and values to future generations of citizens. Another function of the school is to produce intellectual competence, so many educators have studied the school's influence on children's achievement. Relatively less information is available about the effect of school on children's personal, physical, and social development.

U.S. education contains four stages.

Education in the United States is traditionally separated into four stages: nursery school, elementary school, secondary school, and college or university. This sequence assumes that knowledge can be assimilated by the student in more breadth and depth as he matures. In the nursery school a child's primary responsibility is to get along in a group, to pay attention, to follow instructions, and to interact with his peers. During the elementary-school years primary emphasis is placed on reading, mathematics, and social studies. Near the end of elementary school students are separated into two main groups: Those who cannot profit from a college education are guided into vocational training; while students who show academic talent and interest are placed in a college preparatory program, stressing English, physics, chemistry, mathematics, biology, and history. The college or university is used as preparation for more advanced training in professional or graduate schools, or to qualify for a good job.

The Purpose of School

Two views of education exist.

Two different views of education exist. A traditional theory assumes that the purpose of school is to teach reading, computing, and other academic subjects. Traditional theorists believe in reward for improvement and punishment for failure. The progressive education theory assumes that if children are given an opportunity to learn, they will become educated. Traditional programs of education yield higher achievement scores, while progressive schools produce children who are happier and better adapted.

School children are different.

Not only is there variation in school atmosphere but there are enormous differences among children in maturity, intelligence, and ability to handle interpersonal relations. The average elementary teacher has about thirty children in the classroom. About half are boys and half girls. On the average girls are physically more mature than boys, as we learned earlier, and among these thirty children there may be one or two with IQs around 80 and one with an IQ score of over 140. The teacher may have one pupil from a poor farm family and another who is the offspring of a physician. Some children will come from families who may not enjoy reading books at all, while other children may see a morning and evening paper and three or four weekly magazines. Many of the children may have seen only a few miles outside of the town in which they live, while a few may have traveled around the world. The average class contains large intellectual, cultural, and racial variation. Large individual variation is the rule among schools where the neighborhood provides a mix of family backgrounds. Compared with elementary pupils, populations are more homogeneous in high schools, because disadvantaged students tend to drop out at this level. The student population in college is even more similar.

Teachers must consider the needs of different children.

In elementary school the slow learner is often frustrated by not being able to understand his lessons. Very bright children, who can learn two or three times as fast as anyone else, are often bored by elementary school. To produce a reasonable curriculum for such large individual variation, a teacher must consider all the needs. She must present work materials with a sufficient range so that the dull child is not overwhelmed nor the bright child bored.

As an alternative, the class may be grouped according to ability. How is this process handled in other countries? Consider early childhood education in the U.S.S.R.

The U.S.S.R. trains children communally.

Urie Bronfenbrenner (1970) reported that communal facilities for child-rearing and early education have been common for a long time in the U.S.S.R. He found that over 10 percent of all children under two years of age are enrolled in preschool programs, and there are long waiting lists of parents who want to enroll their offspring in the programs. Bronfenbrenner argues that the Soviet experiments in early childhood communal upbringing represent a wave of the future, as industrialization increases and more women enter the labor market. He points out that Project Head Start has enrolled over 2 million children in preschool programs in the U.S., and that number is expected to climb rapidly over the next several years. Bronfenbrenner explains that in the Soviet Union the early education of the child is much more than just babysitting. Soviet educators try to develop moral behavior and character in their young charges. They emphasize the virtues of respect for elders, self-discipline, modesty, and manners.

Soviet education is collective.

Soviet education is based on collective living and learning—even the infant finds himself in a communal playpen. Adult discipline is not needed in the classroom because order is kept by peer pressure. The Soviet educational system emphasizes professional care and leadership, and believes that parents and family are subordinate to other types of social institutions.

More mothers are working.

No one is quite sure whether the Soviet experiment in collective development could or should be adopted for children in the U.S., but the trend seems clear that as women enter the work force and more females demand an independent life, some sort of day-care centers will be needed and the duty of the school expanded to handle moral education and character training. It must also continue to perform its traditional purpose of educating and evaluating pupils, which is a complex and sometimes controversial task.

Evaluating Pupil Performance

There are three ways to evaluate children.

There are at least three ways to evaluate a child's understanding of school subjects. The standard procedure is to award students who master most of the material high grades and to assign students who fail to master the material low marks. Another way to evaluate children is in relation to their own potential, or how they are achieving compared to national standards. The first way concerns low or high achievement, while the question about national standards is more relevant to college admission or school-system evaluation. To determine whether a child is under-achieving, an educator should compare his IQ with his progress in school. The teacher should be satisfied with minimum achievement from a child who scores 80 on an IQ test, but would expect more from average or bright students.

Bright children gen-
erally earn high
grades.

Typically, bright children earn A's, the highest scores in a given class, and children at the bottom are failed. However, suppose the local class is very superior. Then, a moderately bright child in a superior class may come to believe that he is not qualified for college because his grades are not superior. A modestly bright child in an isolated rural community may feel he is a very superior student because the local comparison group is low. The variation in local schools is so large that within the same state school system the top-ranking student in some high-school graduation classes actually scores lower on standardized tests of achievement than the lowest-ranking student in other high schools. Two problems occur as a result of this local variation in norms: The top-ranking student from a poor high school may go to college and be unprepared to compete with students who are much better trained; and a student who ranks near the bottom of a rigorous high school may not even go to college, although he might find that he could do very well there by comparison with his very difficult high school.

Evaluation should be
appropriate for the
pupil's goals.

The main thing to remember is that the evaluation of a pupil should be appropriate for the purpose of the evaluation. Under- or overachievement is primarily related to motivation and it should be determined if this is influencing the scores. The student's relative ranking on standardized tests in a local school system will determine the types of classes he should attend. His rank is also relevant when he is being counseled about whether he should go on to college or stop his education at the high-school level.

School Achievement and Failure

IQ mostly determines
academic success.

Many studies have explored the reasons for success or failure in the classroom. As you might expect, the most important cause of success or failure is variation in IQ and we will discuss this a little later. However, other factors contribute to academic success or failure. During the first years of school a child may be hampered by immaturity or dependence on others. Emotional and motivational factors can also affect school achievement.

Motivation can affect
achievement.

The relation between emotions and academic achievement is complex. No one is sure whether low achievement creates emotional stress or whether emotional problems cause poor achievement. Children with a poor self-concept often do not achieve according to their abilities. Yet overachieving children are under strong pressure from their parents to succeed. By the time an *overachiever* reaches the fifth or sixth grade he often shows signs of hostility and resentment toward his parents for this reason. By contrast, underachievers are either rejecting the demands of parents, or their parents are making no demands. One thing is clear about achievement in school: Failure breeds demoralization and *fear of further failure.* Children with a history of failure set unrealistically high or low goals for themselves; children with a history of success set more realistic goals. This probably happens because the successful child is better able to understand the consequences of his actions, while the unsuccessful child fears failure so much that he will perform any irrational act to finish the task quickly and relieve his anxiety. Children who are encouraged to be independent tend to do well in school. This is another factor in school success.

Several factors determine school success.

Intelligence is also important for school success, as we know. Numerous studies show a strong positive relation between intelligence test scores and measures of academic achievement. IQ scores are not the whole answer, because a student also must be motivated. A lack of either intellect or motivation can produce low achievement. Children can be motivated by external reinforcement or internal reward derived from understanding. Studies of reward and punishment suggest that positive rewards are better than punishment, which is negative, because rewards motivate the child to repeat a learning behavior, whereas punishment merely shows the child what to avoid. Although school attendance has grown (*see* Table 11.4) lower-class children are dropping out. Ninety percent of the children in the lowest social class drop out of high school, while very few children in the top socioeconomic classes do so. The main causes of lower-class dropping out are:

1. Lower intellectual ability.
2. Poor achievement motivation.
3. Poor health care.
4. Insecure personal development.
5. Negative teacher reactions.

TABLE 11.4 Percent of school-age population enrolled in school, 1954 to 1964*

	Age groups							
Year	*5*	*6*	*7–9*	*10–13*	*14–15*	*16–17*	*18–19*	*20–24*
1954	57.7%	96.8%	99.2%	99.5%	95.8%	78.0%	32.4%	11.2%
1955	58.1	98.2	99.2	99.2	95.9	77.4	31.5	11.1
1956	58.9	97.0	99.4	99.2	96.9	78.4	35.4	12.8
1957	60.2	97.4	99.5	99.5	97.1	80.5	34.9	14.0
1958	63.8	97.3	99.5	99.5	96.9	80.6	37.6	13.4
1959	62.9	97.5	99.4	99.4	97.5	82.9	36.8	12.7
1960	63.7	98.0	99.6	99.5	97.8	82.6	38.4	13.1
1961	66.3	97.4	99.4	99.3	97.6	83.6	38.0	13.7
1962	66.8	97.9	99.2	99.3	98.0	84.3	41.8	15.6
1963	67.8	97.4	99.4	99.3	98.4	87.1	40.9	17.3
1964	68.5	98.2	99.0	99.0	98.6	87.7	41.6	16.8

* From *NEA Research Bulletin.*

Educational Problems

Schools have several problems.

The people of the U.S. demand many things of their schools. Often, when these expectations clash with educational realities, the schools are blamed in such areas as a high dropout rate, cheating, competition between television and school, and violence in the classroom or on the school grounds.

Dropouts

One serious problem is dropping out.

Many authorities feel that one of the most serious problems confronting U.S. secondary schools is the large number of students who quit school. Almost one-third of all adolescents fail to graduate from high school. Often, soon after students drop out, they have difficulty with the law, with their employers, and with their parents. Lower-class children drop out because they receive little encouragement to stay in a school system they cannot understand. The traditional way to handle school dropouts was to establish two curricula: A college preparatory course, for the student who plans to go on to higher education, and a vocational course, for the student who will go to work right after high school. A more recent solution is the mixed work-study program, where students go to school mornings and work afternoons, or work during the day and attend classes in the evenings. The Youth Studies Center at the University of Southern California designed an experiment to test whether the following program might be effective in stopping dropouts:

1. A curriculum consisting primarily of English, mathematics, and social studies, with special emphasis on practical applications.
2. Small classes of fifteen students each, where the same teacher taught all of the classes.
3. A counselor was made available to talk to each of the students.
4. Jobs that would earn school credit and money.

The experiment ran for three years. Seventy-five potential dropouts attended the special classes and an equal number of potential dropouts were exposed to a regular school program. Unhappily, the special programs had no significant effect on the dropout rate: 57 percent of the experimental subjects in the special classes dropped out as compared with 60 percent from the regular classes.

Competition and Cheating

Another problem is cheating.

Almost all public schools give their students grades, and these are a source of information about the student. They let the pupil know how well he's doing in comparison with others in his class; grades also inform parents about their child's progress. They are one indicator of whether the student should think about attending college or enter a technical training school. Grades also can be a source of motivation. Students may work to earn good grades or to avoid failure. However, competitive grading means that only a few students can receive A's, and that they must earn comparable grades year after year. A continual negative evaluation of poor students can make them drop out.

Academic pressure causes cheating.

Competition and cheating on examinations are both serious school problems. Academic pressure is one cause of the problem. If children are equal in intelligence and achievement but, because of differing school policies, some are promoted to the next grade while others are retained for a second year in the same grade, a natural experiment in which the promoted children are under greater pressure to achieve is underway. Studies report that the self-concept and personal maturity of the promoted children are positive as compared with children who are not promoted. However, children who are promoted cheat more than children who are retained for another year in the same grade. Apparently, children who are moved ahead experience difficulties staying up with their classmates, and so resort to cheating as a way to meet the academic pressure.

Moral knowledge has no effect on cheating.

Do children cheat because they don't know what is expected, or do they know the rules but ignore them? Hartshorne and May (1928) found a low correlation between awareness of rules and children's practice of these rules. The researchers studied cheating and rediscovered a fact which is well-known to many children but forgotten by many adults: Noncheaters are simply more cautious, not more honest. Most children felt it was wrong to be caught, not wrong to cheat. Hartshorne and May also reported that cheating in some classrooms was very high, while cheating in others was very low, even among the same children. Apparently, subjects had no internal morality against cheating, but their chances of getting caught varied from one classroom to the next. The experimenters concluded that the moral education which does occur in school is almost totally ineffective and has no impact on the conduct of pupils.

Piaget thinks cheating is natural for children.

Piaget feels that cheating is a defensive reaction demanded by modern educational practices. He argues that schools isolate a child against his natural preference for cooperation with his peers, and makes him compete against them.

A child's sense of fairness affects cheating.

Another factor which affects cheating is the child's sense of "fairness." Mischel and Liebert (1966) studied this on seven-to-eleven-year-old children's willingness to cheat. An adult alternated with a child in a game of bowling in this study. The experimenters used differences between the performance standards necessary for the adult to reward himself and the standards used to reward the child. Mischel and Liebert presented four conditions:

1. Both the adult and child faced a stringent reward standard.

2. The adult rewarded himself for low achievement, but rewarded the child only for high achievement.
3. Both were rewarded for low achievement.
4. The adult rewarded himself only for high achievement and rewarded the child for low performance.

Following several sessions under one of these four conditions, children were asked to teach the game and the reward system to another, younger child. Their results showed that:

1. If both players were on a stringent standard, then the child adhered to this standard and transmitted it to the younger child.
2. If both had a low-reward criterion, then the child did not keep to that standard well nor did he transmit it to the younger child.
3. If there was a discrepancy, the child did not adhere to the original standard imposed on him, but he did learn to use differing criteria for others.

Thus, children will be unfair if they are shown examples of unfairness.

Television versus the Classroom

Television takes pupils' time.

Television, comic books, radio, and movies absorb a substantial amount of children's attention. The mass media can be so attractive to some children that dinner or homework may suffer. Ask any mother who tries to pull her child from his favorite television program.

Does TV affect school-work?

What are the effects on a child of exposure to mass media? Is he primarily entertained, or does he absorb ideas which affect his later acts or emotions? Critics in the past have suggested that even fairy tales are too violent, while defenders of children's stories say that some excitement is necessary to arouse interest, to entertain, and to allow the child an opportunity to deal with new thoughts and social patterns.

Does TV violence produce aggression in children?

Systematic research into the effect of movies on children's attitudes and actions was started when the Payne Fund explored children's social attitudes, delinquency, and emotional responsiveness. Current concern with the mass media stems from adult fears that delinquency is related to violence on television or in comic books. It is true that young delinquents are addicted to violent programs. Do the mass media *cause* violence or are they simply a by-product of delinquency? Do children learn to be violent by watching violence on television? Are there hostile feelings which last after the program is over? Do emotional reactions weaken or do they last for some time? Does it make a difference who is violent? Some theories proposed that substitute aggressive experience as in the media may reduce the need to be aggressive (Feshbach, 1971). It may be true that children experience a release of tension when they are aggressive, but is that same release available when they experience aggression at second hand?

Imagined aggression can decrease violence.

Work with children shows that imagined aggression may increase or decrease violence. In one study Albert Bandura and his colleagues (1963) showed children aggressive film scenes and then frustrated the subjects. These children imitated the filmed aggression. However, when older children and adults were frustrated, and then allowed to write stories about their aggressive feelings, they produced less hostility. Why are these two results different? Possibly because the young children were frustrated after they had seen the violent movies. If they had been frustrated before seeing the movies, their aggressive impulses might have been diminished by experiencing second-hand aggression.

TV-viewing has no effect on school achievement.

The average child spends eighteen hours a week watching television, almost as much time as he spends in the classroom. Children who watch television go to bed later, listen to the radio less, read fewer comic books, and see fewer movies than children who do not watch television. Does television-watching help or hinder schoolwork? Schramm and his colleagues (1961) showed that children who grow up with television are a year advanced in the use of words as compared with children of similar IQ who do not see television. However, this difference disappears by the sixth grade. Later, there is a negative relation between IQ and the amount of time spent viewing television. However, Himmelweit found that when IQ is matched among children who watch television there is no relation between amount of television viewing and school performance. Television-watching it seems does not affect school performance, but does it influence social relations?

Rejected children watch TV a lot.

Research proves that children who are rejected or punished by their parents and children from broken homes watch a great deal of television. Many of these unhappy children are trying to escape a difficult situation by withdrawing into a world of fantasy. Shy, withdrawn children who have few friends spend a great deal of time in front of the television as well. The conclusion seems to be that television-watching is a result of social maladjustment rather than a cause of it, and that watching television does not interfere with school performance and has only a minor influence on the development of violence in children. But what are the causes of hostility and violence? There are many.

Violence

Children are aggressive.

Children not only affiliate, they also fight. One apparent cause of violence is frustration. If something or someone blocks the path to a goal, most children become angry—especially if the blocking seems to be deliberate. Frustration may not cause anger or hate if the frustrated child believes the act which blocked his goal was random or beyond anyone's control. It therefore does not always produce aggression, but may call forth various reactions such as withdrawal or regression. Whether a child responds to frustration by fear or anger is a complex result of his heredity, sex, the amount of encouragement he has received for aggression, the amount of guilt associated with aggression, whether he has seen successful aggression by others, and the child's age. John Poppy argues that *exploration* and *aggression* are healthy and necessary characteristics of man, but *violence* is not. Summarizing a report from the Stanford School of Medicine, he concludes that there are several constructive steps society should take to end violence on the playground, in the schools, and on the streets of our communities, among them to stop encouraging or admiring violence, to have fewer children, to control gun sales, to remove much of the violence shown on the mass media, and to keep learning about change so that we can be comfortable with it.

Summary

During the child's early years the dominant influence on his development is his parents. However, after the child enters school, his teachers and peers come to exert more and more control over his behavior. The child's peers influence him by social pressures toward conformity and positive social interactions through cliques and friendships. Children's groups are highly structured into crowds, cliques, and friends. The teacher's social-class background and personal traits jointly determine how he or she will react to and interact with the pupils. The abilities and personal traits of these pupils influence whether they stay in school and profit from the educational setting or drop out and reject education as a springboard to success.

SUGGESTED ADDITIONAL READINGS

Bandura, A., and A.C. Huston. "Identification as a Process of Incidental Learning," *Journal of Abnormal and Social Psychology*, Vol. 63 (1961), pp. 311-318.

Garvey, W.P., and J.R. Hegrenes. "Desensitization Techniques in the Treatment of School Phobia," *American Journal of Orthopsychiatry*, Vol. 36 (1962), pp. 147–152.

Glasser, W. *Schools Without Failure*. New York: Harper & Row, 1969.

Hewett, F.M. *The Emotionally Disturbed Child in the Classroom*. Boston: Allyn and Bacon, 1968.

12 Personality

Factors in Personal Development
  The Biological Bases of Personality
    Genetics and Personality
    Physiological Development
  Environmental Influences
    Social Influences on Personality
    The Self-concept
    Imitation and Social Feedback
    Social Symbols
    The Healthy Person
      Acceptance of Reality
      Autonomy
The Measurement of Personality
  Projective Tests
    The Rorschach
    The CAT
  Objective Tests
    The MMPI
A Theory of Personal Development—
Sigmund Freud
  Oral Egocentrism

  Anal Period
  Oedipus and Identification
  Latency
  Genital Puberty
  Mechanisms of Ego Defense
    Repression
    Projection
    Sublimation
    Rationalization
    Reaction Formation
    Regression
    Displacement
Challenges to Personal Growth
  Childhood Dependency
  Autonomy versus Discipline
  Aggression and Hostility
  Sex-role Development
  Moral Development
    Moral Knowledge
    Guilt
    Shame
Summary

PREVIEW

Having a "good" personality has become so important to all of us that by the time a child leaves elementary school, he is worrying more about social acceptance and peer popularity than about schoolwork. A little later in life sexual attraction and mating are based largely on a "pleasing" personality. The adult learns that getting along with his fellow workers and making a good impression on the boss are often more important than the quality of his work, when promotion time rolls around. In fact, success in business depends more on personality and motivation than on intellect, college graduates who majored in "athletics and social activities" tend to be more likely to head large corporations than those who earned top grades in school. The strong emphasis on having a "good" personality has caused many older children to worry about self-development. In fact, a majority of adolescents say they are more concerned with self-development than with any other single thing.

The derivation of a word can often reveal something about its hidden meanings. Our word "personality" is derived from the Latin word *persona*, which means "mask." The popular uses of personality include two separate meanings: the skill with which a person handles social situations and the impressions he makes on others. The scientific study of personal development stresses the organization of human behavior, the changing nature of personal growth, the physiological and genetic bases of actions, and the motivational and emotional determinants of personality.

There are many theories of personality.

Psychological history abounds with theories of personality development. One of the earliest was proposed by Hippocrates, a Greek physician who lived around 400 B.C. He believed that a person's body-fluid balance determined his behavior. Twenty-five centuries later William Sheldon (1954) suggested that people's personality depends on their *body type*. Between fluid balance and body types hundreds of theories about personality were proposed. Hippocrates speculated that too much black bile generated melancholy, depression, and pessimism. He noted that an excess of yellow bile produced quick temper and aggression. He also believed that abundant blood brings optimism and cheer; while excess phlegm produces passive, withdrawn people (*see* Figure 12.1). Although his specific theory of body fluids is incorrect, the traits Hippocrates selected to describe human behavior are rediscovered time and again.

FIGURE 12.1 Hippocrates' four personality types. He believed the balance of body fluids determined personality. His theory developed the first physiological explanation of character.

Psychoanalyst Carl Jung described people as *introverted* or *extroverted*; while the originator of Freudian psychology believed people may be trapped in states of dependency, depression, or hostility. The American psychologist Henry Murray proposed a long list of human motives which he believed determine personal behavior (*see* Table 12.1). His major motives include aggression, self-abasement, and achievement, which all appeared on Hippocrates' original list.

Sheldon based his theory on body type.

Harvard scientist William Sheldon associated various personality characteristics with three main body types: the *endomorph*, who is overweight; the *mesomorph*, who is muscular; and the *ectomorph*, who is thin (*see* Figure 12.2). Sheldon believed that endomorphic people would enjoy body comforts, are jovial, and are relaxed; that mesomorphs would be active, competitive, energetic, and aggressive; while ectomorphs are thoughtful and sensitive. Most people believe endomorphs like to eat, mesomorphs to compete, and ectomorphs to think.

TABLE 12.1   Major motives of man.

Motive	Definition
Abasement	To seek or accept blame or criticism
Achievement	To strive; to accomplish
Affiliation	To enjoy friends
Aggression	To overcome frustration forcefully
Autonomy	To be independent
Deference	To yield to others
Dominance	To control others
Nurturance	To assist others in trouble
Play	To laugh and be gay

(From Murray, 1938.)

Factors in Personal Development

Biology and social experience both determine personality.

Today's psychologists believe that personal development is based on two primary factors: a biological foundation and a social history. Biology is important in personal development because the child's genes help determine whether it will be male or female; introverted or extroverted; bright or dull; and normal, neurotic, or psychotic (Eysenck, 1967). But biology is not the whole story. The individual child's unique social history may modify these inherited biological tendencies.

Consider first what is known about the physiological foundation of personal development and then how the foundation may be modified by experience.

FIGURE 12.2 Three body types described by Sheldon. Endomorphs are overweight; mesomorphs are muscular; and ectomorphs are thin, nervous types.

The Biological Bases of Personality

A child's personality is the joint result of genetic predispositions, physical growth, and interaction with a social environment. The most basic factor is the child's heredity. Genes determine such developmental traits as sex, emotionality, and aggressiveness.

GENETICS AND PERSONALITY The child does not inherit a personality directly. His genes contain certain physical and neurological predispositions which make him more or less able to cope with stresses and demands. Long before Gregor Mendel proposed his gene theory of heredity there were scientists who argued that retardation, psychoses, and some personality disorders are passed on from generation to generation. Even today, much of our knowledge about the genetics of personality concerns abnormal development.

Studies by F.J. Kallman (1946) and others on familial trends in schizophrenia and depressive mental illnesses strongly suggest that genes primarily determine who will develop these disabling mental disorders. H.J. Eysenck (1967) and others claim that neuroticism and alcoholism are genetically determined to some extent. Even very primitive personal traits, such as smiling and fear of strangers, show much higher agreement and similarity among identical twins as compared with fraternal twins or siblings. Irving Gottesman (1972) has investigated the inheritance of social responsiveness among males and females. His results state that genes control about 80 percent of the individual variation in sociability among males, but only about 60 percent of the social variation of females. He suggests that females are subjected to stronger social pressures than males, and that these environmental influences suppress some genetic variation in social responsiveness among them. Raymond Cattell (1961) has analyzed responses from thousands of college students and believes that traits like tenderness, self-control, and general neuroticism are primarily environmentally determined; that conformity and dominance are influenced about equally by genetics and environment; but that schizophrenia, manic-depressive psychoses, and general intelligence are determined primarily by hereditary factors.

Not only are some types of behavior programed into the child's central nervous system but other behavior patterns are triggered by variations in the hormone level.

PHYSIOLOGICAL DEVELOPMENT There is a close link between physiological functions and personality. If the thyroid gland secretes too little thyroxine, the active hormone of the gland, the child will exhibit a low metabolic rate, sluggish behavior, and little endurance. Too much thyroid will produce restless, nervous, frantic behavior. Hormonal secretions from the gonads, the reproductive organs of both sexes, trigger sexual growth and to some extent sexual behavior, although human sexuality is influenced by environmental factors as well. Secondary sexual characteristics—facial hair, female breasts, for example—and body build can also exert some influence on personality development.

Environmental Influences

Environmental factors may impede personal development.

There are other biological factors which may affect a child's personality. General nutritional deficiency, illness, injury, or a physical handicap may impede the child's personal development. Prolonged physical illness makes a child withdraw from his environment, causes him to be concerned about his body, and thus makes him self-centered and less sociable. Physical handicaps or illness can cause peers to reject the child, which will affect his personality to a large extent.

Social factors also influence personality.

SOCIAL INFLUENCES ON PERSONALITY Personality is determined by many things. Every child develops some consistent traits which characterize how he handles emotions, frustrations, and challenges. Early personal development is influenced by how the child handles social relations. It is the joint result of innate tendencies and interaction with significant others in the child's life. These two factors produce a child's self-concept.

The child's self-concept changes when he enters school.

THE SELF-CONCEPT One important characteristic of a child's self-concept is his age. A young child's activities are less competitive, compared with those of his later school years, and so he faces fewer threats. Most young children are also treated kindly by parents and other adults. A crucial period in the development of a child's self-concept occurs when he enters school. This marks a shift from parental care to a world of competition where the child must try to succeed and interact with his peers. Another serious challenge to his maturity occurs at adolescence, when the young adult must establish a sexual role, consistent moral values, and make career choices. Let us consider first the young child's concept of self and the effect of social feedback on his personal adjustment, and then the various symbols which the child and adolescent use to project or hide their personalities.

Young children are egocentric.

Almost everyone agrees that young children are concerned with themselves and have little awareness of others. Most people also agree that a sure sign of personal maturity is the ability to differentiate between the self and others. Young children have great difficulty taking the position of another. If a child is shown a picture of three different sized mountains, as we have learned, and is then asked to imagine what the mountains would look like from a different position, he will maintain that any other view will look just like the view he now has. The transition from this egocentrism to an awareness of others' needs and views usually happens at around eight years of age, and no one is sure exactly why.

One requirement for an awareness of self is a memory of your own actions. When do children first recall their existence? Many psychologists

First memories begin at 3.

have asked that question, and most studies find that the first memory of childhood begins at around thirty months of age. Few adults can recall personal events from an age earlier than two-and-one-half years. Does that mean the self-concept begins at that time? Again, no one knows, but it is clear that the capacity to remember past events and to generalize from them is a prerequisite for the development of a child's self-concept.

Social feedback influences the self-concept.

IMITATION AND SOCIAL FEEDBACK   Self-evaluation and social feedback also affect the development of a person's self-concept. Social feedback in the form of praise or blame probably develops first and self-evaluation comes later. The young child's behavior is approved or disapproved by significant others, and he takes his cues from them. Somewhat later, the child incorporates moral standards into his self-concept and that is when he begins to feel guilt. The development of guilt shows that the child can assume more independent control of his actions. However, too much guilt can cripple the child. A positive evaluation of self is necessary for happiness, so if a child is constantly reminded that his performance is inadequate or that his parents do not care about him, this negative feedback will be disastrous to his personal development.

Boys think disobeying is bad.

What sort of values do children express about their own behavior? Table 12.2 shows what children think are bad and good things for them to do. Note that bad behavior includes disobeying, acts of violence, and saying bad words. Little boys feel that helping mother is the most important good behavior and that doing nice things is important. Little girls think that playing is most important.

TABLE 12.2   Children's standards of bad and good behavior

	Percentage of responses	
	Girls	Boys
Bad behavior		
Doesn't do what mother asks	28	7
Doesn't do what other people tell him	0	14
Commits overt acts of violence (spits, scratches, snatches, hits, breaks windows, throws mud, and so on)	47	55
Cries, says bad words, is cross, isn't nice	12.5	17
Good behavior		
Helps mother (specific items such as dusts, washes, cleans, and performs other household tasks)	20	40
Takes care of own routine (dresses self, goes to toilet, picks up toys, cleans up, and so on)	13	6
Plays (gently with dolls, colors, and so on)	28	6
Does nice, kind things (good things, does things for people and so on)	13	30
Obeys mother (does what mother says, and so on)	8	6

Young children are most affected by parents.

Early in the child's life his parents' appraisal is very important to him. Later on, teachers and peers exert social control over the child. If the parents belittle the child, they can create a negative self-image for him. If they react in an open, accepting way, the child can realistically evaluate both his positive and negative features, and incorporate all his abilities into a single coherent self-concept.

Later, teachers and peers control the child.

As the child matures, he is evaluated more by teachers and peers and less by his parents, as we have said. A child who is average for his age but younger in years than the rest of his class may come to believe he is small in stature, and his final self-concept may be biased as a result. Many late-maturing children see themselves as much smaller and weaker than their peers, when in fact their final height and weight may be average or above. Once a child's self-concept begins to develop, it may acquire a life of its own. If a little boy begins to see himself as an athlete, he will try to fulfill that particular expectation of himself. If a little girl sees herself as an actress, she's likely to do everything she can to meet that particular role.

The child's basic attitudes come from his parents.

Parents rarely set out to teach their children specifically about the world, yet children acquire their basic personal attitudes from parents. Parents do not tell their children which political party to join, but hundreds of studies show that children usually vote as their parents do. Why does this happen? Most psychologists believe that children tend to imitate significant people in their lives. Parents often serve as models because they have a great deal of power. Children observe things their parents do and the outcomes of their parents' acts. Also, parents reward or punish their children for certain things. Parents, teachers, and peers influence the child by social feedback, but the child also influences the type of reactions he receives by the symbols he displays. These symbols may reflect or hide the person's inner needs and problems, and the symbols can match or contrast with the parents' and peers' expectations.

Social symbols are for communication and deceit.

SOCIAL SYMBOLS Every child displays *social symbols* which reflect or mask his personality. These symbols may signal financial or social status, or one's cultural group. Among young children concrete symbols like grades are most visible, while later a proper address or good manners become important symbols of personal status. Usually, children learn to select symbols which accurately reflect their personal characteristics and are not misinterpreted by others. This is because social symbols perform two functions: they give information to others, and they serve to reinforce the self-concept by feedback from others.

Clothes are an important social symbol.

One important personal symbol for children is the clothes that a child or adolescent wears. Strong interest in clothes can be a sign of social insecurity, and total disdain for dress standards suggests the child may have an unfavorable attitude toward himself. Clothes can signal a sexual role, economic success, or the person's maturity. Women tend to pay more attention to fashions than men; the peak of female interest in clothes occurs during early adulthood when sexual attractiveness is important. Males become interested in dress during their middle age, when they enjoy economic success and worry about aging.

One's name is a social symbol.

Another symbol of self is your name. Most people have little choice about their given names, since parents choose it. But people do change their names, or use a nickname if they dislike the original choice. In the U.S. the family surname is always the name of the father; the middle name is selected by the family and usually reflects personal choice or family relations; and the first name is a primary identification of the individual. Names come in and out of fashion, so they vary in frequency with time. Usually, nicknames are given to people for racial, ethnic, social, or personal traits—Fatso, Red, and so on. There are stereotypes associated with people's names. Archibald is generally considered a sissy name for a boy, while Jack is more masculine. By the same token Anne is a feminine name, but Gertrude is not. Nicknames can reflect popularity, glamour, sex appropriateness, or ridicule. Thus, a name affects the child because it reflects how others view him, and to some extent how he views himself.

Reputation is a personal symbol.

Another personal symbol is an individual's reputation—those characteristics used to judge him as good or bad. The person may be bright or dumb, lazy or energetic, pretty or ugly, and rich or poor. Probably the most important factor determining reputation is the initial impression that a person makes on others by his behavior, and how that impression conforms to social norms. There is a lasting effect of these initial impressions. Once a reputation is acquired, it often spreads by gossip and may last for years. Overcoming a bad reputation is often difficult, but it can be done. One way is to change behavior. Moving to another locality is an easier way to change a reputation, or, rather, to build a new, more favorable one.

The healthy child should satisfy his own needs and some needs of the people around him.

THE HEALTHY PERSON   A child is well adjusted when he can function in many social situations with relative ease, is self-assured, is comfortable with himself, and can handle stress or conflict without undue emotion. A healthy child must have two things: a life pattern that meets most of his needs, and one that meets the needs of significant people close to him. If the child is constantly disappointed with his own performance, or is constantly scolded by his parents and peers, there is little chance he will acquire a healthy personality. If the child has realistic expectations about himself and lives with parents who share his goals, then he has a fair chance of happiness.

Psychologists study normal and abnormal behavior.

One reason psychologists study personal behavior is to understand normal and abnormal development. The first step in this diagnostic process is to determine the characteristics of healthy children. Psychologists have studied literally hundreds of children and adults who were judged to be well adjusted. On the basis of his observations Abraham

Maslow (1954) argued that healthy personal development includes self-acceptance, interest in outside problems, possession of some independence, definite goals, and some imperfections of character or personal adjustment.

The healthy child must accept reality.

ACCEPTANCE OF REALITY   The first, and many argue most important, characteristic of a well-adjusted child is the ability to accept reality about oneself. This means there is good correspondence between a child's "real" and "ideal" self. A well-adjusted child uses neither defense mechanisms nor psychological avoidance mechanisms to handle his personal problems. He can accept negative evaluations for what they are — either healthy constructive criticisms, which can be met best by some change on his part, or unreasonable demands, which must be resisted. The healthy child realizes that success is earned by hard work rather than hope. He does not simply accept barriers in his environment but tries to overcome or go around them. A well-adjusted child sets realistic goals and expectations and has a plan for achieving them. Very high or very low goals signal fear of failure and probable maladjustment. A healthy child can gain information from defeat as well as victory. He does not take every setback as a personal rejection, but sees failure as a challenge to work harder, plan more carefully, and do better next time. He accepts the notion that life is a series of challenges, and relishes new and exciting tasks. A maladjusted child fears the future and tries to avoid challenges.

Another sign of health is autonomy.

AUTONOMY   Beyond reality, the next important achievement of a well-adjusted child is autonomy, or independence, and personal responsibility. The healthy child eventually breaks his dependency on parents or peers, and begins to govern his life with self-directed goals and actions. He begins to make decisions without undue worry, and once he makes a decision will stick with it unless new information indicates a change.

The major traits of a well-adjusted child include: realistic expectations about himself, a clear picture of his strengths and weaknesses, the absence of serious frustrations, favorable social attitudes from his parents, and a reasonable number of successes along with some failures. If a child never fails, it may be because he is afraid to try something new or difficult — which may make failure possible. If he always fails, then he may be trying to attain the unreachable. Balance is the main key to health.

How has modern psychology set about diagnosing adjusted or abnormal personal development? The answer is primarily by means of tests. We turn next to the structure and function of personality tests.

The Measurement of Personality

Psychologists measure personality two ways.

There are two ways in which contemporary psychologists study personal development. Some prefer intensive understanding of single cases, while others produce standard tests and measure many individuals with them. Sigmund Freud gathered information used in formulating his theories by interviewing about two dozen patients in great detail. This *idiographic* method yields rich data and generates many hypotheses. However, a few cases may paint a misleading picture of normal personality.

Because of this weakness, recent work in personality development has concentrated on measuring many normal and abnormal personalities through standardized testing. There are two main types of personality tests: projective and objective. In a projective test the child is shown an ambiguous design and asked about what he sees; in an objective test a child answers a series of simple questions about himself. Each type has strengths and weaknesses.

Standardized tests are used to measure personal development.

Projective Tests

Projective devices are disguised so that a child taking a personality test is often unaware of what his answers mean. It is difficult to shirk or give false answers in such a test. The assumption behind projective tests is that their ambiguity causes the child to be guided by his unconscious wishes and desires. The ambiguous situations of this kind of test are assumed to release unconscious thoughts and drives, and the responses can be used to measure the strength and type of conflicts.

Projective tests use ambiguous situations.

THE RORSCHACH The best-known projective test was invented by Hermann Rorschach (*see* Figure 12.3). He was the first to use inkblots for the study of personality (Rorschach, 1942). Five of his inkblots have only shades of gray, two include bright red with gray, and the remaining three inkblots contain several colors. When taking the Rorschach test, the child is asked to look at each inkblot and tell what he sees. The tester

One projective test utilizes inkblots.

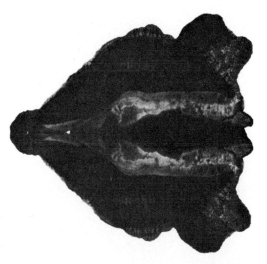

FIGURE 12.3
An inkblot similar to the original Rorschach designs. The subject is asked to tell what he sees and where it is.

keeps a verbatim record of responses and the amount of time required for the answer. Following presentation of all ten cards, the child is questioned about which part of the inkblot he used for each response and the meaning of each item. The major scoring categories of the Rorschach include location (part of the inkblot used), determinant (form, color, or shading), content (human, animal, anatomical diagrams, landscapes, food, art, or abstractions), and frequency of response. Rorschach assumed that longer response times reflect stronger emotional conflict and blocking—so those cards which take a long response time are studied most carefully to uncover the child's fears and conflicts. From these categories, response times, and the examiner's theory of personality comes a picture of the child's unconscious motives and conflicts.

There are problems with the inkblot test.

The main problems with the Rorschach inkblot test include the difficulty of scoring responses, and the lack of experimental support for the predictions derived from Rorschach's theories of unconscious motives. This test is popular with many clinical psychologists, who believe that in the hands of a sensitive examiner it will reveal important things about a child's personality development.

In another projective test pictures are used.

THE CAT   Another projective instrument is the *Children's Apperception Test* (CAT), which uses pictures like the one illustrated in Figure 12.4. The child is shown one picture at a time and is asked to describe what is happening, how the people in the picture feel, and what is the outcome of

FIGURE 12.4
A picture like those used in the Thematic Apperception Test (TAT). The person taking the test is asked to make up a story about the picture.

the situation. The CAT shares many problems and possibilities with the Rorschach inkblot test. Responses are often difficult to categorize, and little experimental evidence supports the notion that unconscious wishes determine the content of the CAT stories.

To overcome these problems, more objective measures of personality development were assembled to assess normal and abnormal personalities. These objective tests include checklists and short questions about the child which can be answered yes or no.

Objective Tests

Objective tests ask questions.

A variety of objective self-report questionnaires have been used to measure personal development. Some require the child to point out his symptoms from a list, while others ask him to point to those adjectives which describe his personality.

One objective test is the MMPI.

THE MMPI   One widely used personality test is the children's version of the Minnesota Multiphasic Personality Inventory (MMPI). It is an objective test designed to measure normal personality and introversion, extroversion, schizophrenia, paranoia, and delinquency. The test has 566 statements like those shown in Table 12.3. In the children's form of the test, the statements are read to the child from cards, and he indicates whether each item is true or false about himself. The MMPI is scored on nine scales, which measure personality traits, and four scales, which reflect the test-taker's attitude and honesty about his answers. The various parts of Figure 12.5 show the profile of scores associated with neurotic or psychotic personality development. The normal child scores in the middle range on all the scales; the neurotic child is high in scales He, D, and Hs; while the psychotic child is high in scales Pa, Pt, Sc, and Ma. The ?, L, K, and F scales reflect how careful and honest the child was in making his responses. High ?, L, or F scores indicate that the test is not a good measure; while high K scores are used to adjust other scales in giving a better picture of the child's total personality.

TABLE 12.3   This is a list of items similar to typical MMPI statements. Subjects mark whether a statement is true or false about themselves.

At times I feel like swearing.
I have engaged in petty thievery.
I sometimes tease animals.
I like dramatics.
My memory seems to be all right.
I am afraid of losing my mind.
I sweat very easily even on cool days.
I worry about catching diseases.

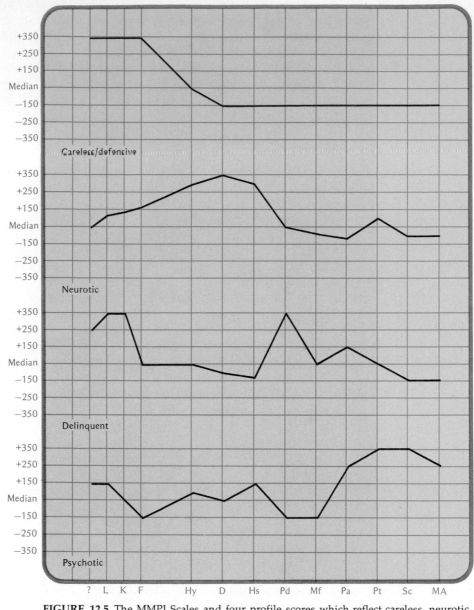

FIGURE 12.5 The MMPI Scales and four profile scores which reflect careless, neurotic, delinquent, or psychotic personalities.

Normal children score along the middle range on all scales. The careless/defensive test-taker's score is the top illustration; next comes the neurotic child's score; then the delinquent's score; and finally the psychotic child's score.

Objective tests also have problems.

Two problems plague objective personality tests: Often items are ambiguous or too difficult for children to understand, and some children say "yes" or "no" to everything without thinking about it. To solve these difficulties, ambiguous or difficult items can be rewritten to make them clearer, and children can be asked to choose between two items rather than merely saying "yes" or "no" to one statement. In this way ambiguities and the tendency not to think about the answer will not affect the outcome as directly.

Personality tests measure many factors.

Psychologists have analyzed these objective tests statistically to find the minimum dimensions which describe most people. Table 12.4 lists some factors which appear in many objective personality inventories. Most clinical psychologists don't interpret single scores, but look at the total test pattern. For example, a high score in emotional stability is favorable if connected with high general activity. If the child is lazy, sluggish, or withdrawn, a high stability score may indicate poor adjustment.

One of the most controversial and influential theories about personal development was proposed by Sigmund Freud. Consider his notions about children and behavior.

TABLE 12.4 Factors of personality

General activity—hurrying, liking for speed, liveliness, vitality, production, efficiency versus slow and deliberate, easily fatigued, inefficient.

Restraint—serious-minded, deliberate, persistent versus carefree, impulsive, excitement-loving.

Ascendance—leadership, speaking in public, bluffing versus submissiveness, hesitation, avoiding conspicuousness.

Sociability—having many friends, seeking social contacts and limelight versus few friends and shyness.

Emotional stability—evenness of moods, optimism, composure versus fluctuation of moods, pessimism, daydreaming, excitability, feelings of guilt, worry, loneliness, and ill health.

Objectivity—thick-skinned versus hypersensitive, self-centered, suspicious.

Friendliness—toleration of hostile action, acceptance of domination, respect for others versus belligerence, hostility, resentment, desire to dominate, and contempt for others.

Thoughtfulness—reflective, observing of self and others, mental poise versus interest in overt activity.

Personal relations—tolerance of people, faith in social institutions versus fault-finding, critical of institutions, suspicious, self-pitying.

Masculinity—interest in masculine activities, not easily disgusted, hard-boiled, inhibits emotional expression, little interest in clothes and style versus interest in feminine activities and vocations, easily disgusted, fearful, romantic, emotionally expressive.

The items in the Guilford-Zimmerman Temperament Survey (1956) are expressed in the form of affirmative statements rather than questions. Most concern the examinee directly. A few represent generalizations about other persons. Three examples are given below:

You start work on a new project with a great deal of enthusiasm.	Yes	No
You are often in low spirits.	Yes	No
Most people use politeness to cover up what is really "cutthroat" competition.	Yes	No

A Theory of Personality Development—Sigmund Freud

Freud believed development proceeds by stages.

Freud viewed personal growth as a sequence of stages (*see* Table 12.5). He defined each period of development by the object a child invests with energy. Freud believed that each child has a store of energy which he can transfer from one goal to another, and that by desiring various objects the child learns about reality. By wanting everything, a child learns what he may have and what he cannot possess. Freud believed that the baby's only interest is himself, but later the child is fascinated by objects; finally, people become his main interest. Babies are intrigued by simple pleasures like sucking, eating, and cuddling; but the young child realizes how weak he is, and comes to identify with stronger others. Freud felt that identification meets two needs: security and competence. Imitation lets the child learn new responses and helps him feel secure by becoming more like a stronger person. Let us consider Freud's proposed stages of personal development.

Oral Egocentrism

The first stage Freud called oral egocentrism.

According to Freud, during the oral stage of development a baby cannot differentiate between himself and the world. His instinctive impulses determine all his behavior. Later, when the baby does differentiate, his ego is born. The child is then aware of himself as "I" and everything else as not me. The oral stage, for Freud, is characterized by an intense preoccupation with self, so that the young infant is often a tyrant with no consideration for parents or siblings.

Anal Period

Freud's second stage was called the anal period.

Freud believed that at some point parents or peers begin to control the child's behavior. During this anal stage parents place limits on the child, and at the same time give him security and comfort. The child trades independence for security and guidance. Without some structure, Freud argued, the infant remains a tyrant; while with reasonable restraints he can become secure and feel competent.

Oedipus and Identification

Freud believed that children love their parents.

One of Freud's most startling statements was that at about the age of four the child becomes attracted to his opposite-sexed parent. This sexual attraction encounters a universal taboo against incest, so children must learn to express their affections indirectly. Freud argued that the little girl *becomes* like her mother so she can enjoy her father at second hand; and the little boy *becomes* like his father so he can vicariously enjoy his mother. According to Freud, there are two basic motives behind identification: one is fear of a more powerful adult, the other is desire for the opposite-sexed parent. Both motives compel boys to identify with their fathers and girls with their mothers. Identification with the same-sexed

TABLE 12.5   Freudian stages of personality development

Stage	Natural mode of pleasure	Object relation	Personality structure	Defense mechanisms operating
Oral stage (0–8 months)				
Early oral phase	Sucking, swallowing	Dependence	Id and beginning of ego	Fixation by gratification or deprivation
Late oral phase	Biting	Ambivalence	Id and ego	Regression
Anal stage (8–18 months)				
Early anal phase	Expelling	Ambivalence	Ego strengthened	Denial
Late anal phase	Retaining	Competence	Anxiety (superego)	Guilt
Phallic stage (2-6 years)	Touching and looking at genitals	Oedipus complex	Superego and ego emerge in full form	Beginning of ego defense mechanisms Sublimation Repression Reaction formation Displacement
Latency (6–11 years)	Loss of sexual interest	Sublimation	Consolidation of ego, superego, id	Reaction formation present
Genital stage (11–18 years)				
Prepubertal phase	Revival of infantile modes of pleasure	Reactivation of childhood	Disruption of organization	Intellectualization
Pubertal phase, heterosexual-genital	Adult modes of pleasure finding	New sexual relations	Reorganization into adult personality	

parent initiates a latency period in U.S. culture when young children's sexual feelings are repressed.

Latency

The latency period was asexual according to Freud.

Freud noted that following identification, boys associate with boys and girls with girls. School-age children suppress their sexual feelings and become interested in sports, games, and school. Sexual reawakening occurs at puberty.

Genital Puberty

Sexual feelings re-appear during puberty.

During puberty strong sexual feelings recur and can no longer be ignored. Since it is still unacceptable for the pubertal child to possess his opposite-sexed parent, he must seek other relations. Freud believed that adolescents are likely to form a very close attachment with one or two significant peers who replace the parents in the process of socialization. At the same time the young person wants to make his own independent decisions and assume more responsibility for his life. At this stage in life parental control is finished—although some parents cannot accept that fact. Adolescents must reject parental control if they are to mature into complete, independent persons. The adolescent finds homosexual interactions tend to bring incomplete satisfaction, so, sooner or later, most adolescents seek relations with members of the opposite sex. The ultimate purpose of a mature sexual relation is love and, possibly, children.

Freud proposed three mechanisms for personality.

Freud hypothesized that human personality develops through conflict between primitive innate impulses (id) and social restrictions (super-ego). He felt that the ego grows to reconcile these forces. Impulses may be so strong or social restrictions so severe that the ego is threatened. In these extreme cases ego-defense mechansims are utilized, most often unconsciously, to prop and protect a battered self-concept. Freud postulated several such defenses.

Mechanisms of Ego Defense

Defense mechanisms help the child cope with stress.

Under everyday circumstances culture and biology determine personal behavior, but unusual stress or severe training may present the child with overwhelming emotional upset. In the theory of Freud, when a child faces really serious difficulties, frustrations, or conflicts, his ego-defense mechanisms begin to operate. If the child uses the defenses only occasionally, he is healthy. Habitual use of such defenses indicates that the child is developing abnormally. Reliance on defense mechanisms to maintain personal stability means the child has few healthy reactions to stress and maintains his ego only by constant struggle or distortion of reality. Freudian ego defense mechanisms include repression, projection, sublimation, rationalization, reaction formation, regression, and displacement.

Repression means to forget an unpleasant experience.

REPRESSION   If a child can't tolerate thinking about something, his most likely solution is to push the thought into the unconscious. Painful or anxiety-provoking thoughts are suppressed. Blocking thoughts from consciousness, particularly emotion-laden thoughts, requires a great deal of energy. Assume that a small child has just been spanked by mother and immediately hates her. He may also recognize the danger of saying he hates his mother, since he is dependent on her for love, security, and comfort. The child may feel his mother would desert him if he showed hate, because some mothers can't tolerate rejection from their children. For this reason some mothers discourage all expressions of anger or hate by their children, so the child's only alternative is to repress his angry feelings. Many children segregate their feelings and thoughts into two compartments: "good" and "bad." The bad thoughts are repressed to keep away anxiety, but the child spends a lot of time feeling guilty. He really *wants* to be good, but he keeps having "bad" thoughts.

Freud felt that repression can create psychosomatic disorders.

Many Freudian psychoanalysts believe that repressed feelings of anger and hate are one cause of psychosomatic disorders. They argue that when anger and hate are repressed, the physiological processes which accompany these feelings may continue to occur: The stomach secretes extra acid; the heart beats faster; and the entire body is geared for fight or flight. These scientists assume that prolonged repressed feelings may cause hypertension, ulcers, and high blood pressure. A child may be started on the path of repression and subsequent psychosomatic disorder by being forced to inhibit his emotions rather than expressing them.

Projection means the attribution of one's own feelings to another.

PROJECTION   Another defense mechanism, used to handle unacceptable thoughts and feelings, is the transfer of such thoughts to another person. "Nice" children are taught not to attack others unless they have been attacked first. The angry child must somehow see his peer as an aggressor because then he can attack the other child who threatens him. If the angry child learns attack is not socially acceptable, he may repress his wishes and come to believe, through projection of his repressed feelings, that it is the other child who is about to attack *him*. Then he can "defend" himself and attack first without feeling guilt, for the other child is really the aggressor. (Or was about to be!) He can be completely sincere when he claims, "He was going to hit me first!"

Sublimation means socially acceptable need satisfaction.

SUBLIMATION   A child who seeks substitute satisfaction for his needs and desires is sublimating them. Freud believed that basic needs are satisfied by instinctive action patterns early in life, and that these early instincts often come into conflict with social taboos or family power. Socialization requires learning new means of gratifying basic instincts. Changing from one satisfaction to another requires that a child give up old pleasures and find new ones. Freud argued that when a primitive mode of satisfaction is blocked, other means of expression must be found. The substitution of a new mode of satisfaction for an old instinctive pattern is called sublimation. This process converts primitive instinctive response patterns into socially acceptable behavior systems.

The fox who called the grapes sour exemplifies rationalization.

RATIONALIZATION   Another common defense mechanism is rationalization. The fable about the fox who couldn't reach a bunch of grapes and said they were probably sour anyway is a good example. Rationalizations are attempts to reduce frustration by deciding that the unreachable goal is not worthwhile. Children use rationalization when they decide that the friend who rejected them wasn't very nice; or, in adolescence, when they are put off by a member of the opposite sex, they come to think that person wasn't really very interesting after all.

Reaction formation means to do what you fear.

REACTION FORMATION   The sexual athlete, daredevil, or spendthrift may be driven by reaction formation. They are acting contrary to their fears. If they are afraid of heights, daredevils may parachute from airplanes; if afraid of sex, they may seduce everyone who is willing. Reaction formation can produce either a lifetime of excess or healthy *counterphobic* behavior, in which the fear is lessened because of constant exposure to the object of the fear. By confronting fears, the person may overcome them and achieve a better adjustment.

Regression means going back to more immature behaviors.

REGRESSION   Regression is the opposite of maturation, because the child retreats to earlier forms of satisfaction and simpler, more primitive pleasures. A regressed child asks others for help rather than trying to help himself; he sucks his thumb or cries rather than trying to handle his frustrations directly.

Displacement means directing anger at a weaker person.

DISPLACEMENT   When a child displaces his feelings, they are directed at an object unrelated to the initial frustration. Suppose a child is angry at a parent. He may yell at his younger sibling rather than the parent, who might spank him. Lower animals also show displacement. If two rats are placed in a closed cage and given painful electric shocks, they will attack each other. If one animal is then placed alone in the cage, he will fight an innocent bystander.

Erikson believes life is a challenge.

Freud was concerned with the child's personal and emotional development. He and others (Erik Erikson, 1950) argued that five main challenges to personal growth occur during the early years. Most psychologists now agree that five areas of development are especially difficult during childhood: the attainment of independence, control of behavior by parents and peers, development of a sex role, development of a moral code, and learning to handle aggression or hostility.

Challenges to Personal Growth

There are several problems to overcome in early childhood.

Let us rename and simplify the main problems of early personal development:

1. Independence.
2. Discipline.
3. Aggression.
4. Sex role.
5. Moral development.

These areas produce strong emotions that often tax young children's adaptive abilities. Dependence happens during the first years of life.

Then, every child struggles with social discipline. The goal of socialization is to strike a compromise between the growing child's requirements for autonomy and the parent's responsibilities to instill manners and self-control in the child. Sexual growth has three phases in our society: a childhood period, a long latency, and puberty. This pattern is probably not universal, since in some cultures there does not seem to be a latency period. Aggression is a constant problem because the young child must come to accept his own hostile impulses, convert them into productive energy, and learn to handle fear and hurt from the aggression of others. We have seen how frustration often leads to aggression, and how social factors may determine the ways in which people express hostility. Finally, the child must develop a sense of moral values by which to live.

Childhood Dependency

Babies are helpless.

A human baby is helpless, completely dependent on adult care. Infants are self-centered, as we have learned, and concentrate on the satisfaction of their primitive hunger, thirst, and oral needs. Feedback from these early experiences reflects the world as a place where a baby can cry a little and get what he wants, or, perhaps, cry forever and get nothing. There are several ways to harm human infants during this period, and some ways to make them healthy. Freud wrote that a child who is gratified during the oral stage would become optimistic, while frequent deprivation would produce pessimism. Erik Erikson called this first period the state of trust or mistrust. According to his theory, if the infant develops a sense of trust, he can later become independent and self-reliant with no feelings of bitterness or isolation. Erikson also argued that if the baby mistrusts others and still becomes independent and self-reliant, he will feel alienated and angry. Parental deprivation and rejection are an insecure base for later independence.

Child-centered homes produce dependency.

Robert Sears, *et al.* (1957) discovered that child-centered homes produce dependent children, because parents control the offspring, reinforce dependency, and discourage independent action. Paradoxically, parental rejection also produces dependency, but rejection leaves the child with a sense of helplessness.

Males and females handle dependency differently.

Males and females handle dependency differently as they mature. Jerome Kagan and Howard Moss (1962) found that boys' dependency during the early years is unrelated to their later behavior, while dependent girls remain so throughout their lives. The researchers proposed that in the U.S., dependency is more acceptable for females, so their early inclinations in this direction may be encouraged or ignored. Men in the U.S. are not supposed to be dependent, and so little boys' early dependency may be punished or he may be pushed toward more independence. Sexual maturity may also change a male's hormone balance in favor of aggressiveness. Both social pressure and biological process combine to more actively drive males from their parents' homes.

Portrait

Margaret Mead was born in 1901 and spent her early years moving from place to place with her father, who was a professor at the University of Pennsylvania. She describes her early education as a collage of ideas served by her mother and grandmother, who were both interested in how the mind works. By the time Mead was ten years old, her mother had her following around a younger sister to record language development. Mead completed her master's degree in Psychology at Columbia University; she then took a Ph.D. in anthropology at the same school. Mead moved into the Samoan culture in 1924, and spent the next several years studying various groups and writing about them. Each of her books had a major impact on psychology. Her first work, *Coming of Age in Samoa*, showed that adolescence is not necessarily a time of storm and strife. Next, she wrote *Growing Up in New Guinea*, which argued that Jean Piaget's notion of animism was limited. *Sex and Temperament in Three Primitive Societies* was based on the thesis that males are not necessarily natural aggressors and females always passive. Mead found some tribes in which the male-female roles are reversed from those of our own culture, another culture in which both sexes were aggressive, and one in which neither sex was aggressive.

Mead had become interested in anthropology while working with Ruth Benedict and Franz Boas. Boas wanted Mead to stay in the United States and work with the American Indians, but she made a deal with him. She said she would do research on the problem of the biological and cultural aspects of adolescence, if he would let her study the culture she was interested in. When Boas agreed, she began her famous study of the Samoans. Another major idea that interested her was the notion of animism as proposed by Piaget. He believed that primitives are animistic (that they think that all living creatures have souls separate from their bodies) because primitives are convinced that all objects are alive. Mead discovered that the Manus tribe of the South Seas did not believe that everything is alive, thus at least one primitive culture was not animistic.

Margaret Mead stands before an enlargement from her 1966 book, *Family*. The stick in her left hand is a famous trademark. (The Granger Collection)

Early in her career Mead had wanted to be a painter. She was told by her parents that if she wanted to be an artist, she would not be able to attend college, so she decided to become a writer instead. Later in life she published a number of novels and popular books on anthropology. Her more recent work and writing is concerned with the social problems of the post-World War II generations, and the difficulties that parents and their children have in communicating with each other. In *Culture and Commitment* she argues that the younger generations have been reared in a culture that is more fragmented than their parents experienced. As a result, she believes there is little common ground for communication between generations. She has also published a volume of autobiography, *Blackberry Winter*.

Margaret Mead at age sixteen. (The Granger Collection)

Formal Sex Relations

The first attitude which a little girl learns towards boys is one of avoidance and antagonism. She learns to observe the brother and sister taboo towards the boys of her relationship group and household, and together with the other small girls of her age group she treats all other small boys as enemies elect. After a little girl is eight or nine years of age she has learned never to approach a group of older boys. This feeling of antagonism towards younger boys and shamed avoidance of older ones continues up to the age of thirteen or fourteen, to the group of girls who are just reaching puberty and the group of boys who have just been circumcised. These children are growing away from the age-group life and the age-group antagonisms. They are not yet actively sex-conscious. And it is at this time that relationships between the sexes are least emotionally charged. Not until she is an old married woman with several children will the Samoan girl again regard the opposite sex so quietly. When these adolescent children gather together there is a good-natured banter, a minimum of embarrassment, a great deal of random teasing which usually takes the form of accusing some little girl of a consuming passion for a decrepit old man of eighty, or some small boy of being the father of a buxom matron's eighth child. Occasionally the banter takes the form of attributing affection between two age mates and is gaily and indignantly repudiated by both. Children at this age meet at informal *siva* parties, on the outskirts of more formal occasions, at community reef fishings (when many yards of reef have been enclosed to make a great fish trap) and on torch-fishing excursions. Good-natured tussling and banter and co-operation in common activities are the keynotes of these occasions. But unfortunately these contacts are neither frequent nor sufficiently prolonged to teach the girls co-operation or to give either boys or girls any real appreciation of personality in members of the opposite sex.

Two or three years later this will all be changed. The fact that little girls no longer belong to age groups makes the individual's defection less noticeable. The boy who begins to take an active interest in girls is also seen less in a gang and spends more time with one close companion. Girls have lost all of their nonchalance. They giggle, blush, bridle, run away. Boys become shy, embarrassed, taciturn, and avoid the society of girls in the daytime and on the brilliant moonlit nights for which they accuse the girls of having an exhibitionistic preference. Friendships fall more strictly within the relationship group. The boy's need for a trusted confidante is stronger than that of the girl, for only the most adroit and hardened Don Juans do their own courting. There are occasions, of course, when two youngsters just past adolescence, fearful of ridicule, even from their nearest friends and relatives, will slip away alone into the bush. More frequently still an older man, a

From Margaret Mead, *Coming of Age in Samoa* (New York: William Morrow & Co., 1928), pp. 86–109.

widower or a divorced man, will be a girl's first lover. And here there is no need for an ambassador. The older man is neither shy nor frightened, and futhermore there is no one whom he can trust as an intermediary; a younger man would betray him, an older man would not take his amours seriously. But the first spontaneous experiment of adolescent children and the amorous excursions of the older men among the young girls of the village are variants on the edge of the recognised types of relationships; so also is the first experience of a young boy with an older woman. But both of these are exceedingly frequent occurrences, so that the success of an amatory experience is seldom jeopardised by double ignorance. Nevertheless, all of these occasions are outside the recognised forms into which sex relations fall. The little boy and girl are branded by their companions as guilty of *tautala lai titi* (presuming above their ages) as is the boy who loves or aspires to love an older woman, while the idea of an older man pursuing a young girl appeals strongly to their sense of humour; or if the girl is very young and naïve, to their sense of unfitness. "She is too young, too young yet. He is too old," they will say.

Besides formal marriage there are only two types of sex relations which receive any formal recognition from the community—love affairs between unmarried young people (this includes the widowed) who are very nearly of the same age, whether leading to marriage or merely a passing diversion; and adultery.

Between the unmarried there are three forms of relationship: the clandestine encounter, "under the palm tree," the published elopement, *Avaga*, and the ceremonious courtship in which the boy "sits before the girl"; and on the edge of these, the curious form of surreptitious rape, called *moetotolo*, sleep crawling, resorted to by youths who find favour in no maiden's eyes.

In these three relationships, the boy requires a confidant and ambassador whom he calls a *soa*. Where boys are close companions, this relationship may extend over many love affairs, or it may be a temporary one, terminating with the particular love affair. The *soa* follows the pattern of the talking chief who makes material demands upon his chief in return for the immaterial ser-

vices which he renders him. If marriage results from his ambassadorship, he receives a specially fine present from the bridegroom. The choice of a *soa* presents many difficulties. If the lover chooses a steady, reliable boy, some slightly younger relative devoted to his interests, a boy unambitious in affairs of the heart, very likely the ambassador will bungle the whole affair through inexperience and lack of tact. But if he chooses a handsome and expert wooer who knows just how "to speak softly and walk gently," then as likely as not the girl will prefer the second to the principal. This difficulty is occasionally anticipated by employing two or three *soas* and setting them to spy on each other. But such a lack of trust is likely to inspire a similar attitude in the agents, and as one over-cautious and disappointed lover told me ruefully, "I had five *soas*, one was true and four were false."

In the strictly clandestine love affair the lover never presents himself at the house of his beloved. His *soa* may go there in a group or upon some trumped-up errand, or he also may avoid the house and find opportunities to speak to the girl while she is fishing or going to and from the plantation. It is his task to sing his friend's praise, counteract the girl's fears and objections, and finally appoint a rendezvous. These affairs are usually of short duration and both boy and girl may be carrying on several at once. One of the recognised causes of a quarrel is the resentment of the first lover against his successor of the same night, "for the boy who came later will mock him." These clandestine lovers make their rendezvous on the outskirts of the village. "Under the palm trees" is the conventionalised designation of this type of intrigue. Very often three or four couples will have a common rendezvous, when either the boys or the girls are relatives who are friends. Should the girl ever grow faint or dizzy, it is the boy's part to climb the nearest palm and fetch down a fresh cocoanut to pour on her face in lieu of *eau de cologne*. In native theory, barrenness is the punishment of promiscuity; and, *vice versa*, only persistent monogamy is rewarded by conception. When a pair of clandestine experimenters whose rank is so low that their marriages are not of any great economic importance become genuinely attached to each other and maintain the relationship over several months, marriage often follows. And native sophistication distinguishes between the adept lover whose adventures are many and of short duration and the less skilled man who can find no better proof of his virility than a long affair ending in conception.

Often the girl is afraid to venture out into the night, infested with ghosts and devils, ghosts that strangle one, ghosts from far-away villages who come in canoes to kidnap the girls of the village, ghosts who leap upon the back and may not be shaken off. Or she may feel that it is wiser to remain at home, and if necessary, attest her presence vocally. In this case the lover braves the house; taking off his *lavalava,* he greases his body thoroughly with cocoanut oil so that he can slip through the fingers of pursuers and leave no trace, and stealthily raises the blinds and slips into the house. The prevalence of this practice gives point to the familiar incident in Polynesian folk tales of the ill fortune that falls the luckless hero who "sleeps until morning, until the rising sun reveals his presence to the other inmates of the house." As perhaps a dozen or more people and several dogs are sleeping in the house, a due regard for silence is sufficient precaution. But it is this habit of domestic rendezvous which lends itself to the peculiar abuse of the *moetotolo,* or sleep crawler.

The *moetotolo* is the only sex activity which presents a definitely abnormal picture. Ever since the first contact with white civilisation, rape, in the form of violent assault, has occurred occasionally in Samoa. It is far less congenial, however, to the Samoan attitude than *moetotolo,* in which a man stealthily appropriates the favours which are meant for another. The need for guarding against discovery makes conversation impossible, and the sleep crawler relies upon the girl's expecting a lover or the chance that she will indiscriminately accept any comer. If the girl suspects and resents him, she raises a great outcry and the whole household gives chase. Catching a *moetotolo* is counted great sport, and the women, who feel their safety endangered, are even more active in pursuit than the men.

Two motives are given for this unsavoury activity, anger and failure in love. The Samoan girl

who plays the coquette does so at her peril. "She will say, 'Yes, I will meet you to-night by that old cocoanut tree just beside the devilfish stone when the moon goes down.' And the boy will wait and wait and wait all night long. It will grow very dark; lizards will drop on his head; the ghost boats will come into the channel. He will be very much afraid. But he will wait there until dawn, until his hair is wet with dew and his heart is very angry and still she does not come. Then in revenge he will attempt a *moetotolo.* Especially will he do so if he hears that she has met another that night." The other set explanation is that a particular boy cannot win a sweetheart by any legitimate means, and there is no form of prostitution, except guest prostitution in Samoa. As some of the boys who were notorious *moetotolos* were among the most charming and good-looking youths of the village, this is a little hard to understand. Apparently, these youths, frowned upon in one or two tentative courtships, inflamed by the loudly proclaimed success of their fellows and the taunts against their own inexperience, cast established wooing procedure to the winds and attempt a *moetotolo.* And once caught, once branded, no girl will ever pay any attention to them again. They must wait until as older men, with position and title to offer, they can choose between some weary and bedraggled wanton or the unwilling young daughter of ambitious and selfish parents. But years will intervene before this is possible, and shut out from the amours in which his companions are engaging, a boy makes one attempt after another, sometimes successfully, sometimes only to be caught and beaten, mocked by the village, and always digging the pit deeper under his feet.

The attitude towards virginity is a curious one. Christianity has, of course, introduced a moral premium on chastity. The Samoans regard this attitude with reverent but complete scepticism and the concept of celibacy is absolutely meaningless to them. But virginity definitely adds to a girl's attractiveness, the wooing of a virgin is considered far more of a feat than the conquest of a more experienced heart, and a really successful Don Juan turns most of his attention to their seduction. One youth who at twenty-four married a girl who was still a virgin was the laughing stock of the village over his freely related trepidation which revealed the fact that at twenty-four, although he had had many love affairs, he had never before won the favours of a virgin.

The bridegroom, his relatives and the bride and her relatives all receive prestige if she proves to be a virgin, so that the girl of rank who might wish to forestall this painful public ceremony is thwarted not only by the anxious chaperonage of her relatives but by the boy's eagerness for prestige.

In premarital relationships, a convention of love making is strictly adhered to. True, this is a convention of speech, rather than of action. A boy declares that he will die if a girl refuses him her favours, but the Samoans laugh at stories of romantic love, scoff at fidelity to a long absent wife or mistress, believe explicitly that one love will quickly cure another. The fidelity which is followed by pregnancy is taken as proof positive of a real attachment, although having many mistresses is never out of harmony with a declaration of affection for each. The composition of ardent love songs, the fashioning of long and flowery love letters, the invocation of the moon, the stars and the sea in verbal courtship, all serve to give Samoan love-making a close superficial resemblance to our own, yet the attitude is far closer to that of Schnitzler's hero in *The Affairs of Anatol.* Romantic love as it occurs in our civilisation, inextricably bound up with ideas of monogamy, exclusiveness, jealousy and undeviating fidelity does not occur in Samoa. Our attitude is a compound, the final result of many converging lines of development in Western civilisation, of the institution of monogamy, of the ideas of the age of chivalry, of the ethics of Christianity. Even a passionate attachment to one person which lasts for a long period and persists in the face of discouragement but does not bar out other relationships, is rare among the Samoans. Marriage, on the other hand, is regarded as a social and economic arrangement, in which relative wealth, rank, and skill of husband and wife, all must be taken into consideration. There are many marriages in which both individuals, especially if they are over thirty, are completely faithful. But this must be attributed to the ease of sexual ad-

justment on the one hand, and to the ascendency of other interest, social organisation for the men, children for the women, over sex interests, rather than to a passionate fixation upon the partner in the marriage. As the Samoans lack the inhibitions and the intricate specialisation of sex feeling which make marriages of convenience unsatisfactory, it is possible to bulwark marital happiness with other props than temporary passionate devotion. Suitability and expediency become the deciding factors.

Adultery does not necessarily mean a broken marriage. A chief's wife who commits adultery is deemed to have dishonoured her high position, and is usually discarded, although the chief will openly resent her remarriage to any one of lower rank. If the lover is considered the more culpable, the village will take public vengeance upon him. In less conspicuous cases the amount of fuss which is made over adultery is dependent upon the relative rank of the offender and offended, or the personal jealousy which is only occasionally aroused. If either the injured husband or the injured wife is sufficiently incensed to threaten physical violence, the trespasser may have to resort to a public *ifoga,* the ceremonial humiliation before some one whose pardon is asked. He goes to the house of the man he has injured, accompanied by all the men of his household, each one wrapped in a fine mat, the currency of the country; the suppliants seat themselves outside the house, fine mats spread over their heads, hands folded on their breasts, heads bent in attitudes of the deepest dejection and humiliation. "And if the man is very angry he will say no word. All day he will go about his business; he will braid cinet with a quick hand, he will talk loudly to his wife, and call out greetings to those who pass in the roadway, but he will take no notice of those who sit on his own terrace, who dare not raise their eyes or make any movement to go away. In olden days, if his heart was not softened, he might take a club and together with his relatives go out and kill those who sit without. But now he only keeps them waiting, waiting all day long. The sun will beat down upon them; the rain will come and beat on their heads and still he will say no word. Then towards evening he will say at last: 'Come, it is enough. Enter the house and drink the kava. Eat the food which I will set before you and we will cast our trouble into the sea.' " Then the fine mats are accepted as payment for the injury and the *ifoga* becomes a matter of village history. . . .

If, on the other hand, a wife really tires of her husband, or a husband of his wife, divorce is a simple and informal matter, the non-resident simply going home to his or her family, and the relationship is said to have "passed away." It is a very brittle monogamy, often trespassed and more often broken entirely. But many adulteries occur—between a young marriage-shy bachelor and a married woman, or a temporary widower and some young girl—which hardly threaten the continuity of established relationships. The claim that a woman has on her family's land renders her as independent as her husband, and so there are no marriages of any duration in which either person is actively unhappy. A tiny flare-up and a woman goes home to her own people; if her husband does not care to conciliate her, each seeks another mate.

Within the family, the wife obeys and serves her husband, in theory, though of course, the hen-pecked husband is a frequent phenomenon.

Autonomy versus Discipline

Young babies are spontaneously active.

Every young baby is spontaneously active—following things with his eyes, exploring and experimenting with his hands, and trying to integrate his sensory-motor acts. One-year-old infants spend more time exploring and playing than eating. The three-year-old is outgoing and increasingly curious. This early shift from the dependency of the infant to the autonomy of the preschooler may conflict with a parent's need to control the child. However, for healthy personal growth a child must develop a sense of his own competence (White, 1959). This good self-concept results when the child produces something by his own effort. If the child is denied competence, he may remain insecure and dependent for an unhealthy length of time.

Too much or too little discipline creates problems.

Two possible disciplinary problems concern the indulged child, who may experience no restriction, and is demanding and defiant and the overprotected child, who is often subjected to total control. The over-controlled child—who is tricked, ridiculed, shamed, or threatened with pain and punishments if he does not conform—can find no middle ground between hopeless resistance and unconditional surrender. Excessive control produces two distinct patterns: *anxious conformity*, in which all personal resentments and desires are suppressed so the child is considered to be a model child by adults, or *negativism*, when he rejects even reasonable demands.

Maturity should bring achievement motivation.

As a child matures in U.S. society his needs for independence, competition, and achievement increase (*see* Figure 12.6). One sign of maturity is a shift from dependence to achievement, which means the child evaluates himself against an external standard of excellence. M.R. Winterbottom (1958) studied the effects of early child-rearing patterns on achievement motivation. She found that high-achievement boys receive early independence training. For example, mothers of nine-year-old high-achievement boys expected early self-reliance and placed few restrictions on them. These mothers gave large and frequent reinforcements for independence.

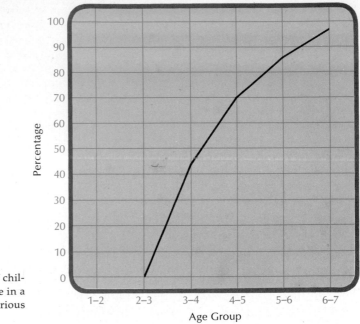

FIGURE 12.6
The percentage of children who compete in a simple game at various ages.

Early independence training also produced high-achievement motivation during adolescence. By contrast, scientists find that encouragement of independence during the period of adolescence is associated with dependency and lack of achievement. Whether the late encouragement of independence causes low-achievement needs or whether it is the result of ongoing adolescent dependency is not known.

High need achievement children are bright.

Several characteristics distinguish high- and low-achieving children. Those who expect to do well are brighter; and they persist longer, try harder, and succeed more often than children who do not expect to perform well. Low-achievers believe others are responsible for their successes and failures; high-achievers feel they control their own destinies. Children who achieve will choose to delay immediate gratification, so that they receive a larger reward later. Academic and economic success requires the ability to work for long-range goals rather than immediate tangible rewards. High-achievement children prefer moderately difficult tasks or risks which involve challenge to very easy or very difficult assignments. Successful children do not gamble, but in fact prefer tasks where skill or ability is involved.

Aggression and Hostility

The goal of aggression is dominance.

The aim of aggression is usually mastery or dominance. Hostility is associated with anger, frustration, and pain. The frustration-anger-hostility link does not seem to be present at birth. A young infant's response to unpleasant situations is undifferentiated. He cries when he is hungry or hurt. Anger does not emerge until the beginning of the second year. Then anger and hostility become cyclic in children, and most outbursts occur around lunch, dinner, or bedtime (*see* Figure 12.7).

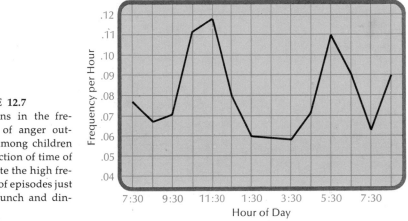

FIGURE 12.7
Variations in the frequency of anger outbursts among children as a function of time of day. Note the high frequency of episodes just before lunch and dinner.

Two theories about aggression exist.

There are two views about how aggression develops: Some experimenters see it as an instinctive biological response to frustration, while others think aggression is learned. Freud believed aggression is the product of instinctive energies, while Skinner and others think it is maintained by reinforcement. Freud believed aggression must occur, but could be controlled and channeled into productive activities through social pressure. Skinner thinks aggression happens primarily because we reinforce hostility (*see* Figure 12.8).

Freud believed that aggression is innate.

Scholars often debate about whether aggression is innate or learned. Freud believed that people can learn to handle frustration and the resultant aggression in several ways: by overt aggression, self-aggression, regression, sublimation, or displacement. Once aggression is triggered, he asserted, it must be expressed—and hopefully in a nondestructive manner—or turned inward.

Ethologists believe aggression is instinctive.

Ethologists also stress the innateness of aggression. Konrad Lorenz speculated about human aggression on the basis of his work with animals. He defined aggression as readiness to dominate, and felt the trait is crucial for survival of a species. He pointed out that innately aggressive animals like lions respond well to appeasement or submission signals from a defeated rival. A defeated wolf will submit and show its throat, a sure sign to stop another wolf from attacking. Man also responds to submission signals, although his inhibitions, or stopping signals, are less than perfect. In the modern world much human aggression is impersonal and too far removed from the individual for submission signals to be effective.

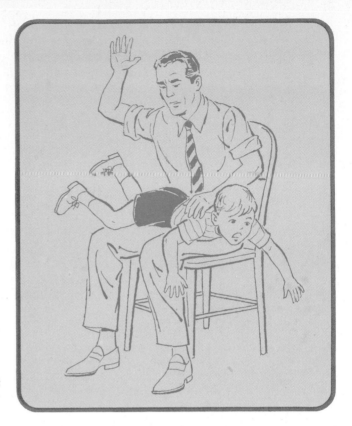

FIGURE 12.8
An example of how punishment may teach the child to be more aggressive.

Overcrowding creates hostility.

Recent studies of animals in experimental and in free territorial situations suggest that pathological or extreme hostility may result from territorial overcrowding. Early experiments used rats as subjects and manipulated the amount of territory available for use by the animals. These studies were criticized because rats are much more primitive than humans and also because the experimental situation was artificial. More recent field studies of monkeys show that the population density among these animals seriously affects their social relations. The results are frightening in their implications for those who live in cities.

Learning theorists believe aggression is acquired.

Robert Ardrey argues that much of man's aggressiveness results from biological processes. According to this view, overcrowding and lack of communication are certain to produce social chaos. This biological view of hostility is challenged by theorists who believe environmental events control humans. They argue that man learns to fight just as he learns to read—by being reinforced. Albert Bandura, one of the leading exponents of the social-learning view, showed that children will imitate aggressive acts which they see others perform (Bandura *et al.*, 1963).

Bandura's subjects were forty-eight boys and forty-eight girls of nursery-school age. A male or a female adult served as the aggressive

Bandura studied
aggression.
model in each of three experimental groups. One group observed an aggressive model in a "real-life" situation; a second experimental group saw the same model portraying aggression on film; and a third group saw an aggressive cartoon. The groups were further subdivided into boys and girls. Half the children were exposed to a same-sex model; the other children saw an opposite-sex model. A comparison or control group of children did not view the adult aggression at all. During the study each child was brought into the experiment room and asked to play with toys while the adult model played with other things. After a minute the adult model became very aggressive toward a plastic doll—sitting on the doll, punching it in the nose, raising it above his head, hitting it with a mallet, tossing it in the air and kicking it about the room (*see* Figure 12.9). The adult model shouted, "Sock him; hit him in the nose; kick him down, pow!" Children exposed to the film or cartoon aggression watched ten minutes of adult violence on film. Following exposure to the adult aggression, and prior to a test phase, each child was put in a frustrating situation. The children were shown beautiful toys and allowed to play with them for a short while, but once they became interested, they were told that these toys were for others as they were the best toys. They were told they could play with toys in the test room—plastic dolls, mallets, and other items just like those the aggressive adult model had used. Each child played for twenty minutes in this test session.

Two observers judged the amount of aggression each child expressed. They found significant increases in aggression as a result of viewing the

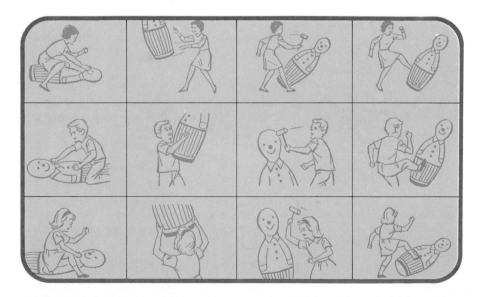

FIGURE 12.9 (*Top*) A model portraying aggression; (*middle and bottom*) children imitating the model.

Frustration increases aggression.

real-life aggressive model, a film of the aggressive model, or the cartoon aggression. Boys were more aggressive than girls. The male model was more influential with boys; while girls were more aggressive after viewing a female model. Thus, viewing aggression *and* experiencing frustration do increase the incidence of specific aggressive acts.

Several factors affect aggression.

Most social scientists argue that several factors jointly influence human aggression. Among them are hereditary predisposition, environmental frustration, anxiety associated with aggression, visual exposure to aggression, and social reinforcement for aggression. Since little can be done about innate predisposition, most students of behavior have concentrated on the social control of hostility.

We know little about the control of aggression.

Although we know a good deal about how to increase aggression, there is little information on how to stop hostility. A few studies exist—for example, verbal punishment decreases aggression in the punishing situation, but increases it in other encounters. Parents who punish their children for being aggressive produce children who are nice to their parents and hostile toward others. Probably the best way to reduce aggression is by removing environmental frustration, showing the child a passive model to imitate, and reinforcing nonaggressive acts.

Sex-role Development

Are sex roles innate or acquired?

A fundamental characteristic of personality is sex role—the masculine or feminine pattern of behavior which colors all social relations. A continuing and long-standing controversy surrounds the origins of human sex roles. Some argue that sex role is only biologically given, while others insist that only cultural pressures determine whether a human being is masculine or feminine. There is little doubt that personality differences exist between males and females. Whether these variations are simply the result of early training or reflect deep biological differences, beyond primary and secondary sexual characteristics is open to question. The reading by Tom Alexander explores innate sex differences, the influences of social pressure on sex role, and the consequences for man and woman.

human sex roles

TOM ALEXANDER

Few of the brickbats that have recently been sailing through the fragile greenhouses of our society have sprayed out more flinders of emotion

and self-doubt than the women's liberation movement. With so many sharp edges flying about, it is understandable that some important distinctions have been generally overlooked. The many-faceted movement embraces a diversity of contentions, with very different implications for both

From Tom Alexander, "There Are Sex Differences in the Mind Too" (*Fortune Magazine,* February 1971).

women and men. The demands put forward by many of the feminists—probably the majority—seem quite reasonable: changes in male-oriented attitudes and arrangements so that women can enter upon and advance in a greater variety of careers and, if they wish, combine these careers with motherhood. Progress in these directions is not only possible but inevitable; and, to an extent that might surprise some of the fiercer soldiers of women's lib, a great many men will applaud.

But some of the more radical spokeswomen of the movement are asserting a much more questionable, and potentially much more momentous, set of contentions and claims. They maintain that innate differences in temperament and ability between men and women are nonexistent or insignificant, and that the differences in the roles performed by men and women in our society are *entirely* due to social indoctrination and discrimination. The solution proposed by many radical feminists is an "androgynous" society—one in which the treatment accorded to, and the performance expected from, males and females would be essentially identical, whether at home, at school, or at work. "For the sexes are inherently in everything alike," writes Kate Millett, one widely known philosopher of the movement, "save reproductive systems, secondary sexual characteristics, orgasmic capacity, and genetic and morphological structure."

As it happens, such assertions about fundamental alikeness are being advanced at the very time when research from many scientific fields has been converging to suggest quite the opposite—that there are some inborn differences between the sexes in temperament and inclination. The most general finding of all, to be sure, is that aside from obvious differences in anatomy, physiology, and reproductive behavior, no characteristic belongs exclusively to one sex. Some differences are much more sex-specific than others, but in general, no matter what nominally male psychological trait is under consideration, some women exceed the male norm; and vice versa for nominally female traits. Some of the uncertainty in psychology is merely about the extent of these overlaps. More of the uncertainty is about the extent to which the traits have biological or social origins or some combination of both.

Differences in behavior are evident very early in life. Male infants are generally more active than females. They cry more, sleep less, and demand more attention. Female babies, while apparently more sensitive to cold, touch, and sounds, are more passive and content. They smile more often, appear to learn more rapidly, and generally seem more mature. At the age of only twelve weeks, according to some experiments, girls look longer at pictures of faces than at geometrical figures, while boys show no preference (but later they come to prefer the geometrical forms). On the average, however, boys look longer at *all* kinds of pictures than girls do.

At so early an age, it seems, females are already expressing the preferences and behavior that, for whatever reason, will develop more completely later. Girls, research predicts, will find their satisfactions in relationships with people to a greater extent than boys. They will learn to talk earlier and more fluently, and this superiority will persist through life. They will be more concerned with having companionship than boys. They will be more docile, will strive harder to please both at home and at school.

Later on, the work women select will usually involve close interaction with people. Social scientists apply the term "nurturant" to typical female professions such as child care, teaching, nursing, or social work. The feelings and the opinions of others matter more to women than to men; words of encouragement and praise often elicit more dogged effort than the prospect of promotion. One of the persistent problems of women in careers is that as they rise to high levels they often enter realms where competition is keener and praise is rare. An even more basic female handicap in the pursuit of careers is distraction: the single overriding preoccupation of most women, psychologists agree, is marriage.

A Negative Image of Success

Rightly or wrongly, women often come to suspect that too much intellectual achievement or success in male-dominated fields can impair their marriage prospects. An examination of the attitudes of Harvard law graduates by psychologist Matina Horner revealed that the women as a group had a considerably more negative image of a successful woman lawyer than the men. Moreover, the present generation of students exhibits more, not less, of this attitude than former generations did. Horner has also found that even girls in elite colleges demonstrate a powerful "motive to avoid success" in careers. It appears to arise from what they perceive as a conflict between career success and feminine identity.

There is evidence, indeed, that women who do well in male specialities tend to be a good deal more masculine in other respects than most women — they show, for example, less interest in marriage and children. A set of experiments carried out by psychologist Brian Sutton-Smith (now at Columbia) revealed that girls who are able to work out successful strategies in ticktacktoe — which is usually a male specialty — also display personality traits of an aggressive and domineering sort, more so even than boys who quickly get the hang of ticktacktoe.

In contrast to girls, boys will maintain and develop their early dissatisfactions and quarrelsomeness and their greater interest in "things." They will give their teachers more trouble and get lower grades through high school. They will tumble and wrestle more; they will instigate catastrophes involving blocks and toy cars, and ultimately real automobiles and real implements of war. Economic considerations aside, males will work more often than females for victory over others, for power, or for achievement in workmanship or intellect. When they work for approval it will often be for those peculiar forms called prestige or fame or glory. And no matter what level they attain, males will be less content with it than their female counterparts. In short, their drive and persistence and self-motivation are likely to be greater; and, psychological experiments show, they are likely to be spurred by competition and difficulty rather than discouraged by it as females tend to be.

Tests of particular mental abilities sometimes show striking disparities between the sexes. Only about one girl in twenty, for example, demonstrates the boys' average level of ability at mechanical aptitude or certain kinds of spatial reasoning, such as is required for solving mazes. And only one male in five equals the average female in ability to perform certain kinds of perceptual tasks involving accuracy and rapid shifts of attention in the face of monotony.

Among characteristics in which the sexes show the *smallest* differences is intelligence, as measured by ordinary I.Q. tests. One thing often overlooked, however, is that this indistinguishability is a deliberate artifact of the tests themselves. The test compilers, from Alfred Binet on, found that males tended to score better on certain kinds of test items, such as those calling for a wide store of information or for arithmetical or spatial reasoning. Girls, on the other hand, consistently excelled on items involving symbol manipulation (as in encoding) and recognition of similarities between different things. On virtually all standard I.Q. tests in use today, the mix of such items is deliberately adjusted to equalize the average male and female scores.

Beyond Nature versus Nurture

Despite wide agreement that differences exist, the social and behavioral sciences have been sharply — often emotionally — divided over whether the differences are biological or social in origin. "Science really hasn't answered the question of nature versus nurture," comments University of California psychologist Frank Beach, a long-time investigator of sex differences. "This probably means that the question has never been asked properly." But at least it is becoming clear that "nature versus nurture" is the wrong formulation. The current trend is away from contentions that sex differences are entirely attributable to nature *or* to nurture. What goes on, it appears, is a complex interaction between the two.

Until roughly a hundred years ago, scarcely anyone questioned the assumption that along with their obviously inherited bodily differences, the two sexes had inherited differences in temperament and intellect as well. But in the last decades of the nineteenth century there emerged a basic shift to the opposite view. Egalitarianism, coeducation, the feminist revolt, and the high achievements of women in male fields began chopping the ground out from under male claims to a God-given dominance and superiority. Pavlov's revealing experiments in the phenomenon of conditioning and the subsequent rise of the behavioral psychologists' views of the child as *tabula rasa* — the "blank slate" upon which over time the environment writes — led psychologists, anthropologists, sociologists, and popular opinion to view innate sex differences as insignificant and to emphasize cultural influences.

For a long time these views amounted to dogma. Frank Beach sums up the way things were: "When I was a graduate student in the early Thirties the problem of sex differences was extremely sensitive, as it is today. At that time the psychologists were all environmentalists, and it was simply unthinkable to say that the sexes could differ psychologically for any reason except conditioning. Nobody argued that a woman's size, general body formation, or reproductive anatomy were not strongly influenced by genetic factors. But the curtain dropped when it got to psychology, as though the brain, which controls behavior, was totally unaffected. I can recall getting scolded when I even raised the issue, because if you said that boys and girls differed, it seemed automatically to mean that one was inferior and the other superior. Even then tests were coming out showing that boys did better in math and girls did better in English, but if you ever suggested that this kind of thing had genetic origins at all it somehow suggested that girls were inferior. Why English should be inferior to math, I don't know."

By now, however, most adherents of the environmental explanation of sex differences have shifted away from older behaviorist ideas that externally imposed reward and punishment — i.e., approval or disapproval by parents or society — were the principal shapers of male or female personality. Now widely held is the "role modeling" theory, which stresses some sort of motivation in the individual to shape himself according to the society's prevailing stereotypes. Once a child begins to identify itself as male or female — that seldom happens before the age of eighteen months, psychologists think — it is driven to search the world around it for clues as to how to assemble a personality appropriate to its sex and culture. In effect, this need to establish an "identity" is akin to the innate and irrepressible drive to learn the culture's language.

Both science and common sense lead inescapably to the conclusion that some form of role modeling is a major shaper of personality. The roles of the sexes differ widely from one culture to another. Among the Tchambuli of New Guinea, the males are raised to be passive and emotionally dependent. Anthropologists who studied a large number of cultures found that in more than half of them the accepted role of women included doing practically all the heavy carrying. In some West African societies women control much of the commerce. Even modern nations show striking differences in the extent to which women do various kinds of work. In the U.S.S.R., for example, some 75 percent of the medical doctors are women.

The Beat of Inner Drums

Even so, any simple version of the role-modeling hypothesis faces certain logical difficulties that clearly point to limits in the malleability of the sexes. One problem, for instance, is that traits such as male aggressiveness or female verbal superiority display themselves at a very early age, presumably long before the child knows which parent to imitate. Similarly, it seems unlikely that, for example, male children are able to discern subtle differences in their parents' intellectual styles by the early age at which males begin to evidence signs of their superiority at spatial reasoning. So, while males and females need to respond to their culture's peculiar orchestration, they hear the beat of inner drums as well.

Two developments in the 1950's helped to breed a new industry of speculative writing about innate components of behavior. One was the flowering of ethology, the study of animal behavior. The other was the discovery in Africa of fossil remains indicating that man is a direct descendant of weapon-wielding, tool-using, ground-living, hunting primates whose emergence may date as far back as twenty million years or more. Putting together findings from these two areas of research, a number of scientists have concluded that much more of human behavior may have genetic roots than was previously imagined.

For the closest living analogues to mankind's

predecessors, scientists have looked to other primate species. Virtually all of the ground-dwelling primates have some sort of social structure in which the leaders are male. Because of their vulnerability to predators, baboons and rhesus and Japanese macaque monkeys appear to have evolved defensive cultures complete with intricate hierarchies of dominance and submission and considerable differentiation in sex roles and traits. In general, a groundling primate troop of whatever size has a single dominant leader (ethologists refer to him as the "alpha" male), with lesser males arrayed in a rank order beneath him. The male hierarchy favors organized action for the defense of the females and their young.

It is a notable aspect of these primate societies that the basic social format of each species is transmitted at least partly in the form of a genetic program, a program that permits a limited range of variations in behavior to accommodate changes in the environment. The definitive experiments have yet to be carried out, but there is suggestive evidence that if infant members of these "culture-forming" primates are placed together before they have had a chance to learn the society's norms, they will nevertheless eventually sort themselves into a fair copy of the social order characteristic of their species. Primate young also display behavioral sex differences that appear to be innate. Males are more aggressive and indulge more in playful sexual mounting. Females perform more "grooming" of other members and show more interest in still younger infants.

As a ground-dwelling primate, man must have received a good deal of genetic programming from many millions of years of hunting ancestors. Though wide variations in behavior patterns are evident in various cultures, there do appear to be quite a few cultural "universals" for the human species. The most obvious, probably, are male dominance and aggression and, of course, female nurturance, or maternalism. Despite much speculation in fable and feminist literature about ma-triarchal — i.e., female-governed — societies, there is no evidence that such have ever really existed. There have been, and are, quite a few "matrilineal" cultures, in which descent is reckoned by the blood line of the female, but even in these societies governance is largely or entirely a male domain.

Man, the Domesticated Animal

Those who emphasize innate sex differences often encounter the objection that it is useless or deluding to try to extrapolate from the etho-logical or fossil evidence to human behavior. "In general," cautions Frank Beach, "the higher you go on the evolutionary scale, the more behavior is determined by environmental factors and learning than by biological influence directly. Susceptibilities and predispositions may be genetic; complex behavior patterns are probably not."

The well-known ethologist, Konrad Lorenz, contends that humans are more closely analogous to domesticated animals than to wild animals. Usually, wild animals express their genetically transmitted behavior in direct, unambiguous ways. But in a state of domestication, those adaptations that were once necessary for survival in a perilous environment are gradually bred out or distorted or become dangerously inappropriate, as may be the case with the human will to violence.

Nevertheless, like many other ethologists, Lorenz believes that a large and perhaps dominant source of our behavior is genetic or instinctual. Even when it does not express itself in the complicated behavior patterns of lower species, it shows up in propensities, mainly as strong emotions — such as love, anger, maternalism, and probably yearnings to dominance or affiliation as well. Most of these propensities in humans, it is true, can be modified or overriden by cultural influences. But a persistent question keeps occurring to ethologists and psychiatrists: What are the costs — to the individual and to society — of overriding them? Do these costs, for example, include what in some instances we mean by neurosis?

Altered in the Womb

Major contributions to the understanding of sex differences have come from the field of endocrinology. Scientists have long known that sex hormones—the female hormones, such as progesterone and various estrogens, and the male hormones or androgens such as testosterone—must be involved in behavior. But prior to puberty, it is thought, roughly equal amounts of androgens and estrogens are present in the blood stream of male and female children alike, and this originally lent support to the role-modeling theorists' views that whatever differences in behavior were to be found in children must be due to learning.

Beginning in the 1950's, however, animal experiments have clearly shown that not only anatomical differences between males and females but also certain aspects of male and female behavior are determined prior to birth. In the late Fifties, for example, a group of University of Kansas scientists, including Charles Phoenix, Robert Goy, and the late William Young, injected female guinea pigs with small amounts of masculinizing hormone before birth and found that the animals' anatomical and behavioral futures could thereby be altered for all their lives. That is to say, these genetic females proceeded to develop not only the genitalia but also the mating behavior typical of males. Subsequent experiments have revealed that the same effects hold for animals higher than the guinea pig.

The fundamental organization of mammalian brains and bodies, it appears, is female first and only secondarily male, a reversal of the sequence assumed in the story of Adam and Eve. In human fetuses during the early stages of gestation, the brain of either sex possesses, in effect, the "blueprints" and latent neural circuits to develop and behave either as a female or a male. But if left hormonally alone, the fetus will always develop into a female. What happens in the case of males is that the male sex chromosome triggers a brief spurt of androgen from the fetal gonads. This spurt, in turn, somehow triggers a chain of chemical and organizational events that result in maleness. These include activating the neural circuits that will generate masculine behavioral propensities in the later presence of male hormones.

The female circuits, however, are not completely turned off; they continue to make a greater or lesser contribution to the behavior of even a "normal" male all through life. Experiments with rats, for instance, have shown that even a normal adult male rat can be induced to simulate female mating and maternal behavior by injections of hormones at certain sites in the brain. The reverse holds for females.

An Unhappy Bunch of Boys

Recent experiments reveal not only how the sex hormones influence the behavior of individual rhesus and macaque monkeys but also how the very composition of the monkey "culture" is partly subject to the hormonal balance of one or two individuals. These experiments were conducted at the Oregon Regional Primate Research Center near Portland, one of seven federally funded research centers set up in the U.S. to take experimental advantage of the kinship between monkeys and men. Psychologists Goy and Phoenix, who had taken part in the pioneering experiments at Kansas, are now at the Oregon center. They and several of their colleagues have altered the direction of development of fetal female monkeys by means of male hormone injections prior to birth. After birth these masculinized females behave more like males than females. That is to say, from infancy onward they indulge in much of the rough-and-tumble play and threatening grimaces of males of their species, as well as imitating the male-type infantile mating play.

It sometimes happens that by dint of sheer aggressiveness one of these masculinized females will work her way up to become the "alpha" individual in her troop. So far as human observers are able to judge, the members of these troops are quite happy with their unorthodox leaders. But the results of some other hormone experiments at the Oregon center have been less happy for the monkey communities involved. In one study, instead of masculinizing the fetus, a researcher has injected male hormones into normal females after birth but prior to puberty. These monkeys too become aggressive, and sometimes one emerges into alpha status. The day this happens is a dark one for the males; from that time on she absolutely prohibits her male subjects from playing their rough-and-tumble games or engaging in their mock-sexual play. "She makes the boys sit quietly in the corners," says Goy, "and they're obviously a very unhappy bunch of boys."

These experiments with guinea pigs, rats, and monkeys clearly signal that temperament is related to sex hormones. Recent research reveals that this is true of people too. At Johns Hopkins Hospital, for example, psychologists John Money and Anke Ehrhardt have investigated several varieties of human hermaphroditism—ambiguities in sexual development. Hermaphroditism occurs in a fetus because of some congenital inability of the cells to respond to sex hormones, or because of hormone therapy to the mother during pregnancy. Occasionally, therefore, a genetic male is born indistinguishable in infantile appearance from a female (though possessing no uterus and with internal testes in place of ovaries). Naturally, parents often unknowingly raise these infants as girls. Usually, these children grow up happily into women. They may like dolls, they often date boys, and they frequently marry. Though sterile, of course, they adopt children and display normal maternal affection.

Mysterious Programs

Initially, evidence of this kind was seen by some psychologists as support for the view that social upbringing was the all-important shaper of behavior. But later studies by Money and others now suggest a different interpretation: in the feminized-male hermaphrodite, the brain as well as the body has failed to receive the normal hormonal stimulation toward maleness. Support for this view comes from investigation of another form of hermaphroditism. It involves genetic females who because of therapy or a glandular malfunction are supplied before birth with excessive amounts of androgen-like substances after their ovaries and female internal reproductive organs are already formed, but before the external genitalia have stopped developing. In many such cases, surgery and hormone treatments can be employed early to bring about the development of a completely normal-appearing fertile female. But this intervention apparently comes too late to offset completely the effects on the brain. The girls often act more like boys than girls. They tend to display an unusual degree of interest in outdoor athletics, a preference for boys' toys instead of dolls, and even a pattern, in Money's words, of "giving priority to career over marriage or at least combining the two in future expectancies."

Very early in the development of any human being, the evidence suggests, the presence of minute amounts of one hormone or the other activates some as yet mysterious program that, together with later hormonal activity, will partly determine what kinds of experiences and social molding a given individual will tend to prefer, ignore, or reject. Some researchers go further and propose that differences in cognitive "style" between males and females are traceable to hormonal influences upon the central nervous system. Psychologists Donald and Inge Broverman, a husband and wife team who work at Worcester State Hospital in Massachusetts, draw upon a great deal of psychological and biochemical research in arguing the controversial hypothesis that such intellectual differences are due to the differential stimulating effects of male and female hormones upon different nervous subsystems.

Why Women Feel Hurt

The Brovermans maintain that estrogen increases the acuteness of many sensory perceptions. This may account for the observations reported by various researchers that females tend to show more acute hearing, taste, and tactile sense than males. By the same token, according to Broverman, this lower sensory threshold may also cause most women to hurt more under punishment, and to have a greater need than most men to avoid stressful situations. From an evolutionary standpoint this would make sense, for lower levels of fear and sensitivity to pain would be of benefit to males engaged in the rigors of hunt or combat.

The greater sensitivity of women leads Broverman to speculate that females can be conditioned more quickly to respond to stimuli than males. This might help explain some of the male puzzlement at the feminist contentions that our patriarchal society will not "let" women practice male pursuits and occupations. The explanation may be that women tend to respond to the conditioning pressures of society more acutely than do men.

Better Living through Chemistry?

The large and growing body of evidence of the existence of inborn differences in temperament between men and women does not deny the validity of feminist demands for changes in existing social arrangements. All aspects of society should be subject to re-examination and readjustment to ensure that all citizens enjoy the right to optimal development of their human potentialities. But Kate Millett was much too dolorous when she wrote: "If human sexual temperament is inherent, there is really very little hope for us."

Indeed, innate differences need not stand in the way even of the homogenized androgyny that some radical feminists call for. If that were what society really wanted, it might one day be possible to use hormone pills to make males and females think and behave very much alike. (A side effect might be to suppress women's menstrual cycle, which has pervasive debilitating effects. A British study reports, for example, that schoolgirls' performance on written examinations declines by roughly 15 percent during the few days prior to menstruation.) A more efficient approach to androgyny would be to intervene in the early stages of pregnancy when the male or female neural circuits were being activated. By means of hormone implantations or deletions in this period, it should be perfectly feasible to masculinize the female fetus or feminize the male. The society thus created would be undeniably androgynous, and—most people would agree—awful.

Short of such measures, education and social pressures could undoubtedly bring about a considerable narrowing of the differences between the roles of the two sexes. Several educational researchers have demonstrated that special encouragement can offset much of women's lack of interest or ability in certain kinds of creative problem solving. It also seems clear that social influences can reduce overt male aggressiveness.

Competing at Men's Own Games

It is far from clear, however, that the use of training and indoctrination to make the sexes behave more alike would foster optimal satisfaction for either males or females. Edward Zigler, formerly a psychologist at Yale and now director of the federal Office of Child Development, puts the matter this way: "All that behavior geneticists have taught us suggests that genetic variation is an important component in many of the male-female behavioral differences we observe. Perhaps many of these genetically influenced behavioral differences could be overridden through training, but only at some considerable psychological cost. I think that such a thing as being true to one's self makes sense genetically as well as making for a much more interesting society."

What does seem clear is that deliberate blindness toward the evidence of innate differences is likely to lead to greater strains and dissatisfactions among women—and men as well. So long as feminists measure their progress in terms of how well they as a class compete with men at men's own games, their cause is likely to be damaging to women's self-esteem. For there will always be fewer high-ranking jobs than there are people who want them, and society has found no effective—or fair—way of filling them except through some kind of competition. Individual women, of course, should be free to decide which of these kinds of games they want to play, as well as how hard. But given the psychological evidence on male needs for achievement, together with the female distractions of marriage and maternity, it seems likely that there will always be more men than women at the top.

On the other hand, the importance of men's special traits may be on the decline. Aggression, preoccupation with technology, even competitive ambition itself, seem to be counting for less and less as our society matures. Conversely, the especially feminine qualities of nurturance and concern for people may be assuming more importance in a society threatened with disintegration. If in their quest for a more androgynous world, feminists lop off the feminine end of the behavioral spectrum, the operation could well be fatal.

Moral Development

Cognitive theories of moral development claim a universal sequence.

Do moral principles really exist or are human ethics and morality nothing more than cultural habits imposed on the child by his parents and peers? Freudian theories of human development argue that moral development involves internalizing parental morals. Behavior theory assumes that morality is the search for pleasure and the avoidance of pain. Both these important theories of humans reject the possibility of universal ethical principles which go beyond individual cultures. Both regard ethics as relative to the particular cultural history of the individual child. Cognitive theories of moral development argue that all children, regardless of their particular cultural experiences, pass through the same sequence of moral stages and arrive at a universal moral understanding.

There are three factors involved in moral growth.

It is possible to reconcile these diverse views of morality if we assume that each theory only explains part of moral development. Suppose there are three factors involved in moral growth: ethical knowledge, feelings about ethical knowledge, and actions based on moral knowledge and ethical feelings. Within this scheme of moral behavior, cognitive theorists are concerned with ethical knowledge; Freudian theorists explain ethical emotions; and social learning theorists predict how humans react to their knowledge and feelings.

Many psychologists have studied moral knowledge.

MORAL KNOWLEDGE   Many developmental psychologists have studied the growth of moral knowledge. The most prominent theorists are John Dewey, J.M. Baldwin, Jean Piaget, and Lawrence Kohlberg (1971). For over a dozen years Kohlberg followed the development of moral knowledge among seventy-five boys in the U.S., and observed moral knowledge in other cultures as a comparison with his U.S. sample. Kohlberg's results suggest that all children pass through three stages of moral knowledge in a fixed, universal sequence that is independent of cultural teachings. These three major stages are:

1. *Preconventional* — the child is concerned with punishment or satisfying his own needs.
2. *Conventional* — the child is concerned with being good or enforcing the social order.
3. *Autonomy* — the child is concerned with the social contract or the possibility of universal moral principles.

Three stages of moral knowledge exist.

Figure 12.10 shows the age trends of these three stages among boys in the U.S. Note that Stage I knowledge is most frequent among boys during their early years; Stage II knowledge predominates in adolescence; and Stage III begins to make its appearance at maturity. Kohlberg found that only a small percentage of his samples ever attained the third stage of moral knowledge. He believes that happens because people are incapable of such complex moral understanding.

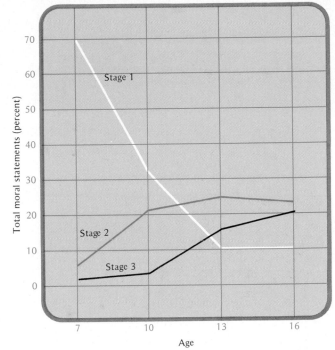

FIGURE 12.10
How three stages of moral development accompany certain ages of a child's life.
(After Kohlberg, 1963.)

Children base their moral judgments on moral knowledge.

Cognitive theorists of moral comprehension believe that children base their moral judgments on the highest current moral knowledge, but that children also make moral choices based on lower levels of understanding. For such theorists, children occasionally make judgments based on the next higher moral level as they continue to mature.

Many cultures show similar stages of moral development.

Kohlberg found that his three stages of moral knowledge occurred among children in Taiwan, Mexico, and Turkey, suggesting that the development of knowledge about morality is not based simply on the particular experiences of the individual child in his culture but is somehow inherent in all children. A study by Kohlberg and Ramer (1971) showed that the development of moral understanding is related to social class. More middle-class adolescent boys attain Stage II and III knowledge than their lower-class age peers. If all children must develop cognitive ability before they can understand abstract moral principles, then one would expect:

1. Universal age trends of morality.
2. That brighter people would attain higher stages of moral knowledge earlier.
3. That brighter, older people would ultimately attain a more complex morality than their duller or younger peers.

Freud argued that the feelings and emotions associated with moral

Punishment affects
resistance to tempta-
tion.

knowledge come out of early experiences between the child and his
parents. Freud believed that children identify with their same-sexed
parent, adopt the moral system of that parent, and then feel guilt whenever there is a discrepancy between the child's overt behavior and the
incorporated moral system. The parent's moral system becomes the child's
conscience, called his superego by Freud, as we have learned. The super-
ego monitors the child's every act and makes moral judgments of good
and bad about his behavior. When the child lives within the moral principles of his parent, the child feels good. But, when the child acts against
these moral principles, the child feels guilt. Recent research by Richard
Solomon, and others (1964) on the effect of punishment delay is related
to this theory. Solomon and his students exposed puppies to a choice
between horsemeat or canned dog food. Whenever a puppy approached
the horsemeat, he was swatted on the nose with a newspaper. Soon the
puppies learned to ignore the horsemeat and eat only the dog food. The
experimenters then presented each puppy with a choice between horsemeat and dog food while they were not present. Their measure of conscience or guilt was the amount of time it took the puppy to approach the
horsemeat.

Early punishment
produces more in-
hibition.

One of the things Solomon and his students studied was the relation
between *when* the puppy was hit on the nose, and his later resistance to
temptation. Some puppies were hit when they first approached the horsemeat, while others were allowed to eat before they were punished. The
puppies who were punished when they approached the horsemeat
waited longer before finally eating, but they enjoyed the meal when it
was finally consumed. In contrast the puppies who were punished only
after eating nearly all the meat approached it quickly, ate it, and then began
to show signs of tension or anxiety. Apparently, the choice is one of a
happy sinner, who feels bad after he has sinned, or an anxious moralist,
who feels fine after finally giving in to temptation.

Similar studies were run by Ross Parke (1967) using children, toys,
and loud noises. The results were remarkably similar. Early punishment
produced greater resistance to temptation and fewer feelings of anxiety
and guilt.

Moral knowledge and
moral behavior are
independent.

SHAME   We have discussed moral understanding and feeling, now let us
turn to moral behavior. Is there a strong association between the child's
cognitive understanding, emotions, and what he actually does in a tempt-
ing situation? Studies of moral acts show there is no relation between
moral thoughts, emotions, and acts. A massive study by Hartshorne and
May (1927) discovered that moral behavior is specific to the situation.
The cognitive and Freudian theories about morality cannot explain why
these situational changes in moral behavior happen. However, a social
reinforcement theorist like Skinner has no difficulty predicting situational
variations in morality. The social learning theory assumes that rewards

and punishments from the social environment determine ethical behavior. Skinner and others argue that social pressure and shame are most important for understanding morality.

Human ethics are complex.

Probably all three kinds of theories are needed to comprehend the complexity of human ethics. A Stage I child is probably most controlled by punishment and reward, and a Stage II child by guilt and peer pressure. Only the few who attain Stage III can be expected to govern their actions by universal moral principles.

Summary

Many theories of personal development exist. Some, like Eysenck's theory, emphasize genetic factors in development; others, like Skinner's, argue that reward and punishment control all of development; still others, like Freud's, assume that instinctive needs and social inhibitions jointly determine how a person will grow. There are several ways to measure personal development: by projective tests (like the Rorschach or the Thematic Apperception Test) and by more objective scales (like the Minnesota Multiphasic Personality Inventory). No matter how personal development is measured, two factors seem to appear in most development studies. One concerns how stable or emotional the person seems to be; the other factor concerns whether the individual is outgoing or withdrawn in social relations. Freud argued that personal development proceeds through several stages and that there are many challenges to maturity.

SUGGESTED ADDITIONAL READINGS

Kagan, J. and H.A. Moss. *Birth to Maturity*. New York: Wiley, 1962.

Miller, N.E., and J. Dollard. *Social Learning and Imitation*. New Haven, Conn.: Yale University Press, 1941.

Sears, R.R., E. Maccoby, and H. Levin. *Patterns of Child Rearing*. New York: Harper & Row, 1957.

Solomon, R.L. "Punishment," *American Psychologist*, Vol. 19 (1964), pp. 239-253.

13 Abnormal Development and Therapies

Causes of Abnormal Behavior
  Genetic Evidence
  Biochemical Evidence
  Environmental Theories
Neuroses
Childhood Disturbances
  Anxiety
  Phobias
  Obsessive/Compulsive Reactions
  Conversion Reactions
  Dissociation
  Hypochondria
  Depression
  Psychosomatic Problems
Personality Disorders
  Delinquency
Psychoses
  Schizophrenic Reaction

Childhood Autism and
  Schizophrenia
Affective Reactions
Organic Psychoses
Physiological Therapies
  Narcosis
  Shock Therapy
  Surgery
  Nutrition
  Drug Therapy
  Hospitalization
Individual Psychotherapy
  Freudian Psychoanalytic Therapy
  Behavior Modification
    Systematic Desensitization
    The Token Economy
Group Therapies
Evaluation of Therapies
Summary

PREVIEW

Even well-adjusted children are not always happy. Everyone experiences physical illness, social rejection, or loneliness sometime in their early years. Initial hereditary differences and later experiences give some children a head start toward happiness and point other, less fortunate children to a good deal of anxiety, withdrawal, or confusion. How can a parent or child tell if there is maladjustment? Probably not by looking into their own feelings, because self-diagnosis is often unreliable. Neither the mentally-ill parent nor the young child are accurate observers of their emotional balance. To decide whether someone is adjusted, there must be some objective criteria of happiness and there should also be an objective observer to decide about the degree of adjustment.

The most elementary criterion of adjustment is survival, but this is a very limited goal. Often, adjustment has been defined as the absence of distress, so if a child is not anxious, lonely, depressed, nor unhappy he is assumed to be maturing normally. More recently, clinical psychologists have argued that healthy adjustment should include achievement, zest for life, and compassion. It is unfortunate that not all children develop normally. Some children experience anxiety and fear, others simply feel apathy and despair. Chapter 13 covers some of the problems and outcomes of abnormal personal development.

Some authorities say
no behavior is
abnormal.

Is any behavior really abnormal? Some authorities say no (Laing, 1970). Not only is there cultural variation in what is considered normal or abnormal, but within the same culture we find class differences in what is designated as abnormal behavior. In the United States lower-class children are more likely to be labeled as psychotic, while those from the middle or upper class are more likely to be diagnosed as neurotic (*see* Figure 13.1). There are several possible explanations for these class differences:

1. The child-rearing practices and environmental deprivations of being poor dispose lower-class children toward psychoses.
2. The label assigned to a child's development may reflect ability to pay rather than behavior.
3. Psychotic behavior may be debilitating, so that seriously abnormal families automatically fall to the bottom of the social hierarchy.

No matter what the cause, mental illness is a serious problem among children and adults in the U.S.

How frequent are mental disorders? Surveys suggest that over one million adults occupy mental hospitals in the U.S.—more than for all other illnesses combined. One in every ten U.S. citizens is hospitalized for mental illness some time during his life. Are these statistics also true of children? Figure 13.2 shows that children's emotional problems are usually first recognized when they enter school, and children are more likely to receive treatment as they mature. In the case of adults one-quarter of all first admissions to public mental hospitals are labeled *schizophrenia*, which appears most often during early adulthood (twenty-five to thirty years) and is rarely fatal. This diagnostic category constitutes over half of

FIGURE 13.1
The relative rate of psychoses and neuroses as a function of social class. The most striking difference is that psychoses become much more frequent with lower-class status. (After Hollingshead and Redlich, 1958.)

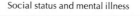

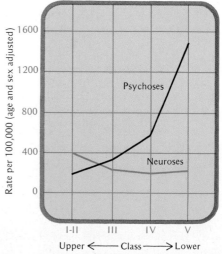

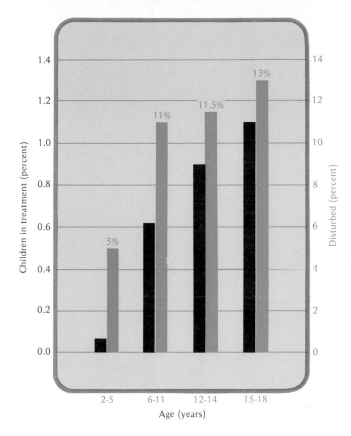

FIGURE 13.2
The number of children by age who
are in treatment for mental illness,
and the proportions of U.S. children
who are disturbed.

all mental hospital patients in the U.S. Another large group of mental
patients suffer from *senile diseases* of aging. By contrast, their death rate
is high, so they occupy only 15 percent of the available hospital beds. The
hospitalization rate for neuroses is low, because most neurotics remain at
home. Several surveys suggest that about one-third of the U.S. population
(children and adults) show neurotic symptoms that disturb their lives to
a significant degree, but are not serious enough to require institutionalization. Although there is some consensus about the major types of mental
illness, there is a growing debate among psychiatrists and psychologists
of what causes abnormal behavior. Some psychologists see abnormal behavior as the result of faulty learning, while others think mental illness is
a symptom of biological malfunction or that it is caused by genetic factors.
Let us consider these divergent theories.

Causes of Abnormal Behavior

There are three
theories about abnor-
mality.

Currently, three explanations of abnormality exist: genetic, biochemical, or environmental. The *genetic theory* implies that defective
genes are passed from parent to offspring. The *biochemical hypothesis*

assumes that genetic or environmental events produce biochemical defects which produce abnormal behavior. The *environmental position* argues that the social history of the individual determines his behavior—including his abnormalities.

Some babies are innately difficult to handle.

Two things are evident from recent studies of parent-child relations. Some babies are easy and others more difficult to handle from the day they are born; and most parents love their babies more after they receive positive feedback from the infant. These results suggest that babies train their parents at the same time the parents are training the child. Thus, some of the bizarre parent-child interactions found in the history of psychotic children may be the result of bizarre child behavior rather than its cause.

Genetic Evidence

Psychoses run in families.

There is strong indirect evidence that some psychoses are hereditary. Simple Mendelian genetic theory predicts that relatives of schizophrenic patients are more likely to become schizophrenic than the general population, and that the likelihood of relatives developing a psychosis increases with familial closeness (*see* Table 13.1; *also see* Table 10.1). The grandparents, cousins, nephews, and nieces of a schizophrenic patient are more likely to develop the disorder than the general population, but less likely to become afflicted with psychoses than are siblings of a psychotic. Children who have two schizophrenic parents are more likely to develop schizophrenia than children who have only one schizophrenic parent. Siblings and fraternal twins who have a schizophrenic brother or sister are less likely to develop the affliction than an identical twin of a schizophrenic. The observed frequencies of the incidence of schizophrenia as related to family members are somewhat different than those predicted by simple recessive Mendelian genetic theory. This means there may be recessive or dominant genes involved in susceptibility to the

TABLE 13.1 Similarity in various types of criminal, antisocial, and asocial behavior among twins

	Number of twin pairs	Identical	Fraternal	Proportion of similarity Identical	Fraternal
Adult Crime	225	107	118	71	34
Juvenile Delinquency	67	42	25	85	75
Childhood Behavior Disorder	107	47	60	87	43
Homosexuality	63	37	26	100	12
Alcoholism	82	26	56	65	30

Source: Adapted from H.J. Eysenck, *Crime and Personality* (Boston: Houghton Mifflin, 1964). Used by permission.

disease, and that environmental stress may be associated with the development of schizophrenia. Or it may be that psychoses are based on many genetic factors and that some of the genes are recessive. In any case, these data are strong indirect evidence for some genetic basis of schizophrenia.

Often heredity and environment are confused.

The fundamental problem with most genetic studies of schizophrenia is that the effects of heredity and environment are confused, as we have seen. The same parents who may pass on defective genes may also rear their child in such a way as to obscure the cause of the disorder. One way to separate the effects of heredity and environment is to study children separated from their parents at birth and reared in another family. If children born to schizophrenic parents are reared in nonschizophrenic adoptive homes and exhibit schizophrenic disorders far in excess of those exhibited by comparison with adopted children from biologically normal families, that would be strong evidence of an hereditary basis for schizophrenia uncomplicated by environmental factors.

Heston studied adopted children.

The most comprehensive study of adopted children from schizophrenic mothers was reported by L.L. Heston in 1966. Heston followed fifty-eight children born to schizophrenic mothers between 1915 and 1945 at the Oregon State Psychiatric Hospital. All apparently healthy offspring born of schizophrenic mothers were included in his study if the mother's record:

1. Specified a diagnosis of schizophrenia.
2. Contained sufficient description of thinking disorder or bizarre behavior to substantiate that diagnosis.
3. Contained negative test results for syphilis and no evidence of other diseases during pregnancy.
4. Showed that mother and child were separated at birth.

Heston found that adopted children of schizophrenic mothers often become schizophrenic.

All the experimental children were placed in a local foundling home within three days of birth. An equal number of comparison children were selected from the same foundling home, and they were matched with the experimental offspring of the schizophrenic mothers by sex, type of eventual placement, and length of time spent in the foundling home. The two groups were evaluated as adults with a personal interview, a Minnesota Multiphasic Personality Inventory, a Menninger Health-sickness Rating Scale, and an IQ test by two psychiatrists who were unaware of the subject's status in the study. Heston found statistically significant differences for the MHSRS scores, incidence of schizophrenia, number of years in penal institutions, and number of psychiatric discharges from the armed forces between the two groups of children. Eight of the experimental subjects exhibited schizoid personalities, while none of the control subjects did. These data show that schizophrenia is at least partly hereditary and not entirely the result of early parent-child interactions. Karlsson (1966) confirmed Heston's finding in another adoptive study of schizophrenia. His results showed that six of twenty-nine adopted children born to schizophrenic mothers developed schizophrenia, while no member of a matched comparison group showed schizoid signs. These studies represent the most conclusive evidence to date concerning the heritability of schizophrenia; they strongly imply that schizophrenia is partly caused by genetic factors.

Schizophrenia is probably a polygenic trait.

Several theories concerning the genetics of schizophrenia have been proposed. One theory assumes that a single recessive or dominant gene is responsible for the illness. However, the simple theories cannot be completely correct because the incidence rates found by F.J. Kallman (1953) and others do not agree with a single-gene theory. Schizophrenia does not show the 25 percent expectancy rate that a single-gene theory would predict among offspring of schizophrenic parents. A single-gene recessive theory predicts that all children of two schizophrenic parents should become schizophrenic, while the actual rates are around 65 percent. Also, by any single-gene theory, identical twins should show identical abnormal behavior, and this is not always the case. The best explanation for the incidence of schizophrenia is probably a multi-gene theory combined with some environmental effects. Schizophrenia is almost certainly genetically determined, but may be modified by environmental events.

Biochemical Evidence

Psychoses may result from biochemical defects.

Several experimenters have found that the blood of schizophrenic patients contains less of a substance called *glutathione* than does the blood of nonschizophrenics. Other studies show that if a substance called *daraxein* is extracted from the blood of schizophrenics and injected into monkeys or people it will produce abnormal brain waves and disorganized behavior. This does not happen when serum from normal human subjects is used. Thus, there seems to be some biochemical basis for psychotic behavior. Many people have speculated that schizophrenia results from a chemical failure in the central nervous system, probably due to an inherited deficiency. Children are not born with schizophrenic symptoms, but a particular part of schizophrenic children's central nervous systems are fragile and wear out relatively early or are stressed by anxiety and tension.

One explanation of psychoses involves competitive inhibition of enzymes.

When a person is angry or afraid, adrenalin is released and his heart rate goes up to make him ready for fight or flight. Once the emergency is over, the body is supposed to regain its normal activity level by rapidly neutralizing the adrenalin. This is done through an enzyme called *amine-oxydase,* which combines with adrenalin to deactivate it. But suppose this enzyme is already being used. Enzymes can be trapped by other molecules related in chemical structure to their true target. This phenomenon is called "competitive inhibition" and it can be serious. When an enzyme combines with a proper target molecule, it performs the reaction called for, and then moves on. But if an enzyme combines with an improper molecule, it may become permanently stuck, like a key broken off in a lock. The psychoticlike effects of adrenachrome and mescaline probably result from competitive inhibition, since these compounds are so similar to adrenalin that they tie up the enzyme which would normally neutralize adrenalin. The result is a build-up of adrenalin which leads to hallucination.

Body fluids of schizo-phrenic and normal persons differ.

Many scientists are exploring the blood and urine of schizophrenics trying to find unusual metabolic products. Using a technique called *paper chromatography* in which different molecules in body fluids are separated and allowed to precipitate on pieces of porous paper; several investigators have found differences in the urine of schizophrenic and non-schizophrenic patients. One difference turned out to be *dimethoxyphenyl-ethylamine,* whose chemical structure is similar to both adrenalin and mescaline. Some scientists think that schizophrenics have their adrenalin-destroying enzyme locked up, and that this contributes to the manifestation of the disease.

Environmental Theories

Many psychologists believe interpersonal relations produce psychoses.

A number of environmental theories have been proposed to explain the development of schizophrenia. They generally assume that distortions in the social or emotional environment of the family are the primary cause of schizophrenia. L. Kanner (1957) argued that the child becomes psychotic from impersonal parent-child relations and severe conflicts within the family. Several other psychologists suggest that abnormal communication patterns within the family are associated with schizophrenia. Laing and Esterson (1970) proposed that the behavior of a schizophrenic child even makes sense within this distorted communication system in a schizophrenic family, and that the schizophrenic child's behavior only appears bizarre when taken out of context.

One environmental theory is called the double bind.

Watzlawick, Beavin, and Jackson (1967) summarized a great deal of research and speculation about the causes of schizophrenia and concluded that psychotic development is associated with a family communication system in which the child is *told* he is loved, but is *treated* as if he is hated. According to this *double-bind* hypothesis, one or both parents continually confront the child with conflicting verbal and nonverbal messages and this discrepancy produces psychotic behavior. One problem with these environmental explanations is that the same abnormal communication system is used with other children in the same family, but these siblings often do not become psychotic.

Social stresses may interact with heredity.

The findings do not mean the environment is wholly innocent, because everyday stresses and strains (*see* Table 13.2) may well determine when and how serious a child's mental disability becomes. However, there is growing evidence that early environmental events are not as important in the development of psychoses as researchers once thought. Currently,

TABLE 13.2 Life change events which might occur to the average person. A total of around 150 is usual and totals over 350 are often associated with physical illness or psychological stress.

Stress	Values
Family	
Death of spouse	100
Divorce	73
Marital separation	65
Death of close family member	63
Marriage	50
Marital reconciliation	45
Major change in health of family	44
Pregnancy	40
Addition of new family member	39
Major change in arguments with wife	35
Son or daughter leaving home	29
In-law troubles	29
Wife starting or ending work	26
Major change in family get-togethers	15
Personal	
Detention in jail	63
Major personal injury or illness	53
Sexual difficulties	39
Death of a close friend	37
Outstanding personal achievement	28
Start or end of formal schooling	26
Major change in living conditions	25
Major revision of personal habits	24
Changing to a new school	20
Change in residence	20
Major change in recreation	19
Major change in church activities	19
Major change in sleeping habits	16
Major change in eating habits	15
Vacation	13
Christmas	12
Minor violations of the law	11
Work	
Being fired from work	47
Retirement from work	45
Major business adjustment	39
Changing to different line of work	36
Major change in work responsibilities	29
Trouble with boss	23
Major change in working conditions	20
Financial	
Major change in financial state	38
Mortgage or loan over $10,000	31
Mortgage foreclosure	30
Mortgage or loan less than $10,000	17

most authorities agree that the best prospect for a cure to psychoses probably derives from recent biochemical and genetic investigations. They point out that if the particular biochemical basis of abnormal behavior can be found, then chemical supplements or special diets may be developed to alleviate abnormal behavior.

Genetic counseling of schizophrenic couples could lead to a drop in the number of schizophrenic babies born each year. The issue is not settled, but the available evidence favors a genetic/biochemical theory of psychoses rather than a strictly environmental cause.

Neuroses

Hans Eysenck has argued that human personal development can be explained by the independent opposing dimensions which he called neuroticism-normality and introversion-extroversion. He also proposed that the child's position in this two-dimensional space (vertical and horizontal) is determined primarily by his genetic endowment, but that this can be modified to some extent by early experience. There are a number of childhood situations where neurotic processes may show up or be reinforced by parental handling. Among these are toilet training, eating, and sleeping. These important functions of the infant and young child can give early clues to later problems.

Childhood Disturbances

An early sign of an emotional problem may occur when a child encounters toilet training for the first time. Most children attain bladder and bowel control by two-and-one-half years of age, but occasionally they refuse training or regress to wetting (*enuresis*) or soiling (*encopresis*) because of emotional problems. Most clinical authorities agree that bedwetting more than once a week at four years of age should receive attention from a competent therapist. Enuresis is about twice as frequent among little boys as girls, and some clinicians believe that if bed-wetting is a boy's only problem, it may not be serious. If enuresis is accompanied by other problems—like an inability to control impulses, overaggressiveness, or disobedience—then the child certainly needs treatment. Psychoanalytic theories argue that enuresis is a sign of regression to an earlier mode of behavior and is usually caused by severe stress. Behavior theories argue that enuresis results from faulty learning. Behaviorists believe that a child with enuresis simply has not learned to pay attention to body cues about toilet habits and that a proper training schedule will solve the problem with little difficulty. O. Hobart Mowrer (1938) experimented with classical conditioning techniques and developed a machine which rang a bell whenever a few drops of urine were released by the child. Mowrer found that about 70 percent of all childhood cases of

Genetic counseling could reduce psychoses.

Eysenck proposed two dimensions of personality.

Early emotional problems may appear during toilet training.

enuresis could be helped with this device. However, enuresis is not the only toilet-training problem.

There are two kinds of toilet-training problems.

There are two types of bowel-training difficulties: Some children exhibit problems after toilet training is completed; while others never successfully control their bowel movements, and were usually given little or no training by their parents. Children who lose bowel control often experienced very severe training followed by emotional stress. These children understand that they alone can control the time and place of bowel movements, so if they want to resist their parents bowel control is one area where they have power. Some behavior theorists argue that the best way to handle toilet-training problems is to reward the child when he is cooperative and punish or ignore him when he is uncooperative. This regime works well with children who have had little previous toilet training. Psychoanalytic techniques of uncovering emotional conflicts and fears work more effectively in cases involving loss of toilet control after training.

Feeding can also produce problems.

Another area where problems can occur is feeding. Most babies have little trouble taking food, and it is only a rare baby who is starved. However, around two years of age a variety of feeding difficulties may appear. The most frequent is refusal to eat or vomiting of food after it has been swallowed. Freudian theorists argue that food rejection occurs at about two years of age because the child is beginning to invest the oral zone with important emotional content, so anything which upsets him at that time will be reflected as a feeding problem.

Overeating is another problem.

Another type of feeding disturbance is overeating. There is sharp disagreement among clinical psychologists about the causes of obesity. Psychological explanations of obesity and overeating stress the fact that feeding is a way to handle stress and compensate for parental rejection. Other scientists argue that constitutional factors, like heredity or the alteration of hormonal or neuronal factors, are the main causes of obesity.

Fear of eating can occur during puberty.

Fear of eating can be a serious problem during puberty, and is frequent among young females who are frightened by sexual maturity. Apparently they come to believe that if they do not eat, they will not mature and be forced to face the problems associated with sexual maturation. In families where there is conflict between parents and children, refusal to eat is one way the child can strike back at his parents. Since most parents show serious concern over a child's rejection of food, the child may continue not eating so that he can manipulate his parents.

Some children have difficulty sleeping.

In addition to toilet training and eating, a third early problem area concerns sleeping. If a child's sleep is regularly disturbed by nightmares, restlessness, or *night terrors,* he has serious problems. All children occasionally resist going to bed because they are excited or believe they may miss something important. That type of sleep avoidance is not serious. The best way to avoid serious sleep problems is for the parent to begin a regular nap and sleep program, and stick to it without much variation. If children still experience nightmares, then professional consultation is advised. Children who experience nightmares are more suggestible, show greater fearfulness, and have a higher incidence of eidetic imagery (*see* Chapter 4) than a comparable clinical population without sleep disturbances. The main treatment for sleep problems is to uncover latent fears through free association. A new sleep schedule can also be established by retraining the child.

Consider next the problems associated with later development—neuroses, psychoses, and personality deviations.

Childhood and adolescent mental illness may take the form of severe anxiety, irrational fears of objects or events, obsessive thoughts or compulsive acts, hysterical illnesses with no physiological cause, loss of memory, excessive worry about health or death, and depression which can lead to suicide.

Neurotic childhood behavior is uncomfortable and sometimes bizarre, but it is not often serious enough to require hospitalization. Life for the neurotic child is difficult, and is an emotional strain on his family. If neurotic behavior is so distressing to children and their parents, why is it so difficult to change? Some psychologists believe neurotic behaviors persist in the face of pain and fear because the abnormal acts relieve the unfortunate child of even greater pain and fear. Consider a young child who becomes deaf or paralyzed at the thought of attending school. He is temporarily deaf or helpless to move, but at the same time he escapes the more dreadful fear of leaving his home and attending a competitive school. Neurotic problems afflict many children during their early lives. The most frequent single type of neurosis is anxiety or fear of the unknown.

Anxiety

According to Sigmund Freud, many childhood and adult neuroses are caused by repressed fear. Freud believed that once fear is repressed it becomes unconscious, and then the child does not know why he is anxious, yet his fears persist. Anxiety may take the form of worry, depression, mood swings, physical illness, headaches, or tension. The source of much early anxiety is repressed hostility, Freud believed, and he and his followers theorized that when forbidden feelings of anger threatened to reappear in the child's consciousness, a sense of doom overcame the child. Freud argued that neurotic anxiety is similar to the fear a child would feel in response to a real threat, except that the child has no notion of why he is afraid and has no idea of how to escape from or handle his anxiety. Anxious children are often taken to visit a physician, who usually cannot find anything physically wrong with the child. He may then prescribe a tranquilizing drug or an inactive *placebo* (a sugar-coated "pill" without actual medication) to relieve the parents' concerns.

Anxiety can be a serious problem in childhood.

Neuroses may relieve immediate anxiety.

Freud believed that neuroses are caused by repressed fear.

Fear is a natural
emotion.

Fear is a natural reaction to danger and is a common part of the young child's life. Studies by Arthur Jersild (1933) showed that most children are seriously concerned about their fears. Jersild and his colleagues reported that early childhood fears are of immediate things, like large dogs and strangers; while in later childhood these same children expressed fears of more remote events like ghosts, witches, or sharks. The investigators also found that rational treatment of fears by explanation—ghosts do not exist; sharks only live in the water—are not likely to change the child's fears. Jersild believes that the child's fear is based on irrational associations, rather than rational facts; and he proposes a direct approach to the child's fear of parental punishment or rejection as most likely to be successful.

Phobias

Sometimes children
fear strange things.

When children attach their fears to particular objects or events, they exhibit a phobia. The particular object or event the child fears may be harmless or dangerous, but it is very unlikely that he will encounter it. Sometimes the phobic object has a symbolic association with unconscious neurotic conflict. If a child's conflict concerns hostility, his phobia may be of guns or knives.

There are many differ-
ent phobias.

There are several common phobias. *Claustrophobia* is a strong fear of small enclosed rooms; *acrophobia* is a fear of high places; *nyctophobia* is fear of the dark; and *zoophobia* is irrational fear of animals. Phobias enable the neurotic child to handle his internal conflict by externalizing the fear to an improbable object or event. If he can avoid the feared object, he can avoid the associated terror.

The most common is
school phobia.

The most common fear among children is *school phobia*. This phobia, characterized by a morbid dread of school, is much more common among girls than boys. Most clinical psychologists believe that school phobia is caused more by parent-child separation anxieties—which are often shared by the parent—than by fear of school itself. Specifically, the child is afraid of leaving home and entering school, but the parent is threatened by loss of the child's dependency through teacher and peer influences. Another source of school phobia is the school's possible threat to the parent's and child's self-concepts. The school is a competitive situation in which the child is compared with his peers and judged on his performance. School competition and evaluation may threaten a child's unrealistic self-concept and it may also threaten the parents if they encourage the child's unrealistic self-evaluation.

Another common
phobia is of death.

Another common phobia among children is fear of death. This particular phobia is most frequent among eight-year-old children. Both Freud and Piaget suggest that at around eight there is a mental and emotional transformation during which the child develops a whole new set of cognitive and emotional abilities. As a result he can appreciate possibilities and problems which were not available to him before. With this increased ability to appreciate, Piaget and Freud argue that the child comes to fear dying because he can begin to appreciate what death means. Actual experience with death does not seem to be necessary for the child to develop a death phobia, although the death of a relative may trigger the fear.

Psychologists believe phobias are learned.

Many U.S. psychologists believe that phobias are learned. Behaviorists point out that fear may be connected to new objects by repeated association of painful events and previously neutral stimuli. Following such repeated association, the previously neutral event automatically brings forth fear. These psychologists point out that learned fears can be overcome by counterconditioning or extinction. *Counterconditioning* involves doing something pleasant in the presence of the fearful situation; while extinction requires that the child experience his fear over and over without accompanying pain. Thus, the learning theorist believes most phobias can be overcome.

Phobias may be a bargain.

Freudian theorists believe that phobias are a bargain. They think that the neurotic whose fear is directed toward one specific object can overcome his anxiety by avoiding that one object, so most of the time he functions well because the fearful object is rare. The evidence suggests that some phobias can be overcome by counterconditioning or extinction; but the specific causes of phobias are still unknown.

Obsessive/Compulsive Reactions

Obsessive-compulsive problems are related to sex or hostility.

Obsessive/compulsive problems are the next most frequent type of neurosis after phobias. *Obsessions* are things a child can't stop remembering, while *compulsions* are an irresistible urge to perform a ritualistic act again and again. Obsessive thoughts often concern aggression in the child or sex in the adolescent. The obsessive child may continually think about pushing his mother down the stairs or drowning his brother, while the obsessive adolescent may imagine walking naked in the street or raping his sister. Freudian psychoanalysts believe that compulsive acts are performed to counteract and rid oneself of these unacceptable impulses. Washing the guilt off one's hands or locking the sin outside the door are common compulsions among children and adolescents. Obsessive thoughts are usually disturbing, while compulsive acts are often absurd.

Obsessive-compulsive children are afraid of impulses.

The obsessive/compulsive child may be so overwhelmed by his impulses and defenses against these feelings that he cannot concentrate on normal development. Some psychologists believe that obsessive/compulsive children can be helped by emotional insight or awareness of why he does or says such things. They point out that the obsessive/compulsive child is usually inhibited and afraid of his impulses. Giving him insight into his conflict and acceptance of his emotional impulses of hate or sex can help relieve the symptoms.

Portrait

Sigmund Freud was born in Moravia, now part of Czechoslovakia, in 1856, and spent his professional life in Vienna. He entered the University of Vienna at seventeen to study biology, physiology, and medicine. Freud received his M.D. in 1881, and reluctantly entered private practice as a clinical neurologist in order to support himself. During the course of his life Freud initiated a revolution in psychological thought. His theories grew from observing and treating neurotic patients, and his theory of unconscious conflicts changed people's minds about rationality and emotion.

Freud's training in neurology and medicine gave him a strong scientific background. His early work concerned the anesthetic properties of cocaine and created a minor scandal when he prescribed the drug for his friends. Later, he performed several experiments on nerve impulses.

Freud's main interest became psychological paralysis and neurotic anxiety. He witnessed a demonstration of hypnosis by the French neurologist, Jean Martin Charcot, and immediately tried it on his own patients. It didn't cure them, but, in the course of his studies with hypnosis, Freud discovered that his patients could recall events, fears, and desires from their childhood that they were unable or unwilling to experience while awake. Freud concluded that unconscious memories of early conflicts or traumas could cause neurotic behavior. Earlier, Wilhelm Wundt and William James had defined psychology as the science of human consciousness, but Sigmund Freud showed that unconscious processes are also part of man's character and personality.

Freud left Vienna for England when the Nazis took control of Austria before World War II. He died there in 1939.

The founder of psychoanalysis, Freud regarded sexuality as a primary motivating factor in human behavior. Among his most important works are *The Interpretation of Dreams* (1909), *Totem and Taboo* (1918), and *The Ego and the Id* (1927).

Freud's concepts of the id, the ego, and the superego, and his division of a child's early years into psychosexual stages of development have widely influenced the thinking of twentieth-century theorists in the Western world—even when they disagree violently with him. In addition, Freud's work strongly affected much of our contemporary art and literature.

Sigmund Freud, who first formulated many of the theories of psychoanalysis. (Courtesy of Mrs. E. L. Freud)

Anxiety is an affective state—that is to say, a combination of certain feelings in the pleasure-unpleasure series with the corresponding innervations of discharge and a perception of them, but probably also the precipitate of a particular important event, incorporated by inheritance—something that may thus be likened to an individually acquired hysterical attack. The event which we look upon as having left behind it an affective trace of this sort is the process of birth, at the time of which the effects upon the heart's action and upon respiration characteristic of anxiety were expedient ones. The very first anxiety would thus have been a toxic one. . . . There is a distinction between realistic anxiety and neurotic anxiety, of which the former was a reaction, which seemed intelligible to us, to a danger—that is, to an expected injury from outside—while the latter was completely enigmatic, and appear to be pointless.

We . . . turned to neurotic anxiety . . . under three conditions. We find it first as a freely floating, general apprehensiveness, ready to attach itself temporarily, in the form of what is known as 'expectant anxiety', to any possiblity that may freshly arise—as happens, for instance, in a typical anxiety neurosis. Secondly, we find it firmly attached to certain ideas in the so-called 'phobias', in which it is still possible to recognize a relation to external danger but in which we must judge the fear exaggerated out of all proportion. Thirdly and lastly, we find anxiety in hysteria and other forms of severe neurosis, where it either accompanies symptoms or emerges independently as an attack or more persistent state, but always without any visible basis in an external danger. We then asked ourselves two questions: 'What are people afraid of in neurotic anxiety?' and 'How are we to bring it into relation with realistic anxiety felt in the face of external dangers?'

For we consider that what is responsible for the anxiety in hysteria and other neuroses is the process of repression. We believe it is possible to give a more complete account of this than before, if we separate what happens to the idea that has to be repressed from what happens to the quota of libido attaching to it. It is the idea which is subjected to repression and which may be distorted to the point of being unrecognizable; but its quota of affect is regularly transformed into anxiety—and this is so whatever the nature of the affect may be, whether it is aggressiveness or love. It makes no essential difference, then, for what reason a quota of libido has become unemployable: whether it is on account of the infantile weakness of the ego, as in children's phobias, or on account of somatic processes in sexual life, as in anxiety neurosis, or owing to repression, as in hysteria. Thus in reality the two mechanisms that bring about neurotic anxiety coincide.

In the course of these investigations our attention was drawn to a highly significant relation between the generation of anxiety and the formation of symptoms—namely, that these two represent and

Sigmund Freud, "The Nature of Anxiety" from *New Introductory Lectures on Psychoanalysis* (New York: W.W. Norton & Company, 1965), pp. 81-94.

replace each other. For instance, an agoraphobic patient may start his illness with an attack of anxiety in the street. This would be repeated every time he went into the street again. He will now develop the symptom of agoraphobia; this may also be described as an inhibition, a restriction of the ego's functioning, and by means of it he spares himself anxiety attacks. We can witness the converse of this if we interfere in the formation of symptoms, as is possible, for instance, with obsessions. If we prevent a patient from carrying out a washing ceremonial, he falls into a state of anxiety which he finds hard to tolerate and from which he had evidently been protected by his symptom. And it seems, indeed, that the generation of anxiety is the earlier and the formation of symptoms the later of the two, as though the symptoms are created in order to avoid the outbreak of the anxiety state. This is confirmed too by the fact that the first neuroses of childhood are phobias — states in which we see so clearly how an initial generation of anxiety is replaced by the later formation of a symptom; we get an impression that it is from these interrelations that we shall best obtain access to an understanding of neurotic anxiety. And at the same time we have also succeeded in answering the question of what it is that a person is afraid of in neurotic anxiety and so in establishing the connection between neurotic and realistic anxiety. What he is afraid of is evidently his own libido. The difference between this situation and that of realistic anxiety lies in two points: that the danger is an internal instead of an external one and that it is not consciously recognized.

In phobias it is very easy to observe the way in which this internal danger is transformed into an external one — that is to say, how a neurotic anxiety is changed into an apparently realistic one. In order to simplify what is often a very complicated business, let us suppose that the agoraphobic patient is invariably afraid of feelings of temptation that are aroused in him by meeting people in the street. In his phobia he brings about a displacement and henceforward is afraid of an external situation. What he gains by this is obviously that he thinks he will be able to protect himself better in that way. One can save oneself from an external danger by flight; fleeing from an internal danger is a difficult enterprise.

I hope you have not lost the thread of what I am saying and remember that we are investigating the relations between anxiety and repression. In the course of this we have learnt two new things: first, that anxiety makes repression and not, as we used to think, the other way round, and [secondly] that the instinctual situation which is feared goes back ultimately to an external situation of danger. The next question will be: how do we now picture the process of a repression under the influence of anxiety? The answer will, I think, be as follows. The ego notices that the satisfaction of an emerging instinctual demand would conjure up one of the well-remembered situations of danger. This instinctual cathexis must therefore be somehow suppressed, stopped, made powerless. We know that the ego succeeds in this task if it is strong and has drawn the instinctual impulse concerned into its organization. But what happens in the case of repression is that the instinctual impulse still belongs to the id and that the ego feels weak. The ego thereupon helps itself by a technique which is at bottom identical with normal thinking. Thinking is an experimental action carried out with small amounts of energy, in the same way as a general shifts small figures about on a map before setting his large bodies of troops in motion. Thus the ego anticipates the satisfaction of the questionable instinctual impulse and permits it to bring about the reproduction of the unpleasurable feelings at the beginning of the feared situation of danger. With this the automatism of the pleasure-unpleasure principle is brought into operation and now carries out the repression of the dangerous instinctual impulse.

The theory of the instincts is . . . our mythology. Instincts are mythical entities, magnificent in their indefiniteness. In our work we cannot for a moment disregard them, yet we are never sure that we are seeing them clearly. You know how popular thinking deals with the instincts. People assume as many and as various instincts as they happen to need at the moment — a self-assertive instinct, an imitative instinct, an instinct of play, a gregarious instinct and many others like them. People take them up, as it were, make each of them do its particular job, and then drop them again. We have always been moved by a suspicion that behind all these little *ad hoc* instincts there lay concealed something serious and powerful which we should like to approach cautiously. Our first step was modest enough. We told ourselves we should probably not be going astray if we began by separating two main instincts or classes of instincts or groups of instincts in accordance with the two great needs—hunger and love. However jealously we usually defend the independence of psychology from every other science, here we stood in the shadow of the unshakable biological fact that the living individual organism is at the command of two intentions, self-preservation and the preservation of the species, which seem to be independent of each other, which, so far as we know at present, have no common origin and whose interests are often in conflict in animal life. Actually what we are talking now is biological psychology, we are studying the psychical accompaniments of biological processes. It was as representing this aspect of the subject that the 'ego-instincts' and the 'sexual instincts' were introduced into psychoanalysis. We included in the former everything that had to do with the preservation, assertion and magnification of the individual. To the latter we had to attribute the copiousness called for by infantile and perverse sexual life. In the course of investigating the neuroses we came to know the ego as the restricting and repressing power and the sexual trends as the restricted and repressed one; we therefore believed that we had clear evidence not only of the difference between the two groups of instincts but also of the conflict between them. The first object of our study was only the sexual instincts, whose energy we named 'libido'. It was in relation to them that we sought to clarify our ideas of what an instinct is and what is to be attributed to it. Here we have the libido theory.

And here, at an unexpected point, we have emerged from the psychical underworld into the open market-place. I cannot lead you any further, but before I take leave of you for to-day I must detain you with one more train of thought. It has become our habit to say that our civilization has been built up at the cost of sexual trends which, being inhibited by society, are partly, it is true, repressed but have partly been made usable for other aims. We have admitted, too, that, in spite of all our pride in our cultural attainments, it is not easy for us to fulfil the requirements of this civilization or to feel comfortable in it, because the instinctual restrictions imposed on us constitute a heavy psychical burden. Well, what we have come to see about the sexual instincts, applies equally and perhaps still more to the other ones, the aggressive instincts. It is they above all that make human communal life difficult and threaten its survival. Restriction of the individual's aggressiveness is the first and perhaps the severest sacrifice which society requires of him. We have learnt the ingenious way in which the taming of this unruly thing has been achieved. The institution of the super-ego which takes over the dangerous aggressive impulses, introduces a garrison, as it were, into regions that are inclined to rebellion. But on the other hand, if we look at it purely psychologically, we must recognize that the ego does not feel happy in being thus sacrificed to the needs of society, in having to submit to the destructive trends of aggressiveness which it would have been glad to employ itself against others. It is like a prolongation in the mental sphere of the dilemma of 'eat or be eaten' which dominates the organic animate world. Luckily the aggressive instincts are never alone but always alloyed with the erotic ones. These latter have much to mitigate and much to avert under the conditions of the civilization which mankind has created.

Conversion Reactions

Conversion reactions have no physiological basis.

Conversion reactions are physical symptoms which have no physiological basis. The symptoms may be sensory (such as blindness), motor (paralysis in a limb), or visceral (choking, sneezing, hiccuping, nausea, or coughing). The hysterical child handles his anxiety by converting it into a physical symptom. He is not simply shirking; in fact, he often shows almost complete loss of pain sensitivity. Conversion reactions allow a child to avoid anxiety by letting him escape difficult situations, and at the same time they gain parental attention. Most hysterical symptoms are inconsistent with medical facts, and so are fairly easy for a physician to differentiate from real ailments. Unless the hysterical child has studied anatomy, his loss of feeling will not correspond with neural pathways. No physical damage is present in hysteria and such symptoms usually disappear under hypnosis. In emergencies the hysteric will recover and escape. If his house is burning, a paralyzed hysterical child will manage to get out the door.

Conversion reactions can be a cry for help.

Many clinical psychologists believe that conversion reactions are both a cry for help and a way out of emotional conflict. They think the child who develops a conversion reaction is emotionally immature and has been reinforced in the past for using physical symptoms to obtain love and avoid anxiety.

Dissociation

Dissociative reactions can produce amnesia.

Dissociative reactions occur when a part of the personality splits off and produces such symptoms as amnesia or multiple personality. The child suffering from amnesia may not know his own name, where he is, who his parents are, or what he has been doing for the past several hours. Amnesia can be caused by brain injury or emotional conflict. Brain damage usually produces a permanent loss of memory, while repressed thoughts are not forgotten but are simply blocked from the child's awareness.

Another outcome of dissociation is multiple personality.

Another possible outcome of dissociation is multiple personality. The Freudian psychoanalyst believes dissociation develops when unacceptable impulses are compartmentalized by the child into a second self and find expression only through that second personality. The fictional case of Dr. Jekyll and Mr. Hyde—in which one personality was good, the other evil—is an example of multiple personality. Personality switches can occur during sleep or following an emotional upset. Psychoanalysts believe multiple personality begins when socialization is so complete that all overt aggressive or later sexual impulses are stifled. Analysts theorize that the only way such a child can express his natural impulses is through the second self.

Hypochondria

The hypochondriac is obsessed with illness.

It is quite normal for parents to be concerned about a child's physical illness, but neurotic children often worry excessively about their health. When every minor discomfort or pain becomes exaggerated, natural worry has turned into hypochondriasis. The *hypochondriac* child derives satisfaction from his symptoms, and may carry his neurosis to the point of excessive visits to the doctor and even unneeded surgery.

Depression

Depression is a serious mental problem.

Depressed children are sad for no obvious reason. They are unable to concentrate; lack self-confidence; are bored, irritable, and often can't sleep (*see* Table 13.3). The Freudian theory of *depression* argues that it results from unexpressed hostility turned inward. The child blames himself for his problems and is overwhelmed by self-doubt and self-hate. Depression can even bring on attempted suicide, although most children don't try to kill themselves but express their need for help. Suicide is a risk primarily for older persons. More than one thousand adults in the U.S. kill themselves every day—about one-half million a year. More than eight times that number try to commit suicide. Age, sex, and race are all related to suicide rate (*see* Figure 13.3). White males over fifty-five are most self-destructive, while nonwhite females have the lowest incidence of suicide. Freedom and responsibility seem to be associated with a higher suicide rate. Suicide occurs most often in the Spring, in the late afternoon, on a Monday, and at home.

Suicide is difficult to stop.

Can a potential suicide be stopped? Sometimes. The most successful tactic at this time is a suicide-prevention center. However, these systems rely on the suicidal person calling for help. To really prevent self-destruction a way must be found to identify potential suicides. In theory, identification of potential suicides is not that difficult, because people give many signals before they make such an attempt. The two most important signs are depression and talk of self-destruction. The practical

TABLE 13.3 Four sets of characteristics which signal serious depression in children.

1. Motivational-Emotion

    Dejection
    Crying
    Self-hate
    Lack of motivation

2. Cognitive

    Suicidal thoughts
    Indecisive
    Low self-image

3. Physiological

    Loss of appetite
    Sleeplessness
    Constipation

4. Appearance-Behavior

    Slow speech
    Gloomy
    Stooped posture

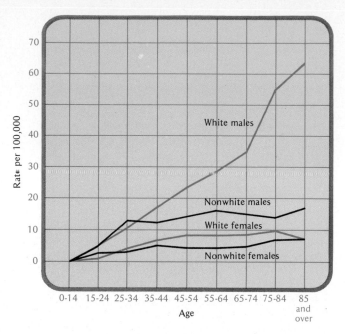

FIGURE 13.3
The suicide rate separated by sex, age, and ethnic group. The startling finding is the extraordinary increase in suicide among white males in the United States. (After Maris, 1969.)

problem is how to contact such people at frequent intervals and persuade them to seek personal help when the first signs of depression appear. Invasion of privacy and cost are two problems in making such a widespread survey.

Psychosomatic Problems

Emotional problems can cause physical illness

Another way the child may channel his fears and feelings into physical symptoms is through psychosomatic illness. Some psychologists believe that if the child's normal emotional processes are blocked, serious physical illness can result in later life. They point out that repressed hostility or fear can keep the child's autonomic nervous system in constant turmoil, and they think that continued autonomic activation may produce gastrointestinal disturbances in the child.

Neuroses result from heredity, severe socialization, and fear.

Clinical psychologists believe that the child's neurotic problems are caused by his particular genetic makeup plus too much socialization and fear. The result is strong emotion felt but overcontrolled. By contrast, psychopathic personalities are characterized by lack of self-control and emotions. These psychopathic children are more dangerous to society.

Personality Disorders

Delinquency

The psychopath feels little guilt.

The child delinquent or psychopath feels little guilt; forms few intimate personal bonds; is irresponsible, emotionally shallow, self-centered, and often gets into trouble with the law. He cannot tolerate frustration, shows poor judgment, and is often impulsive. Some psychologists believe that psychopathy can be inherited. These theorists point to the occurrence of abnormal chromosomal structures in criminals, for example (XXY instead of XY), and the fact that criminality runs in families—although this could also be due to environment. Other authorities argue that early emotional deprivation produces psychopathy. They theorize that an absent or hostile father and an indulgent mother can produce a psychopathic child who will mature into a criminal adult.

Psychopaths lack emotional responsiveness.

There is some evidence that delinquents differ from others in emotional responsiveness. If such children have been emotionally deprived, a difference in emotional reaction could easily result. The delinquent child's autonomic nervous system is much less reactive than the average child's in a tension-producing situation, and delinquent children show little concern about their futures—perhaps because it is so uncertain.

Delinquents often come from broken homes.

Early studies of delinquent children originated in the Chicago juvenile courts, where it was found that their family backgrounds were marked by marital discord or family disintegration. Homes broken as a result of divorce, death, separation, or desertion were twice as frequent among delinquent children as in the nondelinquent population. Families of delinquents also physically punished their children more often. Boys reared by a passive father do not become delinquent, possibly because imitation of a timid, withdrawn father produces a timid, withdrawn boy. Delinquent boys, in contrast, are reared by hostile fathers and indulgent mothers, and their family lives often include immorality, cruelty, alcoholism, and parental quarreling. A more disturbed family background is required to produce a delinquent girl than a delinquent boy. Disruptive factors occur twice as often in the homes of delinquent girls, for example, and female delinquency is associated more often with parental immorality, sexual molesting of the female child, and parental drunkenness. Male delinquency is generally related to parental hostility. Delinquent girls most often commit sexual offenses, like prostitution, when they mature; while delinquent boys are more likely to be involved in violent crimes like robbery or murder when they are adults.

No one knows how to cure delinquency.

Not only is there little agreement about the causes of juvenile delinquency but no one is sure about how to handle the problem. Should the juvenile delinquent be put in prison or in a hospital for rehabilitation? What is the effect of placing young offenders in jail or reform school or on probation? The outcome often seems to be a more skilled criminal rather than rehabilitation. No one has a workable solution to this problem at the moment. Often the sentence is based on the delinquent's ability to differentiate between right and wrong. U.S. laws concerning mental disorders and criminality are based on the English McNaughten decision of 1834, in which a Scotsman suffered paranoid delusions and thought the Prime Minister of England was out to kill him. In retaliation, he killed the Prime Minister's secretary and tried to assassinate the Prime Minister himself. The English court judged that McNaughten was insane, so it committed him to a mental hospital instead of putting him to death for murder. Thus, English law evolved the notion that a defendant may be considered *not guilty* by reason of insanity if he is so severely disturbed that he does not know what he was doing or could not know his act was wrong. Some psychologists, psychiatrists, and criminologists think that mere knowledge of right and wrong is too narrow an interpretation of insanity, but the problem of legal responsibility is complex. What about the rights of society to be protected from insane criminals?

Psychoses

Psychoses are serious mental problems.

Beyond childhood neuroses and personality problems is a third class of abnormal behaviors called psychoses, which are the most serious mental abnormalities that afflict children and adults. Some theorists argue that psychotic reactions are simply variations in the intensity of abnormal behavior, while others point out that the history and outcome of neuroses and psychoses are very different (*see* Figure 13.4). In any case, psychoses are very serious mental health problems.

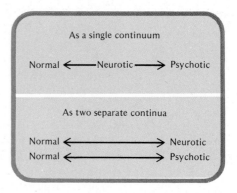

FIGURE 13.4
Some psychologists believe that neuroses and psychoses are different degrees of a single disorder; while others believe that neuroses and psychoses represent two distinct disorders.

Neurotic children improve much more often than do psychotic children.

Neurotic children certainly improve in mental health much more often than psychotic children do. A neurotic child may be tense and anxious, but he is still attempting to cope with life; while the psychotic child has often given up. Psychotic children and adults are characterized by a collection of symptoms which place them in serious psychological trouble. There is strong indirect evidence that genetic factors predispose some children toward developing psychotic reactions, particularly when these predispositions are triggered by emotional stress, as we have seen in the case of schizophrenia. Yet some therapists believe psychoses are caused exclusively by traumatic early childhood experiences. This controversy is by no means settled.

The psychotic child is typically withdrawn and does not respond to his surroundings; his thought processes and communications are dis-

Psychotic children are withdrawn.

torted; and he often experiences images which have no sensory base, and may hold to ideas which have no foundation in fact. Psychotic children are egocentric and often autistic. The classification of psychoses is complicated, although most authorities agree there are at least three kinds:

1. Schizophrenic reaction.
2. Affective reaction.
3. Organic psychoses.

Schizophrenic Reaction

There are five kinds of schizophrenic reactions.

Schizophrenic reaction includes severe emotional, intellectual, and perceptual disturbance. There are five kinds of schizophrenic reactions: childhood autism, simple, hebephrenic, catatonic, and paranoid (*see* Table 13.4). The onset of schizophrenia may be gradual or it may occur suddenly. Gradual development is called *process* schizophrenia; the chance for recovery is extremely poor because process psychotic behavior is securely established and very pathological. *Reactive* schizophrenia appears suddenly and is often triggered by stress in the child's life. The reactive psychotic has a more favorable chance of recovering.

Autistic children are asocial.

Childhood schizophrenia (autism) is defined as an inability to interact with others. Autistic children show obsessive behavior and do not attend to stimulation. They rarely recover.

Psychologists disagree about autism and schizophrenia.

CHILDHOOD AUTISM AND SCHIZOPHRENIA   There is still controversy among clinical psychologists and psychiatrists about whether childhood autism is a separate affliction or simply a form of childhood schizophrenia which appears particularly early in life (Rimland, 1964). The evidence is confusing at the moment. However, we do know that autistic development may be gradual during the first year of infancy or it may appear suddenly during the third year of life. The outstanding feature of childhood autism is a rejection of or disinterest in human interaction. Beyond this primary abnormality the autistic child also lacks personal awareness, exhibits pathological preoccupation with objects, strongly resists any change in his environment, is often indifferent to heat or pain, is extremely afraid

TABLE 13.4   Five types of schizophrenia.

1. *Childhood autism*—This disorder is characterized by stereotyped behavior, self-destruction, lack of coherent speech, and general emotional withdrawal.
2. *Simple schizophrenia*—Simple schizophrenics show apathy, withdrawal, alcoholism, and general inability to cope with life situations.
3. *Hebephrenia*—This most serious psychosis shows incoherent thought, speech, and action, plus hallucinations and regression to primitive behavior patterns.
4. *Catatonia*—Catatonics are able to remain in one stereotyped position, without food or drink, for weeks. However, these schizophrenics are more likely than any other group to recover.
5. *Paranoia*—This disorder is characterized by suspicion, hostility, and delusions of omnipotence.

TABLE 13.5 A comparison of autistic and schizophrenic children.

Autistic child	Schizophrenic child
Autism develops early in life.	Normal early childhood development.
Good physical health.	Various physical ailments.
Absence of social interaction.	Dependency on adults.
No hallucinations or delusions.	Hallucinations and/or delusions.
Good motor coordination.	Poor motor coordination.
Stable home life.	Often unstable family life.
Low family incidence of psychoses.	High family incidence of psychoses.

of many common objects or of strangers, shows only primitive communication, may be overactive or sluggish in movement, confuses personal pronouns, and lacks normal social skills. The existence of one or two autistic symptoms is generally not conclusive evidence of childhood autism, but if several signs are present, and linked to a pattern of abnormal development, there is a strong possibility of autism. Parents of autistic children report that their offspring rarely show anger, affection, or pleasure; but they sometimes have great skill at dismantling and reconstructing common household articles at an early age. Autistic children often repeat the same act over and over in a stereotyped manner, like rocking or stepping back and forth. They exhibit poor speech development, and finally begin talking by automatically repeating what they hear, a process called *echolalia*. Bernard Rimland has argued that there are differences between childhood autism and schizophrenia (*see* Table 13.5). Some other clinical psychologists disagree with Rimland's differentiation, and theorize that there is only a difference in degree rather than in kind between autism and schizophrenia in childhood. This issue is in doubt and must wait on more conclusive evidence.

Many psychologists believe that autism is innate.

There is also disagreement about the cause of autism or childhood schizophrenia. Some scientists, like Rimland (1964), support a genetic hypothesis, while others argue that complex family communication systems and cold interpersonal relations cause early childhood psychoses. At the moment the genetic evidence seems stronger, but further research on the exact mechanisms and their interactions with the environment are needed. For some reason there are around four times as many autistic boys as girls, and only about one-quarter of the children diagnosed as autistic during their early years develop into normal adults. Thus, over three-quarters of all autistic children continue to develop abnormally. The best single predictor of normal adult maturity among autistic children is the development of language before five years of age.

Schizophrenic children can be shaped.

Recently, Ivar Lovaas (1965) and his colleagues have modified the behavior of childhood schizophrenics by shaping them with environmental rewards and punishments based on the child's behavior. This technique holds promise as a way to make the caretaking of such children much simpler. In particular, the psychotic child's self-destructive tendencies may be modified by operant-conditioning techniques.

Affective Reactions

Affective reactions involve severe mood shifts.

About 15 percent of all patients admitted to mental hospitals suffer from *affective reactions,* which reflect severe changes of mood or emotion on the part of the patient. Almost 75 percent of such patients are female. One-third of all manic-depressives, one of the serious affective reactions, are excited, while the rest are depressed. Manic psychotics exhibit a speeding up of thought processes, so that their speech and eating habits may be excited and they cannot sleep. The final stage of mania can be complete delirium, in which the patient's actions are frantic and purposeless. Sometimes this frantic activity is merely an attempt to ward off depression.

The emotions may be cyclic or depressed.

In another affective pattern, mania and depression may alternate throughout a child's life in cyclic rhythms. Those affective psychotics who are cut off from social contacts become apathetic and sink deeper and deeper into despair. On occasion, mania and depression can be merged into a single state called agitated-depression, where the child's mood is depressed, but his activity level is excited. In this state the patient may wring his hands in frantic activity, but be sad and despairing.

Another type of childhood psychosis is caused by physical damage to the brain either by trauma or birth defect.

Organic Psychoses

Organic psychoses are caused by brain damage.

Abnormal behavior caused by brain dysfunction is most frequent in old age, but there are a singificant number of brain injuries among children. Organic psychoses account for one-third of all patients admitted to mental hospitals. Factors causing organic brain damage include infection, nutritional problems, and trauma from auto accidents or other injuries. The child's preinjury personality development and the amount of brain damage jointly determine how he responds to an injury of the central nervous system. Bright, well-integrated children tolerate brain damage better than dull, disorganized children; and the more serious the brain injury, the greater the abnormal behavior. Chronic symptoms can be caused by physical blows, interruption of blood supply, tumors, drugs, or infection. Unhappily, recovery from serious brain damage is difficult.

Psychological Therapies

Various psychological therapies exist.

Psychologists believe that there are many psychological abnormalities like anxieties, obsessions, compulsions, phobias, psychosomatic disorders, depressions, and psychoses. To combat these disorders various therapies have been proposed. Treatments for abnormality come in four main forms:

Physiological therapy—drugs, electroshock, or psychosurgery.
Individual psychotherapy—a therapist talks directly to the child to affect a cure.
Behavior modification techniques—learning-theory procedures.
Family group encounters—children are encouraged to express their emotions and try new ways of interacting in a social setting.

Let us consider some specific physical treatments first.

Physiological prescriptions come in various forms like narcosis, convulsive shock, surgery, nutritional supplementation, chemotherapy, and hospitalization. Such treatments have cured some abnormal behaviors. Vitamin therapy has virtually eliminated those behavior problems associated with pellagra or other deficiency diseases. More recently, antibiotics have controlled the mental deterioration associated with many infections. Barbiturates control many types of epilepsy and, occasionally, brain surgery can permanently relieve or help control epileptic seizures in some children. Let us look at some specific physiological treatments.

Physiological thera-pies cure some behavior problems.

Narcosis

Narcosis is used to aid diagnosis.

This label is derived from a Greek word meaning "to benumb." Drugs like sodium amatol, sodium pentothal, and scopolamine produce narcosis. Before the discovery of tranquilizers, these chemicals were used to control agitated or depressed children and adults in hospitals. They are used now primarily during diagnosis, because in a narcotic trance the child will talk about or act out traumatic and unpleasant experiences which he cannot face in an unsedated condition. This re-experiencing of an event can relieve the child's emotional tensions and give the therapist insight into the patient's problems.

Shock Therapy

Shock therapy is used to treat depression.

Convulsive *shock therapy* usually renders the patient unconscious or produces seizures and muscular convulsions. Convulsive shock therapy was discovered by accident when a severely depressed patient received an overdose of insulin, which first produced unconsciousness and then, when the patient had recovered from the shock, had dispelled his depression. Insulin shock proved to be dangerous and hard to control, so other ways of inducing unconsciousness were explored. A drug called metrazol was tried, but it produced violent convulsions causing patients to break bones or experience violent emotions during the course of therapy.

Electricshock is used today.

The current form of convulsive shock is a carefully regulated dose of electrical current passed through electrodes directly into the patient's brain. A regulated current of somewhere between 70 and 130 volts is

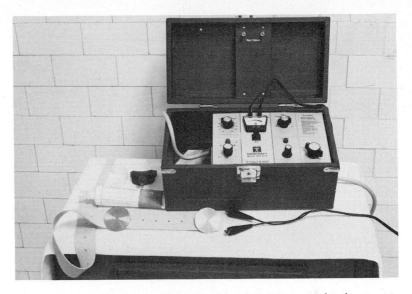

FIGURE 13.5 Electroshock therapy equipment used to administer a regulated current to a patient to relieve feelings of depression.
(LamMediflex Photo Lab.)

applied for a fraction of a second to produce unconsciousness. The child retains little memory of events right before and during the shock session. There is some evidence that electro-convulsive shock relieves depression and eliminates feelings of guilt or suicide. No one knows why or how electroshock works, but many believe it is one important way to relieve depression. Figure 13.5 shows how electroshock is administered.

Now that psychic energizing drugs are available, there is every reason to believe that electroshock therapy will be replaced by chemical therapy.

Surgery

Surgery can help some mental disorders.

The practice of drilling holes in the skull in the course of brain surgery has existed for a long time. The treatment of mental illness by surgery is undertaken for two reasons: relief of symptoms and removal of diseased or damaged brain tissue. When tumors or brain injury exist, the surgeon can cut away the tumor to limit damage or remove scar tissue which may trigger an epileptic seizure. These forms of corrective surgery often have beneficial effects on behavior.

Prefrontal lobotomy is no longer used to control agitated patients.

A distinctive form of brain surgery called prefrontal lobotomy was used at one time primarily to calm and control mentally disturbed patients. Neurologists believe the frontal lobes of the brain are involved in planning, anticipation, and emotional expression. By severing nerves in these frontal lobes the neurosurgeon hopes to keep patients from worrying about the future, thus making them less overly emotional. Experiments with monkeys demonstrated that anxiety is reduced following prefrontal lobotomy. The experimenter measured a monkey's anxiety by giving him a lever to press which would deliver food, and then associating electric shock with a light and the food. Eventually the light became a distressing signal to the monkeys, and when it was turned on the animal stopped pressing the lever for food. Following prefrontal lobotomy the previously distressing light no longer disturbed these animals. They continued to press the lever and eat even in the presence of the light.

As you might expect, prefrontal lobotomy produces some negative side effects in human patients. Following *prefrontal lobotomy* patients may lose interest in their bodies, fail to foresee the consequence of events, care little about the opinions of others, become impulsive, have no feelings of guilt, maintain a weak self-image, and lose interest in their futures. Prefrontal lobotomy is irreversible.

Lobotomy produces many side effects.

This kind of surgery has been almost completely supplanted with tranquilizing drugs, which reduce emotional tone, quiet agitated patients, and can be stopped if the patient begins to recover.

Tranquilizers have replaced the lobotomy.

Nutrition

Studies at the Mayo Clinic, a research hospital, demonstrated that the behavior of some psychiatric patients who were given a double dose of a vitamin called thiamine without their knowledge improved. A variety of mental disorders are associated with deficiencies of vitamins B_1, B_3, B_6, B_{12} and C. These known vitamin deficiencies can come from genetic irregularities in metabolism or from poor nutrition. Many scientists believe that the brain is particularly sensitive to vitamin concentrations, and they propose that some behavior disorders may be due to vitamin deficiency. If so, these disorders can be helped by vitamin supplements. We do not yet know whether vitamin deficiency is a serious source of current behavior problems, although many authorities are skeptical at the moment.

Some studies suggest that vitamin supplements may help psychoses.

Drug Therapy

Many chemicals change behavior. Barbiturates relieve anxiety or induce sleep; while stimulants, like amphetamines, can relieve depression or paradoxically calm the hyperactive child. The assumption underlying drug therapy is that mental illnesses come from biochemical abnormalities, and that the abnormal behavior will disappear if the biochemical imbalance is corrected or counteracted by chemical means. Many psychiatrists assume that the causes of psychoses are biochemical and that the best way to treat them is with drugs. The drugs used most often to combat abnormal behavior are tranquilizers like reserpine and chlorpromazine (*see* Figure 13.6). These drugs have replaced physical restraints and surgery as methods of patient control. Tranquilizing drugs probably

Many drugs are used to treat abnormal behaviors.

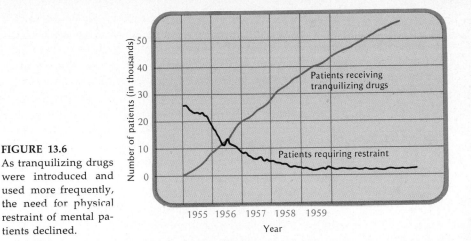

FIGURE 13.6
As tranquilizing drugs were introduced and used more frequently, the need for physical restraint of mental patients declined.

don't cure abnormal behavior, but they do calm the agitated child and make it easier for him to live within a family or institutional setting. Also, drugs are a much less radical way to handle the agitated or aggressive child than restraints or surgery.

Hyperactivity is most frequent around 8 years of age.

One particularly frequent problem among school-age children, especially boys, is hyperactivity. Overactive children are characterized by restlessness, short attention span, and distractability. The frequency of *hyperactivity* peaks during the first and second grades. Some psychologists argue that hyperactive children suffer from minimal undetectible brain damage, which makes them difficult to control.

Drugs are used to quiet hyperactive children.

A study by Burks (1960) revealed no IQ difference between hyperactive and normal children in the classroom. As we have learned, the most effective treatment for hyperactive children seems to be the administration of amphetamines, a central nervous system stimulant. For some reason, which is not understood, this stimulant seems to quiet many hyperactive children. Drug therapy has enabled many hyperactive boys and girls, who could not profit from normal instruction, to continue their educations. However, there is strong criticism of drug use to control these children. Some critics argue that the drugs may interfere with the child's ability to learn; while others say that the overactive child should not be made to conform to the demands of the classroom through drugs. This is an issue which promises to be with us for some time.

Hospitalization

Many disturbed patients are hospitalized.

Physiological therapies are often administered in a mental hospital because physicians believe the protective environment is needed to handle seriously disturbed or suicidal children. Other authorities argue that hospitalization removes the child from his family and settles him into an institutional routine from which it is difficult to break loose. For some children separation from a destructive environment is probably healthy. But the hospitalized child can become so entrenched in this protective setting that he may not want to go back to his family. To avoid this problem, hospital administrators now try to discharge children as soon as possible, and then readmit them if they cannot tolerate living outside of the institution. As an alternative to hospitalization, a variety of community mental health clinics, rehabilitation centers, halfway houses, day hospitals, and therapy groups have been established to help children and adults move back into their families.

A medical view of abnormality has good and bad features.

The medical view of abnormal behavior has good and bad features. Positive aspects include the development of effective physical therapies, humane treatment of patients, money for research, and the solid foundations associated with professional medicine. The bad features are isolation of the child from his family and ignorance of social pathologies. Physiological treatment and hospitalization are costly forms of treatment, although often no more expensive than individual psychotherapy.

Individual Psychotherapy

There are many kinds of psychotherapies.

Two people: a *therapist* and his *patient* interact in the course of individual psychotherapy. The process can be simple or complex depending on the therapist, the nature of the child's problems, and their joint treatment goals. Often the family of the child also helps to set these goals, especially if the child is irrational. The goals may change during the course of individual therapy. In the initial interview a therapist usually collects a life history of his patient. Then the child is given a medical examination to rule out the possibility of physical problems. Psychological tests of intelligence and personality may also be given. Finally, the therapist summarizes the child's problems and outlines his treatment procedure and the goals of therapy. These depend partly on the therapist's theory of mental illness. He may believe a child's problems stem from:

1. Environmental frustrations.
2. Motivational conflicts.
3. Faulty learning.
4. Biochemical imbalances.
5. Genetics.

If a therapist believes environmental frustrations, motivational conflicts, or faulty learning are the underlying cause of mental illness, he will try to change the child's attitudes and habits and perhaps instruct the family in behavior-modification techniques. If he believes the patient's problems are biochemical, diet or drug therapy is indicated. If the problem is heritable, perhaps he can do little for the child, but genetic counseling is in order so that future offspring of the same family may be spared the same affliction.

Insight often allevi-
ates psychological
distress.

Changing the child's environment is often a simple way to change his behavior. If the child's problems are emotional, sorting out his family experiences by gaining insight into and awareness of his conflicts and fears may help. The techniques of insight and talking out emotional problems were developed by Sigmund Freud in the last century.

Freudian Psychoanalytic Therapy

Freud invented free
association.

Freud developed psychoanalytic theory and the process of free association during the course of treating his patients. Freud's students extended or modified the original techniques. He assumed that neurotic behavior derives from unresolved emotional conflicts which begin very early in life and are repressed into unconsciousness so that the child is no longer aware of his difficulties. Freud felt that unconscious conflict produces anxiety, and that relief from fear can come by uncovering and working through these early conflicts in a mature way. He proposed two means of uncovering buried emotional conflict: *free association* and *interpretation* of symbols. Let us consider how these two techniques work.

Psychoanalysts try to
uncover hidden fears.

Psychoanalysts see their patients for fifty-minute sessions one or more times a week—sometimes for years. The first several sessions are used to review the child's problems, fears, or symptoms and produce a personal biography. Next, the child is taught how to free associate and is encouraged to express all his fears, feelings, and dreams. The purpose of free association is to uncover buried thoughts and feelings.

Freud believed the
child censors his
thoughts.

According to Freud, the main impediment to free association is the child's censoring of his thoughts. Freud believed that this resistance must be overcome so that a child can express his emotions freely and gain insight into and awareness of his conflicts. Freud noted that often during the course of free association a mental block would develop and his patients could produce no more associations. The patient's mind was blank and he could think of nothing further. Freud felt that a mental block indicates that the free associations had branched into important repressed emotions and stopped there. He noted further that his patient could often gain insight into the repressed feelings through an analysis of dreams or the thoughts which had immediately preceded the mental block. These repressed emotions were so unacceptable to the patient that he had to deny their existence. Violence was often involved in the repressed emotional material of children and sex in the conflicts of older patients. Freud argued that neuroses came from this repression of unacceptable feelings.

There are two con-
tents to dreams.

When exploring dreams which came out of repressed feelings Freud looked at two levels: the *manifest content,* which is what the child actually remembers, and the *latent content,* which is the distorted hidden motive that is too painful or frightening for the child to acknowledge. As an example, suppose a child dreams of killing a dog. The manifest content is killing the dog, while the latent content might be that he thinks his mother is a bitch and he wants to kill her. The distortion occurs because the child can't admit his feelings of hate for his mother.

Freud felt that the child must face his emotions.

Freud wrote that the aim of psychoanalysis is to break through this resistance and help a child face his unacceptable desires, feelings, and conflicts. Freud tried to clarify his young patient's conflicts by calling attention to resistances, asking about blocked associations, or pointing out missed appointments when the material being covered was proving too "dangerous" for the patient. Occasionally, Freud deduced the nature of a child's problem from the content of interviews and pointed such a problem out directly; on other occasions, the child would hint at the problem and then the analyst would expand that hint into a clearer interpretation of the conflicts involved.

Often the child treats his therapist as a parent.

As a child faces his emotional conflicts, the therapist is often thrust into the center of them. Freud wrote that often the therapist is put into the role of the patient's father, mother, or sibling. If this role is positive, the patient's feelings toward his therapist will be those of love and admiration. If the patient's role *transference* is negative, the patient may become hostile toward the therapist.

Catharsis means the expression of emotion.

During the final phase of psychoanalysis three things are assumed to happen: catharsis, insight, and working through. *Catharsis* occurs when a patient begins to express his repressed emotions and to relive forgotten experiences. The expression of emotion brings temporary relief and can lead to insight and understanding. During catharsis, memories of repressed experiences and feelings may occur and the child often reports dramatic events that he has forgotten but which deeply affected him. Following catharsis, personal understanding may continue with a gradual accumulation of self-knowledge. This is *insight*. Freud believed the final job for the patient was to handle his emotions in a more mature way. To become mature, Freud wanted his patients to face reality, not deny it. With emotional maturity, he felt the child would become independent of his analyst and eventually of his parents. It was this final phase that was designated as *working through*.

Many new therapies have evolved from Freud's technique.

Many individual therapies have evolved since the days when Freud established his new science. These therapies have one thing in common — they reject the notion that some underlying illness produces abnormal behavior. Rather, they postulate various alternative causes of abnormal acts. Clinical psychologists, who use behavior-modification procedures believe that most abnormal human behavior results from faulty learning. Client-centered therapists think that the discrepancy between a child's self-image and his actions produces neuroses. Most group therapists assume that unsatisfactory peer relations, rather than internal conflicts, are the cause of children's personal problems.

Psychologists advocate relearning.

These varying assumptions about abnormal behavior have generated many different treatments. Psychologists who advocate behavior modification argue that proper relearning procedures can change neurotic behavior, since abnormal acts were acquired the same way—through learning—as any other kind of behavior. Behaviorists strive to modify *acts*, not the mind, personality, or a mental disease. Let us consider the methods and goals of behavior modification in more detail.

Behavior Modification

Pavlovian and Skinnerian theories have been applied to treatment.

Two different theories of learning have been applied to modifying behavior: *Pavlovian classical conditioning* and *Skinnerian operant conditioning*. Classical-conditioning theory assumes that all stimuli—like the sight of food or the child's mother—which immediately precede biologically important events come to signal those events after a few associations. A previously neutral sign can come to elicit conditioned fear if the neutral stimulus is consistently associated with pain or loud noises, as we have learned. To reduce learned fear, the Pavlovians argue you must break the connection between the conditioned stimulus and the acquired anxiety. They do this by a procedure called desensitization.

Systematic desensitization can reduce acquired fears.

SYSTEMATIC DESENSITIZATION   Systematic reduction of anxieties by classical-conditioning procedures is called *desensitization*. It's based on the notion that a child can't be happy and sad at the same time. Desensitization therapy begins by asking the child about things that make him anxious. Then, the therapist asks his young patient which of these listed items makes him most fearful. Next, the child is trained in how to relax. Then desensitization itself begins by asking the child to imagine doing something that makes him only a little anxious. When the child begins to feel afraid he is told to stop thinking about the fearful thing and again go through the relaxation procedure. When the child can think about a moderately fearful item without anxiety he is instructed to imagine a yet more fearful act, and the desensitization process is repeated. Gradually, he is able to think about more and more fearful events, until he can finally approach previously unthinkable fears in a reasonably calm state. Systematic desensitization is an effective treatment for specific fearful reactions (*see* Figure 13.7).

Behavior modification is based on reward and punishment.

By contrast to the treatment based on Pavlovian classical conditioning, Skinnerian behavior-modification techniques manipulate the rewards which follow types of behavior. To modify abnormal behavior the classical-conditioning therapist tries to break the association between neutral stimuli and painful happenings and substitute a pleasant association. Behavior modification therapists argue that to change behavior you must change the outcome of acts. They believe that misbehavior will decrease if parents or teachers ignore the child when he acts in a negative manner and reward him when he is being positive. They point out that behaviors have a variety of consequences—some negative, some positive. The behavior-modification therapist theorizes that positive reinforcement can

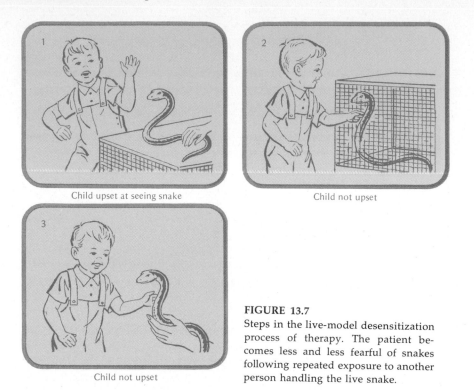

Child upset at seeing snake

Child not upset

FIGURE 13.7
Steps in the live-model desensitization process of therapy. The patient becomes less and less fearful of snakes following repeated exposure to another person handling the live snake.

Child not upset

support abnormal behavior and that these unworkable social responses can be changed by instituting rewards for positive acts and punishments for improper ones. Behavior-modification therapists treat everything from crying to aggression by rewards and punishment. In order for punishment to work, it must be intense, predictable, and occur immediately after the undesirable act.

The token economy rewards good behaviors.

THE TOKEN ECONOMY   Another approach to altering human behavior is called the "token economy." This form of behavior modification is organized to systematically dispense rewards and punishments based on people's performance. Token economies make two simple assumptions: if an act is followed by reward the act will increase in frequency, and if it is not followed by reward or results in punishment the act will stop. Therapists, hospital administrators, teachers, and parents give children toys; attention; or tokens, stars, or poker chips to purchase sleeping time, passes, television time, or food. The "tokens" are earned by engaging in social activities, cleaning up, being on time for meals or other work, and so on; and the process of behavioral change is gradual. At first the child is rewarded for merely approximating the act; later only more complete acts leading directly to the goal are rewarded. This process is called *shaping*.

To establish a token economy, the parent, therapist, or teacher must have almost absolute control of the child's environment. Proponents of the token economy argue that it provides clear feedback, introduces consistency into almost every situation, and allows the learner a choice in determining where and when he will work. Critics argue that token economies simply reduce human interaction to a marketplace. Members of the economy learn "what's in it for me," rather than achieve intrinsic satisfaction. Opponents of the token system argue that learning is more effective if reinforcement is part of the task rather than externally applied. However, those who favor the system believe that some children can't learn from such rewards; they need clear external feedback.

Group Therapies

In a parallel effort to make treatment more efficient and less costly, many therapists have moved from treating children one at a time to interacting with several simultaneously in a group. Consider how this group therapy might work.

The intensive group experience is a recent phenomenon. It has many names: drug addicts live at Synanon, executives attend "leadership conferences," teenagers go to "encounters," college students frequent "T-groups," and housewives and business people flock to "sensitivity groups." Intensive group experiences occur in churches, industry, government, universities, penitentiaries, and schools. This explosion of intensive group experience apparently meets a strong need.

Therapy groups began in the United States right after World War II. Two people were primarily responsible for their development: Kurt Lewin at the Massachusetts Institute of Technology and Carl Rogers at the University of Chicago. Lewin thought that the ability to get along with other people would become increasingly important in modern society, so he set up Training Groups (T-groups) for the purpose of teaching and understanding socialization. At about the same time, Carl Rogers was asked by the Veterans Administration to train people with Master's degrees as counselors for Vets. Rogers thought that ordinary classroom experience would not be adequate preparation for counseling, so he set up intensive group interaction sessions. These group sessions lasted several hours a day for several days, and intense human interactions and personal attitudes were explored by the members. During the course of this interpersonal counseling, some of Roger's students experienced personality changes. He wondered if this might be a new form of psychotherapy. The result has been a spectacular growth in group meetings.

Current groups come in many forms and they vary in emphasis, leadership, and intensity. Some groups for youngsters are composed only of children, while others include members of one or more families. Group therapy rests on the assumption that most problems come from dealing

---

Critics say the token economy reduces interaction to a marketplace.

Group therapies are efficient.

The group experience is a recent development.

Lewin and Rogers pioneered groups.

There are many group therapies.

with peers or from feeling isolated, rejected, and inadequate. Group therapists believe that together children can see the kinds of problems others have and they can also discover how others cope with their difficulties. The advantages of group therapy include:

1. The child learns he is not alone with his problems.
2. He can explore his own attitudes and reactions to other children.
3. He receives feedback from others.
4. Group therapy is inexpensive compared with other forms of psychotherapy.

Family therapy can be effective.

Sometimes disturbed parents bring their child to a mental health facility for treatment because it is easier for the adults to project their frustrations and conflicts onto a child than to accept the fact that they may have problems themselves. Parents usually claim: "This child is so difficult, I don't know what to do with him!" To solve this type of problem a group therapist must study the interactions of the entire family. Two ways are available to the therapist: he can watch the family in a variety of situations, or he can study the child alone. Group interviews between the therapist and the parents and child can bring out many problems. However, children are not very articulate at describing their feelings, so

FIGURE 13.8 Believe it or not, this child is playing. He is being encouraged to express his emotions about his family through play. Apparently his primary feeling at the moment is anger.

therapists need other ways in which to let them reveal their anxieties. Role-playing and play therapy are used most often to bring out children's emotions.

Role-playing helps the child see other points of view.

To act out a role, the child may be asked to imagine he is a mother or father or sister or brother, so that the therapist can understand the child's view of family interaction. Role-playing also gives the child practice in handling difficult situations and seeing other points of view. Play therapy lets the child express thoughts and feelings through actions (*see* Figure 13.8). A popular form of play therapy uses dolls. The therapist gives a child furniture, a house, a doll mother, doll father, and some doll children and the child is asked to make the dolls "act like a family." Family doll play lets the child express his own unfulfilled wishes and fears about his family.

Thus, we have a bewildering variety of techniques for alleviating mental illness. Do they work? How can we know?

Evaluation of Therapies

Does therapy work?

How can anyone know if therapy really works? Psychologists have questioned children who were former patients, measured personalities, tabulated how long children stay in hospitals, and interviewed individual therapists. The results show that former patients almost always say therapy helps, and therapists universally claim their favorite methods work. The problems with any evaluation is that many children get better, even if nothing is done for them (*see* Figure 13.9) and the therapist earns his living by providing his particular method of psychotherapy.

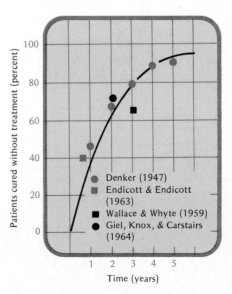

FIGURE 13.9
When neurotic patients get well without therapy they are said to have remitted spontaneously. The remission rate, shown as a curve in the figure, fits data from four studies of patients who went untreated but were cured.

Almost any therapy helps neurotics.

The data currently available show that almost any technique will help neurotics, and that specific fears can be changed by punishment and reinforcement. Chemotherapy, surgery, and hospitalization are moderately effective in treating some psychotic behaviors, although the long-term outlook for these patients is still uncertain.

How does one measure a cure?

Two ways of evaluating therapy exist. One is called *process research,* the other *outcome studies.* Process research looks at what happens in a therapeutic situation; outcome studies ask how effective one therapy is compared to others. When is a child cured? How can we know? How do you measure a cure?

Therapists and patients are not good judges of therapy.

Therapist and patient are not the best judges of effectiveness, since they have a vested interest in success. Many measures have been used to evaluate the outcome of psychotherapy. These include the therapist's judgment, the patient's feelings, personality test scores, interviews with the patient before and after therapy, information from parents and peers about the child, and the frequency of specific acts by the child before and after therapy. The particular measures taken and their meaning depend on the therapist's theoretical orientation. For some, success means the child is now manageable in an institution or school setting. Others believe that eliminating a kind of objectionable behavior is satisfactory. For psychoanalysis, success means the development of an integrated, healthy personality for the child.

Eysenck claims that no therapy is effective.

Cure rates between 75 and 90 percent are claimed by most behavior therapists. However, these success rates incorporate a bias. Only patients who remain in therapy are counted, while those who drop out are not included. This stacks the cards in favor of a high success rate. An additional problem with evaluating therapy is that often techniques are so mixed, that it's difficult to know what specific therapy causes the change. A number of years ago Hans Eysenck outraged the clinical profession by claiming that cure rates for patients receiving no therapy are often as good or better than cure rates for psychotherapeutic or specialized situations. This particular controversy has not been resolved to anyone's satisfaction.

No psychotherapy works well on psychoses.

Psychoanalytic therapy is expensive, time-consuming, and works best for bright, motivated, upper-middle-class neurotic children. For those "fortunate" few, psychoanalysis can relieve repressions, open emotional reactions, and produce a more healthy human being. However, individual therapy is *not* the answer to all mental-health problems, because there are neither enough well-trained psychiatrists nor are all patients bright, rich, neurotic children. Most treatments seem successful with neurotic behavior, but none work very well on psychoses. Probably the best hope for eliminating psychoses is research into the metabolic bases of abnormality, and genetic counseling of psychotic parents about the dangers involved for any children they may have.

Finally, there are ethical issues which must be resolved by any therapist, and these judgments may influence his choice of therapy and patient.

Should the therapist try to change a child's fear of school or simply accept his fear? Suppose a boy fears heights and wants to be cured so he can grow up to be a bomber pilot. Is the therapist helping the boy protect his country or is he helping a killer? What about the adolescent who thinks society is corrupt and wants to destroy the military-industrial complex. Is the student a paranoid schizophrenic or a progressive idealist? Should the therapist try to change society to fit the child, or the child to fit society? These are problems no therapist can ignore and there are *no* easy answers.

Summary

Abnormal behavior runs in families and the probability of developing abnormally increases with the genetic relation between the offspring and an abnormal person. Thus, serious abnormality seems to be inherited, although there is considerable controversy about the extent and generality of the genetic constraints on abnormal development. There are various types of abnormal development: most frequent are neuroses like phobias, obsessions, and depression; next come the personality disorders like delinquency; and, finally, the most serious abnormal behaviors like schizophrenia or manic-depressive affective reactions. Abnormal development can also be caused by injury to the developing central nervous system. There are three types of therapies used to treat abnormal behavior: physiological therapies that include shock, surgery, drugs, and hospitalization; individual therapies that include psychoanalysis and behavior modification; and group therapies. There is some controversy in psychology about whether any of the talking therapies are effective.

SUGGESTED ADDITIONAL READINGS

Bandura, A. "Behavioral Psychotherapy," *Scientific American,* Vol. 216 (March 1967), pp. 78–86.

Caplan, G. *Principles of Preventive Psychiatry.* New York: Basic Books, 1964.

Eysenck, H.J. "Learning Theory and Behavior Therapy," *Journal of Mental Science,* Vol. 105 (1959), pp. 61–75.

Freud, A. "Assessment of Childhood Disturbances." In R. Eisler *et al.,* eds., *The Psychoanalytic Study of the Child,* Vol. XVII. New York: International Universities Press, 1962.

Freud, S. *The Disposition to Obsessional Neurosis,* standard ed., Vol. XII. London: Hogarth Press (1913, 1958).

———. *General Theory of the Neurosis.* Standard ed., Vol. XVI. London: Hogarth Press (1917, 1963).

Karlsson, J.L. *The Biologic Basis of Schizophrenia.* Springfield, Ill.: Charles C Thomas, 1966.

part IV

Adolescence

(Magnum Photos)

14 Adolescence

A Definition of Adolescence
  The History of Youth and Adolescence
  Cross-cultural Perspectives
  The U.S. Adolescent's Parents and Peers
Physical Development during Adolescence
  Physical Changes during Puberty
  The Adolescent Growth Period
The Peer Group
  Friendship and Peer Acceptance
    Sex-role Determinants
  Sexual Attitudes and Behaviors
    Sexual Attitudes in the U.S.
    Female Sex Attitudes
    Male Sex Attitudes

Vocational Choice
  Parent Influences on Career Choices
  Peer Influences on Career Plans
Problems of Adolescent Development
  Dropping Out
  Delinquency
  Drugs
    Causes of Addiction
    Alcohol Use and Abuse
    Marijuana Use and Abuse
    Hallucinogenic Chemicals
    Opiate Addiction
    Amphetamine Dependence
    Drugs and the Law
Summary

PREVIEW

Historically, adolescence was a time when youth assumed the responsibilities and enjoyed the pleasures of maturity. Extended education and marriage later in life (after the teenage years) increased the interval between childhood and adulthood, and in the process created difficult social and emotional adjustments for parents and their adolescent offspring. Prolonged financial dependence has delayed emotional and social maturity among some adolescents, and has created friction between the generations. Later marriage produces sexual frustration or premarital experimentation with its accompanying guilts, diseases, or unwanted pregnancies. Is the storm and strife of modern adolescence a necessary part of growing up or the result of postponed marriage and independence? No one is sure, but most authorities on adolescence feel that granting financial independence and social recognition to youth when they mature sexually would lead to less conflict and stress than is true of the current system in the United States. They argue that the primary cause of adolescent discontent is a disparity between feelings of maturity, on the one hand, and a reality of dependence, on the other. Social scientists point out that most adolescents and their parents manage to coexist a good deal of the time with mutual respect and few ill feelings, but the transition to adulthood could be much smoother.

Human development
covers four periods.

Human development is traditionally divided into four periods: infancy, childhood, adolescence, and maturity. The principal task during infancy is growth, while childhood is occupied with school and play. Adolescence is a period for choice and change, and maturity is based on all the earlier periods. During infancy and childhood, offspring are nurtured and guided by parents and other adults, but the adolescent is expected to begin going out on his own. This transition from dependence toward responsibility occurs for several reasons: The adolescent is maturing physically, intellectually, and sexually so he is ready to accept responsibility for his actions. The adolescent shifts his focus from parents to peers, and they expect independence from him. Most adolescents want to accept responsibility for their own lives and naturally begin thinking about their careers, marriage and the future away from parental control. The rapid physical, emotional, and social changes that occur during adolescence produce some conflicts for the average teenager. Chief among these difficulties are disillusionment, questions of obediency, and problems of competency. Before we review the problems associated with adolescence, let us consider society's changing conceptions of this period through time and across cultures, taking into account the physical and emotional developments which thrust a child into maturity.

A Definition of Adolescence

The History of Youth and Adolescence

Our view of youth as
a separate stage is
quite recent.

Most historians agree that society's current view of adolescence as a separate human stage is quite recent. Apparently, even the notion of childhood as a separate period was absent during the Middle Ages, although earlier civilizations, like Greece and Rome, believed that children between six and twelve years of age should be in schools. Most historians believe that both our theories of human development and our treatment of children are strongly affected by economic realities. They point out that before the appearance of a wealthy middle class, children were needed to work on the farms and tend the shops with their parents. Only when wealth and leisure increased, and the need for educated clerks and shopkeepers became acute, did childhood become a time for learning rather than a time for apprenticeship in a factory or on a farm. Once universal primary education became an institution, childhood changed from hard work under hard conditions into a protected time of play and education (*see* Figure 14.1). Even after childhood was well established as a period of growth, the concept of adolescence as a separate period of human development required additional time to be implemented. In fact, modern theories of adolescence as a time of physical and psychological development date only from the nineteenth century. In earlier times, Western societies acknowledged the fact of sexual maturity, but paid

FIGURE 14.1 Children working in an American vegetable cannery. They were photographed in 1912 by Lewis W. Hine.
(Courtesy of The Granger Collection.)

little attention to teenage problems and did not expect the period to have a unique psychological meaning.

Modern adolescence is prolonged due to extended career preparation.

Recent images of the adolescent depict him as insecure and awkward, angry and wild, or idealistic and withdrawn. Probably the average teenager is all these things and more at various times during his growth. The main reason that modern societies recognize adolescence as a special period is the long educational preparation now required for employment in our more sophisticated world. The average adolescent is faced with longer and longer intervals for education. A generation ago less than half of the youth in the U.S. finished high school, while now almost that many finish college. Adolescents have grown more and more dependent on their parents for financial support, and at the same time have begun to experiment with alternate life styles. The result has been increasing concern and attention given to the ideals, emotions, and the acts of youth in the U.S.

Cross-cultural Perspectives

Adolescence is a time of storm and stress in the U.S.

Since at least the beginning of this century adolescence has been viewed as a time of storm and stress. Some authorities even argue that adolescence is necessarily a difficult period because the person is sexually mature at a time when he is still emotionally and socially dependent. Two facts argue against such a simplified interpretation of adolescent problems. First, the storms and stress appear at least a year after the period of rapid sexual and physical maturation has begun. And in some cultures there is no storm or stress associated with sexual maturity. Let us consider the treatment of adolescents among primitive societies.

Adolescent storm and stress does not exist in all cultures.

In many primitive groups the notion of adolescence does not even exist. They mark the transition from child to adult by a short, significant ritual called the *puberty rite*. Generally, these rituals coincide with sexual maturity, and the decision about when the young members of a tribe are prepared to undertake the ceremony is left to the individual or delegated to tribal elders. Whatever the procedure, all young males and occasionally young females must endure an initiation into maturity. Some rituals are little more than a simple ceremony; while others involve complex periods of isolation and fasting, elaborate markings of the face and body, and in some cases painful ordeals which must be overcome or endured with grace. Some tribes require a young male to prove himself a hunter or a warrior. He may have to slay a lion or a man to be thought of as an adult.

FIGURE 14.2
An aboriginal Australian boy is painted ritualistically before entering the adult tribal world via a puberty rite.

Anthropologists argue that the existence of these clear demands and a specified time for maturity make the transition less traumatic for primitive adolescents. But the Western adolescent is faced with a long interval during which he is neither child nor adult, but is only in a state of becoming mature.

The U.S. Adolescent's Parents and Peers

Modern adolescents believe the world is changing too fast.

The current generation of Western adolescents believe that the world is changing too fast, becoming more and more impersonal, is too competitive, and presents them with conflicting and complicated beliefs and values. In response to this change and ambiguity, a minority of adolescents have vowed to basically alter the system by active opposition or have dropped out and given up. The majority of adolescents have done neither, but have remained in the mainstream of society and continued to work for success, marriage, and advancement within established institutions.

Adolescents mature in different ways.

There are two extremes in the way adolescents mature. Some are upwardly mobile, achievement-oriented, interested in higher education, and able to delay immediate gratification for later rewards. Others are socially static, not achievement-oriented, learn practical skills, and require immediate gratification of their needs and wishes. There are as many variations of such patterns as there are adolescents. The middle-class adolescent usually believes that he has some control over his future, and he is oriented toward making a place for himself in society with education as the path to his future success. Lower-class adolescents are more fatalistic about the future, and often believe that luck is responsible for their successes and failures.

Many teenagers understand the purposes of government.

Several investigators have reported increased interest in political activities among adolescents. J. Adelson (1971) found that U.S. adolescents answered the question, "What is the purpose of laws?" with a good understanding of the abstract principles and governmental institutions which control social interaction. The change in political and social awareness among adolescents is closely related, and probably caused by, cognitive development. By late adolescence the person is much better able to comprehend the complexities and abstractions of political and social life, as compared with his younger peers. Studies carried out in the 1950's and 1960's showed that few adolescents were concerned about social and political issues, and that they read few newspapers and books concerned with everyday events. Current surveys show strong political awareness and serious social concern among adolescents.

Modern adolescents are politically aware.

F. Kline (1972) concluded that the main cause of increased political awareness and social concern among today's adolescents is the democratic upbringing they have received from their parents. He argued that ideas of justice and principles of democracy used within the family foster a sense of outrage toward injustices and authority badly used. Kline's theory of political awareness based on democratic upbringing contradicts earlier Freudian interpretations of political activism, which assumed that activism and dissent were caused by rejection of parental authority or rebellion against parental dominance. It is true that few families are totally democratic or authoritarian, so some combination of democratic unbringing and rejection of parental authority probably best explains the increased political awareness among today's adolescents. One direct result of this new political awareness has been the lowering of the voting age to eighteen years, which gives many young Americans more of a voice in their government, and a chance to have an impact on the events in society.

Portrait

Erik Erikson was born during 1902 in Frankfurt, Germany, of Danish parents. His father died when Erikson was quite young, and his widowed mother married a prominent pediatrician. Erikson's stepfather wanted the boy to become a physician, but the young man decided to become an artist instead. During these early years as an artist in Vienna, Erikson met Sigmund Freud on several occasions. He must have been impressed by what Freud had to say, for Erikson entered an American School in Vienna and undertook psychoanalytic training with Freud's daughter, Anna. After his analytic training, Erikson met and married a young American artist named Joan Serson and came to the U.S. in 1933 to practice psychoanalysis. Over the next two decades Erikson held clinical and academic appointments at Harvard, Yale, and Berkeley.

Erik Erikson has always had broad interests. He initiated early field work on American Indians by observing the Sioux of Pine Ridge, South Dakota, and the Yurok Indians of northern California. He attributes much of his understanding about normal personal development to the cross-cultural perspective he gathered from these diverse peoples. During his cross-cultural observations, Erikson came on several personal problems among the Indians which could not be explained by classical Freudian theory. For example, the Indian's feeling of discontinuity with their past could not be attributed to sexual frustrations.

Erikson's most influential book is titled *Childhood and Society,* and it integrates fifteen years of research and thinking about personal development. He believes that personal development contains not only the psychosexual stages of oral, anal, phallic, and genital development developed by Freud, but in addition parallel stages of ego development. He argues that the various stages of ego development are opportunities for the child to establish a new orientation between himself and his world.

Following the publication of *Childhood and Society,* Erikson applied his theory of ego development to the biographies of great men. He published comprehensive studies of the early development of men like George Bernard Shaw, Sigmund Freud, and Martin Luther.

Currently, Erikson spends his fall in Cambridge, Massachusetts, where he teaches a course on the human life cycle to Harvard seniors. He moves back to his home in Stockbridge, Massachusetts, in the spring to participate in seminars at the Austen Riggs center. His summers are spent on Cape Cod. He is studying preschool children's play in different countries. His major contribution has been a rejuvenation of psychoanalysis as a workable alternative to humanistic and behavioristic views of man. He brought new life to a discipline which many considered to be dead or dying.

Erik Erikson believes that early childhood is only one stage of human development.

Perhaps because he had been an artist first, Erikson has never been a conventional psychoanalyst. When he was treating children, for example, he always insisted on visiting his young patients' homes and on having dinner with the families. Likewise, in the nineteen-thirties, when anthropological investigation was described to him by his friends Scudder McKeel, Alfred Kroeber and Margaret Mead, he decided to do field work on an Indian reservation. "When I realized that Sioux is the name which we [in Europe] pronounced "See ux" and which for us was *the* American Indian, I could not resist." Erikson thus antedated the anthropologists who swept over the Indian reservations in the post-Depression years. (So numerous were the field workers at that time that the stock joke was that an Indian family could be defined as a mother, a father, children and an anthropologist.)

Erikson did field work not only with the Oglala Sioux of Pine Ridge, S.D. (the tribe that slew Custer and was in turn slaughtered at the Battle of Wounded Knee), but also with the salmon-fishing Yurok of Northern California. His reports on these experiences revealed his special gift for sensing and entering into the world views and modes of thinking of cultures other than his own.

It was while he was working with the Indians that Erikson began to note syndromes which he could not explain within the confines of traditional psychoanalytic theory. Central to many an adult Indian's emotional problems seemed to be his sense of uprootedness and lack of continuity between his present life-style and that portrayed in tribal history. Not only did the Indian sense a break with the past, but he could not identify with a future requiring assimilation of the white culture's values. The problems faced by such men, Erikson recognized, had to do with the ego and with culture and only incidentally with sexual drives.

The impressions Erikson gained on the reservations were reinforced during World War II when he worked at a veterans' rehabilitation center at Mount Zion Hospital in San Francisco. Many of the soldiers he and his colleagues saw seemed not to fit the traditional "shell shock" or "malingerer" cases of World War I. Rather, it seemed to Erikson that many of these men had lost the sense of who and what they were. They were having trouble reconciling their activities, attitudes and feelings as soldiers with the activities, attitudes and feelings they had known before the war. Accordingly, while these men may well have had difficulties with repressed or conflicted drives, their main problem seemed to be, as Erikson came to speak of it at the time, "identity confusion."

David Elkind, "Erik Erikson's Eight Ages of Man" in *The New York Times Magazine,* April 5, 1970.

It was almost a decade before Erikson set forth the implications of his clinical observations in "Childhood and Society." In that book, the summation and integration of 15 years of research, he made three major contributions to the study of the human ego. He posited (1) that, side by side with the stages of psychosexual development described by Freud (the oral, anal, phallic, genital, Oedipal and pubertal), were psychosocial stages of ego development, in which the individual had to establish new basic orientations to himself and his social world; (2) that personality development continued throughout the whole life cycle; and (3) that each stage had a positive *as well as* a negative component.

Much about these contributions—and about Erikson's way of thinking—can be understood by looking at his scheme of life stages. Erikson identifies eight stages in the human life cycle, in each of which a new dimension of "social interaction" becomes possible—that is, a new dimension in a person's interaction with himself, and with his social environment.

Trust vs. Mistrust

The first stage corresponds to the oral stage in classical psychoanalytic theory and usually extends through the first year of life. In Erikson's view, the new dimension of social interaction that emerges during this period involves basic *trust* at the one extreme, and *mistrust* at the other. The degree to which the child comes to trust the world, other people and himself depends to a considerable extent upon the quality of the care that he receives. The infant whose needs are met when they arise, whose discomforts are quickly removed, who is cuddled, fondled, played with and talked to, develops a sense of the world as a safe place to be and of people as helpful and dependable. When, however, the care is inconsistent, inadequate and rejecting, it fosters a basic mistrust, an attitude of fear and suspicion on the part of the infant toward the world in general and people in particular that will carry through to later stages of development.

It should be said at this point that the problem of basic trust-versus-mistrust (as is true for all the later dimensions) is not resolved once and for all

during the first year of life; it arises again at each successive stage of development. There is both hope and danger in this. The child who enters school with a sense of mistrust may come to trust a particular teacher who has taken the trouble to make herself trustworthy; with this second chance, he overcomes his early mistrust. On the other hand, the child who comes through infancy with a vital sense of trust can still have his sense of mistrust activated at a later stage if, say, his parents are divorced and separated under acrimonious circumstances.

This point was brought home to me in a very direct way by a 4-year-old patient I saw in a court clinic. He was being seen at the court clinic because his adoptive parents, who had had him for six months, now wanted to give him back to the agency. They claimed that he was cold and unloving, took things and could not be trusted. He was indeed a cold and apathetic boy, but with good reason. About a year after his illegitimate birth, he was taken away from his mother, who had a drinking problem, and was shunted back and forth among several foster homes. Initially he had tried to relate to the persons in the foster homes, but the relationships never had a chance to develop because he was moved at just the wrong times. In the end he gave up trying to reach out to others, because the inevitable separations hurt too much.

Like the burned child who dreads the flame, this emotionally burned child shunned the pain of emotional involvement. He had trusted his mother, but now he trusted no one. Only years of devoted care and patience could now undo the damage that had been done to this child's sense of trust.

Autonomy vs. Doubt

Stage Two spans the second and third years of life, the period which Freudian theory calls the anal stage. Erikson sees here the emergence of *autonomy*. This autonomy dimensions builds upon the child's new motor and mental abilities. At this stage the child can not only walk but also climb, open and close, drop, push and pull, hold and let go. The child takes pride in these new accomplishments and wants to do everything himself, whether it be pulling the wrapper off a piece of candy, selecting the vitamin out of the bottle or flushing the toilet. If parents recognize the young child's need to do what he is capable of doing at his own pace and in his own time, then he develops a sense that he is able to control his muscles, his impulses, himself and, not insignificantly, his environment—the sense of autonomy.

When, however, his caretakers are impatient and do for him what he is capable of doing himself, they reinforce a sense of shame and doubt. To be sure, every parent has rushed a child at times and children are hardy enough to endure such lapses. It is only when caretaking is consistently overprotective and criticism of "accidents" (whether these be wetting, soiling, spilling or breaking things) is harsh and unthinking that the child develops an excessive sense of shame with respect to other people and an excessive sense of doubt about own abilities to control his world and himself.

If the child leaves this stage with less autonomy than shame or doubt, he will be handicapped in his attempts to achieve autonomy in adolescence and adulthood. Contrariwise, the child who moves through this stage with his sense of autonomy buoyantly outbalancing his feelings of shame and doubt is well prepared to be autonomous at later phases in the life cycle. Again, however, the balance of autonomy to shame and doubt set up during this period can be changed in either positive or negative directions by later events.

It might be well to note, in addition, that too much autonomy can be as harmful as too little. I have in mind a patient of 7 who had a heart condition. He had learned very quickly how terrified his parents were of any signs in him of cardiac difficulty. With the psychological acuity given to children, he soon ruled the household. The family could not go shopping, or for a drive, or on a holiday if he did not approve. On those rare occasions when the parents had had enough and defied him, he would get angry and his purple hue and gagging would frighten them into submission.

Actually, this boy was frightened of this power (as all children would be) and was really eager to give it up. When the parents and the boy came to realize this, and to recognize that a little shame and doubt were a healthy counterpoise to an inflated sense of autonomy, the three of them could once again assume their normal roles.

Initiative vs. Guilt

In this stage (the genital stage of classical psychoanalysis) the child, age 4 to 5, is pretty much master of his body and can ride a tricycle, run, cut and hit. He can thus initiate motor activities of various sorts on his own and no longer merely responds to or imitates the actions of other children. The same holds true for his language and fantasy activities. Accordingly, Erikson argues that the social dimension that appears at this stage has *initiative* at one of its poles and *guilt* at the other.

Whether the child will leave this stage with his sense of initiative far outbalancing his sense of guilt depends to a considerable extent upon how parents respond to his self-initiated activities. Children who are given much freedom and opportunity to initiate motor play such as running, bike riding, sliding, skating, tussling and wrestling have their sense of initiative reinforced. Initiative is also reinforced when parents answer their children's questions (intellectual initiative) and do not deride or inhibit fantasy or play activity. On the other hand, if the child is made to feel that his motor activity is bad, that his questions are a nuisance and that his play is silly and stupid, then he may develop a sense of guilt over self-initiated activities in general that will persist through later life stages.

Industry vs. Inferiority

Stage Four is the age period from 6 to 11, the elementary school years (described by classical psychoanalysis as the *latency phase*). It is a time during which the child's love for the parent of the opposite sex and rivalry with the same sexed parent (elements in the so-called family romance) are quiescent. It is also a period during which the child becomes capable of deductive reasoning, and of playing and learning by rules. It is not until this period, for example, that children can really play marbles, checkers and other "take turn" games that require obedience to rules. Erikson argues that the psychosocial dimension that emerges during this period has a sense of *industry* at one extreme and a sense of *inferiority* at the other.

The term industry nicely captures a dominant theme of this period during which the concern with how things are made, how they work and what they do predominates. It is the Robinson Crusoe age in the sense that the enthusiasm and minute detail with which Crusoe describes his activities appeals to the child's own budding sense of industry. When children are encouraged in their efforts to make, do, or build practical things (whether it be to construct creepy crawlers, tree houses, or airplane models—or to cook, bake or sew), are allowed to finish their products, and are praised and rewarded for the results, then the sense of industry is enhanced. But parents who see their children's efforts at making and doing as "mischief," and as simply "making a mess," help to encourage in children a sense of inferiority

During these elementary-school years, however, the child's world includes more than the home. Now social institutions other than the family come to play a central role in the developmental crisis of the individual. (Here Erikson introduced still another advance in psychoanalytic theory, which heretofore concerned itself only with the effects of the parents' behavior upon the child's development.)

A child's school experiences affect his industry-inferiority balance. The child, for example, with an I.Q. of 80 to 90 has a particularly traumatic school experience, even when his sense of industry is rewarded and encouraged at home. He is "too bright" to be in special classes, but "too slow" to compete with children of average ability. Consequently he experiences constant failures in his academic efforts that reinforces a sense of inferiority.

On the other hand, the child who had his sense of industry derogated at home can have it revitalized at school through the offices of a sensitive and committed teacher. Whether the child develops a sense of industry or inferiority, therefore, no longer depends solely on the caretaking efforts of the parents but on the actions and offices of other adults as well.

Identity vs. Role Confusion

When the child moves into adolescence (Stage Five—roughly the ages 12-18), he encounters, according to traditional psychoanalytic theory, a reawakening of the family-romance problem of early childhood. His means of resolving the problem is to seek and find a romantic partner of his own generation. While Erikson does not deny this aspect of adolescence, he points out that there are other problems as well. The adolescent matures mentally as well as physiologically and, in addition to the new feelings, sensations and desires he experiences as a result of changes in his body, he develops a multitude of new ways of looking at and thinking about the world. Among other things, those in adolescence can now think about other people's thinking and wonder about what other people think of them. They can also conceive of ideal families, religions and societies which they then compare with the imperfect families, religions and societies of their own experience. Finally, adolescents become capable of constructing theories and philosophies designed to bring all the varied and conflicting aspects of society into a working, harmonious and peaceful whole. The adolescent, in a word, is an impatient idealist who believes that it is as easy to realize an ideal as it is to imagine it.

Erikson believes that the new interpersonal dimension which emerges during this period has to do with a sense of *ego identity* at the positive end and a sense of *role confusion* at the negative end. That is to say, given the adolescent's newfound integrative abilities, his task is to bring together all of the things he has learned about himself as a son, student, athlete, friend, Scout, newspaper boy, and so on, and integrate these different images of himself into a whole that makes sense and that shows continuity with the past while preparing for the future. To the extent that the young person succeeds in this endeavor, he arrives at a sense of psychosocial identity, a sense of who he is, where he has been and where he is going.

In contrast to the earlier stages, where parents play a more or less direct role in the determination of the result of the developmental crises, the influence of parents during this stage is much more indirect. If the young person reaches adolescence with, thanks to his parents, a vital sense of trust, autonomy, initiative and industry, then his chances of arriving at a meaningful sense of ego identity are much enhanced. The reverse, of course, holds true for the young person who enters adolescence with considerable mistrust, shame, doubt, guilt and inferiority. Preparation for a successful adolescence, and the attainment of an integrated psychosocial identity must, therefore, begin in the cradle.

Over and above what the individual brings with him from his childhood, the attainment of a sense of personal identity depends upon the social milieu in which he or she grows up. For example, in a society where women are to some extent second-class citizens, it may be harder for females to arrive at a sense of psychosocial identity. Likewise at times, such as the present, when rapid social and technological change breaks down many traditional values, it may be more difficult for young people to find continuity between what they learned and experienced as children and what they learn and experience as adolescents. At such times young people often seek causes that give their lives meaning and direction. The activism of the current generation of young people may well stem, in part at least, from this search.

When the young person cannot attain a sense of personal identity, either because of an unfortunate childhood or difficult social circumstances, he shows a certain amount of *role confusion*—a sense of not knowing what he is, where he belongs or whom he belongs to. Such confusion is a frequent symptom in delinquent young people. Promiscuous adolescent girls, for example, often seem to have a fragmented sense of ego identity. Some young people seek a "negative identity," an identity opposite to the one prescribed for them by their family and friends. Having an identity as a "delinquent," or as a "hippie," or even as an "acid head," may sometimes be preferable to having no identity at all.

In some cases young people do not seek a negative identity so much as they have it thrust upon them. I remember another court case in which the defendant was an attractive 16-year-old girl who had been found "tricking it" in a trailer located just outside the grounds of an Air Force base. From about the age of 12, her mother had encouraged her to dress seductively and to go out with boys. When she returned from dates, her sexually frustrated mother demanded a kiss-by-kiss, caress-by-caress description of the evening's activities. After the mother had vicariously satisfied her sexual needs, she proceeded to call her daughter a "whore" and a "dirty tramp." As the girl told me, "Hell, I have the name, so I might as well play the role."

Failure to establish a clear sense of personal identity at adolescence does not guarantee perpetual failure. And the person who attains a working sense of ego identity in adolescence will of necessity encounter challenges and threats to that identity as he moves through life. Erikson, perhaps more than any other personality theorist, has emphasized that life is constant change and that confronting problems at one stage in life is not a guarantee against the reappearance of these problems at later stages, or against the finding of new solutions to them.

Intimacy vs. Isolation

Stage Six in the life cycle is young adulthood; roughly the period of courtship and early family life that extends from late adolescence till early middle age. For this stage, and the stages described hereafter, classical psychoanalysis has nothing new or major to say. For Erikson, however, the previous attainment of a sense of personal identity and the engagement in productive work that marks this period gives rise to a new interpersonal dimension of *intimacy* at the one extreme and *isolation* at the other.

When Erikson speaks of intimacy he means much more than love-making alone; he means the ability to share with and care about another person without fear of losing oneself in the process. In the case of intimacy, as in the case of identity, success or failure no longer depends directly upon the parents but only indirectly as they have contributed to the individual's success or failure at the earlier stages. Here, too, as in the case of identity, social conditions may help or hinder the establishment of a sense of intimacy. Likewise, intimacy need not involve sexuality; it includes the relationship between friends. Soldiers who have served together under the most dangerous circumstances often develop a sense of commitment to one another that exemplifies intimacy in its broadest sense. If a sense of intimacy is not established with friends or a marriage partner, the result, in Erikson's view, is a sense of isolation—of being alone without anyone to share with or care for.

Generativity vs. Self-absorption

This stage   middle age—brings with it what Erikson speaks of as either *generativity or self-absorption,* and stagnation. What Erikson means by generativity is that the person begins to be concerned with others beyond his immediate family, with future generations and the nature of the society and world in which those generations will live. Generativity does not reside only in parents; it can be found in any individual who actively concerns himself with the welfare of young people and with making the world a better place for them to live and to work.

Those who fail to establish a sense of generativity fall into a state of self-absorption in which their personal needs and comforts are of predominant concern. A fictional case of self-absorption is Dickens's Scrooge in "A Christmas Carol." In his one-sided concern with money and in his disregard for the interests and welfare of his young employee, Bob Cratchit, Scrooge exemplifies the self-absorbed, embittered (the two often go together) old man. Dickens also illustrated, however, what Erikson points out: namely, that unhappy solutions to life's crises are not irreversible. Scrooge, at the end of the tale, manifested both a sense of generativity and of intimacy which he had not experienced before.

Integrity vs. Despair

Stage Eight in the Eriksonian scheme corresponds roughly to the period when the individual's major efforts are nearing completion and when there is time for reflection—and for the enjoyment of grandchildren, if any. The psychosocial dimension that comes into prominence now has *integrity* on one hand and *despair* on the other.

The sense of integrity arises from the individual's ability to look back on his life with satisfaction. At the other extreme is the individual who looks back upon his life as a series of missed opportunities and missed directions; now in the twilight years he realizes that it is too late to start again. For such a person the inevitable result is a sense of despair at what might have been.

These, then, are the major stages in the life cycle as described by Erikson. Their presentation, for one thing, frees the clinician to treat adult emotional problems as failures (in part at least) to solve genuinely adult personality crises and not, as heretofore, as mere residuals of infantile frustrations and conflicts. This view of personality growth, moreover, takes some of the onus off parents and takes account of the role which society and the person himself play in the formation of an individual personality. Finally, Erikson has offered hope for us all by demonstrating that each phase of growth has its strengths as well as its weaknesses and that failures at one stage of development can be rectified by successes at later stages.

The reason that these ideas, which sound so agreeable to "common sense," are in fact so revolutionary has a lot to do with the state of psychoanalysis in America. As formulated by Freud, psychoanalysis encompassed a theory of personality development, a method of studying the human mind and, finally, procedures for treating troubled and unhappy people. Freud viewed this system as a scientific one, open to revision as new facts and observations accumulated.

The system was, however, so vehemently attacked that Freud's followers were constantly in the position of having to defend Freud's views. Perhaps because of this situation, Freud's system became, in the hands of some of his followers and defenders, a dogma upon which all theoretical innovation, clinical observation and therapeutic practice had to be grounded. That this attitude persists is evidenced in the recent remark by a psychoanalyst that he believed psychotic patients could not be treated by psychoanalysis because "Freud said so." Such attitudes, in which Freud's authority rather than observation and data is the basis of deciding what is true and what is false, has contributed to the disrepute in which psychoanalysis is widely held today.

Adolescents are influenced by three groups: parents, peers, and teachers or employers. As the adolescent acquires various skills he incorporates the family's values and beliefs into his own self-concept. The influence of parents, peers, and teachers can help the adolescent acquire maturity, identity, and purpose; or it can get in the way of his maturing. Most adolescents have few real difficulties, but their path is not always smooth and straight. As we have already pointed out, the amount of time that modern adolescents spend in preparing for a career has dramatically lengthened their financial dependence on the family. This gives parents more control over their children. In previous generations the adolescent might already have left home, taken a job, and even be married by the age of seventeen.

What effect does this prolongued dependence have on parent-teenager relations? Modern parents handle their increased power in at least two ways: Some encourage independence and responsibility from their children; others try to prolong the control well beyond its usual limits leading to the so-called generation gap.

Once a teenager rebels against his parents, he generally conforms even more religiously to the patterns he sees in his peers. Most authorities agree that the lower-class adolescent is more likely to experience extended parental authority and consequently to rebel against his family compared with his middle-class peers. To be accepted and popular with his group requires conformity to their customs. Among males for the most part this means athletic ability, standing up against aggression from others, and a strong sexual interest in females. For girls, it may mean she must be physically attractive, be popular with males, and be socially poised and natural.

How can this problem be avoided? If parents train their children for both independence *and* responsibility at an early age and then have the courage to let the child make his own mistakes and learn from them, the generation gap need never appear.

Physical Development during Adolescence

One characteristic of adolescence is rapid physical and sexual growth.

Next to uncertainty and rebellion, the most characteristic trait of adolescence is physical and sexual growth. And, although there is general agreement that physical and psychological maturity are not the same, the growth of primary and secondary sexual characteristics transform boys and girls into men and women. For females, the definite symbol of such maturity is her first menstruation. Several less-dramatic events signal manhood. These male signs include the appearance of pubic hair, increased body size and muscular strength, and the growth of his penis and testicles.

Physical Changes during Puberty

Hormone ratios
change during ado-
lescence.

During childhood both boys and girls produce male (androgen) and female (estrogen) hormones. As they near puberty, the proportions of these two hormones change, and there is a sharp increase in the production of androgen among boys and estrogen among girls. Female menstruation is anticipated by cyclic variation in the level of estrogen. Female sexual maturity is characterized by:

1. Growth of the breasts.
2. Appearance of straight, pigmented pubic hair.
3. Rapid body growth.
4. Appearance of kinky public hair.
5. Menarche—the beginning of menstruation.
6. Growth of underarm hair.

Females mature sexu-
ally around 13 years
of age.

The age at which U.S. American females mature sexually varies from nine to seventeen years, with an average at around thirteen years of age. Menarche does not necessarily signal fertility, because most females begin to menstruate at least a year before their ovaries produce fertile sex cells. Frank Beach has cited evidence which suggest that most human females are not fertile until about fifteen years of age, and many authorities agree that the optimum age for producing babies is between nineteen and thirty years in females.

Males mature sexually
around 15 years of
age.

For males, the signs of sexual maturity are:

1. Growth of the testes and penis is accelerated.
2. The soft hair on the upper lip becomes more coarse and dark.
3. The pubic region becomes covered with hairs.
4. The voice begins to deepen.
5. The penis and testes reach adult proportions and size.
6. The body reaches full size and strength.
7. Body hair appropriate for the young adult is fully developed.

Most authorities agree that males reach sexual maturity about two years later than females. Several studies of physical and sexual development among U.S. males place their average age of maturity at around fifteen.

Maturation average
age has lowered over
the last century.

The average age of sexual and physical maturity has gradually lowered over the last century from around sixteen years of age to about thirteen years of age among Western females. This earlier sexual maturity comes at a time when education and social independence is taking longer and longer, and the two trends have caused a serious displacement in the social development of adolescents in the U.S.

Adolescents' expec-
tations and status are
quite discrepant.

The legal age for drinking, driving, induction into the armed forces, and the age of consent for sexual intercourse for females have not been lowered for over a century. At the same time, young people are maturing physically at an earlier and earlier age. The voting age was recently lowered from twenty-one to eighteen in an attempt to bring more young people into the political process in recognition of their need to enter adult society. But there is still a large discrepancy between the adolescents' maturity and adult status.

Adolescents vary in their reactions to sexual maturity.

The adolescents' psychological reaction to sexual maturity ranges from joy to horror. A female is most likely to be happy about menstruation and sexual maturity if her mother has prepared her for the event, if she has a wholesome image of herself as a female, and if she is accepting of a feminine role. If she is not so prepared, and her feelings about femininity are ambivalent, a young girls' reaction to the thought of menstruation, sexuality, and marriage may be negative.

Females are concerned about breast development.

Males are much less likely to reject or dread sexual maturity, probably because young females worry about their physical development much more than do boys. During adolescence, both males and females are concerned about whether their bodies are attractive or not to the opposite sex. For a female, the development of her breasts is an extremely important characteristic of sexual maturity. Female breast development begins before other signs of sexual maturity, and is usually complete by the onset of menstruation. In a systematic study of several hundred females E.L. Reynolds and J.V. Wines (1948) reported that the growth of breasts requires about three years on the average and is usually complete by fourteen years of age. They found that most female breasts could be classified as either small, medium, or large; and flat, rounded, or conical. Figure 14.3 shows the frequency of various breast types among U.S. females classified by these researchers.

As you might expect, young males are concerned about the size of

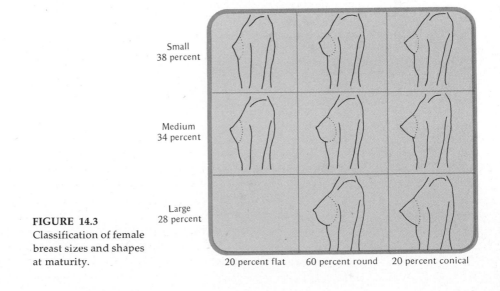

Small
38 percent

Medium
34 percent

Large
28 percent

FIGURE 14.3
Classification of female breast sizes and shapes at maturity.

20 percent flat   60 percent round   20 percent conical

their bodies and, in particular, the relative size of the penis. Actual measurements of penis length show considerable variation with age and individuals. For example, the range of penis length when stretched but not erected is about 2.4 to 4.8 inches at thirteen years of age, and 4.2 to 6 inches at eighteen years of age. Often, young males with small sexual organs feel that their bodies are also going to be small, but in fact there is little relation between body size and penis length. W. Masters and V. Johnson (1966) report that the ability to satisfy a female partner sexually is not related so much to penis size as to other factors like sexual technique and understanding of the partner.

Overweight can be a serious problem during adolescence.

Another problem for maturing boys and girls is that they are likely to be overweight during the middle stages of adolescence. In the total population about 10 percent of people are judged overweight. In contrast, 12 percent of fifteen-year-old white males, 7 percent of black males, 15 percent of white females, and 21 percent of black females are judged to be overweight. Young white males have fat deposits around their thighs, lower trunks, and genital areas which will disappear with maturity, but which can be embarrassing while it exists. Overweight is the result of many factors: Chief among them are overeating, poor dietary balance, and a genetic predisposition toward overweight.

The Adolescent Growth Period

Maturity is controlled by the pituitary gland.

During the adolescent years an average youth's height increases about 25 percent and his weight almost doubles. There is wide individual variation in the rate and timing of this growth period, but it is orchestrated by a gland of the endocrine system called the *pituitary*. This master-control gland is located at the base of the brain in human beings. Its hormonal secretions stimulate the adrenal glands to produce other hormones which stimulate gonadal and growth hormones to accelerate the body's growth and sexual maturity. Once sufficient growth and gonadal hormones are produced, they inhibit further production of pituitary hormones—a good example of balanced feedback control. The particular timing and sequence of hormonal changes in growth and sexual maturity is primarily genetically controlled.

Numerous physiological changes happen during adolescence.

During this growth period, the teenager's neck, arms, and legs grow faster than the rest of his body, making him look long-legged and coltish. Boys' shoulders grow broader and girls hips enlarge. There are also numerous internal physiological changes during the adolescent growth period. Male blood pressure increases and his total metabolic rate increases relative to the average female. During the adolescent growth period there may be asynchrony, or lack of sameness, in the rate of body growth between two halves of the body. Any differential growth rate between one side of the body and the other can make the adolescent feel very self-conscious. Not only does the body change, but the head proportions of boys and girls also shift during adolescence, with particular

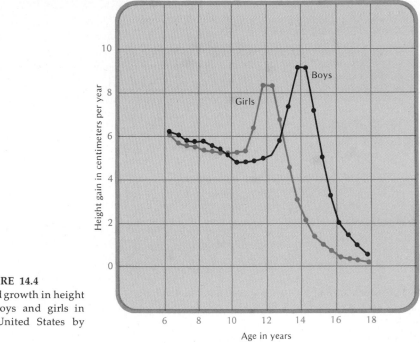

FIGURE 14.4
Rapid growth in height for boys and girls in the United States by age.

changes occurring in the forehead, mouth, and lips. Figure 14.4 shows the periods of rapid growth between eleven and thirteen for girls, and fourteen and sixteen for boys in the U.S.

Many psychological changes happen.

During this period of rapid physical change, there are also psychological shifts happening to the adolescent which have far-reaching consequences. For one thing, as we have seen, he is shifting from parental to peer guidance and control.

The Peer Group

Adolescent groups contain three levels of structure.

An adolescent group really contains several interrelated levels of organization. The most inclusive peer group structure is the *crowd*; next comes the *clique*; and, finally, there are individual *friendships*. The crowd is composed of many adolescents who congregate to pursue mutual interests or activities. Individuals in cliques are emotionally much closer, and clique formation is based primarily on personal attraction rather than simply shared activities. Most social scientists believe that the relation between crowds and cliques is reciprocal. A crowd contains the cliques, whose primary functions are talking, planning, and evaluating social activities; while the crowd actually participates in the social acts. A clique may plan, organize, and prepare a party; the entire crowd participates in the party; and then the clique reforms to evaluate and communicate about what happened. As you might expect, cliques function most during the week and the crowd comes together on weekends. There are several stages of clique and crowd development throughout the adolescent years. Stage One is composed of primarily all boy or all girl cliques, with almost no heterosexual interaction. Stage Two begins with the formation of heterosexual crowds for interaction at dances and the like, but the cliques are still primarily all male or all female. Only during Stage Three, with the beginning of sexual maturity for males and females, do heterosexual cliques form. During Stage Four these heterosexual cliques begin to break up into loosely associated couples.

Friendship and Peer Acceptance

Friendships are important.

Beyond the crowd and cliques, friendships are also important to the adolescent. In fact, many social scientists argue that adolescent friendships are the most important part of peer relations. They point out that instead of playing a role or trying to impress others with his sophistication, the adolescent can be more open and honest with a friend. They believe that close friends contribute to an adolescent's social and personal maturity in ways similar to those the child's parents performed at an earlier time.

Friendships allow true feelings to surface.

Adolescents are struggling to understand themselves and their relations with others at a time when their bodies and social roles are changing rapidly. Friendships help this process along by allowing true feelings and fears to surface and be talked about, so that they can be evaluated and handled constructively. The alternative to self-examination is denial, fear, and misunderstanding between an adolescent and his peers. Adolescence is a time when even the self-concept is open for evaluation and possible revision based on friendly feedback from an intimate friend.

Friends have similar social backgrounds and tastes.

Adolescent friendships occur most often between teenagers of similar intelligence, social-class background, age, tastes, sex, and career goals. Occasionally, there is attraction between opposites, but not often. Girls have more friendships that last longer, and they invest more emotional and social importance in their friends, than boys do. This difference probably occurs because females pay more attention to interpersonal relations, are more concerned about love and nurturance, and fear rejection and loss of love more than most males. Whether this difference is social or biological is not the main point. The differences exist, and they can help us understand adolescents.

Popularity is caused by many factors.

Many factors are associated with popularity or rejection by peers. Adolescents describe a popular peer with words like tolerant, flexible, cheerful, goodnatured, sympathetic, has a sense of humor, and is self-confident. By contrast, their descriptions of unpopular peers include words like ill-at-ease, lacking in self-confidence, timid, nervous, withdrawn; or aggressive, conceited, and demanding. Adolescents who have personal traits that make others feel comfortable are liked by their groups, while people who make others uncomfortable are rejected.

Intelligence and social class affect friendships.

A number of other characteristics affect peer acceptance or rejection. Chief among these are intelligence, social status, and ethnic group membership. Studies show that bright, middle-class, or white children are more socially accepted than dull, lower-class, or minority adolescents, depending on the peer group or social institution. Unhappily, the socially rejected adolescent is often caught in a vicious circle—he is rejected, feels isolated, withdraws or acts hostile, and then is rejected even more strongly because of the withdrawal or hostility. There are no easy ways to break this cycle. Intervention by an older friend, a parent, or an understanding peer can sometimes stop the decline and begin a more constructive interpersonal relationship for a rejected adolescent.

There is a difference between liking and loving someone.

Zick Rubin (1973) has recently argued for a fundamental difference between liking a friend and loving a mate. He developed the internally consistent but independent pair of scales in Table 14.1, and found that males liking and loving scales are more highly correlated (.56) than are girls liking and loving scales (.36). He speculated that this difference occurs because men tend to be the task specialists in our society, while women are more the social-emotional specialists. Because of this, Rubin argued that women are more sensitive to interpersonal relations than men, and thus women make finer discriminations than men between loving and liking others.

Loving scores are associated with marriage plans.

Another interesting finding of his study was that while the average love scores of men for their women friends and women for their men friends were almost identical, the liking scores of men for women were much lower than the liking scores of women for men. Rubin also found that women tend to like their same sex friends more than males do; and he discovered a much higher association between the *loving* scores of couples and their estimates of marriage prospects as compared with the association between *liking* and marriage prospects. This finding probably reflects the idea in our society that marriage should be based on love rather than liking for the mate.

Money argues that sex role is determined by experience.

SEX-ROLE DETERMINANTS   John Money (1965), a long-time student of sexual development, argues that the primary determinant of human sexual behavior is experience rather than genetic endowment. Money believes that human babies are neutral about sex role at birth, and only after they pass through two critical periods of sexual imprinting, in which irreversible gender roles are acquired, do they become differentiated into men and women. He suggests that one of these critical periods of sexual imprinting occurs between birth and three years of age, while the second happens during puberty.

Money and his colleagues base their critical-period hypothesis on

TABLE 14.1   Love-scale and Liking-scale Items

Love Scale

1. If _____ were feeling bad, my first duty would be to cheer him (her) up.
2. I feel that I can confide in _____ about virtually everything.
3. I find it easy to ignore _____'s faults.
4. I would do almost anything for _____.
5. I feel very possessive toward _____.
6. If I could never be with _____, I would feel miserable.
7. If I were lonely, my first thought would be to seek _____ out.
8. One of my primary concerns is _____'s welfare.
9. I would forgive _____ for practically anything.
10. I feel responsible for _____'s well-being.
11. When I am with _____, I spend a good deal of time just looking at him (her).
12. I would greatly enjoy being confided in by _____.
13. It would be hard for me to get along without _____.

Liking Scale

1. When I am with _____, we almost always are in the same mood.
2. I think that _____ is unusually well-adjusted.
3. I would highly recommend _____ for a responsible job.
4. In my opinion, _____ is an exceptionally mature person.
5. I have great confidence in _____'s good judgment.
6. Most people would react favorably to _____ after a brief acquaintance.
7. I think that _____ and I are quite similar to one another.
8. I would vote for _____ in a class or group election.
9. I think that _____ is one of those people who quickly wins respect.
10. I feel that _____ is an extremely intelligent person.
11. _____ is one of the most likable people I know.
12. _____ is the sort of person whom I myself would like to be.
13. It seems to me that it is very easy for _____ to gain admiration.

From Zick Rubin, *Liking and Loving: An Invitation to Social Psychology* (New York: Holt, Rinehart and Winston, Inc., 1973), p. 216.

Diamond argued that sex role is innate.

observations collected from over a hundred cases of persons with contradictory sexual characteristics, like *hermaphrodites* with both male and female sex traits, chromosomal patterns, or internal reproductive organs. The investigators interviewed and observed their subjects for mannerisms, interests, and life histories. They determined the particular sex role that each hermaphrodite assumed, and how that sex role was related to various other factors like chromosomal sex, gonadal sex, hormonal sex, internal sexual organs, external genitalia, and assigned social role. They reported that, without exception, the assigned social role of the person matched the person's adopted rather than his chromosomal sex. Other investigators have criticized these conclusions. M. Diamond (1965) argued that for man to be sexually neutral at birth would make him different from all other animals, and that seems unlikely. Instead, Diamond argued, biological and environmental factors jointly determine the sex role of a human infant or adult.

Sexual Attitudes and Behaviors

Sexual attitudes vary between cultures.

Probably the most critical and potentially difficult adjustment for an adolescent is his developing sexuality. The urges and desires associated with biological maturity are strong and cannot be ignored, while the manners and customs of sex vary greatly from culture to culture and class to class. Among the Zuni Indians of New Mexico there is little sexual play before adolescence, and young children are not encouraged to explore sexuality until they are physically mature. Among the Melanesian cultures of New Guinea sex play is encouraged and taken for granted among even very young children. Cultural attitudes vary all the way from complete acceptance of sexual intercourse at a very early age to punishment of sexual play by death for both parties. Some African and Indian groups encourage sexual intercourse among children so that by the age of ten years, there are no virgin females in the tribe. Other groups try to prevent intercourse until after marriage.

Sexual relations probably reflect basic cultural values.

This enormous variation in cultural attitudes and behaviors seems to have strong consequences for personal feelings about sex. Some anthropologists argue that sexual relations within a culture simply reflect the general attitudes of that culture. If interpersonal relations are honest, open, and cooperative, the researchers assert, then sexual feelings and acts can also be open, honest, and cooperative. If cultural relations are dishonest, competitive, and hostile, then sexual relations in that culture will also be dishonest, competitive, and hostile. Given this cultural variation in sexual customs and attitudes, where do the attitudes of U.S. adolescents fit?

Male and female sex attitudes are different.

SEXUAL ATTITUDES IN THE U.S.   When young adolescents are asked whether there has been a revolution in U.S. sexual attitudes, they will almost all say yes. They are often quick to add that the change has been in what people say about sex, rather than in actual sexual behavior. Adolescents believe that the main difference between sexual attitudes in the U.S. now and a generation earlier is in the willingness of young people to be honest and open about it instead of hypocritical as their parents were. This adolescent honesty about sexuality is reflected in a desire for sex education courses in schools and a concern about the personal factors of sexuality rather than public morality.

Most psychologists believe that sexual attitudes are made up of three components: information, feelings, and actions. They find that male and female attitudes about sex are quite different.

Females desire more sex education.

FEMALE SEX ATTITUDES   Surveys show that practically all teenage girls want more detailed and explicit information about sex. Figure 14.5 shows the frequency of various facts about sex in contemporary sex-education courses, and also the percentage of females who want these items included in a comprehensive sex-education course. These young women

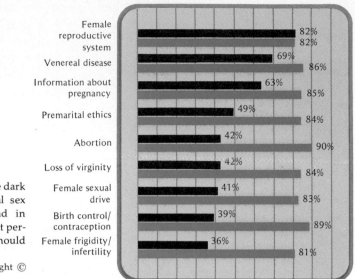

FIGURE 14.5
Sexual attitudes and behavior. The dark bars show the amount of formal sex education young girls have had in school. The yellow bars show what percentage of girls feel the subject should be taught in school.
(From *Seventeen* ® July 1970. Copyright © 1970 by Triangle Publications, Inc.)

are most interested in learning more about venereal disease, pregnancy, abortion, and birth control. In fact, they are strongly interested in all aspects of human sexuality.

Girls learn about sex from many sources.

Where do young girls learn about sex? Figure 14.6 shows they receive most of their information from mothers, books, friends, and schools; but that they believe their mothers, schools, doctors, and fathers much more than other sources. Interestingly, young girls believe their peers are unreliable sources of information about sex.

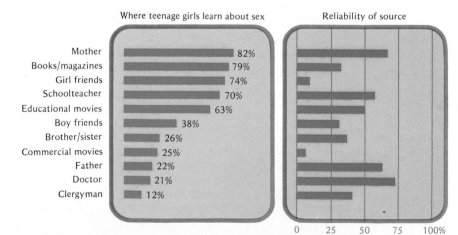

FIGURE 14.6 Sources of sex information among adolescent girls.
(From M. Hunt, Copyright © 1970 by Triangle Publications, Inc.)

Young girls are inter-
ested in love and
security.

How do young females feel about sex? Most surveys show that adolescent girls are interested in love and security rather than sexual intercourse. Most males are more interested in sexual intercourse, and only later in love and marriage. Many authorities agree that young females are encouraged from an early age to use sexual enticements to attract and keep males interested in them. At the same time, they are advised to refrain from sexual intercourse because coitus is supposed to make the male lose interest and respect for the female and it is supposed to lower her ability to get married.

Many adolescents
enjoy premarital
intercourse.

Table 14.2 shows the frequency of various sexual experiences reported by adolescent females from five Western countries. Note that almost all these young females report that they engage in deep kissing, and about half admit that they engage in sexual intercourse before marriage. Apparently many young females are neither taking their parent's advice

TABLE 14.2   Percent of females reporting experiencing respective sexual behaviors.

Type of sexual behavior	United States	Canada	England	Germany	Norway
Light embracing or fond holding of hands	97.5	96.5	91.9	94.8	89.3
Casual goodnight kissing	96.8	91.8	93.0	74.0	75.0
Deep kissing	96.5	91.8	93.0	90.6	89.3
Horizontal embrace with some petting but not undressed	83.3	81.2	79.1	77.1	75.0
Petting of girl's breast area from outside her clothing	78.3	78.8	82.6	76.0	64.3
Petting of girl's breast area without clothes intervening	67.8	64.7	70.9	66.7	58.9
Petting below the waist of the girl under her clothing	61.2	64.7	70.9	63.5	53.6
Petting below the waist of both boy and girl, under clothing	57.8	50.6	61.6	56.3	42.9
Nude embrace	49.6	47.6	64.0	62.1	51.8
Coitus	43.2	35.3	62.8	59.4	53.6
One-night affair involving coitus; didn't date person again	7.2	5.9	33.7	4.2	12.5
Whipping or spanking before petting or other intimacy	4.5	5.9	17.4	1.0	7.1
(N)	(688)	(85)	(86)	(96)	(56)

From E. Luckey and G.A. Nass, 1969. By permission.

nor finding it applicable to the contemporary youth culture. Based on these data, it appears that a majority of adolescent females no longer require marriage as a precondition for coitus, but almost all say they want love and a strong emotional attachment to their sexual partner.

Males and females have endured a double standard of sexual behavior.

MALE SEX ATTITUDES   Traditionally, males and females have been subjected to a double standard about sexual behavior. Earlier generations assumed that males like sex more, act on their sexual impulses more often, and know more about sexual matters than their female peers. However, recent surveys suggest that this double standard of sexual behavior is changing, because modern females are behaving the way males were allowed to act in the past. Table 14.3 shows the relative frequency of reported coitus among college females and males in five Western countries. These data indicate that there is still a bias toward more frequent male sexual experience (except among German adolescents), but the difference is smaller than in earlier generations. Whether this change reflects a real shift in actions or merely a willingness to admit sexual behaviors now which were denied earlier is not known. Sexual behavior among adolescent males usually begins with masturbation at around the age of fourteen, and continues to heterosexual contact at around sixteen years of age. By the age of twenty-five, 65 percent of unmarried males report that they have engaged in premarital intercourse.

TABLE 14.3   College students who have experienced sexual intercourse (1969).

Country	Boys (percent)	Girls (percent)
United States	58.2	43.3
Canada	56.8	35.3
England	74.8	62.8
Germany	54.5	59.4
Norway	66.7	53.6

Adolescents express several fears about sexual behavior.

What are the current problems associated with sex? A majority of teenagers admit to guilt about some sexual behaviors, and fears of venereal disease, worries about pregnancy and loss of love. In particular, females are concerned about the last three. The most serious concern among adolescents is what to do about an unwanted pregnancy. The traditional solution was for their parents to insist that the young couple marry immediately. The alternative was an illegal and dangerous abortion. Unhappily, neither of these solutions worked very well. For one thing, a young married couple often became financially dependent on their parents, or were forced to drop out of school in order to earn a living and care for the baby. They might neither like each other nor be mature enough for marriage.

One proposed solution for an unwanted pregnancy is to make abortions available to teenage girls without their parent's consent, and to provide effective contraceptive techniques to them so that an unwanted pregnancy will not occur in the first place. Such a solution is attractive to many teenage girls, but parents often find the prospect of adolescent contraception or abortion distasteful. Teenage sexual behavior is potentially a very troublesome problem for children and their parents. Disagreements about proper acts can strain understanding and mutual respect to the breaking point.

One solution for unplanned pregnancy is abortion.

Vocational Choice

Career choice is a challenge.

Another challenge that must be met by adolescent boys and girls is the choice of a career. What are the vocational alternatives available to the modern teenager?

Careers have been more important for males.

A career has generally been more important for adolescent males than females because even in this age of woman's liberation more men than women are employed and among employed persons, men have been working more years of their lives than women of comparable skills and education. This may be changing, however.

Career choices are based on many things.

The choice of what to do about a job is crucial to the long-term satisfaction and maturity of adolescents. A career choice and the preparation necessary to achieve that goal meet many needs beyond the obvious one of money. Chief among these are self-satisfaction, self-esteem, independence, security, and development of a self-concept. Since career choices are very important to U.S. adolescents, what type of information is available and what factors help determine their careers?

Career choice is becoming more and more complex.

Most authorities agree that occupational choice is becoming more and more complex in modern society. As machines assume more menial tasks, people are being shifted into service occupations and more sophisticated jobs. The result has been that higher levels of education are being required for entrance into top occupations. The extract below illustrates ratings given to various careers over the past decades. Note that doctor, lawyer, college professor, and engineer have remained high on the list, and that law has gained in attractiveness within recent times, particularly among people under thirty years of age. Also, many people believe they will become teachers after they graduate from college. The common characteristic of all these professions is that they require extensive higher education. Middle-class adolescents recognize the college requirement and agree that college is the most likely route to a high-status occupation. Lower class adolescents are often much less sure that college will help their later careers (*see* Table 14.4).

The following table compares the choices of the American public (18 and older) with those recorded in surveys taken on our earlier occasions during the past 23 years.

TABLE 14.4

	'73 %	'67 %	'62 %	'53 %	'50 %
Doctor	28	29	23	29	29
Lawyer	14	8	6	6	8
Engineer-Builder	13	14	18	20	16
Professor-Teacher	10	12	12	5	5
Business Executive	10	7	5	7	8
Dentist	7	4	4	6	4
Clergyman	7	8	8	7	8
Government Career	5	7	7	3	6
Banker	2	1	2	2	4
Other, none, don't know	4	10	15	15	12

The following table shows the choices of adults under 30 years of age compared with those recorded in 1962:

TABLE 14.5

	Latest %	'62 %
Doctor	25	26
Lawyer	20	8
Engineer-Builder	14	17
Professor-Teacher	14	18
Business Executive	9	3
Dentist	6	5
Government Career	6	7
Banker	2	2
Clergyman	1	4
Other, none, don't know	3	10

The results are based on a nationwide survey of 1,576 adults, 18 and older, interviewed during the period Oct. 6-8.

Here is the question asked:

What field or occupation do you plan to enter when you complete your education?

The results:

TABLE 14.6

	National %	Men %	Women %
Teaching	23	17	32
Medical care	14	10	20
Business	12	13	11
Law	10	13	5
Research and science	8	9	7
The arts (theater, music, painting, writing, crafts)	7	5	9
Social work	6	4	9
Engineering	4	7	x
Accounting/Auditing	3	4	2
Government work	3	4	2
Clergy	2	3	1
Military	2	2	1
Farming	1	2	x
Journalism	1	1	1
Sales	1	2	x
Service (airline hostess, cook, domestic help)	1	2	x
Urban planning	1	1	x
Miscellaneous	4	4	2
Don't know/no answer	6	7	6

x — Less than 1%.
Total exceeds 100% because of multiple responses.

Source: Los Angeles Times.

The results are based on interviews with 1,089 full-time students, representing 60 campuses.

Social class affects occupation.

Regardless of social class, career choices become more realistic and stable with age. There is also a strong relation between social class, intelligence, and occupational choice.

Parent Influences on Career Choices

Family background also influences career choice.

An adolescent's family background influences his vocational aspirations in two ways: by encouragement and example. If IQ and social status are controlled, then adolescents whose parents are ambitious will have higher levels of aspiration than adolescents whose parents are not. An adolescent's father strongly influences his son's but not his daughter's choice of occupation. Sons often follow in their father's footsteps, if they can. Thus, almost 44 percent of physicians' sons choose medicine for their careers, and around 30 percent of lawyers' sons enter law.

Peer Influences on Career Plans

Peers and school can affect occupational choice.

Peers and the school can influence an adolescent's career choices independently of his family. Table 14.7 shows the percent of lower- and middle-class boys who aspire to higher status occupations. These boys were separated on the basis of both peer and family influences. Note that within the four categories, middle-class boys are consistently higher in career aspirations than their lower-class peers. Parents seemed to have more affect on adolescent ambitions compared with peers, but both affect the choice.

TABLE 14.7

| Source and extent of influence | Percent aspiring to high-status occupations | | | |
| | Working-class | | Middle-class | |
	(N)	Percent	(N)	Percent
1. Both high	(28)	71.4	(94)	81.9
2. Parents high, peers low	(45)	55.6	(50)	78.0
3. Peers high, parents low	(70)	35.7	(109)	72.5
4. Both low	(168)	25.6	(113)	30.1

Source: From R.L. Simpson, 1962. By permission of the American Sociological Association.

A career choice should be based on future opportunities.

Any study of career choices should consider both jobs that are currently available and those which are likely to be available in the future. Figure 14.7 shows one set of projections of expanding sections of the U.S. economy. In terms of percentage growth, computer programing, oceanography, social work, and physics are better bets for careers than ele-

FIGURE 14.7
A set of projections by percents of expanding sectors in the U.S. economy. These might be considered good areas for career exploration.

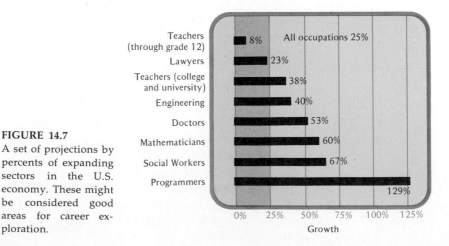

mentary-school teaching or pharmacy. Remember that the actual number of teachers and pharmacists is much larger than the total number of physicists and oceanographers, so there may be many more actual jobs available in large, slower-growing fields compared with the smaller but faster-growing areas of the economy.

Problems of Adolescent Development

Dropping Out

School dropouts face a difficult future.

Most authorities agree that teenagers who are dropping out, are delinquent, or use drugs are all too many. In a complex society, that is becoming more and more technological and specialized, the school dropout is in a difficult position. He has neither the abilities, the skills, nor the motivation necessary to survive in an industrial society. The school dropout is most likely to be from an urban, low-income, minority area.

Many factors influence dropping out.

Many factors are associated with dropping out of school. More dropouts come from low social classes; only one in fifty upper-class adolescents drop out compared with one in two from the lower class. Economic disadvantage is not the only cause of school dropouts, however. Low intelligence, with the resulting frustration and lack of understanding, also contribute to a desire to leave school. The dropout lacks motivation, is two or more years behind his age mates in reading and computation skills, and has failed one or more years of elementary school by the time he reaches the sixth grade. For many lower-class adolescents, school is an academic and social nightmare. They do not participate in as many social activities, share few of the same values as their teachers and middle-class peers, and feel inadequate and resentful about the differences between them and more advantaged peers. The dropout tends to be governed by impulses and is unable to plan ahead or to inhibit his resentments against authority.

Family background affects dropout rate.

Even when social status, intelligence, and income are matched, there are still family differences between dropouts and children who remain in school. Studies show that the families of school dropouts are neither communicative nor close, as compared with families of the children who stay in school. Dropouts say their families care little about them, and they feel distant from their parents and their peer groups. Typical dropouts have friends with similar backgrounds and interests, so they will reinforce the inability to cope with school.

Delinquency

A juvenile delinquent is underage.

Juvenile delinquency is defined as the misbehavior of children or adolescents under the age of seventeen. Although delinquents are generally in their teens by the time they come to the court's attention, their problems began much earlier and there were usually clear signs of trouble to come.

There are differences in male and female juvenile offenses.

There are striking differences between male and female delinquency. Boys used to be five times as likely to run into difficulties with the law or the courts as girls were, although the sex difference is now down to three times more frequent for boys. Boys often engage in violent crimes, while girls are usually arrested for running away from home or for prostitution. Both the amount of juvenile delinquency and the percentage of young people who appear in U.S. courts has increased rather dramatically over the past few decades. Authorities estimate that about 15 percent of all contemporary adolescents and over one-quarter of all male adolescents will come before the juvenile courts before they reach legal maturity at eighteen years of age. Figure 14.8 shows both the increased number of children in the ten to seventeen age range and the even larger increase in juvenile delinquency during the same years.

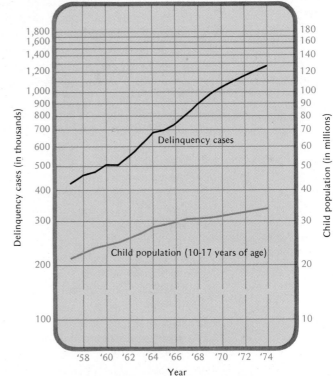

FIGURE 14.8
Numbers of teenage children in the population as compared with numbers of cases of delinquency.

Urban gangs are a serious problem.

One serious urban phenomenon is the emergence of organized juvenile gangs. These gangs engage in territorial defense, organized conscription, and wars among themselves. The gang offers many advantages to a juvenile: fellowship, protection, interesting activities, fun, and status. The costs of gang membership include acceptance of a code of conduct, defense of the territory, and obedience to the gang's leaders.

Adolescent personality also affects delinquency.

In addition to his social class, intelligence, and achievement motivation, the adolescents' personality and family also determine whether he will be delinquent. Healey and Bonner (1926) gathered early information from a sample of delinquent adolescents and compared their personality characteristics with those of their brothers and sisters. The researchers found that delinquents were more personally disturbed, their academic records were significantly lower, they were more discontent, and they felt more deprived of family relationships as compared with other members of the immediate family. A more recent study by J.J. Conger and W.C. Miller (1966) suggested that delinquent boys are less considerate, less friendly, less responsible, more impulsive, and more antagonistic toward authority as compared with a matched group of nondelinquent adolescents of comparable IQ, age, socioeconomic status, and sex. These personal differences among delinquent boys first appeared during early childhood and were followed by poor school performance and bad work habits in later childhood. Similar results were found for delinquent girls; They were less well-adjusted socially, emotionally, and academically as compared with matched nondelinquent peers. The delinquent girls were judged less mature emotionally, less socially poised, less friendly, less liked, and were generally rejected by their peers. The main differences between female and male delinquents occurred in emotional adjustment and conformity. The female delinquents were much more likely to be emotionally disturbed and also were less conforming. The largest differences between delinquent and nondelinquent boys occurred in areas of creative ability, self-reliance, and social relations with peers.

Delinquent juveniles' families are erratic.

The family atmosphere of delinquent boys and girls was characterized by lax, erratic, hostile discipline, and a great deal of physical punishment. Many delinquent boys expressed hostility toward and lack of identification with their fathers. Albert Bandura and Richard Walters (1963) intensively interviewed twenty-six delinquent boys and a similar number of matched nondelinquents. The researchers found that the parents of delinquent boys are rejecting and lack affection. The fathers of delinquent boys used harsh, physical punishment and ridicule to discipline their offspring. Most studies of delinquent boys show that their mothers are unloving and erratic in their application of discipline.

There are two types of delinquency.

An increasing number of investigators argue that there are two quite different types of delinquency: One they call the individual delinquent and the other a social delinquent. These authorities point out that in some sections of society delinquency is a way of life, and the social delinquent is simply identifying and acting on this available social pattern. They contrast the social delinquent with the misfit, who cannot cope with society and has withdrawn into a life of crime, violence, and illicit sexuality, who is an individual delinquent. Many authorities on juvenile delinquency believe that the social delinquent can be rehabilitated, particularly if he is discovered early enough. They are much more pessimistic about the future of individual delinquents, who, they apparently feel is so emotionally disturbed, intellectually under par, and socially debilitated that there is less hope for his rehabilitation. Whatever the merits of this theory, current practices are not working as well as society hoped. New, more effective methods are badly needed if we are to stop the trend toward more and more juvenile violence and crime in the U.S. Associated with this increased threat is the growth of drug use and abuse among young Americans.

Drugs

Drug use is increasing rapidly.

There has been a sharp increase in the use and abuse of almost all drugs by young people in the U.S. over the last few decades. Table 14.5 shows the pattern of general drug use among U.S. college students in 1971. The sharpest increase in drug use has been among college-age and younger adolescents who are experimenting with marijuana, amphetamines, and to a lesser extent barbiturates. However, the increasing use of drugs is not just a problem limited to adolescents.

Mass advertising encourages drug use.

In the United States mass advertising encourages widespread drug use. Billions of dollars are invested by the alcohol and tobacco industries to associate an illusion of happiness with drug-taking. Respectable, acceptable, conventional people take three or four mind-altering drugs each day. Caffeine, alcohol, nicotine, tranquilizers, or sleeping pills are examples. Peer pressure is another source of drug use. "You don't know what you're missing!" is familiar to many. Since young people were told lies about the "horrifying dangers of marijuana" they now believe no one.

The main cause of drug use is unhappiness.

Probably the main cause of drug use is personal unhappiness. Millions are frustrated, dissatisfied, and bored, so they turn to alcohol, tobacco, tranquilizers, or amphetamines to relieve distress. Children simply follow parental examples. Heroin addiction is a conspicuous example of drug abuse. It grows more addictive with use; is more compelling than marijuana, more habituating than tobacco, and more expensive than both.

Many theories of addiction exist.

CAUSES OF ADDICTION   Various explanations of addiction exist. One theory assumes narcotics are used to suppress anxiety, while another suggests drugs are used to produce good feelings. A third explanation assumes that addiction results from therapeutic drug use. Psychoanalysts believe that addicts remained at an early stage of psychosexual development or have regressed to infantile levels. They assume the addict was overindulged or overprotected by his parents, and as a consequence never learned to delay gratification. These unrealistic needs can never be fulfilled, and as a result the addict becomes self-loving, dependent, and hostile. But his dependency prevents the expression of hostility against his parent or others, so narcotics become an escape. According to the U.S. Bureau of Narcotics, addiction is a crime to be stopped by punishment. Probably all these formulations are incomplete. Drug use seems to depend jointly on availability, price, peer pressure, penalties, and personality. In the past addicts in the U.S. were most often sociopathic youngsters from lower-class minority groups. Contemporary drug abuse is spreading throughout all classes and races (*see* Table 14.8).

Drug response is modified by current social interaction and past experience, so certain questions can be explored only within a drug culture. Many things can be learned in the laboratory. One effect which can be studied carefully is the effect of drugs on the physiology of the brain. Central nervous system (CNS) synapses change their activity and chemical composition following drug use. Stimulating drugs produce a decrease in the breakdown of *noradrenaline* (NA), an arousal hormone which increases pulse rate and other internal body reactions. Depressants like heroin result in too little noradrenaline being produced. Following repeated drug use, the human central nervous system compensates for these increases or decreases in noradrenaline thereby producing habituation so that previous dosage levels become ineffective. To achieve a drug effect the user must continually increase his intake to compensate for this habituation. When the drug is no longer available to the body, the central nervous system adaptations tend to swing the person's mood to the opposite extreme. Following withdrawal, the heroin addict gets excited, while the amphetamine addict becomes depressed. The toxicity of morphine and barbiturates is associated primarily with their withdrawal; while alcohol, marijuana, and amphetamine side effects are associated mainly with their existence in the body (*see* Figure 14.9).

The distinction between hard and soft drugs is fuzzy, because massive doses of any drug can produce symptoms. Tobacco and alcohol kill many more Americans than LSD and heroin, yet until recently hallucinogens and heroin were considered *the* dangerous drugs. Variation in drug strength kills some users, while others get depressed and commit suicide.

Drugs can increase or decrease CNS activity.

The difference between hard and soft drugs is not clear.

TABLE 14.8   General drug use among U.S. college students, 1971

	Never use percent	Have used percent	Users who say they will stop percent
Amphetamines	70	30	42
Barbiturates	78	22	48
Mescaline	82	18	38
LSD	87	13	52
Cocaine	93	7	27
Heroin	97	3	45

From "*Playboy's* Student Survey: 1971," copyright © 1971 by Playboy. Used with permission.

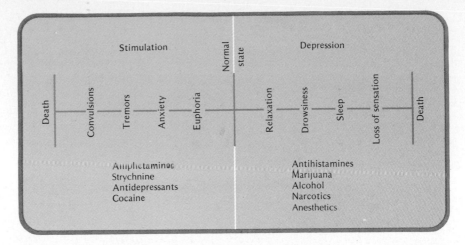

FIGURE 14.9 A continuum of drug effects from stimulation to depression. Abuse of any drug can lead to serious complications or death.

The death rate among male opiate addicts is twenty times the normal population, and the suicide rate among male heroin addicts is fifty times the normal population. Most pharmacologists agree that the number-one drug problem in the U.S. is alcohol abuse.

ALCOHOL USE AND ABUSE During man's history, alcoholism has occurred among all segments of society from the aristocracy to the poor. In early Greece drinking was a pastime of the ruling classes, while during the Middle Ages everyone imbibed. Following the introduction of distilled spirits in the late seventeenth century drunkenness was most common among laborers. Nineteenth-century medical professionals argued that alcoholism was a vice of the poor, but their view probably reflected social bias more than fact. There are traditional class differences associated with the treatment of alcoholism. The Salvation Army aids derelict alcoholics, Alcoholics Anonymous serves the middle class, and private clinics treat the rich. Most people won't admit they have a drinking problem even if classed as a heavy user by an independent observer. They feel drinking helps them socially. Drinking is bad for health, family life, and income. Women who drink excessively are dissatisfied with themselves, their husbands, the neighborhood, their educational attainment, and other women.

Why do some become alcoholics? There is strong evidence that alcohol preference is heritable among animals and that alcoholism runs in families, so alcohol abuse may result from genetic disposition. Social pressure and stress contribute to alcoholism. People handle stress differently. Some rely on the help of others; some rely on drugs; and some organize

(margin notes)

Alcoholism has a long history.

Alcoholism runs in families.

their energies to cope with stress. Reliance on a given approach may reflect a combination of early training and genetic variation.

MARIJUANA USE AND ABUSE   In 1893 the Indian Hemp Commission asked a number of questions:

1. How many use drugs?
2. Where are they used?
3. How do you know?
4. Is use destructive or harmless?
5. Should use of drugs be controlled?
6. How might control be accomplished?
7. Would drugs be consumed illegally?
8. Would prohibition be followed by recourse to alcohol or other drugs?

These are good questions. But we often do not have answers.

Millions use marijuana in the U.S.

Millions in the U.S. use marijuana, but the exact number won't be known while its use remains illegal (*see* Figure 14.10). We do know that marijuana is usually smoked or taken with a group of friends. Most data about marijuana come from clinical interviews during treatment, social questionnaires, and some laboratory experimentation. On the basis of sketchy data many authorities believe that the excessive use of marijuana is proportional to the excessive use of alcohol, and the harmful effect of both seem similar. From these statistics it is argued that marijuana possession by adults should be legal, just as tobacco or alcohol are. Authorities point out that control of marijuana is difficult because it is easy to grow and process. It is assumed that the drug is now consumed illegally by millions, and its prohibition may lead to the use of heroin or amphetamine by young people if marijuana is not available. Some people still think marijuana leads to violence and crime. *Hashish,* a potent form of mari-

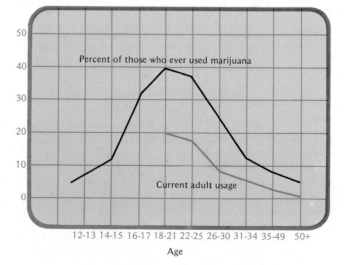

FIGURE 14.10
The percent of those who claim ever to have used marijuana and the estimated current adult usage of the drug.

juana, is associated in the minds of some with assassination, because of its use by a Moslem sect that assassinated Christians during the Crusades. The drugs historically used in connection with hired assassinations were actually wine and opium.

Marijuana is a mild sedative.

Clinical reports suggest that marijuana intoxication causes euphoria, elation, and moderately impaired judgment. Many users believe marijuana is a mild hallucinogen, but the images probably actually result from an increased tendency to fantasize rather than from true hallucinations. As a matter of fact, Humphrey Davies described the same state when he isolated nitrous oxide, the first anesthetic. Chronic use of any sedative-hypnotic produces physical dependence. Hyperexcitability of the central nervous system follows their abrupt withdrawal, since the main action of all sedative-hypnotics is depression of neural activity. Electrodes implanted in the brain of experimental lower animals who have been given the drug show that marijuana mimics many actions of other sedatives, like alcohol and barbiturates.

Marijuana has many physiological effects.

Marijuana has some effect on the circulatory system. Beginning users experience a rise in blood pressure followed by a fall, while chronic users endure only small shifts in their circulatory balance. About 75 percent of marijuana users show congestion of the ciliary vessels in the eye accompanied by yellow discoloration of the conjunctiva of the eye. Some claim this results from marijuana smoke, but the effect accompanies taking it by mouth as well. Smoking marijuana depresses respiratory rate, decreases oxygen consumption, can cause nausea, produces dryness of the mouth, and increases appetite.

Modest marijuana use does not seem dangerous.

Is marijuana dangerous in moderate amounts? Probably not. Among the West Indian population of Birmingham, England, modest marijuana use is not associated with psychological problems. When marijuana is drunk as a tea there is no correlation with mental abnormality. Heavy use of marijuana is, however, associated with mental problems. There is evidence of brain damage among citizens of India who use hashish for long periods of time. These data are somewhat confounded with malnutrition, but most experts believe chronic abuse of marijuana is harmful.

Hallucinogens produce hallucinations.

HALLUCINOGENIC CHEMICALS *Hallucinogens* produce a variety of psychological effects from psychoses to enjoyable hallucinations. Often these images can be differentiated from reality, so they are not true hallucinations. A variety of hallucinogenic drugs exist: *LSD, psilocybin* (extracts of mushrooms), *peyote* and *mescaline* (from the Mexican peyote cactus). Effects of hallucinogens include pupil dilation, increased blood sugar levels, higher heart rate and blood pressure, trembling of the extremities, nausea, headache, and synesthesia (the translation of an experience from one sense to another—the user may say he hears colors, sees sound, and feels light or music). The problem with these drugs is that the type of hallucination is unpredictable for some people; happiness, gloom, or panic can happen.

Hallucinogens do not cure psychoses.

Early enthusiasts supposed LSD might cure sexual abnormalities, schizophrenia, and neuroses. Data are so meager and follow-up studies so inadequate that conclusions about therapeutic effects of LSD are impossible. Under controlled conditions the drug produced psychosis in about 2 percent of a nonclinical sample. Among patients undergoing psychotherapy LSD may induce paranoia or psychopathic tendencies. Adverse reactions to LSD can be reduced sharply by keeping doses below 300 micrograms. Most patients recover from all effects in one to eight days, but 15 percent of the affected 2 percent in the study cited showed persisting abnormalities (.3 percent). Of these, half had no pre-existing psychiatric history. Thus, hallucinogenic drugs are dangerous to some people, although the actual percentage is small.

LSD may be associated with depression of immune responses.

LSD may be an important tool for research into the biochemistry of mental illness, but it can be one kind of Russian roulette for the casual user who is predisposed to psychoses. Some people who use it invite temporary madness or permanent insanity. Recent studies at the University of Illinois show that LSD weakens the body's defenses against infection—a serious problem.

Opiates are very addicting.

OPIATE ADDICTION   Opiate addiction among children is not new. The 1845 commission of inquiry into the state of large towns in England reported rampant opiate addiction among the population. Dr. Godfrey's Cordial was a typical tonic given to children, and its pharmacological activity was based on an extract of opium. Dr. Godfrey claimed his tonic was "excellent for young children who are restless, for it quiets them." Great quantities of Godfrey's cordial were consumed before its use was curtailed by cost and legal prohibition.

The British prescribe heroin to registered addicts.

Three methods of treatment for opiate addiction are used: prescription of heroin, *methadone* substitution, and a therapeutic community. The "British system" assumes that addiction is simply a medical problem, so English physicians are allowed to prescribe modest amounts of heroin to registered addicts. Prescriptions eliminate the black market and keep addicts from stealing. The British system does not stop addiction; it simply maintains the addict in a healthy state at a modest cost. However, the number of addicts in Britain rose from about 500 in 1960 to almost 3,000 in 1968, primarily because some doctors overprescribed heroin to addicts who sold it to others. It should be pointed out that this rate of increase is far below that in the U.S. Whether the difference is caused by this treatment program or other factors is unknown.

U.S. doctors prescribe methadone to heroin addicts.

Another approach to treatment is the methadone maintenance program. Methadone is an inexpensive addicting narcotic which blocks heroin's euphoria. It does not cure addiction to opiates; it is a substitute addiction. Methadone enables an addict to function normally, but he must continue taking the heroin substitute for the rest of his life. The methadone program is about 75 percent successful, according to its founders, although some deaths have occurred.

Synanon is a therapeutic community.

A third way of dealing with drug addiction is through small therapeutic communities like California's *Synanon,* run by former drug addicts. Treatment in a therapeutic community lasts years, and those who leave the community almost always return to narcotic addiction.

Many believe there is no cure for heroin addiction.

Synanon leaders claim there is no cure for heroin addiction. Certainly, the British system and methadone maintenance are not cures. Aging may help, since many older addicts can kick the habit, possibly because only moderately addicted people survive to old age. Federal law enforcement is most concerned about opiates.

Amphetamine addicts may go for days without food or sleep.

AMPHETAMINE DEPENDENCE   The recommended adult dosage of amphetamine is one 25 mg. tablet taken orally twice a day to relieve depression or to suppress the appetite. Serious addicts often take twenty or thirty tablets in one intravenous injection, while some may inject up to four hundred tablets at a time. The common pattern is to take several injections within one day, and then go for a week without sleep or food. Addicts claim they feel elated immediately after an injection ("the rush"), and a few users report sexual orgasm following an injection. To induce relaxation, some amphetamine addicts take barbiturates; others spontaneously fall asleep after several days. These cycles of prolonged activity and sleep may continue for months without interruption.

Crashing is unpleasant.

Amphetamine withdrawal is very unpleasant. Crashing (being without the drug) brings intense depression and discomfort and explains why most users inject more amphetamine even though they feel worn out.

Amphetamine use can produce irritability.

The serious amphetamine abuser's physical condition is often bad. His veins may be scarred and the forearms and hands damaged. If amphetamine tablets are taken orally instead of being injected, they act almost as quickly and are painless. However, needles and syringes have a ritualistic status, and "the rush" only follows intravenous injection.

How may drug abuse be controlled?

DRUGS AND THE LAW   How can people be educated about drugs without arousing their interest? The first thing to do is stop generating exaggerated half-truths. Early pamphlets from the Bureau of Narcotics misinformed people about marijuana. The youth subculture was less wrong than government authorities about the drug, so young people now wonder why they should believe the authorities about any drug. Authorities must face the fact that most parents use mind-altering drugs like cigarettes, coffee, alcohol, tranquilizers, diet pills, or sleeping pills, and so children who use drugs may simply be following parental examples. Many young people argue that marijuana is no more dangerous than alcohol. They ask why is one illegal and the other sold on the open market. To educate children about the dangers of drugs, parents must either change their examples or expect adolescents to use and abuse mind-altering chemicals. A good parental example is most helpful.

No current solution to drug abuse exists.

There is no currently available solution to drug abuse. The entire problem is complex and controversial. Some government officials feel that the best method of drug control is to stop the supply and severely punish all offenders. Others argue that a better method would be to prevent addiction, but no one is sure how to do that. Some drug users feel that mind-altering drugs are an avenue to understanding the human condition which is not available any other way. They say that taking drugs is their right as human beings.

Is drug use simply a search for expanded consciousness?

An important question for science and humans is: Whose reality is correct? Some philosophers argue that all reality derives from sensory experience. Others believe that innate ideas exist. If all truth derives from sensory experience, then altered states of consciousness may lead either to deeper understanding or total confusion. How can the question be decided? One answer to the dilemma is to search all sensory experience for common events and to construct reality based on the widest possible information. This approach would imply that everyone should experience altered states of consciousness. An alternate view suggests that altered states of awareness are simply distortions of reality and add confusion rather than clarity.

Philosophers disagree about reality.

Strong opinions exist on both sides of the question. Western scientific attitudes are for the most part opposed to consciousness alteration as a means to truth. Eastern philosophers and a few Western scientists believe this attitude reflects cultural prejudice rather than reason. The argument will ultimately be solved when one approach produces the most coherent world view. At the moment neither side is clearly winning.

Summary

Modern conceptions of adolescence and youth as separate stages of life are recent developments. There is still some debate whether storm and stress are a necessary part of adolescence, but most agree that the difficulties faced by U.S. adolescents stem from early physical and sexual maturity coupled with prolonged dependence on others. The adolescent faces many problems, chief among them being learning to handle sexuality, choosing a career, deciding whether to stay in school, and handling the temptations of drugs.

SUGGESTED ADDITIONAL READINGS

Coleman, J.S. *The Adolescent Society*. New York: Free Press, 1961.

Kinsey, A.C., W.B. Pomeroy, and C.E. Martin. *Sexual Behavior in the Human Female*. Philadelphia: Saunders, 1953.

———. *Sexual Behavior in the Human Male*. Philadelphia: Saunders, 1948.

Piaget, J. *Play, Dreams and Imitation in Childhood*. C. Gattegno and F.M. Hodgson, trs. New York: Norton, 1951.

Rosenthal, R., and L. Jacobson. *Pygmalion in the Classroom*. New York: Holt, Rinehart and Winston, 1968.

Appendix
Advanced Topics in Child Development

The Ethics of Studying Children

A History of Child Psychology

Some Statistics for Child Psychology

The Scientific Method

Theories of Sensation

Theories of Forgetting

Some Theories of Grammars

Theories of Emotion

PREVIEW

These advanced topics are made available so the student can pursue a particularly interesting topic in more depth and with more sophistication than was possible in the text. The areas covered include the ethical problems of studying children, a history of child psychology, some statistical tools useful in studying human development, an outline of the scientific method appropriate to child psychology, and various specialized theories of child development. One set of such theories concerns how children and adults interpret a stimulus; another discusses why we forget; the third is about grammar, and a final theoretical topic analyzes emotions. Each section of the appendix can be used independently or can be coordinated with the book chapters. For example, the sections on ethics and the history of child psychology might make an interesting introduction to human development; or the methods and statistics sections can be studied whenever a student needs some understanding of central tendency, dispersion, relations, probabilities, or measurements. The methods section also outlines why and how psychologists experiment; and the advanced theories can be read in conjunction with the chapters on perception, learning, language acquisition, and motivation.

The Ethics of Studying Children

Children as research subjects present ethical problems for the investigator different from those presented by adult subjects. Not only are children often viewed as more vulnerable to stress but, having less knowledge and experience, they are less able to evaluate what participation in research may mean. The parents' consent for the study of a child must be obtained in addition to the child's consent. These are some of the major differences between research with children and research with adults.

1. No matter how young the child, he has rights that supersede the needs of the investigator, who should measure each operation he proposes in terms of the child's rights. Before proceeding, he should obtain the approval of a committee of peers. Institutional peer review committees should be established in any setting where children are the subjects of the study.

2. The final responsibility of establishing and maintaining ethical practices in research remains with the individual investigator. He is also responsible for the ethical practices of collaborators, assistants, students, and employees—all of whom, however, incur parallel obligations.

3. Any deviation from these principles demands that the investigator seek consultation on the ethical issues in order to protect the rights of the research participants.

4. The investigator should inform the child of all features of the research that may affect his willingness to participate, and he should answer the child's questions in terms appropriate to the child's comprehension.

5. The investigator should respect the child's freedom to choose to participate in research or not, as well as to discontinue participation at any time. The greater the power of the investigator with respect to the participant, the greater is the obligation to protect the child's freedom.

6. The informed consent of parents or those who act for the parents (for example, teachers, superintendents of institutions) similarly should be obtained, preferably in writing. Informed consent requires that the parent or other responsible adult be told all features of the research that may affect his willingness to allow the child to participate. This information should include the profession and institutional affiliation of the investigator. Not only should the right of the responsible adult to refuse consent be respected, but he should be given the opportunity to refuse without penalty.

7. The informed consent of any person whose interaction with the child is the subject of the study should also be obtained. As with the child and responsible adult, informed consent requires that the person be informed of all features of the research that may affect his willingness to participate; his questions should be answered; and he should be free to choose to participate or not, and to discontinue participation at any time.

8. From the beginning of each research investigation, there should be a clear agreement between the investigator and the research participant that defines the responsibilities of each. The investigator has the obligation to honor all promises and commitments of the agreement.

9. The investigator uses no research operation that may harm the child either physically or psychologically. Psychological harm, to be sure, is difficult to define; nevertheless, its definition remains the responsibility of the investigator. When

the investigator is in doubt about the possible harmful effects of research operations, he seeks consultation with others. When harm seems possible, he is obligated to find other means of obtaining the information or to abandon the research.

10. Although we accept the ethical ideal of full disclosure of information, a particular study may necessitate concealment or deception. Whenever concealment or deception is thought to be essential to the conduct of the study, the investigator should satisfy a committee of his peers that his judgment is correct. If concealment or deception is practiced, adequate measures should be taken after the study to insure the participant's understanding of the reasons for the concealment or deception.

11. The investigator should keep in confidence all information obtained about research participants. The participant's identity should be concealed in written and verbal reports of the results, as well as in informal discussions with students and colleagues. When a possibility exists that others may gain access to such information, this possibility, together with plans for protecting confidentiality, should be explained to the participants as a part of the procedure for obtaining informed consent. . . .

13. Immediately after the data are collected, the investigator should clarify for the research participant any misconceptions that may have arisen. The investigator also recognizes a duty to report general findings to participants in terms appropriate to their understanding. Where scientific or humane values may justify withholding information, every effort should be made so that withholding the information has no damaging consequences for the participant. . . .

16. When research procedures may result in undesirable consequences for the participant that were previously unforeseen, the investigator should employ appropriate measures to correct these consequences, and should consider redesigning the procedures.

It is acknowledged that ethical problems encountered in research with children cannot be solved simply by applying a set of "rules." Rather, the situation in which ethical problems arise is usually:

> . . . one of weighing the advantages and disadvantages of conducting the research as planned. On the one hand, there is the contribution that the research may ultimately make to human welfare; on the other, there is the cost to the individual research participant. Put in these stark terms, the essential conflict is between the values of science to benefit all mankind and the values that dictate concern for the research participant.*

A History of Child Psychology

People study children for various reasons.

People study children for many reasons—parents, because they have children and love and care for them; medical people, because they must advise parents; social scientists, because they want to understand how children develop so as to understand children; and educators, because they are interested in the child's ability to learn. Child development is a way of looking at all of psychology rather than as a separate discipline.

---

* Quoted from the American Psychological Association's report on ethics.

To comprehend current child development we should look at the men who started the field. We'll begin with an examination of the prescientific study of children, followed by the contributions of those who developed the science, and ending with a summary of how child development is regarded today.

Prescientific Child Psychology

Until recently many children died.

Only recently have we begun to appreciate the differences between children and adults. Until the last two centuries the pre-eminent fact about early childhood was death. Childhood diseases claimed many young children. Almost all the increase in man's average life span from thirty years of age during Greek and Roman times through the current seventy-year average is accounted for by the reduction in childhood mortality. Even in early times an infant who lived through his teens and reached sexual maturity could expect a life of seventy years. However, his prospects of reaching sexual maturity were not good.

Darwin began the scientific study of children.

The scientific study of the child can be traced to Charles Darwin's theory of evolution. Many early biologists regarded the human baby as a possible link between animals and people. They proposed that the developing child might pass through the various stages of animal life, and thus give clues to evolution. Darwin's interest in evolution and development led him to observe the growth of his infant son Doddy. He began his observations in 1840, and published a book in 1870 that introduced the baby biography, a chronology of day-to-day observations on a single normal child. One of the most complete baby biographies was published by William Preyer, a physiologist who reported his own son's early mental and physical development. The main difficulty with baby biographies was the size of the sample, and the fact that the child was usually not a typical offspring. Yet these early observations by well-trained minds posed a number of problems to be solved by the study of child psychology.

Hall introduced the questionnaire.

In the 1880's G. Stanley Hall introduced the questionnaire as a way of studying the content of children's minds. He also thought that the early stages of a child's development would recapitulate the early stages of man's evolution, so he asked teachers to question children throughout the primary grades. In Hall's early studies he used carefully selected teachers who uniformly asked standardized questions. Later, Hall's students distributed the questionnaire throughout the country, and teachers or parents used it to study fears, punishments, appetites, dreams, memories, happiness, and motor ability. Hall's questionnaire eventually led to the modern psychological test.

Binet developed the first IQ test.

The first reliable and valuable psychological test of intelligence was developed by Alfred Binet. In 1904 the French Minister of Education had appointed a commission to study ways of insuring that children with low intelligence in the Paris public school system would receive the best possible training. The commission had decided that retarded children should be separated from regular classes on the basis of a special examination. Binet was appalled by the early tests used to make this decision. To improve the tests, Binet made two simple assumptions and developed one important insight into the growth of intelligence. Rather than using artificial laboratory tests—like reaction time, simple discrimination, or memory—Binet looked at what a child does in school and then designed a series of tasks which required these skills. His tests used knowledge of words, names of objects, repetition of digits, drawing of designs, and completing of sentences. The criterion of intelligence was age, because Binet assumed that older children were brighter than younger children. He further assumed that intellectual characteristics go together, so that a child who is bright in one kind of intellectual ability should be bright in others. Louis Terman of Stanford University standardized the original Binet intelligence scale for the United States, and published it in 1916 as the Stanford-Binet IQ test. It became the most used testing instrument for intelligence.

Watson championed behaviorism.

The next major advance in the study of child psychology was the use of Pavlovian conditioning with children. John B. Watson, the first behavioral psychologist, applied classical conditioning techniques to white rats and human babies. Watson found that self-analysis of one's consciousness is not the best way to go about gathering data from animals and children, so he suggested that only observable acts be used in the study of humans. Watson showed that very young infants can be emotionally conditioned. Albert, his most famous subject, was taught to fear a rat and Santa Claus by associating the rat with the sound of striking a large steel bar. Watson produced classical emotional conditioning in Albert with only two trials. These inhibited Albert's reaching for the rat, and six more trials produced crying and withdrawal. Albert would not even reach for a rabbit or a white Santa Claus mask, which had been neutral stimuli. Thus, Alberts' fear of a white rat had generalized to other, similar objects.

Freud had a major influence on child psychology.

Darwin, Preyer, Binet, Terman, and Watson all tried to understand the child and introduce some objectivity and measurement into the study of his behavior. A man from the field of medicine, Sigmund Freud, also had a major influence on child psychology. He molded our thinking about motivation, unconscious processes, and parent-child relations. Freudian psychoanalysis was developed as a way of treating neurosis. Freud had tried a variety of approaches to the treatment of emotional problems in his patients, including drugs and hypnosis. He finally developed a method called free association in which his patients were encouraged to say anything which came into their minds. Freud found that his patients invariably ended up talking about early emotional experiences, and he became convinced that these early experiences were the basis of the adult's emotional problems. Usually the early experiences concerned love or hate of the parent, sexual encounters, or jealousy.

Freud's method of psychoanalysis pointed out the importance of early childhood experiences on later development.

Clinical problems also influenced child psychology.

Three other influences contributed to the early history of the study of child psychology. These forces grew from interest in juvenile delinquency, abnormal development, and education. Child-guidance clinics were founded to enable juvenile authorities to discover why delinquents are antisocial. They came to two basic conclusions: delinquent behavior is the result of psychological process; these psychological processes are modifiable. Child-guidance studies found that poor school and home adjustment was almost always associated with delinquency.

The first psychological clinic opened in 1896.

The first psychological clinic was opened at the University of Pittsburgh in 1896. The clinic received referrals from the school system, and the psychologists there became interested in problems of academic success. Most of the patients came from an educational setting, and these early clinical psychologists concentrated on the diagnosis of intellectually handicapped or emotionally disturbed children.

Education influences child psychology.

Education and child psychology have been influencing each other for most of the twentieth century. Progressive education emphasized the application of social and personal adjustment techniques in the classroom. In recent years education has come to offer a complex array of psychological services, curricula for various kinds of students, psychological tests, counseling for emotional or intellectual needs, and a comprehensive testing program.

Some Statistics for Child Psychology

Psychologists use statistics.

Why are psychologists concerned about statistics, measurement and the significance of their experiments? The answer is primarily because the theories of statistics, measurement, and probability give objective evidence of the reliability, meaning, and stability of the data psychologists collect. Unfortunately, behavior cannot be weighed or measured with a ruler. Psychological phenomena possess special requirements, and psychological measurements are often unreliable. Rarely can the experimenter elicit exactly the same response from his subjects, due to changes in the situation or in the child. Because of this variability, psychologists use large groups of subjects, collect many measurements, and employ statistical analyses.

The field of statistics may be organized into three major areas: measurement, descriptive statistics, and inferential statistics.

Measurement

Measurement means assigning numbers.

Measurement is the assignment of numbers to objects or events by some simple or complex rule. There are four major kinds of measurement:

1. *Nominal*—when numbers are assigned only to reflect qualitative differences.

2. *Ordinal*—when numbers are assigned according to rank.
3. *Interval*—when numbers are assigned to reflect equal differences between events.
4. *Ratio*—when numbers are assigned to reflect equal differences and there is an absolute zero.

In nominal measurement numbers are assigned to objects for descriptive purposes only and no computations should be performed on them. The numbers given to members of a basketball team are examples of nominal measurement.

Ordinal measurement requires that number ref'ect the rank of objects along some characteristic. Ranking means that one object is more than another, but the amount of difference is unknown. As an example, consider the hardness test for gems. If one gem will scratch another it is harder. However, the amount of hardness difference is unknown. Ordinal scales cannot be added or subtracted, but they can be correlated.

By contrast, an interval scale is more informative. As an example, the interval scale can tell you not only that one person is brighter than another but also how much difference exists. Interval scales can be added and subtracted.

The most powerful measurement is a ratio scale, which allows the use of all arithmetic computations including multiplication and division. Unfortunately, psychology provides only a few ratio scales for psychophysical dimensions like brightness or loudness. Most psychological scales are interval measures (such as IQ or anxiety) and ordinal measures (such as neurosis or psychosis).

Once you have a scale of measure, the next step is to summarize observations by computing descriptive statistics. For example, a psychologist may want to know the typical score and the variation of his data. He may also want to say something about how significant his results are in relation to other findings. These analyses require two kinds of statistics: *descriptive statistics*, which tells something about the most common score and how much variation there is, and *inferential statistics*, which describes how significant the data are. Consider these two types of analysis.

Ordinal numbers reflect ranks.

Interval numbers reflect equal differences.

Ratio scales are the best measure.

Descriptive statistics summarize data.

A frequency distribution is a descriptive statistic.

Descriptive Statistics

One of the first things many psychologists do is convert their raw data into a frequency distribution or a histogram (*see* Figure A.1). Frequency distributions show the number of subjects who earn scores which fall within certain intervals. The particular interval is arbitrary and should be picked to display the data sensibly. Psychologists and statisticians usually want to know three things about a distribution:

1. Is it symmetrical?
2. What is its central tendency?
3. What is its variation?

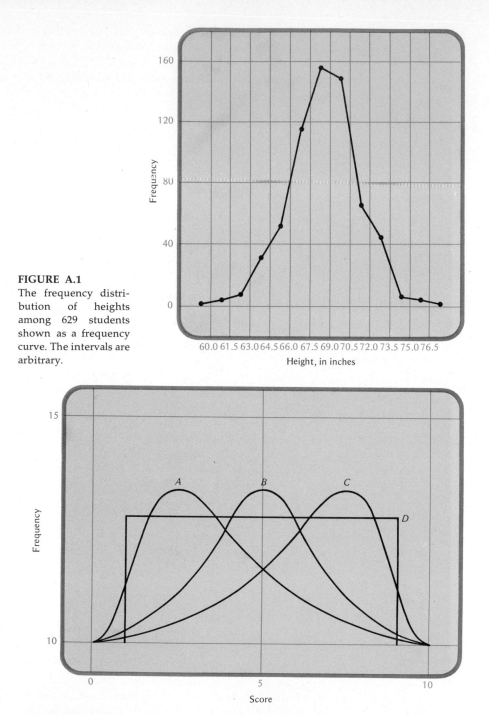

FIGURE A.1
The frequency distribution of heights among 629 students shown as a frequency curve. The intervals are arbitrary.

FIGURE A.2 These curves show symmetrical (*B*) and two skewed distributions (*A* and *C*). In addition, a rectangular distribution (*D*) is shown.

Frequency distributions may be asymmetrical.

Figure A.2 shows three frequency distributions. Distribution *B* is symmetrical, *A* is skewed to the left (which means many people score low on the measure), while Distribution *C* is skewed to the right (which means many people score high on that measure). *D* shows a rectangular distribution in which the frequency of all scores is equal.

There are various measures of central tendency.

The second thing scientists want to know about their data is the central tendency. Central tendencies come in three types: mode, median, and mean. A *mode* is the most frequent score; a *median* divides the distribution so half the subjects fall below the median score and half above; while a *mean* is the familiar arithmetic average, computed by taking the sum of all the scores and dividing them by the number of people earning those scores. Figure A.3 (*top*) shows that in symmetrical distributions the mean, median, and mode are identical. If a distribution is skewed (Figure A.3) (*bottom*) they may be different. In this particular case the mode is

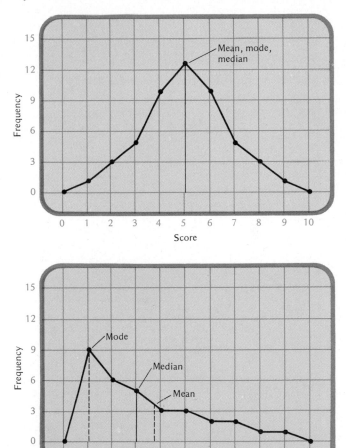

FIGURE A.3
A symmetrical (*A*) and an asymmetrical distribution (*B*). Note that the mean, median, and mode are identical in (*A*) and different in (*B*).

1, the median is 3, and the mean is 3.8. One way you can lie with statistics — although it is frowned upon — is to choose the type of central tendency which shows what you want to prove.

The third thing scientists want to know about a distribution is its dispersion or spread. In symmetrical distributions the amount of dispersion has no effect on the mean, median, and mode (*see* Figure A.3). In asymmetrical distributions central tendencies and variation are related. There are three common measures of dispersion: range, average deviation, and standard deviation. A *range* is the interval between the highest and lowest scores. The range is easy to compute, but is overly influenced by single extreme scores. The *average deviation* is computed by taking the difference of each score from the mean of the group and then

TABLE A.1   Examples of calculating average (A) and standard deviations (B) for two sets of hypothetical data.

	Group I		Group II	
	Scores	d	Scores	d
	8	1	3	6
	8	1	5	4
	9	0	7	2
	9	0	9	0
	9	0	9	0
	9	0	11	2
	10	1	13	4
	10	1	15	6
Σ (sum)	72	4	72	24
M (mean)	9		9	

$$A.D. = \frac{\Sigma d}{N} = \frac{4}{8} = .50 \qquad A.D. = \frac{\Sigma d}{N} = \frac{24}{8} = 3.00$$

Score	d	d²	Score	d	d²
8	1	1	3	6	36
8	1	1	5	4	16
9	0	0	7	2	4
9	0	0	9	0	0
9	0	0	9	0	0
9	0	0	11	2	4
10	1	1	13	4	16
11	1	1	15	6	36
$\Sigma = 72$		4	$\Sigma = 72$		112
M = 9			M = 9		
N = 8		$\Sigma d^2 = 4$	N = 8		$\Sigma d^2 = 112$

$$S.D. = \sqrt{\frac{\Sigma d^2}{N}} = \sqrt{\frac{4}{8}} = \sqrt{.50} = .07$$

$$S.D. = \sqrt{\frac{\Sigma d^2}{N}} = \sqrt{\frac{112}{8}} = \sqrt{14} = 3.74$$

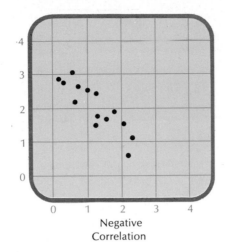

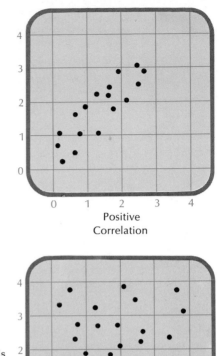

FIGURE A.4
These scatter plots illustrate three kinds of correlations between scores on measures #1 and #2. The first shows there is no relation between the two measures. By contrast, the other two show a strong positive or negative association between measures #1 and #2. This means that for the positive correlation, someone who scores high on measure #1 will also score high on measure #2.

averaging these differences. Table A.1 (*top*) shows the computation of an average difference. A third measure of dispersion is the *standard deviation,* which is computed like an average deviation except that each difference is squared before averaging. Squaring differences makes extreme scores count more heavily than modest deviations in the total standard deviation statistic. Table A.1 (*bottom*) shows the computation of a standard deviation.

Correlation measures association.

In addition to central tendency and dispersion of data scientists may also want to know whether two sets of scores from the same people are related. In addition to cause-and-effect relations, scientists are also interested in the degree of association between two events. One way to measure this association is by correlation. If the correlation between two events is high and positive or negative a person can predict the occurrence of one event from the occurrence of another. A positive correlation between two events means they occur often together; a negative correlation means they do not tend to occur together. A correlation says nothing about the cause of the association; it simply describes relatedness. For example, there is a strong correlation between the number of cigarettes smoked and the incidence of lung cancer, prematurity among pregnant women, and circulatory or digestive problems. The strong association of cigarette smoking with these health problems does not prove they are caused by smoking. However, correlations do suggest causal hypotheses which can be tested by experiment; and the smoker may be foolish to ignore correlational data simply because it is not proof. Mathematically, correlations vary between minus and plus one. The extreme values represent high negative or positive associations between events. A correlation of .90 is much higher than a correlation of .25. Figure A.4 shows three scattergrams which display no correlation, a positive correlation, and a negative correlation. Once the form of the data is known, the next step is to examine how likely it is that these particular scores could have happened by chance. This is a task for inferential statistics.

Statistical Inference

Statistical inference is based on probability.

Descriptive statistics outline the form of a scientist's data, while inferential statistics are rules for determining conclusions from these data. If a psychologist wants to know how much confidence he can place in his results he may ask what is the probability that these data occurred by chance? To know this probability, he needs to understand something of

FIGURE A.5
A device for studying probabilities.
(Courtesy Featherhill Studios.)

chance events. Probability theory deals with the frequency or expected occurrence of events.

Early work on chance theories was supported by gamblers.

Early work in probability theory was supported by a group of gamblers who wanted to know the odds on several games, most notably the roulette wheel (*see* Figure A.5). How does the roulette wheel work? In the ordinary wheel there are eighteen red squares, eighteen black squares, a zero, and a double zero both of which are usually green. If $1 is placed on any one number the gambler can expect to win on the average 1 time out of 38 (18 + 18 + 2). If he wins, the casino will pay him $35 plus the $1 he bet. On the average, every 38 turns of the wheel the player will pay the casino $38 to receive $36. No matter how much a person wins on any particular trial, if enough people play enough times, the casino will win $2 for every $38 bet. People gamble that they can beat those odds and be one of the lucky winners. An honest wheel is one in which the probability of each number is $1/38$th. The wheel is biased if one number has a higher probability than others. If a gambler can find that number he can shift the odds in his favor by always betting on it. This rarely happens, because gambling houses check the probabilities every few days and they interchange wheels, tables, and equipment at every shift.

Probability

Probabilities can be independent or exclusive.

There are two ways to compute the probability of events. First, consider some rules about chance events and biases. Take a "fair coin" in which the odds of getting a head or a tail are each one-half. To find the odds of getting two heads in a row you would simply multiply the probability of getting one head by the probability of getting a second, because the events are *independent*: $1/2 \times 1/2 = 1/4$. If two heads in a row turn up, is the coin biased? Probably not, because the probability is $1/4$ that this could happen by chance. Suppose three heads in a row happen (probability of $1/2 \times 1/2 \times 1/2 = 1/8$). Would this probably be suspicious? Suppose four heads turned up in a row. The odds are $1/16$ that such an event would have occurred by chance alone. At what point should one believe the coin is biased? Psychologists have adopted the arbitary convention that odds of 1 in 20 are not chance; and they report all their inferential statistics in terms of probability levels. For example, when an article in a psychological journal says that the difference between two averages is significant at a probability less than .05 ($P < .05$) it means that the difference in the averages would occur less than 1 in 20 times by chance.

Exclusive probabilities are additive.

When two pennies are thrown they are independent, and the probability of two or more independent events is found by multiplying their *independent* probabilities. If events are mutually exclusive (a head *or* a tail can occur but not both), then the probability of two or more mutually *exclusive events* is found by adding their individual probabilities. Thus, the probability that a penny will show heads *or* tails is $1/2 + 1/2 = 1$.

Sampling

Sampling is about
the selection of
subsets.

One must also know about sampling. Statisticians distinguish between a population and a sample from that population. A *population* is all of the individuals who could comprise a group, while a *sample* is only a selected subset of the total group. Usually a scientist does not have access to the total population, so he tries to represent it by unbiased sampling.

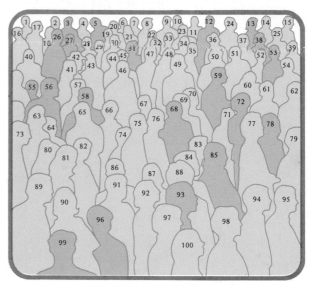

Random sample

Biased sample

FIGURE A.6
The results of random or biased sampling of people in a crowd.

Representative sets of people or events are gathered and inferences about the behavior of the total population are made on the basis of those samples. A random sample is one in which every member of the entire population has an equal opportunity to be included (*see* Figure A.6). A stratified sample is one in which the population is categorized into various groups and sampled in proportion to the size of these various categories. If the total population is 55 percent female and evenly distributed by age, then a stratified sample should be 55 percent female and evenly balanced by age. Precision of estimation is related to the size of a sample. As the number of cases in a sample increase, the amount of error will decrease (by the square root of $N - 1$). However, increasing sampling size follows a law of diminishing returns. An increase in sample size from 50 to 100 will show a sizable drop in the standard error of measurement; but an additional increase to 150 will show a smaller gain in precision. Finally, the addition of more cases will make a trivial difference. The optimum sample size depends on two things: the precision needed and the amount of time and money available. Enough subjects should be measured to establish stable values, but not so many that money and time are wasted.

The Scientific Methods

Psychology studies events, persons, and responses.

Psychology deals with three main things—events in the environment, personal variables, and response measures (*see* Figure A.7). Environmental events and personal variables often can be manipulated by the psychologist. As a result these are called *independent variables.* Environmental variables include stimuli, time, and instructions; while personal variables include age, sex, personal values, intelligence, motivation, and past experience.

Response measures are called dependent variables.

To understand how environmental events and personal variables interact, the scientist collects response measures. The particular data he collects may be physiological changes, speed of response, or complex verbal communications about events and experiences. These measured responses are called *dependent* variables and they are used to test theories and construct new models of humans. There are two major settings in which these responses can be collected. One is called observation and the other experimentation.

Observation

Observation is the first method of scientific study.

Observation is the study of behavior in its normal environment. The method is most often used in clinical, comparative, and social psychology. Naturalistic observation is rich in detail and suggests many ideas which can be tested later in the experimental laboratory. Recording natural behavior can be difficult. To be successful, the scientist needs a plan for

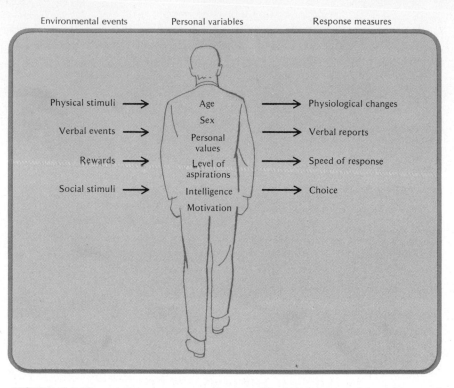

FIGURE A.7 The relation between environmental events, personal variables, and response measures.

collecting facts, and appropriate equipment for recording them. Psychologists use checklists, tape recorders, cameras, charts, questionnaires, and other devices to aid their observations and record-keeping. Naturalistic observations have been made of wasps, ants, seagulls, baboons, and human beings.

Opinion surveys measure beliefs.

To find out how people feel about their environment, social psychologists usually ask questions. Opinion surveys can measure people's beliefs and opinions by mail, telephone, or through direct interview. In general, personal interviews are most reliable. Separating people on the basis of socioeconomic level, age, sex, and other characteristics and then gathering opinions will yield valuable information on how different groups feel about various issues. Opinion surveys are used extensively in political and marketing campaigns.

Tests measure personal abilities.

As another way to observe behavior, clinical psychologists use standardized tests and interviews to measure their patients. Personality inventories, situational tests, and a general clinical interview are standard procedures. Several measures on the same person help determine his difficulties and strengths.

The Experiment

Experiments show
cause-effect relations.

Once the scientist has observed the behavior in question, and develops some ideas about what is happening, he will want to test his theories by producing special conditions and measuring the outcome of these special situations. This is called *experimentation*. Experiments are designed to show cause-effect relations and to test theoretical predictions. They are more expensive than observation, but may yield more valuable data if they are properly controlled.

How would you
study ESP?

Consider an example from extrasensory perception. How might a psychologist go about studying this phenomenon? Should he use naturalistic observation, a survey, the clinical method, or an experiment? For naturalistic observation the psychologist would need people who are said to have ESP, and he might have to wait a long time before he found one. To optimize his chances he might visit a gambling house, since many gamblers wager on the future and thus might believe they have ESP.

Opinion survey is
one way.

Alternately, the psychologist might survey opinions about ESP. He could stratify subjects by age, sex, and socioeconomic status, and ask questions like, "Do you believe in ESP?" "Do you have ESP?" "How do you know?"

Interviewing clair-
voyants is another
way.

To apply the clinical method he would have to find someone who has extrasensory perception and test him in many different situations. To experimentally study extrasensory perception he might design special situations and control any variables which might be giving the person cues to help him guess answers. One procedure would be to use a series of cards with symbols on them. In this situation the person who believes he has extrasensory perception would remain in a separate room to receive messages from a person seated elsewhere who looks at the cards one at a time. The sender might transmit his message as he looks at the cards while the receiver in another room accepts the message and writes it down. To make sure that the sender and receiver are not simply remembering the previous order of the cards, they are shuffled between sessions. Subtle communication and experimenter influence are controlled by physical separation of sender, receiver, and experimenter. The response measure would be the symbols written by the receiver.

Experiments help
decide between
chance and causality.

Suppose this experiment is performed one hundred times. What would convince the scientist that his subject has extrasensory perception? Ten correct? One hundred? Only if the receiver makes no errors? This is a question about the reliability of a phenomenon, and the way to answer that question is to compute statistics and their probabilities. Once it is known how likely it is that the results were produced by chance alone, the experimenter can decide whether extrasensory sending and receiving is superior to guessing. The probability of getting ten binary events correct in a row is about one in a thousand. Thus, if two persons can repeatedly produce a sequence of ten correct ESP responses under controlled conditions, they should be taken seriously.

One trap that must be avoided is the tendency to perform many sequences of tests and only report the one or two which support the experimenter's theory. By running enough trials and selecting "appropriate" ones, a scientist can prove anything. All experiments must be reported, and *not* simply select examples. Using techniques and controls like those just described, experimenters have found that *some* ESP subjects perform well above chance on some occasions. However, most psychologists are skeptical that extrasensory perception really exists, primarily because they cannot see how the process might work. One of the most important parts of any experiment is to control extraneous factors so that the results can be interpreted and understood.

Control of Extraneous Factors

Human behavior is affected by many variables, so psychologists try to minimize irrelevant events that might affect their subject's performances. Control of extraneous variables may be statistical or experimental. For statistical control, several subjects are placed in each experimental condition and random influences are assumed to affect all conditions equally. In this type of study some variables are systematically manipulated and their effects measured and compared with this noisy background of small errors. If the size of an experimental effect is larger than the random variation caused by many uncontrolled factors, the manipulated factor is said to be statistically significant. Many scientists prefer to control extraneous variables by eliminating them rather than using large samples and statistical controls.

Experimental control makes the results more plausible because the error of measurement is much smaller. Consider an example of experimental control in the study of audition, where scientists try to eliminate extraneous noise. Figure A.8 shows a controlled auditory environment called the anechoic chamber. In this artificial environment all echoes are damped and extraneous outside noises are blocked. This degree of control is rare and expensive. More often, psychologists resort to statistical techniques. Usually the scientist compares his experimental group to another set of subjects who have not received the experimental condition. This second group is called a *control group.* The logic of experimental and control groups is simple. By random selection or careful matching, two similar groups of subjects are formed at the beginning of an experiment. Then, one group is exposed to the experimental condition, while the other (control) group is not.

Suppose a psychologist wants to study the effects of early learning on later memory. First, he would collect two groups of children and give the experimental group of children experience in early learning but do noth-

Scientists should report all their data.

Behavior is affected by many factors.

Experimental control reduces extraneous factors.

Most studies need a control group.

FIGURE A.8 The anechoic chamber prevents its occupant from receiving most sensations.

ing with the control group of children. When all the children matured, he would test the effect of early learning on later memory. If the experimental group learns new material better than the control group when both are mature, he could conclude that early experience helps later learning.

Subject's Expectations

Subject's expectations can affect the experimental outcome.

There are two other major problems to control in an experiment: the subject's expectations and experimenter effects. What participants in an experiment believe about a study can significantly affect its outcome. As a result, experimenters attempt to control subject expectations or try to keep participants unaware of the experiment's real purpose. Consider a simple drug experiment. Suppose a scientist wants to test the effectiveness of a new drug. If he simply gave it to some subjects and not to others, everyone would know who received the drug and who did not. If patients expected the drug to alter their behavior, it often would, regardless of whether the chemical has any real effect. To control for subject expectations the scientist should use *two* pills, one which contains the drug and another which looks identical but contains only inert compounds. He would administer the drug-pill to some subjects and give others the inert-pill, which is called a *placebo* in drug research. Thus, subjects won't know whether to expect drug effects or no effects, since the pills look exactly alike. Any differences in behavior between the subjects who received the drug and those who received the placebo can then be attributed to the drug rather than the subject's expectations. This technique is called the *single-blind* experiment—blind because subjects don't know what the pills contain; single because only the subjects don't know, while the experimenter does. In a single-blind study, the experimenter might subtly convey his expectations to the subject, thus causing a problem.

Experimenter Effects

The experimenter may affect his results.

Suppose the experimenter has a vested interest in a drug because he discovered it. He might pass subtle clues to his subjects, letting them know whether they were receiving a drug or a placebo. He might smile when giving the drug and frown when giving the placebo (*see* Figure A.9). In this way his subjects would still know if they were getting a drug or a placebo.

The double-blind controls subject and experimenter effects.

To control for experimenter effects, the experimenter must *not* know which pill is being given. This is called the *double-blind* experiment, because neither the subject nor the experimenter knows which pill contains a drug.

Cross Section versus Longitudinal Measurements

The earliest method of study was a baby biography.

Several unique methods have been used to study human development. The earliest method was the baby biography, as we have seen. The first known biography of a child was commissioned by the court of France. It was a diary describing the growth and behavior of young Louis XIII. Teidemann probably deserves credit for writing the first scientific biography, when he published records of his own son's behavior through infancy.

Baby biographies contain rich detail.

A baby biography is exactly what the name suggests—an account of the day-to-day growth and behavior of a child. The baby biography contains an enormous amount of interesting and relevant data that can be collected and presented in a relatively short interval. Thus, during the early stages of child psychology, when there were few explicit hypotheses or well-established theories, the baby biography made good sense. Descriptions of a single baby brought to light many things which needed explanation. But, as child psychology became more sophisticated, other techniques were developed.

There are three methods of studying development.

Currently there are three methods used to study development: the observation of a single group of children over an extended period of time (longitudinal), the simultaneous observation of several groups of children of different ages (cross-sectional), and a combination of both these methods (mixed). The *longitudinal* method has the advantage that the same children are measured from one age to another. Thus, age changes can be attributed to maturation or experience and cannot be the result of poor

Approving   Disapproving

FIGURE A.9 How an experimenter might influence his subjects' responses by using approving or disapproving expressions.

sampling. The main problems with longitudinal research are its expense and the time required. A longitudinal study of motor development from ages three to ten would require seven years and cost a great deal.

Cross-sectional samples contain different groups of subjects.

To counter these problems, the *cross-sectional* method samples several *different* groups of children at various ages between three and ten to produce comparable information in a relatively short time. In the case of longitudinal measures all variation with age must be the result of maturation or experience. In the case of a cross-sectional sample, some variation may be the result of using different children at the various age levels. The fact that these different age groups cannot be matched may produce spurious age changes in cross-sectional studies. For example, suppose one group in the cross-sectional sample is much brighter than the others. Results from that group would confuse the overall results. Or, suppose an older group has lived through a war. The experimenter won't know whether age changes resulted from genetic differences, historical variation, or sampling.

Longitudinal samples are precise.

The precision of measurement is lower for different groups of children than when the same group is measured several times. Consequently, small developmental changes may be overshadowed by between-group variations.

The mixed method is best.

The *mixed* method of studying development combines the best features of both longitudinal and cross-sectional designs. To perform a "mixed" experiment, different groups of children ranging in age from three to nine years would be selected (for example, three, five, seven, and nine years). Each group is measured immediately and then followed for two years (for example, the three-year-olds until they are five, the five-year-olds until they are seven, and so on). In this way longitudinal data are produced in just two years. The question of adequate sampling can be checked—the five-year-old group is compared with the three-year-old group when they are five to see if their behavior is similar. If all age samples are representative, the three-year-old group at five years of age will look like the five-year-old group did when first measured at five years of age.

Theory and fact should be related.

How are conclusions related to theory and fact, and, in particular, what are the limitations and unknown factors which may influence results or conclusions? Such questions reflect the healthy search for truth and competition among ideas which mark the vigorous, growing field of child development.

Theories of Sensation

Threshold Theory

The threshold is the minimal amount of energy necessary for a sensation.

Early theories of sensation assumed there is a sensory threshold, and that observers were aware of sensations above this threshold and unaware of those below it. The threshold theory proposes that a stimulus causes neural impulses which produce a message in a brain center. The size of the sensory effect is assumed to change with stimulus intensity, receptor state, and the level of background noise. If the sensory effect during a short interval is greater than a certain minimum, the brain center will discharge, yielding a sensation. The stimulus intensity necessary to produce this sensory awareness is called the *threshold*. However, many factors—like stimulus strength, receptor sensitivity, neural efficiency, and noise level—are assumed to vary from moment to moment, yielding a distribution of sensory thresholds. To define a standard threshold, the average of the subjects' threshold distribution is used.

Various methods are used to measure the threshold.

Various methods were developed to systematically measure an average threshold value. In a typical threshold measurement experiment, stimulus strength is varied over a wide range and at some point along this stimulus range the observer's sensation changes. To balance observer errors both high-to-low and low-to-high sequences of stimuli are used. This alternation is necessary because in going from high to low stimulus values the observer tends to overestimate, while going from low to high produces an underestimation. Balancing these two kinds of errors gives an unbiased average threshold. The physical energy that is sensed half the time, averaged over ascending and descending trials, is called the absolute threshold (*see* Figure A.10). Recently, psychologists have expanded the theory of threshold to include a decision process and called this signal detection.

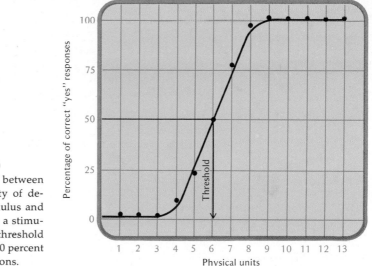

FIGURE A.10
The relation between the probability of detecting a stimulus and the energy in a stimulus. Absolute threshold is defined as 50 percent correct detections.

Signal Detection Theory

Signal detection theory assumes that the decision process affects sensitivity.

This alternate theory of sensory processing uses notions like signal, noise and decisions to explain sensations. *Signal detection* theory assumes that both receptor sensitivity *and* the observer's decision process affect his response to stimulation. Threshold theory, on the other hand, assumes that receptor sensitivity alone determines the person's response to stimulation. Signal detection theory offers a way to separate sensory and decision processes.

There are three necessary parts to a signal detection experiment:

1. Some states of the world (stimuli).
2. Information about these possible states (sensations).
3. A decision.

There are three parts to a detection experiment.

In the typical signal detection experiment the states of the world are the presence or absence of stimuli. The observer looks at a visual display or listens over earphones during defined time intervals to obtain the sensory information he will use to make his decision. The theory of signal detection assumes that two different processes combine to generate an observer's response. One mechanism is assumed to generate sensations which vary in strength as a function of signal intensity, receptor state, and internal processing efficiency. This process is similar to the mechanism assumed by the threshold theory. However, signal detection theory also proposes that observers make a judgment about these varying sensations. Their judgment is based on three things: the strength of the sensation, the costs of errors, and the observer's expectations about signal fre-

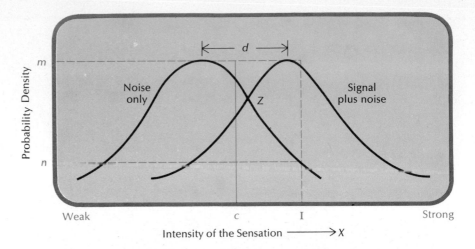

FIGURE A.11 The assumed mental distributions of noise and signal plus noise. The line X, which is related to sensory input, is the observer's "decision axis." He adjusts his criterion to some point along this axis of sensations. The value d, the difference between the means of the two sensation distributions, reflects the strength of the stimulus. As the stimulus becomes stronger, the difference between signal sensations and noise sensations increases.

quency. Observers are assumed to judge that a signal was more likely if the sensation it produced is strong. However, they will be unlikely to say a signal was present if making that judgment and being wrong will cost them a lot of money. The observer will also more likely decide that a sensation resulted from a signal rather than noise if signals are very frequent.

There are two errors and two correct responses in signal detection.

To help him make these decisions it is assumed that an observer establishes some arbitrary sensation level above which he will say the signal was present and below which he will decide the signal was absent (*see* Figure A.11). The particular level of sensation used as a criterion or decision level is affected by a payoff matrix which determines the costs of the various correct and incorrect decisions. In any decision situation there are at least two kinds of correct decisions and two kinds of errors (*see* Figure A.12). The correct decisions are: a *correct rejection*—saying a signal was absent when, in fact, there was no signal—and a *hit*—saying a signal was present when in fact it was. The two errors are: a *false alarm*—saying a signal was present when none was there—and a *miss*—saying no signal was present when in fact one was. An example may help to explain.

The observer's criterion varies with the payoff matrix.

Suppose the observer is a radar operator looking at images of flying objects on a screen. His task is to distinguish hostile aircraft (signals)

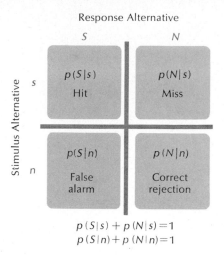

Response Alternative

FIGURE A.12
The stimulus-response matrix of the yes-no procedure.
(From Green and Swets, 1966.)

$$p(S|s) + p(N|s) = 1$$
$$p(S|n) + p(N|n) = 1$$

from birds and planets (noise). If he is worried about being bombed, he will call any increase in radar images a signal (hostile aircraft), and he will produce many false alarms. Suppose after a few days of this "crying wolf" his commanding officer says, "Don't wake me unless you are *sure* it's an enemy plane." In this case the observer will only claim to see an enemy plane when he is absolutely sure one is there. He may miss a few by this criterion, that is a consequence of his "miss." Thus, the observer's decision rule for separating signal and no signal affects the type of errors he will tend to make. The number of false alarms or misses is affected by his goals.

Signal detection theory is an advance over threshold theory because it considers both sensory and decision processes in analyzing a person's response to stimulation.

Colorblindness

There are several tests for color-blindness.

There are several tests for colorblindness and they all measure a person's ability to see color independently of brightness. For example, the dots in Color Plate 4 are balanced for brightness so that the only way to identify the numbers 6 and 12 is on the basis of color. Do you see these numbers clearly? There are at least three kinds of colorblindness. Normal color vision requires that both red-green and blue-yellow opponent cells function. One kind of colorblindness results if the red-green component is absent; such individuals see only blues and yellows. Another kind of colorblindness results if blue-yellow opponent cells are missing; these people see reds and greens but not blues and yellows. The third kind of colorblindness is total, so the person only sees variations in brightness as shades of gray but no color.

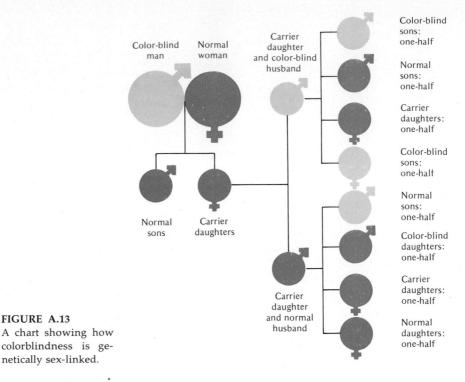

Color-blind man

Normal woman

Carrier daughter and color-blind husband

Color-blind sons: one-half

Normal sons: one-half

Carrier daughters: one-half

Color-blind sons: one-half

Normal sons: one-half

Color-blind daughters: one-half

Carrier daughters: one-half

Normal daughters: one-half

Normal sons

Carrier daughters

Carrier daughter and normal husband

FIGURE A.13
A chart showing how colorblindness is genetically sex-linked.

Colorblindness is sex-linked.

Most forms of partial colorblindness are genetically sex-linked and are passed from father to daughter to grandson. If a man is colorblind and marries a normal color vision woman, their sons will be completely normal while their daughters will have normal color vision but genetically carry a color defect. If the carrier-daughter marries a colorblind husband, their sons will be colorblind half the time and half their daughters will be carriers and half will be colorblind. If the carrier-daughter marries a normal vision husband, half their sons will be colorblind and half their daughters will be carriers, while the rest of their children will be normal. The general principle is that sons receive their color-vision trait from the mother; if she is colorblind then they will be colorblind. If she is only a carrier, then only half her sons will be colorblind. Colorblindness is recessive, so daughters (who all receive duplicate sex cells) will only be colorblind under the condition when the father is colorblind and the mother is a carrier and the daughters receive a colorblind female gene (*see* Figure A.13).

Can people see with their fingers?

Is it necessary to have normal color vision to "see" color? Some people were not so sure a few years ago when sensational reports from the U.S.S.R. and the U.S. claimed that selected people could "see" color and shapes with their *fingers!* However, several magicians showed how easy it is to cheat on this kind of test and how careful the experimenter must be to control all the conditions before he can be sure of his results. If cheating was eliminated, so was the ability to "see" color with the fingers.

We measure infants in several ways.

Scientists have studied the visual ability of newborn infants in several ways: by classical conditioning; observing the habituation of reflexes; measuring visual fixation, total body movement, and physiological functions like heartbeat and respiration rates. For example, Maurice Hershenson (1964) used visual fixation of newborn infants to show that they are sensitive to the intensity of a white light. He found that newborn human infants prefer an intermediate level of light intensity compared with very bright or dim lights.

We know little about infant's color vision.

Although the newborn infant's sensitivity to some visual stimuli has been established, we know little about his response to various hues. A number of investigators have tested infants and young children using lights or colored paper which varied in their dominant wavelength. The experimenters have reported differential responding to various hues. Unhappily, some of the early investigators neglected to control the correlated variation of their stimuli in brightness. Later investigators assumed that the infant's visual system works exactly like the human adults' and they controlled the brightness variation in colored stimuli by using adult standards. For this reason we cannot be sure that very young children are sensitive to color.

Theories of Forgetting

The first theory of forgetting was called decay.

Theories of memory must answer two questions: How are memories stored and why can't they be retrieved? Several theories of forgetting exist. The earliest was called *decay*. According to this notion memory simply faded away with time, so older memories were supposed to be weaker than more recent traces. It's certainly true that information is lost over time. But, simple trace decay won't explain most memory loss because children and adults selectively lose memory traces. Among mature people older memories can often be stronger than what happened yesterday.

Another theory assumes that memories interfere with each other.

A second theory assumes that later learning *interferes* with earlier memories and either destroys these earlier traces or somehow blocks their retrieval. It is true that newly acquired information can be destroyed by later learning, but consolidated, older memories do not seem to be much affected by later events.

A third theory proposes that memories are distorted.

Trace transformation, the third theory of forgetting, assumes that storage is an active process, and the coding imposed on information during learning affects the way items are retrieved. Studies of recall show a strong tendency toward stability and consistency of information within a particular memory production. For example, Figure A.14 shows that

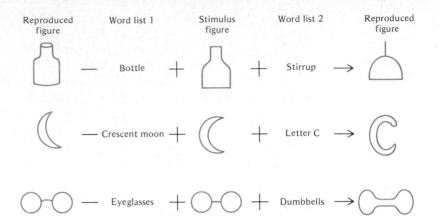

FIGURE A.14 The original stimulus and the reproduced memory following the presentation of various names for ambiguous stimuli. Note that the memory reproductions were distorted to conform with the labels.
(From Carmichael, Hogan and Walter, 1933.)

verbal labels for stimulus events can cause systematic distortions in memory. Specifically, the middle figures were shown to different groups who saw them labeled either as a bottle or a stirrup, a moon or a C, and eyeglasses or dumbbells. Later reproductions of the stimuli from memory were closer to the verbal label than to the original stimulus. Systematic distortions were introduced, and the changes retained some of the original stimulus but enhanced it to conform more with the verbal label.

Freud suggested that we repress unpleasant memories.

Repression, a fourth theory of forgetting, was proposed by Sigmund Freud, who thought forgetting was an active motivational process. He believed that children and adults remember good things and forget bad experiences. Thus, Freud thought memories which provoke anxiety are driven into the unconscious. Repression protects the child from painful memories.

One theory assumes there is no forgetting.

Retrieval, the last theory of forgetting we shall discuss, assumes that humans forget nothing; instead, the reason for loss of information is poor access-labeling. This theory supposes that all experiences are stored, but access to some has been lost, resulting in forgetting.

Penfield was able to retrieve lost childhood memories from patients.

Startling evidence of hidden memory occurred in Wilder Penfield's studies of epileptics. While performing brain surgery on epileptic patients, Penfield exposed the patient's brain and electrically stimulated points of the exposed cortex to test the functions of various areas, so that he would not destroy a vital function. To his surprise, many adult patients recounted experiences of early childhood in great detail following such electrical stimulation. Penfield recorded clear memories of early events that his patients could not remember under normal circumstances. Thus, his data suggest that even forgotten memories are stored in the brain, but only some special event, like direct electrical stimulation, reactivates the memory.

Retrieval is a gradual process.

Retrieval is not an all-or-none phenomenon; many people experience a "tip-of-the-tongue" feeling about a word or event they are trying to recall. Roger Brown tested this kind of memory. When searching for a word a person may have some feeling about the first letter, the number of syllables, the length of the word, and possibly the suffix or prefix, Brown discovered. The results of subjects' guesses about numbers of syllables is shown in Table A.2. Note that the subjects did have considerable information about items even if they could not retrieve the entire memory.

In summary, organization, practice, attention, rehearsal, and sleep help memory; while anxiety, inattention, and disorganization hinder learning and retrieval.

TABLE A.2   Subjects who had a word on the tip of the tongue were often accurate at guessing the number of syllables in the word.

Actual number of syllables	Number of syllables guessed by subjects				
	1	2	3	4	5
1	9	7	1	0	0
2	2	55	22	2	1
3	3	19	61	10	1
4	0	2	12	6	2
5	0	0	3	0	1

Some Theories of Grammars

Two theories of grammar exist.

Two theories exist about the type of grammar children develop. Some believe that the child develops a finite-state grammar, while others argue that he develops a phrase-structure system with transformations. Consider the implications of these different systems.

Finite-state Grammar

A finite-state grammar assumes left to right generation.

What type of grammar will generate a grammatical English sentence? It cannot be a simple memorizing of all sentences, because there are far too many of them. However, a simple communication-theory model suggests one way for a sentence to be constructed. Assume we have a device which may be in any one of several states. Then suppose the machine changes from one state to another by producing a word. Thus, the machine begins in an initial state, runs through a sequence of states producing a word with each transition, and ends in a final condition. We may call the sequence of words that were produced a sentence, and the machine would define a language. As an example, the grammar which produces two sentences—"The boy comes" and "The boys come"—can be represented by

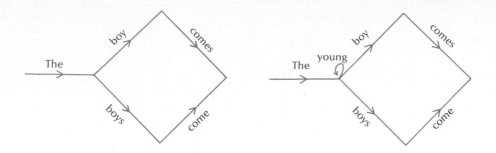

FIGURE A.15 (*Left*) This state diagram shows the paths that can be taken to produce either of two sentences. By taking the upper path the sentence is "The boy comes," while taking the lower path produces the sentence "The boys come." (*Right*) By adding the closed loop ("young") we are now able to produce four sentences. We can produce the two sentences "The young boy comes" and "The young boys come." By not using the loop we can produce the two sentences "The boy comes" and "The boys come." (From Chomsky, 1957.)

the state diagram in Figure A.15 (*left*). We may extend this grammar to produce many more sentences by adding closed loops. We can take "The boy comes" and "The boys come" and add the closed loop "young" to produce "The young boy comes," and so on. All these sentences can be represented by the state diagram in Figure A.15 (*right*).

A finite-state grammar has serious difficulties.

This conception of language is extremely general and if we adopt it, we view the speaker as a finite-state device. However, any attempt to construct a finite-state grammar of English runs into serious difficulties. One can show that English is *not* a finite language by *embedding*. The old nursery rhyme that goes, "This is the cat, that ate the rat, that ate the cheese, that sat on the table, that sat in the house that Jack built," is a good example of embedding. Theoretically, this *one* sentence can be made infinitely long just by adding more descriptive phrases. There is a very large number of possible sentences. It is probably impossible for a finite-state device to produce all the grammatical sentences of English. In addition, a finite-state device is only concerned with single-order left → right sequential events. A finite-state theory of grammar assumes that the speaker looks only at the previous word when considering what the next item should be. Human beings don't speak like that; they seem to operate on several levels simultaneously and take account of more than first-order contingencies among words.

Phrase-structure Grammar

A phrase-structure grammar uses several levels.

A more powerful theory of grammar than a finite-state model is a phrase-structure grammar which assumes there are several levels of language organization. Figure A.16 and Table A.3 show the organization

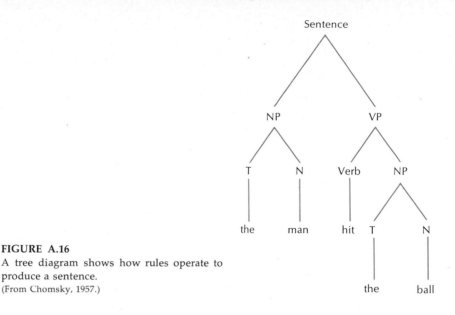

FIGURE A.16
A tree diagram shows how rules operate to
produce a sentence.
(From Chomsky, 1957.)

of a phrase-structure grammar. It begins with an idea for a sentence at the
top level. Next comes two constituents, a noun phrase and a verb phrase.
Each of these can be separated further, because the noun phrase contains
an article like "a" or "the" and a subject. The verb phrase usually contains
a verb, such as "hit" or "fall," and often another noun phrase. The second
noun phrase, contained in the verb phrase, can be further separated into
an article and a noun. Thus, a sentence like "The man bought the tarts"
contains first a noun phrase ("the man") and a verb phrase ("bought the
tarts"). The noun phrase contains an article ("the") and a noun ("man");

TABLE A.3   Constituent-structure analysis of a sentence.

Sentence idea	The man bought the tarts			
Subject-predicate	The man	bought the tarts		
Subject-verb-object	The man	bought	the	tarts
Words	The	man	bought	the	tarts
Morphemes	The	man	bought	the	tart s
Phonemes	The man bought the tarts			

List of rules for generating sentences.

(i) Sentence idea → NP + VP	(a sentence contains a noun phrase and a verb phrase)
(ii) NP → T + N	(a noun phrase contains an article and a noun)
(iii) VP → Verb + NP	(a verb phrase contains a verb and a noun phrase)
(iv) T → the	(T is an article)
(v) N → man, ball, and so on	(N is a noun)
(vi) V → hit, took, and so on	(V is a verb)

and the verb phrase contains the verb ("bought") and another noun phrase ("the tarts"). The second noun phrase contains the article ("the") and another noun ("tarts"). This type of analysis produces the tree diagram shown in Figure A.16, and follows the rules of phrase-structure grammar (*see* Table A.3).

Phrase-structure grammar generates sentences from top to bottom.

As an example of how the system works, run through these rules in the derivation of a sentence: "The man hit the ball." The numbers at the right of each line in Table A.4 refer to the rule of "grammar" used in constructing that line from the preceding line. In this way the second line is formed from the first by rewriting Sentence $\rightarrow NP + VP$ in accordance with rule (i); the third line is formed from the second line by rewriting NP as $T + N$ in accordance with rule (ii), and so on. This kind of grammar is more powerful than a finite-state system because it allows top-to-bottom derivation as a branching tree rather than as left-to-right sequential derivations.

TABLE A.4

Sentence operation	Rule used
$NP + VP$	(i)
$T + N + VP$	(ii)
$T + N + \text{Verb} + NP$	(iii)
the $+ N +$ Verb $+ NP$	(iv)
the $+$ man $+$ Verb $+ NP$	(v)
the $+$ man $+$ bought $+ NP$	(vi)
the $+$ man $+$ bought $+ T + N$	(ii)
the $+$ man $+$ bought $+$ the $+ N$	(iv)
the $+$ man $+$ bought $+$ the $+$ tart	(v)

Transformation Rules

Transformation rules are also required.

Unfortunately, the theory of phrase structure cannot describe all the grammar of English. For example, phrase-structure grammar has only one tense, but English has many forms of a verb. The generation of tenses is crucial to the development of an adequate English grammar. We can, however, easily define the occurrence of variations on a standard declarative sentence by adding to phrase-structure grammar some transformation rules that change verb forms, ask questions, and the like. A phrase-structure grammar adequately handles part of the language, and the remainder may be derived by repeated applications of a small set of transformations to the simple declarative sentences produced by the phrase-structure grammar. This system produces a natural two-way arrangement of grammar. There is a first level of phrase structure, which has rules that change ideas into simple declarative sentences, and a second level of transformational rules, which determine how to ask a question, negate a sentence, and so on.

A sentence is a complex derivation.

To generate a sentence from such a grammar the speaker must perform an extended derivation. He begins with the meaning of the sentence, and then applies rules to construct morphemes. Next the speaker applies proper transformations, using all the obligatory and some of the optional ones. Transformations rearrange, add, or delete morphemes. For example, in asking a question he must reverse the order of verb and object (declaration: we *can;* question: *can* we?).

Current interest is on language acquisition.

At the moment, phrase-structure grammar with transformational rules is the most adequate explanation of grammar. Current theoretical attention is being focused on how these phrase-structure and transformation rules might be acquired by children and others.

Theories of Emotion

Three theories of emotion exist.

Psychologists have long puzzled over the causes of emotions. Three theories of human feelings exist. The oldest, named after William James and Carl Lange, suggests that emotions are caused by physiological changes in the body. A later theory proposed by Walter B. Cannon and Philip Bard assumes that the hypothalamus interprets stimuli and sends impulses to both muscles and glands in response to arousing situations. Cannon and Bard believe that emotions are caused by feedback from the hypothalamus to higher centers of the central nervous system. Recent experiments by Stanley Schachter suggest both theories are incomplete. He found that physiological arousal and cognitive state jointly determine people's feelings. Consider some evidence for each theory.

The James-Lange Theory of Emotion

James argued that behavior causes emotion.

Many believe behavior is caused by emotion. Some people say that a person cries because he is sad, attacks because he is angry, and runs because he is afraid. William James suggested exactly the opposite when he proposed that simuli trigger internal body changes, which feed back information to the nervous system. He thought emotions were simply messages from an aroused body. James proposed that physiological reactions come first and human emotions follow. If emotion is a matter of arousal, then there should be different patterns of arousal for different emotions. To test the James-Lange theory, psychologists have looked for physiological differences between emotions like anger and fear.

Some hormone levels are associated with different emotions.

To measure the body differences that accompany emotion, the experimenter makes a subject angry on one occasion and fearful on another, while he monitors heart rate, blood pressure, and muscular tension. People's physiological measures do show differences. When angry, heart rate goes down, blood pressure goes up, and muscular tension increases. If subjects are afraid, breathing and spasmodic muscular activity increase. Biochemical studies show that the adrenal glands produce noradrenalin when a person is angry and adrenalin when he is afraid. Animals, like lions, that survive by killing produce large quantities of noradrenalin; while animals, like rabbits, that survive by running away produce mostly adrenalin. Young children and females produce more adrenalin; mature males produce more noradrenalin. Thus, some emotional states are correlated with hormone level.

James and Lange were only partly right.

Beyond anger and fear the James-Lange theory of emotion breaks down. Emotions, like joy or happiness, produce no characteristic physiological patterns. The onset of emotion is too fast for complete hormonal control in any case. Cats and dogs that have brain implants may change almost instantly from rage to friendliness, so some neural control of emotions must exist in addition to hormonal control.

The Cannon-Bard Theory of Emotion

Cannon and Bard added a neural component to emotion.

Cannon and Bard proposed a neural theory of emotions to supplement the physiological arousal theory of James and Lange. Cannon and Bard supposed that environmental stimuli enter the hypothalamus, which then arouses the autonomic nervous system, triggering physiological changes. In addition, they theorized that the hypothalamus sends messages to the cortex and that these messages are the emotions. While James and Lange argued that feedback from the body causes emotion, Cannon and Bard believe feedback directly from the hypothalamus is what causes emotions.

Brain stimulation supports this theory.

Support for the Cannon-Bard theory comes from brain stimulation studies. For example, if the hypothalamus of a cat is stimulated, the animal will behave as though it is angry.

A Cognitive-Social Theory of Emotion

Schachter argues that cognition is important in emotions.

Recent studies suggest that both the James-Lange and the Cannon-Bard theories of emotion are incomplete. By manipulating the physiological arousal and social-cognitive states of subjects independently, Stanley Schachter showed that both factors may influence people's emotions. To make sure his subjects did not guess the purpose of his experiment, and thus influence the results, Schachter said he was studying the effect of vitamin supplements on vision. All subjects were told that the vitamin supplements were harmless. However, some subjects were injected with adrenalin while others were given a neutral saline solution that had no effect at all. These two sets of subjects were further separated into three groups that received instructions (*see* Figure A.17). Some were told that the injection would arouse them; others were told it would make them numb; and a third group was told nothing about the possible effects of the injection except it was harmless. All the subjects were individually placed either with a stooge, who would act euphorically, or a stooge who would elicit anger. Under the euphoric condition the stooge did funny

FIGURE A.17 Schematic representation of an experiment with adrenalin and different expectations. Subjects injected with adrenalin gave a different emotional reaction to the stooge who is excited, depending on whether or not they were given appropriate expectations of what the injection would do to them. The visceral reactions, involving organs of the body cavity, were not the only ones produced by adrenalin.

things; under the anger condition the stooge and the subject took a questionnaire and the stooge constantly interrupted the subject and made misleading remarks. Two measures of the subjects' emotions were obtained: observations through a one-way glass and self-reports on their moods.

Schachter found that social-cognitive factors influence emotion.

The major finding was that subjects who are aroused but have no explanation of their physiological state are influenced by the social situation. Subjects with no explanation of their arousal reported and behaved as though they were angry or euphoric, depending on the particular social situation. Subjects with an explanation for their physiological arousal did not feel either angry or happy. Subjects injected with adrenaline and told how they would feel were immune to the effects of the stooge's behavior. In the angry conditions these subjects did not report or show anger. In the euphoric conditions they reported themselves as less happy than subjects with identical body states but no knowledge of why they felt that way. Thus, when physiological arousal exists without an appropriate explanation, human subjects can be manipulated into states of euphoria, anger, or amusement by social interaction. Apparently, human emotional states are a composite of autonomic arousal *and* surrounding social-cognitive factors. Either factor alone cannot adequately explain feelings.

Even false beliefs can affect emotions.

Are physiological changes necessary for feeling or can a person be fooled into simply thinking body changes are occurring to experience an emotional shift? To test this notion men were shown pictures of semi-nude women from *Playboy* magazine. While viewing the pictures they heard an amplified heartbeat, which they believed to be their own. For half the pictures the heartbeat was actually from the participant. For some pictures the experimenter manipulated the amplified heartbeat artificially. Following the viewing, each man rated the pictures for pleasantness. The results showed that those pictures associated with higher heart rates were judged more pleasant than those pictures which did not change the heart rate; and this was true even in those cases where the heart-rate change was artificially induced by the experimenter. Simply believing body changes are occurring apparently can change attitudes.

Glossary *

acceptable sentence—a sentence which is within the ability of actual speakers and listeners to understand.

accommodation—a second function from Piaget's theory which assumes that the child will develop a new cognitive category if he is unable to fit a particular stimulus into any existing schema.

achievement motivation—an internal need to achieve one's own goal or to set and meet an internal standard of excellence.

acrophobia—a fear of heights.

American sign language—a sign language used by most deaf children and adults in the U.S. and also taught by Gardner and Gardner to a chimpanzee.

amniocentesis—the procedure of extracting amniotic fluid from the pregnant mother to test for genetic abnormalities in her unborn child.

animism—the tendency of young children to attribute life to all things.

anxious conformity—the result of overzealous socialization, in which the child must conform to the parents' wishes or suffer the consequences in terms of punishment and rejection.

approach-avoidance conflict—a conflict in deciding whether to accept something which has both positive and negative aspects to it.

articulation—a smooth coherent pattern of behavior which runs its course in an uninterrupted manner (Warner).

assimilation—the notion from Piaget which assumes that children will try to fit a stimulus into an existing cognitive category if they can.

association—the connection of stimuli and responses by repeated presentation.

audiogram—the standard form on which the results of a hearing test are plotted. The differential sensitivity of the subject to varying frequencies is corrected so that the person's sensitivity is graphed as a flat line when he hears normally.

autism—an early childhood form of withdrawal and rejection of interpersonal relations. Many clinical psychologists feel that autism is simply another form of schizophrenia which happens at a very early age; while others argue that it is a different mental illness.

autonomy—the final stage of moral development in which the child is concerned with the social contract and universal principles of moral development.

base mental age—the mental age below which the child passes all items on the intelligence test.

behavior modification—changing the patient's behavior by manipulating rewards and punishments in his environment.

behaviorist—a scientist who deals in observable actions and speech rather than in thought or emotions which cannot be seen.

* Terms which are cross-referenced in the Glossary are marked with the words *which see* in parentheses.

biofeedback—the collection, transformation, and presentation of biological information (such as one's own heart rate or blood pressure) visually or auditorily so that one becomes more aware of internal physiological states.

body type—the theory proposed by Sheldon that the personality and behavior of the individual is partially determined by the shape of his physique. Sheldon proposed three types: the mesomorph, the ectomorph, and the endomorph.

CAT—children's apperception test.

catharsis—an emotional expression which leaves the patient feeling relieved about his anxieties and fears.

centering—the tendency of young children to concentrate their attention on one aspect of a perceptual or conceptual problem to the exclusion of other relevant features.

cephalocaudal—the principle of growth which suggests that the infant's growth and motor development proceed from the head toward the caudal or tail end of the body.

cerebral dominance—the theory which says that one side of the human central nervous system is dominant over the other side for any particular task. For example, for most human beings, the left side of the brain contains the major center for speech.

CFF—critical fusion frequency; the frequency at which a flickering light becomes fused into a constant lower brightness.

classical conditioning—the automatic association of a previously neutral stimulus with an unconditioned reflexive response by repeated pairing of the neutral conditioned stimulus with an innate unconditioned stimulus.

claustrophobia—a fear of enclosed places.

clique—formally, a close subgroup of a crowd which is emotionally bound together and shares confidences much more than the crowd.

closure—the Gestalt ability to complete a figure when only part of the outline is present.

cocktail party phenomenon—the ability of some people to follow a single conversation in the midst of many distracting noises and events.

comparative psychologist—a social scientist who is primarily interested in the relative learning abilities of different species.

competence—a linguistic term, which means the ability of the native speaker to understand the rules of the language without attention to limitations like memory capacity, attention span, articulation, and so on.

compulsion—a recurring act which often follows an obsessive thought in an attempt to expiate the guilt associated with the obsession.

conditioned response—the response which is elicited by the conditioned stimulus after several classical-conditioning trials.

conditioned stimulus—any neutral stimulus which can be paired with an innate unconditioned stimulus to produce classical conditioning.

conductive impairment—a hearing problem caused by a loss of conductance in the middle ear, often due to otosclerosis (the depositing of calcium in the bones of the ear).

conformity—the suggestibility of an individual by group pressure to conform with the group decision in the face of conflicting information.

connotative meaning—the emotional, often unconscious evaluative meaning of words or sentences.

construct or **theoretical validity**—a test has theoretical validity if results from the measurements are in agreement with a particular theory.

content validity—a test has content validity if the items on the instrument are representative of the type of process that is being measured.

conventional moral development—the second major stage of moral development in which the child is concerned with being good.

conversion reaction—a paralysis or other malady caused by psychological stress and conflict rather than physiological injury.

cooperative play—play in which there is interaction and cooperation between the members; for example, playing in a band.

counterconditioning—the association through classical conditioning of positive, rather than negative, primary unconditioned stimuli with previously negative stimuli.

counterphobic—an action taken by a person to counteract a strong fear; for example, a person who is afraid of snakes might take a job at a zoo so he could work closely with snakes and overcome his initial fears.

creative thinking—an attempt to develop a novel and important solution to a problem.

critical thinking—the process of evaluating the products of other modes of thought.

cross-sectional measurement—the simultaneous collection of age-related data from several groups of children at different ages to assess developmental trends.

crowd—technically, a loose group of people who join together for mutual activities like dancing, watching a game, and so on.

cumulative recorder—a device which traces the cumulative number of responses an animal makes in an operant-conditioning situation as a function of time; the slope of the cumulative record indicates the rate of responding.

declarative—a sentence which states a direct subject-action object relation; for example: The girl hit John; as opposed to a passive, indirect sentence: John was hit by the girl.

delinquent—the result of negative feelings and autonomy from the family; usually defined as a child or youth in trouble with the law.

denotative meaning—the objective, reality-based meaning of words or sentences.

depression—a lowering of mood so that the person or child is deeply disturbed.

desensitization—the process of extinguishing a classically-conditioned fear by gradually presenting the person with the fearful object in the absence of any pain or other discomfort.

detour task—a Lewinian task in which the path between the child and his goal is blocked by a barrier which cannot be overcome but can be bypassed.

developmental quotient (DQ)—$\dfrac{\text{sensory motor score}}{\text{chronological age}}$; the developmental quotient is a measure of how rapidly the infant is progressing through the early stages of sensory-motor development. The DQ is *not* correlated with IQ.

directed thinking—information-processing which has the solution of a particular, well-formed problem as its goal.

disassociative reaction—the cause of amnesia or multiple personality; the person segregates some of his thoughts from the rest.

displacement—the channeling of hostility from a superior to an inferior so that the person will have both the satisfaction of venting his anger and the security of not being attacked in return by the superior. Most familiar, is the wife attacked by the husband when he has had a hard day at the office, then the wife in turn yelling at the children, who kick the dog, who attacks the cat, who attacks the mouse.

distinctive feature—the assumed binary features of sounds which make up phonemes and, ultimately, all of spoken language; for example, nasal or not nasal.

dominance (1)—the asymmetrical relation between two or more individuals in a group such that one member is higher on a hierarchy than the other.

(2)—the genetic characteristic by which one of a gene pair determines the phenotypic structure of the organism when the two genes on the same chromosome are not identical.

double bind—a situation in which the parent or person communicates two inconsistent messages, such as a positive one with vocal language and another negative one with body language.

dwarfism—small stature and weight associated with the lack of growth hormone from the pituitary gland.

echolalia—the automatic repetition by a child of what he hears without understanding what the words mean.

ectoderm—the primitive germ layer from which skin and most sensory organs derive.

ectomorph—a body type proposed by Sheldon to be thin, nervous, and active.

egocentrism—the tendency of young children to assume that everyone sees the world the same way that they do; the inability to take another's view of reality.

eidetic imagery—the ability of some young children to recall almost all the perceptual information from a display even after the stimulus is removed from the child's vision.

empiricism—the theory which assumes that all knowledge is gained through experience and nothing is preprogrammed in the organism.

enactive representation—the picturing of an object or event by motor movement.

encopresis—uncontrolled bowel movements.

endoderm—the primitive germ layer from which most internal organs of digestion and circulation derive.

endomorph—a body type proposed by Sheldon to be fat and sluggish in behavior.

enrichment—the notion that perceptual ability can be enhanced by giving the child or animal extra stimulation during the early years of development.

enuresis—bed wetting.

estrous cycle—the cyclic variation in amount of the hormone estrogen in the female's bloodstream. This variation in estrogen level is correlated with behavioral variations in many animals.

ethologist—a biologically-oriented student of behavior who studies primarily instinctive acts among lower animals and human infants.

expanding—repeating the utterance of a child with grammar that is more clear and complete than he used.

extending—repeating a child's sentence with more facts or information, but no attention to the grammar of the utterance.

extinction—the dimunition of a conditioned response following the presentation of several conditioned stimulus trials without the unconditioned stimulus.

extraversion—one end of a bipolar dimension which describes whether an individual is directed toward or away from people; the extrovert is directed toward others.

fear of failure—the tendency of some children to set unrealistic high or low goals because they fear they will fail. If they fail with high goals they say they could not do it anyway; if they succeed with low goals they can do so easily.

figure-ground—the Gestalt notion that parts of a perceptual field are seen as the important central figure and the rest of the perceptual field is seen as ground or background to the central figure.

Fixed Action Pattern (FAP)—the programed pattern of responses elicited when an instinct is triggered.

fixed interval schedule of reinforcement—a pattern of reward which delivers reinforcements to the organism after a fixed interval of time independent of the response rate of the organism.

fixed ratio reinforcement schedule—a pattern of reinforcement which delivers a reward after a set number of responses.

fraternal twins—a pair of individuals who are conceived and carried by the mother at the same time but who are no more alike genetically than siblings.

free association—a Freudian technique for uncovering hidden conflicts and emotions by allowing the mind to freely associate ideas until there is blocking. Blocking is supposed to be associated with conflict or emotion.

free thinking—revery, daydreaming, and other types of wishful thinking with no particular goal except entertainment.

friendships—a very close relationship between two or more individuals, which allows them to share emotional experiences without the usual masks of crowds and cliques.

generalization—spreading of responses from one original stimulus to other similar stimuli without further practice or reward.

genetic counseling—the technique of following a couple's family tree to determine whether they run a high risk of producing genetically abnormal children.

genotype—the hidden genetic structure of the individual organism, opposed to the phenotype (*which see*), which is the observable characteristics of the same individual organism. In the case of purebred (homozygous) genetic materials, there is perfect correspondence between genotype and phenotype; in the case of mixed genetic materials (heterozygous) genotype and phenotype are not the same.

Gestalt—a school of psychology which theorizes that perceptions occur in consciousness as wholes and not as bits and pieces.

glutathione—a chemical substance found in the blood and urine of many schizophrenic patients which, when injected into the bloodstream of normal human beings, produces many of the same symptoms experienced by the psychotic person.

good continuation—the Gestalt notion that lines which continue along an expected path are more likely to be seen as a single line than lines which diverge into unexpected directions.

good form—the Gestalt notion that simple, symmetrical forms are more likely to be seen than more complex forms when both are possible from the same stimuli.

Graduate Record Exam (GRE)—a difficult, high-level test of intelligence given to students who are applying to graduate school.

grammar — the general rules which allow any native speaker to produce all the utterances of his language.

grammatical — judgment of the correctness of utterances by native speakers in terms of rules, but without attention to whether the sentences can be understood or have meaning.

group therapy — psychological treatment dispensed and associated with group interactions.

habituation — the gradual dimunition of a reflexive response following repeated presentation of the stimulus.

hallucinogens — any of a family of chemicals which produce visual and occasionally auditory hallucinations; for example, LSD, psilocybin, peyote, and mescaline.

hashish — a very potent form of marijuana.

hatchet man — the second most powerful man in a group and the one who is feared and disliked by all the other members of the gang. He usually does the punishing for the task leader in order to keep the group in line.

hate-autonomy — a family in which the parents do little to control their children and dislike them.

hate-control — a family in which the parents use punishment and fear to control their children.

hermaphrodite — technically, a person who possesses the sexual characteristics of both males and females; this may be at the chromosomal, hormonal, or genital level.

heterozygous — an animal or person with two different genetic characteristics, of the genotype; of mixed breeding.

homozygous — an animal or person with similar genetic characteristics of the genotype; purebred.

hyperactivity — a distractable and irritable state also characterized by short attention spans.

hypochondriac — a person who is overly concerned with his physical health.

iconic representation — the picturing of an object or event by perceptual or image processes.

identical twin — a pair of individuals who result from an early splitting of a single fertilized egg and thus are genetically identical.

idiographic — the intensive study of single cases to understand the workings of a human mind or self-concept.

imprinting — the strong, immediate, and almost irreversible attachment to the caretaker or other objects in its environment which the young of many species form during an early critical period; imprinting is usually initiated by locomotion and ended by the development of fear.

inbreeding — the process of reproducing organisms within a small group so that all the members of the group approach similar genetic constitutions. The technique is used primarily for behavior genetic studies.

independent assortment — the notion that genes are segregated independently of other genes. This is, in fact, only partially true, since many genes are located on the same chromosome and are only arranged independently at the level of the chromosome.

individual therapies — treatment which involves talking between the trained specialist and his patient.

innate releasing stimulus (IRS) — the particular pattern of stimulation necessary for the release of an instinct when the organism is in the appropriate physiological state.

insight — understanding a problem by mental operations or thinking rather than trial and error or random behavior.

instinct — a more complex innate pattern of stimuli and responses which are internally programed to occur when the animal is in a particular physiological state; for example, the sexual behavior of many species.

institutionalization — when a child is cared for in a hospital or other establishment by several caretakers rather than one or two or his own mother in the home.

intelligence quotient (IQ) — $\dfrac{\text{mental age (MA)}}{\text{chronological age (CA)}}$

intentionality — the state in which the individual is striving toward some particular goal and is not simply reacting to the environment or behaving randomly.

interpretation — the therapists' statements about the meanings and implications of what a patient has been doing and dreaming over the past several days, usually designed to give the patient some insight into his emotional problems.

introspection — the technique of observing the workings of one's own mind to find out how various cognitive and perceptual processes work. This method was rejected by the behaviorists as unscientific.

introversion — a bipolar (opposite-valued) dimension which describes whether people are directed toward or away from others; the introvert is directed away from others into himself.

latent content — the hidden, symbolic meaning of a patient's dreams.

latent learning — the notion that learning can occur in the absence of direct reinforcement and will only show up in the organism's performance after he is motivated to actually perform the task.

life space — the notion from Lewin's theory that an internal representation of reality is what guides people in their relations with the world and others.

longitudinal measurement — the assessment of the same group of children over time to determine developmental trends.

long-term memory — a function of the brain with almost unlimited storage capacity which holds information for later use by the central processor of the nervous system.

love-autonomy — an atmosphere in which the family is loving and permissive with the child.

love-control — a family atmosphere in which the parents are loving and controlling with their children.

manifest content — the obvious material in the patient's dreams.

maternal deprivation — the hypothesis that the lack of a single caretaker during the early life of an infant will hamper his development.

maternal separation — the notion that an infant comes to recognize his mother at about six to eight months of age, and that after that time he will feel separation anxiety (*which see*) if the mother leaves for an extended period of time. Before six months of age the emotional reaction from maternal separation is impossible, because the baby will not recognize that his mother has left.

mating — one sign of dominance among animals in a group.

meditation — the voluntary change of awareness by restricting sensory inputs and attending primarily to internal states and thoughts.

mesoderm—the primitive germ layer from which most muscular and supportive tissue derive.

mesomorph—a strong, muscular body type proposed by Sheldon as energetic and aggressive.

methadone—an addicting chemical used in the U.S. to substitute for morphine and heroin in the treatment of addiction.

MMPI—Minnesota Multiphasic Personality Inventory; an objective test of personality containing about 550 items, which are answered as true or false about the self.

mnemonic—any of a large number of devices which take advantage of rules or patterns to aid the storage and retrieval of information from long-term memory (*which see*).

morpheme—the smallest meaningful unit of a language. There are three types of morpheme: *free,* which stand alone; *bound,* which must be connected to another morpheme to be used; and *combined,* which are free and bound morphemes together. For example, cat (free), -s (bound), and cats (combined).

mutation—a permanent biochemical change in the genetic structure of the organism caused by some physical or chemical agent acting directly on the genetic material.

narcosis—a state of numbness associated with the administration of a drug.

nativism—the notion that a number of human behaviors are controlled by genetic processes rather than acquired by experience.

nearness—an idea from Gestalt psychology that perceptual is influenced by the close relationship of the elements.

negative reinforcement—outcomes which either suppress the rate of responding when they occur or increase the rate of responding when they are withdrawn; for example, electric shock.

negative sentence—a sentence which contains a negation and thus states that the action described is not true or did not happen.

negativism (1)—according to Freud, the adjustment of a child who is bullied by his parents to the point where he will do nothing that they ask, even if it is reasonable.

(2)—the obstructive, denying attitude and behavior of children in institutions; according to Ribble, the result of a lack of mothering.

neural impairment of hearing—a loss of hearing ability due to nerve damage.

neurotic—a form of psychological disturbance characterized by anxiety, fears, or peculiar behavior patterns and often depression; milder than psychosis (*which see*).

night terrors—a recurring nightmare from which it is difficult to wake the child, although he appears to be somewhat awake and is often crying and quite upset.

nomothetic—studying large groups of people to find out what the usual or average response is.

nonstandard English—variations in the transformations (*which see*) and pronunciations of the English language which comprise local dialects. For example, Black English, the blending of Spanish and English, and American-Indian languages and English are all nonstandard English forms.

noradrenalin—a chemical related to central nervous system activity and the emotion of anger.

nyctophobia—fear of the dark and night.

obedience—willingness to obey an authority even if the authority is telling the person to do something against his professed moral feelings and principles.

object concept—the child's understanding that a particular set of perceptual events is a coherent whole, and that the perceptual events do not cease their existence when the child looks away.

obsession—a recurring thought which the person cannot get out of his mind; usually related to violence in children and sex or violence in adults.

operant conditioning—the rules of learning which govern the effect of reinforcement and punishment on the performance of animals and men.

overachiever—someone who is accomplishing above what would be expected on the basis of his IQ score.

overprotection—the result of love and control in which the child is kept dependent well beyond the usual age.

parallel play—amusements or games in which two children are next to each other on the playground, but do not interact.

paranoid—a form of schizophrenia (*which see*) in which the victim is frightened of others and feels that he is being persecuted. These individuals are usually brighter than average and often dangerous.

pedigree—the study of familial similarities done by following the family tree of individuals who share common genetic and environmental backgrounds. This was the first method used in behavior genetics, but it is *not* utilized extensively now because of the confounding of genetics and environment.

performance (language)—the actual ability of a human speaker to say sentences and understand them.

penetrance—a genetic notion similar to dominance but referring to the effectiveness of many genes which each have a small effect rather than to the dominance or recessiveness (*which see*) of a single gene.

perceptual set—the expectation induced in a person's apparatus of sense observation when it is exposed to several items of the same general class. This perceptual set can influence how a person sees and interprets an ambiguous situation.

phenotype—the measurable physical and behavioral characteristics of the individual, differentiated from genotype (*which see*).

phoneme—the basic sound unit of all languages; comparable in some ways to letters but more general.

phylogenetic skills—those motor abilities which all individuals of a particular species develop in the natural course of maturation without the necessity of training; for example, walking in the human being.

physiological therapy—treatment which involves drugs, electric shock, or surgery.

pivot word—the stable word which children begin to use to anchor two- or three-word sentences when they first begin to speak *grammars*.

placebo—a sugar or other inactive pill which may have a beneficial effect because the patient *thinks* it will help him. The cure is psychological rather than physiological.

positive reinforcement—rewards which increase the probability of those responses which they follow.

postpartum—the interval immediately after the birth of a baby, a time of emotional and physiological stress for some species.

preconventional moral development—the early stage of ethical understanding in which the child is primarily concerned with escape from pain and acquisition of rewards.

prefrontal lobotomy—an outdated surgical treatment for the handling of psychotic patients. The surgery involved cutting the connections between the frontal lobes of the cortex and the rest of the central nervous system, and the result was a docile patient.

premenstrual—the interval immediately before the beginning of the menstrual cycle in females.

primary circular reaction—a reaction which is chained into a sequence of acts and is centered about the child's own body; for example, sucking the thumb.

primary reinforcement—the innate class of stimuli which are rewarding to organisms; for example, sex and food.

process psychosos—a psychotic reaction which develops over an extended period of time and seems unrelated to external stressful situations.

projection—the attribution of one's own hostility and fears to another person to justify attacking the other person before he can attack.

projective test—a disguised test designed to allow the person to throw his own wishes and fears into ambiguous pictures and other materials. These tests are designed to uncover hidden fears, conflicts, and anxieties.

proximodistal—the principle of growth which suggests that size and developmental differentiation begin at the proximal or inner parts of the body and only later do the extremities become mature and differentiated.

pseudohermophrodite—the apparent masculinization of a female baby by the ingestion of too much androgen by the mother during the early stages of pregnancy.

psychoanalysis—a treatment of mental illness developed by Freud which consists of bringing repressed material into the consciousness through such methods as free association (*which see*), investigation of dreams, and so on.

psychosis—a major mental disorder which impairs the functioning of the person and divides him from reality.

puberty rite—a ceremony which marks the transition from childhood to adulthood in many primitive societies.

punishment—any stimulus which produces pain.

Rapid Eye Movement sleep (REM)—a period during which the sleeper moves his eyes rapidly and, if awakened, will usually report a dream.

rationalization—the logic used by people to debase those things which they cannot attain by their own efforts. For example, the fox who could not reach the grapes said they were probably sour anyway.

reaction formation—the development of an opposite personal trait. For example, the person who appears sexually adequate but is afraid of the opposite sex, who seems aggressive when he is really dependent, and so on.

reactive psychoses—a psychotic response precipitated by environmental stress.

realism—the tendency of young children to attribute reality to psychological processes like dreams and imagination.

recessive—the genetic characteristic by which one part of a gene is overwhelmed or dominated by the other when they are different. The recessive gene does not affect the phenotype (*which see*) of the individual.

reflex—the innate association of a specific stimulus to a particular response. These early fixed behaviors were assumed to be the basis of all later learning by the behaviorists (*which see*).

regression—the disintegration of personality so that a person moves back to earlier, more primitive forms of behavior; for example, when a child cries helplessly rather than attacking a frustration directly.

reinforcement—the positive or negative events which follow responses and are assumed by operant-conditioning theorists (*which see*) to increase or decrease the strength of response probabilities.

reliability—a statistical measure of the repeatability of testing results; usually assessed by giving the same test on two separate occasions or giving two forms of the test and correlating them over a number of people.

repression—the unconscious pushing of emotional or fearful materials into the unconscious so that they will no longer bother the person.

reticular activating system—part of the brain stem of the central nervous system concerned primarily with activating and quieting the brain during cycles of sleep and wakefulness.

reversibility—the ability of the concrete-operational child to retrace the logical steps of an argument and thereby return to his original premise.

scapegoat—the person in the group who is rejected and disliked by most of the other members. They do not, however, fear him, since he is at the bottom of the power ladder.

schema—for Piaget, the notion that the child has cognitive structures and operations stored in his memory which will help him to understand the world; for example, the ability to add.

schizophrenia—any of several types of severe psychoses (*which see*) which are characterized by hallucinations, delusions, and disturbed emotions; often also accompanied by severe thought disorganization.

school phobia—a fear of schools.

secondary circular reaction—a reaction in which behaviors are chained into an integrated sequence. In the case of secondary circular reactions, the behaviors are related to the person's body and external events.

secondary reinforcement—reward value derived from associating a neutral stimulus with a positive reinforcer; for example, money.

segregation—the genetic notion that genes act like marbles which can be combined at conception and then retrieved again unchanged during sex cell production.

selection—the differential reproduction or survival of individuals which makes for changes in the genetic pool of a species.

selective breeding—a behavior genetic technique in which animals with similar phenotypic characteristics are mated and the resulting offspring are also selected for the same characteristic and mated again. The result is a gradual change in the genetic and phenotypic characteristics of the group, if there is genetic constraint on the characteristic.

semantics—the study of the meaning of words and sentences.

senile psychoses—a psychosis (*which see*) of aging, usually caused by degenerative brain damage.

sensoritonic—a theoretical construct from Werner. Sensoritonic factors are internal sensations which affect the person's perception of the horizontal.

sensory information storage—the device in the brain which stores large amounts of sensory information for a short interval while it is being processed and transferred to short-term memory (*which see*).

sensory isolation—the separation of a person from stimuli, restricting sensory information to the point where he is almost completely cut off from all input. Most people find isolation extremely difficult to handle for extended periods.

sensory motor abilities—for Piaget, the notion that the early integration of sensation and movement abilities into a single schema (*which see*) is basic to all later cognitive abilities.

separation anxiety—a fear of separation from the mother which develops in babies at about twelve months of age and lasts for about one year.

shaping—an operant-conditioning technique (*which see*) in which the organism is gradually shifted from a series of simple approximations of a complex act into the performance of a complex sequence of events by reinforcing such approximations and then gradually defining the acceptable acts more and more precisely.

shock therapy—the treatment of depression by the administration of electric or chemical shock.

short-term memory—a device in the brain which stores about six items of information for a few seconds while they are either processed or transferred to long-term memory (*which see*).

silent member—a member of the group who is at the bottom of the power ladder, but is not disliked or rejected. Feelings toward him are neutral.

similarity—a Gestalt (*which see*) notion that similar items are grouped into a single percept.

socialization—the process of instilling manners, morals, and social consciousness into the child.

social symbol—the symbols by which we all display status, personal traits, and wishes. For example, clothes, cars, addresses, and so on are all social symbols.

solitary play—play in which the child is alone.

standardization—the process of collecting a representative sample of the total population for use as a comparison yardstick against which to interpret the scores of individuals who take a test.

stimulus generalization—the elicitation of a response by a similar stimulus to the original conditioned stimulus.

stranger anxiety—a fear of new objects and people which appears in human babies at about six months of age and lasts for three or four months.

structured classroom—a school room in which the fundamentals of reading, writing, and mathematics are emphasized rather than socialization and group cooperation.

sublimation—the changing of a drive satisfaction from primitive to more socialized and sophisticated satisfaction. For example, writing love poetry rather than gaining sexual satisfaction directly.

syllogism—a logical statement of the form if-then, in which both the premise must be true and the reasoning valid in order for the conclusion to be valid and true.

symbolic representation—the calling forth of an object or event by linguistic means.

Synanon—a theraputic community dedicated to the treatment of heroin and morphine addicts.

syncretic—the fusion of sensory images and impressions from one modality into another. For example, hearing lights and seeing sounds.

task leader—the person in a small group who determines what the group does and who is assigned various jobs.

taxis—the most primitive type of behavior which is an innate programed turning of the body into or away from a particular stimulation. For example, a moth into the flame.

teacher's expectations—an unproved notion that what a teacher thinks about the potential of a child can have a significant effect on his subsequent academic and intellectual development.

tertiary circular reaction—a sequence of behavior in which the child comes to integrate means and goals into a smooth pattern of behavior.

transference—the investment of emotions and expectations of a patient in the therapist. Usually the patient treats the therapist as if he were a member of the patient's family.

transformation—a rule which may be applied to a sentence or phrase which can change the voice of the sentence from active to passive; or if applied to a word can change it from singular to plural or present to past. When applied to sentences it can change a statement to a question or negation.

truth value—for a statement to be true it must be based on true premises and logical arguments.

unconditioned response—the innate behavior produced by an unconditioned stimulus (*which see*).

unconditioned stimulus—any biologically important stimulus which elicits a reliable reflex. For example, food in the mouth which elicits salivation, or a loud noise which elicits fear in the infant.

underachiever—someone who is accomplishing below what would be expected on the basis of his IQ score.

unstructured classroom—a schoolroom in which children are allowed to discover things for themselves, and there is much greater emphasis on the social and moral development of the child than his intellectual development.

valence—the geometric solution of two forces having both a direction and a size (Lewin).

validity (1)—the degree to which a test measures the concept it is supposed to assess. There are two different types of validity: *face validity* (a test has face validity if it seems to be a measure of what it is supposed to measure); *predictive validity* (a test has predictive validity if it will significantly increase the precision with which decisions can be made about people on the basis scores on the test).

(2)—the logical structure of an argument.

variable interval schedule of reinforcement—a pattern of reward which delivers reinforcement to the organism after a changing period of time independent of his response rate.

variable ratio reinforcement schedule—a pattern of reward which delivers reinforcements after a changing number of responses.

visual cliff—the apparatus developed by Gibson and Walk to measure the depth perception of babies or young animals that can locomote.

white noise—the particular noise used by psychologists to mask other sounds; it is composed of a random sample of frequencies and loudnesses.

working through in therapy—once a patient has an insight (*which see*) into his difficulties, working through is the next stage, where a person, re-educates his emotions so that he can handle conflict in a more mature way.

zoophobia—a fear of animals.

Selected Bibliography

Adelson, J. "The Political Imagination of the Young Adolescent," *Daedalus: Journal of the American Academy of Arts and Sciences,* 100 (1971), pp. 1013–1050.

Adler, A. *Social Interest* (London: Putnam, 1939).

Anastasi, A. *Psychological Testing* (New York: Macmillan, 1968).

Asch, S.E. "Studies of Independence and Submission to Group Pressure: I. A Minority of One against a Unanimous Majority," *Psychological Monographs,* 70, no. 416 (1956).

Bakan, P. "The Eyes Have It," *Psychology Today* (April 1971).

Bandura, A., and A.C. Huston. "Identification as a Process of Incidental Learning," *Journal of Abnormal and Social Psychology,* 63 (1961), pp. 311–318.

Bandura, A., D. Ross, and S.A. Ross. "Imitation of Film-mediated Aggressive Models," *Journal of Abnormal and Social Psychology,* 66 (1963), pp. 3–11.

Bandura, A. and R.H. Walters. *Social Learning and Personality Development* (New York: Holt, Rinehart and Winston, 1963).

Bayley, N. *Bayley Scales of Infant Development* (New York: The Psychological Corp., 1969).

Bower, T.G.R. "Slant Perception and Shape Constancy in Infants," *Science,* 151 (1966), pp. 832–834.

Bower, T.G.R. "The Development of the Object Concept." In J. Mehler, ed., *Handbook of Cognitive Psychology* (Englewood Cliffs, N.J.: Prentice-Hall, 1970).

Braine, M.D.S. "The Ontogeny of English Phrase Structure: The First Phase," *Language,* 39 (1963), pp. 1–13.

Broadbent, D. "Flow of Information within the Organism," *Journal of Verbal Learning and Verbal Behavior,* 4 (1963), pp. 34–39.

Bronfenbrenner, U. *Two Worlds of Childhood: US and USSR* (New York: Russell Sage Foundation, 1970).

Bronowski, J., and U. Bellugi. "Language, Name and Concept," *Science,* 168 (1970), pp. 669–673.

Brophy, J., and T.L. Good. *Teacher-student Relationships* (New York: Holt, Rinehart and Winston, 1974).

Brown, R.W. *Selected Papers of Roger Brown* (New York: The Free Press, 1970).

Brown, R.W. *Social Psychology* (New York: The Free Press, 1965).

Brown, R.W., and J. Berko. "Word Association and the Acquisition of Grammar," *Child Development,* 31 (1969), pp. 1–14.

Bruner, J. *On Knowing: Essays for the Left Hand* (New York: Atheneum, 1965).

Bruner, J. *Processes of Cognitive Growth: Infancy* (Worcester, Mass: Clark University Press, 1968).

Burks, H. "The Hyperkinetic Child," *Exceptional Children,* 27 (1960), pp. 18–26.

Butcher, H. *Human Intelligence* (New York: Harper and Row, 1968).

Cameron, J., N. Livson, and N. Bayler. "Infant Vocalizations and Their Relationship to Mature Intelligence," *Science,* 157 (1967), pp. 331–333.

Cattell, R.B., and I.H. Scheier. *The Meaning and Measurement of Neuroticism and Anxiety* (New York: Ronald Press, 1961).

Cazden, C. "Environmental Assistance to the Child's Acquisition of Grammar," Unpublished doctoral dissertation, Harvard University (1965).

Chomsky, N. *Aspects of the Theory of Syntax* (Cambridge, Mass.: MIT Press, 1965).

Claiborn, W. "Expectancy Effects in the Classroom: A Failure to Replicate," *Journal of Educational Psychology,* 60 (1969), pp. 377–383.

Cline, V., J. Richards, and W. Needham. "Creativity Tests and Achievement in High School Science," *Journal of Applied Psychology,* 47 (1963), pp. 184–189.

Coleman, J.S., *et al. Equality of Educational Opportunity* (U.S. Department of Health, Education and Welfare, 1966).

Conger, J.J., and W.C. Miller. *Personality, Social Class and Delinquency* (New York: Wiley, 1966).

Copi, I. *Symbolic Logic* (New York: Macmillan, 1954).

Costanzo, P.R., and M.E. Shaw. "Conformity as a Function of Age Level," *Child Development,* 37 (1966), pp. 967–975.

Cronbach, L. *Essentials of Psychological Testing* (New York: Harper and Row, 1970).

Cronbach, L., N. Rajaratman, and A. Gleser. "Theory of Generalizability: A Liberalization of Reliability Theory," *British Journal of Statistical Psychology,* 16 (1963), pp. 137–164.

Dale, P.S. *Language Development* (Hinsdale, Ill.: The Dryden Press, 1972).

Darwin, C. *Origin of the Species* (London: Murray, 1859).

Davis, A., and R.J. Havighurst. "Social Class and Color Differences in Child Rearing," *American Sociological Review,* 11 (1946), pp. 698–710.

Dennis, W., and M.G. Dennis. "The Effect of Cradling Practices upon the Onset of Walking in Hopi Children. *Journal of Genetic Psychology,* 56 (1940), pp. 77–86.

Dennis, W., and P. Najarian. "Infant Development under Environmental Handicap," *Psychological Monographs,* 71 (1957).

Diamond, M. "A Critical Evaluation of Ontogeny of Human Sexual Behavior," *Quarterly Review of Biology,* 40 (1965), pp. 147–175.

Ebbinghaus, H. *Memory: A Contribution to Experimental Psychology* (New York: Teachers College, Columbia University, 1913).

Erikson, E.H. *Childhood and Society* (New York: Norton, 1950).

Erlenmeyer-Kimling, L., and L. Jarvik. "Genetics and Intelligence: A Review," *Science,* 142 (1963), pp. 1477–1479.

Estes, W. "An Experimental Study of Punishment," *Psychological Monograph,* 263 (1944).

Eysenck, H. *The Biological Basis of Personality* (Springfield, Ill.: Thomas, 1967).

Falconer, D.S. *Quantitative Genetics* (New York: Ronald Press, 1960).

Fantz, R. "The Origin of Form Perception," *Scientific American,* 204 (1961), p. 66.

Feshbach, S., and R.D. Singer. *Television and Aggression* (San Francisco: Jossey-Bass, 1971).

Flavell, J. "Concept Development." In P.H. Mussen, ed., *Handbook of Child Psychology* (New York: Wiley, 1970).

Flavell, J. *The Developmental Psychology of Jean Piaget* (Princeton, N.J.: Van Nostrand, 1963).

Freud, S. *A General Introduction to Psychoanalysis* (New York: Liveright, 1916).

Fuller, J., and W. Thompson. *Behavior Genetics* (New York: Wiley, 1960).

Furth, H.G. "On Language and Knowing in Piaget's Developmental Theory," *Human Development,* 13 (1970), pp. 241–257.

Gardner, R.A., and B.T. Gardner. "Teaching Sign Language to a Chimpanzee," *Science,* 165 (1969), pp. 664–672.

Gesell, A. *The First Five Years of Life* (New York: Harper, 1940).

Gesell, A. "The Ontogenesis of Infant Behavior." In L. Carmichael, ed., *Manual of Child Psychology,* 2nd ed. (New York: Wiley, 1954).

Getzels, J.W., and P.W. Jackson. *Creativity and Intelligence* (New York: Wiley, 1962).

Gibson, E., A. Pick, H. Osser, and M. Hammond. "The Role of Grapheme-morpheme Correspondence in the Perception of Words," *American Journal of Psychology,* 75 (1962), pp. 554–570.

Gilmore, J.B. "Play: A Special Behavior." In R.N. Haber, ed., *Current Research in Motivation* (New York: Holt, Rinehart and Winston, 1966).

Goldfarb, W. "Variations in Adolescent Adjustment of Institutionally-reared Children," *American Journal of Orthopsychiatry,* 17 (1947), pp. 449–457.

Gottesman, I., and J. Shields. *Schizophrenia and Genetics* (New York: Academic Press, 1972).

Graham, F., R. Matarazzo, and B. Caldwell. "Behavioral Differences between Normal and Traumatized Newborns," *Psychological Monographs,* 70 (1956).

Greenberg, J.H., C.E. Osgood, and J.J. Jenkins. "Memorandum Concerning Language Universals." In J.H. Greenberg, ed. *Universals of Language* (Cambridge, Mass.: MIT Press (1966), pp. xv–xxvii.

Grimes, J., and W. Allinsmith. "Compulsivity, Anxiety and School Achievement," *Merrill-Palmer Quarterly,* 7 (1961), pp. 259–261.

Groos, K. *The Play of Animals* (New York: Appleton-Century, 1915).

Guilford, J.P. *The Nature of Human Intelligence* (New York: McGraw-Hill, 1967).

Gutteridge, M. "A Study of Motor Achievements of Young Children," *Archives of Psychology,* 34, no. 244 (1939).

Haber, R., and R. Haber. "Eidetic Imagery: I. Frequency," *Perceptual and Motor Skills,* 19 (1964), pp. 131–138.

Haggard, E. "Social-status and Intelligence: An Experimental Study of Certain Cultural Determinants of Measured Intelligence," *Genetic Psychology Monographs,* 49 (1954), pp. 141–186.

Haith, M., F. Morrison, K. Sheingold, and P. Mindes. "Short-term Memory for Visual Information in Children and Adults," *Journal of Experimental Child Psychology,* 9 (1970), pp. 454–469.

Harlow, H. "On the Meaning of Love," *American Psychologist,* 13 (1958), pp. 673–685.

Harter, S. "Discrimination Learning Set in Children as a Function of IQ and MA," *Journal of Experimental Child Psychology,* 2 (1965), pp. 31–43.

Hartshorne, H., and M.A. May. *Studies in the Nature of Character,* 3 vols. (New York: Macmillan, 1928–1930).

Hayes, C. *The Ape in Our House* (New York: Harper and Row, 1951).

Haynes, H., B. White, and R. Held. "Visual Accommodation in Human Infants," *Science,* 148 (1965), pp. 528–530.

Healy, W., and A.L. Bronner. *Delinquents and Criminals: Their Making and Unmaking* (New York: Macmillan, 1926).

Hebb, D. *The Organization of Behavior* (New York: Wiley, 1949).

Heber, R. "Rehabilitation of Families at Risk for Mental Retardation," *Progress Report* (University of Wisconsin, Madison, 1972).

Held, R. "Plasticity in Sensory-motor Systems," *Scientific American,* 213 (1965), pp. 84–94.

Hershenson, M. "Visual Discrimination in the Human Newborn," *Journal of Comparative and Physiological Psychology,* 58 (1964), pp. 270–276.

Hess, E. "Imprinting," *Science,* 130 (1959), pp. 130–141.

Heston, L. "Psychiatric Disorders in Foster Home Reared Children of Schizophrenic Mothers," *British Journal of Psychiatry,* 112 (1966), pp. 819–825.

Hetherington, E.M. "Girls Without Fathers," *Psychology Today,* 6 (1973), pp. 47–52.

Hewett, F. *The Emotionally Disturbed Child in the Classroom* (Boston: Allyn and Bacon, 1968).

Hilgard, E., and D. Marquis. *Conditioning and Learning* (New York: Appleton-Century-Crofts, 1940).

Honzik, M. "Developmental Studies of Parent-child Resemblance in Intelligence," *Child Development,* 28 (1957), pp. 215–228.

Hooker, D. *The Prenatal Origin of Behavior* (Lawrence, Kansas: University of Kansas Press, 1952).

Hubel, D., and T. Wiesel. "Receptive Fields of Cells in Striate Cortex of Very Young, Visually Inexperienced Kittens," *Journal of Neurophysiology,* 26 (1963), pp. 994–1002.

Ingalls, T.H. "Environmental Factors and Terratogenesis." In G. Wolstenholme and C. O'Connor, eds. *CIBA Foundation Symposium on Congenital Malformations* (London: Churchill, Ltd., 1960).

Jakobson, R., G. Fant, and M. Halle. *Preliminaries to Speech Analysis* (Cambridge: Acoustics Laboratory, MIT, Technical Report No. 13, 1952).

Jencks, C. *Inequality: A Reassessment of the Effect of Family and Schooling in America* (New York: Basic Books, 1972).

Jensen, A.R. "IQ's of Identical Twins Reared Apart," *Behavior Genetics* 1 (1970), pp. 133–148.

Jerison, H.J. "Brain Evolution: New Light on Some Old Principles," *Science,* 180 (1970), pp. 1224–1225.

Judd, C.H. "Practice and Its Effects on the Perception of Illusions," *Psychological Review,* 9 (1902), pp. 27–39.

Kagan, J., and H. Moss. *Birth to Maturity* (New York: Wiley, 1962).

Kallman, F. "The Genetic Theory of Schizophrenia: An Analysis of 691 Schizophrenic Twin Index Families," *American Journal of Psychiatry,* 103 (1946), pp. 309–322.

Kallman, F. *Heredity and Health in Mental Disorder* (New York: Norton, 1953).

Kanner, L. *Child Psychiatry* (Springfield, Ill.: Thomas, 1957).

Kaplan, B.J. "Malnutrition and Mental Deficiency." *Psychological Bulletin,* 78 (1972), pp. 321–334.

Karlsson, J.L. *The Biologic Basis of Schizophrenia* (Springfield, Ill.: Thomas, 1966).

Keen, R., H. Chase, and F. Graham. "Twenty-four Hour Retention by Neonates of an Habituated Heart Response," *Psychonomic Science,* 2 (1965), pp. 265–266.

Kline, F.C. "New Life Styles versus Political Activism," *Current,* 137 (1972), pp. 23–28.

Kohlberg, L., and E. Turiel. *Research in Moral Development: The Cognitive-developmental Approach* (New York: Holt, Rinehart and Winston, 1971).

Labov, W. "Academic Ignorance and Black Intelligence," *Atlantic* (1972), pp. 59–67.

Laing, R.D. and A. Esterson. *Sanity, Madness and the Family: Families of Schizophrenics,* 2nd. ed. (London: Tavistock, 1970).

Lenneberg, E. *Biological Foundations of Language* (New York: Wiley, 1967).

Lesser, G.S., F. Fifer, and D.H. Clark. "Mental Abilities of Children from Different Social Class and Different Cultural Groups," *Monographs of the Society for Research in Child Development,* 30 (1965), no. 4.

Lewin, K., R. Lippitt, and R. White. "Patterns of Aggressive Behavior in Experimentally Created Social Climates," *Journal of Social Psychology,* 10 (1939), pp. 271–299.

Lindsley, D. "Emotion." In S.S. Stevens, ed., *Handbook of Experimental Psychology* (New York, Wiley, 1951).

Lipsitt, L., and H. Kaye. "Conditioned Sucking in the Human Newborn," *Psychonomic Science,* 1 (1964), pp. 29–30.

Locke, J. "An Essay Concerning Human Understanding." In W. Dennis, ed., *Readings in the History of Psychology* (New York: Appleton-Century-Crofts, 1948).

Lorenz, K. *On Aggression* (New York: Harcourt, Brace and World, 1966).

Lovaas, O.I., G. Freitag, V. Gold, and I. Kassora. "Experimental Studies in Childhood Schizophrenia: Analysis of Self-destructive Behavior," *Journal of Experimental Child Psychology,* 2 (1965), pp. 67–84.

Lubchenco, L., F. Horner, L. Reed, I. Hix, D. Metcalf, R. Kohig, H. Elliot, and M. Bourg. "Sequelae of Premature Birth," *American Journal of Diseases of Children,* 106 (1963), pp. 101–115.

Maccoby, E. *The Development of Sex Differences* (Palo Alto: Stanford University Press, 1966).

Maccoby, E., and J. Hagan. "Effects of Distraction upon Central vs. Incidental Recall: Developmental Trends," *Journal of Experimental Child Psychology,* 2 (1965), pp. 280–289.

Mandler, G. "Subjects Do Think," *Psychological Review,* 72 (1965), pp. 323–326.

Marx, J. "Drugs during Pregnancy: Do They Affect the Unborn Child?," *Science,* 180 (1973), pp. 174–175.

Maslow, A. *Motivation and Personality* (New York: Harper and Row, 1954).

Masters, W., and V. Johnson. *Human Sexual Response* (Boston: Little, Brown, 1966).

Mateer, F. *Child Behavior* (Boston: Badger, 1918).

McCall, R.B., P. Hogarty, and N. Hurlbort. "Transitions in Infant Sensorimotor Development and the Prediction of Childhood IQ," *American Psychologist,* 28 (1972), pp. 728–748.

McCall, R.B., and J. Kagan. "Attention in the Infant: Effects of Complexity, Contour, Perimeter and Familiarity," *Child Development,* 38 (1967), pp. 939–952.

McClelland, R., *et al. The Achievement Motive* (New York: Appleton-Century-Crofts, 1953).

McGaugh, J., and M. Herz, eds. *Controversial Issues in Consolidation of the Memory Trace* (New York: Atherton Press, 1970).

McGraw, M.B. *Growth: A Study of Johnny and Jimmy* (New York: Appleton-Century-Crofts, 1935).

McNeill, D. *The Acquisition of Language: The Study of Developmental Psycholinguistics* (New York: Harper and Row, 1970).

Mendel, G. "Letter to Carl Nageli." In M. Gabriel and S. Fogel, eds. *Great Experiments in Biology* (Englewood Cliffs, N.J.: Prentice-Hall, 1955).

Milgram, S. "Some Conditions of Obedience and Disobedience to Authority," *Human Relations,* 18 (1965), pp. 57–76.

Miller, N., and A. Banuazizi. "Instrumental Learning by Curarized Rats of a Specific Visceral Response, Intestinal, or Cardiac," *Journal of Comparative and Physiological Psychology,* 65 (1968), pp. 1–7.

Milner, P. *Physiological Psychology* (New York: Holt, Rinehart and Winston, 1970).

Mischel, W., and R. Liebert. "Effects of Discrepancies between Observed and Imposed Reward Criteria on Their Acquisition and Transmission," *Journal of Personality and Social Psychology* (1966), pp. 45–53.

Money, J. *Sex Research: New Developments* (New York: Holt, Rinehart and Winston, 1965).

Montagu, A. *Prenatal Influences* (Springfield, Ill.: Thomas, 1962).

Morris, D. *The Human Zoo* (New York: McGraw-Hill, 1971).

Moss, H. "Sex, Age and State as Determinants of Mother-infant Interactions," *Merrill-Palmer Quarterly,* 13 (1967), pp. 19–36.

Mowrer, O.H., and W.M. Mowrer. "Enuresis, a Method for Its Study and Treatment," *American Journal of Orthopsychiatry,* 8 (1938), pp. 436–459.

Mueller, J. "The Specific Energies of Nerves." In W. Dennis, ed., *Readings in the History of Psychology* (New York: Appleton-Century-Crofts, 1948).

Munsinger, H., and M. Banks. "Pupillometry as a Measure of Visual Sensitivity among Infants, Young Children and Adults," *Developmental Psychology* (1974).

Munsinger, H., and W. Kessen. "Uncertainty, Structure and Preference," *Psychological Monographs,* 78 (1964), pp. 1–24.

Needham, J. *A History of Embryology* (New York: Abelard-Schuman, 1959).

Neisser, U. *Cognitive Psychology* (New York: Appleton-Century-Crofts, 1967).

Nisbitt, R. "Determinants of Food Intake in Human Obesity," *Science,* 159 (1968), pp. 1254–1255.

Norman, D., ed. *Models of Human Memory* (New York: Academic Press, 1970).

Osgood, C. *The Measurement of Meaning* (Urbana: University of Illinois Press, 1957).

Parke, R.D., and R.H. Walters. "Some Factors Influencing the Efficiency of Punishment Training for Inducing Response Inhibition," *Monographs of the Society for Research in Child Development,* 32 (1967), pp. 1–45.

Parrish, M., R. Lundy, and H. Leibowitz. "Hypnotic Age-regression and Magnitudes of the Ponzo and Poggendorf Illusions," *Science,* 159 (1968), pp. 1375–1376.

Parten, M.B. "Social Participation among Preschool Children, *Journal of Abnormal and Social Psychology,* 27 (1932), pp. 243–270.

Patterson, G., R. Littman, and W. Bricker. "Assertive Behavior in Children: A Step toward a Theory of Aggression," *Monographs of the Society for Research in Child Development,* 32 (1967), no. 113.

Peterson, L., and M. Peterson. "Short-term Retention of Individual Verbal Items," *Journal of Experimental Psychology,* 30 (1959), pp. 93–113.

Piaget, J. *The Psychology of Intelligence* (London: Rutledge and Kegan Paul, 1950).

Piaget, J. *Play, Dreams and Imitation in Childhood* (New York: Norton, 1962).

Premack, D. "The Education of Sarah." In *Time* magazine (September 21, 1970).

Rahe, R.H. "Subjects' Recent Life Changes and Their Near Future Illness Reports," *Annals of Clinical Research,* 4 (1972), pp. 250–265.

Reynolds, E.L., and J.V. Wines. "Individual Difference in Physical Changes Associated with Adolescent Girls," *American Journal of Diseases of Children,* 75 (1948), pp. 329–350.

Rheingold, H. "The Effects of a Strange Environment on the Behavior of Infants." In B.M. Foss, ed., *Determinants of Infant Behavior, IV* (London: Methuen, 1969).

Rheingold, H. "The Modification of Social Responsiveness in Institutional Babies," *Monograph of the Society for Research in Child Development,* 21 (1956).

Ribble, M. *The Rights of Infants,* 2nd ed. (New York: Columbia University Press, 1965).

Rimland, B. *Infantile Autism: The Syndrome and Its Implications for a Neural Theory of Behavior* (New York: Appleton-Century-Crofts, 1964).

Roffwarg, H.P., J.N. Muzio, and W.C. Dement. "Ontogenic Development of the Human Sleep-dream Cycle," *Science,* 152 (1966), p. 608.

Rorschach, H. *Psychodiagnostics: A Diagnostic Test Based on Perception,* P. Lemkau and B. Kronenberg, trs. (Berne: Huber, 1942).

Rosenthal, R., and L. Jacobsen. *Pygmalion in the Classroom: Teacher Expectation and Pupils' Intellectual Development* (New York: Holt, Rinehart and Winston, 1968).

Rubin, Z. *Liking and Loving* (New York: Holt, Rinehart and Winston, 1973).

Rumbaugh, D., T. Gill, and E. von Glaserfeld. "Reading and Sentence Completion by a Chimpanzee (Pan)," *Science,* 183 (1973), pp. 731–733.

Ryan, D. *Characteristics of Teachers* (Washington, D.C.: American Council on Education, 1960).

Sackett, G. "Effects of Rearing Conditions upon the Behavior of Rhesus Monkeys (Macca Mulatta)," *Child Development,* 36 (1965), pp. 855–868.

Sameroff, A. "The Components of Sucking in the Human Newborn," *Journal of Experimental Child Psychology,* 6 (1968), pp. 607–623.

Schaefer, E.S. "Converging Models for Maternal Behavior and Child Behavior." In J. Glidewell, ed., *Parental Attitudes and Child Behavior* (Springfield, Ill.: Thomas, 1961).

Schaefer, E.S., and N. Bayley. "Maternal Behavior and Personality Development: Data from the Berkeley Growth Study," *Child Development,* 13 (1960), pp. 155–173.

Schaffer, H.R., and W.M. Callender. "Psychological Effects of Hospitalization in Infancy," *Pediatrics,* 24 (1959), p. 538.

Schaffer, H.R., and P.E. Emerson. "Patterns of Response to Physical Contact in Early Human Development," *Journal of Child Psychology and Psychiatry,* 5 (1964), pp. 1–13.

Schramm, W., J. Lyle, and E.B. Parker. *Television in the Lives of Our Children* (Stanford, Calif.: Stanford University Press, 1961).

Scott, J.P. "Critical Periods in Behavior Development," *Science,* 138 (1962), pp. 949–957.

Sears, R.R., E.E. Maccoby, and H. Levin. *Patterns of Child Rearing* (New York: Harper and Row, 1957).

Sheldon, W. *Atlas of Men: A Guide for Somatotyping the Adult Male at All Ages* (New York: Harper and Row, 1954).

Sherif, M., and C. Sherif. *Social Psychology* (New York: Harper and Row, 1969).

Sherman, M., and I. Sherman. *The Process of Human Behavior* (New York: Norton, 1929).

Simpson, G., and W. Beck. *Life: An Introduction to Biology* (New York: Harcourt, Brace, Jovanovich, 1965).

Skinner, B.F. *The Behavior of Organisms* (New York: Appleton-Century, 1938).

Skinner, B.F. *Verbal Behavior.* (New York: Appleton-Century-Crofts, 1957).

Shodak, M., and H. Skeels. "A Final Follow-up of One Hundred Adopted Children," *Journal of Genetic Psychology,* 75 (1949), pp. 3–19.

Slobin, D.I. *Grammatical Transformations in Childhood and Adulthood,* unpublished doctoral dissertation (Harvard University, 1963).

Snow, R. "Unfinished Pygmalion," *Contemporary Psychology,* 14 (1969), pp. 197–199.

Solomon, R.L. "Punishment," *American Psychologist,* 19 (1964), pp. 239–253.

Sperling, F. *Information in a Brief Visual Presentation,* unpublished doctoral dissertation (Harvard University, 1959).

Sperry, R. "Mechanisms of Neural Maturation." In S.S. Stevens, ed., *Handbook of Experimental Psychology* (New York: Wiley, 1951).

Spitz, R.A., and K. Wolf. "Anaclitic Depression: An Inquiry into the Genesis of Psychiatric Conditions in Early Childhood," *Psychoanalytic Study of the Child,* 2 (1946), pp. 313–342.

Spock, B. *Baby and Child Care* (New York: Pocket Books, 1946).

Stein, Z., M. Susser, G. Saenger, and F. Marolla. "Nutrition and Mental Performance," *Science,* 178 (1972), pp. 708–713.

Stodolsky, S., and G. Lesser. "Learning Patterns in the Disadvantaged," *Harvard Educational Review,* 37 (1967), pp. 546–593.

Tanner, J.M. "Earlier Maturation in Man," *Scientific American,* 218 (1968), pp. 21–28.

Tanner, J.M. "Physical Growth." In P. Mussen, ed., *Carmichael's Manual of Child Psychology,* I (New York: Wiley, 1970).

Tanner, J.M. "The Regulation of Human Growth," *Child Development,* 34, (1963), pp. 817–847.

Taylor, C. "The Expectations of Pygmalion's Creators," *Educational Leadership,* 28 (1970), pp. 161–164.

Terman, L., and M. Oden. *The Gifted Child Grows Up* (Stanford, Calif.: Stanford University Press, 1947).

Thompson, R., and W. Spencer. "Habituation: A Model Phenomenon for the Study of Neuronal Substrates of Behavior," *Psychological Review,* 73 (1966), pp. 16–43.

Thompson, W., and J. Grusec. "Studies of Early Experience." In P. Mussen, ed., *Manual of Child Psychology* (New York: Wiley, 1970).

Thorndike, E., E. Bergman, J. Tilton, and E. Woodyard. *Adult Learning* (New York: Macmillan, 1928).

Thorndike, R. "Review of Pygmalion in the Classroom," *American Educational Research Journal,* 5 (1968), pp. 708–711.

Thurstone, L. "Primary Mental Abilities," *Psychometric Monographs,* no. 1 (Chicago: University of Chicago Press, 1938).

Tinbergen, N. *The Study of Instinct* (Oxford: Clarendon, 1951).

Tolman, E.C. *Purposive Behavior in Animals and Men* (New York: Appleton-Century, 1932).

Travers, R., *Handbook for Research on Teaching* (New York: Rand-McNally, 1972).

Tryon, R. "Genetic Differences in Maze-learning Abilities in Rats, 39th Yearbook, *National Society for the Study of Education* (Chicago: University of Chicago Press, 1940), pp. 111–119.

Tyler, L. *The Psychology of Human Differences* (New York: Appleton-Century-Crofts, 1956).

Velten, H.V. "The Growth of Phonemic and Lexical Patterns in Infant Language," *Language,* 19 (1943), pp. 281–292.

Vygotsky, L.S. *Thought and Language* (Cambridge, Mass.: MIT Press, 1962).

Walk, R., and E. Gibson. "A Comparative and Analytical Study of Visual Depth Perception," *Psychological Monographs,* 75 (1961).

Wallach, M., and N. Kogan. *Modes of Thinking in Young Children* (New York: Holt, Rinehart and Winston, 1964).

Watson, J.B. "Psychology as the Behaviorist Sees It," *Psychological Review,* 20 (1913), pp. 158–177.

Watson, J.D. *Molecular Biology of the Gene* (New York, Benjamin, 1970).

Watzlawick, P., J. Beavin, and D. Jackson. *Pragmatics of Human Communication: A Study of Interaction Patterns, Pathologies and Paradoxes* (New York: Norton, 1967).

White, B.L., and R. Held. "Plasticity of Sensory Motor Development." In J.F. Rosenblith and W. Allinsmith, eds., *Readings in Child Development and Educational Psychology* (Boston: Allyn and Bacon, 1966).

White, R. "Motivation Reconsidered: The Concept of Competence," *Psychological Review,* 66 (1959), pp. 297–333.

Whitehead, A., and B. Russel. *Principia Mathematica,* 2nd ed. (Cambridge, Eng.: Cambridge University Press, 1925).

Whorf, B. *Language, Thought and Reality* (New York: Wiley; and Cambridge, Mass.: MIT Press, 1956).

Wickman, E.K. *Teachers and Behavior Problems* (New York: Commonwealth Fund, 1928).

Winterbottom, M. "The Relation of Need for Achievement in Learning Experiences, in Independence and Mastery." In J. Atkinson, ed., *Motives in Fantasy, Action and Society* (Princeton, N.J.: Van Nostrand, 1958). pp. 453–478.

Zubin, J., and J. Money. *Contemporary Sexual Behavior: Critical Issues in the 1970's* (Baltimore: Johns Hopkins University Press, 1973).

Indexes

Name Index

Adelson, J.,	499
Adler, A.,	351
Albert,	539
Alexander, T.,	440
Allinsmith, W.,	399
Anastasi, A.,	268
Ardrey, R.,	304, 438
Asch, S.,	377
Bakan, P.,	137
Baldwin, J.,	448
Bandura, A.,	407, 438, 525
Banks, M.,	126
Bard, P.,	567
Bayley, N.,	201, 266
Beavin, J.,	459
Berko, J.,	203
Binet, A.,	254, 538
Borke, H.,	18
Bower, T.G.R.,	115, 152–153
Braine, M.,	207
Bricker, W.,	370
Broadbent, D.,	136
Bronfenbrenner, U.,	371, 401
Bronowski, J.,	195
Brophy, J.,	398
Brown, R.,	197, 203, 563
Bruner, J.,	189, 227
Burks, H.,	481
Butcher, H.,	253
Callender, W.,	340
Cameron, J.,	201
Cannon, W.,	567
Cattell, R.,	413
Cazden, C.,	206
Chase, H.,	128
Chomsky, N.,	210–215
Claiborn, W.,	398
Claus, S.,	539
Coleman, J.,	215
Conger, J.,	525
Copi, I.,	234
Cronbach, L.,	264
Darwin, C.,	41, 294, 307, 538
Darwin, D.,	538
Davis, W.,	359
Dennis, W.,	96, 357
Dewey, J.,	448
Diamond, M.,	514
Ebbinghaus, H.,	190
Erikson, E.,	24, 428, 500–506
Erlenmeyer-Kimling, L., and	
L. Jarvik,	57
Esterson, A.,	459
Estes, W.,	178
Eysenck, H.,	335, 412, 461, 490
Fantz, R.,	137, 148
Feshbach, S.,	406
Flavell, J.,	188, 225
Freud, S.,	15, 24, 306, 389, 424,
	428, 437, 463, 466–469,
	483–585, 539, 562
Furth, H.,	221
Galileo	27
Galton, F.,	52–55
Gardner, A.,	195
Gesell, A.,	86, 266
Getzels, J.,	288
Gewirtz, J.,	369
Gibson, E.,	144, 145
Gilmore, B.,	392

Goldfarb, W.,   355
Good, T.,   398
Goodenough, F.,   324
Gottesman, I.,   413
Graham, F.,   128, 338
Greenberg, J.,   200
Grimes, J.,   399
Groos, K.,   389
Guilford, J.,   285
Gutteridge, M.,   94
Haber, R.,   151
Haggard, E.,   279
Haith, M.,   185
Hall, G.,   538
Harlow, H.,   313
Harter, S.,   282
Hartshorne, H.,   405, 450
Havighurst, R.,   359
Hayes, C.,   195
Haynes, H.,   126
Healey, W.,   525
Hebb, D.,   145, 306
Heber, R.,   275
Held, R.,   112, 126
Herrnstein, R.,   253
Hershenson, M.,   149
Hess, E.,   313, 339
Heston, L.,   457
Hetherington, E.,   354
Hippocrates,   411
Hooker, D.,   62
Horse, S.,   69
Hubel, D.,   137, 144
Hyde, Mr.,   470
Ingalls, T.,   69
Jackson, D.,   459
Jackson, P.,   288
Jakobson, R.,   201
James, W.,   567
Jekyll, Dr.,   470
Jencks, C.,   282
Jensen, A.,   282
Johnson, V.,   510
Judd, C.,   191
Jung, C.,   411

Kagan, J.,   201, 429
Kallman, F.,   336, 413, 458
Kanner, L.,   459
Kaplan, B.,   97
Karlsson, H.,   457
Keen, R.,   128
Kessen, W.,   320
Kinsey, A.,   29
Kline, F.,   499
Koch, H.,   351
Kogan, N.,   285, 288
Kohlberg, L.,   22, 448
Kohler, I.,   156
Laing, R.,   454, 459
Lange, C.,   567
Lenneberg, E.,   198
Lesser, J.,   215
Levin, H.,   342
Lewin, K.,   381, 382–385
Liebert, R.,   405
Lipman, R.,   370
Lipsitt, L.,   167
Livson, N.,   201
Locke, J.,   144
Lorenz, K.,   297, 304, 305, 437
Lovaas, I.,   476
Maccoby, E.,   136, 318, 342
Mandler, G.,   189
Masters, W.,   510
Mateer, F.,   167
May, M.,   405, 450
McCall, R.,   201, 265
McClelland, D.,   321
McGaugh, J.,   189
McGraw, M.,   94
McNaughten decision,   473
McNeill, D.,   197
Mead, M.,   430–435
Mendel, G.,   42, 43
Milgram, S.,   378
Miller, N.,   179, 180
Miller, W.,   525
Mischel, W.,   405
Milner, P.,   303
Money, J.,   513

Monis, D.,	373	Sherman, M., and I. Sherman,	73
Montagu, A.,	65	Skeels, H.,	281
Moss, H.,	201, 429	Skinner, B.F., 163, 168–173, 197, 437	
Mowrer, O.,	461	Skodak, M.,	281
Mueller, J.,	141	Slobin, D.,	215
Munay, H.,	411	Snow, R.,	398
Munsinger, H.,	126, 281, 320	Solomon, R.,	450
Neisser, U.,	218	Sperling, G.,	185
Nisbitt, R.,	298	Sperry, R.,	295
Oedipus,	424	Spitz, R.,	340
Osgood, C.,	227	Spock, B.,	358–365
Parke, R.,	450	Stein, Z.,	66
Parrish, M.,	156	Stodolsky, S.,	215
Parten, M.,	392	Tanner, J.M.,	26, 97, 302
Patterson, G.,	15, 370	Taylor, C.,	398
Pavlov, I.,	162	Terman, L.,	276, 539
Penfield, W.,	562	Thompson, W., (IQ)	280
Piaget, J.,	13, 16, 22, 99, 145,	Thorndike, R.,	187, 398
	197, 225, 228–234,	Tinbergen, N.,	306, 307–311
	236, 306, 389, 448	Tolman, E.,	182
Poppy, J.,	408	Travers, R.,	393
Premack, D.,	196	Tuddenharn, R.,	25
Rank, O.,	73	Velten, H.,	201
Rat, W.,	539	Vygotsky, L.,	221
Reynolds, F.,	509	Walk, R.,	145
Rheingold, H.,	341, 356	Wallach, M.,	285, 288
Ribble, M.,	356	Walters, R.,	525
Rimland, B.,	475, 476	Washoe	195
Rorschach, H.,	419	Watson, J.,	55–56, 130, 162,
Rosenthal, R.,	398		219, 539
Rubin, Z.,	513	Watzlawick, P.,	459
Rumbaugh, D.,	197	Werner, H.,	99, 117
Ryan, D.,	394	White, B.,	111, 126
Sackett, G.,	304	White, R.,	435
Samaroff, A.,	184	Whitehead, A.,	234
Schachter, S.,	567	Whorf, B.,	220
Schaffer, H.,	337, 340, 345	Wickman, E.,	395
Schramm, W.,	407	Wiesel, T.,	137, 144
Sears, R.,	342, 429	Wines, J.,	509
Segal, J.,	327–329	Winterbottom, M.,	435
Sheldon, W.,	411	Wolf, K.,	340
Sherif, M.,	381	Wolff, C.,	41

Subject Index

abnormal behavior,	335	birth order,		351
abstract thinking,	27	birth rate,		351
achievement motivation,	321	brain damage,		199
adolescence,	26, 496–497	brain dominance,		137
adopted children,	51	breast development,		509
adoptive families,	281	CNS,		38
affective reaction,	477	canal-boat children,		280
aggression,	14, 302, 436–440	career choice,		519
alcohol use,	528	castrati,		300
American Sign Language,	195	catharsis,		484
amine-oxydase,	458	"catch-up",		97
amniocentesis,	58	cause and effect,		114
amphetamine use,	532	central tendency,		543
anal stage,	424	centration,		242
Anglo-Saxon,	399	cephalo-caudal,		87
animism,	238	cerebral dominance,		91
anxiety,	463	cheating,		404
articulation,	118	childhood fears,		21
attention,	132	childhood illnesses,		98
audition,	126	Children's Apperception Test,		420
autism,	475	children's games,		21
babbling,	10, 201	children's groups,		370, 381
baboons,	372	circulation,		72
bad behavior,	415	classical conditioning,		165–167
balance,	129	clique,		511
Bayley Infant Scale,	89, 267	closure,		142
Beagle,	307	cloth mother,		314
behavior genetics,	48	cognitive motives,		319
behavior modification,	485–487	color blindness,		559
behaviorism,	162	color mixing,		126
bilingual children,	207	color vision,		126
binocular cues,	146	comparative psychology,		294
biofeedback,	332	competence,		216
birth,	70, 338	competition,		22, 404
birth cry,	73	conception,		4

concrete operational,   240, 243–246
conductive impairment,   128
conflict,   324, 385
conformity,   377
content validity,   265
control groups,   552
convergence,   146
conversion reaction,   469
cooing,   9
correlation,   545
counter-conditioning,   465
creativity,   285–290
cretinism,   65
criminality,   337
cross-sectional method,   554
crowd,   511
crying,   9
culture fair test,   278–279
curiosity,   320
deaf children,   198
deafness,   128
defense mechanism,   426
delinquency,   30, 472
dependency,   429
depression,   471
depth perception,   145
detour,   387
dialect,   209
digestion,   72
discipline,   341, 343
dispersion,   544
displacement,   428
dissociation,   470
distorting lenses,   112
divorce,   353
dominance,   19
dominant (genetics),   42, 43
double bind,   459
double-blind,   554
dreams,   238, 483
drive,   297
dropouts,   30, 404, 523
drug abuse,   31
drugs,   66, 526–533
drug therapy,   480
Dutch famine,   66

echolalia,   476
ectoderm,   60
ectomorph,   411
EEG,   79
ego,   426
egocentrism,   241
eidetic imagery,   151
Embryonic phase,   4, 60
emotion,   322
emotions,   567–570
empathy,   18
empiricism,   144
encopresis,   461
endoderm,   60
endomorph,   411
enuresis,   461
environmental deprivation,   280
environmentalism,   162
ESP,   551
ethics,   536
ethology,   294
evolution,   34
eye,   124
expansion,   206
experiment,   551–554
experimenter effect,   554
extinction,   174
extension,   206
extrovert,   411
face validity,   265
facial expressions,   323
fairy tales,   406
family atmosphere,   345
farsightedness,   125
father absent home,   353
fatty,   96
fear,   304
fear of failure,   322
feedback,   187
feeding problems,   462
female sex attitudes,   515
fetal phase,   4, 61
field observation,   302
figure-ground,   143
fixed action pattern,   296
forgetting,   561–563

formal operations,	240
fraternal twins,	51
free association,	483
frequency distribution,	541–543
friendship,	379, 511
generalization,	174
genetic counseling,	59, 461
genetic theory of psychoses,	456
genetics and personality,	413
genotype,	34, 42
germinal phase,	4, 60
gestalt,	142, 220
glutathione,	458
good behavior,	415
good continuation,	142
good form,	142
grammer,	204, 207–209, 563–567
grasping,	91
group therapy,	487
growth curves,	84
habituation,	164–165
hallucinogenic drugs,	530
handedness,	91
hatchet man,	372
head banging,	361
Head Start,	274
hermaphrodite,	514
history of child psychology,	537–540
hospitalization,	481
human memory,	185–192
Human Zoo,	373–376
hunger,	298
hyperactivity,	481
hypochondria,	470
id,	426
identical twins,	56, 282
identification,	14
illusions,	154
imitation,	113, 205, 341
immunity,	73
imprinting,	306, 339
inbreeding,	49
incubation,	286
independence,	11
independent assortment,	46
infant,	7
infant tests,	266
innate feeding pattern,	298
innate releasing stimulus,	296
insight,	108
instinct,	295
institutionalization,	355
intelligence,	335
interposition,	146
interpretation,	483
introvert,	411
intuitive thought,	16
IQ,	24
and age,	276
tests,	252
irreversibility,	17
isolation,	332
juvenile delinquency,	523–526
kibbutz,	317
kinesthesis,	129
language,	12
language universals,	221
latent learning,	182
latency,	24
leadership,	371
level 1 brain functions,	79
level 2 brain functions,	81
life change events,	460
life space,	385
liking,	513
linear perspective,	146
logical thinking,	246–249
longitudinal method,	554
loving,	513
male sex attitudes,	518
malnutrition,	97
manic depressive,	477
marijuana use,	529
maternal age,	69
maternal attachment,	313
maternal care,	313
maternal deprivation,	317, 340
maternal emotions,	65
maternal infection,	67
maternal nutrition,	65
maternal separation,	317, 340
meaning,	219, 225

measurement,	540	operant conditioning,	175–182
meditation,	330	Opiate addiction,	531
mental retardation,	274	oral stage,	424
mentally gifted,	276	organic psychoses,	477
Merrill-Palmer Scales,	268	orienting response,	133
mesoderm,	60	otosclerosis,	128
mesomorph,	411	overachievement,	402
Minnesota Preschool Scale,	269	overeating,	298
MMPI,	421	overprotected child,	347
mnemonics,	190	overweight,	96
mongolism,	69	ovum,	40
monocular cues,	146	pacifier,	363
moral development,	22, 448	pain,	131
morpheme,	200, 203–205	pedigree,	49
motor development,	87	peer aggression,	370
motor sequence,	89	penetrance,	48
Mueller-Lyer illusion,	154	percentile values of IQ,	273
multigene theory,	47	perception,	17
multiplication of classes,	244	theories of,	137
narcosis,	478	perceptual distortion,	156
nativism,	141, 162	perceptual learning,	144
Nazi,	378	perceptual set,	135
nearness,	142	performance,	216
nearsightedness,	125	personal development,	24
negativism,	356	personality,	20, 335
neonate,	7	personality tests,	418–423
nervous system,	34	phenotype,	43
neural impairment,	128	phobia,	464
neurotic,	347	phoneme,	200
neuroses,	461	phrase-structure grammar,	564–567
newborn,	6, 72	phylogenetic skills	94
newborn brain,	77	physical growth,	26
night tenor,	462	patterns,	85
non-standard English,	209	problems,	96
nonverbal communication,	221–222	physical handicap,	99
nuclear family,	350	pituitary,	510
nursery school,	18, 281	pivot word,	13
nutrition,	480	placebo,	463
obedience,	377	play,	11, 109, 388, 489
object perception,	147	associative,	392
object permanence,	108, 115	cooperative,	392
objective test,	421	independent,	392
observation,	549–550	parallel,	392
obsessive-compulsive,	465	unoccupied,	392
Oglala Sioux,	501	political activism,	499

Ponzo illusion,   154
post partum,   301
predictive validity,   265
prefrontal lobotomy,   479
prejudice,   25
prematurity,   71, 388
premenstrual,   301
prenatal life,   4, 64
preoperational thought,   240–243
preschool child,   16
preschool tests,   268
primary addition of classes,   244
primary circular reaction,   104
Primary Mental Abilities,   253
probability,   547
projection,   427
projective test,   419
proximo-distal,   87
pseudohermaphrodite,   301
psychoses,   474
psychosomatic illness,   472
psychosurgery,   479
psychotherapy,   477, 482–486
puberty,   426
puberty rite,   498
punishment,   178
pupil evaluation,   401
pupil size,   323
purpose of school,   400
pygmalion in the classroom,   398
rationalization,   427
reaction formation,   428
short-term memory,   186
signal detection theory,   557
similarity,   142
single gene theory,   47
size constancy,   151
sleep,   74, 326–329
smell,   129
smiling,   8, 325, 369
smoking,   67
social change,   28
social class,   277, 357
social development,   371
social feedback,   415

social relations,   13, 19
social symbols,   417
socialization,   344
Soviet education,   401
space,   111
space perception,   145
specific skills,   95
speech,   218
sperm,   40
spontaneous recovery,   174
standardization,   262, 265
Stanford-Binet,   12
statistical inference,   546
statistics,   540–547
storm & stress,   497
stranger anxiety,   9, 340
structured school,   398
stuttering,   218
subject's expectations,   553
sublimation,   427
sucking,   299
suicide,   471
  rate of,   472
super-ego,   426
superstition,   182
syllogism,   234
synanon,   487
syncretic,   118
T-group,   487
task leader,   372
taste,   128
taxis,   295
teacher,   392
teacher background,   397
teachers,
  fearful,   393
  impulsive,   393
  self-controlled,   393
television,   406
temperature,   131
tertiary circular reaction,   108
realism,   238
recessive,   42, 43
reflex,   104, 163, 295
reflexes,   78

regression,	356, 428	sex role,	15, 440–447
reinforcement,	176	sexual maturity,	302, 507–510
schedules of,	180	shame,	450
rejected child,	348	shape constancy,	153
rejection,	379	shaping behavior,	179
reliability,	262, 264	shock therapy,	478
REM,	74, 330	thalidomide,	66
repression,	426	theoretical validity,	265
reputation,	417	thirst,	297
response speed,	93	threshold theory,	556
retinal disparity,	146	thumb sucking,	362
reversibility,	243	time,	113
Rh sensitization,	68	tip-of-the-tongue,	563
risk taking,	322	toddler,	11
rod and frame test,	121	toilet training,	366
Rorschach test,	419	token economy,	486
rote learning,	190	touch,	130
roulette,	547	tranquilizers,	481
rule learning,	191	transference,	484
sampling,	548–549	transformation,	204
scapegoat,	372	transformation rules,	566
schizophrenia,	454, 475	trial and error,	109
school achievement,	402	truth,	234
school child,	22	twins,	49, 336
school phobia,	464	twitching,	361
scientific method,	549–556	underweight,	96
secondary circular reaction,	105	unstructured school,	398
segregation (genetic),	46	U.S.S.R.,	355
selection,	34	validity,	262, 264
selective breeding,	49	violence,	407
selective listening,	136	visual cliff,	145
self-concept,	414	visually-directed reaching,	8, 111
semantic differential,	227	WAIS,	272
semantics,	219	walking,	89
semi-circular canals,	130	whole-part perception,	149
senile psychosis,	455	Who's Who,	276
senses,	124	wire mother,	314
sensory-motor,	240	working mother,	351
sensory motor coordination,	107	WISC,	269
sensory information storage,	185	wug,	204
separation anxiety,	9, 340	x words,	13
sex,	300	XYY,	473
sex differences,	318	Zuni,	515
sex, premarital,	29	Zygote,	40
sex relations,	431		

About the Author

Harry Munsinger took his undergraduate degree at the University of California at Berkeley. He had already decided on a major in biology and was taking a premedical course when he became fascinated by psychology and developmental biology and changed his major. After graduation, and a short time in the armed forces, he entered the University of Oregon at Eugene for graduate study in experimental psychology. Having completed his doctorate in two years, he took a postdoctoral clinical internship program at the veteran's hospital in Palo Alto, California. It was only after he joined Dr. William Kessen, Professor of Psychology and Research Associated in Pediatrics, at Yale that Harry Munsinger began his absorbing work in the areas of infancy and child development. After a year at Yale, Dr. Munsinger moved to the University of Illinois at Urbana-Champaign, where he taught for three years. But when a job offer came from the newly opened University of California campus at San Diego, where he still teaches, Dr. Munsinger moved back to California. Currently his research is concerned with the biological causes of human development. Partially because of his daughter, Brita, whom he calls "the joy of my life," he wants to work in the areas of learning how children develop intelligence and personal behavior.

WESTMAR COLLEGE LIBRARY